NINETEENTH CENTURY GERMAN PROTESTANTISM

The Church as Social Model

John E. Groh

UNIVERSITY
PRESS OF
AMERICA

Copyright © 1982 by

University Press of America, Inc.

P.O. Box 19101, Washington, D.C. 20036

Printed in the United States of America

ISBN (Perfect): 0-8191-2078-2
ISBN   (Cloth): 0-8191-2077-4

Library of Congress Catalog Card Number: **80-6286**

TO THOSE WHO FOUGHT

WHEN AUTHORITY VIOLATED CONSCIENCE

IN 1973

6715A

iii

CONTENTS

INTRODUCTION

I have tried to compile a comprehensive account of
nineteenth century German Protestantism that recognizes the
role of Protestantism in culture, education, society,
economics and politics. My goal has been to record this
story of German Protestants for a variety of readers.
Because these Protestants functioned rather consistently
throughout the century, the book saves no punch lines for
the last paragraphs.

The study is designed for the generalist as well as the
specialist. Hopefully, the person who is broadly
interested in German culture will enter some of
Protestantism's long caverns and hidden anterooms through
this door. Historians of modern Europe, church historians,
theologians, and historians of dogma will find a composite
review of church life, and a conclusion or two that may
stimulate further research. The book also provides data
for comparative studies of religious life in the Atlantic
community, and on the continent.

Who were these nineteenth century German Protestants? They
were people who were proud of their Reformational heritage.
After tnat shattering schism in Christendom, their
religious history was stamped by orthodoxy, rationalism,
pietism, the "Auflkaerung," and other movements. But their
most marked characteristic was their membership in more
than thirty churches, rather than a single German church.
Even in tne Second Empire, each state had its own
Protestant church, or churches, counting Roman Catholic.
After it became legal for a person to withdraw from the
territorial church, citizenship and membership were no
longer coterminous, at least in theory.

Half of the Protestants in Germany were Prussians, and that
is one reason why this volume traces developments in that

state in some detail. It may be somewhat wearisome to review a listing of each state's Protestant population at this point, but the following table shows Prussia's predominance, and explains why the phrase "church and state" actually means "churches and states." Statistics published in 1865 provide this information on the number of souls, parishes, pastors, and pastor-to-parishioner ratios in the German states in 1862:

STATE	SOULS	PARISHES	CHURCHES	PASTORS
PRUSSIA	11,026,608	———	8,181	6,193
SAXONY	2,171,148	925	1,186	1,096
HANOVER	1,630,618	1,102	1,195	1,165
BAVARIA	1,283,867	1,062	1,414	1,165
WUERTTEMBERG	1,178,501	909	1,114	996
HESSE-CASSEL	614,688	456	833	470
HESSE-DAMRSTADT	601,611	439	641	477
HOLSTEIN	546,486	143	142	196
MECKLENBERG-SCHWERIN	536,198	315	458	341
BADEN	443,187	355	438	368
GERMAN AUSTRIA	308,451	175	201	182
BRUNSWICK	280,938	231	335	238
SAXE-WEIMAR	262,295	302	510	311
NASSAU	236,728	196	239	209
OLDENBERG	226,111	109	119	122
SAXE-HILDBURG-HAUSEN	168,379	149	242	167
ANHALT-DESSAU	121,681	93	148	101
LIPPE	105,175	45	43	47
MECKLENBERG-SRELITZ	98,266	62	149	68
REUSS YOUNGER LINE	75,830	62	92	54
SCHWARZBURG-RUDOLSTADT	73,591	66	117	76
SCHWARZBURG-SONDERSHAUSEN	63,179	67	94	74
ANHALT-BERNBURG	57,443	41	58	48
WALDECK	56,642	54	88	58
LAUENBURG	50,655	29	29	31
SAXE-COBURG	46,382	38	54	49
FRANKFURT	44,119	14	14	20

LUEBECK	37,547	12	12	22
SCHAUMBURG-LIPPE	30,819	19	19	21
HESSE-HOMBURG	20,066	18	26	19
TOTALS	23,464,609	7,632	18,443	14,550

No single set of statistics from this convoluted century is definitive, but in 1862, Prussia's eleven million evangelicals made her a leader among German Protestants. She boasted five times as many evangelicals as any other state, and Protestants outnumbered Roman Catholics by a ratio of eleven to seven in her provinces.

What have I discovered about German Protestants in this century? They were willing partners in an unwritten agreement with the states or state governments. The agreement provided that the Protestant churches would serve as the states' chief model for the larger society; the accepted paradigm, "freedom within authority," mutually benefitted them and the states. I have called this consensus between churches and states the "unwritten Protestant charter," or "religious charter." While circumstances and events modified the uncodified agreement, its early design persisted throughout the century. In the reactionary fifties it reached its apex of public recognition, when social theorists described the "Christian state" as the major goal of church-state interaction. These and other proponents of the unwritten Protestant "charter" argued that the church's primary role was to encourage people to use and enjoy the freedom given to them by authorities.

Assigned to the task of modeling "freedom within authority" for the wider society, the churches were perpetuating a long German Protestant tradition of submission to lawful secular authorities. This tradition was rooted in Luther's teaching, and his substitution of princes for bishops at the time of the Reformation. During the nineteenth century, a wide range of biblical and doctrinal material was used to support this practice. But social, political and economic developments, including greater political power for the territories and the drive toward national unification, powerfully reinforced and partially reshaped this doctrinal proclivity among Protestants between 1815 and 1914. This study concentrates on the process of reinforcement, rather than the theological underpinnings or long history of the submissive attitude among German Protestants. The "unwritten charter" between churches and states, namely, that the churches' primary social role was to model "freedom within authority" for the wider society, provided a unique channel for traditional submissiveness to manifest itself among German Protestants.

As one of the states' models for society, the churches were responsible for inculcating much more than moral and civic virtue. In sum, the Protestant moral and civic order was not the model for society that the German states proposed, programmatically speaking, from around 1815 to 1914. Rather, they intended that the life and work of the churches should demonstrate for society how persons and institutions could and should live "freely" within an authoritarian structure. This nebulous assignment permitted the state to continue defining "freedom" and delineating its limits, but at the same time, it gave the impression that true freedom was available for the taking. The assignment process explains how the Protestant churches continued to serve as a model for society in the North German Confederation and the German Empire, despite the fact that neither of these political entities had constitutional "state churches," though their constitutive territories did. It also explains how the "Kulturkampf," a general assault on all organized religion, paradoxically reinforced the churches' modeling function.

It would be a mistake, however, to think that the churches were the only social model used by the states to inculcate a sense of freedom, whose limits were defined by structural authority. The army, bureaucracy, and schools also showed the broader society how to function in varying degrees of "freedom." In a broad sense, the same was true for the development of the modern political process in the German states, including parties and constitutional monarchies. The states did not make the mistake of relying solely on the slender reed of the territorial churches, but neither did they ignore this powerful instrument of social control.

A church's assignment as model for society did not depend on its being constitutionally or administratively "free" or

independent in a territory. In fact, more often than not
the "freedom" granted to Protestants in an authoritarian
context was a spiritualized freedom, rather than a form of
legal or administrative freedom. But the fact that the
churches were not constitutionally disestablished, or
administratively free, did not make them less effective
modeling instruments for the state. In view of the image
they were expected to reflect to society--"freedom within
autnority"--it was assumed that constitutional or
administrative independence would not in and of itself
remove the church from the control and supervision of
"authority." This ironic ambivalence lies at the center of
the story of German Protestantism in the nineteenth
century.

To the two thirds of the population that was Protestant,
then, the territorial churches' primary social role carried
a powerful message: the "freedom" of social institutions
was to be exercised within narrow limits defined by
political authority, not the society. Naturally, the
lesson had more impact on some than others. The Roman
Catholic segment of the population could profit as well
from this Protestant model since it was part of the wider
society, although the Roman Catholic Church was a more
immediate religious influence for its members. While this
study concentrates on the Protestant experience, it
indicates how the Roman Catholic Church sometimes resisted
the state's imposition of a modeling function more
successfully than the Protestant churches.

To understand the story of nineteenth century German
Protestantism from the inside, one should also examine the
"Grossdeutsch-Kleindeutsch" debate from the perspective of
the church's modeling function for society. This is
especially true since religion was an intricate part of the
debate. The "religious charter" informs this study's
discussion of the problem, most clearly when it examines
the confessionalist opposition to the Prussian Union
Church, Ernst Ludwig von Gerlach's opposition to Bismarck's
foreign policy, the revolutions of 1848-50, and Protestant
responses to the war against Austria in 1866.

I have also discovered that the churches exhibited little
of the prophetic zeal--what H. Richard Niebuhr called
"Christ against culture"--that sometimes stirs within

xiii

organized Christianity. They did not counterbalance the state's power, and engaged in social criticism only with great hesitancy. The church was seldom the state's "loyal opposition," nor did it encourage its own "loyal opposition" in the free (non-territorial) churches.

In sum, German Protestants failed to set an agenda for the century. In such major questions as national unity, social oppression, church polity, and even theology, they were largely reactionary. The basic reason for this orientation was that the churches failed to secure their independence early in the century, when that may have been possible. Why they did not, and what the circumstances were, is the study's plot. It is the story of the unwritten religious "charter."

There are subordinate themes, of course. The "charter" linked Protestant church life to the century's social, economic, and political developments. It was one reason why the churches were anti-revolutionary during the revolutions that "failed to turn the corner" in 1848, and in the liberal national revolution that failed to achieve national unification. But the churches provided religious support and theological justification for the conservative nationalism that helped unify Germany "from above"; in the new Empire, the annual Sedan Festival symbolized their continuing interest in this assignment. Protestant involvement in Christian and anti-Christian anti-Semitism, as well as the churches' relations with Jews throughout the century, were other implemental phases of the unwritten "charter."

That Protestants agreed to give higher priority to the national question than to the social problem is not difficult to understand, though the consequences were enormous. In general, the churches responded in a reactionary way to problems accompanying industrialization and urbanization. The unwritten "charter" explains the limited extent of social consciousness among Protestants, as well as their inability to battle materialism and Social Democracy effectively.

Another sub-theme is the interrelation between political and ecclesiastical particularism, namely, each state's propensity to maintain local prerogatives. Why did German

Protestants never achieve a national church? How did states use church polity on behalf of the unwritten "charter?" How did a revolution in church polity help forge the consensus about the church's social role? How did territories begin levying church taxes? How were the religious awakenings deeply rooted in territorial particularism, and how did the surrogate nationalism of these awakenings help defuse liberal nationalism? In what ways did territorial particularism influence Protestant-Roman Catholic relations in the Cologne Troubles, and the "Kulturkampf?" These and other questions demand answers, and the unwritten Protestant "charter" provides a helpful set of hermeneutics.

I have weighed the monarch's influence on Protestant church life, and found it to be substantial. For example, royal treasuries financed a sizable number of new churches and church renovations. In material terms, the monarch's concern for church buildings was a clear signal of his interest in the "charter."

Church life at all levels bore the imprint of the consensus about the church's social role. It was stamped on preaching and liturgy, liturgical books and vital records, ceremonial unions between Lutheran and Reformed confessions, and the free churches' many problems. The problem of compulsory religious instruction was a nerve nodule of special importance. Naturally, pastors were the major functionaries in local church life. They were a rather docile lot, bureaucratic in outlook. But could one expect more of a man who usually waited five to ten years after theological training before the "candidate" became the "pastor," with all attendant rights and responsibilities? The clergyman was living proof that social modeling was the chief component of the church-state consensus.

Protestant church life was more like a symphony than a train, and in this "century of the masses" the theme of the "charter" recurred on every page of the musical score. True to form, German Protestants produced their share of new voluntary organizations for philanthropy, moral reform, evangelization, foreign missions and other purposes. But "authorized" voluntaryism worked best, as ecclesiastical authorities and others ensured that voluntary organizations

served the wider society as examples of "freedom within
authority." The "charter's" most serious attacks came from
individuals and groups that resisted such cooptation, such
as the theoretical challenge of the Young Hegelians, or the
confessional challenge of the Old Lutherans.

But the century belonged to the broad middle, not the
radicals on either side. Three major clerical groups
mirrored the larger social structure. More often than not,
the conservatives were allied with aristocratic and peasant
groups; the liberals with academicians, the "educated," and
politically oriented liberals; and the mediating party with
the rising middle class or bourgeoisie. Church periodicals
helped advance their causes.

Conservatives usually endorsed the working arrangement
between church and state, though they sometimes sought a
more rigid theological orthodoxy than others could bear.
Some liberals called for church disestablishment, or even
the church's dissolution, but seldom did they seize the
cudgel and translate words into actions. The mediating
group was an intermediary between the others. Its
adherents were heavily responsible for implementing the
unwritten "charter," since their efforts to reconcile the
conservatives' emphasis on authority and the liberals' on
freedom epitomized the church's modeling function. It was
their century for upward mobility, but not at too great a
cost to the conservatives' aristocratic-agrarian alliance.
These three groups danced with different partners in the
mid-century revolutions, until circumstances forced them
into a threesome stepping to the right.

The study also asks the question of the "charter's"
theoretical and theological foundations. The impact of the
romantic movement, Schleiermacher, and Hegel, as well as
the important work of cultural Protestant theologians,
should not be underestimated. Nor can we ignore the close
relation between theological conviction and political
opinion among many Protestant churchmen. Also important is
the fact that Lutheran confessionalism was at times an
expression of antagonism toward Prussia's growing hegemony;
that was evident in the late sixties, when Prussia annexed
several Lutheran territories while confessionalists
resisted being taken into her union church.

Special consideration is also given to the interrelation of national and social problems, and their impact within Protestantism; the effects of social diversity and social change; and historical factors behind the Protestant response to National Socialism in the twentieth century. I have tried to illuminate aspects of church life that sometimes are overlooked, using statistical evidence where helpful, and have saught to fill some of the gaps in English literature on the awakenings, the "Gemeinschaftsbewegung," eschatological zeal, and military chaplains. Also included are thumbnail sketches of the lives and thought of Wichern, Ritschl, Rothe, Hegel, Harnack, Schleiermacher, Stahl, Bismarck, Ludwig von Gerlach, Hengstenberg, Draeseke, Hanstein, the Young Hegelians, Frederick William IV, William II, Stilling, Claus Harms, Stoecker, Nauman, Christoph Blumhardt, Weitling, and others who significantly influenced church life.

This is not the place to broach the problem of periodization, but a comment is in order on the study's chronological limits. For me, "nineteenth century" signifies the period between the War of Liberation and World War I, roughly from 1806 to 1914, although the narrative reaches beyond these boundaries when necessary. Without doubt, this period was a political unit in German history. I agree with Friedrich Meinecke and Hajo Holborn that 1819, 1848 and 1866 were three tragic turning points in modern German history; World War I was unquestionably another.

But since politics is not an end in itself, this political century was also a social and economic unit. Industrialization, urbanization, and other significant social changes set apart this segment of the German calendar as an identifiable whole. The churches' responses to social and economic developments, and their political ramifications, made the churches an integral part of this centenary unit. For example, the rapid spread of voluntary groups, the Inner Mission's social programs, and efforts to find rapprochement with Social Democracy could not have occurred in a previous period.

Theologically, too, these years cohere as a unit. Historians speak of the "cultural Protestantism" that

Schleiermacher engendered early in the century, by
proposing to investigate the theological ramifications of
Kant's philosophical work. Liberal and mediating
theologians propagated this theological strain most
consistently, and it held the field until the Great War.
In sum, the confluence of social, economic, political, and
theological currents led me to focus on the decades between
1800 and 1920. They make up the century of the Protestant
"charter" in Germany.

Several personal experiences have left their imprint on
this work. My first acquaintance with nineteenth century
German theologians brought the mistaken impression that
they lived and worked in a vacuum. Further efforts to find
relevant material in English on their church-historical
context were largely unfruitful or unsatisfying. Even
today, the number of works in English on nineteenth century
German Protestantism is very limited. Among them are
several chapters in two older works, Andrew Landale
Drummond's GERMAN PROTESTANTS SINCE LUTHER (London, 1951),
and Kenneth Scott Latourette's second volume of
CHRISTIANITY IN A REVOLUTIONARY AGE (New York, 1959), as
well as two specialized studies, William O. Shanahan's
GERMAN PROTESTANTS FACE THE SOCIAL QUESTION; THE
CONSERVATIVE PHASE (Notre Dame, 1954), and Robert M.
Bigler's THE POLITICS OF GERMAN PROTESTANTISM: THE RISE OF
THE PROTESTANT CHURCH ELITE IN PRUSSIA, 1815--1848
(Berkely, 1972). Several volumes have recently appeared on
individual theologians, but relevant information on church
life is still inadequate.

Another formative experience was my graduate work in the
history of Christianity at the University of Chicago. My
disseration, which examined the idea of God's kingdom as a
propaganda symbol among nineteenth century German
Protestants, gave impetus to this work, although it was
much more restricted in scope. Professor Martin E.
Marty's enduring interest in the place of religion in
culture and society, and Professor Leonard Krieger's THE
GERMAN IDEA OF FREEDOM (2nd ed.; Chicago, 1974), influenced
me appreciably.

The third was my involvement in a bitter ecclesiastical
controversy. Despite talk about religious freedom in the
United States, I experienced oppression and legalistic

pressure in ways that illuminated for me the complex history of German Protestantism. The administration of The Lutheran Church--Missouri Synod displayed many of the characteristics of state governments, as they manipulated the fortunes of Protestant churches in nineteenth century Germany. After being terminated as a college teacher because of my theological views, I found the community of Concordia Seminary in Exile (Seminex, later also called Christ Seminary) stimulating and refreshing. But the experience left its imprint.

A glossary of German terms and a brief annotated bibliography are appended to the text. All titles of books and journals are fully capitalized, and foreign language words have been placed in quotation marks.

ACKNOWLEDGEMENTS

The American revivalist Henry Ward Beecher warned that "a church debt is the devil's salary." Presumably a church historian's debt is also tainted—better paid than not! And while a list of liabilities never pays one's debt in full, it is a beginning.

I owe much to many for information, stimulation and encouragement, and in a rather impersonal way the bibliography catalogs the names of some of these persons. Among others who have provided special guidance and encouragement over the years are three scholars at the University of Chicago: Martin E. Marty, Leonard Krieger, and Jerald C. Brauer. Colleagues at Christ Seminary—Seminex in St. Louis, MO, sometimes asked what I was doing in my spare time. Dr. John Tietjen and Dr. John Damm showed special interest in the work's progress.

A number of German scholars made important contributions in correspondence and during my visit to Germany in 1973. They include Paul Ernst, Fritz Fischer, Werner Jochmann, Hermann Kuhlow, Gerhard Schaefer, Hans-Joachim Schoeps and Horst Weigelt.

Nancy Asher Groh did a yeowoman's job typing and proofreading the original manuscript. Her continuing interest and evenhanded encouragement added to the debt that love alone can seek to repay.

Several students at Seminex, including George Gehant, Thomas Becker, Don Flaxbart, and Martin Pauschke, read all or parts of the manuscript and offered helpful comments. Also helpful were the criticisms and comments of Professor Martin E. Marty, Bishop Stephen C. Neill, Professors Kurt Hendel and Edward Schroeder of Seminex, and several others who read all or parts of various drafts.

During 1973-74, a National Endowment for the Humanities Younger Humanist Fellowship provided time for research and writing. The Endowment's concern for all phases of the humanities, including religion, is one of its most positive features.

Debts to libraries are usually as difficult to pay as church debts. Behind every library stands the governmental unit, university, or private donors that support it, and I acknowledge my debt to them, as well as to the libraries. The following libraries and staffs provided valuable assistance during my research: Regenstein Library of the University of Chicago, which houses the Hengstenberg Collection; Christ Seminary-Seminex; Eden Theological Seminary; St. Louis University; the university libraries of Tuebingen, Erlangen, Goettingen, and Hamburg; Free University in West Berlin; Humbolt University in East Berlin; Berlin Hochschule for Evangelical Theology; Deutsche Staatsbibliothek in East Berlin; the Archives of the Baden-Wuerttemberg Evangelical Church in Stuttgart; the Blumhardt Family Archives in Stuttgart; the Institute for the History of National Socialism in Hamburg; and the Seminar for Religious and Intellectual History in Erlangen.

I also want to thank the JOURNAL OF CHURCH AND STATE for permission to use copyrighted material from my article on Friedrich Naumann, entitled "Friedrich Naumann: From Christian Socialist to Social Darwinist," XVII,1 <Winter, 1975>, 25-46.

No longer young enough to know everything, I know that I have forgotten some important creditors. But I ask their pardon, just as I ask that the errors and mistaken judgments found in this work not be attributed to those whom I have remembered. The errors are mine alone.

J.E.G.

CHAPTER I

LIMITED OPTIONS

As the nineteenth century opened, there was some
possibility that German Protestants might view the church's
role in ways that differed from the past. In the century's
early decades, church-state relations, as well as the
church's role in society, were discussed at length in
German society, culture and politics. While there were few
options in the real world, people with fertile minds
debated the issues in these years of change and upheaval.
For most of them the more important question was not, "What
should be the church's role?", but rather, "What should be
the relationship between state and society?" The answer to
the second question significantly shaped the answer to the
first.

At least three groups tried to answer the question. The
first based its arguments on societal considerations.
Representing societal spokesmen who saw the benefit of a
national church in a unified nation, the nationalist
"Turnvater" Jahn envisioned a "single German church
independent in faith." Speaking for culture and its loving
critics, the philosopher Johann G. Fichte proposed the
second option when he described the church as a colony sent
from heaven, to "enroll citizens for that foreign state,
wherever it can take root." More pragmatic, more forceful,
and ultimately more influential were the political answers
of monarchs and state servants. In 1806, for example, the
Bavarian king provided an "answer" of sorts when he ordered
the city officials of Nuremberg to conduct special church
services on the day that Bavaria assumed control of the
formerly imperial city. "The sermon should comment on a

1

suitable text referring to the change in government," he wrote, "and it should be followed by a singing of the solemn Te Deum Laudamus."(1)

In the first group, liberal convictions lay at the base of the national liberals' nationalism. They thought that a unified society should mirror itself in a unified German nation, and they often spoke of the church as a unified national institution, with its basis in society. Leaders in the second group were more apt to stress cultural rather than social values; they tended to view the church as the state's moral agent. In the realm of politics, monarchs, princes, and their bureaucrats usually looked on their territorial churches as a unit in the political structure, whose function it was to inculcate social, cultural and political views.

For the history of German Protestants, then, the decade between 1806 and 1817 is the story of how political developments overshadowed national liberals and the proponents of cultural philosophy, as well as their role descriptions for the church. After reviewing the scripts they proposed, we will examine three political developments that encouraged Protestants to see the church as the state's model for society. Most of the chapter concentrates on the formative events that brought consensus about the church's role as a social model: a state-imposed revolution in church polity, religious facets of the War of Liberation, and the formation of church unions between Lutheran and Reformed congregations. This process laid the foundation of the "unwritten charter," or agreement, between churches and states that persisted throughout the century.

ONE SOCIETY, ONE CHURCH, ONE NATION?

One vision of the church's place in society arose among those who wanted a national church to personify the unity and solidarity of German society—and hopefully of the German nation. Many of these visionaries were national liberals who, like most European liberals before 1848,

sought to liberalize the whole society in one fell swoop
through national unification. There was a consistent
conservative quality about their liberal ideas on limited
suffrage, respect for education, civility and property, and
acceptance of monarchy as the proper form of government.
They understood the deep religious roots of German
territorial particularism, and they hoped for a national
church rooted in a national society

The Enlightenment's ideal of one evangelical church for all
of Germany seemed to have new appeal in all the German
states after the German Empire collapsed in 1806.
Protestants in all the German states lost their only
institutional bond in August of that year with the end of
the "corpus evangelicorum," an imperial board with
representatives from all the evangelical churches. The
commission's problems became a matter for decision on the
territorial level.

One response was a number of suggestions for a national
church. In 1810, "Turnvater" Jahn proposed the formation
of a German church that would serve as a tool of statecraft
and provide information on national unity, while also
stressing morality, reason and humanity. Six years later
the theologian Gottlieb J. Planck complained that "we have
no church, only churches; as an ecclesiastical community we
have no central administration." His proposed national
church was to take the place of the defunct "corpus
evangelicorum," while the Weimar theologian Alfred Mueller
wanted to renew the commission without its imperial
trappings.

Others endorsed the idea of a sacred religious place to
symbolize German or evangelical unity on a national level.
The nationalist poet Ernst M. Arndt wanted to build a
temple—a sacred place for all Germans—on the battlefield
near Leipzig where Napoleon was routed in 1813; he also
suggested a "German Society" for Germans of all
confessions, and a songbook with the best of Christian
hymnody from the last three hundred years. The future
senator from Hamburg, Karl Sieveking, wanted to memorialize
the victory at Leipzig with a "cathedral for all Germans,"
and the Berlin theologian Wilhelm DeWette asked that each
town build a Gothic church for all confessions, in memory
of the "newly resurrected faith and liberated fatherland."

3

Many talked of a national monument to Luther, though after 1815 the Reformer lost his stature as a universal figure for all confessions.

The three hundredth anniversary of the Reformation in 1817 was a focal point for agitation about a national church. The Swabian theologian Johann F. Bahmaier, called the "southern Arndt" because of his collection of nationalist songs, said that God had a great future for Germany if the nation renewed itself in Him. His periodical, entitled CAECILIA, included a program for full national revival and unity; its tricentennial Reformation issue urged readers to fan the glowing coals of unity among Germans who had recently tasted victory in 1813.

In 1817, Student Unions ("Burschenschaften") at various universities led the way in celebrating the anniversary of the Reformation, as well as the recent victory over the French. Attacking the territorial particularism that flourished on university campuses, the unions revised membership qualifications to admit males from all territories. All "Germans and Christians" could join, including converted Jews.

Universities had become centers of dissent after the War of Liberation in 1813-14. Some professors campaigned for human rights and national unity, and especially at Jena and Giessen, students protested the "business as usual" atmosphere. They viewed the war not only as a campaign against alien Frenchmen, but also as the start of a struggle to liberalize and unify the German states. Their black, red and gold flags symbolized the bloody transition from the night of slavery to the golden day of freedom.

Jena's romantic, youthful enthusiasm complemented the rather stern and exclusivistic spirit of the Student Union at Giessen, where previously no liberal tradition was to be found. The chief agitator at Giessen, named Karl Follen, recruited students to discuss the writings of Moeser, Schiller, Koerner, Arndt, Fichte and other nationalist writers. Clothed in black velvet coats and daggers, long haired student cultivated physical fitness and opposed such traditions as dueling. Follen's religious views contributed to his preference for republicanism over monarchism; he also hoped for a national church based on

Christ's teachings.

In August of 1817, a representative from Jena invited twelve other societies to a mid-October celebration of the Reformation and the Battle of Leipzig. The date coincided with the battle's anniversary, but did not conflict with official Reformation ceremonies later that month. Many hoped that this cultic celebration of national unity would demolish confessional barriers between Roman Catholics and Protestants.

Three hundred and sixty-six students and faculty members from a score of universities registered for the event in historic Wartburg, Thuringia. The states most heavily represented were Thuringia (117), Prussia (69) and Mecklenberg (40). About 40 percent of the students were law students, and another 40 percent were students of theology; Jena had the largest delegation of theological students with sixty-nine, followed by Goettingen (16) and Erlangen (8).(2)

This celebration of national unity in 1817 was filled with songs, speeches, protest activities and a communion service. Students and professors hailed Germany's high calling and the need for national unification; they discussed the role of the Student Unions, as well as the relationship between Luther's "inner" liberation and Germany's liberation from Napoleon. A philosophy student from Jena urged those present to form an alliance that breathed Luther's spirit. Professor Jakob F. Fries of Jena challenged his audience to do God's will by freeing and uniting the German states. Reenacting a scene from Luther's life, the students put the torch to old books inscribed with the titles of recently published conservative books. Arndt had earlier suggested that bonfires should be used to observe the victory at Leipzig, but governmental athorities were terrified by this juvenile act at Wartburg.

The Student Union festival in 1817 was an effort to strengthen the spirit of national identity and freedom. It stressed that a national church was an important element in the struggle; nationalist sentiment, social integration, and feelings of camaraderie—not dogma—were to be the confessional basis of this church. But this vision of the

5

church's place in society held little attraction for most because it would radically restructure church-state relations. The academicians who gathered at Wartburg had an extremely narrow support base in society, and soon the states' reactionary policies cut short their movement. They were no more successful than other proponents of a national church in posing a viable option for the church's role description.

THE CHURCH AS BENEFACTOR OF HUMANITY?

Cultural leaders were less concerned with the church's place in society than with the relation between church and state, although they broached this issue indirectly. For them, the church found its identity in the context of the state, as guardian of society and benefactor of humanity.

When he claimed that religion was the "highest humanity," the "essential blood of the human soul," the Lutheran pastor and philosopher of history Johann G. Herder (1744-1803) added individuality, feeling, and religion to the idea of "humanity" that was espoused by the enlightened poet and playwright, Gotthold E. Lessing (1729-91). Herder viewed man's history as God's revelation, the pedagogical process that gave growth to humanity. The church's task was to preach Jesus' philanthropic message: the fatherhood of God and the brotherhood of man.

Not all were so religious in their emphasis. Some called this man a pantheistic determinist, and true to that description, the great poet Goethe (1749-1832) advised men to ignore religion and find strength in humanity. In a short couplet, the Apostle of Eros asked the question, "What religion do I confess? None from all those That you name! 'And why none?' Without religion."

But in his discussion of God's kingdom, the pivotal philosopher Immanuel Kant (1724-1804) provided more specific instruction about religion and the church's nature. As he understood it, this kingdom of virtue was a moral community that drew the individual toward morality, fulfilling a task which the state could not accomplish with its limited geography and political structure. Since Kant made no distinction between religion and morality, he thought that God's kingdom was the foundation of the moral community called the church. The church's function was to complete the work of Jesus and his apostles, and to enable men to obey the law of moral freedom by exercising their autonomous will. Ultimately, the moral kingdom would conquer evil and inaugurate an aeon of perpetual peace.

The thought of the idealist philosopher Johann G. Fichte (1762-1814) was equally complicated. The biblical text that was inscribed on his tombstone--"Those who are wise (teachers) shall shine like the heaven's splendor"—presumed that visitors to his grave knew that he tried to deduce everything from the nature of consciousness. He thought that insight into moral activity provided the fullest understanding of man and nature; God's kingdom consummated the long struggle to unify human and divine in personality, but the kingdom was also an indeterminate future point without explicit content, since reality itself was infinite activity. Religion showed that man secured freedom by reflecting on his use of reason, realizing in the process that his consciousness of humanity was knowledge of God in man. Religion enabled man to reach his full potential; his first moral act, the perfection of subjectivity, removed the barrier separating him from God. Christianity's purpose was to educate people in the dual nature of the kingdom, its cosmic and its personal ramifications. Sent from heaven as a colony to "enroll citizens for that foreign state, wherever it can take root," the church provided "education for salvation in heaven."

These and other German thinkers used the idea of "Humanitaet" (humanity) to collect such major themes of the German Enlightenment as government by law, self-fulfilment, intellectual self-reliance, and man's unity in nature and morality. They argued that social and political action would not provide a system of values, and so they turned to the unifying idea of "Bildung" (formation, cultivation) to monitor and control the advances of the Enlightenment. One modern scholar defines the term as a "painstaking, precarious process of individual growth and self-definition whereby a person might bring his nascent humanity to

7

fruition in a society that offered few aids and still fewer human models worthy of imitation."(3)

Cultural idealists generally conceded that the cultured individual needed to progress from the "representation" of religion to the logical "notion" of philosophy. And although the idealists implied a highly pluralistic ethic for personal development, they offered no significant social ethic. Supposedly, one's absolute obedience to the state's positive law eliminated the need to wrestle with the question of social ethics, while still allowing a place for Christian charity in the state.

In this way, German idealism, together with its description of cultural formation, tried to infuse life with new "religious" meaning, but in the process it transferred responsibility for ethical and spiritual life and behavior from the church to the state. The idealist philosopher Georg W. F. Hegel (1770-1831) found the church to be no more important for the political realm than did the Lutheran historian Leopold von Ranke (1795-1886), a devout Christian who defined the church as a mysterious community with no positive influence on human events, as long as it did its proper work of providing and defending an unchanging religious rule. Ranke contended that the church lost spiritual power when it claimed secular power.

In sum, for many of these spokesmen the church was an unnecessary but desirable appendage to culture and state. The educated viewed institutionalized religion as a wet nurse for children who were unable to drink the spirits of philosophy. As educated adults abandoned religion in favor of aesthetic culture, a chasm divided German culture from the churches, while drama and music became the new cult's preaching and liturgy.(4)

By 1815, idealists began discarding the idea of "Bildung" by turning the question of self-definition into a cosmic question, for which the individual's resources were inadequate. This approach to philosophy, one modern scholar observes, was "well suited to a people for whom almost any alternative was preferable to actuality and for whom almost no alternative to actuality existed but such a philosophy."(5) But it brought little advantage to religion, and even less to the institutional church,

8

neither did it offer a constructive answer to the question of the church's identity and role in times of change. Cultured people continued to suggest that the church should function as the political system's moral teacher, but it should derive its teachings from the state's high priest, the philosopher. This option also failed as a role description for the Protestant churches in the German states.

THE STATE'S MODEL FOR SOCIETY

Shattering political events occurred in Germany in the century's early decades. The social and political elite involved in these events--not the spokesmen for a national church, or the cultured men of letters--spoke the definitive word about the church's role. Realigning and intensifying traditional beliefs on the subject, they delineated the church's relation to the state and its place in society. Their decisions and actions before 1819 etched the outline of an "unwritten charter" for the Protestant churches. In this area, as in many others, they retained the initiative over spokesmen for society, as well as the cultural critics and philosophers.

During several decades of reform and administrative centralization, the church became the state's model for society. Prussia's reform campaign between 1806 and 1813 was the mainspring for important changes in church polity, for religious involvement in the controlled revolt against the French (the "Erhebung"), and for the creation of church unions between Lutherans and Reformed. These developments firmed up the emerging consensus that the church was to serve as the state's model for social institutions, and for society at large. This unwritten agreement about the church's role I have called the Protestant "charter."

The primary challenge facing the Prussian reformers in 1806 was to redefine the proper relationship between state and society. The Revolution in France, as well as French occupation of some German states, once again raised the ticklish question of society's traditional role as servant of the state. Rapid social change intensified the question. During the period of bureaucratic reform, the Prussian reformers tried to implement social and political reforms that would encourage social groups to provide more effective assistance for an occupied and humiliated state. Their reform efforts reached to the church, where they resulted in extensive polity changes. The reformer Hardenburg liked to say that reforms were aimed at implementing democratic principles in monarchical disguise, but his reforming knife had two edges in the religious area, as well as in others. The collapse of the old Empire in 1806 also stirred reforming zeal in other states.

As rulers formed supra-confessional territorial churches, so-called "union churches," especially in the largest Protestant state, Prussia, they based their efforts on the foundation laid by the revolution in church polity. These two pivotal developments, together with religious involvement in the War of Liberation in 1813-14, clearly signalled that the states intended for the churches to nurture a spirit of service and submission to the state. The evangelical church was not to be a vibrant social force, manifesting German solidarity in a national unit, nor was it merely to serve as the state's moral teacher. It was to be the state's chief model for society, a model that showed how a major social institution attained a degree of freedom by living responsibly within boundaries set by state authority.

REVOLUTION IN CHURCH POLITY

When the German Empire came to its end in 1806, evangelical churches in the German states came under the direct and unrestrained supervision of the territorial rulers. Protestants no longer had any appeal to the imperial commission for Protestant religious affairs, the "corpus evangelicorum." As each territory tried to assume the functions of the Empire, a revolution in church polity shook the evangelical churches. In Prussia, the reform movement was part of an effort to fill the gap left by the Empire, and to throw off French control as well. This movement had a direct effect on church polity.

Signs of the polity revolution were visible as early as 1803, and by 1817 it extended to the area of interconfessional relations, when ecclesiastical unions were formed between Lutheran and Reformed Protestants. The convoluted history of this revolution—and it is not an easy story to tell—must be laid out, since it was an important element in the emergence of the state-imposed consensus about the church's social assignment. We will investigate the religious repercussions of the Empire's collapse, and then turn to the largest Protestant state, to see how the Prussian reform movement between 1806 and 1813 had long range effects on the church's political structure.

Imperial Collapse and Church Polity

Military defeat, French occupation, the hope of liberation, and liberal agitators helped stimulate a spirit of social and political reform in the German states. But in some cases, the most immediate stimulus for alterations in church polity came from the realignment of old borders, and the formation of new states when the Empire neared its end, and when Napoleon assumed administrative control of some areas in the Rhenish Confederation (1806). Various reforms were required to collect new revenues and incorporate new geographical areas into old political units.

As early as the year of 1803, for example, the "Reichsdeputationshauptschluss" (Final Recess), a meeting of imperial representatives, authorized princes to expropriate church property, but required that they provide "adequate and permanent support for all cathedral churches and pensions for all dispossessed canons." Free to use monastic property to subsidize their general revenue funds, and to finance religion, education, and charitable efforts, the princes assumed full responsibility for church finances, public welfare, and education. The Final Recess substantially reduced the number of imperial principalities (then over 300 in number) by secularizing church lands. The borders of Hesse-Kassel, Hesse-Darmstadt, Nassau, and Bavaria shifted appreciably, while Prussia received the bishopric of Paderborn, parts of Muenster, areas around the

11

Harz and north of Thuringia, and the imperial cities of Muehlhausen, Nordhausen and Goslar. One sure sign that the Empire was in serious trouble was the fact that for the first time in years, Protestant rulers attained a majority in the council of imperial electors.

These border adjustments, as well as others inaugurated by Napoleon, raised the fervor for change in church polity. The enlarged state of Baden required rather substantial realignments after the settlement of 1803 increased her Roman Catholic population to over 600,000 people, while there were 230,000 Lutherans and 60,000 Reformed. In 1807, Baden merged the Palatinate's Reformed Church Council with the Lutheran Church Council at Karlsruhe to form the Evangelical High Church Council, subsequently absorbed into the state's Ministry of Interior in 1809. Meanwhile, in Bavaria the Roman Catholic king took personal charge of the Protestants transferred to his realm in 1803. Five years later he transferred the responsibility to the Ministry of Interior, and this arrangement prevailed until 1818, when a Supreme Consistory of four clergymen and two laymen assumed control. In 1811 the king announced that the sale of Lutheran hymnals and Protestant school books would provide a pension for clergymen and their widows. Protestant preachers were addressed as "royal clergy," but not until 1824 did the Protestant communion receive the offical title of "church." Their minority status, and the administrative structure of their territorial church, were special burdens for evangelicals in Bavaria.

The policies of King Frederick I of Wuerttemberg were no less oppressive. With Napoleon's help, Frederick scaled the ladder of success from duke (1797) to prince (1803), and finally king (1806-16). He looked on the windfall of the Final Recess as conquered territory; "new" Wuerttemberg included 400,000 Roman Catholics added to his realm. He assigned to the Spiritual Department of the Ministry of Interior the administration of the Roman Catholic Church, and also the religious affairs of the remaining two-thirds of the population, the Protestants. Although he insisted on equal rights for all, he took away much of the Lutheran Church's independence, and controlled the endowment funds it had collected to support churches, schools and charities. The king made few friends in 1804 when he ordered the clergy, his "religious teachers," to encourage good health, and to urge parishioners to be vaccinated against smallpox. Royal orders in 1806 and 1811 set standards for clerical dress in the street and in the chancel, and proposed fashions for beards and haircuts. Frederick also eliminated the reading of the Augsburg Confession during Lutheran Reformation services, and in 1809 he gravely offended pietists by promulgating a rationalistic liturgy purged of all references to the devil.

Prussian Reform and Religion

Prussia launched a zealous reform effort after her army suffered a humiliating defeat to the French at Jena in 1806. Baron Karl Stein and other reformers suggested that if the state wanted to rally all classes to its defense, it would have to eliminate a number of social abuses. His plan to implement reform through a strengthened ministerial system included a prominent place for religion, and that is why we must take a closer look at the reform movement as a backdrop for radical changes in Prussian church polity.

In view of his interest in religion, Stein might well have penned these anonymous lines from a brochure entitled PRUSSIA'S FUTURE, although, of course, he did not: "From you, you preachers, we demand that the spirit of greatness and goodness be returned. You have killed it, destroyed the kingdom of truth, and instead preached yourselves—poor and powerless--to the people." Heavily influenced by the Enlightenment, he felt that the state would benefit greatly if it fulfilled its responsibility of revitalizing popular religious zeal. In 1811 he wrote these words to another major Prussian reformer, Hardenberg:

> <Such popular support for the state> can only be stimulated by institutions that kindle religious sentiments, and by such political institutions as absorb all the forces of the nation. How to arouse such a religious sense, and how to direct it toward the love and defense of the fatherland, what liturgical measures to take—about that you will hear proposals by the spirited Professor Schleiermacher.

The reformers clearly salvaged one of the legacies of the Enlightenment, namely, the state's responsibility for cultivating religion. In theory at least, religion was for them purely a private affair, the inner fountain of life, not confessional groupings that collected individuals into larger circles of faith. This view made religion a unifying instrument for a weak and threatened state, but it also assumed that the government could effectively administer the territorial church, with little or no ecclesiastical interference or self-government. The Prussian Territorial Law ("Landrecht") took a somewhat different position; it did not refer to a territorial church since it had been adopted in 1794, while the Empire was still functioning. And even Stein may have preferred provincial churches over a single territorial church for Protestants. But these differences were a matter of degree rather than kind, and church polity reform soon became a item on the reformer's agenda.

Set on using bureaucratic machinery for semi-liberal purposes at the turn of the century, the reformers confronted the reliable core of German conservativism: the territorial ruler, the aristocracy and the army officer corps it provided, the city patriciate, guild masters, and the peasantry. The bureaucracy's success was limited, since the monarch was more interested in preserving aristocratic privileges than in achieving middle class ideals. Another related problem was the cleavage between army and society, since the officers' training institutions were not related to the civil system or higher education.

The bureaucrats were the shock troops of the reform movement, which also included the army's reform between 1806 and 1814. They were attracted to administrative work as long as the state retained the initiative in charting a course of social development. Their work was a commitment to a novel element in German history: the "conscious ideal" of the state as bearer of culture. Composed of civil servants, professors, secondary teachers, and some clergy, the middle class was less interested in destroying the authoritarian state than in reforming it; it was to be a state based on justice and cultural values, but not deficient in raw political power. Challenged to determine which social authorities were required to cultivate this new spirit, and trained to screen out inconsequential social forces and conditions, the bureaucrats forged a political theory with power at the center. Instead of overcoming class distinctions in German society, this theory imposed what Hajo Holborn called a "sharp ideological rigidity" on class distinctions.(6) In addition, the bureaucrats accented the rights and responsibilities of accepted social institutions—including the church—that supported the state's common goal. In the name of a liberal objective, namely, social and political reform, they made administrative control a decree of state for regulating social life at all levels.

The reform of town governments was one of the few enduring successes of the Prussian reformers, although it did not appreciably affect church life. The diversity of practice and tradition in peasant ownership complicated efforts at agrarian reform. Peasants made up three-fourths of the population of Prussia and most of the other states. Between 1799 and 1805, the Prussian crown freed its peasants, while 50,000 freehold farms were formed in the eastern provinces, excluding Silesia. But the reformers did not succeed in extending their coverage to serfs on noble property. As a result, the agrarian settlement of 1816 set the terms of ownership for the next fifty years. While reducing the number of medium-sized peasant farms and increasing the number of large noble estates, the settlement failed to create a large class of prosperous peasants who could have pulled Prussia to the left during the period of industrialization.

Prussia's unsuccessful attempt at agrarian reform precipitated an aristocratic resurgence, which in turn affected the church's fortunes directly. The periodical published by the aristocratic Christian-German Table Society in Berlin vigorously opposed the reformers' proposals. Nobles were afraid of being offered on the altar of state survival. Their renewed interest in religious matters, especially in the religious Awakening, was partly due to local alliances between patrons and preachers. The country squire's right to serve as patron of the local church persisted until 1918, and throughout the century, the running battle between centralized (royal) and local control of ecclesiastical polity was one facet of

15

the continuing squabble over patronage rights. But the nobility held firm. For example, in 1789 the province of East Prussia had 243 parishes (62 percent of the total) under royal patronage, 138 (35 percent) with noble patrons, ten parishes supported by towns, and only two independent parishes. The percentages changed little in the course of the century.

As part of Hardenberg's response to fiscal crisis, the Prussian king took control of the income and property rights of all Protestant and Roman Catholic institutions on October 30, 1810. The Prussian state now had access to revenues previously channeled to high officials in church and state, although it also had to assume financial responsibility for the churches. Seven days later the monarch's Spiritual and Educational Deputation in each province instructed all Lutheran, Reformed and Roman Catholic clergymen to give public recognition to the royal decree scheduled to be issued on November 11, which would guarantee each subject's "holy rights of personal freedom." Pastors were instructed to use the Gospel pericope for November 25 to comment on human rights and duties, authority, and the monarch's welfare. Observing that the clergy's public prayers for the king would be a good example for the people, this carefully worded directive showed the reformers performing their high wire act: they tried to maintain firm monarchical control, while securing popular support by reforming social abuses. In Prussia, the church's refined social role was emerging; the church served as the state's moral mouthpiece, while the government coopted and exploited new social movements.

Ecclesiastical Polity Reform

In Prussia, the polity revolution associated with the reform movement gave a clear signal about the church's appointed role as model for society. In the course of a decade, the evangelical church was stripped of most self-government, and made a department of state. That unilateral process pointed up the significance of the "political" option, and contributed to the emerging understanding that the church's primary task was to model "freedom within authority" for the rest of society.

Prussia's ecclesiastical reform movement centered in the polity decisions of 1808. For all practical purposes, the reforms rendered inoperative the religious sections of the "Allgemeine Landrecht," or Territorial Law, of 1794. When eventually the Ministry of Interior assumed control of ecclesiastical affairs, the church partially ceased to exist as an independent organization; the "Landrecht's" recognition of congregational and individual freedom was largely ignored.

The reformers' first step in 1808 was to abolish the Lutheran and Reformed consistories, administrative church boards on the provincial and territorial levels. For the first time since the Reformation, the state assumed full responsibility for administering the churches. In 1808 as well, Prussia formed provincial boards for ecclesiastical and educational affairs, called "Geistliche und Schuldeputationen" (Spiritual and Educational Departments), to manage religious affairs for all three confessions in a province of the state. On the territorial level, the Ministry of Interior housed a Section of Public Worship and Instruction, headed after 1810 by Ludwig Nicolovius, a close friend of Stein and other reformers.

The elimination of confessional consistories had a direct impact on Prussia's chaplain corps and military church. In 1811, the provincial boards for ecclesiastical and educational affairs, together with the Section of Public Worship and Instruction in the state's Ministry of Interior, assumed full administrative control of chaplains and military churches. Since the military consistory and field provost were phased out, army chaplains found their niche within the civilian church's provincial structure. Inasmuch as the king considered the army his private domain, this organizational transfer gave him another entree into the civilian church, and signalled that his interest in the church might be as intense as his supervision of the army. Confessional consistories no longer supervised the witness of Lutheran and Reformed chaplains to men in uniform.

Implementing the provisions of the "Landrecht," the king retained control over external ecclesiastical affairs, called "jus circa sacra," including administrative matters, such as buildings and personnel. But in addition, he claimed the right to administer internal church affairs such as liturgy and doctrine, the so-called "jus sacrorum," which Lutheran and Reformed consistories previously controlled. The king and his chief ecclesiastical advisor, Frederick Sack, wanted to inaugurate a confessional union of sorts between Lutheran and Reformed Protestants at this time, but the reformers restrained their zeal. Their proposal was opportune, since the abolition of consistories was a decisive step toward union. All that remained of the previously identifiable Lutheran and Reformed churches were the individual congregations.

The elimination of consistories and of provincial boards for all three confessions was the high water mark of state church absolutism in Prussia. The monarch's control over "jus sacrorum" invalidated the state's claim that it was "confessionless." But at the same time, the reformers recognized that administrative fiat would not reignite religious zeal. Religious renewal probably hinged more on their ability to create congregational and ecclesiastical self-government, in moves that might have paralleled Stein's reform of town governments. But this possibility faced tremendous obstacles, ranging from the monarch's hesitancy, to the reticence of Lutheran churchmen in the east.

The loss of consistories was bemoaned more for the damage it was expected to bring to piety and spiritual religion than for the state's blatant usurpation of church rights. For example, early in 1809 Superintendent Ewald of Rathenow asked the king to restore the old system, or incorporate consistorial personnel in the new, so that their spiritual leadership might be salvaged. When the king finally answered his letter in May, the suggestion was rejected.

The resurgence of aristocratic influence affected polity developments in 1815 when, once again, each province formed a single consistory to administer all religious life in that governmental unit. But the consistories' new lease on life did not mean that bureaucratic absolutism had lost momentum. The king's continuing influence in matters of "jus sacrorum" was painfully clear to Protestants all too soon when he promulgated a new liturgical agenda, as the next chapter explains. At the same time, the clergymen and lay governmental officials who were members of the

18

consistories were effectively made part of the province's governmental structure, since the chief administrator of the province, the "Oberpraesident," served as the consistory's presiding officer. Because he functioned as the chief executive of territorial policy for the province while also supposedly representing regional interests, we can assume that the provincial consistory's role was equally ambiguous. The ambiguous nature of dual-hat appointments was a favorite Prussian tool for retaining centralized control, while giving another impression.(7)

At the same time that provincial consistories were reestablished in 1815, the state's central bureaucracy also created a more refined administrative structure for religious affairs. Chancellor Hardenberg kept both the Ministry of Interior and the Ministry of Finance in his own portfolio after 1808, but in 1813-14 each post received its own minister, with a more careful delineation of the responsibilities of the Ministry of Interior. It included a section of Public Worship and Instruction. Finally in November of 1817, the government formed a separate Ministry of Public Worship and Education, with separate sections for religion, education and medicine. Freiherr von Altenstein headed the new ministry; he was the first in a long string of department heads who were trained primarily in law.

The reconstitution of consistories, and the formation of a new central ministry, followed on the heels of the Congress of Vienna, the peace conference held in 1814-15 after the Napoleonic Wars. Against her wishes, Prussia received substantial holdings in the Rhineland at the Congress, but in return she had to yield a sizable portion of her Polish territory in the east. This trade-off assured that she would be deeply involved in western German affairs for years to come. As part of the new Prussia, a number of Reformed families in the Rhineland, such as the Stumms, Boeckings, Kraemers, and Roehlings, played significant roles in the area's economic development. They also took the lead in forming evangelical congregations in the new province. But since vast numbers of Roman Catholics in the western region also entered the Prussian kingdom, they gave the lie to the traditional description of the Prussian king as "foremost member" of a homogenous Protestant community. The same thing was happening elsewhere as well, but at least the Congress reduced the number of German states by over 90 percent, to a manageable figure of thirty-eight. Twelve states still had fewer than 50,000 inhabitants, but seven could boast of 50,000 to 100,000 people, while ten had 100,000 to 500,000 people, and nine counted their population at more than half a million.

In Rhineland-Westphalia, one of the areas given to Prussia, the reintroduction of consistories on a provincial level in 1815 did little to strengthen congregational autonomy. Lutheran and Reformed Protestants in the area had a long history of presbyterial and synodal self-government, and now consistories were used for the first time in some years. In the rest of Prussia, congregational patrons continued nominating candidates for parish openings after 1808, but the state retained the right of appointment. Some Prussian squires argued that this arrangement infringed on their rights, and congregations in the new western regions disapproved of the practice, since it violated their longstanding tradition of having congregations elect their pastors. In 1815, for example, only forty-seven of the 789 pastors in the Rhine province had not been elected by the 627 congregations. The new policy deprived some of the rich families in the area of the opportunity to influence the selection of pastors. The state's right to appoint and dismiss pastors was also a sore point in some urban parishes, which only recently showed interest in electing pastors.

The Congress of Vienna indirectly influenced the polity revolution when it set up a loose union of German states, called the German Confederation. The Federal Diet's "Law of Citizens" guaranteed equal rights for the Christian churches, and required that its Plenary Council cast a unanimous vote on any act affecting religious matters. Clearly the states had no intention of the Confederation's meddling with their rulers' control over religious affairs.

Article Thirteen of the Confederation's constitution required each state to adopt a constitution. Nassau (1814), Bavaria (1818), Baden (1818) and Wuerttemberg followed the stipulation, but the giants, Austria and Prussia, ignored with aplomb. The Bavarian and Swabian constitutions hinted that churches might be granted independence and autonomous polity sometime in the indeterminate future.

Because Prussia's church government was generally restrictive, if not oppressive, governmental officials interpreted pressure for representative church government as a back-door effort to force a territorial constitution on Prussia. The opposite was equally true. Altenstein, the Minister of Public Worship and Education, reminded the monarch that the divine right of kings made it difficult to justify representative institutions in church no less than state. In 1815, a court preacher named Eylert warned the famous theologian Friedrich Schleiermacher, and other proponents of representative church polity, that they served the king, not the people. But Schleiermacher replied that the "king has said more than once that he would give an acceptable constitution to his state. Are you insinuating that this was not in any sense his intention?" Two years later, East Prussia's general superintendent reminded his clerical colleagues that above all else, a "soldier of the king" was obedient.

Frederick William III established a church life study commission in 1814, and in the process stirred false hopes for representative church government. Twenty-two territorial superintendents met in June to study options for church polity in Prussia, although the king tried to direct their energies toward liturgical reform. The commission finally offered its recommendation in 1816; it urged that the consistorial system integrate elements of presbyterial and synodal polity. Its proposal included no plans for lay involvement, and provided that the church's governmental structure remain under the state's ecclesiastical bureaucracy. This church polity plan had points of contact with efforts to write a constitution in Prussia based on the prevailing system of classes and estates ("Staende").

Implementing the study commission's recommendation, but also coopting moves to create a viable representative church government, the king acted in 1817. He ordered the formation of consultative bodies of clergy on district, provincial, and territorial levels. The district synods lacked legislative power, but served the state's purposes by venting discussion about religion in schools, pastoral education, and doctrinal and liturgical matters. Among

21

other things, the delegates discussed discipline cases that finally were decided by bureaucratic authorities. But since Lutheran and Reformed pastors worshipped together at these meetings, the district session provided a form of church union prior to the union declaration of 1817.

The province's superintendents made up the provincial synod. It forwarded the district's recommendations to the consistory, which in turn took the matter to the Minister of Public Worship and Education. Some eastern provinces were not required to create district and provincial synods because conservative Lutherans opposed them. But the king insisted that a territorial synod would meet in five years, although this did not occur until 1846.(8)

It is clear that by the end of 1817, the Protestant churches in Germany were experiencing a revolution in polity. Repercussions from the Empire's collapse, as well as the Prussian reform movement, deprived the churches of the initiative for self-government, and made them departments of state. Their relations with the states determined their role in society, since the states imposed on them an administrative structure that regulated church-state relations. One reason for these conditions, at least in Prussia, was the church's involvement in the "Erhebung" (revolt), that primal experience of bureaucratic absolutism during which the reformers fomented a revolt against the French.

PRUSSIA'S ERHEBUNG

Religious involvement in the controlled revolt against the French, the "Erhebung," put ligament and muscle on the church's skeletal assignment as paradigm for society. During the War of Liberation in 1813-14, religion showed a new vitality in several social classes; it was important for the states to channel this energy appropriately, in order to strengthen the church's paradigmatic role in society.

The story of Protestant involvement in the war falls into

three sections: fast-moving events that led to the war, the chartered response of religious figures, and awards for work well done. But first we shall provide a brief overview of the religious spirit that accompanied the war.

Religious renewal during the War of Liberation pointed to the breakdown of the theological rationalism of the "Aufklaerung." Especially in Prussia, people once more acknowledged God's involvement in human affairs; conceptions of an inscrutable, static, mechanistic World Controller yielded to imagery of a God acting in history. Men—especially Frenchmen—were no longer seen as virtuous creatures, but as animals of unbridled hate who attracted the lightning bolt of divine wrath and judgment. Faith in providence no longer signified reliance on the natural order as much as reliance on God's truth and justice, and people believed that God acted on behalf of the group, not the individual, as He defeated evil with good.

This religious vitality entered two streams, both of which reinforced the emerging consensus about the church as a model for society. Largely attracting academic and middle class people, the first stressed the religious significance of contemporary events. Its followers tended to lump folk, fatherland, nation, freedom and religion under the same nationalist-Protestant umbrella. They believed that God's redemptive sovereignty showed itself in history as He accomplished His will for Prussia and Germany, the "Urvolk." Repentance meant that one returned to the old German virtues while following the model of Christ's suffering.

The second stream of piety seemed to hold more attraction for the nobility and peasantry. It soon flowed into the religious Awakening, as a succeeding chapter explains. Its proponents stressed the experience of a guilty conscience, and occasionally argued that a decisive military defeat might help bring repentance. They dramatized the gulf between God and man, and the need for divine redemption.

Agreeing on their reinterpretation of divine providence and on the conviction that God acts in history, people in both camps contributed to the emerging consensus about the church's social role. The one laid greater stress on the smallest social unit, the individual, while the other

23

stressed the largest, the state. Together, they deepened
the religious zeal of the "Erhebung" and enabled the state
to benefit from these resources, although of course not all
religious practices of the period fell into one or the
other or these groups.

Call to Arms

Up to 1806, Napoleon's forays into Germany did not threaten
Prussia, and in general, public opinion opposed war with
France. But Frederick William III was not able to keep
Prussia neutral. When Napoleon smothered Prussia in his
arms, some Prussians began to realize that they were
subjects rather than allies. After war with France erupted
in 1806, Prussia's inept high command suffered major
defeats at Jena and Auerstadt, while fortresses toppled
like dominos. Prussia's foreign policy was bankrupt, and
by late October Napoleon occupied Berlin and forced
officials to swear allegiance to him. Largely in deference
to the Russian Czar, he allowed the Prussian state to
survive. With an army of only 42,000 men and a population
of five million, less than half of what it was before the
war, Prussia played no part in the Peace of Tilsit (1807),
when the French and Russians signed an alliance.

Simple poster messages in Berlin announced the defeat of
Jena in 1806: "The king has lost a battle. The citizen's
first duty is to remain calm <subject>." The governor
failed to mention that the king did not participate in the
battle, nor did he indicate that the monarch fled to East
Prussia. The first sentence was a falsity since in reality
the king had lost his state. The second summed up the
state's political philosophy, which also governed its
relations with the church: the subject's primary duty was
to nurture his consciousness of service and subjection.

But before long, those Germans who wanted relief from the
French were less inclined to look toward Austria and the
free cities in the south and west, and more inclined to
turn to Berlin for leadership in the struggle for
liberation. If Berlin became the nerve center of the
effort, it was certain that it would use all the weapons in
the Protestant arsenal, since Berlin was the capitol of
German Protestantism. And since Prussia was dependent on

Russia in so many ways, the Russian commitment to legitimacy was sure to influence the development of German nationalist sentiment during the struggle, and for decades to follow. And it did.

Prussia did not disappoint those who looked northward for help. With the Czar's cooperation, Frederick William III gave chase to the French army as it retreated from Russia. In March of 1813 he issued a proclamation from Breslau entitled "To My People," which conflated two divergent ideologies, monarchical legitimacy and controlled revolution. The document signalled the start of the War of Liberation, even though its tone was not passionately nationalistic. Addressing Prussia's four remaining provinces by their provincial titles, the king called on them to stand their ground for king and fatherland. The final paragraphs of the proclamation were eschatological in tone; the king described the impending battle as the "final, decisive battle that we will pass through for our existence, independence or well-being; there is no exit except through honorable peace or glorious defeat." The announcement included the traditional appeal to God for victory, but added a new twist when it said that victory comes from God "and our firm will."

That spring Prussia mobilized 280,000 men, fully six percent of her population. The poorly equipped army had good morale, and the state's new military organization and striking force gave her an influence beyond her size. Hatred of the French and a yearning for economic stability fed the war spirit, and the peasantry did not falter in its great loyalty to the crown, the apex of divinely ordained authority on earth.

The people's militia and the professional army joined forces during the mobilization. This relieved tension between the two groups to some degree, but the credibility gap between state and people persisted. That was why the uprising in Prussia was a controlled exercise, not an insurrection, as in Spain; one English observer reported that "young people consider it necessary to have a uniform and to be drilled before they can be soldiers." Nevertheless, the mobilization welded some popular elements into the old aristocratic system.

25

At first, most German states were in no rush to join the Russian-Prussian phalanx. Many states sided with Napoleon as late as the summer lull of 1813, and pro-Napoleonic sentiment was strong in ducal Saxony until 1815. The Castle Church in Wittenberg, St. Peter's Church in Hamburg, and a number of other churches served as stables and supply depots; sometimes they were scarred in battle. After the decisive victory against Napoleon near Leipzig in October of 1813, most of the German princes rushed to the winners' side.

Preachers Respond

We have seen that Prussia's reforms were aimed at igniting a controlled revolt against the French, later known as the War of Liberation. The reformers wanted to mobilize all the state's resources, including its religious institutions. Churches, preachers, and some cultural leaders turned on the French, and in the process they helped clarify and validate the emerging consensus about the church as social model.

Prussian clergymen were accustomed to serving as royal errand boys. Pastors traditionally performed a number of administrative chores, especially in rural areas. Few Prussians would have been surprised if they had learned of the plan that the military reformer Gneisenau proposed to the king in 1811. He urged that the state's pastors preach a crusade against the French, like the Maccabees did against the Romans. But the king rejected his memorandum with a marginal note, "Good as poetry," adding that if a single pastor were shot, the affair would end. Gneisenau indignantly replied that "religion, prayer, love of the monarch and of the fatherland are nothing but poetry!" Insult was added to injury in 1812, when France forced Prussia to invade Russia as her ally. All that the reformers stood for seemed to be lost.

The response of churchmen to the state's crisis was largely dependent on what the state allowed or encouraged at one time or another. French censorship and prohibition of public meetings made churches one of the few places where political views could be discussed, although not always without recrimination. Before 1813, the Prussian government seemed to distrust clergymen who discussed political views openly, but some preachers persisted in preaching about Prussia's disastrous defeat in 1806, the French occupation, and other salient issues. Some pastors also had problems with the French. An imperial order deported Pastor Niemeyer of Halle because of his continued allegiance to Prussia, and Pastor Saalfeld was put under surveillance in Hameln. Pastor Koehler of Silesia was forced to flee, and the French banned Pastor Kottmeier from Bremen for nearly a year. Popular patriotism posed another problem for pastors. For example, a pastor in Wolfenbuettel dutifully prepared a sermon for the birthday of King Jerome, Napoleon's relative, but never delivered it since no one came to the service.

Some religious figures inched toward an expression of patriotism in their sermons by suggesting that the French embodied Evil. There were exceptions, of course, such as those Rhenish and Westphalian pastors who bowed to the inevitable, and welcomed the French as liberators, or the pastor in Barmen who favorably compared Napoleon and Christ as the princes who had "done most for justice and equality." But the powerfully cohesive emotion of revenge imprinted itself indelibly on the age. Francophobia seemed more attractive to preachers than to politicians; Stein was one of the few governmental officials who maintained a Francophobic posture from 1792 to 1815. The patriotic preacher Friedrich Schleiermacher and several other pastors entered the citadel of revenge through the door of anti-Catholicism, portraying Napoleon as protector of the Roman Catholic faith. Schleiermacher's revised edition of ON RELIGION; SPEECHES TO ITS CULTURED DESPISERS (1806) appealed for a religious war against the French. In constant battle with the censors, the press also stirred anti-French sentiment. Berlin's NEW GERMANY published lists of reasons for hating the French; a homiletical journal recommended that the rite of confirmation be revised to include new vows to the fatherland; the Badenese lay theologian Jung-Stilling openly opposed the French in his devotional paper, although he rejected the claim of some pietists that the Antichrist had begun to reign. In northern and western towns, Napoleon received the dubious royal title of "Prince of Darkness."

The leading patriotic preacher in Prussia was Friedrich

Daniel Ernst Schleiermacher (1768-1834), the son of a military chaplain, and the first Reformed professor to serve on the all-Lutheran theological faculty at Halle. Deeply influenced by Moravian pietism and romanticism, he tried to make romantic individualism serve a communal purpose. He stressed that the individual attained his potential only as he served the common cause. This was one reason why he aimed his political sermons at the educated upper classes rather than the common man.

After 1804, Schleiermacher filled a teaching post at Halle and preached by invitation at the Reformed cathedral church. Assuming the position of preacher for the newly formed student congregation two years later, he attacked the spirit of cosmopolitanism in a powerful sermon just after Prussia mobilized against the French in 1806. He argued that universal love was an abstraction apart from patriotism; a cosmopolitan person was as much a stranger and pilgrim in God's kingdom as in his native land. Just before the battle at Jena that year, he advised students to seek the dialogical peace of God's kingdom by moving from external strife to divine peace, and from inner peace to total warfare against Evil. He was saddened when French soldiers closed the university at Halle, and confiscated his quarters and some personal belongings during what he called the "reign of Attila."

The next year he left Halle, reportedly because he refused to make public intercession for the new royal couple of Westphalia. Working as a tutor and preacher in Berlin, he also engaged in amateur spying operations aimed at allying Austria and Prussia against France. In August of 1807 he traveled to Koenigsberg for the Berlin conspirators; meanwhile, Stein hurriedly commissioned him to prepare a reorganizational plan for territorial church government. His patriotism did not flag in these dark days; he wrote a friend that there was no room for despair since Prussia was a "chosen instrument and people of God." In 1809 he became the chief preacher at the Reformed Trinity Church in Berlin; as a member of the Section for Public Instruction in the government's Ministry of Interior, he helped make plans for Berlin's new university.

At long last, in the spring of 1813 Schleiermacher and the

other pastors in Prussia received an official invitation to join the war effort. Many felt that it was time. The director of the ecclesiastical section in the Ministry of Interior issued a "Plea to the Clergy of the Prussian State"; it included a prayer on behalf of those fighting "for freedom and independence, for God, fatherland and king." Clergymen could "contribute greatly to the victory of our weapons . . . by awakening the patriotic spirit of every soldier and civilian," Nicolovius wrote. He instructed pastors to base their Palm Sunday sermon on Jeremiah 30:7-9, a text in which God promised to remove the yoke from Israel's neck, burst her bonds, and release the Israelites from service to strangers. The director ordered pastors to include the royal proclamation from March in their sermons, even if it had been read to the congregation previously. Another royal decree ordered church officials to prepare tablets that listed the names of military casualties, and to honor their sacrifices in memorial services after the war. Each pastor was asked to recount the dead man's heroic acts, and to publicize the survivor benefits that came to widows and children.

Less than two weeks after the king issued his proclamation in March, Schleiermacher conducted a farewell communion service for new recruits from Berlin University. Unable to secure a chaplain's position in the army, he had enlisted in one of Berlin's pseudo-national guard units. He said in his sermon that the king's proclamation was both an admission of repentance for royal selfishness, and a call to action in God's kingdom, since selfishness and sectarianism had no place in that kingdom or in the Prussian nation—which was no longer merely a monarchical state. Listeners heard him say that God would sanctify this holy war as people returned to sincerity and strong will; soldiers were summoned to courage, and all citizens were called to the personal war against indifference and narrowmindedness. King and people together would reassert their independent and aspiring spirit, in this way "seeking the kingdom," and eliminating divisive selfishness.(9)

Like Schleiermacher, some pastors took up arms in local guard units in 1813, while others served as army chaplains. "Konsistorialrat" Offelsmeyer took command of Prussia's mobile chaplains as the state's sixth military provost. By the end of the year, the Saxons had chosen as field bishop

the theological professor Heinrich Tzschirner; he
accompanied Saxon troops to the Netherlands, even though
Saxony hesitated in joining the alliance. Pastors who
faithfully performed their parish duties often quoted a
popular verse about Russia's defeat of the French: "With
man and horse and weapon, the Lord has destroyed them."
Berlin newspapers glowingly reported on religious services
conducted for recruits on the way to the front, and
favorably compared Russian religious practices over against
the French.

Clearly, Schleiermacher did not stand alone in efforts to
rally the Prussians during their humiliation after the
defeat of 1806. Superintendent Ernst Ludwig von Borowski
(1740-1831) in Koenigsberg, Professor J. C. Gass in
Breslau, and Pastor C. G. Ribbeck made notable patriotic
pleas. In 1807, the Immediate Peace Executive Commission
publicly acknowledged the pulpit oratory of four Berlin
preachers, including Ribbeck, J. P. F. Ancillon, and
Gottfried August Ludwig Hanstein (1761-1821), the Lutheran
provost at St. Peter's Church after 1805.

Hanstein edited one of the "new style" homiletical journals
that encouraged preachers to meet political issues head on,
and he actively supported the military effort in 1813. A
popular preacher in Berlin, he had a reputation among
civilians and soldiers alike. During the summer battle
lull, he asked his hearers to become part of God's rule by
committing themselves wholeheartedly to national duty.
Commenting on the victory at Liepzig, he noted that through
contemporary events, the believer had immediate access to
the virtues of faith, hope and love; that was why citizens
of God's kingdom were ready to die for their brothers, for
their king, and for the fatherland.

The Lutheran preacher Johann H. B. Draeseke (1774-1849)
tried to rally resistance against the French in Ratzeburg,
in Schleswig-Holstein. After the town was plundered in
1806, Draeseke attacked the "political catechism" that
Napoleon had imposed on schools and churches; its
explanation of the Fourth Commandment said that "to honor
and serve our Emperor Napoleon means to honor and serve God
Himself, since he is the one whom the Lord raised up."
Soldiers passed handwritten copies of Draeseke's sermons
from hand to hand. He and Hanstein were among the first to

30

use Jahn's term "Volkstum" (nationhood), although most preachers preferred the term "Deutschheit" (Germanhood). But Draeseke's favorite motif was the Christian idea of rebirth, a concept that he applied to Germany in his widely read sermonic collection, entitled GERMANY'S REBIRTH (1814). The motif was appropriate for Ratzeburg since the French controlled the town until late in 1813. During the war, preachers often interpolated new meaning into this term and others, including "redemption," "resurrection," and "revelation."

The flaming patriot and poet, Enst Moritz Arndt (1769–1860), also issued a call to arms against the French. Arndt was trained as a clergyman, although he never served in that office. He often portrayed God as an omnipotent Force of hatred and vengeance, who stirred up mass nationalistic comradeship among Germans. To be religious, he wrote in 1807, a "united people" had to have a "single conviction about a common task, to join together with the bloody sword of vengeance" against hell and the devil. His supposed reconversion to Christianity between 1808 and 1810 brought a number of pseudo–Christian references to his writings, but it is doubtful that he materially changed his rationalistic convictions. His PHANTASY OF A FUTURE (1812) echoed themes from Second Isaiah, and showed the influence of renewed Old Testament study. THE RHINE, GERMANY'S RIVER BUT NOT HER BORDER (1813) interpreted the curse at Babel as a blessing, since language differences prevented the enslavement of humanity. His articles in the PRUSSIAN CORRESPONDENT, a paper edited by Schleiermacher and an associate, discussed hate as a Christian virtue planted in man's soul by God.

Arndt's remarkable ability to interweave patriotic and religious emotions attracted more admirers from the younger generation than from his contemporaries. As a result, he made a larger impact in later years. But some of his material was included in the mass of propaganda that inundated soldiers and civilians alike in 1813. His CATECHISM FOR GERMAN SOLDIERS AND MILITIAMEN went through eleven editions by 1815; one edition in Berlin ran to 50,000 copies. The tract blamed Napoleon's defeat in Russia on the "fearful punishment" of the God who "works to destroy bloody tyrants."

31

University recruits were among the readers of this propaganda. New nationalistic poems written to musical accompaniment were among some of the most interesting material. As substitutes for traditional military songs that sometimes offended moral sensitivities, the new patriotic hymns tried to stir people through the use of religious imagery. The most popular song writers—Arndt, Friedrich Schlegel, Max von Schenkendorf, and Theodor Koerner—compared Napoleon's defeat with Pharaoh's, altered Luther's "A Mighty Fortress" in its last line to read "the kindom remains for Germans," portrayed the national awakening as a new Pentecost, and pictured Napoleon as the Antichrist and Paris as Babylon. Some church hymns were altered slightly to give new meaning, and in 1814 a collection of over 800 compositions commemorated the first anniversary of the victory at Leipzig.

Memorials, Awards and Promotions

About the time that the first anniversary of the victory at Leipzig was observed, the Prussian king received plans for a Gothic cathedral to commemorate Prussia's success in war. To be built near Berlin, it was supposed to serve as a monument of thanksgiving and a memorial for past blessings. Statues of princes, great religious leaders, and apostles were to grace its interior according to the plans, and representations of the iron cross would adorn its entrances.

This "award" for the faithful involvement of religious forces in the war did not become a reality for nearly a century, but the plan's inclusion of decorative iron crosses was no anachronism in 1814. When the war began the previous year, the iron cross was struck as a medal of honor for Prussian service. Since all Christians could perform patriotic and courageous service for the state, combatants and non-combatants alike could receive and wear this cross. The creation of the medal showed how effectively Prussia cojoined religion and patriotism during the war.

No less important were the awards and promotions given to preachers "in recognition of outstanding services" to the state, as the Prussian king noted. Borowski of East

Prussia became the chief court preacher; Sack was given the rank of bishop, which was equivalent to the provincial "Oberpraesident," and in 1817 he became the first clergyman to receive the Order of the Red Eagle, first class; the Reformed court preacher Ruhlemann F. Eylert (1770-1852) was also named bishop in 1818 and appointed to the "Staatsrat," while Hanstein and the Berlin theologian Konrad Marheineke (d. 1846) received the second class Order of the Red Eagle. Some of the titles carried additional income as well.(10) But these awards and plans for memorials could not hide the fact that the war was largely the work of the state's bureaucracy, and an educated elite. Most military volunteers were students, and the educated elite personified the intellectual and religious arguments about God's providential concern for national identity, an idea proposed earlier by Herder and Hamann. While the so-called War of Liberation threw off the French yoke, it also enabled princes to ignore the demands of the educated middle classes.

Already by mid-1813, for example, Schleiermacher began questioning Prussia's commitment to the unification of the German states along liberal lines. He argued that the state was not acknowledging its debt to its citizens. For some time, he thought that it would be easier to cure Prussia's ills by unifying the German states, rather than by reforming society through a more painful process; but up to this point he had tended to ignore Prussia's authoritarianism.

ECCLESIASTICAL CONGLOMERATIONS

After the war ended, the Congress of Vienna in 1814-15 doubled Prussia's population. As part of the agreement, Prussia traded three million Polish serfs for three million free peasants and townspeople in the west. Two new provinces were created as a result in the Rhineland. People joked that the only integrative force in the "Prussian states" was the crown. It was more than obvious that a united evangelical church could help to bring a sense of unity to the far-flung provinces that stretched across northern Germany. A ceremonial church union could also give a sense of community to the Protestant minority in the new Rhineland provinces, while legitimating union movements in that area.

The dignified hierarchy and liturgy of England's national church probably impressed Frederick William III when he visited there in 1814. In any case, he soon used his position as the church's "summus episcopus" to proclaim a voluntary cultic union between Lutheran and Reformed Protestants, which he effected in 1817. In the process, Germany's largest territorial church showed that its role in society was determined by its existence as a state institution, not by its confessional commitments.

But this was not the full story of Protestant union in Prussia, nor was the Prussian union the only ecclesiastical conglomeration for Lutherans and Reformed in the German states. The Enlightenment planted the seeds of the union movement, and other factors played a part as well, including the revolution in polity described above. The pre-history of church unions illuminates what happened in Prussia and elsewhere, when united Protestant churches modeled religious freedom within the confines of state authority. A brief summary of this pre-history precedes our discussion of the union in Prussia and elsewhere.

Impetus for Church Union

Three important influences paved the way for cultic unions during the second decade. They were the legacies of the Enlightenment, French administrative reforms in the southern and western states, and the patriotic piety that appeared during the War of Liberation.

During the Enlightenment, political theorists were interested, among other things, in a more precise definition of the monarch's role in a well-ordered state. Pragmatic utility was a major motif. In Prussia, that definitional process sharpened the monarch's role as "summus episcopus" (chief bishop) of the territorial church, and stimulated interest in a religious union between Lutheran and Reformed Protestants. In addition, two of the Enlightenment's major religious currents, theological rationalism and pietism, pressed Protestants toward union by stressing common articles of faith, and de-emphasizing confessional landmarks that distinguished the two evangelical traditions. When the Empire ended in 1806, the way was clear for rulers such as Prussia's Frederick William III to initiate religious reforms that were advantageous to the state, while supposedly respecting the individual's freedom. In the process, the state seemed to be reforming church life through a voluntary religious union. Thus, the introduction of a union between evangelical groups can be seen as the final business of the "Aufklaerung," and as a reform movement that fit the spirit of the age. The Enlightenment's effects could not be ignored.

One important legacy of the Enlightenment was a rash of publications early in the century in support of ceremonial union. One contribution came from the Prussian court preacher, Sack; Schleiermacher and the historian Gottlieb J. Planck added their contributions to the list. Another of the Enlightenment's legacies was the movement to form a national church, discussed above. A third was a number of monuments dedicated to the ideal of toleration. A Reformed preacher, Benedictine abbot, and a Lutheran general superintendent jointly consecrated one of these monuments in 1811 in the Thuringian Forest. The largest of three flames that illuminated this sandstone column in Altenburg represented the Lutheran territorial church.

A final legacy was Prussia's Territorial Law (1794), and the enlightened religious views which the Prussian king absorbed. Frederick William III was quite well at home in the religious atmosphere of the Enlightenment. He had been baptized, confirmed, and married by the Reformed court preacher, Friedrich S. G. Sack (1738-1817), whose theology was strongly influenced by the Enlightenment. During his confirmation examination in 1787, the crown prince showed that his mentor's instruction had been effective. In the examination the future king endorsed the traditional spirit of toleration, adding that the Reformed Church gave him the best perspective on things. He lamented the continued separation of the two Protestant church parties, since "in all essentials of the Christian faith" they were already united. Some scholars call Sack the "spiritual father" of the union because of his influence on the king, but no less important were the lectures on toleration delivered to Frederick by the legal scholar, Suarez.

Soon after he was crowned in 1798, Frederick received a memorandum from Sack urging that the two branches of Protestantism be united. As the first step, the court preacher recommended the creation of a common liturgy. Like him, the Reformed monarch came to see opponents of the union as enemies of religious peace and toleration. In 1812, Sack rehearsed his arguments in a book entitled ON UNITING THE TWO PROTESTANT CHURCH PARTIES IN THE PRUSSIAN MONARCHY. The king reiterated his views early the next year when the crown prince was confirmed. Notes from the occasion indicate that he reprimanded the clergy in attendance. They stood "together as brothers" and preached a "Gospel of peace," he said, but they were "still separated from one another by confessions . . . . Miserable! <You> should be united with one another."

In the fall of 1814, the king formed the liturgical commission that two years later provided a provisional liturgical agenda for the Court and Garrison Church at Potsdam, and the Garrison Church in Berlin. At that point the king decided to inaugurate the ceremonial and cultic union first and only where his absolute authority would meet no resistance—in military congregations. At long last, he was acting to overcome the pain at not having been able to commune with his deceased wife, a Lutheran. Broader reform had to wait until church union was declared for the whole territory in 1817.

Theoretically, at least, the king's plans had to take into account the "Allgemeines Landrecht" of 1794. A product of the Enlightenment, this legal code included more than 1,200 paragraphs on ecclesiastical affairs. They did not mention a territorial church, or legally sanctioned confessions, but only religious parties composed of like-minded citizens, who cooperated in pursuit of legitimate religious goals. Since religion was construed as a private matter, individuals could adopt confessional statements of faith, but the code made no provision for confessional parties. The code did not permit a religious society to exclude members "for mere opinion deviating from the common confession of faith"; the state had the last word in all disputes. This was why evangelical canon law in Prussia did not discuss the right of church membership until the nineteenth century. Traditionally, citizenship and church membership were coterminous; the church was conceived as the religious side of the state, not an autonomous corporation within the state.

Given these conditions, it seemed nearly impossible for the king to proclaim a ceremonial union, without violating the description of the Reformed and Lutheran confessions as the embodiment of the "doctrina evangelica" (evangelical doctrine) that distinguished evangelicals from Roman Catholics. At least Schleiermacher and other proponents of the union offered this interpretation, when they tried to derive the binding power of confessional standards from the church's communal spirit, not from their status as legally required norms.(11) But the king and his advisors were not persuaded.

The second major impetus for cultic union, especially in southern and western territories, were the administrative reforms effected by the French. Napoleon's Rhenish Confederation (1806) and reforms laid the groundwork for later unions by bringing evangelicals together across confessional lines, and encouraging grassroot efforts that sometimes led to confessional unions.

Along the Rhine at Mainz, a mixed evangelical congregation of 1,000 persons was organized in 1802, under the liberalized administration of the French. Even though the group was a minority in the city's largely Roman Catholic population of 21,000, Lutherans did not commune with Reformed until 1809. On the left bank of the Rhine, the French gathered all Protestants into Lutheran or Reformed "consistory churches" of 6,000 souls. France's Organic Articles simplified the ecclesiastical map of the Rhineland, prior to Prussia's takeover in 1815, by eliminating over seventy-five principalities, and even more knightly parcels. This action paved the way for subsequent union efforts. Near the French border, in Aachen, Protestants got permission to use St. Anne's Church for worship in 1802; when they met for the first time in nearby Cologne, they organized an evangelical communion that was not specifically designated as Lutheran or Reformed. In sum, Napoleon made two lasting contributions to evangelicals in this area: he stabilized the salaries of clergymen, and encouraged the idea of union.

The third influence in the emergence of unions was the patriotic piety that accompanied the War of Liberation.(12) Especially in Prussia, the largest Protestant state, these religious experiences constituted a kind of "religious baptism" of fire for the Enlightenment's emphasis on the state's practical use of religion. Prussia's church union appropriated these elements in a distinctive way.

The Prussian Union

In the spring of 1817, the Prussian king told his ministers in a cabinet order that union between the two confessions would be an appropriate way to observe the 300th anniversary of the Reformation that year. Sack and Hanstein, two members of the royal church consistory, argued unsuccessfully that a new plan of representative church polity should precede such a union. In June, the consistory provided information on the anniversary to "churches and congregations of both confessions." The order promised that a "special liturgy" would be produced, although it did not refer directly to the proposed union celebration. At one point it glossed over confessional differences by referring to the "pure knowledge of Christian truth" achieved by the Reformation.

In the preceding decade, the Prussian state's polity revolution created the necessary substructure for implementing a ceremonial or liturgical union. It is unnecessary to review this story, but it should be noted that in 1813, the state's Section of Public Worship and Instruction relieved patrons of the responsibility of providing parishes with appropriate confessional books. In addition, the decision to conduct unified district synods--including worship services--for clergy of both confessions was meeting with success. In the western region of Prussia, joint meetings occurred in Cologne and Trier before the union was announced, and at Aachen and Trier soon thereafter.

The most significant polity development of 1817 was unmistakably related to the union proclamation. We noted earlier that in the first days of November, the Ministry of Public Worship and Education assumed a life of its own. Thus, less than a month after the new evangelical union was proclaimed, it had institutional representation and administration at the highest level of government. The king waited five more years to use this machinery to issue his new liturgical agenda, which became the instrument of compulsory cultic uniformity among evangelicals. But it was clear at a much earlier date that his announcing a "voluntary" union was a contradiction in terms.

The king issued his union proclamation for the territory on September 27, 1817, although public circulation to consistories, synods and superintendents was delayed until October 9. He wrote that while sectarianism delayed his predecessor's efforts to bring the two confessions together, their goal would finally be achieved. He added that only externals divided the two churches, and their reunification was an act of deep Christian significance. The spirit of Protestantism and the reformers supported the union; it was a responsible act of churchmanship that would nurture piety and improve conditions in church and school. The king rejected any intolerant zeal for compulsion, and insisted that Reformed would not become Lutheran, nor would Lutheran become Reformed. Nevertheless, he appealed not only for a union in external forms, but a union "in the unity of hearts." By uniting Lutheran and Reformed congregations at the Court and Garrison Church at Potsdam on Reformation Day, he hoped to point the way for others, until in the near future the One Shepherd would feed His flock in one faith, hope and love.

On the first of October, forty-six Berlin pastors met to discuss plans for union. The Lutheran majority elected the famous Reformed theologian, Schleiermacher, as chairman. Then participants agreed to give a unified witness to the whole state by holding joint services in all of Berlin's churches on Reformation Day. The pastors also expressed a desire to be called "evangelical" clergymen, not Lutheran or Reformed. This decision came as no surprise, in part because the widespread practice of intermarriage between confessions had also invaded parsonages.

The first congregation in Berlin to take a favorable stance toward the union was the Reformed Cathedral Church, whose edifice was being renovated between 1816 and 1820 at a cost to the state of 120,000 "Thaler." Early in October, the congregation dropped its traditional confessional status in favor of the union. Sometime earlier, Hanstein recommended that the Lutheran congregation of St. Peter's unite with the Cathedral Church, after its remodeling program was finished.

On October 30, the king joined city officials, sixty-five pastors, Berlin's church consistory, teachers from five gymnasium schools, and theological professors from the new university, for a special Reformation service in Berlin. This cultic act of state began with a march from the Town Hall to St. Nicholas Church, where Lutheran and Reformed celebrants conducted a joint communion service.

The next day, Reformation Day, while westernmost towns in the kingdom conducted their first Protestant service in Marx's home town of Trier, the churches of Berlin celebrated the new union while the king attended services in nearby Potsdam. His chief of chaplains, a Lutheran named Offelsmeyer, preached the sermon at the Court and Garrison Church; during the communion, Frederick received the bread from the Reformed court preach Eylert, and the cup from Offelsmeyer. The next day he traveled from Potsdam to Wittenberg, to lay the cornerstone of a Luther monument. When the monument was finally completed in 1821, the atmosphere was so different that it could not serve as a "national monument" for a great German leader for all confessions, as some had hoped when plans were first laid in 1815. Instead, the movement became a Prussian-Protestant-monarchical symbol, a fitting memorial to the king's proclamation of a ceremonial union.

Neither did the king forget the other major Protestant reformer, John Calvin. He soon authorized a medal to commemorate the union; Luther and Calvin graced one side, and on the other, Mother Church clutched her two sons to herself. For his support of the union, Schleiermacher was among the first to receive the medallion. In due course, the court preacher Eylert called the union a "heavenly kingdom on earth, in which Christ's spirit reigns," and soon the king was donating crucifixes and candelabras to congregations that joined the union, such as the 2,800 Lutherans and fifty Reformed Protestants in Oranienburg, who created a united congregation in 1819.

The Prussian union clearly demonstrated the state's capacity to use what it wanted for its own purposes. In the Rhineland, where union efforts had become somewhat popular, the state coopted the movement, and used it to integrate the new region into the realm. Elsewhere, the state inaugurated a cultic union based above all else on the pragmatism of the Enlightenment. The religious parties described in the "Landrecht" were first to serve the state, and only then their own members, since the "voluntary" union had a compulsion all its own.

Other Church Unions

A variety of circumstances surrounded the unions that were created in the other German states. Some were formed more democratically than Prussia's, such as in Baden. French influence was a significant element there, and, as we have seen, a series of administrative reforms paved the way for the confessional union. Church bureaucrats had been using the same checklist to inspect both Lutheran and Reformed congregations, but especially in Heidelberg, Reformed pastors and congregations were less than enthusiastic about union since they had a higher social status than Lutherans, and feared loss of property. The search for union came on hard times in 1809-10, when the Section of Public Worship was absorbed into the Ministry of Interior. Church officials made no reference to union in the liturgy prepared for the 300th anniversary of the Reformation in 1817. In Heidelberg, the two confessions observed the event separately, but pastors in Mannheim conducted joint services. In December of that year, laymen seized the initiative by preparing a petition which they presented to church officials the next spring. After bureaucrats legitimated the search for union, Baden's first elected "Landtag" (Assembly) requested a canvass of all clergy on the subject.

Local synods met in Baden in 1820, and a general synod convened the next year. Despite the Lutherans' four to one majority in the state, the synod was almost equally split

41

between the two confessions (11 Lutheran clergy and 12 laymen, 10 Reformed clergy and 11 laymen). The synod nearly lost its chance to form a confessional union while bickering whether to inform the prince of its actions before or after the last session. Bowing to princely pressure, it enabled the prince to call synodal meetings at will, instead of requiring that an assembly meet every five years. In fact, the next synod did not convene for thirteen years. But the general synod that met in 1821 rejoiced that the Grand Duke's edict on church union referred to the Scriptures as the "inexhaustible source of evangelical faith," and prescribed the use of the Augsburg Confession, Luther's Small Catechism, and the Heidelberg Catechism as the confessional symbols of the confessionally united church. Baden joined the Palatinate region of Bavaria as the second state with a confessional--as contrasted with a cultic, or ceremonial--union when evangelicals celebrated the new rite of union on October 28, 1821, with little noticeable resistance.

In the Palatinate, the union occurred under the auspices of the Bavarian crown, since Protestants there remained under the control of Munich's High Church Council until 1849. Bavaria's constitution (1818) carefully provided for state supervision of churches, but some possibility for church autonomy remained. Impetus for union in the Palatinate flowed up through synodal channels, until finally the king gave his approval. Several united congregations had been formed as early as 1817, including those in Zweibruecken and Bergzabern, but the king asked the consistories to test popular support for the move. Votes were taken on four successive Sundays in 1818; the tally showed 40,000 in favor, and only about 500 persons--primarily Reformed--in opposition. Then at the king's request, the general consistory convened a meeting of clergy and laymen. After this synod of forty-eight delegates met for two weeks in the summer, the king in October approved the decision to form a united church.

Synodal or congregational approval was an integral part of the process that brought unions to Baden, the Bavarian Palatinate, and Nassau. Church union was a political necessity in Nassau, a state created out of thirty-nine smaller principalities between 1809 and 1816. In 1817, twenty-eight pastors meeting as a synod voted to consummate the union, and in August the prince's edict made the union official, and set the celebration for Reformation Day. He ordered pastors to instruct congregations on the value of combining the groups during September, and to explain on October 26 that the union festival would be observed five days later. Church bells rang for more than an hour on the 30th, and for a quarter hour the next day as paraders marched from parsonages to churches, carrying Bibles, copies of the Augsburg Confession, parish chalices, and other items. Meanwhile, in Frankfurt am Main four thousand school children celebrated the new union on All Saints Day.

Except for Hanover, Mecklenberg, Saxony and the rest of Bavaria, where the number of Reformed Protestants was negligible, unions sprouted in most of the states and principalities of Germany. Prussia's declaration stimulated unions in Saxony-Weimar (1818), Hanau, with Isenburg and Fulda (1818), Waldeck-Pyrmont (1818), Anhalt-Bernburg (1820), Lichtenberg (1820), Waldeck (1820), Rhine-Hesse (1823), Hildburghhausen (1823), Hesse (1823), and Anhalt-Dessau (1827), in addition to those mentioned above. People called the union in Hanau and Fulda the "bookbinder's union," because the pertinent confessions were published in a single volume.

As 1817 drew to a close, two rather different movements must have attracted the attention of many German Protestants. In one, a small band of students and professors gathered for a cultic festival of national union at Wartburg in mid-October. In the other, Prussia and Nassau inaugurate ceremonial church unions between two evangelical confessions on the Festival of the Reformation.

At the time, it may not have been clear which of the two movements would have more enduring significance. But the keen observer could not have ignored the active involvement of the state in one. Nor, for that matter, could one forget that in the last decade, many cultured intellectuals pointed to the state as the driving force for the full development of human potential.

Some doors still stood ajar, but in 1817, German Protestant

churches seemed to have fewer open options than in 1806. The possibility of a national church in a unified nation appeared to be slim. And because of its programmatic imprecision, the proposal that the church serve as benefactor of humanity did not catch hold. In fact, with their emphasis on absolutist political values, proponents of this view ended up lending support to the idea of the church as a social model.

Since this was a tumultuous decade in the political realm, it is not surprising that the states retained the initiative in determining the role of the churches in a society that would soon become "modern" Germany. Especially in Prussia, the largest Protestant state, but also in other states, the territories used the churches as educative models for a changing society, one that now had to absorb new elements without doing violence to traditional society and its political structures. The revolution in church polity, religious involvement in the "Erhebung," and the formation of church unions, were instructive experiments on two levels. For Protestants, they were building blocks in the emerging consensus--what we have called the unwritten charter--that the church's primary social role was to be the state's model for society. For society, Protestants showed how one lived freely and responsibly—and with finesse—within boundaries prescribed by state authority.

Any number of circumstances had changed since 1770, but the new century perpetuated the pattern perfected by the Old Regime in one important respect: the bureaucracy continued to transfer important issues between state and society into areas that lay under immediate state control.(13) As a result, few people--at least in Prussia--should have doubted that the states would continue to dominate the Protestant churches in the century to come, even though all the conditions of the unwritten charter were not yet clear. One thing was unmistakably clear: for the church, the future held fewer options than before.

NOTES

CHAPTER I

(1) Klaus Epstein, THE GENESIS OF GERMAN CONSERVATISM (Princeton: Princeton University Press, 1966), pp. 648–52.

(2) Among the students from Jena were two brothers well known later as clerics in the religious Awakening, Friedrich Wilhelm and Emil Wilhelm Krummacher. In the registry their signatures bracketed the name of Karl Ludwig Sand, a theological student from Erlangen whose assassination of the conservative Russian playwright Kotzebue helped precipitate the politically oppressive measures of the Carlsbad Decrees (1819). After the festival, state authorities tried to draw up a full list of registrants in order to subject them to harrassment and legal action.

(3) Robert Anchor, GERMANY CONFRONTS MODERNIZATION; GERMAN CULTURE AND SOCIETY, 1790—1890 (Lexington, MA: D. C. Heath & Company, 1972), p. 10.

(4) Hajo Holborn, "German Idealism in the Light of Social History," in GERMANY AND EUROPE: HISTORICAL ESSAYS (Garden City, NY: Doubleday & Company, Inc., 1970), pp. 14–15, 19–20, 25–26.

(5) Anchor, pp. 14, 51.

(6) Holborn, pp. 3–4, 8–11.

(7) In 1829, all ten Prussian provinces inaugurated ecclesiastical superintendencies patterned after the model used in the eastern provinces. Labelled the "ecclesiastical bodyguard of the Prussian kings" by the German historian

Gerhard Ritter, the general superintendents served under the "Oberpraesidenten" as directors of the provincial consistories. They ordained clergymen, and fit perfectly Schleiermacher's description of them as "the government's ecclesiastical prefects" by regularly reporting clerical activities and consistorial decisions to higher echelons. In recognition of faithful service, most eventually received the title "bishop," which added glamor to their bureaucratic duties. Frederick William III designed their silk gowns and crosses. See Robert M. Bigler, "The Rise of Political Protestantism in Nineteenth Century Germany: The Awakening of Political Consciousness and Beginnings of Political Activity in the Protestant Clergy of Pre-March Prussia," CHURCH HISTORY, XXXIV (1965), 435-36.

(8) In short order, Brandenburg's provincial synod met and offered a radical constitutional plan. It urged the creation of a political system that would substitute provincial synods for provincial consistories, and transfer the functions of the Minister of Public Worship to the territorial synod. Naturally, the proposal was uncacceptable to the king. The ecclesiastical bureaucracy continued to administer church affairs, while churchmen implemented the king's plan. But, as indicated, the eastern provinces were exempted from this requirement because most clergymen there feared any form of representative polity.

(9) Karl von Raumer, later a well-known confessional Lutheran, reported that the sermon made "the deepest impression on me, as certainly it did on all who were present." The stenographer for many of Schleiermacher's sermons noted that during this sermon his emotions frequently interrupted his work. Later the novelist Theodor Fontane incorporated parts of the sermon almost verbatim in his work, BEFORE THE STORM.

(10) Bigler, pp. 434-35. See also his study, THE POLITICS OF GERMAN PROTESTANTIbM; THE RISE OF THE PROTESTANT CHURCH ELITE IN PRUSSIA, 1815—1848 (Berkely: University of California Press, 1972), pp. 35-36.

(11) As the century progressed, a growing number of confessionalists opposed liberal and middle-of-the-road, or mediating, theologians who supported this view. They reverted to the previous interpretation of confessional

writings as statutes of church fellowship, especially for church leaders.

(12) As mentioned above, one strain of this piety flowed into the early religious Awakening. Before it hardened into confessionalism, the Awakening was supra-confessional and ecumenical in character, and this encouraged the union movement.

It should also be noted that in the early decades, the prevailing intellectual spirit paralleled political efforts to restore order after the upheaval of the French Revolution. Thinkers tried to construct massive, all-encompassing systems of thought that would harness reality into manageable philosophical and theological categories. As I understand it, the search for union between Lutheran and Reformed confessions was compatible with this effort.

(13) See Leonard Krieger, THE GERMAN IDEA OF FREEDOM; HISTORY OF A POLITICAL TRADITION (Boston: Beacon Press, 1957), pp. 3-80.

CHAPTER II

IMPLEMENTATION AND THEORY

Early in the century, Protestants in Germany found the
states using their churches as models for society.
Although a fair amount of political pressure was involved
in arriving at a consensus on this point, the unwritten
charter had less the force of law than of a working
agreement between two parties, church and state. But the
pressure persisted, so much so that by the twenties
Schleiermacher made a joke of the royal favors that came to
those who adopted the king's new liturgical agenda. A new
set of criteria now governed who received patriotic awards,
he said. Playing on the Latin word "agenda," he noted that
the Order of the Red Eagle no longer was awarded "propter
acta" ("for things that have been done") but "propter
agenda" ("for things that should be done")—for adopting
the new liturgy.

This chapter reviews the practical ramifications of the
unwritten charter in the years between 1817 and the early
thirties, as well as theoretical arguments advanced in
support of the consensus. We will delay for now our
investigation of the so-called "religious Awakening" of
these years, and concentrate on Protestant church life
during the restoration. This epoch spawned the Holy
Alliance, restorational movements in politics, and massive,
unitary systems of theology and philosophy. It was a
breathing period, a time to settle down, return to
normalcy, and reprogram institutions to ensure social and
political tranquility. The general cultural and political
atmosphere was compatible with the restricted social

assignment the churches had accepted in the unwritten charter.

The far-reaching effects of the agreement became more noticeable as it touched more areas of church life. One early sign was the response of churchmen to the Holy Alliance, but there were others as well. The restorational impulse brought new changes to church polity in Prussia, and the church's governmental machinery guaranteed a healthy response to the king's liturgical agenda. But when he faced open resistance to church union, the king changed the emphasis from a confessional to a confederative union, in order to keep the unwritten contract intact, and to facilitate its implementation in other areas. The civil servant status of pastors, as well as prevailing social and economic restraints, helped keep clergymen attuned to the emerging consensus. And while the Prussian state revised educational curricula so the church could more effectively support monarchical legitimacy, evangelical missionaries worked to fulfil part of the church's assignment, by bringing Jews into the "Christian state."

The unwritten charter needed theorists to evaluate its ramifications and to trumpet its cause among intellectuals. Many of the themes of the romantic movement, which had close affinity with restorational thought, influenced the chief theorists, who included Schleiermacher, Hegel and the "mediating" theologians.

The church in Prussia stressed the king's right to act unilaterally as the church's union, agenda and polity structure assumed the force of habit among the clergy. We will have much to say about Prussia, not only because it was the largest state with the greatest number of Protestants. Tagging after Austria, she was also a leader of the restoration among the German states. But by the fourth decade, even in Prussia the church's right and left wings were clamoring for revision of the religious compact—which had no legal force—since it coopted liberal and conservative power in ways that benefitted the state. This development will be considered in greater depth in a later chapter, but we should note that the seeds were planted during the restorational period, and in the vigorous implementation of the charter that was part of the restoration.

A RESTORATIONAL MODEL: THE HOLY ALLIANCE

The Holy Alliance of 1815 became a symbol of the restorational era that followed France's defeat. While the circumstances of its origin were less conservative and restorational than fanatical and pious, references to the document by German authorities transformed it into a conservative manifesto.

The response of churchmen to the Alliance was an early sign that they were grasping the basic thrust of the unwritten agreement between church and state. In fact, their responses helped implement the church's assignment, since they were acknowledging the state's right to shore up monarchical legitimacy with religious jargon.

In an age inclined toward massive, unitive systems of theology and philosophy, Czar Alexander of Russia proposed that the victorious monarchs of Austria, Prussia and Russia pledge themselves to an international alliance based on Christian principles. His original draft of the proposed Holy Alliance assumed a supra-confessional and all-embracing piety, demanded a total break with all previous political theory and practice, including the French Revolution, and emphasized Christian brotherhood in common eschatological zeal, not in natural rights.(1)

Receiving Alexander's draft document on September 11, 1815, the monarchs signed the draft fifteen days later, after Prince Metternich made several significant alterations that tempered its tone and diluted its indictment of the European state concert system. According to Henry Kissinger, the revised version was an "attack on the transformations wrought by the revolution . . . a promise to return to order . . . an assertion of the primacy of law over will." Metternich used the Czar's programmatic conception of the Holy Alliance as the "proclamation of a new era transcending the pettiness of history," to announce "the end of a revolutionary period and re-entry into history."(2) In 1819, when Austria and Prussia fabricated a grave crisis over student unrest, authorities were able to use the document to support

51

legitimacy because of these changes. As a result, international conservatism presented a coherent vision of world order for the first time in the Alliance. The document contained seeds of many of the restoration's guiding principles, including the political role of supra-confessional moral tenets, commitment to a paternalistic order, reliance on God's gracious will, affirmation of the overwhelming importance of stability and peace, and the hope that Christ's banner would unite all people.

The restorational impulse that was emerging helps us understand the religiously motivated responses offered to the Alliance by churchmen and other significant figures. Soon after it was signed, Frederick William III of Prussia issued a prayer for days of special patriotic importance. It was to be used in all Prussian churches. The prayer asked God to pour "the spirit of wisdom, counsel and harmony" on all European rulers, and included these petitions as well: "Especially bless and protect the Holy Alliance and the monarchs who created it, in order to rule and give happiness to their peoples in Thee and in Thy Son, the world's Savior. Let their holy work redound to the praise of Thy Holy Name and the advancement of common good, so that peace, order and justice may prevail everywhere."

At Reformation time in 1817, the newly formed Swabian Bible Society in Stuttgart made special reference in its annual report to the Czar's interest in Bible distribution. It added that while its distribution program was not intended to convert the whole world, it helped to implement the Holy Alliance by combatting revolution in local areas.

The ideas of the Alliance influenced a number of Christian spokesmen. A pious layman from Nuremberg named Georg F. Hillmer wrote in his periodical, entitled CHRISTIAN MAGAZINE FOR CHRISTIANS (1816), that his journal ordinarily had little interest in secular affairs. But, he added, the current issue discussed the Alliance because it was a memorial reaching to heaven, sanctifying the victory of a holy people interested in peace on earth, and God's honor in the heavens. "Yes, amen! a Holy Alliance! Holy since truth is sanctified! Holy since it issues from holy sources," he wrote. Three years later, his book THE HOLY ALLIANCE once more demonstrated the magnetic power of the

Alliance.

The influential German-Swiss theologian, Johann Jakob Hess, wrote in 1819 that in their Alliance the three monarchs encouraged recognition of God's "absolute power." People who identified this power would more readily eliminate the distinction between church and state, and then the City of God would "unite the two into itself," he added. Four years later, the popular Prussian theologian and preacher Franz Theremin (1780-1846) constructed a veritable utopia in his DOCTRINE OF THE DIVINE KINGDOM, which focused on the Alliance as a significant step in the universal process uniting national churchs and states into national kingdoms, and finally into one "great republic of states" that coincided with the advancement of God's kingdom on earth.

At the Congress of Aachen in 1818, Czar Alexander presented a memorandum that some saw as an effort to substitute the sweeping principles of the Holy Alliance for the defined obligations of the Quadruple Alliance. Another pamphlet was published at the same time, entitled MEMORANDUM OF THE CURRENT SITUATION IN GERMANY. Probably written by a Russian diplomat, it assumed that political history coincided with the history of salvation or redemption, and that religion snould serve political ends. Composing as it were a brief for the new religious charter in Germany, the author urged authorities to pay closer attention to the spirit of the Alliance. Religion should be used more forcefully as a stabilizing influence, the author wrote, and authorities should dismiss theologians who undermined this policy.

Under Metternich's leadership, the German states acted in the Carlsbad Decrees (1819) to censor the press and keep closer watch on universities, which after the Wartburg Festival were considered to be seedplots of liberalism and revolution. The nobility in particular wanted to clamp down on the breeding ground of the "Gebildte" (The Educated), who were using the bureaucracy to try to bring change to Prussia. Some of the most outspoken champions of a constitution for Prussia were professors, and it was said that these "demagogues" were ready and willing to sacrifice Prussia—and her nobility—for Germany.

Authorities were given a striking opportunity to stiffen

their control that year--the same year that de Maistre published his reactionary DU PAPE in France--when in Mannheim a deranged theological student named Karl Sands stabbed to death August von Kotzebue, a reactionary playwright, and part time literary correspondent for the Russians in Prussia. Sands took the Student Unions' calls for radical action seriously, and his attendance at the Wartburg Festival in 1817 gave authorities even more reason to act. They beheaded him for his crime, but the issue was not settled, even after the Student Unions came in for attack under the Decrees.

When the theological professor from Berlin, Wilhelm M. L. DeWette (1780-1849), consoled Sand's mother in a letter made public without his permission, he was condemned by a rash of publications and dismissed from office. One pamphlet's title page bristled with the biblical injunction to obey authority. Another urged clergymen to be "true demagogues," by reconciling the rich and poor in times of stress; this was the real problem, according to the author, not the supposed cleavage between rulers and subjects. DeWette's firing had social and political overtones, since the middle classes respected professors and were taken aback when they were not admitted to the royal court. The uproar also brought governmental officials to Schleiermacher's sermons, to monitor his preaching.

But the Alliance showed remarkable tenacity in conservative circles, especially among Prussian aristocrats pledged to preserve the Christian state. Later in the century, the well-known conservative lawyer-churchman, Ernst Ludwig von Gerlach, remarked that the pact was "the most sublime creation of the nineteenth century" since it "embodied and portrayed the idea of Christendom as a family of peoples." August F. Fuehle, in a biblical commentary (1828), showed in mathematical calculations that Napoleon was the Antichrist, and Czar Alexander a messianic figure whose Alliance was an important eschatological sign. Little wonder that Eylert, Prussia's chief court preacher, and a recent appointee to the "Staatsrat," preached at the Potsdam chapel early in 1819 that political opposition to the government was nothing short of treason! The next year the Final Act of Vienna ("Wiener Schlussacte") of May 15, 1820 sharpened the focus of the reactionary movement already underway. The age of revolt had been followed by the age of submission.

MACHINERY SET FOR ACTION

Two clear signals announced that the restoration was underway in earnest: the first was the creation of a central investigatory body at Mainz as a result of the Carlsbad Decrees (1819), and the second the formal dismissal of the last Prussian reformer. But flowery romanticism, and sugary Biedermeier culture, could not blur the sharp lines of a new religious charter etched in the polity and worship of Prussia's union church. Made more responsive by repressive alterations, the machinery of church government stood ready to enforce the king's new liturgical agenda as the basis for a ceremonial union between confessions. Some accomodation was made for the confessionalist surge that issued from the religious Awakening. But since the foundations were firmly laid, reactionary impulses ensured that construction would proceed on schedule.

After a brief examination of changes in Prussian church government, we will turn to new questions raised by the king's liturgical agenda, as well as the old problem of church union. These themes will lead us inside the bureaucratic maze of Prussia's church administration; its leaders consistently held to the unwritten charter between church and state, even in such sensitive areas as the church's worship, and relations between evangelical confessions. In Prussia, at least, the church's primary social role was molded by a prior relationship with the state.

In 1818, Prussia's monarch flexed his muscles and removed all internal tariffs within the state, a move that jeopardized the individual identities of the separate provinces. That same year as well, the clergy synods that had just been formed in 1817 were shelved until 1843. The state's central Ministry of Public Worship made all important decisions on the ordination and placement of clergy, and also consistently exercised general supervision and discipline, although consistories could initiate disciplinary action, and dismiss clergymen subject to the ministry's final judgment. The government shared with consistories such administrative powers as the examination of pastoral candidates, and deliberation on specifically theological matters. Provincial consistories supervised evangelical, Roman Catholic, Jewish and sectarian groups in each province until 1825, but the "Oberpraesident" then took responsibility for all religious groups except evangelicals.

After 1829, the general superintendent became the province's chief ecclesiastical executive. As he traveled about ordaining clergy, dedicating churches, and visiting congregations, he personified the idea of a united evangelical church. Like the king on the territorial level, he epitomized a "personal union" between the religious party, represented by the consistory, and the state, represented by the Ministry of Public Worship. Hence, he chaired the consistory, but also served as an administrator for the whole ministerium. Some general superintendents were named "bishops" in the union church, and Borowski of Koenigsberg even became an archbishop.

The consistories continued to slide into oblivion, with responsibilities not commensurate with their status. For example, in the early twenties the consistory at Brandenburg busied itself deliberating the case of Pastor Gottlob C. Baetzer. He was fined thirty "Thaler" for conducting an afternoon prayer meeting on the Day of St. Michael, after an administrative decree declared that the festival could not be observed in the afternoon.

In general, the state's bureaucratic structure continued to set the pace for church government. After taking control of the Rhineland in 1815, Prussia first set up two provinces, with headquarters in Koblenz and Cologne. The consistory in each province cared for the whole province's religious needs, even though the attachment of Aachen to the provincial headquarters in Koblenz interrupted a longstanding connnection with Cologne, and caused grave problems. After the two provinces were united in 1822, a provincial consistory was created in Koblenz (1826).

While practices varied, evangelicals in this province had a

long traditon ot administering their own church. As a result, they stiffened their resistance to the king's new liturgy until eventually an accomodation on church polity was worked out. In the interim, the state channeled the spirit of self-administration toward its own ends by using rewards and promotions to win the goodwill of Rhenish church leaders. In 1818, an eccelesiastical assembly in Duisburg elected as its respected "president" the new superintendent, William J. G. Ross. By 1820 he was playing a pivotal role in extended plans to incoporate Rhenish-Westphalian Protestants into the union church. In 1826 he strongly supported the government in the provincial "Landtag," and soon the king shrewdly named him as the Rhineland's first general superintendent. Gerhardt F. A. Strauss and F. W. Krummacher, both of Elberfeld, and K. W. Snetlage of Wuppertal also received significant political appointments.

Reformed clergymen in the western provinces had strongly opposed the heavy-handed administrative structure imposed by the Prussians, as well as faltering attempts to create a skeletal form of synodal polity, which they judged inadequate. Meeting in Duisburg in 1817 to respond to the proposed synodal constitution, the pastors in Cleve, Berg and Mark acknowledged their willingness to make minor changes in order to achieve geater unity with other provinces, but for them, the most pertect constitution unequivocally remained the "presbyterial church constitution." Specifically, they wanted lay participation in synodal meetings and the proper use of elections in church administration. The next year they asked Hardenberg for permission to retain their presbyterial constitution, since "the evangelical church rejects all hierarchy among pastors." In 1819 the Westphalian Provincial Synod offered a similar response to the proposed synodal constitution, taking issue with the restricted power of an all-clergy provincial synod, and the curtailment of lay participation on the local level. We will pursue this challenge below.

By 1822-23 in territorial Prussia and most other states, the possibility of a synodal or presbyterial-synodal system of church government seemed remote. One grave result was that the churches did not train an effective corps of lay leaders when they needed them most. In many areas, the organized church was farther removed from the people than it had been during the Enlightenment. In Prussia, the king abandoned plans for autonomous ecclesiastical polity at the same time that he scrapped Hardenberg's constitutional plans.

The only places in Prussia with potential for developing some degree of autonomous church government seemed to be the towns and cities, whose administrative structures the reformers had refurbished. But like most of the major issues of the century, the problems of church polity were not open to solution on this level, although these communities reflected such problems in their life and work. Since the people who were attracted to national issues—and here we might add, the problems of church polity as well—did not devote themselves to municipal politics, "the character of city government was largely determined by that section of the solidly conservative propertied class whose interests were centered around local affairs."(3) Efforts to develop autonomous church government floundered in the towns no less than in the country while the restoration pushed ahead, arresting all moves toward representative polity.

United in Prayer

Sitting on the pinnacle of Prussia's ecclesiastical structure, the king in 1822 promulgated a new liturgical agenda for use in the state's union church. This precipitated a long struggle over acceptance of the new service book. The ensuing battle—and the king's ultimate victory—more sharply focused some points of the unratified agreement between church and state about the church's social role as model for society.

Even though at first the agenda's use was not obligatory, it drew fire from those who were embittered by lack of progress in securing representative church polity. Others had their own reasons for joining the fray, but the efficient church bureaucracy in Prussia made it extremely difficult to wage an effective war of resistance. After the initial shock wore off, the king squared off against separatist confessionalists, who attacked the union church by concentrating on the agenda's inadequacies, as we will discover in a later chapter.

The state's assuming control over church registries earlier in the century pointed the way toward the king's promulgation of the new church service book, or agenda. Until the end of the eighteenth century, church consistories supervised the care and management of church registries, which were assumed to be a spiritual responsibility associated with the pastor's cure of souls. State officials were not involved. But this was before the role of the consistories changed, and before the self-conscious state began collecting vital demographic statistics such as births, deaths and marriages. When the church's old administrative structure was scuttled in 1808, the Spiritual and Educational Boards of the Ministry of Interior began to inspect and supervise church registries in each province of Prussia. Unlike the French model, clergymen continued to post the records. The revival of consistories in 1815 made little difference: the consistory supervised bookkeeping connected with purely spiritual matters, while the Ministry of Interior retained responsibility for tallying the statistics. Two years later, the Ministry of Public Worship assumed control of both functions.

But the church's guidebook for worship life was its liturgical agenda, not its registries. The agenda was certain to be an interest of the Prussian king, since he viewed divine services as the church's equivalent of the army's parade. When he named himself the church's "summus episcopus" (chief bishop) in 1798, he noted in a cabinet order that the time was ripe for a common agenda to bring Lutheran and Reformed confessions closer. War and political upheaval interrupted the work of a commission appointed to draft a new agenda, and a new committee had to be formed in 1814. The king inspected the finished product in 1816; it had been designed for use in military church services at the Court and Garrison Church in Potsdam, and the Garrison Church in Berlin. The king's spokesman, Sack, responded to Schleiermacher's strong protest against this provisional agenda.

At least the Prussians' "summus episcopus" was not a Roman Catholic, as were the kings of Saxony and Bavaria, or a notorious adulterer, like William I of Wuerttemberg. But much to his dismay, many clergymen were unable or unwilling to distinguish between his supposed sovereign right, under "jus circa sacra," to promulgate a church liturgy for use by all Protestants, and his moral exhortation that the two confessions should join in a voluntary religious union. The fact of the matter was that from the start his interest in evangelical union was largely cultic and ceremonial, but since he could control the latter, he could also control the former.

The king's attraction to high church liturgical practices seemed somewhat out of character for a Reformed monarch, but he persisted nonetheless, donating crucifixes and candleabras for the Garrison Church at Potsdam and the Cathedral in Berlin in 1816. His recent acquaintance with Anglican and Russian Orthodox practices led him to deck the altar black on Good Friday—a day the Reformed scarcely observed—and to encourage laymen to kneel for communion, and clergymen to sign themselves with the cross. Five years earlier, he ordered clergymen to wear pleated gowns with wide arms. Soon some of the Prussian practices were adopted in other states; a white surplice augmented the black gown during altar services and, in Wuerttemberg, during Communion.

After 1817, the king personally studied the liturgical agendas in use during the Reformation period. Perhaps Stein's earlier plans for a new liturgy and hymnbook, using hymns from before the year 1700, intensified his interest. In any case, almost singlehandedly he compiled an agenda that was based largely on Luther's masses of 1523 and 1526, and Joachim of Brandenburg's Agenda of 1540. When the new agenda appeared at Christmas in 1821, its introduction noted that with God's help, its use by military congregations would promote "Christian fear of God, true virtue, and true love of the fatherland." An early revision corrected a major error and enabled the congregation to pray for the crown princess, as well as for the crown prince.

On February 12, 1822, a royal cabinet order directed that all clergy receive copies of the agenda that had been prepared for military use. Its mandatory usage in institutions funded directly by the state, such as boarding schools, hospitals, and prisons, was an unmistakable sign in the middle of Prussia's constitutional battle—which occurred between 1815 and 1823—that the one unchanging reality was the monarch, not a constitution. Administrative control was being tightened in all areas, including the church's divine liturgy, and the ordinand's oath in the new agenda gave a clear witness to the monarch's undisputed legitimacy: "With my life and blood, with doctrine and example, word and deed, I will defend royal power . . . as it is established in our wholesome monarchical form of government. Likewise, at the appropriate time I will make it know if I discover anything that aims to abolish or alter it . . . ." This part of the ordinand's oath was totally new in the history of German Protestantism.

One of the agenda's rubrics restricted the sermon to a half-hour maximum. This irritated long-winded rationalists no less than some neo-pietists, who sometimes preached for two hours in fresh, vibrant language. Some argued that the agenda removed the sermon from its central position in the service, but this probably did not bother the king since he had become increasingly disenchanted with preachers. Once he left a service in Potsdam because the sermon was a paean of praise for him and his army's courage, remarking to a clerical aide that he had no use for preachers who forgot that "God's Word never flatters man."

The time limit on sermons was only one of several irritants. Rubrics dealing with music and choirs made little sense to small congregations unequipped to implement them. The choir seemed to overshadow the congregation, and congregations seemed to sing more responsories than hymns. The new prayers and pericopes were unfamiliar to clergy and laity alike. Some complained that the agenda's supposed liturgical frills and Romanizing tendencies might transform the preacher into a priest, and encourage a misunderstanding of the liturgy as an "opus operatum." But for the king, the agenda's most important virtue covered a multitude of deficiencies: it nurtured the development of a cultically uniform church, even when a Lutheran congregation had no neighboring Reformed congregation with which to break bread. And bread breaking was no small matter, since now the liturgy required the use of the Reformed custom of breaking the communion bread. An appropriate biblical text justified this practice.

61

Generally speaking, initial reaction to the agenda was mixed. The consistory at Koenigsberg indicated in 1823 that some fifty pastors appreciated the Christian spirit and biblical language of the agenda, and planned to use it without revision. But it added that a much larger group would continue to use the so-called Prussian Church Agenda, published most recently in 1789, because worshippers could follow its prayers in their hymnals. A pastor in Brandenburg reported that when he and another pastor announced at a synod meeting in 1827 their decision not to use tne agenda, he spoke last since he was the youngest one present. After he finished, the superintendent conducting the meeting vented his full anger on him, and lashed out even more vehemently after other pastors indicated that they were changing their position. Some days later the consistory invited this young man to meet with the hierarchy. Immediately after it was distributed, the agenda was used without alteration by only six percent of the Prussian clergy.

Fears ran high that the agenda was to become an instrument for sanctioning a confessionally based union of consensus. The king continued to insist that confessional documents were private matters without significance for religious parties, but some Lutheran and Reformed pastors would not accept this logic. One Reformed preacher in Berlin flatly declared that no king could release him from his ordination oath to the Confession of Sigismund, and until that occurred he would continue to use the Reformed agenda of 1713. The king wisely refused to exercise his power as "summus episcopus" in such a direct confrontation; his politics paid off, and eventually the majority of the clergy adopted the agenda with deliberate speed.

But for some the problem remained. The incorporation in the ordination formula of a nebulous statement on confessional commitment led 500 of the 744 pastors in confessionally sensitive Silesia to reject the agenda as late as 1827. As early as 1818, on the other hand, a cabinet order had abolished the traditional promissory commitment of Reformed pastors to the Confession of Sigismund (1614), and the electoral edicts of 1614, 1662 and 1664; and in 1813, the Section for Public Worship had relieved Lutheran pastors of their obligation to the sixteenth century Lutheran Confessions.

The ordination oath in the agenda bound the ordinand in an ambiguous way to the "symbolical books of the Evangelical Church of the Prussian monarchy." The ordinand was free to fill this phrase with appropriate meaning, but some argued that one could not take an oath simultaneously to all the Reformed and Lutheran confessions, since they did not agree in all points. In 1826, four prominent clergymen proposed a compromise that would permit the ordinand to vow allegiance to scriptural doctrine and the creeds, and then affirm his loyalty to the other symbolical writings in accordance with the type of congregation he would be serving—Lutheran, Reformed or union. But the king's next edition failed to include this revision in the agenda.

Despite the growing acceptance of the new service book, the king and his party had to pray for the patience of Job, especially after a pamphlet war erupted. Since the government was beginning to appreciate the power of the press and the increasing role of public opinion, it was no surprise when the king came to his own defense, after Schleiermacher and several other prominent figures attacked the agenda in print, with an anonymous publication entitled LUTHER IN RELATION TO THE EVANGELICAL CHURCH AGENDA IN PRUSSIA'S ROYAL LANDS (1827, 2nd ed., 1834). Writing as "Sincerus Pacificus," Schleiermacher demonstrated his allegiance to the union, but questioned the sovereign's right to promulgate a liturgical book that was strictly the church's prerogative. Ordered in 1825 to use the new book or follow the old book verbatim, he joined twelve other respected preachers from Berlin in criticizing the work as defective in literary style, and out of harmony with evangelical freedom. The king refused to act on their petition, but neither did he follow the recommendation of the Minister of Public Worship to take them to court. The government warned that in the future their behavior should improve.

By 1824, encouraged in part by royal gifts of costly crucifixes and expensively bound copies of the agenda, 5,343 of Prussia's 7,782 congregations were using the agenda in some form. In the province of Pomerania, 1,136 of 1,311 congregations had the service book on their altar, although many incorporated local revisions. The king offered two alternatives: use the new agenda, or follow the old agenda to the letter. Many clergymen were caught on the horns of a dilemma, since traditionally they had been free to adapt liturgical services in the old agenda to fit local conditions. The new agenda abrogated this freedom, just as it eliminated "ex corde" prayers. The king insisted that he did not want "every foolish pastor to bring his muddled brainstorms to market, to mold and change as he saw fit what the immortal reformers, Luther and Melanchthon, composed and arranged."

But in the real world of church politics, the king modified his position on the agenda in order to attain his goal, namely, its widespread acceptance. He began in Pomerania. Since, as noted, most of the congregations accepted the agenda, he permitted the addition of a supplement (1827) containing old Lutheran prayers and other formulae. He also allowed other provinces to create editorial commissions and make revisions, and in 1829, the third edition contained provisions for provincial supplements. In the Rhineland and Westphalia, the acceptance of a common agenda in the early thirties was part of the compromise that led to royal approval for a modified form of representative church order in 1835.

Prussia's Evangelical Church

With his Ninety-Five Theses, Claus Harms of Kiel, a non-Prussian, had offered an inauspicious greeting to the king's proclamation of union in 1817. Soon more than two hundred publications attacked or endorsed the union. Unlikely bedfellows, such as Christoph F. von Ammon, the rationalist court preacher in Saxony, and H. L. Huebner, the director of the seminary in Wittenberg, rallied to support Harms' anti-union position, though for different reasons. But in Prussia, proponents of the union continued to be rewarded; Borowski was named archbishop in 1829, and ennobled in 1831 at the age of ninety-two. Prussia's Evangelical Church was there to stay.

The king kept careful account of pastors and congregations that adopted the union. Between 1817 and 1823, he signed fifteen commendations for those helping to advance the union. The preponderance of Reformed congregations in the west explains why the union was more widely accepted there than in the eastern plains, which were largely Lutheran. To help things along, a cabinet order officially substituted the term "Evangelical" for "Protestant" in 1821; the name of the union church, the "Evangelical Church," now had the ring of full authenticity. Altenstein, the Minister of Public Worship between 1817 and 1838, gave his full support to the union with a hard line on the agenda and resistance to any form of representative polity. He was convinced that the state had to retain the initiative in religious matters, and his policies brought some financial savings to the state. The unification of Lutheran and Reformed congregations between 1817 and 1840 eliminated 205 clergy positions, while only 105 new positions were added.

The king remained ambiguous about the interrelation of union, agenda, and confessional subscription so that the politics of his union effort had time to work. For example, in 1822 he said that evangelical pastors were obliged to proclaim no other doctrine "than that which accords with Holy Scripture, and the confession of faith contained therein and in the symbolical books." While he personally thought that the confessions of the two churches overlapped, opposition to his views centered in freedom of conscience, and loyalty to one's confessional commitment.

The three hundredth anniversary of the Augsburg Confession in 1830 intensified the confessional question for some, but Altenstein used the occasion to support the union's advance. In a letter late in 1829, he wrote that "the anniversary of the Confession's presentation <to the emperor in 1530> aims at permitting the Evangelical Church to honor itself in such an observance by ordering its most important affairs," especially the matter of union. The next April he warned the king that efforts to support the union and agenda independently would endanger both, but in view of the agenda's wide use, the anniversary was a "propitious moment" for giving new impetus to the union. Two weeks later the king instructed him to intensify efforts among general superintendents and other church officials, so that the clergy would fully accept the practice of breaking bread during Communion, an act regarded as the "symbolic expression of entrance into union." These same officials were to recommend that preachers and congregations stop using the names of the two confessional groupings, Lutheran and Reformed.

Altenstein issued his circular order in six days. An earlier royal order dealing with the anniversary emphasized the ecumenical nature of the Augsburg Confession, and advised that, alongside the Bible, the document was "regarded as the fundamental basis of the Evangelical Church." Neither directive mentioned the sixteenth century squabble over the "alterted" and "unaltered" versions of the Confession.

By 1834 the king felt secure enough in the union to proclaim the compulsory use of the agenda. While the cabinet order hailed the nearly twenty year history of the Prussian union, its tone differed sharply from the first proclamation in 1817. Earlier, the king discussed the possibility of combining the two confessional groups into a single "united evangelical church," but in 1834, he referred to two evangelical confessions. Now the goal was "external ecclesiastical communion" between the two churches, not, as it had been, their "inner union." One informed scholar notes that "no longer was the goal a union of consensus, but confederative, union whose distinctive traits were partnership in church, chancel and Holy Communion."(4)

Among the forces that turned the tide against a union of consensus by 1834 were the continuing resistance of some evangelicals in Silesia and Pomerania, and the growing power of confessionalism even among "New Lutherans," who were willing to make their confessional witness within the union church.(5) The king's cabinet order that year emphasized that entrance into the union was a free choice, totally unrelated to the agenda's use, which was not obligatory in view of the provincial supplements. The order said in part, "The union intends and signifies no surrender of the prevailing confession of faith, nor does it abolish the authority that the symbolical books of both evangelical confessions have had to date. Entrance only expresses the spirit of moderation and gentleness, a spirit that no longer permits differences with the other confession on specific doctrinal points to be the basis for refusing external church fellowship." The agenda was "based on the directives that I released," the king added, but the union issued from "each one's free decision." He insisted that one could not reject the agenda out of dislike for the union.(6) It appears that he thought he was giving churchmen an opportunity to practice freedom within boundaries set by authorities, although not all of them interpreted the matter this way.

Where the union created no doctrinal sparks of its own, "Firebreather" Altenstein played the role of arsonist. He won few friends in the Rhineland with his insistence that the union would be administered from the top. Although more than half of the province's congregations had entered the union by 1828, Rhenish evangelicals played hide and seek, withholding full endorsement until they received a new church order in 1835. In the area administered from Duesseldorf, less than a third of the 152 churches, and only sixty of 172 pastors, remained outside the union. More than two-thirds of the churches were unionized by 1830, when negotiations for the new church order showed good promise. Some Lutheran pastors in the area feared that the union would bring defections and subsequent loss of personal income; they were accustomed to adding to their meagre incomes through gifts and perquisites, but Reformed pastors usually did not share in this good fortune.

After difficult negotiations, Prussia in 1834 formed a "Zollverein" (tarrif union) among a number of northern states, extending to them the benefits and opportunities she experienced after abolishing inter-provincial tariffs in 1818. Was it mere coincidence that the same year the king publicly changed his views on the nature of the Evangelical Church's union, from a confessional union to a union of consensus, or confederative union? One receives the impression that by design or force of circumstances, Prussia's leaders were preparing to absorb the other German states, and the process left no room for confessional loyalties to undercut royal control of the church. In point of fact, most confessionalists soon discovered that they could continue to function within the union, so long as they recognized the king's prerogative to control the agenda of what might be called their holiest hour, the hour of worship. But above all, they had to acknowledge the king's approval of their status.

The supposed "confessionless" character of Prussia's union church was a knotty problem. Those who wanted Prussia to resuscitate the old imperial "corpus evangelicorum," or to assume leadership as Protestantism's protector in Germany, approached the question indirectly. Pursuing this remote possibility, Prussia sent invitations to Karlsruhe, Kassel, Darmstadt and Stuttgart in 1833, but the proposed conference of Protestant representatives never materialized. In 1830 as well, a royal order indirectly broached the problem of an officially "confessionless" church. It directed all officials to favor orthodox preachers in filling vacant positions, but failed to define orthodoxy or describe its confessional basis, despite the monarch's apparent dissatisfaction with rationalism and some strains of contemporary philosophy.

As the century progressed, the supposed "confessionless" nature of Prussia's Evangelical Church adversely affected a number of strong confessionalists in Germany. It turned them against Prussia. Some found confessionalism to be a convenient channel for their expression of anti-Prussian--and sometimes pro-Austrian and pro-particularist—sentiments, especially as Prussia began exerting positive leadership in the cause of German unification. No less valid for others, including "New Lutheran" confessionalists in Prussia, was the accepted formula: to be a good Prussian meant to be a supporter of the union. Throughout the century, Prussia was called the "mother of the union," a phrase that had political as well as church-historical significance.

Church polity was the one factor under constant monarchical monitoring between 1817 and 1834. The monarch's second line of control was the union and the agenda, since their implementation depended on the church bureaucracy and a polity of limited representation. Confessionalism—within defined limits--was the third way for the church to live a life of "freedom" within authorized boundaries. Thus, "confessionless" seemed to be a more positive term in 1817 than in 1834, when the king's order stressed that confessions had the right to live, as long as they did not violate the state-enforced rights of others.

In his support for the union church and the agenda until the early thirties, the king stressed the unity of the

Protestant communion in Prussia. His unitive emphasis on behalf of these two projects paralleled prevailing philosophical currents, and the restorational politics of the second and third decades. When he made the agenda compulsory at the same time that he clarified the union's confederative character in 1834, the king was mirroring a shift in cultural currents. Generally speaking, from about 1830 to about 1848, intellectual currents and political thought in Germany stressed the parts of the totality under consideration, while not ignoring their basic unity; the period up to 1830 was characterized by comparatively more emphasis on the element of unity. This shift in emphasis, from the whole to the parts, found its counterpart in Prussia's Evangelical Church; polity structure and agenda assured unity, but the union was now admittedly confederative.

In 1840, Frederick William III composed a testimonial for his son while preparing for his death. He recommended that the prince preserve the agenda at all costs since it was a protective shield for Christ's revealed religion. What he failed to say was that, as long as the agenda's rubrics prevailed, there was living proof that Prussia's vast northern plain was truly united—if only for one hour each Sunday. Through the agenda, Prussia's church continued to be a model for society, even if some degree of confessional adherence was permitted.

VOCATIONAL PRESSURES

Among other things, church union in Prussia and several other states were cooperative efforts between monarch and nobility to regain or retain the initiative in church life. Especially in Prussia, the union and its supporting apparatus relied on accrued respect for the Enlightenment's pragmatic approach, and this neutralized in part the growing influence among the clergy of the religious Awakening and its new daughter, confessionalism. As professional religious middlemen, pastors were susceptible to all sorts of social and economic pressure. The crown and upper class pressed their joint effort relentlessly, in a way that resembled their recourse to restorational politics in the face of a restive society. Clergymen were to become model functionaries in a model institution.

The Prussians usually avoided the kind of open pressure the Bavarians used to force Protestant soldiers to attend Roman Catholic services, and kneel as the "Corpus Christi" tabernacle passed by. Nevertheless, they were skilled masters at cooptation, the genius mark of their state since its inception. Prussia had the capacity to manipulate the state church, especially its clergy, while on the way to a party of cooptation and unification she was hosting for the other German states. And the king's unilateral control of the church enabled him to display it as a model for a society on the way to discovering industrially-based freedoms. This society would have to learn and exercise its newfound liberties within an authoritarian context.

It was no accident that Prussia's efficient clergy and ecclesiastical bureaucracy—and not merely the size of her Protestant community—made Prussia the undisputed leader of German Protestantism. Her clergy were state officials, and state officials recognized that the state's foundation was not its physical resources or national culture, but its power—the army's, and the intellectual resiliency of the bureaucracy. Prussia was an idea that had to take on reality, and power played a key role.

As bureaucrats of sorts, clergymen in most of the German states were in no position to write their own job descriptions. Herder earlier described the pastor as the "preacher of morals, district magistrate, registrar, and secret police agent under state authority." Generally, the social status of pastors was lower than that of their English counterparts because their positions were not financially independent; most of them came from peasant or middle class stock. The "black police," as they were sometimes called, had to carry out their ruler's orders meticulously, especially in Prussia. At the turn of the century, the typical Badenese pastor performed administrative tasks under the magistrate's supervision. He knew all about brook dredgings and roadway repairs; he reported epidemics and the deaths of property owners, whose holdings would be taxed; he kept records of births, deaths, marriages, and the number of blind, lame, deaf, dumb and

70

aged people, illegitimate children, and homeless orphans; he provided population statistics and lists of available recruits for the military--and he was present when new recruits were conscripted. To round out his day, he supervised the village school, and assisted the magistrate in caring for the poor.

In the period before 1848, Prussia's numerically stable group of about 6,000 Protestant clergymen were socially differentiated in position, income, ability, education and life-style. But like their counterparts elsewhere, they were subtly pressured to follow directives by an overabundant supply of replacements. Many theological "candidates" waited as long as ten or fifteen years for a permanent parish assignment, and sometimes "marrying the boss's daughter" was a prerequisite for securing the patron's approval for a position. But all during the period, theological faculties continued to train too many students. In Prussia, for example, a report indicated in 1833 that the number of Protestant theological students had doubled in a few years, while students for the priesthood had tripled. Since only one-third of the graduates were needed, a kind of pastoral or spiritual proletariat was formed; it eventually included such candidates as David F. Strauss, Ludwig Feuerbach, and Johann H. Wichern—men who, through their writings and institutional activities, contributed their fair share to theological and ecclesiastical upheaval and reform in Germany.

The wage of most German pastors put them slightly above the poverty level. During the early "Goethezeit," the average pastor collected 50 to 70 "Thaler" annually; when the era closed, he was earning 350 to 800 "Thaler" if he lived in the country, and 450 to 1,000 if he worked in town. Many clergymen supplemented their income with other work, while wives and children took to the fields to gather the tithe already included in their income. Some of the most popular moonlighting trades were tutoring, writing, horsetrading, farming, vegetable gardening, the cultivation of silkworms, and brokering money.

We can begin to understand, then, why most clergymen were ready to follow orders in implementing the new religious charter in the German churches. It was not easy to slough off financial, bureaucratic, theological and political pressures, with two or three candidates standing in the wings, ready to take one's place. And it was almost ironic that clergymen were called upon to implement the unwritten charter in the field of education, the source of so much of their own vocational uneasiness.

RELIGION IN THE SCHOOLS

In the years before 1830, the Prussian state acted vigorously to ensure continuing close cooperation between the church and the elementary school. The state's concern for religion in the schools was additional evidence that the acknowledged, but unwritten contract between church and state was generally acceptable to both parties. For state authorities, the teaching of religion and the teaching of morality, especially the virtue of obedience, seemed to be coterminous in elementary schools. Through religious and moral instruction, the church inculcated the spirit of legitimacy among the masses, more successfully in the lower schools than in the "gymnasia," or upper schools. A student who failed to enroll in one of these institutions by the age of nine or ten forfeited his chance for university training. Many of the teachers in the old Latin school, which were the "gymnasium's" immediate predecessor, had been second rate theologians. Early in the century the Prussian reformers replaced them with state-examined teachers who were graduates of philosophical faculties. The examination procedure adopted in 1810 seemed to assure that the "gymnasium" would subordinate Christianity to Greek ideals. Religion continued to play a fairly important role in the Protestant "gymnasia," but the historian Hajo Holborn notes that that religion "inevitably competed with humanistic values."(7)

In 1825, the central educational administration in Prussia took full responsibility for the "gymnasia." Although church consistories were relieved of their work in this area, Minister of Worship Altenstein continued to show a great interest in the upper school's religious curriculum. The typical student had thirty-two contact class hours each week; two were in religion, six in mathematics, three in

72

geography, and twelve to nineteen in classical languages. The course of study extended over six years. In 1826, Altenstein issued a memorandum urging directors of "gymnasia" to conduct religious instruction in the morning, although all classes that opened and closed morning and afternoon sessions were to begin or end with prayer. All major ceremonies, including graduation, induction of new teachers, and retirements, were to include religious exercises. Boarding schools were to conduct morning and evening table devotions, and teachers were to attend divine services and Holy Communion with their students. According to Altenstein, "gymnasia" teachers were to remember that "it is the state's responsibility to train up Christians in the pupils of its schools . . . the teacher must struggle toward a God-fearing, moral way of thinking that rests on faith in Jesus Christ, and the well-founded knowledge of the Christian certainty of salvation," not on some flighty morality without a foundation.

In 1829, an order directed the general superintendents of the church, who were responsible for evangelical schools in their province, to re-reform the "gymnasia" as much as possible. Altenstein asked them to give special attention to religious instruction, reminding superintendents that elementary schools were "institutions of preparatory training for the church."

In elementary schools, zeal for "throne and altar" permeated all grade levels. Frederick William III launched a private war against liberals seeking a constitution when he rejected their preferred term, "Freedom War," in textbooks in favor of the term "War of Liberation." An even greater challenge to the system was the effort to establish "Simultantschule," non-denominational elementary schools that included children of both evangelical and Roman Catholic parentage. In 1819, Hesse-Nassau began to educate children without regard for their religious affiliation. But this model did not fit Prussia's reactionary needs. A non-denominational school would diminish the stature of the local pastor, and deprive him of the chance to explain the nuances of the throne-altar alliance to little children.

The Prussian king's edict on education in 1822 did not outlaw non-denominational schools. It merely called them undesireable since "the chief ingredient of education, religion, is not suitably cultivated there, and it is in the nature of things that this cannot occur." The code word "suitably" was softened somewhat by the provision that non-denominational schools could be formed if local congregations and civil and religious education authorities approved.

The major regulation for Prussia's elementary and teacher training schools was issued in the year of the reactionary Carlsbad Decrees, 1819. It deeply reflected the spirit of restoration and legitimacy. While the order provided that no child had to participate in the religious instruction of another confession against the will of his parents, it perpetuated the dangerous myth that the school was confessionless--except for this hour of religious instruction--with the provision that "Jewish children may enroll in Christian Schools." But, interestingly, it added that "Jewish schools may not admit Christian children." Schools educated the whole person, providing knowledge, skills, and especially that discipline that was inseparable from others, "religious faith, which must provide the keystone for the school's entire educational effort."

The school's most important function was to help the student develop insight into the nature of his eternal destiny, and man's relationship with God, on which it depended. The school must "firmly anchor the student in the spirit of true religious faith and piety at an early age, and fortify it in him," the regulation noted. The plan stipulated that each day begin and end with prayer and pious meditation. In larger schools with students of mixed confessions, a teacher was to lead the students in a common devotional exercise. The goal of discipline was to inculcate virtue, but the teacher's "most holy duty" was to nurture "devotion for king and state, and definite obedience to law and legal authority."

CONVERTING THE JEW

The religious charter was also implemented by those who tried to give full citizenship status in the "Christian state" to Jews—by converting them to Christianity. Since Francophobia played a role in the incipient nationalism that flourished during the War of Liberation, it is probable that evangelism efforts among Jews during the restoration also molded the character of German nationalism as an "anti-X" movement, with the "X" quotient changing from time to time. In any case, this might help explain why so much effort was expended to convert Jews, although the long history of anti-Semitism should not be discounted. It also highlights the proto-nationalistic element in the idea of the "Christian state," which was integral to the unwritten religious charter.

Jews received full citizenship in all the German states in 1848. Earlier they had been emancipated in Westphalia and Baden (1808), Hamburg (1811), Mecklenburg-Prussia (1812), and Hesse (1833). Despite emancipation in Prussia, they could not hold office, partly because the nobility greeted Hardenberg's reform with little enthusiasm. Some years later a prominent Prussian legislator said that widespread unbelief showed who needed emancipation—"the Christians' emancipation from Judaism!" The Jewish thinker Spinoza was assigned responsibility for the decline of Christianity.

Since the restoration involved attempts to rejuvinate the Christian faith, and cleanse it of rationalistic accretions that led to revolution, to make and to keep the Christian state "Christian" was perceived an act of religious patriotism. One of the restoration's chief spokesmen, Adam Mueller, explained that the persistence of Judaism in Christian society produced "patholigical tumors or boils" on the body of the state. Some conservatives held that since the Christian monarch derived from God, paralleling Christ's incarnation, good citizenship implied commitment to Christianity. It followed that admitting an outspoken foe of Christianity into the body politic was nothing less than "false humanitarianism." Especially in the thirties and forties, conservatives interpreted the liberal and radical theories of Hegel and the Young Hegelians as expressions of a Jewish spirit that was out of step with Christianity. Even the reknowned rationalist theologian H. E. Paulus offered frequent anti-Semitic statements between 1819 and 1831.

The Prussian king did not lag behind in steering Jews

75

toward Christianity. About the time he announced the creation of the union church, he dispatched a cabinet order prohibiting doctrinal and liturgical reform in Jewish synagogues. He offered Jews essentially two options: to stay with their old and mostly outdated forms, or desert their faith. A cabinet order in 1821 prevented interfaith ceremonies by outlawing the participation of Protestant clergy in Jewish religious ceremonies. Six years later the king asked the Berlin churches to arrange for one of their number to conduct a special service for Jews each Sunday. Another cabinet order in 1833 allowed Jewish mission societies to conduct an annual meeting with a divine service and an offering. A second directed that no one interfere with the work of missionaries to the Jews; at the same time, the missionaries could be fined or dismissed for throwing suspicion on any pastor, congregation, or member who disagreed with them. In 1834, the Silesian consistory ordered missionaries in that area not to seek permission to make addresses where no Jews lived.

The programmatic instrument for Jewish conversion was Christian baptism. The historian Friedrich Ruehs set the tone in 1816, when he wrote that all Jews should "be induced to <accept> Christianity through gentleness, and thereby fully acquire the distinctive character of the German people, so that in time the elimination of the Jewish people is accomplished in this way." A pious, high ranking finance official in Prussia claimed that if Jews resisted baptism, all that remained was "to exterminate <them> in violent fashion."(8)

Between 1822 and 1840, 2,200 Jews in Prussia's old provinces felt sufficient pressure and incentive to become evangelicals. August Neander, later known for his biographies of famous Christians and a history of Christianity, symbolized his change of heart by taking the name "Neander," Greek for "new man." He credited Schleiermacher's ON RELIGION, SPEECHES TO ITS CULTURED DESPISERS with a major role in his conversion. The Bavarian legal and political scholar Friedrich Julius Stahl also was a convert. In 1840 the Prussian king called him to Berlin as professor of law, and he became one of the most reknowned theorists and proponents of the "Christian state." In the old Roman Catholic town of Trier in western

Prussia, the father of Karl Marx showed his support for Protestant Prussia—and perhaps displayed a self-seeking spirit—by having his seven children baptized as evangelicals in 1824.

The history of "The Society for the Furtherance of Christianity among the Jews" tells the story concisely. Formed in 1822, fully two years before any foreign mission society in Prussia, the Society received royal approval only eight days after it was organized. Its central committee included such famous clerics as August Tholuck, Philipp K. Marheineke, and Franz Theremin, but in 1832, only 24 of the 144 members of the Society were clergymen, including two superintendents. Total membership dropped from 119 in 1837 to 81 in 1840. Military officers, lawyers, professors, members of the royal family, and others from the upper class, provided leadership in the early years; they composed nearly a fourth of the members in 1832. The central committee elected army officers of general rank as the first three presidents of the Society.

Eight auxiliary units, two of them in Potsdam, supported the Society's work in 1832. By 1839 the number rose to ten, while sister societies sprouted in Breslau, Posen, Minden, Koenigsberg, Olotzko and Dresden. But success was slow in coming. The first baptism occurred in 1822; 60 were performed between 1822 and 1824, 73 between 1830 and 1834 (19 in 1830), 32 in 1836, 39 the next year, 22 in 1838, and 13 in 1840. In 1838, nearly twice as many women were baptized as men. An upswing in the number of conversions followed the lean years of 1836 to 1840. Many of the Jewish converts were not native Berliners, but pilgrims who journeyed to Berlin for baptism.(9)

UNDERGIRDING THEORY

Germans have been known to examine an idea theoretically, and pursue its ramifications to their radical (from the Latin "radix," root) conclusions. While it should not be overemphasized, especially in theology this Teutonic tendency—if we can excuse such a nationalistic phrase for the moment--has been a prominent cultural trait. As a result, we might expect to find some intellectual articulation of the religious charter's foundations and ramifications.

The romantic movement contributed a number of key supports to the charter's intellectual foundations. Its most important contribution was an indirect one: it provided impetus for the restorational movement, the shakedown period for testing the consensus about the church's role in a society rendezvousing with change.(10) It also encouraged the development of nationalism, which affected the charter for decades. Romanticism's more direct influence on the church, as we will see in the next chapter, came through the religious Awakening and confessionalism.

The influential theologian, Schleiermacher, made important theoretical contributions to the consensus. We are more apt to understand his activities as a patriot and university professor if we examine those elements in his thought that led to the so-called "mediating school" of Protestant theology. While sometimes his position seemed at odds with the "chartered" position, we should not leap to the conclusion that Schleiermacher was a maverick. As I understand it, he made substantial contributions to the theoretical basis used by others later in the century to affirm the church's role in German society.

The most radical theorist was Hegel. More a philosopher of religion than a Christian theologian, he forged an all-encompassing philosophical position of idealism that provided for the state's absorption of the church. This radical extension of the charter's ramifications was too extreme for some, but in the forties, the Left Wing Hegelians used Hegel's ammunition to launch a massive intellectual assault on the Protestant consensus, namely, that the church was the state's model for society.

The Romantic Movement

Romanticism in Germany was neither a unified nor a highly organzied movement. Its leaders' itinerant habits stimulated diversity, and major emphases differed from one center to another. Jena was the first home for romantic

78

figures, followed in turn by Berlin and Heidelberg between 1804 and 1808. Wherever they traveled, they left a trail of art work, restorational political theory, nationalist emphasis, and a strong interest in history or nostalgic data.

The romantics' fascination with organic thought grew out of a desire to locate the individual in a community or collective unit, in which one could fully extend oneself without becoming a solipsist. They preferred an organic theory of state over the social contract, and viewed the individual's relation to state or nation as a highly personal matter. The romanticists of the 1790's, especially Novalis and Schlegel, were convinced that the cosmos was an inherently infinite source of individuality, and this increased rather than diminished the harmony of the universe. An important corollary was that the worth of each German state increased in proportion to its relationship to the total nation. In this light, the German historian Friedrich Meinecke noted that "it was no accident that the era of modern nationalistic thought was preceded by an era of individualistic freedom-movements. The nation drank as it were the blood of free individuality in order to take personhood into itself."(11)

The romantics' yearning for the past, and inchoate vision of the future, helped prepare the soil for nationalism. They realized that history conditioned them and their national traditions, which differed from the traditions of others; as the national community assumed some of the divinely imputed characteristics of the individual, it seemed to be invested with a divine mission.

The shift from cosmopolitan nationalism to political nationalism was only one of the consequences of the eventual politicization of romanticsm. Some romantics soon allied themselves with political conservatism. The theory of a continent-wide conspiracy associated with the French Revolution, as well as their own stress on social and political structures in history, pulled many of them toward political conservatism. The romantic Renaissance was so successful in "reviving the natural order" that by 1830 some people equated romanticism and reactionary politics, although originally the movement was politically liberal. The movement's attraction to reactionary and restorational politics comes as no surprise, since nostalgia seemed to be its most popular sentiment.

Many romantics were repulsed by certain aspects of contemporary life. They looked for meaning and direction to the distant pasts of nonclassical civilizations, especially Germany's. Lord Acton observed that their Renaissance revived the natural order, while doubling Europe's horizon; India achieved equality with Greece. They gave impetus to the study of psychology, early Christianity, comparative religions, literary criticism, historical criticism, and the history of art. Novalis' Jesus-poems helped spawn the century's quest for the "historical Jesus," and by the twenties, a new edition of Luther's works was at the printers.

In sum, German romantics did not appreciate the Enlightenment's tendency to universalize history. Convinced that human will could alter the course of history, they stressed the difference between nature and history. Some "enlightened" thinkers used the discipline of geography to force history into the natural mold, but as an assist to romantics, Karl Ritter severed the connection between history and geography, redefining geography so that the earth became the arena for human action.

This emphasis on the force of human will in the thought of Johann G. Hamann (1729-1786) was echoed by Fichte, Schelling, Schlegel, and the young Hegel while he was under Hoelderlin's influence. Romantic thinkers grappled with the identity crisis that came from realizing that the traditional formula about "man in nature" no longer applied. Engaging the problem much earlier than Darwin, and lacking the challenge of scientific Darwinism to absorb their energies, they turned to history to ameliorate their deprivation and "felt loss," and to answer the pertinent question: How did we come to feel this estrangement, also our estrangement from nature? Their slowly industrializing world no longer undulated to the natural rhythms of a natural society, but ticked to the time of a mechanical clock called history. To fill their void, they offered alternatives to nature that included national community and the arts.

The advantage of the arts was that they helped fill the

void, while satisfying the yearning for mystery so deeply embedded in the romantics. Since artistic endeavors seemed to hide mystery better than religion, the arts in fact became a substitute, as Hajo Holborn explains.(12) This search for synthesis was one reason why, in his later period, Schelling turned from philosophy to art, in search of a theosophical synthesis broad enough to encompass all nature, history and art. Literature could no longer merely "provide higher entertainment or moral examples; it became itself an instrument of exploration, a tool in the search for truth," much like the romantic, Frederick Schlegel, demanded.(13) Felix Mendelssohn Bartholdy (1809-1847) tried unsuccessfully to revive church life through musical art. He is remembered for dusting off the works of Bach, but his own oratorios were usually judged as too subjective for Christian worship, although the concert hall was more receptive. Devotees of the "Kulturkirche," or esthetic church, gathered for communal worship in temples built for opera, music and drama; musical culture and the dramatic arts took the place of church and religion for many. And after the show, the German bourgeoisie returned home to listen to piano and chamber music.

The romantic movement's emphasis on the past, and on the organic state, provided a broad intellectual framework for the emerging agreement about the church's role in society. Its eventual politicization in favor of conservatism was another influential factor. But to see how deeply it affected life and culture, we must look more closely at one of the charter's theoreticians who drank from its well.

Schleiermacher

Friedrich Schleiermacher, whom we met in the previous chapter as a patriotic preacher, was a geniuine romantic, and a theoretician of the new religious charter. His romantic bent was evident in the way he distinguished metaphysics and morals from religion, the "contemplation of the universe," but he was as much at home in the pulpit as in the lecture hall. In the course of the century, the theological faculty in which he taught at the University of Berlin included such luminaries as DeWette, Marheineke, Neander, Tholuck, Hengstenberg, Nitzsch, Dorner, Weiss, Kaftan, Harnack, Gunkel, Holl and Deissmann. But the title "church father" is reserved for him, since he was the fountainhead of the theological development in Germany in the nineteenth century.

Schleiermacher unmistakably broke new ground by moving beyond rationalism and supernaturalism to the sphere of feeling, as the context and content of religion. His treatment of the doctrine of God delineated the feeling of absolute dependence, or inchoate awareness, as the representation of God's being within man. His dogmatic explanation of this concept showed that consciousness of absolute dependence is basic to all religious consciousness.

His seminal work, ON RELIGION, SPEECHES TO ITS CULTURED DESPISERS (1799), claimed that religion (piety) is an original and autonomous form of self-consciousness, not to be identified with doing and morality on the one hand, or with knowing and science on the other. He rejected the traditional dichotomy between natural and supernatural, arguing that such a closed circle would permit oscillation only between rationalism and biblicism, on the one hand, and naturalism and supernaturalism on the other. His denotation of the word "God" contradicted the view that one's feeling of dependence "is itself conditioned by some previous knowledge about God." In his view, "natual knowledge" of God anchored in the intellect was neither possible nor necessary, since it would destroy the receptivity of self-consciousness. This same argument was equally applicable in the sphere of self-consciousness. With this tour de force, Schleiermacher sought to assure the autonomy of religion in the face of science and morality.

His dogmatics incorporated the particularized phenomena of the individual's piety, as well as the universal character of piety. The title of his major work, THE CHRISTIAN FAITH (1821), contained the crucial elements of a definition of dogmatics, whose function it was to provide a structured, systematic account of the "Christian faith" manifested in the community of believers. The church brought growing awareness of the kingdom of God, which was the consummate point of mankind's development. Thus, dogmatics was a churchly science, since the individual's self-consciousness could be born only in a community. Since religion was distinct from metaphysics and morals, in practical terms to reform the church meant to reawaken the living community by separating church and state.

According to Schleiermacher, one's universal perspective allowed one to view the three circles of individuality that assume identifiable form in mankind as a whole, in the various peoples of the earth, and in individuals. Each circle is contiguous to the other structually, though not temporally. He posited the state as the "material side" of the "Volk" or folk. The folk precedes the state, but the state is the "natural development of a higher rung of consciousness" in the folkish reality. "The state is the form of the people; the folk is only fully developed if this form presents itself clearly and perfectly in it."

In the problems he faced day by day, Schleiermacher rather consistently strove to put his principles into practice. He supported a representative synodal church polity; opposed attempts to impose a liturgy on the church except through its own choice; approved the union as a step toward autonomy; resisted efforts to make confessional subscription binding, or to create a new confession; and strongly opposed efforts to remove rationalists from the church. His work as a patriotic preacher was consistent with his views, as was his description of the folk-church as the desired form of the religious community.

But the evidence shows that he was no revolutionary. In fact, since he was coopted by the Prussian state and his own nationalist sentiments, he must share responsibility for providing part of the theoretical basis for the church's new charter, by works of omission if not by commission. It would be less than charitable to suggest that he was a major contributor to the charter's theoretical foundations, soley because he added to the overabundance of thinking and talking that kept theologians and churchmen occupied, when they should have been seizing the initiative from the state. A more responsible accusation is that he engendered and nurtured the idea of an inner freedom and peace that no extraneous circumstance could disturb.

This was an alternate way of speaking about submission, of having freedom within authority. Schleiermacher never

83

tired of confronting power with critical questions, but he was ill prepared to follow through at all costs after "speaking truth to power." In this regard, his example provided little inspiration, and no valid alternative, to the many theologians and churchmen who came to respect him through the century.

He continued to insist that a healthy tension existed between critical insight and religious certainty. This paradox—a familiar one for the romantics—allowed the theologian and preacher-churchman to function side by side. But was it possible to maintain such a high-strung paradox without yielding on either side at some critical point? Schleiermacher lived and worked at the dawn of a new century when a number of changes were imminent, and his was the responsibility of spelling out critical questions in the most helpful way. It was true that in terms of religious certainty and critical insight, his delineation of issues provided a reprieve for theology, which was under attack from all sides. But was it not also, in final analysis, an admission that while the state could not interrupt or damage the church's religious certainty, it could legitimately examine, influence and guide the church's decisions?

Schleiermacher's decision to work in the system must be judged a failure on another account as well. His primary interest lay with the educated middle class, which served the state zealously, since it hoped that the state would fulfil its social ideals. But Schleiermacher's theology was unable to bridge the gap between the educated and the church. He had to accept this defeat, and recognize as well that he had succumbed to the state's design for the church in Prussia.

Schleiermacher was at home in the early decades of the century. His notion of an organic system of dogmatics, derived in part from his appreciation of dialectics, was compatible with the mentality of system builders such as Hegel and others, who tried to reintegrate the multifaceted experiences and events of these decades. But like others, he sowed the seeds of dissolution in his system. Salvaging historical theology to edify the church, he gave impetus to a kind of rampant biblical criticsm, and more devastatingly, to reckless criticism of the historical

Jesus. His inclination to restrict dogmatic propositions
to the primary type opened the way for a devolution that
would not permit men to speak of God, or any absolute in
any sense, even in the sense of subjective apprehension.

This is not to deny his greatness. With Chateaubriand and
Lamennais, he "sought to show the Church not only as a
defunct relic of barbarism, but as a living organism;
religion not as antiquated superstition, but as an
expression of life, integral to man's individual psyche or
to his social well-being; doctrine not as a static,
timeless set of propositions declared once for all in the
Protestant Bible, or the Catholic's tradition, but as a
progressive, developing revelation in history."(14) For the
first time since Calvin, Protestantism had a theologian who
attempted to construct an organic system of dogmatics. On
a broader level, his philosophy of religion owed something
to Rousseau. The more immediate influence, of course, were
the German romantics, whose persistent efforts to fully
penetrate the transcendent ego by interrelating human egos,
especially through human institutions, found a parallel in
his emphasis on dogmatics as a churchly discipline.

The "mediating school" of theologians, sometimes mistakenly
called the "Schleiermachian school," also made distinctive
contributions to the theory and practice of the religious
charter. In one place, Karl Barth called them
"world-surveyors" who "knew how to place each thing nicely
in its place," but they were also "born churchmen" who
steered a middle course between right and left, "positive"
and "liberal," "supernatural" and "rationalist" theology.
For example, the theological faculty at Bonn's new
consolidated university (1818) followed this mediating
course, and favored the union until mid-century. Nitzsch,
Luecke, Sack, Gieseler, Augusti and Bleek also influenced
the area surrounding Bonn through their graduates, but at
that point the split between "positive" and "liberal"
occurred. In other areas as well, the conditions that gave
rise to this brand of theology also prevented it from
succeeding in full; the rise of the Ritschlian school at
Goettingen around 1870, for example, signalled that the
movement was dead.

But along the way, this school included powerful spokesmen

for the state's right to influence church life in a
substantial way. The movement included representatives on
most theological faculties. August Twesten (d. 1876) of
Kiel and Berlin walked the narrow path between criticism
and repristination as he sought to preserve churchly
religious faith. At Bonn and Berlin, Karl I. Nitzsch (d.
1868) provided heavy support for the union; in 1846 he
proposed a new confession for ordinands that summarized the
essentials of Christianity, while opponents joked about the
"Nitzschean" substitute for the Nicean Creed. In THE
SINLESSNESS OF JESUS, Karl Ullmann (d. 1865) of Heidelberg
and Halle explained that Jesus' singularity manifested
perfected divine humanity; the modern formulation of the
"idea of the holy" probably owes something to him. He
stressed individuality as the chief motif in Christianity,
and this explains his preoccupation with Jesus as an
individual. Julius Mueller (d. 1878) of Halle was
nicknamed "Sin Mueller" because of his theories about the
individual's decision to sin before the beginning of time.
Isaak A. Dorner (d. 1884) taught at a number of
universities before settling in Berlin. "Judaism," he
wrote in his proposal for a national church, "is a
corrosive that is able to bring about the deterioration of
the Christian communion." His mediational theology focused
on Christology. Richard Rothe (d. 1867) of Heidelberg is
sometimes included in this group, but his clear thinking
and systematic ability places him in a class by himself.
We will hear more about him later.

The list could continue, but these men are representative.
The mediating theologians were rather well reputed among
church authorities and state officials since they worked to
keep peace in the church, without scuttling strong churchly
and confessional theology. Particularly between 1828 and
1835, they flexed their muscles against certain rationalist
theologians, who seemed to be questioning the form of
church life that the state safeguarded, in return for other
duties rendered by the church.

Hegel

Georg W. F. Hegel (1770–1831) assuredly provided the most
comprehensive supporting theory for the church's unwritten
charter. A graduate of the same theological faculty at

Tuebingen that produced Schelling, Strauss, and several other important figures, he was a faculty colleague of Schleiermacher's at the University of Berlin, although the two had little in common. Hegel's most zealous disciple on the theological faculty, Marheineke, liked to flaunt his Iron Cross medal in Schleiermacher's presence, and Hegel himself lashed out at Schleiermacher's theology with the remark that "if the feeling of dependence is the ground of religion, then a dog makes the best Christian."

Accepting the validity of a dialectical relation between rationality and reality, Hegel formulated an ascending dialectic in which human personality fully realized itself in a social context. Since moral sanctions became moral imperatives in the state, the state was in no sense a dispensable commodity. Hegel reached these conclusions in part because the growing impact of historical consciousness forced the question of history upon him. In addition, he was also heavily influenced by the political restoration of the day.

For Hegel, the Absolute Spirit continued to manifest itself more and more fully in the dialectic of history. This process entailed the advancement and development of God's kingdom as well. The idea of the kingdom had two interconnected meanings: it denoted a purely spiritual entity, the condition of interior human perfection; and it characterized the developmental historical process. As Karl Loewith observed, Hegel effectively secularized Christian eschatology: "Hegelian Christianity . . . <transformed> the will of God into the spirit of the world, into the World Spirit and folk spirit."(15)

Since man was the instrument of the Absolute Spirit, the attainment of God's kingdom was a human task. But men could not act on their own accord. To develop his freedom fully, a man had to abide by the state's codified and regulative law; obedience to the state fully manifested the spirit's true freedom. As it rushed on toward the realization of God's kingdom, the state integrated man's highest activity; its rigorous morality and summons to obedience advanced the cause of the kingdom on earth.

Like history, man too was divided between the spiritual and the natural, some form of good and evil, according to

87

Hegel. His real task was to become spirit, not just to
transmit spirit. His escape from the purely natural would
come by subsuming his will to common morality, for in this
way alone God's kingdom would be attained. Man's task was
to isolate and expose his dichotomy, and in the process
identify the need for reconciliation, which came from God.
With the realization that the division between good and
evil was actually a polarity within the Absolute Spirit,
man would sense the appearance of a new religion, a
reconciliation of God and man that brought God's kingdom.
Jesus' cross and resurrection aptly portrayed the "kingdom
of love for God" into which man was introduced by this
understanding. Church and state served as the mediator of
history as it brought consciousness of reconciliation to
the fore. Christ's entrance into history, the Spirit's
reversion from the external to the internal, helped men
grasp their ultimate purpose: they were citizens in God's
kingdom.

Proposing to reconcile elements of classicism ("objective
idealism") and of romanticism ("subjective idealism") in
his system, Hegel succeeded in formulating the kind of
system that romantics envisioned: the absolute state with
no basis in natural law, which, like Savigny's historical
school of law, was the product of the Absolute Spirit
unravelling itself in history. This theory gave
respectability to the way the state handled the church in
Prussia and elsewhere. Hegel's prominence in Germany
coincided with the age of restoration; his greatest
following came after 1815, and his influence lasted well
into the thirties.

Hegel portrayed the church, then, in terms of its role in
the state. The principle of Christianity was the spirit's
undying ascent toward simple purity. The "pure heart" to
which Jesus referred was the prerequisite for realizing
God's kingdom, because the pure heart was the place of
God's dwelling. Jesus' revelation was the first important
moment in the church's history; the second came when the
community carried his message to the world. But if and
when the church succeeded in its mission, it would
ultimately be absorbed by the state. "Through the
consciousness-shaping activity of the church," one
commentator explains, "the state's morals and law will be
recognized as 'regulations of the divine nature' which

88

produce the actual, conclusive form of God's <eternal> kingdom; obedience of respected constitutional law is then the realization of this idea."(16)

Hegel unabashedly elevated philosophy above theology, and state above church. His power-state was a secularized version of the "Christian state," and his philosophy held a special attraction for those who supported the superiority of reason, while still seeking progress toward freedom within the authoritarian state. His philosophy of self-confidence made some conservatives uneasy, but in the age of restoration, it provided the most comprehensive intellectual formulation of the church's unwritten agreement with the state.

In the usual course of events, the sieve of time effectively strains out many of the trivialities and irrelevancies of history. But on some occasions, the "Zeitgeist" marks a period so indelibly that even hundreds of years later it presents a clear impression to the mind's eye. In Germany, the restoration was such a period.

No less distinct is the impression one receives of Protestant church life in this period. As Protestants held up their part of the bargained agreement, the restoration stamped its image on one area after another. Wherever one casts the eye--to favorable comments about the Holy Alliance in religious periodicals; to empty halls where clergy synods once convened; to uniform worship services in Prussia's thousands of churches; to pastoral candidates waiting in line for the office-holder to falter; to an elementary classroom, where a pastor patiently teaches children about God's gift of legitimate authority; or to evangelistic efforts among Jews--the deep imprint of the restoration is evident. And for good measure, theorists of the religious charter incorporated romantic, restorational motifs in their unitive systems of thought.

NOTES

CHAPTER II

(1) Max Geiger, AUFKLAERUNG UND ERWECKUNG; BEITRAEGE ZUR ERFORSCHUNG JOHANN JUNG-STILLINGS UND DER ERWECKUNGSTHEOLOGIE, Basler Studien zur historischen und systematischen Theologie, ed. Max Geiger (Zurich: EVZ Verlag, 1963), pp. 384-410. While useful in forming public opinion, the Alliance had little significance for the practicing statesman.

(2) Henry A. Kissinger, A WORLD RESTORED (New York: Grosset & Dunlap, 1964), p. 189.

(3) Hajo Holborn, A HISTORY OF MODERN GERMANY, 1648—1840 (New York: Alfred A. Knopf, 1964), p. 404.

(4) Walter Delius and Oskar Soehngen, DIE EVANGELISCHE KIRCHE DER UNION, ed. Walter Elliger (Witten: Luther-Verlag, 1967), pp. 64-65.

(5) We will examine the growing confessional movement more fully in a later chapter, but several items should be noted here. Among factors contributing to the resurgence of confessional commitment were romanticism, the religious Awakening, resistance to the king's agenda in Prussia (which seemed to point toward consensus at all costs), and the rather phenomenal recovery of Roman Catholicism after the Napoleonic wars. Many were shaken by such a minor event as the conversion to Roman Catholicism of Anhalt-Coethen's ruler in 1826, and his subsequent designation of Catholicism as the territorial church.

(6) Nagging problems did persist. For example, since the agenda included the Apostles Creed in the divine service of worship, the creed's use was mandatory in

90

confirmation and ordination ceremonies. As a result, a conflict erupted near the end of the century as the "Struggle over the Apostles Creed." Other skirmishes occurred in the intervening decades, including strenuous debate on liturgical formulations.

(7) Holborn, pp. 475-77.

(8) Elinore Sterling, ER IST WIE DU; AUS DER FRUEHGESCHICHTE DES ANTISEMITISMUS IN DEUTSCHLAND, 1815—1850 (Munich: Chr. Kaiser Verlag, 1956), p. 127.

(9) Other conservatives found ways to incorporate Jews into the cosmic process through eschatological theory. After several liberal Jews concluded that the day's events signaled the arrival of the Jewish messiah, some conservative Christian theologians charged that their conclusion was an assault on the Redeemer, whose imminent arrival would overwhelm the Antichrist (see Sterling, pp. 122-23). Nonetheless, they reserved a place for Jews in their apocalyptic scenario—in Palestine! Early in the century the "patriarch of the Awakening," Johann Heinrich Jung-Stilling, wrote that the Jews' rapid conversion and return to Palestine pointed to the millennial kingdom. He and others believed that when the terrestial kingdom in Jerusalem broke in over converted Jews and Christians of all nations, Christ would form a new and pure Christian state. Some periodicals regularly reported conversions of Jews and Jewish rabbis.

(10) The reactionary-romantic forces that influenced Jews to become Protestants also encouraged some Protestants to convert to Roman Catholicism. While each conversion was different, most certainly the romantic movement contributed to the conversions of such important cultural, literary and academic figures as Friedrich Schlegel and his wife Dorothy, Adam Mueller, Count Leopold von Stolberg, Zacharias Werner, Josef F. Overback, Karl F. Rumhor, Heinrich Mueller, Ferdinand von Eckstein, Karl Ludwig von Haller, and later in the century, Julius Langbehn and Georg F. Daumer. Some Jews, such as the two physicians Emanuel and Nikolaus Veit, converted directly to Catholicism; unlike most, the two bypassed Protestantism. The Prussian court offered support and diplomatic protection to the first evangelical congregation established in Rome in 1819, but cabinet orders

in 1809, 1825, and 1826 outlawed any religious activity or pressure designed to convert Roman Catholics or Protestants to the other faith. The conversion of the royal couple in Anhalt-Coethen was a stunning victory for Catholicism; in the early decades, one-third of this state's population was Lutheran, and the remaining two-thirds Reformed.

(11) Friedrich Meinecke, WELTBUERGERTUM UND NATIONALSTAAT, STUDIEN ZUR GENESIS DEUTSCHER NATIONALSTAATES (3d ed.; Munich: R. Oldenbourg, 1919), pp. 9, 63. Meinecke's classic has recently been translated by Robert B. Kimber as COSMOPOLITANISM AND THE NATIONAL STATE (Princeton: Princeton University Press, 1970).

(12) Holborn, pp. 346-47.

(13) Erich Heller, "Imaginative Literature," in THE NEW CAMBRIDGE MODERN HISTORY, Vol. X, The Zenith of European Power: 1830—70 (Cambridge: Cambridge University Press, 1960), 158.

(14) NEW CAMBRIDGE MODERN HISTORY, Vol. IX, War and Peace in an Age of Upheaval: 1793—1830 (Cambridge: Cambridge University Press, 1965), 160-61.

(15) Quoted in Christian Walther, TYPEN DES REICH-GOTTES VERSTAENDNISSES; STUDIEN ZUR ESCHATOLOGIE UND ETHIK IM 19. JAHRHUNDERT, Forschungen zur Geschichte und Lehre des Protestantismus, ed. Ernst Wolf, Zehnte Reihe, Band XX (Munich: Chr. Kaiser Verlag, 1961), p. 61.

(16) Ibid., p. 85.

CHAPTER III

RESISTANCE AND AFFIRMATION

Not all Protestants appreciated the way that strong
political leaders were molding church life in the early
decades of the century. In the southern states, sectarian
activities, emigration "harmonies," and religious
settlements were signs of resistance against what we have
called the unwritten religious charter. But the religious
Awakening in Germany more than compensated for these
variegated forms of discontent. This movement of renewed
religious zeal flourished at the same time as the political
restoration, and drew its life-breath from the same
"Zeitgeist."

Religious people in the Awakening affirmed the viability
and validity of the emerging consensus, namely, that it was
the state's legitimate right to determine the church's
social role. During these decades, awakened church people
interpreted theological rationalism as the religious
counterpart of political liberalism. They concluded that
rationalism endangered the foundations of the monarchical
system, just as it did the church's theology. Their
struggle against the Enlightenment, rationalistic theology,
and political liberalism was an affirmation of the
unwritten agreement, with which the awakened had few
problems.

A vignette from Wuerttemberg summarizes the story well.
With British assistance, the awakened established a new
Bible Society there in 1812. It soon received the king's
approval, together with a contribution of two hundred royal

"Gulden." During the War of Liberation, the society
distributed tracts and Bibles to soldiers; later, free
postage helped deliver Bibles to poor people and children
throughout the state. In 1816 the king sent his usual
contribution, together with a note that read, "The
undertaking has a very salutary purpose, one suited to the
religious needs of the people." In subsequent years, the
society often reminded him of the Bible's
anti-revolutionary character.

In this chapter our focus shifts southward from Prussia's
vast plains, to emigration groups that registered
disapproval of increased state control over the church. We
will also visit a Swabian settlement that helped muffle
dissent at home among old-line pietists. Then we will see
how the religious Awakening reinforced the church's
assignment as a model for other social institutions. The
early Awakening's relation to old-line pietism, and its
attacks on theological rationalism, throw into sharp relief
the distinctive theological motifs of the movement. These
factors also pulled the awakened into the camp of political
conservatism. In turn, through the good graces of the
unwritten charter, a two-way linkage developed between the
Awakening and the restorational movement. The Awakening
spawned a kind of surrogate nationalism that diluted the
appeal of liberal nationalism. And it gave birth to a host
of voluntary agencies, which modeled
"freedom-within-authority" for the larger society.

SEEKING A NEW COUNTRY

Emigration was one way to show displeasure with the state's
increasing control of the church. Several religious
leaders and their small flocks made this choice. While
they were part of the surge of religious sentiment that was
eventually called neo-pietism, or the "religious
Awakening," their roots lay in old-line pietism, to which
they were more closely related than to the Awakening.
These southern Protestants were among the first to give a
clear witness against the emerging consensus, although most
German evangelicals did not hear their message.

In some cases, the economic situation contributed to emigratory zeal. The devastation of the Napoleonic Wars, and the economic depression from 1815 to 1827, created hard times for many. In Wuerttemberg, 1816 was the last in a series of bad crop years; the meteorological flukes of this period made weather forcasters run for cover, while the price of rye reached nearly three times its level of 1814.

Political and religious pressures exacerbated the economic problem. Wuerttemberg's "good old law" was replaced by a new constitution early in the century, while the king's new hymnal and liturgy eliminated many familiar hymns and prayers. It was rumored that Napoleon opened the era of the Antichrist; some radicals recommended that parents keep their children home from school, while others turned to vegetarian diets, avoided military service, and emigrated. In neighboring Baden, Johann Heinrich Jung-Stilling, called the "patriarch of the Awakening," published ambiguous articles in his devotonal periodical, THE GRAY MAN, portraying emigration as a religious act. He argued that the Russian Czar played an important role in the game of geographical chess, through which God was creating a new and powerful religious base in the East. Later, an English tourist reported that several leaders of German settlements in southern Russia attributed their decision to emigrate to Stilling.

Wuerttemberg provided the bulk of the emigrants to southern Russia, fully 90 percent in 1816-1817. In response, the government commissioned Friedrich List, who later became famous for his program of national economics, to study emigration. He concluded that religious fanaticism and economic difficulty were secondary factors; at the top of his list were political pressure and lack of freedom, followed by taxes, military costs, excise taxes, local oppression, and judicial delays. He did not suggest—though he might have—that many in Wuerttemberg saw an interrelationship between political and religious policies.

The fact of the matter was that religion was a factor. While only about 300 of the 6,000 who left the territory for Transcaucasia in 1816-17 were separatists who had withdrawn from the state church, others among the emigrants felt the heavy hand of political oppression most personally in the state's religious policies. An official report in Wuerttemberg showed that in February of 1817, "religious enthusiasm <drove> 380 to distant regions; 2,874 <including children sought> to overcome famine, shrinking means and unfavorable prospects." If these 380 were adults, they composed 28 percent of the adults who emigrated that month. Together, the East's millennial magnetism, and opposition to the new religious service books, made a powerful team.

In the second decade, the number of Swabian emigrants to Russia climbed rapidly, from 3,067 in 1804, to 9,294 in 1817 (only 1,071 left the state in 1816). In 1817, the Czar opened his empire to Swabians, Bavarians and Swiss. He intended to witness the influx into the sparsely settled area around Odessa firsthand, but finally appointed a German overseer instead. Nearly half of those who emigrated from Wuerttemberg in 1816-17 failed to arrive at their destination because of death and desertion, but the remnant settled in Russian Georgia. The settlers allowed no clergyman in the Georgian settlements; some set up an isolated colony on the eastern coast of the Black Sea, far from the main Lutheran settlements around Odessa, to escape the tentacles of clerical control. The 17,879 emigrants sent by Wuerttemberg to Russia between 1804 and 1842 included some who waited for the millennium in earthen huts. Ten thousand more came from Baden (4,984), the Palatinate (2,674), Alsace (1,580), Rhine-Hesse (420), Hesse (400) and Bavaria.

Many of the new emigratory "harmonies," or journeying communities, formalized the traditional pietist emphasis on brotherhood by adopting a constitution. One group that eventually settled in Hoffnugsthal, in southern Russia, called its charter, "An Appeal . . . to the Faithful Who Wait and Hope for the Promised, Imminent Kingdom of Jesus." The document lamented the corruption of the institutional church, and warned that the harmony's communal ownership of property should not result in a reenactment of the story of Ananias and Sapphira.

CONTROLLED DISSENT AT HOME

Taking a softer line, some groups remained in Wuerttemberg, and expressed their displeasure at the ruler's increased control of the church. But since the church was largely controlled by rationalists, its bureaucracy gave them little comfort or relief. As a result, some people preached full equality among all, called high officials by their first names, refused to doff their hats, and willingly suffered imprisonment. Meanwhile, the king gave approval for a small settlement in Korntal that provided a haven for certain troubled people in the state. Korntal helped pacify some of the discontent that grew out of the working agreement between church and state.

Before he emigrated in 1817, a master brickmaker named Johann Leibbrand organized a separatist band in 1809 with chiliastic, and sometimes anarchistic views. Johann G. Frick whipped the passions of his followers in Wuerttemberg to a feverish pitch, and the separatists who gathered around Barbara Grubermann in Rottenacker had to be restrained by soldiers in 1805. Local officials characterized their lifestyle as a "strange mixture--but still suitably concocted for the encouragement of their wickedness—of fantastic and religious 'Sanculotism,' and mystical-chiliastic, cabalistic nonsense."

Before he emigrated to Pennsylvania and Indiana in 1803, Georg Rapp (1757-1847) was one of the more important lay leaders among separatists in Wuerttemberg. After leaving the territorial church in 1785, he preached to three or four thousand followers in the region of Maulbronn. His apocalyptic slogans condemned the institutional church: "Against Babel!", "Down with the hellish whore!" Johann Hoernle took charge of the small remnant that stayed in Wuerttemberg, while 700 emigrated with Rapp. Gathering at night in large groups, those in the remnant wore distinguishing clothes, called one another by first names, followed vegetarian diets, refused to marry, and opposed ordinary worship services, infant baptism, confirmation, and school attendance for children. The group called the prince of the state an "apocalyptic beast," and refused to take civil oaths, since they saw the state as the church's protector. Their greeting--"Praise be to God and His son Napoleon Bonaparte!"--summarized their view that Napoleon paved the way for the return of Christ.

The Michaelites and Pregizerians were two of the less radical chiliastic groups in Wuerttemberg. Johann Michael Hahn (1758-1819), a layman who ignored the law prohibiting lay preaching, gave his name to the first group. A prolific writer of commentaries, doctrinal statements and hymns, he used as his major theological motif a concept as old as the Christian father Iraeneus: "Widerbringung" (restoration). Opponents of the territorial church, the Michaelites had spread throughout Wuerttemberg and Bavaria by mid-century, although avoidance of marriage resticted their natural growth.

The Pregizerians, a group that still numbers around 6,000 members, took their name but not their origin from a pastor, Christian G. Pregizer (1751-1824). Along with the Michaelites, they waited with anticipation for the millennial kingdom. In contrast to the Michaelites' social and theological conservatism, the Pregizerians emphasized the immediacy of the conversion experience, and the intensity of the converted Christian's love. These precursors of the modern holiness movement held that even a true Christian was not able to forgive fully; as a result, they dropped the fifth petition of the Lord's Prayer. They set traditional hymns to snappy contemporary melodies, and used a creed with theosophical overtones. Despite occasional strained relations with the territorial church, the group did not become separatist. But it did not support foreign missions, since missions belonged only to the time of Christ—"no longer" and "not yet."

In 1819 a religious community was organized in Korntal, Wuerttemberg. On the one hand, the settlement was a signal of resistance against the state's encroachment of church rights. But on the other, it discouraged people from taking direct action to express dissatisfaction at the state's using the church as a model for society. Thus, many of the separatists who adamantly opposed what they called the church's rationalism, but who still wanted to show obedience to the state, were met halfway. Those separatists who wanted no compromise continued to emigrate, but Korntal enabled others to register their displeasure witnout leaving Wuerttemberg.

Although the king eased emigration restrictions as part of a reform effort early in his reign, he became concerned in 1816-17 when the rate of emigration held steady at about two percent of the population. He asked local officials in Wuerttemberg to warn citizens about the dangers of emigrating, and to provide him with their insights about the problem. Early in 1817, Leonberg's imperial notary and parish overseer, a layman named Gottlieb W. Hoffmann (1771-1846), wrote a reply in which he described three types of emigrants: outspoken enthusiasts and separatists; impoverished citizens; and those whose convictions "do not find a new liturgy introduced seven years ago patterned after the old Lutheran faith." He added that "a great and influential part of this group could be restrained from emigrating if permitted to establish their own communities in the kingdom." In ten days, Hoffmann secured the names of 700 family heads interested in such a community; in some villages, 20 percent signed his petition.

After the king approved Hoffmann's project in 1819, sixty-eight families settled on the estate used for his settlement in Korntal. Eight thousand people attended the dedication of the Great Hall sanctuary in 1819. Its solid construction contrasted markedly with the rather poorly built homes, which were designed to last only until the End. Liturgical and confessional idiosyncracies, including the use of the old hymnal and liturgy, and some Moravian rites, were responsible for some of the criticisms brought against the new colony.

The settlement's constitution provided for distinct spiritual and secular leaders, and while Hoffmann tended to emphasize the community's religious character, the royal privilege that created the colony stressed civil affairs. Members were exempt from oaths, but not from military service, as Hoffmann had requested. "Independent" members signed the rules as adults; "non-independent" members included children who were baptized and raised in the settlement. The association held all property in trust; it had the first option to buy any shares up for sale if no other acceptable buyer was found.

From 1819 to 1827, a chiliast named Johann J. Friedrich occupied the chief ecclesiastical office. After a six year vacancy, Sixt Karl Kapff assumed the office until 1843, when he took a powerful post in the territorial church. Kapff's pastorate coincided with the period during which the territorial church gravitated from rationalism toward neo-pietism. As relations with the church improved, the colony became a center for the neo-pietist spirit. Popular preachers, lay leaders, confirmands, and Roman Catholics who were part of the religious Awakening made pilgrimages to the estate.

Korntal's well-known educational institutions owed much to Johannes Kullen, their first superintendent. The colony also opened a home for war orphans, and supported the Basel Mission Society. But in 1836 the Korntalians, along with many other chiliasts in Wuerttemberg, experienced a psychological shock when the year passed uneventfully, without the expected End. Hoffmann continued to conduct "news hour" briefings for the men of the colony, during which he discussed the interrelationship between daily events and millennial "signs of the times."

The formation of the colony at Korntal signalled an important shift in Swabian pietism. Those separatists who would not compromise with the world, or with the territorial ruler when he imposed new religious regulations, continued to leave the church or emigrate, although by the early twenties the stream of emigrants dwindled to a trickle. But those who opposed the church, and still wanted to obey civil authority, now had a place in which to settle until the End came. They were soon attracted to that other major branch of pietism, which found its identity in creating Bible, tract, mission, and philanthropic societies, rather than separating or emigrating. Channeling their energy toward common causes, they set out to wrest control of the territorial church from the rationalist bureaucracy. As the new pietists eventually gained control of the church bureaucracy, what had begun at Korntal as a sign of religious opposition ended as part of the established state church.

THE EARLY AWAKENING

100

Above all else, the religious Awakening in Germany was a heterogeneous and pluralistic phenomenon, and we create insurmountable problems if we try to squeeze all its adherents into a rigid conceptual mold, with little room for the diversity of their views. A precise definition of this multifaceted movement is nearly impossible. But the first half of the nineteenth century, called the "charistmatic century" by the church historian Alfons Rosenberg, bears the indelible imprint of this movement. My own reasoned conclusion is that, despite a wide range of beliefs and practices in the Awakening, most of its participants affirmed the validity of the social role that the German states were prescribing for their Protestant churches.

The following pages will explain precisely how and why most of the awakened approved the unwritten charter—though not always forthrightly, or with unmistakable zeal. We will describe their theological motifs; their tendency to equate political and redemptive history; their support of a kind of surrogate nationalism; and their voluntary agencies and societies, which provided authoritarian-voluntarist models for society. But first we must determine how two forerunners, old-line pietism, and theological rationalism were formative for the people of the Awakening.

For the historian who is concerned with forerunners and runners-up, one of the most vexing questions about the German religious Awakening is a simple one. Precisely when did it begin and end? No simple answer can be given, but it can be argued with some authority that the movement extended from around 1780 to around 1860, with a noticeable intensification of zeal after the turn of the century. Certain developments clearly gave impetus to the movement, including the emergence of nationalist sentiment in the north between 1806 and 1813. The 300th Anniversary of the Reformation (1817) and of the Augsburg Confession (1830) were important benchmarks in the history of Lutheran confessionalism, which drained away much of the Awakening's theological flexibility. But many of the awakened felt that their star had finally risen in 1840, when the pious and romantic king, Frederick William IV, ascended Prussia's throne.(1)

A discussion of the movement's "forerunners," or "early

figures," underscores the complexity of the chronological question. Many scholars agree that the theologian Johann G. Hamann (1730-1788) made a significant contribution with his insistence on a return to Luther and the Bible. But equally important were Johann G. Herder (1744-1803), Friedrich H. Jacobi (1743-1819), Johann K. Lavater (1741-1801), Mattias Claudius (1740-1815), and Johann F. Oberlin (1740-1801).

A number of Roman Catholic priests and laymen were also involved in the early stages of the Awakening. The leading figure in the early Roman Catholic awakening in Bavarian Swabia, Johann M. Sailer (1751-1832), provided the spark for awakenings among evangelicals in Bavaria and Wuerttemberg through his association with Johann M. Feneberg, Martin Boos, and Johann E. Gossner. Three students from Berlin, Carl von Lancizolle, a student of law, Adolf von Thadden-Trieglaff, a student at the war college, and Moritz von Bethmann-Hollweg, a student of Savigny, visited Johann Josef von Goerres in Munich and carried home the news of a great spiritual revival. Also influential was the political and philosophical writer, Franz von Baader.

A lay theologian in Baden, Johann Heinrich Jung-Stilling (1740-1817), was an important transitional figure between old pietism and neo-pietism, and also one of the most influential Protestant forerunners of the Awakening. Working as a schoolmaster, tutor, and medical doctor before he taught political economics at Kaiserlautern, Heidelberg, and Marburg, he exhibited his skills as a lay theologian in HOMESICKNESS (1794), SCENES FROM THE SPIRIT WORLD (1795), and a sporadic journal, THE GRAY MAN (1795-1816). After 1803 he worked in Heidelberg and Karlsruhe as a religious advisor to the Grand Duke of Baden.

His vast correspondence and literary activity earned him the title "patriarch of the Awakening." He added the name "Stilling" to his surname Jung to honor the "Stille im Lande" ("quiet ones in the land"), since these pietists were his people, his correspondents, and readers. His lively correspondence with all kinds of people, including court figures, formed a web of interpersonal relations among those of similar persuasion. In 1808-1809, his postage bill amounted to more than his rent.

According to his book entitled HOMESICKNESS, the atheism
and materialism of the French Revolution showed that the
church's geographical center was shifting to "Solyma" in
the East. In preparation for Christ's return, God's game
of geographical chess was moving history eastward, not
westward as expected. Stilling continued to hint at the
desirability of eastward emigration in VICTORIOUS HOPE OF
THE CHRISTIAN RELIGION (1799), and his journal THE GRAY
MAN, which portrayed Russia as the promised land of hope.

He abhorred the Enlightenment and the French Revolution,
but thought that God was awakening new religious life
through both. He viewed Napoleon's defeat in Russia, and
the victory of the Germans at Leipzig, as preliminary
skirmishes in the millennial battle, but refused to say
that the final conflict with the Antichrist was underway.
With many others he shared the feeling of an approaching
deluge, and relied on the rather amorphous symbol of God's
kingdom to publicize his calculations about the millennium.
His ambiguous attempts to pinpoint the year of the
millennium piqued his readers' interest without portraying
the author as a religious fanatic. Since conceivably God's
visitation could strike in one year or another, he beckoned
people to emigrate eastward with one hand, but cautioned
them to stay at their posts with the other.

His eschatological interpretation of Russia perpetuated a
tradition with roots in the Swabian pietist, Johann Bengel.
The Russian Czar played a preparatory apocalyptic role in
his thinking, and although he did not see Alexander I as a
messianic figure, he wanted to meet him nonetheless. When
they finally met in southern Germany in 1814, they agreed
that the End was near. Stilling later said that he could
not divulge all of their conversation, but he felt free to
report that the Emperor "has set his mind to live and die
as a true Christian, and to propagate true Christianity in
every possible way," as his support for the fledgling
Russian Bible Society attested.

Stilling soon became an important link between Germany's
awakened people and leading statesmen and churchmen in
Russia. His friendship with the Russian prophetess,
Julianne von Kruedener, whom we will discuss below, and his
opinions about Russia's role in redemptive history helped

prepare the way for the Holy Alliance and for closer cultural relations. Four of his works were translated into Russian between 1813 and 1823 for readers affiliated with the Russian Bible Society.

Stilling held that three activities would help pave the way for the millennium. He issued a ringing call for foreign missions, the "hour hands of God's clock." More ambiguous was his emphasis on a gathered religious community that would precipitate Christ's return. But his heroes in the Moravian settlement of Hermhut, as well as emigration groups that moved eastward, performed this function. Finally, his bitter attacks on sectarianism, and his plea for spiritual unity, echoed the Awakening's motif of Christian unity, as well as contemporary calls for national unity.(2)

Another important figure in the early Awakening was a woman named Julianne von Kruedener (1764-1824), also known as "Frau Kruedener." This Russian baroness experienced a religious awakening in Riga, the capital of Baltic Livonia. In 1807, a visit to the Moravian community of Hermhut in upper Saxony led to a contact with Stilling. She then contracted a "mystical marriage" with the visionary prophet from Markirch, Jean Frederick Fontaines, and moved with his group from place to place until returning to Riga in 1810.

After several years she revisited southern Germany, concentrating much of her preaching around Basel and Grensacher Horn in Baden. Her ominous chiliastic warnings attracted a sizable following. With several assistants, she performed acts of mercy, preached Christ's imminent return, and stirred up governmental opposition. Eventually she was chased from one German state to another until she reached her native Russia.

During these years of famine and unrest, her work with the poor did not endear her to governmental officials, or strengthen the working agreement that was emerging between state and church. Many officials viewed her as subversive, despite her contacts with the Russian Czar. One small tract she distributed in 1817 was especially disturbing. Entitled TO THE POOR, it promised impoverished peasants that "the Lord will lead you by means of this famine and persecution out of the land where His judgments strike—hunger, war, pestilence, earthquakes, where you are treated so inhumanely, where people no longer obey God's commands . . . where human laws oppose the laws of God. The Lord your God has already prepared a new land for you, and to this end He has chosen a man <Alexander I> who must lead the people of God in the Lord's name." The poverty of the poor was the first stage of the unfolding drama of apocalyptic redemption. Frau Kruedener's NEWSPAPER FOR THE POOR appeared only once, in May of 1817. But this issue instructed peasants to sell copies to the rich for money that could be used for food; God's kingdom offered them protection, but brought retribution to the rich.

The Common Enemy

While the forerunners and early figures of the Awakening showed no clean break with old pietism, they hinted that something new was in the air. At times it is difficult to distinguish between the two movements, but there is general agreement that, despite their similarities, the awakened were not pietists in new disguise. For this reason, some scholars refer to them as "neo-pietists." In their time they were also called "mystics," proponents of "new piety," and apologists for "positive Christianity." Comparing the two groups, we will more readily identify the enemy that all the awakened abhorred, namely, rationalism.

Influenced heavily by romanticism, the awakened usually looked for a deeper emotional religious experience than the old pietists. The pietist characteristically found God in the Bible, but neo-pietists searched for His tracks as well in nature and personal experience. While the pietist tended to be involved in the world and to exercise limited moral judgment in public, the awakened were more concerned with contemplation and private reflection, although they too organized a host of charitable societies and mission agencies. In sum, the awakened figures who criticized pietism had good reason to claim that they were different. They were attuned to many of the day's cultural and intellectual emphases, and that required some distancing from old pietism. They engaged in dialog with a number of cultural leaders, including those who had a new interest in history. The eminent German historian Franz Schnabel pointed out that the Awakening contained "many elements that in the separatist movement, or in natural philosophy, or in pantheistic and theosophical speculation, could lead to occultism and spiritual prophesying, or even withdrawal from Christianity."(3)

Also novel was the Awakening's flat rejection of the "Aufklaerung," the intellectual consequences of the Enlightenment in Germany. The awakened attacked theological rationalism and its proponents in the institutional church; in their appraisal of the "Aufklaerung," the Enlightenment was a tool of the devil, a satanic disguise set on destroying God's kingdom. Morality was not tne basis of religion, nor was reason the foundation of the state. Their common opposition to "enlightened" rationalism was, on the cognitive level, the single most important integrative force in the movement.

Clearly, their attack on theological rationalism had some anti-intellectual markings, since rationalism centered in the theological faculties of universities, especially at Halle and Heidelberg. As the century progressed, the awakened were able to gain control of church leadership posts more easily than teaching positions on theological faculties. This was possible because state officials such as Altenstein, Prussia's minister of worship, defended the academic freedom of such rationalist professors as Wegscheider and Gesenius.

For this reason, Julius Wegscheider (1771-1849) and his colleague at Halle, Heinrich F. W. Gesenius (1786-1842), aroused deep suspicion among the awakened. Wegscheider's dogmatic studies, and Gesenius' Old Testament works, led awakened figures to campaign for their dismissal in the EVANGELICAL CHURCH NEWS in 1830, but without success. The chief target at Heidelberg was a New Testament scholar, Heinrich E. G. Paulus (1761-1851). The arid lectures of some rationalist teachers did comparatively little to stimulate theological inquiry early in the century, although Halle remained the citadel of rationalism well into the thirties, while Paulus lectured to large classes at Heidelberg until his death. Interestingly, the enrollment patterns of the more conservative theological faculties at Erlangen, Leipzig, Tuebingen, and Griefswald did not parallel the rationalist centers, where enrollments peaked in 1825, 1860, and 1888, and troughed in 1850 and

1870. Rationalism provided basic impulses for German idealism, but persisted longer than its offspring, and reasserted itself as a popular movement in the forties.

For the awakened, the rationalists were a target that would not stand still. Their chief organ was the UNIVERSAL CHURCH NEWS (ALLGEMEINE KIRCHENZEITUNG), a paper published two or three times a week after 1822 by its editor, Ernst C. P. Zimmermann (d. 1832), the gifted court preacher at Darmstadt. Its masthead symbols consisted of a cross, anchor, chalice and Bible, signifying faith, hope, love, and the gospel. After Zimmermann's death, Christian Palmer and Daniel Schenkel turned the paper into a forum supporting the theology of church union.

Parish pastors with a rationalistic orientation were also a target for the awakened. In Silesian Hirschberg, the number of communions dropped from 16,500 in 1786 to 4,873 in 1836, and 4,498 in 1837, reportedly because of rationalistic preaching in the village church. This may also have been a factor at St. Catherine's Church in Hamburg, where 10,052 communions were served in 1750, but only 2,343 a century later, despite heavy growth in the surrounding population. Rationalistic preachers often used old proverbs as texts for their sermons. In one instance, the preacher on Christmas Day discussed the need for good stable fodder, and on Good Friday dwelt on the advantages of a will. One man in Silesia reported hearing a sermon on hog butchering and the preparation of sauerkraut. In some areas, these moralistic and "practical" sermons were merely an extension of the parson's role as chief governmental administrator on the local level. But they ingratiated the sensibilities of those whose faith had been newly reignited.

The awakened zealously attacked church authorities who protected these preachers, as well as other religious figures in the rationalist party. Among the more prominent were Christoph F. von Ammon (1766-1850), the chief court preacher in Dresden, who was known for the "elasticity" of his spirit and character; and Karl G. Bretschneider (1776-1848), who served for the last thirty years of his life as general superintendent in Gotha. One of the first to question the historicity of John's gospel, Bretschneider is best known for his New Testament lexicon, and his editions of the works of Calvin and Melanchthon. On a popular level, his books and novels lamented the general absence of religion in society, and stressed the differences between Protestants and Roman Catholics. The ever-popular SCHOOL TEACHER'S BIBLE (1826-30) in nine volumes was written by the rationalist Gustav F. Dinter (1760-1831), an educationalist in Koenigsberg. One devotional piece widely read among Protestants and Roman Catholics was the rationalistic HOURS OF DEVOTION, published weekly between 1806 and 1816, and then republished in thirty-six editions. After his death, a preacher from Lucerne named Johann H. D. Zschokke (1771-1848) was credited with being the anonymous author of this popular work.

The bitter struggle between rationalists and the awakened often surfaced in pamphlet wars and local squabbles. One spark was the series of theses issued by Claus Harms in 1817, condemning union between Lutherans and Reformed. And there were other squabbles too. When he was called to teach at Leipzig, a major rationalist stronghold, August Hahn (1792-1863) asserted that rationalism and Christianity were incompatible. His success at polemics won him a subsequent position in Breslau. In Jena, the church historian Karl A. Hase (1800-1890) launched an attack on Herder's rationalistic successor at Weimar, Johann F. Rohr (1777-1848), who had earned the animosity of Schleiermacher's followers. In Bavaria, the HOMILETICAL-LITURGICAL CORRESPONDENT (1827ff.) was published, it was said, to overcome the Goliath of rationalism with David's sling, the word of God. In the Hamburg "church battle" of 1839-40, the forces of the North German Awakening were pitted against rationalism. A young activist named Johann Hinrich Wichern found himself at the center of the fray; this was the start of an illustrious career for Wichern, and we will meet him again as the founder of the Inner Mission. Rationalistic church authorities in Wuerttemberg did not look kindly on the exorcism and healings performed by a young preacher in Moettlingen named Johann C. Blumhardt. Removed from office in the thirties by rationalist church bureaucrats in Koenigsberg, the fanatical preacher Johann W. Ebel (1784-1861) found refuge in the Swabian settlement of Ludwigsburg, a daughter of the colony at Korntal.

Although it owed a great deal to the rationalism of the Enlightenment, German idealism proved to be a faithful ally of the early Awakening. The two movements differed in many respects, but both disapproved of the excesses of rationalism, and emphasized the joy of personhood, the inner life, and life in the eternal world. Between 1806 and 1813, people in both groups attributed Prussia's collapse to religious and moral decay, and some blamed the lack of national spirit on the mechanistic world view of "enlightened" thinkers. In positive terms, the idealists relied on the notion of the world spirit acting through history, while the awakened anticipated the final conquest of evil under God's direct action.

Idealism had a much more mystical and "irrational" view of man's relationship with nature than the Enlightenment, and this encouraged the awakened to investigate the depths of soul and universe from a theological perspective. The awakened stressed man's sinfulness and need for redemption more than idealists, but idealism reinforced their efforts to relate to the Divine Being through mysticism, and in some cases, through theosophy and occult practices.

Hegel's idealism allowed the two groups to explore areas of disagreement while mounting a joint attack against the old rationalism. But especially after 1830, awakened figures rallied against the "pantheism" of idealism. In the meantime, the 300th Anniversary of the Augsburg Confession prompted demonstrations at Rostock, Halle, and at other universities against the convoluted "mysticism" of the Awakening. The death of most major idealist thinkers in the thirties foreshadowed the eclipse of the Awakening as a religious movement of primary importance. Its influence trailed off into dogmatic emphases in confessionalism and, as we shall see, into voluntaryism, which created a spate of religious societies and agencies.

Even though awakened figures attacked theological rationalism with enthusiastic vigor, the Enlightenment left its mark on them. People of the Awakening agreed that their "enlightened" predecessors were correct in one respect: differences in doctrine did not require sectarian division. In addition, enlightened thinkers were more inclined than the Reformers to emphasize mankind's better qualities. We can begin to understand why Stilling called

109

Christianity the "true" "Aufklaerung."

Theological Motifs

Theologians in the Awakening, including Gottfried Menken (1768-1831), August Neander (1789-1850), and Friedrich A. Tholuck (1799-1855), agreed on the need to combat theological rationalism. But their positive theological statements contained a great diversity of opinion. This is one reason why no brief summary of their leading theological motifs can be exhaustive. Nonetheless, it is safe to assert that the theological currents of the Awakening were compatible with guiding principles of the political restoration. But the Awakening's motifs were more than reactionary attacks on theological rationalism. They were, in addition, the theological coordinates of the ecclesiology implied by the unwritten charter. They were the theological assumptions and consequences of the unwritten agreement between church and state that elevated—or relegated—the church to the role of a social model.

Biblical literalism marked the Awakening. For example, Menken perpetuated Bengel's approach to the Scriptures with three fundamental principles: the Bible, God's final and absolute revelation, is the sole authority for faith and life; the kingdom of God must be understood from a chiliastic perspective; and there is no distintiction between the God of the Old Testament and the God of the New.

The Awakening also gave careful attention to the ideas of sin, evil, and the devil, a concern that occasionally led to demonology. Similarly, its adherents put great stress on God's graciousness. Piety involved the whole person—body, soul and mind; the individual's subjective experiences were central to the formation of one's religious beliefs. It was held that God rewarded the seeker with moving experiences. The awakened exhibited a strong urge to convert others from irreligion, and to cultivate works of Christian love on a wide scale. Many attached great importance to charismatic gifts, occult phenomena, and eschatology. Gossner, Blumhardt, Nicklaus Wolf, Dorothy Trudel and others—Protestants and Roman

Catholics alike—reportedly performed healings, and Georg Blum published a two volume study on the subject, entitled THE MOST HOLY NAME OF JESUS, THE MOST CERTAIN MEDICINE IN ILLNESSES WHERE NO DOCTOR CAN HELP; OR, EXAMPLES OF HEALINGS THROUGH FAITHFUL PRAYER (1842-44).

Many of the awakened welcomed the nickname "mystic" since it distinguished them from the rationalists. But the northern awakenings had a more tenuous relationship with classical Christian mysticism than the other outbreaks, although even in the north, Tholuck published a study of mysticism. The "little people" and their awakened leaders read the reissued works of Boehme, Paracelsus, Tersteegen, Madame de Guyon, and 'a Kempis to recover a missing dimension in their lives. More than anything else, it was a common mystical interest that forged the working alliance between idealists and the awakened during Prussia's "Erhebung." Later, Ernst W. Hengstenberg, and others with definite distaste for the mystical tradition, helped move the Awakening toward a more rigid kind of Lutheran orthodoxy.

The passionate exploration of time attracted the interest of many people during the first half of the century, and the awakened joined this quest in their eschatological doctrines. Eschatology was sometimes associated with mysticism, so it held a natural attraction for the awakened. Eschatology enabled the awakened to find in the End the denouement of the battle between reason and revelation. Some were satisfied with reaffirming the importance of eschatological doctrines; others, such as Stilling, discussed the millennium in detail. The German church historian Max Geiger insists that this forceful consciousness of eschatological deliverance was an important difference between the Awakening and old pietism. He adds that "the entire circle around Jung-Stilling, Lavater, and Hess was intensely preoccupied with the 'when' and the 'how' of the fulfilment of apocalyptic hope, with pragmatic knowledge of the signs of the times, with the problems of the Antichrist, the first and second resurrection, the final apostacy, hell, the millennial kingdom, and the imminent, sovereign reign of God."(4) A strong eschatological note permeated the settlement at Korntal and the Moravian community at Herrnhut; elsewhere economic hardship, and social and political developments, at times contributed to renewed eschatological zeal.

The awakened also explored the nature of time by sensitizing their consciousness to history. They showed great interest in the way "salvation history" manifested itself in secular history down to their time. The first issue of an awakened paper, PILGRIM FROM SAXONY (1835), noted that the journal would have a healthy respect for creation and history; the comment proved to be more than gratuitous. History was a means for reestablishing contact between man and nature, the connection so carefully guarded during the Enlightenment, but severed by the intellectual upheaval at the turn of the century. Renewed faith in a God who acts had its corollary in the conviction that He acts in history, and that all history—to the End—is divine history.

Community was another prominent theological motif among the awakened. Although it also had its strongly individualistic side, romanticism made a heavy contribution in this area, and the awakened did much to transmit the idea to the common folk. Their meetings and conventicles throughout the land were reminiscent of the old pietist "circles." Sunday afternoon and weekday evening gatherings gave welcomed relief to the regular fare of dull services and rationalistic sermons. As late as 1828, over 30,000 evangelicals in Wuerttemberg regularly attended Bible study groups, or "Stunden," meeting on Sundays and two weekdays. The time together was passed in conversation, devotional readings, prayer, introspection, confession, and reports from the mission fields.

Awakened preachers nurtured the sense of community and participation in their worship services. Some asked each hearer to decide whether he supported or opposed God and His people; the preachers gave a sense of urgency to the proclamation by using contemporary metaphors. For example, during the railway boom, more than one preacher talked about making the "journey to paradise" by train.

A sense of loneliness and despair drove the awakened together, since the rationalists controlled most of the influential positions in the organized churches. The inter-confessional character of the Awakening seems to have been a foregone conclusion, inasmuch as the movement could not ignore the Enlightenment's leveling effects upon confessional identity. Lavater and the Roman Catholic Sailer were both strong proponents of the "una sancta" movement, while Goerres, Johann K. Passavant, Baader, and Oberlin were strong ecumenical figures in their own right. Reporting on the awakened circle that functioned in Augsburg in the mid-twenties, the Lutheran confessionalist Gottfried Thomasius wrote that "all were one--Moravians, pietists, Lutherans, Reformed, Catholics." Stilling insisted that God's church was composed of "neither Greek, nor Roman, nor Protestant, nor any single Christian party exclusively, but all of those in these ecclesiastical communities who have been reborn through water and the Spirit." His contemporary, Frau Kruedener, attracted Lutherans, Reformed, and Roman Catholics to her troupe. And lay people, who played leading roles in organizing conventicles, mission societies, and charitable organizations, helped to nurture a conciliatory spirit among confessions.

Political Conservatism

In the political realm, the most important contribution of the Awakening was that many adherents rallied to the cause of the restoration engulfing Germany after Napoleon's defeat. Even before the political restoration reached its apex, men in the Awakening stimulated the restorational impulse by providing theological interpretations of contemporary events. This implies that the awakened offered public assurances about the soundness of the church's unwritten charter. And they did, adding for good measure that it was divinely approved.

The knot that tied things together was their equation of political and salvation history. In their view, what happened politically was what God wanted to happen as He molded and guided universal history towards its goal, His kingdom, and the full redemption of mankind. Given this assumption, it was easy enough to conclude that the divinely ordained political system--in this case, monarchical and territorial in nature--was not open to modification. And so, while the early Awakening may indeed have kept German Protestantism from being swallowed by secularism early in the century, the turnabout to the Old Faith actually strengthened the conservative impulse in state and society, and helped build a wall of defense against revolutionary liberal movements. Conservatism and religious romanticism--or the Awakening--were able to capture the people's moral imagination because they both had the same governing premise: "that of the intrinsic and irremediable imperfectness, incomprehensiveness, and inconclusiveness of all human existence."(5) This kind of sin needed redemption, political and religious redemption. That was why Tholuck said that before Germany would hear God's voice, she had to be covered with blood.

One of the Awakening's eschatological emphases was soon placed in the service of conservatism and reaction. We noted above that Stilling and others interpreted Russia as the new center of Christendom, and the proper destination of the emigrant in the eschatological age. Cranked into the conservative propaganda machine, this understanding emerged as a description of Russia as the model religious and anti-revolutionary state. It was more than coincidental that many Prussian conservatives espoused such views about the Russian state for many decades into the century.

Those among the awakened who were ardent chiliasts helped polarize the body politic for or against God's political activity. Early in the century this implied a position for or against the French Revolution, as well as Napoleon's expansionary policies. Many used the symbol of God's kingdom, or such negative counterparts as "antichrist" or "Babylon," to voice opposition against Napoleon and his armies. At the turn of the century, Menken claimed that revolution opposed God's kingdom since it was based on human, not divine wisdom. About the same time, a two volume study by the Lutheran court preacher at Darmstadt, Johann A. Stark, explained that the French Revolution occurred through a conspiracy of "philosophers and Illuminati." Stilling said in 1814 that the "man of sins" learned much from his failure, but he would probably return in a religious disguise and wreak havoc since atrocity, tyranny, and attempts to create a world monarchy had been inadequate disguises for him.

One of the magnets that attracted the awakened to political

conservatism was Austria's keen interest in the movement of political restoration. We recall that Metternich rearranged the wording of the Czar's religious treaty, the Holy Alliance, to read like a tract on legitimacy. One reason for Metternich's restricting brotherhood to monarchs, instead of peoples, was his fear of the Awakening in the southern states. His fears bordered on paranoia; he claimed that British and American "mysticism" could inundate the continent, warned the Czar against Frau Kruedener, and in 1817 stated his belief that an Austrian Bible Society would be undesirable.

For most of the awakened, the ruler functioned in the political system much as the Bible did in theology. As the highest religious authority, the Bible provided knowledge about God for head and heart. A person's subjective interpretation of the Bible provided divine validation of his faith, and this permitted the awakened person to exercise a great deal of interpretive freedom within the confines of the faith-validating Bible.(6) Like the Bible, the ruler was an intermediary with the highest authority, God. But he also provided opportunities to exercise freedom within authoritarian limits, much in the same way that the Bible permitted interpretation; the ruler bestowed the freedom to love one's superiors.

In such an hierarchical structure, the citizen's highest duty was to be obedient, or in religious language, to show loving respect. For the awakened, then, love was the foundational principle in church, state and society. They were not bothered by the fact that sometimes "love" meant little more than enforced respect. They applauded the efforts of the restoration's apologists to establish some theoretical basis for the political order other than reason, and to reincorporate religion into that basis so that legitimacy would be, in fact, divinely legitimate.

By the time that the Rhineland became part of Prussia in the middle of the second decade, the awakened had achieved some degree of political expertise there. The leader of the Awakening in Wuppertal, Daniel Krummacher, extended a warm welcome to the Hohenzollern house, and called it a blessing for both Lutherans and Reformed. At the same time, a colleague in Unterbarmen, Pastor C. G. Wever, advised the people of Europe to "thank God for the rule of

115

such Christian princes as the gentle Tsar of Russia . . . and the pious king of Prussia . . . who . . . have triumphed against the forces of revolt against God . . . and <against> Napoleon, . . . the incarnation of the devil." Other pastors in the area rejoiced that Protestants finally lived in a Protestant state.(7)

Sometimes the awakened moved from reactionary statements to pressure and action in the political realm. After the Berlin professor DeWette consoled the mother of a young theological student executed for murdering a Russian correspondent, the awakened circle in Berlin, especially Baron von Kottwitz, appealed to the king to dismiss him from his position. DeWette was relieved of his post in 1819 because of his liberal views.

The awakened occasionally were able to convert liberals, or would-be liberals, to a more sane form of conservatism. For example, although he was elected as a liberal by the Hessian town of Herzfeld to serve in the state's new parliament, the theologian August Vilmar was influenced by Tholuck, and an awakened circle in Kassel, to desert theological rationalism and political liberalism in 1832. He soon became one of Germany's staunchest Lutheran confessionalists, and never forsook his conservative political position.

The awakened had even more success reassuring those who already agreed with their political views. This was no mean accomplishment, since many who agreed were in positions of power. For example, when Prussia's crown prince toured Elberfeld in the Rhineland less than ten years before his coronation as Frederick William IV in 1840, the awakened preacher Friedrich Wilhelm Krummacher lavishly praised him as a member of Benjamin and Judah's house in the "Israel of the time of the new covenant." Krummacher assured him that God had chosen the New Testament Israel in Germany above all other peoples; he reminded the crown prince that "Israel's theocracy nowhere has found its imitation as truly . . . as in the relationship between the German people and her rulers," a relationship in which "the idea of governing in the name of God—an idea carried in the eternal Word—is firmly and unassailably planted in all hearts." He added that Germans never wavered in the knowledge that the king was divinely

116

invested with the crown, and "nowhere are church and state so closely, so intimately intertwined as in our land." That was reason enough to join in the chorus, "Long live the king!"

The political views of awakened preachers and writers were one reason why the Awakening attracted a sizable following after the War of Liberation. Earlier the movement was restricted to a small coterie of literary and noble figures, but after Napoleon's defeat it spread its influence more widely.

While the movement never claimed more than a small percentage of the total population, and while it was scarcely represented in the theological faculties of Berlin, Halle, Breslau, Kiel, and the preacher's seminary in Wittenberg, its ranks in the north included a sizable number of aristocratic "Junkers," who gave it appreciable political influence. During the "Erhebung," bureaucratic reform efforts roused the Prussian "Junkers" to action. In the process of trying to arrest the bureaucracy's power, the landed "Junker" class was transformed into a "self-conscious, ideologically fortified political group."(8) Some "Junkers" assumed leadership of local religious awakenings on their estates, and in the process found renewed identity in the "counterrevolution from below." Together with the Christian German Table Fellowship in Berlin, they cultivated awakenings of faith that reinforced the old social system, and its political counterpart, as divinely ordained structures. Popular slogans for the program included such phrases as "fromm und feudal" ("pious and aristocratic"), "Patron und Pastor" ("patron and clergman"), and "Thron und Altar" ("throne and altar"). The "Junkers'" life took a turn for the better in the early thirties when Prussia's Tariff Union was established, bringing a larger internal, and a more favorable external market for their agricultural products. In a similar way, the Awakening provided an acceptable religious rationale for their social position and political prominence, just as it legitimated the status of the territorial ruler, who increasingly turned away from reform movements to protect himself against a mounting liberal element in the general populace, including Rhenish Catholics.

117

Thus, for the first third of the century, the Awakening provided substantial support for the day's restorational politics. Early in the century, Stilling advised his readers to "avoid like the plague" those who tried to seduce them with "enlightened" religion or appeals to disobey legitimate authority, "for they will make you miserable in time and eternity." By the thirties, there was little doubt that his advice was being implemented. When a printing press operator in Wuerttemberg criticized the king in 1831, the Bible Society that was using his skills to print Bibles demanded that he be fired. The next year, the society's annual report stressed that Bible distribution "always has a healthy influence on the preservation of order, peace, quietude and contentment."

SURROGATE NATIONALISM

In addition to providing impetus for the restoration, which in turn supported the uncodified agreement governing church-state relations, the Awakening implemented the charter in two ways. First, as the last section of this chapter demonstrates, the goals and organizational structure of many awakened societies showed that the church's place in society was anchored in its relationship with the state. Second, as discussed in this section, it forged a kind of surrogate nationalism through the interpersonal and inter-agency network it created. This web of people intentionally garbled the message of liberal nationalists, and stressed the traditional, conservative particularism of the German states. We will try to understand the significance of local awakenings in the context of their contribution to surrogate nationalism, which was essentially conservative and territorially oriented.

Several scholars have examined the contribution of pietism and neo-pietism to the development of nationalist sentiment in Germany. They conclude that, together with romanticism, these movements heightened the sense of personal identity; in turn, this realization was a prerequisite for identifying the nation's individuality. The sense of national identity increased as some theologians, notably Schleiermacher,

118

pointed to community as the context for examining ethical decisions and implementing solutions.(9)

But that is only part of the story of the relationship between nationalist sentiment and the Awakening. The evidence leads me to think that most of the awakened found state patriotism more attractive than the combination of liberalism and nationalism, which at the time was being promoted by reform-minded bureaucrats and some of the educated middle class, who sought to achieve a liberalized political structure through a unified nation.

Neo-pietism reasserted the classical Christian doctrines of grace and sin, against the idealist and romantic transformation of these ideas into "Ich" (I) and "Nicht-Ich" (that which is not I), in ways that resembled the later formulations of theological fundamentalism. The awakened movement was conservative to the core, and probably state-patriotic, but certainly not liberal-nationalistic. That is why I argue that its brand of nationalism, both inter-territorial and intra-territorial, was essentially a surrogate form of liberal nationalism, no less conservative at the core than its state patriotism on the territorial level.

The surrogate nationalism of the Awakening, its feeling of unity despite distance and territorial affiliations, allowed the movement to flourish within the tradition of German particularism, and, indeed, to nurture it. The marks of an awakening in one territory or region often differed considerably from those of another. In general, then, the local or territorial orientation of each awakening meant that first allegiance went to the state or territory, not to a proposed pan-German nation. In the process, the Awakening made a distinctive contribution to the spirit of legitimacy.

Thus, while leaders in the various awakenings were not nationalists in the sense of being liberal and pan-German, they promoted their own type of surrogate nationalism. It included a firm commitment to the local state, as well as a network of religiously-based interpersonal relations all over Germany. For example, the philanthropic figure Theodor Fliedner (1800-1864) of Kaiserwerth showed little nationalist sentiment in his theological interpretation of

119

Napoleon's career. But careful attention to charitable activities in his institutions, and his wide acquaintance with awakened people all over Germany, were a surrogate for liberal nationalist sentiment that minimized the sentiment's attraction for others. Some of the awakened looked beyond the German states in their search for the borders of the new kingdom God was building. Like Tholuck, they paid little attention to liberal nationalism since their religious experiences and activities integrated them into a larger community, the network of the awakened.

Rooted in eighteenth century pietism, the inter-confessional and inter-faith activities of the Awakening also cultivated a surrogate brand of nationalism. Fellowship among awakened of different confessions and faiths was the rule rather than the exception. This was due in part to the fact that most of the awakened were clergymen, peasants, and aristocrats; of all social groups, these were tied most closely to traditional social values and structures. One scholar reminds us that the aristocracy and peasantry were not inclined to support nationalist sentiment until later in the century, when the aristocracy adopted a modified form of nationalism in order to protect its political preeminence.(10)

It is clear, then, that the Awakening de-liberalized, or at least de-politicized, liberal nationalist sentiment. As we look at local awakenings, we shall see that the Awakening was essentially a particularist movement, and its surrogate brand of nationalism was conservative in nature. The pockets of religious renewal called local awakenings were not a monolith. The Awakening was no less artfully molded to local conditions than were the German states, although its particularist orientation did not prevent the emergence of genuine inter-confessional sentiment in reaction to rationalism. Because of the Awakening's surrogate nationalism, local awakenings gave momentum to social and political conservatism. In turn, this thrust provided renewed legitimacy for the states, and their charter for the churches.

The awakenings in the southern states owed much to renewed vitality in Bavarian Catholicism, but the evangelical awakening in Bavaria differed from movements in Wuerttemberg and the lower Rhineland since it had distinctive confessionalist markings. This was not true in the beginning; it took some time for the confessionalist emphasis to emerge in Bavaria. A pastor in Ansbach named A. Theodosius F. Lehmus battled against the rationalism of Ludwig Pflaum and others, settling on the distinction between Law and Gospel as a powerful weapon. Despite heavy idealist influence in his early years, by the middle of the fourth decade he showed a decisive shift in his theology. He became the mainspring of renewal in Franconia, though others built on the foundations he laid. Pastor Johann G. Schoerner, privy councilor George F. Hillmer, a merchant named Tobias Kiessling, and others, headed the movement in Nuremberg. Another major center was neighboring Augsburg. In Erlangen, Gotthilf H. Schubert and Karl von Raumer helped the theological faculty move to Lutheran confessionalism from idealism, through the awakening. Krafft was a Reformed theologian, and von Raumer taught a non-theological discipline at the university.

We have already noted that emigration groups and religious communities provided some outlet for eschatological zeal in the southern state of Wuerttemberg. The most popular awakened preacher there was a Lutheran, Ludwig Hofacker, who died at the young age of thirty after reaching thousands with his voice. His facial expressions and rhetorical skills influenced crowds in Stuttgart and the neighboring parish of Riel after 1823. He "aimed toward making an impression, that is, to strike the hearer's conscience with a thunderbolt," he said. His brother Wilhelm assisted him, but was also respected in his own right.

The Moravians gave impetus to the awakenings in Wuerttemberg until the late twenties, and Schleiermacher's visit to Tuebingen in 1830 helped move the awakening in theological studies toward maturity. The hymn writer Albert Kapp, the preacher, author and missiologist Christian G. Barth, and the healer Johann C. Blumhardt, also made important contributions to the movement, which was an admixture of pietism and neo-pietism. By 1821, more than half of the state's towns and villages had devotional circles meeting regularly, although the number of neo-pietists probably did not exceed 20,000, or two percent of the population. Their number climbed to thirty or forty thousand by 1860, but fell behind populational growth.

In neighboring Baden, the most popular awakened preacher was a former Roman Catholic priest named Aloysius Henhoefer, who was converted to the evangelical tradition in 1823. He had a sizable following among rural folk, and through his influence a stalwart rationalist preacher named George A. Dietz entered the awakened camp in 1829. The awakening in Baden was restricted largely to smaller villages and the countryside. We noted that Stilling was the Grand Duke's religious advisor early in the century, but the most widely respected prophet was a farmer named Johann A. Mueller. A one-time Roman Catholic priest, Franz J. Helfenreich, was the most prominent figure of the awakening in nearby Rhinehesse, while Johann H. Weisgerber headed the awakening in Dilltal.

One axis of the German Awakening extended from southwest to northwest. The Rhine formed the connecting link. This ligamental connection emerged because of relationships between leading figures of revivals in Wuerttemberg and in the Lower Rhineland, and, in turn, between the Lower Rhineland and such cities as Bremen, Hamburg, Kiel, and Luebeck in northwestern Germany.

Along the Lower Rhine, Samuel Collenbusch paved the way for the three awakened Krummacher brothers, Gottfried Daniel, Friedrich Adolf, and Friedrich Wilhelm. One of the brothers, Gottfried, gave his small but powerful group of followers a useful interpretation of predestination: since they were already predestined to blessedness or damnation, the members of his congregation could smoke pipes during worship services if they pleased. The consistory soon put a stop to this mischief. Ludwig Joergens of Wuppertal took awakened preaching so seriously that he brought his listeners to tears and himself, finally, to suicide. In Bremen and Hamburg, Menken, Johann B. Draeseke, Hermann Mueller, Friedrich Mallet, Otto Funke, Johann Rautenberg, Senator Martin Hudtwalcker, Amalie Sieveking, Henri Merle d'Aubigne, Friedrich A. Perthes, and other laypersons were influential in awakenings. Menken was among the first to enunciate the political overtones of the Awakening, by linking the evils of theological rationalism to the French Revolution. Johann F. Kluecker and Claus Harms were active in Kiel, and Johannes Giebel in Luebeck; Harms later became a revered figure for confessionalists.

In middle Germany, awakened circles of varying strength were formed in Naumburg, Wernigerode, Pforta, Sulza, Duessel, Halle, Wittenberg, Roehrsdorf and Lausa. But awakenings played no major role in the middle and northern states of Oldenbourg, Hanover and Mecklenberg, although awakened pastors and laymen were present in some areas, including the mission proponent Ludwig Harms in Hermannsburg, Hanover.

The awakenings in the north and east radiated from Berlin. Many who were involved in these movements were veterans of the War of Liberation. As early as 1810-12, a renewal of religious interest surfaced in the Berlin cadet corps; furture officers in training at the war college conducted special devotional hours on Saturday before attending Schleiermacher's services on Sundays.

The Moravians stimulated the movement in Berlin and Silesia, as well as in Wuerttemberg. One important link was Johann Jaenicke, the founder of Berlin's first school for missions. Among others influenced by the Moravians was Hans Ernst von Kottwitz, a Silesian baron who moved to Berlin in 1806. The first to organize an awakened circle in the capital, he touched the lives of many theological students; some of them later became influential figures in the church, including Tholuck, Wichern, Rothe and Zahn. He also showed great interest in charitable endeavors, as did another important layman, Samuel Elsner.

Although Kottwitz disclaimed any interest in politics, the awakenings in Berlin and Prussia helped fashion the contours of renewed Prussian patriotism. Awakened figures offered moral and spiritual interpretations of Prussia's humiliation in 1806, and insisted that her renewal hinged on religious rebirth.

The awakening in Berlin seemed to hold special attraction for lawyers and noblemen. By the late twenties, Berlin's upper crust had to reckon with the influence of the awakened, but eventually the renewal touched other groups in society as well. Karl Loeffler was the most popular pastor for women until 1824, when he left the city under strained circumstances. In general the awakening in Berlin was marked by Bible reading, fraternal relations, some disapproval of dancing and the theater, a rather strong fellowship with Roman Catholics, a zeal for organizing all kinds of societies, and firm support of political conservatism.

Two of the most important awakened preachers in Berlin were Schleiermacher and Jaenicke, although Schleiermacher's wife often attended the services of a third, Justus G. Hermes. The mystical interests of the famous scholar of historical law, Friedrich Karl von Savigny, gave him ready admission to the region's pious circle, which included laymen, pastors, and such students as Adolf von Thadden-Trieglaff, Gustav von Below, Ernst von Senfft-Pilsach, August W. Goetze, Karl W. von Lancizolle, Moritz August von Bethmann-Hollweg, the Gerlach brothers, Clemens Brentano, Christian and Anton von Stolberg, Ferdinand Karl von Below, Karl von Roeder, Karl von der Groeben, and Hans Rudolf von Plehme.

But before long the piety of the awakening in Berlin became brown and brittle, like autumn leaves. This was largely due to the polarizing and repristinating activities of a young theologian named Ernst Wilhelm Hengstenberg. He was heavily influenced by the awakening and benefitted from it, also professionally, but was never fully integrated into the movement, despite his close association with some of the leaders. We will examine in a later chapter how Hengstenberg turned the movement to his own advantage, forging a new alliance of orthodox religious forces with his paper, the EVANGELICAL CHURCH NEWS.

Especially in the northern areas of Prussia, east of the Elbe River, the neo-pietists' suspicion of colossal institutions resulted in renewed support for a state organized along the lines of the traditional classes, or "Staende." In Pomerania the noble "Junkers" gave resounding support to the new piety; four important leaders in the Pomeranian awakening were Gustav von Below and his two brothers, together with Adolf von Thadden-Trieglaff. This awakening might appropriately be called the "Von-Awakening," to symbolize its noble lineage.

In 1829 at Trieglaff, von Thadden opened a series of pastoral conferences for awakened Pomeranian clergymen. The annual conferences on his estate faltered momentarily in the mid-thirties, but forty-two pastors attended in 1841, seventy-two in 1842, and up to a hundred in the best years. Especially after the Awakening started to move toward confessionalism, as in Bavaria, the chief agenda item was usually the supposed rationalism of the church. In 1848 von Thadden withdrew from the state church and joined the Old Lutheran sect, but not before influencing the religious faith of the future German chancellor, Otto von Bismarck. Bismarck's family estate was several miles from Trieglaff; it was at von Thadden's estate that he met his future wife, a pious young lady. Bismarck later said that in the forties he once again learned how to pray while standing at the deathbed of the young Marie von Thadden, the wife of his good friend, Moritz von Blankenburg.

The Below brothers, Gustav, Karl and Heinrich, created the first stir in the Pomeranian awakening. Taking their cue from Kottwitz and Jaenicke in Berlin, they brought peasants together in the twenties for lay-led assemblies that included Bible reading, prayer and Holy Communion. Von Thadden and Heinrich von Puttkammer, Bismarck's future father-in-law, belonged to Gustav and Karl's circles; Heinrich's circle in Seehof vacillated in its relationship with the territorial church until finally a group emigrated in 1838. The Below brothers sometimes attracted as many as a thousand people to their services, but eventually they returned to the formal worship of the territorial church.

In East Prussia, where the forces of rationalism were strongly entrenched, only the slightest ripple of an awakening appeared. In Prussian Saxony, Andreas G. Rudelbach and others championed strict Lutheranism against rationalism, and in the kingdom of Saxony, a periodical entitled PILGRIM FROM SAXONY gave the awakening a focus after 1835. This movement rapidly became confessionalist in nature.

AUTHORIZED VOLUNTARYISM

In the first half of the century, a number of forces stimulated the creation of voluntary agencies and societies with religious goals. Romanticism's dual emphasis on the individual's contribution to community, and on community as the context for the individual's full development, helped

125

voluntary organizations become intersecting synapses. Renewed eschatological zeal also played a role. As already noted, one strain of eschatological zeal flowed into the restoration, when theological-eschatological interpretations of Russia and the East became politicized. The second channel of zeal also flowed over conservative terrain, although its course is more difficult to chart; it led to the formation of a host of religious societies and organizations. Like the Moravians, the awakened viewed themselves as a Philadelphian community of love whose voluntary works of mission and charity would help prepare the Lord's return.

No less significant was another function performed by these voluntary agencies and societies: they embodied the model of "freedom-within-authority," which the church was to mirror for the wider society. This is the key to understanding the vitality and importance of voluntary societies in the Awakening. Charitable, humanitarian, missionary, tractarian, and educational in nature, the societies were not designed to knick or cut the social fabric in any way, even where it was rotten. Among the awakened, voluntary societies were a tangible way to affirm the agreement being struck between church and state in the German territories.(11)

Although they were voluntary efforts, the societies of the awakened were deeply influenced by the authoritarian tradition. We have noted that the Society for Mission among the Jews in Berlin was organized along authoritarian and social-class lines. In Wuerttemberg, too, societies had an authoritarian and paternalistic structure since most of their governing boards were self-perpetuating, not elected by the total membership. The more prominent pietists sat on the governing boards of publication houses and societies, while men of lower social stature created policy for the institutions of mercy. This social authoritarianism not only affected the political leadership of societies on a state level, but influenced the selection of local leadership as well. While people in the lower classes, such as weavers, peasants, and shoemakers, controlled the leadership of 220 of 270 local pietist societies ("Stunden") meeting in Wuerttemberg in 1820-21, as time passed and the Awakening gathered strength, pastors and teachers helped swell the number of upper class leaders in these cells.(12)

126

The eschatological zeal in many societies reinforced this authoritarian spirit, which itself was a facet of restorational legitimacy. Chiliasts interpreted contemporary events as signs of the End time; little time remained for debating irrelevancies. In addition, they regularly labelled liberal events as evil, and conservative events as good. The CHRISTIAN MESSENGER FOR SWABIA, a Sunday weekly published after 1831, was led by a number of apocalyptic signals to predict Christ's coming in 1836: the French Revolution of 1830; natural catastrophies and epidemics; the deaths of Hegel, Goethe, and Schleiermacher in the early thirties; the increasing number of defections to Roman Catholicism; reports from the mission fields; and the publication of Strauss's LIFE OF JESUS (1835).

Voluntary societies allowed people to express the old pietist ideal of the brotherhood of all people in a carefully controlled religious environment. Sometimes, brotherhood under the Big Brother became a form of authoritarianism. In any case, the mission, charitable and publishing societies were not based on the liberal political ideal of fraternity.

Mission Societies

The awakened were zealous in their pursuit of foreign missions. The founding of numerous mission societies in Germany in the first half of the nineteenth century was one reason why the eminent missiologist, Kenneth Scott Latourette, called it the "Great Century."

Foreign mission work and mission societies demonstrated that the awakened accepted the church's assigned role in society. Mission work allowed a person to expend a great deal of religious energy without disturbing the local terrain. The faith confessions of newly converted "Hottentots" and Eskimos that were printed in religious periodicals incited no civil riots, and led to few religious disturbances. Then, too, mission work opened the way for the expression of a harmless type of cosmopolitan nationalism. For example, the great historian Leopold von Ranke's brother, a pastor, insisted that missionary societies carried out the special commission God gave to Germans in His kingdom. But most surely he knew that earlier in the century, English societies commissioned German missionaries and placed them in their own mission fields, including seven graduates of Jaenicke's school in Berlin sent to Sierra Leone in 1800.

Like many voluntary groups in the Awakening, the first German mission society, organized at Basel, owed its parentage to the German Society for Christendom. This earlier group was formed in Basel in 1780 to stimulate and coordinate charitable and evangelistic efforts. With strong support from southern Protestants, the German Society played an extremely important role in founding many religious societies, agencies, and institutions in Germany. It hoped to win souls for Christ and to enlarge the number of "institutions" of God's kingdom, and its regular periodical breathed an interconfessional spirit.

The first modern mission society in Germany, the Basel Mission, was founded by Nikolaus von Brunn, Christian F. Spittler, and four others after a steering committee met in the fall of 1815. With headquarters in Basel, the new mission got the bulk of its support from Wuerttemberg, and for years this state provided most of the society's directors, teachers and students, including about one-half of the 1,100 students who entered the mission training school between 1816 and 1882.

Lutheran and Reformed Christians worked side by side in the new society and in its supporting chapters. The constitution provided that "members, retaining sincere and respectful appreciation for their evangelical confessional affiliations, still obligate themselves as such, in their missionary work, to assume the universal perspective of the kingdom of God." The constitution also referred to the society's "apostolic character"; the society would walk in the steps or Jesus' apostles, and do what the institutional church—called an empty human fabrication in 1821—could not do. The first director, Christian G. Blumhardt, was an articulate spokesman for those who had such feelings about the territorial church and foreign missions.

For several years, the Church Missionary Society of London used graduates of the mission institute in its foreign work, but at is annual festival in 1820 the Basel Society finally commissioned four men for its own work. Three went to "serve the kingdom of God in the seacoast territories of the Caspian Sea, and if God's favor disposes, in Russia." The Czar put an end to work in the Caucasian field in the thirties, but the society sent other missionaries to the Gold Coast (1828), Southwest India (1834), and Hong Kong before midcentury. A medical missionary went to the Gold Coast in 1840.

Friedrich W. Hoffmann, son of the founder of the Korntal settlement, assumed the directorship in 1839. He set out to tie the society more closely to neighboring churches, especially in Wuerttemberg, where the church was gravitating toward the Awakening. Hoffmann used the idea of the "Christian folk" to explain the relationship between missions and the institutional church; later, as court preacher for Prussia's Frederick William IV, he descrbed how the institutional church was responsible for mission work. He also confirmed earlier nationalistic references, which were conservative in timbre, when he endorsed a united German evangelical church headed by the Prussian union church.

The Berlin Missionary Society was founded in 1824 by Neander, Bethmann-Hollweg, Leopold and Ludwig von Gerlach, Tholuck, and five other aristocrats, including several high military officials. In the organizational statutes, the society stressed that extending God's kingdom was an important Christian obligation. The society's income rose dramatically, from 3,263 "Thaler" in 1828 to almost 37,000 in 1854; a noticeable decline between 1848 and 1853 was probably related to the economic uncertainties of the revolutionarly years. In 1834 the society decided to make the Cape area of Africa its first field, but its leading mission became Trasvaal, which it entered in 1860.

The Rhenish Mission Society was organized in Barmen in 1827, after an extended pre-history that included a late eighteenth-century mission group in Elberfeld. The society issued a new regulation in 1832 that clarified its confessional position in these words: "We are fully convinced that <confessional differences> are no ground—nor should they become a basis—for hindering our cooperative efforts on behalf of Christ's kingdom." The society sent its first missionary to the Cape in southeast Africa in 1829. The Barmen society showed that mission work could not be blamed for exacerbating confessional differences.

Hamburg was headquarters for the North German Mission Society. It was organized in 1836, when Ludwig Mallet and others gathered several smaller aid societies under a new organizational umbrella. The articles of incorporation included a stringent confessional paragraph endorsing the Lutheran Augsburg Confession, but the paragraph was not so much a confessional endorsement as a protective device against the admission of Baptists and some sectarians, who were greatly feared at the time. The first general meeting substituted for that confessional paragraph a broad statement of purpose committing the mission to extending God's kingdom abroad, not transplanting local confessional divisions to heathen lands. The Bible alone was to be the standard of instruction.

The annual festivals of mission societies were opportunities to make a public commitment to foreign missions, but sometimes local tensions surfaced. This was true at the Basel festival in 1838, when Johann T. Beck, a theologian, charged in the festival sermon that missionaries misperceived things if they thought that the Master's soul-catching net was an enforced system of piety, or an ecclesiastical structure. Following this tact, he warned, they would merely turn heathen people into legalistic Jews, or into others who did not understand Christian freedom. But usually the festivals were joyful celebrations at which the congregation sang mission hymns, such as one written by Albert Knapp for the Basel Festival in 1829:

> You brothers united from south to north,
> For what did you come to see and to hear?
> Behold! Since Jesus has taken His kingship
> His glorious rule multiplies daily!

Offerings at these services helped swell Basel's Swiss franc income from 53,000 in 1823 to 205,000 in 1845, 305,000 in 1852, and 480,000 in 1855. The invocation often echoed themes of unity, universality and peace. "Permit us to identify Thy hand with joy" in the works of kingdom-building beyond the borders of this church and state, the preacher prayed at the Basel Festival in 1821, and "bless all our friends, near and far, who are united with us in the great purpose or Thy kingdom." Local mission festivals followed

130

the same pattern as the society's major festivals, sometimes
even drawing larger crowds. One festival in Baden in 1849
reportedly was attended by 15,000 people, with fifteen
speakers preaching simultaneously.

Tract, Charitable and Reform Societies

The Awakening's religious press was even more openly
supportive than mission societies of the church's chartered
role in society. Many of the new periodicals originated in
response to mediocre handling of religious news in the new
weekly papers. The awakened were interested in showing that
news articles about divine services, personnel changes, and
statistics did not tell all that was involved in church
life. People wanted to know more about activities in God's
kingdom, as the periodical for the German Society for
Christians announced in 1786. "I write as a Christian for
Christians," the editor of the Bavarian CHRISTIAN MAGAZINE
wrote in 1811, "to help extend God's kingdom on earth." Most
other new religious papers served the same purpose, although
their styles and content differed. Wuerttemberg's CHRISTIAN
MESSENGER FOR SWABIA was at first a devotional publication;
the EVANGELICAL CHURCH NEWS in Berlin was a church-political
sheet; the Bavarian JOURNAL FOR PROTESTANTISM AND CHURCH was
a scholarly paper that supported confessionalism.

These periodicals and papers usually limited their coverage
to religious news. When they ventured into social or
political subjects, their conservative views were a foregone
conclusion, as was the case in the POPULIST PRESS FOR PEOPLE
AND LAND in Halle. The religious press, including the
Sunday church papers, affirmed the arrangement that made the
church a model for a modernizing society. The papers seldom
criticized the social structure from a religious
perspective, or challenged prevailing political views. They
threw their support behind religious societies whose
activities did not agitate the water.

The material published by Bible and tract societies showed
their commitment to the emerging consensus as well.
Material that was published spanned the gamut, from the Holy
Bible, to the first five tracts published by the new tract
society in Hamburg in 1821: "The End of Time," "The Good
Mother," "First Evangelical Instruction," "Joseph the

131

Shepherd," and "Faithfulness that Protects." These societies were not apt to tear at the social fabric, or expose the church as the state's hired agent for inculcating authoritarian morality.

This is not to suggest that tract and Bible societies were unneeded. The purchase and reading of Bibles apparently was rare, at least for many in the educated and middle classes. The bookseller Friedrich Perthes of Hamburg reported that in ten years he sold only one Bible, and on that occasion the purchaser was quick to make an excuse, explaining that it was a gift for a confirmand. English money, and the assistance of Karl F. Steinkopf, who was closely associated with the British and Foreign Bible Society, helped to establish a number of Bible and tract societies. Bible societies sprang up in Stuttgart (1812), Berlin (1814), Hamburg (1814), Saxony (1814), and elsewhere. British assistance to groups in Prussia and Wuerttemberg may have been a manifestation of Francophobia, especially since the Russians too were giving thought to Bible distribution, with the Czar's encouragement. The Protestant British had much in common with these areas, and it may have been a matter of pitting the Bible against the Roman Catholic—and republican—tradition of France.

Tract societies such as the Christian Society for Northern Germany (1811), the Lower Saxon Tract Association (1820), and the Evangelical Society in Wuerttemberg (1832), busied themselves with reprints of such devotional classics as Arnd's TRUE CHRISTIANITY, and a wide range of other pietist pieces. In 1833, the 170 members of the Evangelical Society financed and distributed 40,000 tracts, and individuals sometimes made a living peddling tracts. But in general, tracts were neither revolutionary nor liberal in tone, although in 1834 the Prussian government placed stringent restrictions on those tract and mission societies whose members had separated from the church. The source of the problem was the separatist behavior of supporters, not their publishing activities, and to that grievous sin against the charter we shall return in a later chapter.

Equally conservative in outlook were the vast number of charitable, educational, and reform societies organized under religious auspices. Most of their supporters would have affirmed the Jesus-centered cosmic views of a poem from

132

the thirties, written in Elberfeld by a young evangelical confirmand named Friedrich Engels:

> Lord Jesus Christ, God's Son,
> Descend from Thy throne
> And save my soul!
> O come with Thy blessedness,
> Thou Brightness ot the Father's Splendor,
> Make me to choose Thee alone!
> Sweet, splendid, without grief is the joy,
> When there above
> We praise Thee, our Savior.

But this young confirmand's attention soon shifted to the social problems that hovered on the horizon. As a young man, Engels lived for a while in Bremen with the popular awakened preacher Georg G. Trevikanus; he was not invited to join the circle of young men whom Trevikanus gathered to promote foreign missions. It is doubtful that the young Engels would have been any more interested in the campaign for strict Sunday rest that was generated by such papers as the PILGRIM FROM SAXONY. While the drumbeat for observance of the Sabbath increased in intensity as the century progressed, the campaign was a weak, eccelesiastically-centered response to the vast upheaval in society accompaning industrialization and modernization.

Influenced by voluntary societies in England, Germany's new charitable, educational, and reform associations and institutions brought relief and assistance to thousands, although they did not challenge the church's assigned place in society. In Kaiserwerth, Fleidner organized a group of people to systematically rehabilitate prisoners in 1827-28, and his persistence in the Rhineland nurtured an interest in the reform of prisons that later brought the involvement of Johann H. Wichern of Inner Mission fame. Some individuals in the Awakening showed deep personal concern for released prisoners; Ernst Ludwig von Gerlach hired as his personal servant a penitentiary inmate who had been imprisoned for life before his release. But while prison reform and concern for released prisoners were not inconsequential issues, there was little possibility that these activities would address society's basic inequities. Institutions for the aged and indigent, as well as evangelical institutes for the blind established after 1832, were no more likely to alter the basic structure of society.

The temperance movement seized the interest of many awakened laypersons and clergy in the late thirties and succeeding decades. In 1835, the Prussian king arranged for the translation of Robert Baird's HISTORY OF TEMPERANCE SOCIETIES IN THE UNITED STATES, while in many areas, societies were organzied to reduce the consumption of liquor, especially among lower classes. It was thought that the concerted effort of Christians, rather than new laws, would throw off the heavy yoke of liquor. Soon the Prussian government officially recommended the formation of temperance societies to combat overindulgence.

Pastors and teachers in Pomerania painted a gloomy picture of the problem. A pastor reported in 1841 that each of the province's million citizens consumed an average of seventeen quarts of alcoholic drink annually. Progress came slowly, but by 1848-49 the crusaders could boast of twenty-two societies in the province, with 6,000 members, including 200 reformed drunkards. A temperance paper for three provinces helped spread the word.

While colporteurs and traveling preachers warned against the evils of drink, laymen such as the ex-jurist, Baron von Geld, dedicated their lives to the cause of temperance. It was no easy thing to condemn such time-honored traditions as drinking at baptisms, weddings, funerals and house-raisings. But several villages in Pomerania reported complete success in achieving temperance, while others claimed as much as a 90 percent drop in consumption. Not all theologians supported the movement, and once the theological faculty at Griefswald was asked to render an opinion on the question. Although the temperance movement's high water mark was reached before midcentury, some of the awakened still prosecuted the cause in the last quarter of the century.

Women were also involved in philanthropic efforts. In 1831, the daughter of an important politician in Hamburg established a women's society to visit sick and indigent women. She hoped to bring order and hygiene to the lives of these women, and to encourage the use of devotional literature, "which should lead the hearts of the poorest to God." Amalie Sieveking (1794-1859) also helped educate orphans, but she put most of her energy into hospital work in Hamburg, helping the poor with charity.

A more successful training program for women was the deaconess program established by Fliedner in 1836 at his hospital complex in Kaiserwerth. He also used other training institutions to prepare women for work among the sick, the indigent, children, and prisoners. In 1844 the Prussian state authorized the use of the term "deaconess" to identify Protestant women whose work paralleled that of the Roman Catholic nursing orders. Prussia's ambassador to England prevailed upon Florence Nightingale to visit Fliedner's institution.

The awakened sometimes set up a network of auxiliary societies to finance the care of needy children living in residential centers. The leader in this work was Johannes Falk (1768-1826), a bookseller in Weimar who turned to this project after four of his children died in rapid succession. Struggling against great odds, he tried to give shelter and Christian training to the "lost youth" orphaned by the Napoleonic Wars. After taking a vagabond child into his home, and placing others with foster families to keep them out of prison, he finally established a residential community that encountered one crisis after another. The remarkable prose of his diary recounts his tribulations as he tried to interest others in the Society for Friends in Need. One day's entry contained these words: "The butcher has told everyone that since I have paid him merely 25 'Thaler,' he will give me no more credit. I had no more money since the children obtained it from me the day before—to the last penny—for shoes." Despite these difficulties, Falk was an inspiration to others, including the young clerical candidate J. H. Wichern, who established a home for destitute children near Hamburg in 1833. For Wichern, this "Rough House," which still exists, was the start of a lifelong commitment to relieve the suffering of society's cast-offs and misfits.

Along the Lower Rhine, Graf Adalbert von Recke-Volmerstin cared for children on his estate, while in Baden, Christian H. Zeller established a special training school for teachers who worked in "Rettunghaeuser," such as Recke-Volmerstin's. Wichern and others stressed that the moral community of the family imparted the best human virtues; their institutions

135

provided family substitutes and care for society's cast-offs, but without changing the society that produced them. They recognized that the church's social assignment was to inculcate a morality of obedience, and to bandage those injured by society's gristmill.

By midcentury, the awakened had created societies of compassionate concern for the downtrodden. A periodical noted in 1845 that all kinds of institutions and agencies were seeking to ameliorate the problems of the poor, the sick, the drunkard, ophans, lost children, artisans, sailors, indigent and ill school teachers, emigrants, released prisoners, and fallen women, among others. People were also working cooperatively to sanctify the Sabbath. In that year, the Prussian political unit with headquarters in Duesseldorf had 742 societies within its borders that were dedicated to caring for the physical and moral needs of people.

In Prussia, characteristically, the king moved swiftly to seize the initiative, once the movement to create societies began to show signs of success. Frederick William IV issued a cabinet order in 1843, indicating that "it is my will" that people form societies to care for children, the sick, the aged, the poor, and released prisoners, since the best assistance would come from people whose inner resources moved them to act.

We lack the space to recount the works of private mercy that characterized such figures of the Awakening as von Kottwitz and the Gerlach brothers, among others. It is enough to note that the awakened inaugurated the "century of the masses" in German church life by creating a great number and variety of "voluntary" societies. But in the process, they unwittingly affirmed the rather innocuous social role the new religious consensus assigned to the church.

The American church historian Martin E. Marty recounted a conversation between the Jewish scholar Milton Himmelfarb and two historians. The historians had been criticizing American religious figures who always seemed to be reinforcing the status quo. "Ballast. Every culture needs it. Societies need ballast as much as ships or flying balloons do, to steady and control themselves," Marty quoted Himmelfarb as replying. "You fellows are always expecting a Billy Graham . . . to upset things in the name of God," he continued. "He has just the opposite function: he is engaged in ballasting. . . . He assures an uncertain public that its underlying values are proper."(13) The German religious Awakening, too, was "engaging in ballasting." In times of political unrest and social upheaval, it rallied to the side of conservative forces set on reestablishing and reasserting old values.

The few millennialists who jumped ship and emigrated from Germany, partly because they were dissatisfied with religious conditions at home, were more than counterbalanced by the thousands—and perhaps millions—of Protestants we now call "the awakened." Some expressed limited dissent at home, as in the settlement at Korntal. But usually they found positive ways of reaffirming the unwritten religious charter.

The awakened filled society's ballast with attacks against their common enemy, theological rationalism, and with a mixture of theology that had a double weight because it also endeared them to political conservatism. Meanwhile, a surrogate brand of nationalism helped flush out the tanks that bureaucrats and the educated middle class were trying to fill with liberal nationalism. Local awakenings did their part to strengthen ties to the territory, and to reinforce the ballast walls that separated one German state from another. And in the "authorized voluntaryism" of their societies, the awakened provided a ready reservoir of the heavy glue that held an authoritarian society together. While society looked on, this amorphous mixture was poured into the ballast labelled, "freedom within authority."

Himmelfarb said of the ballasting agent that "he helps give society its stability." Translated to fit the times and places of the religious Awakening in Germany, that reads: "They affirmed the viability and validity of the emerging consensus, namely, that it was the state's legitimate right to determine the church's social role as a model." In sum, the Swabian king was talking ballast language when he commended the work of the Stuttgart Bible Society with the comment, "<Your> undertaking has a very salutary purpose,

NOTES

CHAPTER III

(1) While the attempt to chronicle the Awakening is problematic, no less difficult is the effort to schematize local awakenings. In his study of nineteenth century churches, the American church historian Kenneth S. Latourette despaired of offering full coverage because the awakenings were "extraordinarily complex." The foremost German scholar of the movement, Erich Beyreuther, identified three major groups in the movement: the "biblicist," "emotional," and "confessionalist" (see DIE ERWECKUNGSBEWEGUNG, Die Kirche in ihrer Geschichte, ein Handbuch, ed. Kurt Dietrich Schmidt and Ernst Wolf, Band IV, Lieferung R <Goettingen: Vandenhoeck & Ruprecht, 1963>, pp. 29–30). Another writer suggested that a new ascetical ideal prevailed in awakenings in western and northwestern Germany, where Calvinism was strong, including the lower Rhine and Wuppertal. A different strain appeared in the northeast, where conservative political theory coalesced with the romantic inclinations of the Berlin nobility. In the south the clergy led the way to renewed biblical piety, and in northern Bavaria, the JOURNAL FOR PROTESTANTISM AND CHURCH was the focus for theological and confessional formulations that grew out of local awakenings (Horst Stephan and Hans Leube, DIE NEUZEIT, HANDBUCH DER KIRCHENGESCHICHTE, Part IV <2nd ed.; Tuebingen: J. C. B. Mohr (Paul Siebeck), 1931>, p.309). According to Franz Schnabel, the social status of participating laypersons differed from area to area; persons of noble birth were most active in north and east, while in the south and west artisans, peasants, merchants and early manufacturing workers participated (see DEUTSCHE GESCHICHTE IM NEUNZEHNTEN JAHRHUNDERT <4 vols.; Freiburg im Breisgau: Herder and Co., 1927–36>, IV, 388).

(2) The Moravians played an important role in the

emerging Awakening and in the century's religious history; names such as Novalis, Schleiermacher, Kierkegaard, Stilling, and others with Moravian roots or ties, immediately come to mind. The Moravians' world-wide organization, spirit of unity, missionary zeal, theology, and hymnic and devotional corpus provided impetus and a web of interpersonal relationships for people in the early Awakening.

(3) Schnabel, IV, 288-89.

(4) Max Geiger, AUFKLAERUNG UND ERWECKUNG; BEITRAEGE ZUR ERFORSCHUNG JOHANN JUNG-STILLINGS UND DER ERWECKUNGSTHEOLOGIE, Basler Studien zur historischen und systematischen Theologie, ed. Max Geiger (Zurich: EVZ Verlag, 1963), p. 218.

(5) Robert Anchor, GERMANY CONFRONTS MODERNIZATION; GERMAN CULTURE AND SOCIETY, 1790—1890 (Lexington, MA: D. C. Heath & Company, 1972), p. 41.

(6) The way the awakened handled the Scriptures differed markedly from their opponents, the biblical critics, who used tools of reason forthrightly in their interpretive quest. For the critics, the decisive experience grew out of the rational reconstruction of the text's historical context, so that the text could be read and interpreted intelligibly, not in the light of the immediate faith experience that was, for the awakened, coterminous with a subjective trust in the Bible's authority.

(7) Robert M. Bigler, "The Rise of Political Protestantism in Nineteenth Century Germany: The Awakening of Political Consciousness and Beginnings of Political Activity in the Protestant Clergy of Pre-March Prussia," CHURCH HISTORY, XXXIV (1965), pp. 433-34.

(8) See Hans Rosenberg, BUREAUCRACY, ARISTOCRACY AND AUTOCRACY; THE PRUSSIAN EXPERIENCE, 1660—1815 (Cambridge, MA: Harvard University Press, 1958), pp. 221-28.

(9) Friedhelm Wippermann, "Nationalbewusstsein protestantischer Theologen in der Restaurationszeit" (unpublished dissertation, Goettingen University, 1950), pp.

12-16. See also Koppel S. Pinson, PIETISM AS A FACTOR IN THE RISE OF GERMAN NATIONALISM (New York: Columbia University Press, 1934).

(10) Robert M. Berdahl, "New Thoughts on German Nationalism," AMERICAN HISTORICAL REVIEW, LXXVII (1972), 78.

(11) Christoph Maerklin pointed his finger in the right direction in his study of Swabian pietism, entitled PIETISM AND MODERN CULTURE (1838). He commended the involvement of pietists and neo-pietists in foreign missions and charitable work, but argued that these activities were detrimental when they restricted the practice of religion to the religious community, and failed to encourage religious people to take up their social and cultural responsibilities.

(12) Hartmut Lehmann, PIETISMUS UND WELTLICHE ORDNUNG IN WUERTTEMBERG VOM 17. BIS ZUM 20. JAHRHUNDERT (Stuttgart: W. Kohlhammer Verlag, 1969), pp. 256, 262-63.

(13) Martin E. Marty, THE FIRE WE CAN LIGHT; THE ROLE OF RELIGION IN A SUDDENLY DIFFERENT WORLD (Garden City, NY: Doubleday & Company, Inc., 1973), p. 19.

CHAPTER IV

THE LIBERAL CHALLENGE

The year 1835 was filled with excitement for some people in
the German states, and terror for others. The deafening
roar of a locomotive running on Germany's first railway,
between Fuerth and Nuremberg in Bavaria, was both exciting
and terrifying; the same was true for Halley's comet as it
streaked silently through the dark sky. For those who
wanted still more excitement, two scholars attacked the
basic books of Christianity, the Old and New Testaments. In
the spring, David F. Strauss' critical LIFE OF JESUS
appeared, followed in the fall by Wilhelm Vatke's
penetrating RELIGION OF THE OLD TESTAMENT. Some regarded
the books with approval as evidence that theology was being
transformed into humanistic philosophy. At the same time,
writers in the Young Germany movement startled the reading
public with several books that criticized Christianity, and
offered a syncretistic substitute.

The year of 1835 seemed to characterize the decade, which
began with the July Revolution in several territorial
capitals. While the religious Awakening flourished in many
of the states, leading some to believe that 1836 would bring
the End, it also began hardening into defensive orthodoxy,
partly in response to liberals who challenged the value of
the unwritten charter between church and state. For some
people, Halley's comet and the roar of the train were
terrifying phenomena; the liberals' claim that change, not
charter, was the chief item on the public's agenda aroused
terror in the hearts of others.

143

During the decade, liberal men and their movements made the radical assertion that the state was subservient to society. Their views were permeated by a secular spirit that attacked the idea of divine transcendence and its religious, theological, and political corollaries, and stressed man's self-sufficiency in a new humanism. Liberals attacked traditional religion as the basis of a perverted social and political structure, and impugned the unwritten charter that prescribed church-state relations and the church's place in society.

This liberal challenge flowed along the same channel as the social and economic forces that were rushing toward rapid industrialization and massive social change. Problems were sure to arise in the transition from romanticism to realism, and extraordinary pressure would be lodged against ideas and institutions along the way. But change was in the air, and change had to be discussed—theological, political, cultural, philosophical, and social change. Liberals debating the form and function of change struck terror in the hearts of the charter's defenders, and by the early forties the orthodox and the awakened found comfort in one another's arms.

Of course, the challenge did not begin or end in the thirties. The nineteenth century saw the first major shift in Protestant theology in about three hundred years. Signalling among other things a critical adjustment in the church's relationship with society, this development extended over a number of decades. "Enlightened" theologians, rationalists, liberals, and the so-called mediating theologians all made important contributions. But much of the theological spadework passed unnoticed, or at least unchallenged, so long as it did not place liberal theology in the service of politics. When that happened, the liberal challenge was more than serious; it was terrifying.

This chapter examines how various groups challenged different components of the religious consensus achieved in Germany by the 1830s. Moral freedom was a prerequisite for the new humanity sought by the so-called popular rationalists, but was it attainable without major reform? Those evangelicals who joined in political demonstrations for popular sovereignty leveled more direct challenges at the political structure and its religious ally, the church, although they made their romantic appeals in a rather naive way. An artistic movement called Young Germany struggled against the restoration in church and state as it worked to transform culture. But the most serious challenge came from the Young Hegelians, who used history in a critical fashion in their search for a new humanism that would appear, according to their thinking, when theology gave way to philosophy.

POPULAR RATIONALISTS

Rationalist theologians and preachers who tried to make religious truths applicable to daily life, as a sort of folk philosophy, were dangerous to church and state unless held in check. Deriving morality from the idea of moral freedom, they nurtured human responsibility in ways that challenged the status quo, including the cozy relationship between church and state. In fact, success gave rationalism a lease on life so that it was a major popular force until the forties, as we shall see in a later chapter's discussion of the Friends of Light ("Lichtfreunde").

One of the popularizers of theological rationalism was Heinrich Gottlieb Tzschirner (1778-1828), a university professor and preacher in Leipzig. He viewed the connection between religion and culture as fundamental, since Christianity's true mission was to advance civil and religious freedom. In 1820 he sharply criticized those who claimed that the church preached the gospel, but did not orient its members to natural knowledge; that it incorporated people into a holy community, but did not help them establish proper relations with the state; and that it prepared men for heavenly citizenship, but failed to stimulate civic responsibility. He emphasized that the church's function was to provide religious and moral edification, leading mankind into the proper exercise of duty, and thereby transforming humanity into the kingdom of God. Knowledge, the arts, and the state had worthwhile tasks of their own, but

Christianity advances the loftiest, the ultimate
goal for our society, and that through the church
which she has established. For the church intro-
duces faith and love into the world, quickens and
strengthens moral power, and establishes a divine
kingdom on earth.

Tzschirner's Reformation sermons extolled the notion of
freedom and its origins in the gospel; Protestantism helped
men protect themselves against the oppression of spiritual
and civil freedom, and offered a defense against the
renascent powers of darkness, he argued.

A vigorous apologist for Protestantism, Tzschirner
encouraged the prince to allow freedom of speech and action
in his domain, just as freedom prevailed in God's kingdom.
For their part, citizens were to obey the law in order to
attain happiness and freedom, but at the same time, to
recognize the unattainability of perfection in human
affairs. While Tzschirner did not escape the devastating
dialectic between freedom and responsibility that held
Germany in its grip at the time, he used his own type of
rationalist theology to provoke a discussion of the
citizen's moral responsibilities, and a life of spontaneous
love.

Tzschirner was not alone in making muted liberal
suggestions. Some of the rationalist theologians mentioned
in the previous chapter were his allies, including
Wegscheider, Bretschneider, Paulus, Ammon, Dinter, and the
theologian Johann F. Roehr (1777-1848).(1) Appealing largely
to the middle classes after 1830, they argued that just as
theology relied on reason, politics should be reformed by
principles of law and morality, so that civil freedom and
equality before the law became the guiding motifs. In their
eyes, political figures were either liberals or
anti-liberals, or, as Tzschirner wrote, adherents of the
"reform system" or of the "system of reaction." They
asserted that legal protection was necessary to prevent the
state and its bureaucracy from encroaching on civil freedom
and its corollary, religious freedom. The state's primary
function was to protect the individual's rights in order to
safeguard the genius of Protestantism, civil freedom.

Although the popularizers' challenges were covert, theological critics attacked their work by calling it bad theology. The church historian Karl Hase labored tirelessly to undermine the writings of Roehr. As we have seen, the awakened perceived them as their common enemy. The slashing attacks on Wegscheider and Gesenius by Ernst Ludwig von Gerlach and Hengstenberg in the EVANGELICAL CHURCH NEWS in 1829-30 were precipitated as much by the political ramifications of their teachings as by their theological rationalism. Both teachers retained their posts through the good graces of the Prussian minister, Altenstein, but the uproar pointed to the beginning of a tumultuous decade.

Periodicals and devotional materials on both sides spread the struggle beyond academic circles. Stamp returns in Prussia indicate that the circulation of papers increased from 35,516 in 1823 to 41,049 in 1830, including some from both camps. Devotional books carried the claims of freedom into the home; Christoph Friedrich von Ammon edited a work that appeared in its seventh edition in 1839, entitled THE LORD'S PRAYER, A DEVOTIONAL BOOK. In the introduction he noted that the spirit of man is anchored in infinite freedom, light, and truth; God's kingdom fills people with noble virtue, and leads them away from barbarism. Contributors to the volume, including Dinter, stressed liberal themes that emulated the French Revolution. One wrote this verse:

> Come to us, we faithfully pray,
> Thy Love, Thy Kingdom of Grace!
> Those walking before Thee in spirit and truth,
> Rich and poor—we are equals.

The devotions stressed that equality and freedom characterized God's kingdom.

These rationalist preachers and theologians, proto-liberals of sorts, were part of a larger movement with roots in the German "Aufklaerung." Like their "enlightened" predecessors, they assumed that people were basically good and capable of self-sufficiency, if constraints were removed. They hoped to create and educate a new humanity freed from tradition and slavery; this development would be a fitting capstone for the Protestant Reformation. Acting as religious counselors for the emerging middle class, they turned to religion to unleash man's inherent power over his environment. They thought that progress in the spiritual and moral realm would be followed by progress in society and state. They hastened to republish sermons preached by earlier rationalists that could help their cause, reissuing in thirty-nine volumes (1831-36), after numerous earlier editions, the sermons of Franz V. Reinhard, as well as a number of other collections.(2)

While the popular rationalists had no party or set program, they provided an important impetus for the liberal movement in Germany. They refused to limit their struggle against dogmatic constraints and inflexibility to the areas of religion, philosopohy, or pedagogy; their legacy was revived in the forties in a popular religious movement that was as heavily political as religious, the "Lichtfreunde" (Friends of Light, Society of Friends). Most of them would have relished the chance to have heard the Hamburg rationalist, Moritz F. Schmalz, preach in Dresden in 1833, when Saxony's new parliament met for the first time. Schmalz found a striking parallel between Jesus' founding of the kingdom and the new Saxon constitution, soon to be the light of the world. The constitution was part of God's advancing kingdom, he said, just as the well-known scriptural passage was applicable to the present time: "The old has passed away, and the new is at hand."

POLITICAL DEMONSTRATORS

A more immediate and visible challenge to the unwritten religious agreement was the participation of some evangelicals in mass gatherings organized by political liberals. It seemed out of character for churchmen to demonstrate an open interest in popular representation, or popular democracy, especially if they tried to support their position with theological arguments. Reaction came quickly; some were dismissed from their posts, while others were imprisoned.

The Revolution in Paris in 1830 preceded uprisings in the German states of Brunswick, Hesse, Saxony, Bavaria, and

Hanover. National-liberal movements received new impetus, and the Bavarian Palatinate became a hotbed for political radicalism. Finally, in the year that the English Parliament passed a major reform bill aimed at quelling dissent (1832), J. A. G. Wirth and Philipp Siebenpfeiffer organized a mass meeting with others, purportedly to celebrate the anniversary of the Bavarian constitution. In a dramatic departure from tradition, they also invited women to attend the political meeting, scheduled for May 26-27, 1832 at the Hambach Castle in southwestern Germany's Bavarian Palatinate, near Neustadt.

The organizers were amazed at the response, as 25,000 to 30,000 people streamed to the Palatinate from Bavaria, Wuerttemberg, Alcase, Baden, Kurhesse, Hesse-Darmstadt, Nassau, Frankfurt, Saxony, Hanover, and other states. Without the benefit of rail transportation, they gathered to celebrate the connected ideas of national unity and popular representation. On Sunday morning, the twenty-seventh, the first contingent of marchers set out for the castle under the tricolor flag. Accompanying Dr. Wirth and Dr. Siebenpfeiffer was Johann H. Hochdoerfer (1799-1851), an evangelical pastor from Sembach in the Palatinate. Slowly the gigantic crowd assembled in Hambach, including in its ranks 300 students from Heidelberg, nearly half of the university student body. Two major addresses filled the morning hours of this "Liberation Sunday," and then the crowd broke into smaller groups to hear twenty other speakers.

During these years, people still imagined that moral appeals would secure their demands for popular representation, a panacea that in turn would arrest the princely oppression of peoples all over Europe, and bring national unity to Germany as well. One of the afternoon speakers, a physician from Neustadt, concluded his speech with words that echoed the War of Liberation: "Long live Germany's unity, Germany's freedom—and through them, Germany's rebirth!" But the speeches also were peppered with cosmopolitan references, as the liberals tried to find Germany's star without denegrating other peoples, such as the displaced Polish intelligensia and gentry who were so popular in the Palatinate.

The preacher Hochdoerfer also delivered one of the afternoon

149

speeches. A report compiled by the Prussian secret police indicated that he was roundly applauded. Laying bare the extravagances of the royal courts, and charging that rulers impoverished their subjects, he condemned their despotism and caprice in no uncertain terms. He stirred deep emotion with colorful and descriptive phrases such as these: "when the starving citizen comes home with his crippled son, and there finds his parched child lying on the straw bed, on the dry breast of his dying mother . . . ."

But the crowd soon dispersed, leaving behind a steering committee that met the next day to lay plans for the future. This group called for the rebirth of the fatherland through a free press and the "living word in popular assemblies," so that citizens would be equipped to secure "the rebirth of the fatherland in a legal way." These efforts, as well as the proposed Reform Society, came to nothing, but it was not easy to forget the call for a contemporary Bible of sorts in the free press, and liturgical gatherings of sorts in popular assemblies.

The Palatinate church was not only represented by the three Protestant clergymen—one Roman Catholic priest attended—and the three clerical candidates who joined the crowd in Hambach. Many of the thousands who attended were undoubtedly Protestants from the area, and there may have been clergymen from other states as well. Neither should we ignore the fact that the demonstration's chief organizers had deep roots in the evangelical tradition. Wirth's mother was born in a parsonage, and Siebenpfeiffer had served for some years in the twenties as a lay delegate in the Palatinate General Synod, and as a member of a subcommittee on the church's confession. He had a close relationship with his pastor in Hamburg, and it was not surprising to hear him argue before a judge at a later date that "religion, economics and morality are the three bloodstreams of popular life," but "self-government is a people's only true form of government."

Reaction to the festival at Hambach followed quickly. The pietist CHRISTIAN MESSENGER in Wuerttemberg called the meeting "one of the saddest phenomena displayed in our disturbed Germany in modern times." Pastor Hochdoerfer was released from office and sentenced to two years in jail. Although he moved to Switzerland after serving his time, he returned to agitate during the uprisings of 1848. In 1833, Pastor Adolf Berkmann of Einselthum was harrassed with charges of preaching subversion, but was aquitted. He later served in the Frankfurt Parliament and its rump successor at Stuttgart (1849), although this cost him his professional career. Accused of disorderly speech as a sextarian in 1833, Pastor Philipp J. Faber of Alsenborn was imprisoned for nine months. One of the theological candidates who attended the festival was imprisoned as well; after his release in 1833 he went to Peru. Before taking a trip that kept him out of the hands of police, Friedrich W. Knoebel drafted a formal reply to the repressive acts passed by the German Confederation's Federal Diet.(3)

Another response to the Hambach gathering were the "constitutional festivals" held in 1832, including those at Zweibruecken, Weinheim a. d. Bergstrasse, and Badweiler. Only 400 out of an expected crowd of 8,000 gathered in June at Hanauer in Kurhesse. The consistory rebuked the local pastor, named Merz, for greeting the crowd with a short welcoming speech; after he and others defended themselves in print, they were given jail sentences of five to eight months.

The involvement of pastors in the Hambach Festival and in other liberal activities in the Palatinate led to a shuffling of personnel in the church consistory, headquartered in Speyer. As part of the Bavarian government's response to the festival, all but one member of the consistory was retired or moved during the first half of 1833. Two of the old members had worked with Siebenpfeiffer in the General Synod; the one man who stayed was a lay civil servant known for his conservative outlook. The new consistorial members were put in office to combat the kind of liberalism that Prince Oettinger-Wallerstein supposedly found while visiting the Palatinate early in 1833 on a "fact-finding" tour, to determine the cause of the festival. "Liberal principles are incessantly thrown out at the people from chancel and school," he reported.(4)

Late in June of 1832, the Federal Diet passed the Six Article Act, renewing the repressive Carlsbad Decrees of 1819. The articles imposed strict censorship and prohibited political assemblies, especially under the tricolor flag. Prussia had her own repressive decree, and soon a list of subversives made police suveillance more effective. In the Palatinate, the official "Black Book" contained the names of four clergymen from the area, four theological candidates, and nine theological students. Although these men represented only a small fraction of the clergy in the area (2 percent), and of candidates (8-10 percent) and theological students (25 percent), the government's shifting of consistorial personnel at Speyer showed that clergymen in the Palatinate were attracted to liberalism in some numbers.

In April 1833, about fifty students attacked the main guardhouse at the Federal Diet in Frankfurt in an attempt to seize control of the Diet. This brought more repression; the states arrested about 1,800 students, executing thirty-nine. A number of theological students and candidates from the Palatinate were harrassed, arrested, or forced to emigrate, and in the resulting atmosphere of fear, another pastor, Heinrich K. L. Kloeckner of Luthersbrunn, was released from office. His case was not helped by a sermon he published in 1832, entitled "The Free Press as God's Word and Summons to Men for their Illumination and Welfare."

The revolutionary clergyman Friedrich L. Weidig (1791-1837) was also moved to action. At an earlier date, he influenced Karl Follen of the Student Union movement; at this point he joined with the radical writer, Georg Buechner, to publish the HESSIAN MESSENGER. The pamphlet argued that the state's authority came from the devil; it did not deserve the people's obedience. Weidig added biblical references to Buechner's text, and for this he was imprisoned by Hessian authorities at Darmstadt in 1835. Two years later he committed suicide in his cell.

YOUNG GERMANY

Young Germany was a group of writers who placed their art directly in the service of social ideals. Called "subversive doctrinaires" by the Right, and "aimless dilettanti" by the Left, they were seen by most as "un-German" when they challenged the younger generation to save Germany from its bankruptcy.(5) This literary movement contributed to the strain in German culture as it made the difficult transition from romanticism to realism.

One object of their criticism was religion and its support of an oppresive social structure. Since the church was supposed to show society how to function "freely" within limits established by authority, the Young Germans saw religion as the bulwark for an oppressive society. As a result, their criticism included the unwritten agreement between church and state, which set the church up as a model for society.

The movement received its name in 1834 from a participant, Ludolf Wienbarg (1802-1872). One stimulus for the Young Germans' struggle against reaction and restoration in church and state was the Revolution in Paris in 1830; St. Simon and other French socialists, Georg Sand, Shelley, Byron, and Pushkin were also important influences. Social emancipation was the object of the "Tendenzliteratur" written in various genres by Wienbarg, Ludwig Boerne (1786-1837), Karl Gutzkow (1811-1878), Henrich Laube (1806-1884), Theodor Mundt (1806-1861), F. G. Kuehne (1810-1888), and E. A. Wilkomm (1810-1886). Laube had studied theology at Breslau for a time; this experience probably contributed to his vigorous attacks on religious oppression.

Heinrich Heine (1797-1856) was an important model for the group as it attacked censorship and, after 1835, turned on political targets without much effect. Heine had taken the name Heinrich in 1825 when he formally rejected Judaism in Christian baptism. This action enabled him to take his public examinations in law a month later, but he never secured an appointment as jurist or teacher. His hatred of Prussia festered as a result, and he never tired of satirizing this "Jesuit Order of the North." At the time, he interpreted his baptism as a necessary "entrance ticket into European culture," but his role soon proved to be somewhat different than he supposed it would be.

Heine masterfully employed satire and irony to rehabilitate the flesh, making full use of blasphemy, and misquoting biblical passages at will. He provided the basis for Nietzsche's phrase "dead God" when he wrote, "The old

Jehovah prepares Himself for death. Do you hear the bells ringing? Kneel down! Someone brings the sacrament to a dying God." The sincerity of his "re-conversion" to Christianity later in life is much disputed.

But he freely used religious symbols when it was advantageous in his struggle against tyranny, once referring with admiration to the "divine brutality of Brother Martin <Luther>." An emigrant to France in 1831, he expressed his passionate sense of justice in prose and poetry. While he never was able to settle the conflict between paganism and Christianity in his own mind, he remained devoted to his native Germany, appropriating the best in French culture, especially St. Simonian ideals, in his efforts to reconcile spirit and flesh.

Late in 1835 the Federal Diet condemned as dangerous to the public "the literary school known under the name 'Young Germany,' which includes Heinrich Heine, Karl Gutzkow, Ludolf Wienbarg, Theodor Mundt and Heinrich Laube." The Prussian government specifically condemned their works as opposed to "revealed religion"; these "bold assaults on Christianity" could not be tolerated, or for that matter read. In the same year Mundt, published MADONNA, a strange synthesis of social and religious criticism, humanism, and St. Simonian religion. Gutzkow also startled the reading public that year with his novel WALLY THE SKEPTIC. The book wrestled with the question of religious skepticism and the inadequacy of Christianity, although conservatives found it to be little more than a glorification of lustful life. Gutzkow's book championed Jewish emancipation in its description of the religious doubts of a Christian woman, and a Christian man's relationship with a Jewess. He proposed to eliminate all political, religious, moral and racial barriers, and to fuse the purely human core that remained.

The Young Germans experienced and expressed the day's tension between past and present, a tension that leads one observer to call this period before midcentury the "culture of political despair." The apparent impasse between the two led to an indictment of the historical process, and its claim upon living people. While Heine participated in what this historian calls an "Enlightenment of lost illusions," Buechner and Arthur Schopenhauer drew down the veil of

154

pessimism and meaninglessness that was to haunt the century later in Germany.(6)

But supporters of the religious charter in church and state had little time for such criticism and doomsday talk. Reacting with terror to the knife at their throat, they used the methodical machinery of government and censorship to silence the disquieting voices of the Young Germans. They wanted no talk of a cultural transformation that would upset carefully laid plans.

YOUNG HEGELIANS

The Young Hegelians surfaced at a time when the last of the great leaders of German idealism and neohumanism were passing from the scene. Goethe, Hegel, and Schleiermacher died within a span of several years in the early thirties. And although the Young Hegelians did not forget Hegel, they acted as if he had taken to his grave the transcendent elements of his philosophy. William J. Brazill notes in his definitive work that for the Young Hegelians, "the most distinctive feature of Hegel's philosophy was the insistence that history had a purpose and direction, an intrinsic meaning." But history's meaning "was not to be found in reference to transhistorical judgment, to some transcendent force; its meaning lay entirely within itself."(7) They took it as a compliment when they were mocked at the Prussian court as men who "Hegeled their Bible and Bibled their Hegel." Humanistic rather than Christian, they were intent on describing what it meant for God to be immanent, as man. Their charter would be no halfway covenant between institutions of this world and the world beyond, but a blueprint for a new world, created for and by men alone on the basis of their negative criticism.

Meanwhile, in the period between 1830 and 1848 German intellectuals shifted their major concern from the whole to its parts, although, of course, they retained their emphasis on systematic thought and its coherence. Man and his interests and needs became, as it were, the focus, the "data" of the Hegelian Absolute Spirit. New content systems and critical bases were used in conjunction with Hegelian methodology in order to remake the future humanistically, as people tried to decipher the mystery of man as the immanent God. For the Young Hegelians, the form and content of history became the basis of negative criticism.

They held that man, not God, was revealing himself in history. They acknowledged the validity of Friedrich Schlegel's statement that "the universe is not a system, but a history." They thought that by focusing attention on the purported relationship between history and revelation, men would make an advance over earlier efforts to reconcile reason and revelation.

In sum, the Young Hegelians were united by a question that occupied them all: "What were the consequences of the incompatability of Christianity and Hegel's philosophy?"(8) Their answers differed, but they agreed on the question despite the fact that it made no sense to non-Hegelians, and was declared invalid by Right-Wing Hegelians since its premise was false.

For the Young Hegelians, especially David F. Strauss and Bruno Bauer, this question was addressed most advantageously in the area of Christology. They hoped that historical investigations of Christological doctrine would help precipitate the necessary cataclysmic transformation of theology into philosophy. This was for them the logical point of departure for investigating the validity of theology in the modern world. For if it could be shown that traditional Christology erred in portraying Jesus as the human revelation of a transcendent God, the whole structure of theology would collapse. If theology were shown to be a humanistic endeavor, circumscribed by space and time, then the day of full revelation would arrive with the displacement of transcendent theology by humanistic philosophy.

Human progress, the Young Hegelians argued, depended on the ability to crack the seemingly impregnable rock of theology that supported so many human traditions and institutions. They would not accept without challenge Hegel's conclusion that the state was a spiritual reality, attacking both sides of his argument, but especially its basis in transcendence. Feuerbach spoke for them all in 1839 when he criticized

Hegel's philosophy as the "last sanctuary" of theology. They continued to insist that discussion of the reality of reason had to be separated from discussion of the reason of reality, since no Absolute Spirit held the two together. No less than theology, man was the object of philosophy.

Such critical work presented a serious intellectual challenge to theology and, as it became political criticism, to the institutional church. But the Young Hegelians' first target was religion, and that not merely because religious criticism was less likely to be censored than blatant criticism of the state. They attacked religion because they viewed it as fundamental and foundational to the state. They acknowledged the viability of the charter that had been drawn up for the churches, and committed themseves to challenging it with all their intellectual resources.

In his masterful study of the movement, Brazill concludes that the "Young Hegelians both identified and helped create what Nietzsche, at least, saw as the central problem of the age"—that God was dead, and "they provided for most intellectuals of their time the means by which the Immortal became mortal and the Eternal became temporal."(9) They clustered in four geographical areas to do their work: southern Germany, Berlin, Halle, and Cologne. Authorities in Prussia did not move against them or their organ, the HALLISCHE JAHRBUECHER (1838ff.), until 1840, after both Altenstein and Fredrick William III were dead. The new king and his minister of public worship, Johann A. Eichhorn, soon outlawed the journal and took other steps to counteract their influence. The Berlin group eventually became the most radical, insisting that progress could occur only after radical criticism of Christianity ensued, since religion had a stanglehold on academia as well as on the Prussian government.

We will examine their radical challenge in greater detail, beginning with Strauss, who was a close friend of Johann K. W. Vatke (1806-1882) while he studied in Berlin. Vatke's work, cited above, was chiefly of interest to the academic world. He used Hegelian terminology to describe Israel's history from the perspective of comparative literature. His argument that the "P" (priestly) writer was the last of the Pentateuchal writers has been supported by later scholarship. The movement also included Bauer, Vischer,

Feuerbach and Ruge.

Strauss

The broadside attacks of the Young Hegelians were the work
of young men, much as the important scientific discoveries
and technical innovations of the thirties and forties were
the work of the younger generation. Bunsen was thirty-four
when he discovered the natural gas burner, Siemens
thirty-one when he improved the electrical telegraph, and
Abbe twenty-six when he drew up precise construction data
for the microscope. The two-volume, 1,500 page LIFE OF
JESUS, CRITICALLY EXAMINED that was published in Tuebingen
in 1835-36 was the work of a twenty-seven year old
theologian named David Friedrich Strauss (1808-1874). Its
author had gone to Berlin to listen to Hegel, but Strauss
met Hegel only once before Hegel died of cholera in 1831.
Strauss heard the sad news from Schleiermacher in the famous
theologian's home, then tactlessly remarked, "And it was to
hear him that I came to Berlin." But he was telling the
truth; in his work, he wanted to demonstrate that the kind
of mediating course Schleiermacher followed was untenable.

Strauss claimed to show that the unconscious Schleiermachian
synthesis between rationalism and supernaturalism was false
and inadequate. No less tenable was the supernaturalist's
attempt to retrieve the traditional Christ through
historical investigation alone, or the rationalist's attempt
to find Christ by using reason to construct Him on the basis
of rationally unassailable information in biblical
documents. A new synthesis between history and reason was
required that would "immanize" God, and take from Jesus the
burdensome responsibility of touching the transcendent God
in the flesh. No single individual manifested the idea of
unity between God and man, but the idea "comes to distribute
its riches among a multiplicity of instances, which mutually
complement each other."(10) Strauss put his case simply:

> This is the key to the whole of Christianity, that
> as the subject of the predicates which the church
> applies to Christ, we place instead of an individual
> an idea, but an idea that exists in reality, and not
> a Kantian unreal one.

Little wonder why his work aroused such a storm of criticism on all sides!

Strauss was a synthesizer who drew together elements of biblical criticism and the study of myth, and focused them in Christology. He relied heavily on the work of biblical critics, and the distinction they were drawing between revelation and the documents that recorded it. A variety of scholars, including Herder and DeWette, had applied the category of myth to the scriptures, especially the Old Testament and the beginning and end of Jesus' career. Strauss' methodology, a novel feature of his effort, required that the idea of myth be applied to the entire career of Jesus as it was described in the gospels. His original contribution was to combine "the ideas of . . . historical and scriptural criticism within the Hegelian philosophy of development in order to demonstrate the imminence of the Young Hegelian apocalyptic."(11) He hoped that his work in Christology would enable men to attain the plateau of the spirit that lay beyond Christianity, in which the age of religion would yield to the age of philosophy.

Strauss used the category of myth to express the new synthesis. Myth was a state of mind, a representation for an experience; that was why the early Christian community produced myth to talk about Jesus, he argued. Claude Welch indicates that for Strauss, myth

> meant the expression of the IDEA in the form of a historical account. "Evangelical myths" were those narratives relating directly or indirectly to Jesus which might be considered "not an expression of a fact, but as the product of an idea of his earliest followers."(12)

Strauss rejected the miracles of Jesus, not because of his positivistic attitude, but because of his idealism.

Rationalists no less than the orthodox reeled under his attack and reacted with anger, for even they trusted the reliability of some of the gospel records, after they were purged of miraculous elements. Strauss' rejection of John's gospel as a historical record was a direct affront to Schleiermacher's disciples, and to many others. Within four or five years after publication, his LIFE OF JESUS was rejected or defended by forty or fifty books and pamphlets, not to mention articles, in a vigorous literary war. The studies were authored by Franz von Baader, August Tholuck, J. A. W. Neander, Christian G. Wilke, August Ebrard, Daniel Schenkel, Wilhelm DeWette, Christoph von Ammon, and Ernst W. Hengstenberg, among others. Strauss joined the fray in his own defense.

Some claimed that his book should have been written in Latin in order to spare the laity the pain of its heresy. In THE ISCARIOTISM OF OUR TIME, a colleague at Tuebingen, C. A. Eschenmayer, condemned Strauss' book as a betrayal of Christianity. Tholuck conjectured that "Jews and Jew-lovers" bought and circulated copies of Strauss' book in bulk, in order more fully to "propagate Jewish propaganda." The arch-conservative Hengstenberg said that the book showed what happens when Christianity is mingled with Hegelian philosophy, or any other type. Strauss, he said, did a great service when he "calmly and deliberately laid hands on the Lord's Annointed, undeterred by the vision of millions who have bowed the knee, and still bow the knee, before His appearing."

In Strauss' native Wuerttemberg, THE CHRISTIAN MESSENGER published a series of harsh articles in 1836-37 by the pietist leader Sixt Karl Kapff. Gustav Binder and Christoph Maerklin came to Strauss' defense, but C. G. Barth and William Hofacker continued the attack. Soon Wuerttemberg's Council of Education asked Strauss whether he could offer theological lectures at Tuebingen with integrity, while rejecting the historical foundations of Christianity. Dissatisfied with his answer, the government transferred him to a minor teaching job in his native Ludwigsburg, but in 1836 he resigned the post. Officials in Zurich offered him a chair at the university in 1838, but the attempt failed when 40,000 people petitioned against his appointment. He was pensioned without occupying the position.

In Prussia, the government asked the influential awakened theologian, Neander, for advice on the matter. He replied that it was not advisable to ban the book. He wrote that the work

> constitutes a danger to the sacred interests of the Church, but it follows the method of endeavoring

to produce a reasoned conviction by means of arguement. Thus any other method of dealing with it than to meet argument with argument will appear in an unfavorable light, and seem to be an arbitrary interference with the freedom of inquiry.

The government took this advice, but Neander's LIFE OF JESUS (1837) failed to meet "argument with argument."

One of the more tempered responses came from Ferdinand C. Baur (1792-1860), who had been one of Strauss' teachers at Tuebingen. Though not himself a Young Hegelian, he was partly indebted to Hegel for his description of writings in the New Testament as a veritable compilation of Petrine-Jewish-Christian and Pauline-Heathen-Christian sources. A careful scholar who became the center of the "Tuebingen School," he argued that Christ's divinity is seen through His humanity; Christology is the point of departure for discovering the historical basis of Christianity's "positivity." Baur assumed that Christianity was not homogeneous from the start; through careful historical inquiry, one can find theology through history. His use of historical criticism in the Pastoral Epistles had tremendous impact on later New Testament studies, and his work in gospel criticism laid the foundation for years to come as well. But Baur did what Strauss failed to do; he addressed the documents themselves.

Between 1836 and 1838-39, Strauss published the second and third editions of his work. He showed a willingness to modify his position somewhat under attack, particularly his views on the fourth gospel. But the fourth edition in 1840 showed his bitterness at having been rejected at Zurich; in most areas it reverted to the hard line of the first edition. His THE CHRISTIAN DOCTRINE OF FAITH IN ITS HISTORICAL DEVELOPMENT AND ITS CONFLICT WITH MODERN SCIENCE (1841) clearly rejected Bible and church, and placed dogma fully in the realm of historical investigation. In THE ROMANTIC ON THE THRONE OF CAESAR, OR JULIAN THE APOSTATE, he argued that Frederick William IV of Prussia could not retard the historical process; he was tilting windmills in trying to protect an outdated religion. Strauss also busied himself with biographies of the Swabian humanist Frischlin, and of von Hutten and Voltaire. In THE LIFE OF JESUS ADAPTED FOR THE GERMAN PEOPLE (1864), he retracted some of his earlier criticism, and allowed the possibility of an historically identifiable Jesus. But the work was not widely acclaimed. Culture became his new Absolute, and his later writings were eclectic smatterings of bourgeois culture and morality. Nietzsche leveled a telling criticism in 1873 when he called Strauss a "Bildungsphilister" ("Phillistine," or popularizer of culture), especially since he did not like the music of Strauss' friend Wagner.

Strauss' work in 1835 was a new and radical form of rationalism that applied a comprehensive, critical perspective to the gospels. His methodology relegated large amounts of textual material to the categories of myth and legend. He thought that he had demonstrated Jesus to be the creation of a community, not an historical person. But as Karl Barth conclusively argued later, he did not have the stature to be a heretic, neither did he have the power of thought to use and extrapolate the insights of 1835. Claiming that he was an independent thinker, he was really very much a ball of clay molded by circumstances and the desire for acceptance.

Nevertheless, one reason for the widespread rejection of his book was that he touched a sensitive nerve. Although an aristocrat of sorts himself, as his behaviour in 1848 demonstrated, Strauss argued in THE LIFE OF JESUS that the early Christian community played an important role in constructing myth. The implication of this argument was staggering, especially in view of contemporary circumstances: the religious community was responsible for its faith, not the state, or some religious hierarchy. The religious community that Strauss proposed for the present, namely humanity, would indeed have included a leadership elite, with Strauss himself in the forefront; but at least it was something of a change from the hollow, state-controlled church of his day. Strauss held up a vision of a community creating its own myth, and this vision enabled or required people to tear the scales from their eyes and examine the mythical structure they had created for their day, including the unwritten religious charter. That process frightened and angered the people of Strauss' time, and they lashed out angrily in response.

Bauer, Vischer, Feuerbach, Ruge

Bruno Bauer (1809-1882) was a protege of Schleiermacher's opponent Marheineke, and a colleague of both on the theological faculty in Berlin. Like Marheineke, he first pitched his tent in the camp of the Right Wing Hegelians, and dutifully criticized Strauss' work in 1835, claiming that Jesus' incarnation was a philosophical necessity. The Prussian minister Altenstein looked to him as a tool to bring Hegelianism to the theological faculty at Bonn. But suddenly Bauer reversed his public position one hundred and eighty degrees and became, as Arnold Ruge said, the "Robespierre of theology."

In 1839 Bauer was appointed to the theological faculty in Bonn, a citadel of mediating theology. The suspicions of the Bonn theologians, and their refusal to finance his travel expenses and inaugural lectures, led to open conflict about the time that Eichhorn took Altenstein's place in Prussia's Ministry of Public Worship. Bauer published his EVANGELICAL STATE CHURCH OF PRUSSIA AND KNOWLEDGE (1840) anonymously, but he was soon identified as its author. His book argued that since church union in Prussia had brought an end to the confessional churches, the rational state that absorbed them embodied all spiritual life and progress; it was now obliged to fulfil its responsibilities, chief of which was to protect philosophy against theology.

The next year he provided an autographed copy of CRITICISM OF THE GOSPEL HISTORY OF THE SYNOPTIC GOSPELS to Eichhorn. This, his most famous work, attacked the historicity of the gospels and the historical nature of Jesus. Bauer wrote that the gospels were human documents that incorporated the predominant characteristics of the personalities of their authors. They had, in fact, re-alienated man into believing that union between God and man was possible in only one man, Jesus.

In October 1841, the Prussian king ordered his state minister, von Rochow, "to see to it in agreement with Eichhorn that Dr. Bauer does not again return <to Bonn from a visit to Berlin> in his role as unpaid lecturer at Bonn." But Bauer lectured for still another semester before he was forbidden to teach in 1842, partly because Eichhorn had requested judgments from all of the Prussian theological faculties about his right to teach. Eventually he took action against Bauer, even though slightly more than half the responses opposed Bauer's removal on the basis of academic freedom. Bauer returned to Berlin and made sarcastic attacks on religion. His CHRIST AND CAESARS (1877) claimed that Christianity originated with Philo and Seneca; the work soon became authoritative for Marx and his followers. After 1848, this radical atheist worked as a conservative politician and anti-Semite, contributing articles to conservative papers. He continued to write scathing attacks on Christianity, but none was feared as much as UNMASKED CHRISTIANITY (1843), 3,000 copies of which were seized upon publication by Swiss authorities.

The necessity of transforming theology into philosophy was also a major motif for Friedrich T. Vischer (1807-1887), who served as a clergyman in Wuerttemberg for a year before becoming a tutor (1831), and professor of aesthetics and literature at Tuebingen (1835). Vischer demonstrated a continued interest in religious questions, defending Strauss in the radical HALLISCHE JAHRBUECHER, and demanding that the state reject Christianity for humanism. By 1842 he set some distance between himself and this radical journal, but not in time to escape the wrath of the pietists who opposed his appointment as a full professor in 1844. One Sunday late in the year, four preachers denounced him in their sermons simultaneously. The next year the university warned him to stop attacking Christianity, and suspended him from lecturing for two years.

Ludwig Feuerbach (1804-1872) was a Young Hegelian philosopher who called theology anthropology. In an anonymous tract in 1830, entitled "Thoughts about Death and Immortality," he attacked personal immortality. This resulted in dismissal from his academic post in Erlangen, and he never again held a teaching post. But his marriage to a relatively wealthy woman in 1837 relieved him of financial worries.

Feuerbach was free to pursue criticism, based on the idea of man's humanity. That, not history, was his primary focus. In a memorandum on "The Necessity of a Transformation" (1842-43), he wrote that "Hegelian philosophy was the arbitrary unification of various systems, superficialities, with no positive strength, because it contained no absolute negativity. Only he who has the courage to be absolutely negative has the strength to create something new."(13)   His criticism of theology was evidence of a wider trend toward materialism, as many thinkers moved from idealism and Christianity toward Marx.

Feuerbach's most important study was THE ESSENCE OF CHRISTIANITY (1841). He argued that since humanity was God, it was false and offensive to refer to an externalized God when the subject under discussion was humanity.   He added that "atheism—at least in the sense of this work—is a secret of religion itself: that religion itself, not indeed on the surface, but fundamentally, not in intention or according to its own supposition, but in its heart, in its essence, believes in nothing than the truth and divinity of human nature." He advised Christians to "admit that your personal God is nothing else than your own personal nature, that while you believe in and construct your supra- and extra-natural God, you believe in and construct nothing else than the supra- and extra-naturalism of your own self."

But of all religions, Christianity was the "perfect religion" because it assisted men in the full process of negating self and affirming God; that opened the possibility of a full and complete reversal of the process. Most basic of all was the task of finding sensuousness at the foundation of one's thinking, and developing love for fellows who confirm one's way of thinking, since love unites humankind.   The "screen" for man's projection of himself as God was his infinite will to live, the infinite intensity of his love, and the experience of beauty.

Although Feuerbach viewed the state as both the reality of faith and the refutation of faith, he insisted that man must become political because of his faith in man. To prove the point, he ran for election to the Frankfurt Parliament in 1848, and eventually served with two other Young Hegelians, Vischer and Ruge. But in the long run, his major political contribution was made through Marx who, as we shall see in a later chapter, explained projection in terms of its social, not its personal or individual, anchorage.

Arnold Ruge (1803-1880) was the most politically active of the Young Hegelians.   History was absolute for him, but history was restless since it was driven forward by the public spirit of the age.   This spirit was not recognized by many, but its progressive nature had to be made manifest nonetheless, since political humanism meant political democracy. Ruge was convinced, as one commentator notes, that "the philosophy of Hegel could not rest merely on the rejection of Christianity; it had, inevitably, to lead to reforms in the social and political life of Germany."(14) Ruge set out to organize the Young Hegelians around criticism of politics and religion in the HALLISCHE JAHRBUECHER (1838-43), but he met defeat in his effort to form a core party for political action. While he realized that Prussia was not perfect, he continued to support her through Bismarck's time as the state with the greatest potential for democracy.

The impact of the Young Hegelians was tremendous. They sent shock waves of fear through church and state, gave new impetus to scepticism with their denial of transcendence, and advanced the cause of the secular faith of humanism. Theology was forced to come to grips with their challenge, as theologians sought a basis for faith beyond what one writer calls the "contingencies of historical and psychological inquiry." Their effect on socialism was indirect, though no less significant; new socialist thinkers interpreted the apocalypse as a radical change in society deriving from social transformation, not from the transformation of theology into philosophical humanism.(15)

Between 1830 and 1870, each of the four great western European nations was associated with a major scientific advance. In France it was the theory of bacteria, in Britain evolution, and in Italy molecular theory. Germany's contribution was thermodynamics, an appropriate one for a culture so deeply influenced by romanticism's emphasis on history and historical data as a controlled, yet somewhat capricious flow of time.

Thermodynamics is the study of the relation of heat and mechanical energy, and the conversion of one into the other. According to this definition, we might understand the liberal challenge to the unwritten religious charter as a thermodynamic experiment of sorts. Rationalists, demonstrators, and members of the Young German and Young

Hegelian groups generated heat; frightened forces in church and state soon deflected their heat into ineffectual, repetitive mechanical energy. The liberals generated heat, but they were not able to transform it into an energizing process that immediately affected the institutional church. That was prevented by the smoothly operating machinery of the religious consensus between church and state.

But heat invariably transfers its energy elsewhere, and that process cannot be intercepted. Although the liberal challenge was effectively thwarted in the thirties, its long-range effects cannot be ignored in the pages that follow. In sum, the dynamic of the liberal challenge was not as easily arrested as some supposed.

NOTES

CHAPTER IV

(1) Hans Rosenberg, "Theologischer Rationalismus und Vormaerzlicher Vulgaerliberalismus," HISTORISCHE ZEITSCHRIFT, CXLI (1930), 497-541.

(2) See Alexandra Schlingensiepen-Pogge, DAS SOZIALETHOS DER LUTHERISCHEN AUFKLAERUNGSTHEOLOGIE AM VORABEND DER INDUSTRIELLEN REVOLUTION (Goettingen: Musterschmidt Verlag, 1967).

(3) Edgar Suess, DIE PFALZER IM "SCHWARZEN BUCH" (Heidelberg: Carl Winter Universitaets Verlag, 1956), pp. 34-127.

(4) Helmut Kimmel, "Auswirkungen des Hambacher Festes auf die protestantische Kirche der Pfalz," in HAMBACHER GESPRAECHE 1962, Geschichte Landeskunde, Bd. 1 (Wiesbaden: Franze Steiner Verlag, 1964), pp. 41-48.

(5) Robert Anchor, GERMANY CONFRONTS MODERNIZATION; GERMAN CULTURE AND SOCIETY, 1790—1890 (Lexington, MA; D. C. Heath & Company, 1972), pp. 67-68.

(6) Ibid., pp. 77-93.

(7) William J. Brazill, THE YOUNG HEGELIANS (New Haven, CT: Yale University Press, 1970), p. 34.

(8) Ibid., p. 67.

(9) Ibid., pp. 23-24.

(10) Claude Welch, PROTESTANT THOUGHT IN THE NINETEENTH CENTURY, Vol. I, 1799—1870 (New Haven, CT: Yale

University Press, 1972), 50.

(11) Brazill, p. 101.

(12) Welch, I, 148.

(13) Quoted in Karl Loewith, FROM HEGEL TO NIETZSCHE; THE REVOLUTION IN NINTEENTH-CENTURY THOUGHT, tr. David E. Green (Garden City, NY: Doubleday & Co., 1967), pp. 72-73.

(14) Brazill, p. 234.

(15) Ibid., pp. 272-73.

CHAPTER V

CONFESSIONALISM AND TROUBLED DECADES

The thirties and forties produced a number of quotable
quotations from activists responding to the religious
consensus, or in turn responding to responders. In these
decades, Lutheran confessionalism sank its roots; Reformed
Protestants in Prussia's western regions pursued a more
representative church polity, while Roman Catholics there
tangled with the king over mixed marriages. Two radical
groups, the unorthodox German Catholics and the Society of
Friends ("Lichtfreunde"), attracted people to popular
rationalism. And they all had quotable things to say.

The young pastor who helped launch Lutheran confessionalism
provides one illuminating quotation. With his Ninety-Five
Theses, Claus Harms tried to arrest widespread "defection"
from sixteenth century Lutheranism. "Reason races furiously
through the Lutheran Church," he wrote in the seventy-first
thesis; "it rips Christ from the altar, hurls God's Word
down from the chancel, and throws mud into baptismal waters
. . ." Now was the time to recognize that the Lutheran
Church needed no enrichment of this type, since it "has in
its edifice totality and perfection" (thesis ninety).

The struggle between the Prussian king and the German
hierarchy over Protestant-Catholic intermarriage prompted an
ariticle in the EVANGELICAL CHURCH NEWS in the
mid-thirties. A close associate of Prussia's crown prince,
the lay theologian Ernst Ludwig von Gerlach, wrote that "a
clash between the Roman Church and the authorities was

inevitable, since the evangelical prince could not permit the archbishop <of Cologne> to remain in office; with or without his approval, usually a responsive revolutionary body must evolve from this kind of opposition."

Several years later, the journalist Robert Prutz asked rhetorical questions about the supposed religious activities of the German Catholics and Society of Friends: "We conduct politics as we hold Protestant Illuminati <Society of Friends> . . . and German Catholic meetings—Why not politics as politics? Why do we not stop this whole religious masquerade?"

Our last quotation comes from Frederick William IV, crowned king of Prussia in 1840. "There are things," he said, apparently referring to the epistemology of kingship by divine right, "that one knows only as king, which I myself as crown prince did not know."

These comments draw a roadmap for the pages that follow. We will discover that the attacks of liberals in the thirties were not the only challenge to the church's religious charter. Individuals, groups, and movements of a moderate character also nipped at its edges in the thirties and forties. The confessionalism of "Old" and "New" Lutherans was politically rather ambiguous; sometimes they assaulted the unwritten agreement rather openly, and at other times accomodated with demur. Popular rationalist groups, and evangelicals and Roman Catholics in the Rhineland, raised more pointed questions.

Frederick William IV initiated countermeasures to smother these fires and stabilize relations between church and state in Prussia. By the end of the forties, the German governments could rely on their churches to oppose the rising tide of revolution, despite dissonant undercurrents in the culture. But a rocky trail led to that point. In these two troubled decades, new social and religious forces were invited, and sometimes forced, into the religiously chartered society.

Lutheran confessionalists of the "Old" and "New" stripe were somewhat ambivalent in their appraisal of the religious charter, or working agreement between church and state. Some opposed certain policies of the state church, although not the principle of territorial churches. Others were almost reactionary in their support of the throne-altar alliance. The diversity of church-political views in confessionalism was partly due to the movement's origin in the Awakening, with all its complementary, and at times conflicting currents and crosscurrents. But there is little question about the importance of the church politician, Ernst W.) Hengstenberg, a Prussian confessionalist, or about confessionalism's political significance.

Nineteenth century confessionalists were given no reprieve from the pressures of the centuries since the Reformation, or from the cultural and intellectual currents of their own day. As a result, they could not ignore the impact of idealism, romanticism, and a host of other movements and forces. For example, romanticism influenced confessionalism, like the Awakening, to find resources in the past for the present. While the people of the Awakening emphasized their reliance on the Scripture as source and norm of faith and life, confessionalists stressed as well the importance of the sixteenth century Lutheran "confessions," or symbols, contained in the Book of Concord (1580) as a true and faithful exposition of the Word of God.

That is why nineteenth century confessionalism differed from the community of faith among Lutherans at the time of the Reformation. In the first instance, according to public statements, God's Word and the forgiveness of sin knit people together in the same faith. Accepting the sixteenth century confessions as doctrinal standards, the confessionalists had to face in their own day the same question that the Reformers faced: How are confession of faith and experience related? But their attempts to balance objective foundation of faith and subjective belief were complicated by other factors than those of the Reformation era.

173

Some consider the Reformation Day sermon in 1800 of the Dresden preacher, Franz Volkmar Reinhard (1753-1812), as the inauguration of Lutheran confessionalism. But Claus Harms (1778-1855) of Kiel remains the most important of the early trumpeteers. In 1817, his Ninety-Five Theses called on Lutherans to reassert Luther's spirit in the face of efforts to unite them with Reformed Christians, despite doctrinal differences. Several of these theses (numbers 75 and 81) expressed grave doubts about the wisdom of the proposed union, and protested the use of Luther's name to sanction it.(1)

A number of anniversaries and events gave impetus to the confessionalist movement. The Reformation's tricentennial anniversary in 1817, and the three hundredth anniversary in 1830 of the Augsburg Confession, which Harms called the "foundation of the Lutheran Church;" the re-publication of Luther's letters and works, beginning in the twenties; the appearance of Reformation era sources in the CORPUS REFORMATORUM (1834); and new journals and papers, including PILGRIM FROM SAXONY, EVANGELICAL CHURCH NEWS, and JOURNAL FOR PROTESTANTISM AND CHURCH, stimulated the movement. In addition, neo-pietists from Wuerttemberg, such as Korntal's G. W. Hoffmann, attributed more to the notion of confession than the purely legal connotation it bore during the Enlightenment. Confession was a public religious act, and since the individual was called to confess his faith openly before the world, the church had a confessing and confessional character. The preference among many neo-pietists for millennialism and the doctrine of universal restoration was a schematic corollary of their confessional view of the church.

Old Lutherans

The so-called "Old Lutherans" in Prussia were hardline confessionalists who attacked the religious charter where it infringed on their right to worship in conformity with their beliefs. Their theological conception of the church collided with the political conception that undergirded the Prussian union between Lutheran and Reformed. They grappled with what Robert Anchor calls "the most basic problem that modernization poses wherever it makes itself felt," namely, the problem of "self-definition."(2) Theologians in Germany

174

also addressed this problem, but their own authoritarian tradition, and the state's supervision, kept church leaders from examining the question objectively in detail. Especially in Prussia, the state's control over society required that a decision on this question be made at the highest levels, and then the acceptable answer would be filtered down to lower levels for acceptance. Religious groups that worried about self-definition could bring trouble, particularly when the arena was as close to the Prussian king's heart as liturgical practices.

In exhortations to clergy and congregations in the twenties, Frederick Wiliam III stressed the union's voluntary nature, and the new agenda's positive benefits. But he changed his tactics in 1830 in preparation for the anniversary of the Augsburg Confession. Prussia's return to lightly camouflaged authoritarianism was apparent in the statement, which described in detail how to break the communion bread, and emphasized the importance of stated liturgical rubrics. The government was clearly alienating itself from the new popular force of Old Lutheran confessionalists that was emerging in Silesia and elsewhere. The Old Lutherans did not think that the unwritten religious charter demanded their full and unqualified acceptance of new liturgical material. Eventually, they demanded the right to create a free (non-established) church as part of their struggle against rationalism, which they understood as a deviation from the "confessional church" that made the Lutheran Confessions theologically binding within the community of like-minded believers.

Old Lutherans in the province of Silesia had long memories of struggle against Roman Catholic Austrian rulers before they became Prussian. History gave them little reason for hope or comfort as they opposed the Prussian king's agenda and union. Unlike the Old Lutherans in the province of Pomerania, they lacked the kind of noble leadership that was offered by the von Below brothers. The Prussian king was more apt to interpret their resistance as a popular revolutionary or political movement, and that was one reason why he used force to change their habits.

Johannes G. Scheibel (1783-1843), a theological professor and pastor in Breslau, was the recognized leader of the Old Lutherans in Silesia. His opposition to the union came early in a short pamphlet entitled UNIVERSAL INVESTIGATION OF CHRISTIAN STRUCTURE AND DOGMATIC HISTORY (1819), which deplored attempts to unite the Reformed and "Ephesian," or Lutheran, Christians in Breslau. He argued that joint communion could not be celebrated until major doctrinal differences were resolved. In 1830, Scheibel petitioned the king to use the old Wittenberg Agenda instead of the new liturgical agenda. But the king referred him to the chief governmental officer of the province, who in turn ordered that he had to use the new agenda, while securing additional advice from the superintendent.

Scheibel gathered 260 families to create a "pure" Lutheran church in opposition to the union, but soon he was suspended from office, and his church was forcibly opened for celebration of the union rite. In 1830 he fled to Dresden in royal Saxony, after making the unfortunate comparison between Frederick William III and Antiochus Epiphanes. But he continued to support the confessional cause in his homeland, despite his loss of preaching privileges in Saxony in 1832. His congregation in Breslau encouraged fathers to baptize their children, and elders to administer communion in order to sustain sacramental life apart from the territorial church. But the majority waited for the services of an ordained pastor.

By the end of the year 1833, thirteen congregations of the Silesian separatists left the organized church. Members channeled their mission funds to a distinctively Lutheran mission society established in Breslau in 1828. Although the society lacked a legitimate church base, it eventually supported only Lutheran missionaries.

Meanwhile, a war was being waged in periodicals on the subject of the Old Lutherans. A theological professor at Dorpat, Ernst Sartorius, attacked the Silesian separatists in Hengstenberg's popular EVANGELICAL CHURCH NEWS in 1833. He contended that the separatists' argument rested on weak grounds: it was as difficult to prove that secular authority misued its power over the church as it was to prove that the clergy mismanaged its authority in the church. Sartorius was answered by Philip E. Huschke (d. 1886), a jurist in Breslau who supported the Old Lutheran cause.

The influential EVANGELICAL CHURCH NEWS usually supported the Old Lutherans' eucharistic doctrine as based on the Lutheran Confessions, but many of its columns insisted that the union rite should be accepted within the territorial church, in order to preserve a common front against rationalism. The formation of separatist congregations was a foolhardy act under these circumstances, the editor Hengstenberg wrote. While the separatists, especially Scheibel, reaffirmed their total loyalty to the Prussian king, they were viewed as subversives because they held that their ordination oath to the Lutheran Confessions could not be countermanded by a princely liturgy. Finally in March of 1834, the king acted on the advice of his chief ecclesiastical counselor, Altenstein, and ordered Hengstenberg to reject any article that opposed "the agenda, the union, and the existing ecclesiastical structure."

The noose was tightening. In February of 1834 a cabinet order made the use of the agenda compulsory, while admitting that the union was merely a loose confederation of congregations created through joint altar and communion services. The king also tried to put a damper on societies and separatist groups, outlawing all religious meetings and groups outside of the congregational structure, except family devotions. Two cabinet orders in February and March rejected the Silesians' request for permission to establish an independent Lutheran church. Three pastors, four pastoral candidates, and thirty-nine congregational elders met in Breslau in April to protest what they called restrictions against Lutheranism, but their appeal was roundly rejected.

Within six months, armed force was used to browbeat the Old Lutherans in Silesia into submission. On Christmas Day, troops opened the doors of Pastor Eduard Kellner's church in Hoenigern, so that the new pastor could conduct a service in accordance with the new agenda. Kellner and many others, including some pastors, were arrested. Kellner spent four years in jail, but the show of force brought new growth to the Old Lutherans, as eight other pastors in Silesia and Posen joined their ranks. A secret meeting in Breslau in 1835 led to an organization to sustain secret worship among the Old Lutherans, and four candidates were ordained. The government imprisoned lay people who refused to divulge information. Finally, Pastors Kavel, Fritzsche and Grabau

177

led emigration groups from several different parts of Prussia to Australia and the United States, but in 1839 the king sustained the sentences against obstinate Old Lutherans.(3)

The Old Lutherans in Silesia did not resort to emigration until the late thirties, preceded in 1834 by a party of compatriots from Halle and Posen, and somewhat later from Niederlausitz and lower Pomerania. The exodus of Old Lutherans to Australia and America in 1836 was highly publicized. By 1854, slightly more than 7,000 had emigrated, most between 1838 and 1846. Between 1838 and 1839, Prussian officials tried to cut the flow of emigration by distributing free copies of a bureaucrat's book opposing emigration. But more than fifty travel guides were published between 1815 and 1860 by German travelers in the United States, and these books helped stir emigration fever.(4)

The number of Old Lutherans in Silesia held rather steady, increasing from around 8,000 in 1845 to about 13,000 in 1852 and 1865. By 1860 the Old Lutherans' independent, free church in Prussia numbered 55,000, increasing very slightly by the end of the century. In Silesia, at least, the Old Lutherans seemed to have attracted "moral" people; if statistics on illegitimate births mean anything, at least, they were "moral." Between 1858 and 1861, the ratio of illegitimate to legitimate children born to members of the state church in Silesia was one to eight. For the Old Lutherans, the ratio was one to twenty-four. Between 1860 and 1866, some Old Lutheran congregations in Silesia had ratios as low as 1:48 (Waldenburg), 1:55 (Fraustadt), 1:20 (Breslau), and 1:36 (Strehlin). These ratios may have been due in part to a proportionately larger percentage of older people in the Old Lutheran congregations. In the fifties the movement extended itself into the Rhineland, with congregations at Radevormwald (1852), Elberfeld (1858), Alpershofen an der Saar, Fuerth bei Doerrenbach, Ulm bei Braunfels, and Elversberg.

Prussia had to contend not only with the separatist movement in Silesia, but also with a rather sizable Old Lutheran contigent in the northeastern province of Pomerania. Laymen, especially merchants or commercial salesmen, carried some of the separatist literature from Silesia to Pomerania. As

Silesia heated up with strife in the mid-thirties, a number of Old Lutherans moved to Pomerania and established contact with awakened people in Cammin and Wollin. Soon the awakening took on a rather rigid confessionalist cast, and a number of individuals and congregations separated from the organized church, eventually to associate with the church organized in Breslau. Thousands emigrated to America in 1837 and the years that followed, but not before some strange happenings.(5) Laymen distributed the sacrament and baptized children in the face of rigorous countermeasures by church authorities; in Saleske, a child was taken from his mother's arms so that he could be re-baptized by a clergyman of the territorial church. A strict cabinet order in 1834 prohibited the administration of the sacrament of the altar by laymen.

The Old Lutherans who remained behind in Prussia found an accommodating spirit in the new Minister of Public Worship, Eichhorn, who assumed office in 1840 when the crown prince became Frederick William IV. Even as prince, the new king had been interested in their plight. Late in 1840 he released the pastors from prison, and permitted freedom of assembly. In September 1841, representatives of 19,000 Old Lutherans in Prussia met in Breslau to identify themselves as the Evangelical Lutheran Church in Prussia. In 1845 the king offered a general concession to the "Lutherans" who considered themselves separated from the "evangelical" territorial church, although they could not use the name "church" to signify the organization that united their "church congregations."

Moving toward self-identity on the basis of their reading of the Lutheran Confessions, the Old Lutherans concluded that they had to emigrate or organize an independent church. The religious charter was unacceptable without modifications. Ultimately they were able to establish a free church in Prussia, losing the government's financial support in the process. But they secured this minor adjustment in the unwritten charter only after a decade of suffering and strife.

New Lutherans

"New" Lutherans were confessionalists who did not choose to

179

separate from the territorial churches, although they stressed the distinctive identity of the Lutheran Church as constituted by people whose convictions coincided with the writers of the Lutheran Confessions. They held that the church was confessional by its nature: the identification of an objective basis for faith in the Lutheran tradition was a salutory act in a time of deep subjectivism. In regard to the religious charter, New Lutherans seemed generally to embrace it with varying degrees of affection; this showed their roots in the Awakening.

Although the New Lutherans exerted their greatest influence in the fifties and sixties, they prepared for action in the forties. Lutheran confessionalism was particularly strong in Bavaria, Hanover, Mecklenberg, Kurhesse, Saxony, and the Baltic provinces of Prussia. Among the Reformed, a confessional movement flourished under the impetus of F. H. Kohlbruegge (1803-1875), Henrich Heppe (1820-1879), and Gottfried Daniel Krummacher (1774-1837), but Reformed confessionalism never reached the strength of its Lutheran counterpart.

Lutheran confessionalism in royal Saxony was openly critical of the revelatory rationalism, or rational supernaturalism, of the church's titular leader, Christoph Friedrich von Ammon, who portrayed himself as orthodox, and greeted Harms' theses with applause. Andreas G. Rudelbach (1792-1862) used his paper, PILGRIM FROM SAXONY, to work among the laity; it was soon supplemented, with Heinrich E. F. Guericke's aid, by a theological journal entitled JOURNAL FOR UNITED LUTHERAN THEOLOGY AND CHURCH (1839ff.). Rudelbach's Muldenthaler Conference (1830ff.) was a focal point for confessional discussion among pastors, but the greatest boost for New Lutheranism in Saxony came from Adolf Harless (1806-1879) during his short term at Leipzig as professor and preacher, from 1847 to 1852. Harless sharply opposed the state's effort to liberalize the confessional oath required of pastors at ordination. Other confessionalists who joined him in Saxony included Karl F. A. Kahnis (1814-1888), who came from Erlangen and Breslau; Christoph E. Luthhardt (1823-1902), who also attended Erlangen; and Franz Delitzsch (1813-1890), a popular preacher who came to Leipzig via Halle.

In Hanover, the confessionalist camp was led by Ludwig A.

Petri (1803-1873), a pastor in the city of Hannover who had been influenced by Claus Harms. Petri encouraged Lutherans to support "churchly mission" through the confessionalist mission at Leipzig, instead of the less confessionally oriented work of the North German Mission Society. With August F. O. Muenchmeyer (1807-1882), he established the Divine Treasury to finance Lutheran congregations surrounded by Reformed and union congregations. Soon pastors and teachers in Hanover were being asked about their confessional commitment in official church visitations, and the theological faculty at Goettingen struggled to maintain a mediating position. In Hermannsburg, Louis Harms (1808-1865) stirred great interest in mission work with his popular preaching. Although he never became a radical confessionalist, Harms had a high regard for Lutheran teachings. Convinced that ruthless attacks of democracy, liberalism, and secularism would soon destroy all traces of the church in Europe, he looked to mission work to create "free states" outside of Europe where Christians could flee when the church collapsed. In the adjoining city of Hamburg, confessional Lutherans struggled to reassert themselves within the established church.

New Lutherans in Bavaria experienced their richest growth during the reign of a Catholic king, Maximilian II (1848-64).(6) The father of Bavarian confessionalism was Wilhelm K. Loehe (1808-1872), who after 1837 served as the pastor of the small town of Neuendettelsau. While Loehe drew away from the territorial church on several occasions, especially between 1848 and 1850, he never left the state church. His theological education at Erlangen was influened by a Reformed biblical theologian, Christian Krafft (d. 1845), who was the point of contact between Samuel Collenbusch of Barmen in northwestern Germany, and some of the Erlangen theologians, such as Thomasius, Hofmann, and Hoefling, whose teachings on rebirth and the history of salvation owed much to Collenbusch. Loehe claimed that "I owe my spiritual life, humanly speaking, to a Reformed teacher, Professor Krafft of Erlangen. It was he . . . who without knowing it nurtured my love for the Lutheran Church."

A careful student of liturgics, Loehe introduced weekly Eucharists, private confession, and unction in his rural congregation. He denied the charge that he was a Romanist, although his refusal to perform the marriage of a divorcee in 1860 brought a brief suspension from office. He had a very high view of the church and its ministry; he stressed the visible side of the church, and taught that the congregation derived from the ministry. But his studies did not prevent intensive involvement in such practical matters as establishing mission colonies for American Indians in the state of Michigan, and trying to provide for thousands of German immigrants in America who were losing faith and culture. Between 1854 and 1862, Neuendettelsau laid foundations for a deaconess home, a rescue house for the poor, a home for emotionally ill, a home for unwed mothers, and hospitals for men and women.

The theological faculty at Erlangen was the second major force among New Lutherans in Bavaria. Before leaving Erlangen for Leipzig in 1847, Harless had begun publishing the JOURNAL FOR PROTESTANTISM AND CHURCH (1838ff.), which set itself "in decisive opposition to a church . . . that wants to know nothing about Protestantism, and to a Protestantism that wants to know nothing about church." The journal opposed both confessionalist, rationalistic Protestantism, and a unversity theology that was unrelated to the life of the church; it also rebutted the new Catholicism that claimed that Protestantism was the mother of revolution. Harless represented the university in the Bavarian chamber in 1840 when it debated the Minister of War's order of 1838 requiring Protestant soldiers to kneel when the "corpus christi" passed by, and at other critical times. Despite vigorous opposition among Protestants, the order was not changed until 1844. After Harless lost his professorship and was fined for his opposition, he moved to Leipzig. During the years of this struggle, King Maximilian II refused to allow a bust of Luther to be placed in the Walhalla, a temple built as a monument to the great personages of German history. This national museum in Bavaria was finished in 1841, and the exclusion of the great reformer is all the more interesting in view of the inclusion of of Catherine II of Russia, and such representatives of the "Grossdeutsch" spirit as William of Orange.

Harless was assisted in this early period of Erlangen theology by Friedrich J. W. Hoefling (d. 1853), a practical theologian. But the most important representative of confessionalist Erlangen theology, as well as its deepest thinker, was Johann C. K. Hofmann (1810-1877), who taught systematic and biblical theology intermittently between 1838 and his death. Influenced by the historian von Ranke and the covenant theology of the Reformed theologian Krafft, he was preoccupied with the question of the interrelation of theology and history. He pursued a system based on the assertion that "for me the theologian, the express content of my science is me the Christian." The believer's faith coincided with God's objective history of salvation through Christ, recorded in the Scripture; the "present Christ" points back to the historical Christ. Hofmann's use of Luther against Lutherans, in defense of the subjective importance of the objective acts of God, was the beginning of much later Luther research. An active participant in Bavaria's Progressive Party, he was caught up in Germany's search for unity, though not under Bismarck. Before his death, he was ennobled by the Bavarian king.

The second most important figure on the Erlangen faculty of theology was Gottfried Thomasius (1802-1875), dogmatician and historian of dogma there after 1842. Thomasius constructed his dogmatics with Christology as the focus. He stressed the doctrine of Christ's "kenosis," or humiliation, in order to soften the ancient doctrine of Christ's two natures, human and divine, and emphasize the human development of the God-man Jesus. This kenotic theology was in part an effort to respond to the biblical and historical questions raised by Strauss and Bauer, without scuttling the classical two-natured Christology. At the same time, Thomasius wanted to speak of Jesus' human limitations; the divine accepted self-limitation in the incarnation, so that Christ could enter human existence without surrendering his divinity. Other theologians of the Erlangen school included Heinrich Schmid (1811-1885), Reinhold Frank (1827-1894), and Thomasius Harnack (1817-1889), father of Adolf.

Harless was very instrumental in nurturing confessional Lutheran convictions in the territorial church, upon his return to Bavaria from Leipzig in 1852. As president of the Supreme Consistory, he introduced a songbook and liturgy that bore the marks of New Lutheran confessionalism. Although by 1849 union congregations left of the Rhine were treated as an administrative unit distinct from Lutheran congregations, Harless arranged for the separate identity of

Lutheran and Reformed congregations on the right side of the Rhine in 1853, so that Loehe and others could no longer complain about intercommunion. New Lutherans in Bavaria had seen to it that no free or independent church was created there, as in Prussia.

Theodor Kliefoth (1810-1895) was the leading New Lutheran in Mecklenberg. He turned to confessional Lutheranism in the mid-forties after deciding that the age of ecclesiology and eschatology had arrived, since the church had already passed through debates on the Trinity and Christology, as well as anthropology and soteriology. Active in the search for unity among Lutherans, he published CHURCH JOURNAL (1854ff.), later called THEOLOGICAL JOURNAL, to point the way for union movements among Lutherans in the twentieth century. He was well known for a firm grasp of liturgics, but he also nurtured Lutheran consciousness among the clergy of Mecklenberg, and in Rostock's theological faculty. He argued that the church's structure should be based on the pastoral office of the means of grace; the church was a "continuing incarnation of God." His "Lutheranism of office" left no room for presbyterial or synodal structures, which he considered to be gifts of the father of lies, like constitutionalism. He began his rise in the church's hierarchy as cathedral preacher in Schwerin in 1844; after 1850, he became the most influential member of the High Church Council, the group charged with running the church directly under the prince of Mecklenberg. Another important spokesman for New Lutherans was Friedrich A. Philippi (1809-1882).

In Hesse, the most forceful confessional figure was August F. C. Vilmar (1800-1868), a "converted revolutionary" who at one time sympathized with the Giessen Blacks in the "Burschenschaften." Around 1840 he moved from a supernaturalistic to a fixed Lutheran position. He served in various posts, including the superintendency at Kassel, before becoming a theological professor at Marburg in 1855. His views on the church coincided with Kliefoth's. The "objective deeds" of salvation were represented in the church, which as an institution was the "body of Christ." A tight hierarchical church structure flowed from his elevated conception of the ministerial office as a "direct divine institution." Vilmar's theological and political views were complementary; he was a strong supporter of the political reaction after the 1848 revolutions.

As noted above, the Old Lutherans were active in Prussian Pomerania, but the New Lutheran brand of confessionalism also flourished there under impetus provided by Superintendent Otto-Naugard and, later, Superintendent Karl Minhold-Kammin. The Lutheran character of the church was reasserted in unmistakable terms. Baron von Thadden, whom we met in our discussion of the Awakening, gravitated from that movement to confessionalism, like many others; but as an aristocratic layperson, he exerted strong influence through the annual clergy conferences conducted on his estate each year after 1829. One area of concern for him was how the union would affect Lutheranism. He asked the royal consistory in 1839 to tell him what was the legal confession of his congregation, in view of the union, and whether the congregation for which he was patron was Lutheran. The consistory consulted with higher levels before answering, then reported that it was erroneous to think that the union had merged Lutheran and Reformed confessional groups. It added that the union merely permitted evangelicals to hold joint communion and altar services; in Lutheran congregations, the symbolical books of the other confession had no more value than before the union. Thadden seemed satisfied with the answer for a while, although he leaned toward the Old Lutheran position. Finally in 1848 he joined their camp, and separated from the organized church. The pastoral conference meeting on his estate in 1843 wrestled with the question of the value of the Lutheran confessions. As confessionalism took hold, the number of participants in the conferences rose from seventy-two in 1842 to more than two hundred.

Hengstenberg and the Politics of Confessionalism

In Prussia the most important stimulus for the New Lutherans came from Ernst Wilhelm Hengstenberg (1802-1869) and the paper he edited, the EVANGELICAL CHURCH NEWS.(7) He also influenced scores of churchmen outside Prussia's borders, assisting them in making the transition from the Awakening to a rather strict brand of Lutheran orthodoxy. No discussion of confessionalism's political significance in Prussia and elsewhere is possible apart from him. But by the same token, those confessionalists who adjusted rather easily to the unwritten religious charter did not always accept his rabid support of the alliance between throne and altar.

Hengstenberg insisted that the Christian faith had its definite, objective basis in the Bible. The Mosaic authorship of the Pentateuch became an object of faith for him, as did biblical inerrancy. His studies emphasized Christology in the Old Testament, especially in the Psalms, the authenticity of Isaiah's authorship of chapters forty to sixty-six, and Moses' authorship of the Pentateuch. His understanding of the church as a unified community of people with identical dogmatic convictions helped advance the cause of arch-conservative Lutheranism in Prussia.

As a young man of twenty-five, Hengstenberg was appointed editor of the new EVANGELICAL CHURCH NEWS. He served in this capacity while teaching on the theological faculty at the University of Berlin for some time. The paper was the creation of awakened men in Berlin, including the Gerlach brothers, Neander, LeCoq, Tholuck in Halle, and such budding confessionalists as Scheibel, and Rudelbach of Saxony. It was intended to be the polemical counterpart of the rationalists' UNIVERSAL CHURCH NEWS; attacks on the rationalists Gesenius and Wegscheider of Halle, on Schleiermacher, Hegel, Strauss, the mediating theologians, and classicists such as Goethe, Schiller, and Lessing, endeared the paper to many. Soon it was possible to speak of the "EVANELICAL CHURCH NEWS party." The paper was filled with polemics, and the editor's reactionary political articles found their parallel in the repristinated Lutheranism of its pages.

Hengstenberg moved many away from the Awakening to a rigid form of Lutheranism by sharply opposing anything that had the taint of what he called "mysticism." His paper helped channel the zeal of the Awakening into areas that would not harm the organized church. His contention that the church could overcome rationalism only through a united front pulled together three overlapping concerns of the day: changes in Prussian church polity that followed the new king's coronation in 1840; the set views—and high visibility—of Old Lutheran confessionalists; and widespread growth in confessionalist consciousness among Lutherans in the territorial church. More than any other man,

Hengstenberg was responsible for the confluence of neo-orthodoxy and neo-pietism in support of "positive" Christianity and political conservatism, or "throne and altar."

The situation was even more clearly decisive in Prussia than in Wuerttemberg, since in Prussia the new king needed the support of the conservative church party, and agreed as well with the theological position of that party. In Wuerttemberg, as the liberals clamored for more freedom, the pietists increasingly found an ally in the government of King William, while the opposite was also true. Especially after 1840, the king found the pietists to be a more manageable group of subjects than the demanding liberals, even though he was not personally inclined toward their religious views.

Hengstenberg wanted an ecclesiastical administration that was distinct from state authorities. But in his conception of the church's structure, the territorial prince retained primary control. In fact, he urged that the church be placed immediately under the prince's supervision, thereby bypassing the rationalists, who held many important bureaucratic posts, and permitting the new orthodox party to claim seats of power. His idea was to extend reactionary political principles to the sphere of the church, in order to protect the church's doctrine.

Hengstenberg initially supported a church structure that opposed the centralization of the century's early decades, but by 1846 the EVANGELICAL CHURCH NEWS was chanting a different tune. The pressures exerted by the "Lichtfreunde" on behalf of democratic organization for the church, and separation of church and state, as well as the fear that the liberal majorities could change doctrine and liturgy in a synod such as the one planned for mid-1846, meant that the argument for the territorial church's independence had to be refined. The CHURCH NEWS printed articles in May and June of 1846, asserting that the church's freedom consisted of the inviolacy of its faith and teachings; church administration had to be "churchly," but still under the territorial prince.

The radical "Lichtfreunde" were not the only opponents of Hengstenberg's party. Already on August 15, 1845, eighty-eight pastors and prominent laymen issued a declaration in Berlin, later published in the Berlin papers, that charged the CHURCH NEWS with arranging an "inquisition," threatening the unity of the church, and violating the traditional Prussian freedom of belief and conscience. These representatives of the mediating school, many of them students of Schleiermacher, charged Hengstenberg's party with "seeking after dominance in the church" regardless of the consequences. A week later the magistrates of Berlin attacked the orthodox party in an address to the king, forwarded under the chief magistrate's signature. The party, they wrote, was guilty of identifying traditional doctrinal formulations with "the truths of Christianity," while casting aspersions on movements and impulses that diverged from its viewpoint. They added that Hengstenberg's orthodoxy was not representative of most Berliners' faith. The king refused to accept the memorandum until the magistrates delivered it in person; then he condemned them for their point of view, especially their charge that he was partial to one party. Similar correspondence was forwarded by authorities in Koenigsberg and Breslau.

Hengstenberg's persistent polemics contributed to the polarized atmosphere in the Prussian church that produced three distinct parties in Berlin and Brandenburg by 1848. Orthodox and confessional Lutherans regularly attended pastoral conferences at Neustadt-Eberswald after 1846, and eventually they formed the Lutheran Central Society under the leadership of Karl Goeschel. Liberals formed the Berlin Union Society in 1848, later allied with the Protestant Union. Friends of the union met in the Mark's Pastoral Society, and after 1848 in the Society for Evangelical Church Fellowship. Meanwhile, the unsuccessful "Party of August 15," mentioned above, began publishing its own periodical early in 1846.

The political significance of confessionalism is more difficult to delineate in the period before 1848 than twenty years later, but enough hints were given along the way to make a preliminary review worthwhile. Some of the clearest pointers came from the standard-bearer, Hengstenberg, who asserted that conservative politics, specifically the divine right of kings, was firmly rooted in biblical theology. One would expect that as Prussian domination expanded after midcentury, spokesmen for her union church would claim that it should expand to incorporate annexed geographical areas. That claim was made, but not implemented by political authorities. On the other hand, some confessionalists in non-Prussian territories kept their political options open as long as possible. Influenced by the minority status of Lutherans in Catholic Bavaria, Harless claimed that no one political structure was divine; Hofmann worked with the Progressive Party in Bavaria as a constitutionalist. The new Lutheran hymnal accepted for use in Bavaria in 1852 included only two hymns under the heading "Authority," among more than 500 hymns.

But while confessionalists differed in taking "hard" and "soft" political positions, they all seemed interested in recapturing the initiative in religion and morals which they felt now lay with the state. Their theological literature about "church" must be read with a critical eye, since reforms in church administration, and equally so the matter of "confessionalizing" the church, could scarcely be contemplated without considering their state-political ramifications. The unions between confessions that had been declared in many states, and particularly Prussia's promulgation of the liturgical agenda, were signals that the state rather than the church had final responsibility for the church through the chief bishop, the king or prince. The state exercised both "jura circa sacra" and "jura in sacra."

In this light, it is helpful to note that confessionalism's reassertion of the traditional Lutheran Law-Gospel dialectic did not occur in a vacuum. It emerged partly in criticism of the inadequacy of the idealist conception of the state as a moral, as well as a political, entity, and the correlative diminuation of the church's responsibility. Theologians criticized this argument by depriving the state of the theological right to practice "positive" law; they transferred this positive emphasis on law away from the state, and into the theological realm, by attributing to it salvific power via the Gospel. They claimed that the Gospel was to be found only in the true church, whether a state institution or a separate entity, and with it the "positive" side of Christianity, its doctrine and ethic of love and charity. This emphasis, on theological Law and theological Gospel, provided an escape from the moralistic conceptions of religion prevalent among rationalists and idealists; the

189

locus of this religion was the church, not the state. In the process, they reasserted the old pietist distinction between secular and sacred in a new way (in their conceptions of Law and Gospel), in order to overcome the characteristic cleavage in idealism between intellectual and moral. But at the same time, the secular was sacralized, inasmuch as the "Law" in final analysis was a theological entity, driving one to the "Gospel."

Confessionalism did not support radical or "liberal" political principles because, in the main, the Awakening's basic political principle appeared in a new form. That principle was that people should love one another within the existing social and political system. It was "confessionalized" under the basic premise that nothing can be formalized as a "gospel ethic" that has not been previously structured under (theological) law. Luther's doctrine of the two kingdoms—God acting to preserve and judge the world, and to redeem the world—was resuscitated in confessionalism, but unlike Luther, the confessionalists failed to provide an overlap between the two kingdoms.

In the larger national question of the political unification of Germany, most confessionalists—except for some in Prussia, and Hofmann in Bavaria—tended to oppose the "Kleindeutsch" solution which urged unification of the German states under Prussian hegemony. In part, then, confessionalists seemed to be voicing political opposition to Prussia through their rejection of its confessionless union church. That was especially clear in the sixties, as we will see in a later chapter. But even as early as the late thirties, the Saxon paper PILGRIM FROM SAXONY opposed any "small Germany" solution. Most Bavarian confessionalists seemed to support the alliance of the middle states against both Prussia and Austria as long as that was feasible, and confessionalism was one of the cultural forces nurtured by political figures who were interested in this balancing act. When this position later became untenable, the confessionalists provided rallying points for opposition to Prussian hegemony, even after annexation by Prussia.

Thus, when viewed from a later perspective, confessionalism seems to have had a hidden agenda regarding the national question, but this was not at all clear before the midcentury revolutions. What was apparent was that confessionalists adapted rather well to the particularism of the territories, mirroring the Awakening in this regard, and providing little support for liberals, who wanted German unification to serve as a prelude to liberalized state constitutions.

Overall, the confessional movement yields to no easy interpretation, in part because it was a diverse movement influenced by the states in which it flourished. The Old Lutherans' confessional theology had ecclesiological emphases that even Hengstenberg could not accept, despite his repristinating orthodoxy. More than some of the other confessionalists, the theologians at Erlangen, including Hofmann, stressed experience, and the objective verification of experience in Scripture and Confessions.

But in the main, confessionalism confirmed the unwritten religious charter that had been agreed upon earlier in the century, both by perpetuating the conservative political traditions of the Awakening, and by not demanding separation of church and state at that point in time. Although the Old Lutherans provided some excitement, their number was too small to affect significantly the course of church-state cooperation. As governmental leaders in Prussia began to recognize what New Lutherans wanted, they yielded to some requests in return for an even more committed ally. A church with conviction was a better ally than the almost lackadaisical church of the rationalists, and the religious charter was not forfeited in the process of strengthening this alliance.

WESTERN CHURCH POLITY AND TROUBLE IN COLOGNE

On the eastern side of Prussia, confessionalism was the basis of the Old Lutheran challenge to the nature of church-state relations. But church polity was the focus of dispute in the newer western provinces of the Rhineland and Westphalia. Evangelicals there sought a more representative form of church polity, which the state finally granted in 1835 in return for other accomodations. Meanwhile, in

Cologne the Roman Catholic hierarchy confronted Prussia over the issue of Protestant-Catholic intermarriage. These two encounters provide important vignettes into the history of the unwritten religious charter in nineteenth century Germany.

Neither Lutherans nor Reformed had a clear majority among Protestants in the western region. Church polity discussions were complicated by the fact that each group had about 250 congregations, but the Reformed seemed to have more finesse in dealing with church-political questions. That was one reason why the Prussian government finally acceded to their demands in 1835, although not without extracting its own pound of flesh. The almost intuitive political acumen of the Reformed was apparent in the way they interpreted the "eschatological angel" that adorned the steeples of twenty-six congregations in the area before 1815, and four more in the next century. Reformed evangelicals said the figure symbolized their appreciation for the political protection that Holland's House of Orange provided in earlier centuries. Lutherans offered a more theologically oriented interpretation of the symbol: it was the angel who bore the eternal gospel, mentioned in Revelation 14:6.

Generally the union was well received in the Rhineland province, except for some resistance in Jueluch and Berg. Lutherans and Reformed were content to call themselves "evangelicals" in the face of a larger Roman Catholic majority. The agenda caused a good deal more trouble because it seemed to have Romanist leanings. The people opposed the agenda more than the clergy; one parishioner in Elberreld asked a young candidate who used the new agenda whether he would soon also be sacrificing calves and rams in the church.

Prussia's price for more representative church government in this area was acceptance of the agenda. The Westphalians accepted the revised agenda in 1831, and finally in 1834 a revised agenda for the Rhineland and Westphalia was accepted by vote of synods. With this compromise in hand, the government yielded on some earlier points and endorsed the proferred Church Order.

In 1835, after twenty years of waiting under Prussian rule,

evangelicals in the area began practicing a presbyterial-synodal form of church polity more in keeping with their tradition. Local congregations were governed by presbyteries that executed church discipline and called pastors. Circuit synods handled other matters, including the ordination of pastors. The territorial church asserted control at the level of the provincial synod. This body could not pass binding legislation; it could merely forward to territorial authorities the recommendations of lower synods, and "watch over the preservation of the purity of evangelical doctrine in church and schools." Its resolutions took effect upon approval by territorial church authorities. The new Church Order summarized the arrangement well: "The controlling authority of the ecclesiastical body are the minister of spiritual affairs, the provincial consistory, and the government." Some limited lay involvement was permitted at the lower levels.

When the two provincial synods met in 1835 in the Rhineland and Westphalia, an expenditure of 7,000 "Thaler" was required to support the delegate assembly. Following earlier traditions, the Church Order financed this exercise in self-government through a form of taxation based on membership in local congregations. This became a model for other provinces when some degree of self-government was granted to the eastern provinces in 1873, and to the entire territorial church in the old Prussian provinces in 1876. Making arrangements to pay the expenses of self-government was probably as significant a problem as adopting the structure itself.

Much is made of the Church Order of 1835, partly because it served as a model for developments in Wuerttemberg (1854), Saxony (1868), and elsewhere. But it must be remembered that the Palatinate followed a form of synodal government ever since 1818. Nevertheless, the Prussian context within which the Rhenish evangelicals had to operate complicated things, and their accomplishment should not be criticized too severely, although they did yield on the acceptance of the agenda. A compromise was reached at the point where three forces intersected: the Reformed tradition of self-government, the Prussian king's interests in centralizing church authority, and current political pressures for a state constitution. Hengstenberg and some of the awakened in the region strongly opposed this effort to form a self-governing church, since they thought it would give the rationalists even greater control over church administration.

A second problem arose in the Rhineland during the thirties that is significant for our story since it demonstrated a response to Prussian authoritarianism that was quite different from that of most Protestants. It was the case of the "Cologne Troubles" involving the Roman Catholic archbishop of Cologne, Clemens August Freiherr Droste zu Vischering (1773-1845).

Relations were strained between Prussia and the new bloc of Roman Catholic subjects in the Rhineland from the day the area was transferred to Prussian control in 1815. Prussian church authorities made no secret of the state's commitment to Protestantism, although they promised fairhanded treatment to all. In 1819, Minister of Public Worship Altenstein outlined the state's policies in these words:

> The Prussian state is an evangelical state with Catholic subjects making up more than a third of its population. The relationship is difficult. Things are properly arranged if the government looks out for the Evangelical Church with love, and cares for the Catholic Church out of duty. The Evangelical Church should be favored; the Catholic Church should not be neglected.

In 1803, the Protestant government of Prussia had ordered Roman Catholics in the Silesian bishopric of Breslau to raise all children of mixed marriages in their father's religion. This move favored Protestants, since in most mixed marriages the fathers were Protestants who had moved to the area to work in official posts. In 1825, this order was extended to the Rhineland. There it opposed Roman Catholic practice and had the taint of proselytism since, again, most mixed marriages occurred between local Catholic women and Protestant men who worked for the government.

Catholics made up 80 percent of the population of the Rhineland. But preference was given to Protestants for important civil and military posts, and Prussian officials were inclined to raise a heavy hand against Roman Catholicism. One official even censored an advertisement for a translation of Dante's DIVINA COMMEDIA, arguing that divine things should not be comical. A battle was shaping up between those with a Hegelian understanding of church-state relations, and Roman Catholics who held to the older tradition of how Roman Catholicism and the German states interacted. But Prussian expansion and the dissolution of Catholic states made this position largely obsolete.

More was involved than asserting Protestant preeminence over Roman Catholics in mixed marriages. The Prussian government was also struggling against a neohumanist, romantic view that made marriage more than a contractual arrangement. In part, the Cologne Troubles were a struggle for and against the rights of women. For the government, the wife's religious convictions in a mixed marriage held little appreciable significance, not only because she usually was a Roman Catholic, but because she was a woman.

Archbishop Spiegel, Droste-Vischerung's predecessor in Cologne, yielded to Prussian pressure and secretly agreed to take a more conciliatory attitude toward mixed marriages than the Roman pope: children would follow their father's religious faith. But when Droste-Vischerung assumed office in 1837, he refused to abide by the agreement. He soon felt the Prussian whip. "The archbishop," the king ordered in November, "must henceforth refrain from all official functions and proceed to Minden where he must await further orders; otherwise he shall be taken forcibly to the Minden fortress." Droste-Vischerung remained in custody until April of 1839. In that year the government also imprisoned the Polish archbishop, Martin Dunin, for a year over the question of mixed marriages.

In the short run, the decisive action of the government in the Cologne Troubles seemed to boost the fortunes of the religious charter among Prussian Protestants. But in the long run, the victory seemed more apparent than real. A similar decree was by Ludwig I of Bavaria in 1830, ordering that no Roman Catholic priest could insist that children of mixed marriages be raised Catholic, did not create as much trouble as in Prussia. The number of people involved was smaller, Bavaria had not recently assumed political control of the area, and the general political climate was not as repressive as in Prussia—nor was the government Protestant!

Popular Catholic protests in Prussia against the action in Cologne took several forms. Religious pilgrimages were organized for people to view the Holy Robe on display in Trier, near Cologne, especially in 1844. But the most significant response was that the Cologne Troubles helped draw Roman Catholics into a political party through the work of Joseph Goerres of Munich, and his publication of the HISTORICAL-POLITICAL PAPER FOR CATHOLIC GERMANY (1838ff.). The party was born not in opposition to non-Christians, but to Protestants. The Cologne Troubles and the hierarchy's firm stand heightened confessional loyalty among Catholics, and as a result, most Roman Catholics eventually did not join the liberal stream. By the seventies, Goerres' Center Party had captured two-thirds of the Catholic vote in Germany.(8)

In sum, the Cologne Troubles put a dent in the armor of Germany's Protestant establishment. It offered a model for resisting future attacks on the Roman Catholic Church. But the struggle also channeled some Catholic political power toward conservatism since Protestants, not conservatives, were the opposition. In the process, Catholics both protested the Protestant system they opposed, and created a formidable opposition party; the party's basically conservative cast had long range repercussions in Germany's political development.

GERMAN CATHOLICS AND THE SOCIETY OF PROTESTANT FRIENDS

In the thirties and forties, the Prussian government faced enough trouble, even without the agitation of the so-called "German Catholics" and the Society of Friends. These two religious and political movements were the last blossoms of popular rationalism, and for that reason they attracted heavy opposition. Their emphasis on congregational autonomy, and their disregard for the religious charter, were not lost on conservative evangelicals or governmental officials.

It has been indicated that one response to the oppression of Roman Catholics in the Rhineland was a surge of popular piety. In 1844 the bishop of Trier put on display a seamless robe of Christ. This relic attracted over 1,000,000 pilgrims in less than two months, and healings were reported to have occurred. But not everyone was convinced of the garment's authenticity. In Bonn, the Protestant historian Heinrich Sybel greeted the outbreak of devotion with a book entitled THE HOLY ROBE AT TRIER AND TWENTY OTHER HOLY SEAMLESS ROBES.

A more muscular response to the exhibition at Trier came from a suspended Roman Catholic priest named Johannes Ronge (1813-1887), and the "German Catholic" movement he founded. In an open letter to the bishop of Trier, Ronge condemned the pilgrimage as a charade, and soon a congregation gathered around him rather spontaneously in Breslau. Twenty other congregations formed in northern Germany, and by 1848 Ronge's travels and writings had attracted 100,000 people to 259 German Catholic congregations, with the strongest concentration in Silesia. Ronge's rationalistic criticism of this "modern indulgence," as he called the robe at Trier, opened the floodgates of a popular folk movement of religious rationalism among Catholics and some Protestants.

The group evidenced the continuing strength of enlightened thought and rationalism by revising the Apostles Creed, allowing for a married priesthood, and more generally, propagating a religion of immanence based on man's rational faculties. In the province of Silesia and in Leipzig, several evangelical candidates began serving the group as priests; evangelical congregations lent their churches for use in worship, and sometimes provided financial support. A governmental order in 1845 against some of these practices was not implemented everywhere in Prussia; several months later, evangelical churches were officially allowed to open their doors to German Catholic use under certain conditions. In Offenbach am Main, one-half of an evangelical congregation tried to establish an ecumenical pre-Reformation congregation, hoping to forge a "fraternal alliance" with people of all confessions, especially Catholics.

By 1859 most of the remaining German Catholics joined with their Protestant counterparts, the "Lichtfreunde," or Society of Friends (unrelated to Quakers), to create free-thought congregations. In part the two movements were covert political operations, seeking to liberalize state policies in Prussia and elsewhere. Since politics as politics was not yet allowed, a number of radical Jews also joined the German Catholic groups in Breslau, Koenigsberg, Halle, Hamburg, Leipzig, Dresden, and Darmstadt, where they served as baptismal sponsors for German Catholic children and participated in worship services. Often they entered the "Lichtfreunde" or German Catholic congregations without being baptized. In Frankfurt, Jews joined with Catholics and Protestants in a "Luther Foundation Festival"; Luther was portrayed as a "representative of progress," not the founder of a church.

The Society of Protestant Friends originated as a rationalistic reaction to the Awakening, or more precisely, as the last blossom of eighteenth century rationalism in popular form. In 1840, Pastor Wilhelm F. Sintensis published an article claiming that it was idolatrous to pray to Jesus. The awakened in the area around the Prussian town of Magdeburg were shocked after officials merely rebuked him; they began to raise a storm of protest. Pastor Leberecht Uhlich (1799–1872), a rationalist preacher near Magdeburg, felt compelled to organize a pastoral conference to protect such men as Sintensis, and the first meeting of the Society of Friends occurred in mid-1841 at Gnadau under his leadership. The second meeting followed a few months later in Halle. Thanks to the emerging railway system, the group grew rapidly until it reached its peak in the territorial church in 1845. Then, separate and independent "Lichtfreunde" congregations began forming since some of the group's leaders had been removed from their pastoral offices.

God, virtue, and immortality were the major tenents of faith for the "Lichtfreunde." Repeated assemblies were held at a major rail center, Coethen; by 1845 two to three thousand people were attending the open-air meetings. In August the Prussian government prohibited any additional assemblies, but the group continued to grow in middle and southern Germany, while Silesia and Saxony remained its strongholds. Uhlich, Sintensis, Edward W. Baltzer, Friedrich T. Vischer, Gustav A. Wislicenus (1803–1875), Adolph T. Wislicenus, and a military chaplain from Koenigsberg who was suspended from office in 1845, Julius Rupp (1809–1894), helped stoke the fires. The movement primarily attracted people in the educated middle classes for whom it provided an "enlightened" brand of religion, as well as the growing realization that they held much potential political power. The revolution of 1848 was foreshadowed when soldiers fired into a crowd of "Lichtfreunde" at Leipzig in August of 1845; in the revolutionary years, the movement probably numbered as many as 150,000.

In 184/ the Prussian king allowed the "Lichtfreunde" to secede from the state church. They would retain all civil and political rights if the tenets of their religious association were in conformity with the essential points of the confessions identified in the Treaty of Westphalia (1648). The king was attempting to smother the group with freedom by calling it a sect. Conservatives charged that this Toleration Edict struck a heavy blow at the intimate relationship between church and state, although they were happy to see the "Lichtfreunde" leave the territorial church. But the plan did not succeed since the group continued to gain strength, and after the revolution of 1848 new strictures were levelled against it for a time. The radical nature of the group, and its call for the church's democratization, made the idea of an autonomous church all the more unattractive to most conservatives. Increasing pressure led some of the group's leaders to emigrate to the United States, but others, such as Baltzer, served "free" congregations until their death. In the course of his ministry, Baltzer had the distinction of organizing Germany's first vegetarian society in 1867.

ROYAL COUNTERMEASURES

When he issued the Toleration Edict for the "Lichtfreunde" in 184/, the Prussian king had been on the throne for seven years. After succeeding his father in 1840, Frederick William IV moved at once to stabilize relations between church and state, although initially he thought of giving his territorial church greater autonomy. Three of the major projects he undertook were aimed at giving the church new vitality and increasing its social influence. Understood in context, they may be seen as countermeasures against the rising tide of religious dissatisfaction that we have reviewed in this chapter. After informing ourselves about his religious views, we will review his plans and projects for church building and renovation, his creation of a joint Prussian-British bishopric in Jerusalem, and his efforts to reform church polity.

When he mounted the throne as a dedicated, awakened Christian, Frederick William IV faced almost insurmountable odds. Earlier the church had lost the allegiance of the educated upper and middle classes, in the main, and it now was in the throes of losing the masses. In Germany, the alienation of the masses from Christianity is traditionally said to have coincided with the process of industrialization and urbanization in the second half of the century. But the phenomenon was already well underway by that time. In fact, this estrangement probably first occurred between 1820 and 1850; the church's subsequent failure to adjust to rapid industrialization and urbanization was as much a result of earlier difficulties as anything else.(9) Frederick William IV tried to address some of the emerging problems from the obscurantist perspective of such strong conservative supporters as Hengstenberg and the Gerlach brothers.

He is often remembered in history as the king who refused Mexico's offer in 1842 to sell California to Prussia, but his significance for evangelical history in Germany cannot be summarized so succinctly. He can be understood only in the context of the religious awakening he experienced in the twenties, as crown prince in Berlin. He was convinced that Christianity had the responsibility for building God's kingdom in the world, not merely cultivating a form of personal piety, and he felt called to bring to full realization the vision of the true church in a Christian state, with each dependent on the other. The monarch was responsible for ensuring that throne and altar worked harmoniously in serving God's plan for all the people under his control. He was not inclined to bring the church under increased state control, except to the extent that this process would advance God's work in church and state.

It was no surprise that Frederick William IV instructed all evangelical pastors to commemorate Germany's millennial anniversary of unity and independence in their church services on August 6, 1843. Prussian clergymen took up the challenge to examine the role of Providence in the millennium of Teutonic history since the Treaty of Verdun in 843. The "romantic on the throne," as David F. Strauss called him, was an "awakened" king who committed himself to living and serving as a servant of the Most High, uniting in his person the welfare of the state and the well-being of the church. These two institutions, working together, would expand God's kingdom. Frederick believed that he was "king by the grace of God;" he had miraculously been given an ability to rule temporally and spiritually.

Given these predilictions, it is not surprising that the king took the initiative to counterbalance some of the disruptive churchly movements of the thirties and forties. A church building and renovation program, the creation of a joint Prussian-British bishopric in Jerusalem, and efforts to resuscitate some form of synodal church government were priorities on his list. Meanwhile, his friendship with conservative orthodox figures helped preserve Prussia's union church, despite occasionally bitter attacks by his confessionalist friends.

Church Building and Renovation

The activity with the highest public visibility was undoubtedly the church building and renovation program that Frederick William IV set in motion. His romantic inclinations drew his attention to Gothic architecture, and sometimes he took a personal role in preparing architectural plans for the more than three hundred churches that were built or renovated during his reign of nearly two decades.

Immediately after his coronation, he turned his attention toward the unfinished Roman Catholic cathedral in Cologne. His participation in the project to complete this fourteenth century structure showed that he wanted to heal the wounds of the Cologne Troubles, and at the same time give some recognition to nationalist sentiments. He was also attracted to the project because the unfinished cathedral on the banks of the Rhine was a Gothic structure.(10)

When a new German river cult arose in the early forties, after the French threatened to invade the western states, efforts to finish the cathedral carried nationalistic

201

overtones. A new Cathedral Building Society had been organized under the leaderhsip of August Reichensperger, a political spokesman who called the cathedral a "German national monument." In September of 1842, the Prussian king attended the celebration in observance of renewed construction, hoping that his presence and an annual subsidy of 50,000 "Thaler" would help mend relations with his Roman Catholic subjects in the area. He attended both a Catholic mass and an evangelical service on the same day. During the celebration, Goerres, now an old man, called the edifice a "house for all Germans." In his address, the king included these words:

> The spirit that built these doors is the same one
> that broke our chains twenty-nine years ago ....
> it is the spirit of German unity and power. For it
> may be that the cathedral entrances become doors of
> the most glorious triumph! Let it be completed ...!
> May the Cologne Cathedral—I pray God—tower over
> this city, tower over Germany, over epochs, reaching
> toward peace among all men, divine peace, till the
> end of days!

The king expressed the hope that the edifice would symbolize fraternity among confessions, and their unity under one Divine Head.

As renewed construction got underway, the project refuted the poet Heine's anti-ultramontane claim that the cathedral's unfinished state "makes it a monument of Germany's power and Protestant mission." Funds flowed in from many hands; the great Jewish banker Rothschild was criticized for sending 300 "Thaler" while subscribing only ten for the reconstruction of the Jewish synagogue in Leipzig. The cathedral took almost forty years to complete, even with the use of modern steam equipment. But before that day in 1880, men turned to Cologne once again to find there a symbol of German unity. In the revolutionary year 1848, a number of representatives from the Frankfurt Parliament attended the sixth anniversary of the renewed construction project; once more Frederick made the journey to enjoy the festivities, along with the imperial administrator, the archbishop of Cologne, and the president of the Frankfurt assembly.

Soon after his coronation the king showed interest in building a new Protestant cathedral in Berlin. It was to serve as the realm's "chief church" and the "most important national monument of Prussia," as well as the burial place of the Hohenzollern dynasty. A number of architects proposed plans throughout the forties, one taking his cue from Britain's Westminster Cathedral, but the project languished.

The most important Prussian architect in the early part of the century had been Karl F. Schinkel (d. 1841), who was responsible for a number of secular buildings, as well as the Nickolai-Church at Potsdam, and other ecclesiastical structures combining ancient and Gothic motifs. The king's favorite style was Gothic, partly as an architectural signal that differences between Protestantism and Roman Catholicism were not as great as some imagined. At the same time, he showed some inclination toward basilical style because of its affinity with Christian origins. The king took a personal hand in plans being drawn by Schinkel's successor, Friedrich A. Stueler (d. 1865), for the new church in Schirwindt in East Prussia. Completed between 1850 and 1856 entirely at the king's expense, the church had a striking resemblance to the Cologne Cathedral.

In general, Gothic was the leading architectural style for churches built in Germany between 1830 and 1870. Its closest competitor was the roundarched style espoused in Prussia by Schinkel and Persius (d. 1845), as a mixture of early Christian and Italian romanesque architecture. It was inevitable that renovated churches, such as the famous Castle Church in Wittenberg, mirrored the style in vogue. For example, in the first half of the century this church was rebuilt in a style that was at best eclectic; the interior was redecorated with early Christian motifs in accordance with the wishes of Frederick William IV. Some of the artwork was reminiscent of early Christian mosaics. This was one of nearly three hundred churches that Frederick built or renovated in a massive public display of support for the church.

Prussian-English Bishopric

A project more closely identified with the king's plans to

reconstruct ecclesiastical polity was the creation of a joint Prussian-English bishopric in Jerusalem, an arrangement that endured from 1841 to 1881. Early in his reign the king asked the ambassador in London, his good friend Freiherr von Bunsen, to "ascertain in what way the English national church, which already owns a rectory on Mt. Zion and has begun building a church there, might be inclined to grant the evangelical Prussian territorial church a sister's place in the Holy Land." The king seemed determined to use the inclusive character of the Anglican communion and the British fleet's power for his own ends, both to secure the guarantee of apostolic succession for the Prussian church, and to follow the interconfessional inclinations of his awakened heart. Other matters of concern were the spiritual care of Germans living in the Holy Land, and the conversion of Jews.

In September 1841 the king signed an agreement to the effect that "we will contribute half of the endowment of an evangelical bishopric in Jerusalem, which will be established by the Crown and the Church of England." The Prussian contribution was a principal sum of 15,000 pounds sterling. After English church officials and Parliament gave their approval early in October, the queen signed a law empowering the Archbishop of Canterbury to consecrate foreigners as bishops. The Jerusalem bishop would exercise ecclesiastical control over Anglical clergymen there, and any other cleryman who placed himself under his supervision.

The creation of this joint bishopric stirred excitement in some southern parts of Germany, where pietists awaited the conversion of the Jews as a certain sign of the End. One wrote in the Stuttgart OBSERVER that he was extremely fortunate to witness this "sign of the times," as an "unquestioned harbinger of the Lord's imminent return." In Prussia, territorial church authorities followed the king's orders and initiated a freewill offering to finance a hospital for evangelical travelers and inhabitants in the Holy Land. Although these plans were not implemented until the fifties, at least 46,000 "Thaler" was collected in 1842.

The English picked the first bishop, Bishop Alexander, a Polish Jew who converted to Christianity in England. He arrived in the Holy Land in 1842. The British hoped that he would be an effective instrument in the conversion of Jews. Alexander greeted the Prussian king's brother when he traveled to the Holy Land in 1842-43; his sudden death in 1845 enabled the Prussian king to name the next bishop.

Frederick William IV picked Samuel Gobat (d. 1879), a native of Switzerland who was trained at the Basel Mission Society, and was then sent to Malta by the Anglican Church Missionary Society. The king was mindful of Gobat's ties to southern Germany; his wife was the daughter of a Swabian theologian and educator known for his missionary zeal. In succeeding years, Gobat did much to encourage German missionary work and colonization of the Holy Land.

Back in Prussia, the new institution was not greeted with overwhelming approval, especially by such an arch-conservative as Otto von Gerlach, who asked whether the Prussian church was now subservient to the Anglican. The Berlin Pastoral Conference also expressed its disapproval of the project at first, and asked for clarification of several points before cooperating in the financial offering. In Britain, opposition centered in the Oxford Movement; some attributed Newman's coversion to Roman Catholicism to the formation of the new bishopric.

Church Polity

The Jerusalem bishopric showed that the government's initiative in "foreign" church polity could succeed. Foreign activity distracted troubled minds from domestic disruptions of a religious nature, and reminded people that the government still could exert influence in church affairs. The hint was clear enough for some, especially with the provision for apostolic succession that was inherent in the joint bishopric. They took more seriously the king's proposals for a semi-autonomous, but hierarchical church structure.

Frederick William IV's romanticism was the source of his dream to re-create the supposed polity of the apostolic church. He wanted to form provincial churches with a bishop in each province, with pastoral candidates serving as deacons, and with pastors functioning as presbyters.

Provincial and general synods would handle all theological affairs. This proposed structure would be integrated with the territorial church much in the same way that the king, in his person, assumed full responsibility for the church's external affairs, but was not totally responsible for its internal affairs. He wanted each province's bishop to serve as the leading member of the provincial consistory.

Most observers recognized that the king's proposal was little more than what he later called it—a summer night's dream. The king took some steps to form the new structure for a semi-autonomous church, but the dream could not keep pace with the day's many challenges. His appointment of Johann A. F. Eichhorn (1779-1856) as Minister of Public Worship in 1840 at first gave hope to those who were interested in greater freedom for the church. But Eichhorn soon betrayed his reputation as a man interested in freedom, and followed the king's wishes explicitly until he was dismissed during the upheaval of 1848. Eichhorn started to move the church's polity in the direction it had followed during the first two decades of the century, before the restoration settled in. The king hoped that eventually his own plans would materialize, but for the present it seemed advisable to give the church limited autonomy while preventing democratic forces from gaining control.

In 1843, district synods of pastors in the six eastern provinces of Prussia met for the first time since 1810. Demands were made for congregational participation in the selection of pastors, better preparation of candidates, greater confessional commitment, and synodal meetings on the provincial and territorial levels. Provincial synods, predominantly composed of superintendents, met in 1844, but only in Saxony, Posen, and Brandenburg did majorities vote for a stronger enforcement of confessional commitment. Eichhorn said that these synods were "to give the opportunity to a distinguished and intelligent segment of the ecclesiastical teaching office to speak out on everything that interests the church." That did not necessarily imply that confessionalists would be given a high profile. But since some demanded more careful monitoring of confessional commitment, the responsibility of the consistories was widened somewhat in 1845, although all external administrative decisions rested with the government, as usual. Clergymen on the consistories once more assumed control of most spiritual matters, for whatever that was worth.

The apex of the structure was to be a territorial synod. Earlier in the century, synods for the whole territory were frequently promised, but never held. The first one finally convened in Berlin in the summer of 1846, at a cost of 34,000 "Thaler." Some delegates traveled to the capital on Prussia's mushrooming rail system, which the king had wisely supported as crown prince. The first experiment in large-scale troop movements was conducted that same year, but the troops' destination was not the chapel at the royal castle in Potsdam, as it was the delegates.'

Seventy-five delegates gathered there, reportedly to lay the groundwork for the new church constitution desired by the king. Clerical participants included the eight general superintendents, the chief of chaplains, four court preachers, representatives of the provincial synods, and six faculty members. Laymen included the directors of the consistories, some of whom were provincial presidents, six representatives of law faculties, and twenty-four laymen chosen in the provinces, most of whom were aristocrats. Almost equally divided between laymen and clergy, the assembly was indeed a group of notables, as well as a battleground for parties within the church. Friedrich J. Stahl, a law professor at Berlin, and consistorial president Goeschel were the leading representatives of the orthodox party, which was rather lightly represented. Rationalist forces had spokesmen in Pischon, Syndow, and Jonas, but most of the power lay with the "mediating" or union party, whose chief spokesmen were Nitzsch of Bonn, and Mueller of Halle.

Eichhorn's inaugural address stressed the representative character of the assembly, and the opportunity for all to express their views on pressing matters. He walked the fine line betweeen factions with the comment that the "spirit of freedom is the spirit of the evangelical church itself, but naturally, it is a freedom that rests on the foundation that, according to the words of the apostles, has been laid as the Only Foundation." He hoped that the deliberations would heal division and give new life to the Evangelical Church. His speech was followed by the mediating party's first show of force; "Mr. Union," Bishop Daniel A. Neander (1775-1869) of Berlin, was elected vice president, as

207

Eichhorn's pastoral assistant.

Seventeen of the fifty-six sessions dealt with housekeeping matters such as pensions and the status of emeriti, pastoral training, charitable activities, congregational deacons, and similar questions. Another seventeen sessions dealt with the problem of church structure. The king was not happy with the recommendation that emerged, and the orthodox party was antagonized as well. The delegates recommended a presbyterial and synodal structure quite unlike the king's episcopal plans, and called for greater congregational power, with less state control. General superintendents were to be chosen by the church in assembly.

The most significant sessions were the twenty-two that dealt with doctrine and confessional commitment. By a vote of 43 to 23, the delegates turned down a proposal to make the Apostles Creed binding on the ordinand; another resolution, namely, that it be used in liturgical services, passed almost unanimously. By a vote of 48 to 14 the synod approved a declaration of faith for ordination that omitted certain elements of the Apostles Creed that some held to be inopportune, such as Jesus' virgin birth, descent to hell, ascension, and bodily resurrection. The synod urged the church's administration not to require unconditional subscription to certain evangelical confessions on the part of the ordinand. Regarding the nature of church union, the synod's resolution declared that the union was not a third church, but rested on a foundation of doctrine commonly held by Lutheran and Reformed. It is no surprise that the assembly also adopted a proposal to establish an "Evangelical German National Church."

The king adjourned the synod but did not recall it, as some had been led to expect. Conservative and orthodox leaders lashed out at the adopted ordination formula; an old Berlin preacher named Gossner accused the delegates of "tearing down the church's walls, so that the sows can enter and destroy the vineyard." Others called the assembly a "robber synod," much like the one at Ephesus in 449. But the king had the last word. No district, provincial, or general synod was called to meet for some time after 1848, and, most importantly, he did not accept or implement the major recommendations of the synod of 1846. Since the general synod had only the power to recommend, the king could—and did—listen to advisors such as Leopold von Gerlach, and ignored the synod's recommendations.

This experiment in church polity was an unsuccessful one for the king. He neither achieved his own plan for an episcopal church, nor did his orthodox party gain control of the general synod in 1846. But the resolutions of that synod, which he refused to promulgate, showed that the religious charter was alive and well in Prussia, despite unrest. As far as can be measured by representatives at the synod, the union that had come about largely through state initiative was still healthy, even though confessionalist influence was rising.

But the king could not ignore the clamor for a constitution, both in the state and in the church. Five times his father had promised to give the state a constitution. His own rejection of the synod's recommendations showed that he was moving toward a more rigid conservatism, since he could not find "the right hands," as he said, into which to place the controls of the church. Church and society were pitching toward the upheaval of 1848, with left pitted against right, and the majority in the middle. A royal countermeasure in church polity succeeded for a time in tempering discontent, but it also added fuel under the boiling caldron.

CULTURAL DISSONANCE

Religious dissatisfaction was part of the wider cultural uneasiness in Germany in the thirties and forties. We have seen how confessionalism, polity troubles among western evangelicals and Roman Catholics in Cologne, and the activities of German Catholics and "Lichtfreunde," contributed to a sense of malaise. In Prussia, royal countermeasures failed to silence the sounds of cultural dissonance, although they tempered their impact.

To make things worse, other dissonant chords in the culture added to the cacophony. These included scientific challenges to religious faith, upheaval in higher education, anti-Semitism, and the effects of Francophobia and growing nationalism. While religious life in the parish seemed to continue much as in the past, cultural dissonance disturbed sensitive religious people accustomed to living in a "Christian" culture.

One disconcerting factor was the emergence of vocal scientists who challenged the compatability of science and faith. The Association of Natural Researchers and Physicians heard a number of papers in the forties that interpreted the universe materialistically. A scientist named Leupoldt defended the compatability of science and faith in a paper he delivered in 1840, but his approach soon seemed to be in the minority at the group's annual meetings. Younger men were prone to pit science against faith. A mediating group suggested that the truth of the matter lay somewhere between spiritualism and materialism, but it was clear to all that science's growing influence still had to be dealt with.

The states exercised their most immediate influence in the realm of thought by appointing and dismissing faculty members at universities. In 1837, the Hanoverian king dismissed seven professors at Goettingen who protested his revision of the constitution. Included were the brothers Grimm, and the Old Testament Protestant scholar, Heinrich G. A. Ewald (1803-1875). The storm of protest that arose as a result did not convince the king that he was wrong since "professors, actors and whores can always be had," as he said. The governments of the German states also exerted control over the curricula for theological training, by requiring theological candidates to pass state examinations for admission to the church's ministerium.

In Prussia, the new king moved to placate some restless people in 1840 by reinstating the old nationalist warhorse, Ernst M. Arndt, at Bonn after he endured a twenty-year suspension from his professorial post. The king's friend Bunsen also interceded on behalf of the Bavarian jurist Stahl and the philosopher Schelling, who were called to teaching positions in Berlin, to help stem the tide of Hegelianism. Schelling found more eavesdroppers than listeners in his audiences, and soon the rest of Germany was rolling with laughter at the tidbits of information that were divulged. Victor Aime Huber (1800-1869) also came to Berlin in the forties to contend for the "Christian state," although this idea did not reach its apex until the fifties. However, the Prussian Minister of Public Worship, who was also in charge of university appointments, would not make room for Franz Delitzsch (1813-1890), an Old Testament scholar who firmly supported the Old Lutherans. Delitzsch's attempt to secure a theological appointment, with Hengstenberg's assistance, was unsuccessful because he would not assume membership in the union church. He finally accepted appointments at Leipzig and several other non-Prussian universities.

Theological candidates waiting for a parish often worked as tutors. Upon graduation, many candidates were employed by noblemen as house tutors. In this capacity they served as conduits for new fashions and ideas, especially for the ladies, but were in turn themselves influenced by aristocratic values and the cultural atmosphere of the noble estates. By the end of the thirties, 1,200 evangelical students were training under theological faculties, a hundred fewer than the number of students studying law and political economics. Although the total number of university students had dropped from 6,100 to 4,500 in the thirties, there were still more than enough theological graduates. When a candidate finally secured a position as a parson, he immediately became an adjunct teacher in the local elementary school, where he taught religion. The clergy's active involvement in all phases of primary education was considered by Victor Cousin in 1831 as one of the chief reasons for the success of Prussia's schools, which that year enrolled 99 percent of the estimated two million children between the ages of seven and fourteen.(11)

At times, cultural currents reinforced the religious charter in a process that was not always peaceful. The Protestant "Christian state" in Prussia had little room for Jews, although efforts to convert them continued, with the aid of a Jewish Institute organized in Berlin by H. L. Strack in 1833. The proselytizing objective of the Institute persisted until his death. Meanwhile, the rest of the culture seemed to bear with the imagined burden of Jewry. Marriage between Christian and Jew was illegal according to Prussian territorial law, and handbooks for Protestant ministers dutifully reminded them of this fact. In 1847 the first United Prussian Provincial Diet decided against full emancipation for Jews by a vote of 215 to 185. The heavy

majority of conservative Protestants in the diet apparently
gave little credence to a ministerial memorandum of that
year, which noted that Jews were fit recruits with
"unquestionable" moral qualifications for military service.
These Protestants might have felt that the Jews' native land
was Zion, not Prussia, since Jews were not part of their
covenanted community.

In Saxony, the awakened and proto-confessionalist paper
PILGRIM FROM SAXONY included a number of anti-Semitic
reports in the late thirties. The sheet attacked such
developments as the unification of a Christian and a Jewish
school in Thuringia; the inevitability of intermarriage,
with full emancipation of Jews in Hesse-Homburg and
Saxony-Weimar; the election of a Jewish representative by
eighty Christians in Leipzig, and his subsequent battle for
de-christianization of religious instruction in schools.
According to official reports, anti-Semitic hate was stirred
from the pulpit in the Rhineland, Silesia and Bavaria.
District officials in Silesia were instructed to carefully
supervise pastors since "they incite against the Jews." The
mission to the Jews in Schweinfurt was harrassed so badly
that the government took action to prevent violence.

In Prussian Westphalia, the town of Minden was the focus of
anti-Semitic forces stirred by H. E. Macard, the "people's
and peasants' leader." A close associate of V. A. Huber, he
had the support of the Protestant pastors in Minden; his
immediate circle included a student of theolgy and a church
sexton. Thousands of his tracts were distributed, and
petitions prepared to convince the Rhenish Diet in 1843 to
roll back Jewish emancipation. Conservative Protestants
struggled against progressive Roman Catholics in this
battle, until the police put an end to the gathering of
petitions. Then Macard resurrected purported atrocities from
the middle ages as material for posters that were plastered
everywhere.

Political currents reflecting the influence of Francophobia
and nationalist sentiment also contributed to a feeling of
disjointedness in the culture. For example, nationalist
sentiment was partly responsible for the attendance of
representatives from more than twenty-five courts at the
German Evangelical Church Conference in Berlin in 1846. At
the same time that he encountered stiff opposition from

212

Roman Catholic bishops and the Vatican in 1838, the Prussian king had tried to enlist the Protestant princes in a united front against Rome, though with little success. When King William of Wuerttemberg proposed in 1843 that the old "corpus evangelicorum" be reconstituted, with Prussia at its head, his suggestion had little impact, except that Professor C. Ullmann of Heidelberg published a book in 1845 calling for a meeting of delegates from state churches. The six-week meeting in 1846 (the same year that Prussia's general synod met) sounded out the possibility of a union among Germany's evangelical churches; the Roman Catholic states of Austria and Bavaria shut themselves out in the planning stages.

The German Evangelical Church Conference showed that church union would be impossible until political unity was a reality. Under the leadership of the Prussian layman Bethmann-Hollweg, the delegates set up four commissions to deal with future conferences, a unified liturgy, church polity, and confessional concerns. Through diplomatic efforts, Prussia tried to get the proceedings officially adopted by the participating states, but she was unsuccessful since territorial princes were unwilling to yield control over their churches. The only concrete result of the meeting was the Eisenach Conferences that convened in 1852 and succeeding years.

Nationalist sentiment, especially as stimulated by Francophobia, also contributed to the formation of the Gustavus Adolphus Society, an organization to provide financial support to evangelical congregations in predominately Catholic areas. In the thirties, a Saxon pastor proposed the creation of a "living monument" to the Swedish Lion of the North, who had brought relief to seventeenth century German Lutherans. Societies were soon organized at Leipzig and Dresden to assist evangelical congregations financially, but the movement was limited to Saxony.

The war scare with France early in the forties provided new impetus, and in 1841 a pastor in Darmstadt, Hesse, published an article in the UNIVERSAL CHURCH NEWS that brought results. Karl Zimmermann reminded Protestants that some people could not hear the evangelical gospel on Reformation Day, since they had no evangelical pastors, teachers, churches and schools. He later indicated that the formation of a parallel Roman Catholic group in France in 1839 turned his attention to this project. His article carried this appeal:

> Protestants, Lutherans, Reformed, United, Anglicans, and whatever name you may carry; members of the Protestant Church, whatever your specific faith perspective may be—supernaturalist, rationalist, or mediating, whether one calls you Old Lutheran or New Evangelical, Pietist or Mystic, Protestants—and I take that word in its widest sense—dedicate yourselves this day to the decision to establish a society for the support of Protestant congregations in need!

While the society was not supposed to be anti-Catholic, and in later years sometimes received gifts from Roman Catholics, its midwife was nationalistic fear of France, and some degree of anti-Catholicism. In 1842 the Saxon society was re-established with much greater success than before; six hundred representatives from throughout Germany travelled to Leipzig to attend the ceremony. In succeeding years the general assembly met in different cities, moving westward to Frankfurt am Main in 1843. By 1844 the society had more than 150 auxiliary chapters; many people in Prussia joined that year, although it was not until 1846 that the king gave protection to the society. Three hundred and sixty congregations received 864,765 "Mark" in assistance between 1843 and 1848, and twelve hundred congregations by 1882. In 1899, one and a half million "Mark" were distributed among 1,900 congregations.

The society's assembly at Goettingen in 1844 showed how the agency was one ecclesiastical channel for nationalistic sentiment. The Prussian delegation was received with open arms, even though bad weather had delayed its arrival for some time. The aged Saxon court preacher von, Ammon, gave a glowing patriotic speech, and other speeches and activities of the assembly showed the attraction of nationalistic sentiment.

But the disruptive cultural forces of these troubled times did not fail to touch even the Gustavus Adolphus Society. When the assembly met again the next year in Berlin, it faced the difficult question of seating the delegation from Koenigsberg. The problem was so cantankerous that the meeting's minutes were not published. The "Lichtfreunde" leader Rupp had gathered evangelicals, Catholics, Jews and others into his auxiliary society in Koenigsberg, since the group offered him an excellent opportunity to organize a congregation. This "evangelical" society was opposed by a "churchly" society in the same town. When the Berlin assembly decided to seat the latter's delegation rather than the former's, Rupp was essentially forced out of the society. New Lutherans also formed their own aid society in Dresden in 1840, to assist Lutherans in North America. In 1853, Petri and others in Hanover established "God's Treasury" to assist Lutherans, and soon this effort found acceptance in other states as well.

The parish life of most German churches was lived out in the backwaters of the culture and society, that part not yet deeply affected by modernization. The annual statistics of a large urban parish in Hamburg, St. Nicholas, tell us something about how the time of the church's four pastors was occupied in 1844. They married fifty-one couples, and baptized 172 children (89 males and 83 females); the ratio of legitimate to illegitimate children was 34:1. One hundred and thirty-eight children were confirmed, and 2,430 communions administered. Of the 574 funerals, 327 were for children under sixteen (181 males and 146 females), 61 for single adults, 84 for married persons, and 42 for those who had been widowed (14 males and 28 females).

The parish operated under a disadvantage since a fire had recently destroyed its structure, but plans were underway to rebuild. During the interim, the congregation used other facilities. Generally a service of confession and absolution was conducted monthly at St. Nicholas, but during Holy Week, eight confessional services were held. Private confession was available from three of the pastors each Saturday and pre-festival day from 1:00 to 3:00 P.M., but city officials had abolished the practice of conducting private confession on Maundy Thursday and Good Friday mornings in the church. Thirty-six of the parishioners were members of Hamburg's "Collegien," a governmental body of several ranks.

Reporting on religious practices in rural areas, the

Prussian general superintendent Karl Buechsel (1803-1889) noted that in some areas children born to married parents were baptized at home, while illegitimate children were baptized in the church. Weddings almost never occurred on Friday, because custom held that no happy marriage could begin on the day of the Savior's death. As the bride walked into the village church, she was greeted by the pastor's words, "The Lord bless your going in and your coming out from this time forth and forevermore." She, in turn, usually pressed into his hand a piece of gold wrapped in paper as a token of appreciation.

Funerals were occasions of great social importance in rural areas. The service in each case varied in accordance with the social status of the deceased, according to Buechsel. People who committed suicide were often brought to the graveyard by cart and horse, not carried by humans, to be buried outside the wall. The churches generally did not accept the argument of some romantics and "unbelieving humanists" regarding the right to suicide. In some rural areas, congregations were disturbed by one of the Prussian king's orders, namely that graves be dug in the same order as the names of the deceased were recorded in the parish register; this instruction broke the tradition of allowing families to be buried in family plots. It was customary to bury one body on top of another after a period of time had expired, in order to save space, especially where graveyards were small. Buechsel referred to another spacial problem in rural cemeteries when he advised that "no cow, nor the sexton's geese and goats, should feed on the Lord's Acre, neither should the pastor's wife hang her wash to dry there."

Since there are many pitfalls in attempts to periodize, an historian uses the words "troubled decades" with some trepidation. But we have seen in this chapter that the waters were roiled in the German churches between 1830 and 1850. Confessionalism brought a new zeal for orthodox proclamation to churches that—with all due regard for the Awakening—were accustomed to more rationalistic fare. As far as the states were concerned, the scales were balanced on the other side by the conservative political attitudes of most confessionalists. Prussia faced special problems while attempting to reach an accomodation on polity with evangelicals in her western provinces; even more disconcerting for this Protestant state was the challenge of the archbishop of Cologne. The German Catholic and "Lichtfreunde" movements put added pressure on the unsigned agreement controlling relations between churches and states. And the culture itself was not what an Eastern Orthodox theologian might have called a "symphonia" during these decades, since a number of irritants disturbed the equilibrium of institutional religion.

As we near the midpoint of our narrative, we can apply the term "midcentury" to a phase of nineteenth century German Protestantism without in the process becoming self-serving periodizers. And so, as our narrative moves toward midcentury, it may be helpful, at its approximate midpoint, to review the plot of our story.

Facing limited options early in the century, the churches apparently had little choice except to accept the basic social role assigned by the states. They would be a model for society, demonstrating how to live freely within boundaries determined by state authorities. Church unions, religious participation in Prussia's "Erhebung," and a revolution in church polity were important factors in determining the outline of the agreement, or consensus, between church and state that we have called the religious charter.

In the second chapter, we discovered that in the late teens and twenties the Holy Alliance became a symbol for the political restoration, and for religious support that was generated for the restoration. The bureaucratic machinery in Prussia was greased and oiled, in order to implement the religious charter through enforced use of the liturgical agenda, and the union between Lutherans and Reformed. Vocational pressures made it difficult for clergymen to question the basic provisions of the unwritten charter; their work in elementary schools, as well as education in general, manifested the close relationship between government and religion, one of the hallmarks of the restoration era. Theorists for the emerging consensus, including Schleiermacher and Hegel, drew on romanticism to elucidate the charter's undergirding principles.

But casting our eyes over the German countryside, especially to the south, we found a few people who were disillusioned by the coziness between church and state that seemed so dear to some, and so divine to others. A small number emigrated in disgust, attracted by the eschatological magnetism of the East; others registered muted dissent at home. But overwhelmingly endorsing the religious charter, the religious Awakening swallowed this opposition in its wake. It designated theological rationalism as The Enemy, and provided ammunition for political conservatism in its theological motifs. With its own kind of surrogate nationalism, the Awakening stimulated a nationalistic sentiment that was particularist, state-oriented, and conservative in character. The third chapter also indicated that the Awakening's voluntary agencies and societies exemplified what the church was assigned to model: freedom within authority.

The first decidely serious challenge to the unwritten religious agreement arose in the thirties, as the fourth chapter suggested. In comparison with the Young Hegelians, the popular rationalists, political demonstrators, and Young Germans seemed like small-time hucksters, but they also raised questions about the agreement between church and state. The Young Hegelians launched a full-fledged attack on the charter with their claim that man would attain a new plateau in his development when theology became philosophy. Their intellectual challenge to Christianity most often centered in Christology, the traditional intersection of human and divine in theology; that intersection and its institutional counterpart, the working agreement between church and state, was detrimental to human progress.

In this chapter, we have examined other movements and events showing that the consensus of most was not necessarily the consensus of all. "Old" Lutherans wanted freedom from some of the institutional constraints of the agreement; "New" Lutherans were content to make their confessional witness within the territorial church, in most cases a union church. But by submitting, in final analysis, to divinely ordained governmental authority, all confessionalists showed that their ancestry lay in the Awakening; if "ifs" came to "buts," they would rather emigrate than fight.

There is little need to rehearse the other problems of these two decades, or to note the countermeasures of the Prussian king. What is clear is that by midcentury—or by 1848, if we want to avoid periodizing terms—when revolution posed a very serious challenge to the religious charter, the day's confrontation was rooted in problems that had festered for some time. As we shall see, midcentury did not bring the end of trouble for the religious charter, even though "national unification," "industrialization," and "anti-Semitism" were the way to spell "trouble" in the decades that followed.

NOTES

CHAPTER V

(1) Some theologians saw only dogmatic rigidity and schismatic spirit in Harms' writings, but others heard the voice of a prophet. Among Lutherans his theses were a signal for confessional renewal, and the attacks of opponents increased his fame. He rejected rationalism in blunt language; Thesis 27, for example, met the rationalists head to head: "According to the old faith, God created man. According to the modern belief, man creates God, and when he has finished with Him he says, Aha! Is. 44:12-20." Harms urged Bible societies to issue a revised version of Luther's translation to compete with translations such as Nicolaus Funk's, which included rationalistic notes.

Earlier, Harms made the transition from a rationalist stance to awakened views. Schleiermacher's ON RELIGION, SPEECHES TO ITS CULTURED DESPISERS precipitated the move, although the book first brought him to pantheism; in 1814 he wrote that "nature is God, God is nature." By 1819 he stood clear of rationalism, preaching that "to hold Christ dear is better than to know everything." The Awakening's attack on rationalism was a source of strength and identity for Lutheran confessionalists, and like Harms, many of them made the transition to confessionalism through the influence of the Awakening.

(2) Robert Anchor, GERMANY CONFRONTS MODERNIZATION; GERMAN CULTURE AND SOCIETY, 1790—1890 (Lexington, MA: D. C. Heath & Company, 1972), preface.

(3) The Prussian troops that marched on the Old Lutherans were not bereft of religious guidance. In 1832 a new church structure emerged within the Prussian army when the king, acting as chief bishop, integrated the military

church and the territorial church. In 1833, the army's chief of chaplains became a member of Prussia's royal church consistory, an arrangement that endured as long as the monarchy.

(4) The seven hundred persons who emigrated to the United States from royal Saxony late in 1838 were acquainted with an emigration guide written by Gottfried Duden. Martin Stephan (1777-1846) was the leader of this group of Old Lutherans, who settled in Perry County, Missouri. Stephan was the pastor of a bilingual congregation in Dresden for twenty years, ardently opposing the Awakening's subjectivism and the Saxon church's rationalism. He claimed that in the office of the preached Word, the church could find the objectivity to stay afloat in the sea of subjectivism. Since for him pure doctrine was a sign of the true church, he put little credence in the possibility of sustaining a non-territorial church in Saxony; as he understood it, the culture was so permeated by forces antithetical to confessionalism that emigration was the only alternative.

(5) Prussia's loss of the Old Lutherans by emigration did not adversely affect the ratio between immigration to Prussia and emigration from Prussia. Between 1824 and 1848, immigration to Prussia exceeded emigration by nearly 800,000 persons. But at least the Old Lutherans were not deported like the six hundred paupers of Grosszimmern in Hesse, who were shipped to America for good riddance. Local pastors joined town officials in labeling the deportees' complaints as no more than the "sulkiness of good for nothings who will no more work there than they did here, who presume upon their poverty to demand to be cared for."

(6) The publication of Johann Adam Moehler's SYMBOLIK (1832), a Roman Catholic dogmatics, quickened the pace of confessionalism in the area, and focused the attention of Lutherans on the question of their identity. Until about 1833 the Franconian awakening was unionist and interconfessional in orientation, and then an identifiable form of awakened Lutheranism surfaced in the Bavarian environs. The department of theology at Erlangen University began to forge a confessionalist theology out of the awakened motif of rebirth.

(7) Hengstenberg's early career indicates that he

221

was an opportunist (see Friedhelm Wippermann, "Nationalbewusstsein protestantischer Theologen in der Restaurationszeit" <unpublished dissertation, Goettingen University, 1950>, pp. 77-78). Born in a Reformed parsonage, he criticized the Prussian government sharply as a student; letters to his parents displayed allegiance to the Student Union Movement. But he was prepared to shift allegiance if the rewards were high enough. While seeking a theological teaching position in Berlin, he established important contacts in the awakened circle. His theological position shifted to meet the pressures of the moment, and soon he was an adamant foe of rationalism. His "conversion" coincided with maneuvers to appoint him to the theological faculty at Berlin University. Trained as a philologist, he was appointed as a colleague of Schleiermacher and Neander in 1826; his close connections with the awakened and with the court kept Altenstein from transferring him to another university.

(8) Thomas Nipperdey, "Grundprobleme der deutschen Parteigeschichte im 19. Jahrhundert," in BEITRAEGE ZUR DEUTSCHEN UND BELGISCHEN VERFASSUNGSGESCHICHTE IM 19. JAHRHUNDERT, ed Walter Conze (Stuttgart: Ernst Klett Verlag, 1967), pp. 154-56.

(9) See the argument presented in Karl Kupisch, VOM PIETISMUS ZUM KOMMUNISMUS: HISTORISCHE GESTALTEN, SZENEN, UND PROBLEME (Berlin, 1953).

(10) In 1814, the influential Roman Catholic publicist Joseph Goerres offered a counter-proposal to the suggestion of Arndt (a Protestant) for a national memorial to the victory at Leipzig: complete the Cologne Cathedral as an appropriate "thankoffering for liberation from French slavery." Goerres argued that the unfinished cathedral symbolized the disarray of German thought and culture, just as its completion would symbolize "the new empire that we want to build." In 1816 the Prussian king's architectural advisor visited Cologne to secure information on the building, which lacked two steeples and a roof.

(11) Financially and socially, teachers were not as well rewarded as pastors. In 1840 complaints arose in the Rhineland that the Prussian elementary teacher's average wage (78 "Thaler") was inadequate, especially since some

music directors earned as much as 16,000 "Thaler" a year.

CHAPTER VI

VESTED INTERESTS AGAINST REVOLUTION

Many of the churches in Berlin were empty on Sunday, March 19, 1848, one day after revolution rocked Prussia's captial. But one year later, the conservative Prussian lawyer and lay theologian, Ernst Ludwig von Gerlach, jotted this entry in his diary for Sunday, April 22nd: "<Went to> St. Matthew's Church in snow. What people <were> in attendance! Savigny, Uhden, Mathis, Meding, Hengstenberg, Bodelschwingh, Goetze, Kleist, Frau v. Bismarck <Otto's wife>, Senfft II., etc.," his list of important conservative religious and political figures continued. The church was where conservatives met to renew courage; here they heard preachers who talked their language, such as the one in Gerlach's home town, Magdeburg, who late in 1848 thankfully proclaimed that the Father, Son and Spirit were "reactionaries" ("Rueckwaertstreiber").

The German states had little chance of avoiding turmoil during the continental wave of revolution in 1848. But since the territorial system still prevailed, it is more accurate to speak of "revolutions" in the German states, including Austria, than of a single German revolution. Berlin and Vienna were the focal points of these uprisings.

The German revolutions had a long incubation. Widespread dissatisfaction in the forties gave the uprisings form and substance. For example, Berlin's population increased 30 percent between 1841 and 1850, while poor box expenditures nearly doubled by 63 percent in the same period, and almost

40 percent of the city's budget went for the care of the poor. In addition, emigration rose sharply throughout Germany in the mid-forties, and soon this phenomenon became an issue for nationalist agitation. One reason for emigrating was the high cost of living, which peaked in 1847 because of severe crop failure. Nine hundred Silesian weavers starved to death that year. Nevertheless, economic problems were beginning to level off when the revolutions struck. The fifty percent increase in food prices between 1844 and 1847 reversed itself, and by the spring of 1848 a new economic boom started a remarkable economic recovery. This economic shift took some of the pressure off political conservatives, and eventually aided their counterthrust.

Economic conditions did little to create a mass uprising among "proletarian" industrial workers, since the slow advance of industrialization in Germany sharply limited the number of workers in this group. Furthermore, industrial workers made rather substantial economic gains during the forties. When the uprisings occurred, the "desperate proletariat" was composed of unemployed and uprooted artisans, who did not fit the socialist and communist stereotypes of the "revolutionary-prone" worker.

The Prussian king called a United Diet in 1847 to seek consent for a large governmental loan. The Prussian "Junkers" had been agitating for a major railway to the East, arguing that it would facilitate the movement of German culture into Polish areas. Anxious for the track to extend eastward from Berlin, they pressured the king into calling the Diet, which in turn soon demanded constitutional government for Prussia. In 1847 as well, philologists held a national meeting in Luebeck, while radical liberals met in Offenburg, and moderate liberals in Heppenheim. A number of forums issued calls for liberalizing political structures and unifying the nation. Leaders supporting these causes soon forged a temporary alliance with artisans and peasants, who were suffering economic hardship, and ideology joined with force to create a series of revolutions.(1)

The Revolution of 1848 was a continental phenomenon that reached from the English Channel to the Black Sea. Everywhere the same pattern of events repeated itself. A popular uprising forced the old order to capitulate, but after a jubilant celebration, the victors' enthusiasm waned as they recognized serious differences of opinion among themselves. As divisions deepened, conservative forces exerted strong counterpressures until finally the counterrevolutionary forces were able to reestablish the status quo. (2)

In the upheavals of 1848-50, the German churches performed admirably as the conservative camp's reserve forces. Those interested in liberalizing and constitutionalizing the political structures of the German states were portrayed as threats to the unwritten religious charter that governed church-state relations. The upheavals tested the charter's basic validity; if a revolutionary society could claim superiority over the government, the church would be stripped of its assignment to model "freedom" within authority for society.

During the revolutions, the traditional alliance between throne and altar was put to a serious test. Princes and kings regained control of the situation only with great effort, and only after granting major concessions. But throughout the siege, most custodians of the altar remained steadfastly at their ruler's side. The churches made two important contributions to the eventual suppression of revolt: through their theological interpretation of social protest and revolution, they called down upon revolutionaries the full force of divine condemnation and of religious tradition; and they provided organizational conduits and channels for counterrevolutionary zeal. Naturally, both responses were expected of those who accepted the working agreement between church and state.

After summarizing the course of the revolution in Berlin, we will review the difficulties confronting the small number of radical preachers who sided with the revolutionaries. Then our attention shifts southwestward to the German Parliament that assembled in Frankfurt am Main, and we will pursue two themes that emerged there, namely, independence for the church, and a nationwide evangelical church. Protestants who tried to hold the middle ground during the revolutions ended where most middlers are prone to fall—with the conservatives. But they did not receive the plaudits that came to vocal conservative Protestants after the counterrevolution succeeded in all the states. Church polity modifications that paralleled the conservatives' acceptance of written constitutions in some states, the church press, and the phenomenal growth of the Inner Mission, helped make counterrevolutionary ideology more than a series of slogans; these developments also preserved the unwritten religious charter intact. From our perspective, we can understand the nature of the patterned responses to revolution that most Protestant churchmen made in 1848. After living under the provisions of the religious charter for some time, they were well conditioned to make the appropriate response.

THE UPRISING IN BERLIN

Unlike England or France, the German states had no central city where major issues could be decided without forcing local political units to thresh out problems for themselves. But Vienna and Berlin fulfilled this role as nearly as German particularism allowed, and that was why the burial ceremonies for revolutionaries killed in Protestant Berlin had a symbolism that was not easily missed. But before the burials came the uprising, and behind it lay a number of formative influences.

The zoological gardens in Berlin were the favorite meeting spot for would-be revolutionaries. Together with other associates, the "Lichtfreunde" often assembled there for spirited discussion during the early spring days of 1848. At the same time, the conservative churchman, Johann Hinrich Wichern, later of Inner Mission fame, was maneuvering for position; his conversational partner was supposed to be the king. On March 18, Wichern made his way toward Berlin for a 1:00 P.M. appointment with Frederick William IV. The meeting had to be cancelled because of street disorders. For the time being, at least, spirited discussion in the zoological gardens managed to drown out the interminable chatter between throne and altar.

Journeymen and artisans in the traditional trades were largely responsible for the Berlin uprising on March 18. Only a limited number of industrial workers participated. Three hundred citizens were killed in the brief exchange

228

with garrison troops; of this number, only about fifteen belonged to the educated class, and about thirty were master craftsmen. The weather was perfect for the uprising; it was as warm in March as it usually was in May. THE ROWDY, a paper published in Berlin after May 18, made this pithy comment about the weather: "God is the first of revolutionaries since He invariably favors revolutions with the most perfect weather, but usually treats coronations, swearing-in days, and levees with a deluge of rain."

The uprising shook Prussia's royal house to its foundations. In Vienna, the archetypal figure of the old order, Metternich, had already been dismissed from his post on March 13. On March 19, Frederick William IV temporarily capitulated to insurrectionists and ordered his troops away from the barricades. He was a semi-neurotic individual who tried to be all things to all people. By March 21 he was riding though Berlin's streets, dressed in the liberal tricolors, chatting with the people's army, and promising a united Germany.

The upper middle class wanted tranquility no less than the king. Frederick von Bodelschwingh (1831-1910), later famous for his pastoral work at his institution for epileptics in Bethel, described the scene on March 19 in these words: "We youngsters were running about the streets on that Sunday morning (March 19). With the uprising repelled, there reigned a joyful mood among the greater part of our population; everywhere from the houses the troops were supplied with food."(3) When the troops left Berlin that day under the king's orders, most realized that some kind of political realignment was necessary, but the critical question remained unanswered: What kind of political settlement could there be, and how long would it be honored?

In the meantime, the bodies of the dead were decaying above ground. Berlin's clergy rose nobly to the occasion, and buried the revolutionaries in a ceremony that symbolized Prussia's firm unity. The king himself would—or could—have it no other way. On Sunday, March 19, he and his wife were forced to pay honor to the bodies of the slain rebels, laid out row on row in the palace yard; no services were held in the cathedral or in a number of Berlin churches that day. On March 22, twenty thousand people joined the funeral cortege as it wound its way through Berlin and passed the royal palace. Some suggested that the soldiers killed in battle should be buried at the same time, but their advice was summarily dismissed. Three clergymen offered eulogies before the procession began: a disciple of Schleiermacher named K. Leopold Adolf Sydow, a Roman Catholic priest named Ruhland, and a Jew, Sachs. Bishop Neander bestowed the final benediction while one hundred and eighty-three bodies were interred in the cemetery.

The slain revolutionaries were also honored with memorial services in several other towns and cities. In Breslau, H. R. Dietrich praised Berlin's "martyrs" for their sacrifice on behalf of Prussia and Germany. Using Luke 11:14-28 as his text, he observed on March 26 that in recent days, "God's finger" had exorcised an evil spirit from the people's midst; that spirit was the people's fear of princes, and the distrust that prevailed between people and princes. Dietrich took Jesus' statement in the text at face value, suggesting that somehow God's kingdom was at stake when the divine "finger" moved decisively. An ex-army chaplain named Julius Rupp, a vigorous supporter of the "Lichtfreunde" movement, accused the whole population of executing revolutionaries. He said in a sermon that "you deceive yourself, and are in danger of defacing the joy of victory through arrogance, if you maintain that it is the government alone that carries the guilt of blood. It alone has not incurred this misfortune. The guilt of this crime weighs much more on the entire population." The people had been guilty of keeping silence when the Gospel demanded protest.

At the same time, an interesting poster appeared in Breslau. Its left side listed a number of revolutionary demands couched in cautious language. On the right side were printed the petitions of the Lord's Prayer. When read full breadth across, the poster linked revolutionary demands and the prayer's phrases in the following way:

THE LORD'S PRAYER

You, teritorial prince   our father that you are,
you shall have joy and
    blessing with us and   in heaven
if you rule with the people

and through the people;   your name will be hallowed
We hope that your illumina-
    tion and love   comes to us
so that in joy, success and
    happiness flourishes   your kingdom.
Then forever we will be your
    true subjects, and say,   your will be done.
When you have alleviated the
    burdens that oppress us,
    we are   as in heaven;
for oppression is disagree-
    able both in heaven   and also on earth.
Through taxes, fees, and
    other extortion is cut
    short   our daily bread;
the lost commerce   give us today.
That we complain so
    earnestly,   forgive us.
Be the people's father and
    decrease our burdens so
    we can pay   our debts,
and forgive the nation when
    it groans over oppression just as we forgive.
Promote our welfare so we can
    be patient with   our debtors.
Territorial sovereign, we
    beg you,   lead us not into
        temptation;

do not allow your people
    to perish,   but deliver us.
Get ride of your incompetent
    bureaucrats and idle
    gluttons, and thereby
    free us   from all evil;
such men are worthless
    to us,   for the kingdom is yours.
If you grant our demands,
    then we have   the power and the glory.
And you, oh prince, will
    have rest   from now to eternity.
        Amen.

The revolutionaries in Breslau had no qualms about appropriating the most sacred Christian prayer to convince the prince that his kingdom would flourish, if he ruled "with" and "through" the people.

But the mass burial in Berlin, and the memorial services elsewhere, were merely token victories. A number of clergymen in Prussia's provinces voiced their early displeasure that churchmen had been involved in the burial ceremonies. Already at an early date, those who temporarily held power reassessed their resources and re-examined their demands. Rudolf Virchow, a young doctor who actively participated in the March uprising in Berlin, wrote his father less than a week after the melee that "already there begins a reaction among the citizenry ("Bourgeoisie") against the workers (the people). Already they are speaking of rabble, already plans are being made for withholding equal distribution of political rights among the various groups of the nation."(4) Soon the claim was made in print that "one hundred and eighty Jews and other young men, bankrupt artisans and drunkards" had been responsible for the Berlin uprising. Yoked together, throne and altar had tremendous resilience and reserve capacity. Although the throne hesitated momentarily, the second line of defense held firm. Living clergymen spoke the last words at burial rites for the revolutionaries. And as spring turned to summer, and summer leaves turned brown, the lips of evangelicals increasingly formed the word, "obedience."

RADICAL PREACHERS AND THE REVOLUTION

In the revolutionary years, a small number of pastors and religious hucksters participated openly in democratic and anarchistic movements, or served as spokesmen and trumpeteers for revolution. With varying degrees of intensity, they joined the popular clamor for reform, and endorsed the revolutionaries' attacks on absolute monarchs and the established church. They levelled direct attacks at the foundation of the religious agreement.

Foremost among the clergymen who called for a republican form of government was Rudolf Dulon (1807-1887), a popular "Lichtfreunde" preacher who left Prussian Magdeburg for Bremen in August, 1848. Dulon greeted the revolution as

"God's messenger, ambassador of heaven." His understanding of the revolutionary movement as "the Lord's word," and of democracy as the only force that could realize God's kingdom on earth, brought noteriety to him. In Bremen he worked in three organizations that were part of the wider democratic movement; one was a group of cigar makers. He was a popular preacher, and his political activities, gregarious nature, and writings spread his influence throughout northern Germany.

The idea of God's kingdom played a dominant role in Dulon's thought and preaching. He used it to explain that the church's mission was to carry God's plan of socialism into the world. He soon came under fire, and by the spring of 1851, twenty-three pastors petitioned the Senate in Bremen to defend the church against him, since he did not preach "the gospel according to the confessions of the Reformed Church," but the "teachings of God's kingdom on earth construed in accordance with his democratic, socialistic thought." In 1852 the Senate released him from office, after the Reformed theological faculty at Heidelberg advised that his teaching on God's kingdom was a clever camouflage for political rhetoric, and advocacy of a permanent revolution. Dulon eventually emigrated to the United States.

In Kremmen, the congregation's chief pastor, G. Schweitzer, wrote a tract in 1848 describing revolution as part of a continuing process of development through which the people constructed new laws. This publication, and Schweitzer's democratic activities, led to his dismissal without pension in 1850, although he was fully reinstated at Gotha in 1858. In Rhenish Griefenstein, a certain Pastor Schaum led a band of excited peasants as they marched on the castle of the prince of Solms-Braunfels; Schaum was forced to emigrate to the United States.

A popular preacher in Bremen, Friedrich Mallet (1793-1865), helped stir revolutionary zeal in a sermon preached in February of 1848, in which he said that men must assume responsibility for contemporary events. Mallet told his congregation that since God alone, not men—least of all a monarch claiming to embody the state—controls history, no one should fear getting involved in exciting or irresponsible behavior. That fall, a preacher in Dresden named J. E. R. Kaeuffer thanked God for intervening in world affairs, then added these words: "Praise be to God! We live at a time when, generally speaking, men have more zealously arrayed all the standing orders of society according to a standard of perfection than almost any other time on earth. . . . The splendor shines brighter and brighter, though deep darkness still enshrouds the whole earth: the kingdom of God is coming!" This late-blooming rationalist targeted radical criticism at existing moral and religious conditions, and strongly supported the cause of internal political reform.

Several pastors arranged memorial services in honor of Robert Blum, a prominent leftist who was executed at Vienna in November of 1848. The ministers of St. Bernard's in Breslau declared Blum a martyr, while several independent congregations in Koenigsberg observed his execution as a martyr's day; one preacher in Dresden portrayed him as a political messiah. In Leipzig, an unruly crowd gathered at St. Thomas Church soon after his execution became known. The teacher who chaired the meeting led the crowd in singing Luther's "A Mighty Fortress," but soon ecclesiastical officials in Saxony declared churches off limits for political meetings.

In that year of revolution, the pastor of a free congregation in Neumarkt, named E. Herrendoerfer, endorsed constitutional reform in flowing religious rhetoric. One sermon, entitled "The Return of God's Sovereignty," argued that the gospel was infusing new life into contemporary events, and God's sovereignty was gaining strength while monarchical power was slipping. People seeking to destroy the inherently sinful principle of monarchy by divine right were championing the Lord's sovereignty. He added that the "return to God's sovereignty is a return to the people's sovereignty," and that included people of every station and rank.

TREMORS FROM FRANKFURT

The three great problems that occupied many people in Germany in 1848-49 were freedom, national unity, and the

234

Schleswig-Holstein question. Churchmen confronted these issues in arguments over the church's separation or independence from the state, the creation of a unified national church, and the rights of pastors in Schleswig-Hostein to revolt against authority. The national Parliament that met in Frankfurt am Main served as a debating forum for the first two issues.

We will concentrate on these two issues in the remainder of this chapter, describing how the threat of religious freedom and the church's disestablishment fomented debate about a national church. One result was that evangelicals soon created an association of charitable societies, called the Inner Mission, that made major contributions to the conservative counterrevolution. And in other ways as well, evangelical conservatives transformed Frankfurt's questions about religion, and the church's relation to the state, into support for the monarchy and the throne-altar alliance, even after the church became nominally independent.

Organized by a "Vorparlament" whose decisions were ratified by the Federal Diet of the German States, the National Parliament in Frankfurt was a persuasive, not a revolutionary body. It tried to convert the German princes to liberalism rather than overthrow them. Some radicals expected little more from the Parliament than from the thirty-year old Diet, whose meagre accomplishments were touted satirically in a pamphlet early in 1848, entitled DOCUMENTARY EXPOSITION OF THE EFFECTIVENESS OF THE GERMAN FEDERAL ASSEMBLY, WITH REGARD TO THE REPRESENTATION, DEFENSE, AND PRESERVATION OF THE RIGHTS OF THE GERMAN PEOPLE AGAINST THE FORCED MEASURES OF THE GERMAN GOVERNMENTS, FROM ITS INAUGURATION UP TO THE PRESENT DAY. A single blank page summarized the Diet's achievements; some argue that the Parliament accomplished little more.

When the Parliament convened in May of 1848, seemingly too late to be effective, only 330 of the 831 elected delegates attended the opening session. In the months that followed, seldom were more than 500 in attendance, and only 530 delegates participated in the important vote on the emperor. Since the demand for parliamentary representatives throughout Germany exceeded the supply, the delegates at Frankfurt were less radical than those elected to state parliaments, particularly Prussia's.

235

In 1848 the Austrian poet Franz Grillparzer grimly prophesied,

> Modern man's path leads
> From humanity
> Through nationality
> To bestiality.

His words seemed to apply to the Frankfurt Parliament. In the early days the delegates envisioned a new, united Germay that would protect and defend human rights; they spent six months drawing up a bill of rights. But soon the nationalist sentiment of Poles, Czechs, Danes and Germans played havoc with their hopes.(5) Even more importantly, the people who provided the muscle for the revolution were not receiving their rewards from the theoreticians and spokesmen who assumed leadership roles. The frail alliance between artisans and peasants, and their bourgeois leaders, disintegrated because human needs were not being met. Frankfurt soon became a debating society without power.

After months of debate, and efforts to convince the Prussian king to lead a German empire without Austria, the Parliament finally adopted an imperial constitution and law. These were promulgated on the same day in March of 1849 that the assembly elected Frederick William IV of Prussia as emperor. But conservatism had been re-grouping and gathering its strength. Since Austria's constitution was designed for the whole of her old empire, including non-German lands, Frankfurt's only option was to create a "small Germany" with Prussia at the head. Frederick's rejection of the Frankfurt crown as a "pig crown" and "sausage sandwich"—even though his official answer was a curious mixture of "yes" and "no"—sealed the Parliament's doom. German unity was delayed for twenty years, until the time when it was forged with Prussian iron, not a Bill of Rights. In 1870, the same Jewish professor from Koenigsberg carried news of another imperial crown to another Prussian king, but this time as a representative of princes, not the people.

Amid all the political maneuvering at Frankfurt, the delegates also discussed a number of issues that concerned religion and the church. The result was some degree of anxiety among churchmen who feared that the church was not ready for independence, while others felt that the time was ripe for some kind of organizational unity among all German Protestants. In any case, Frankfurt's tremors helped churchmen find one another; when they gathered, more often than not they proposed solutions that advanced the cause of counterrevolution.

Independence for the Church?

One important issue at the National Assembly in St. Paul's Church was the question of the individual's religious freedom and the relationship between church and state. The church-state issue arose in the opening session, when delegates considered the assembly's standing rule on worship. One speaker argued that any worship service for the assembly should be interconfessional, "since we are deliberating a communal matter, and it seems to me therefore that a division of divine services according to confessional differences would be improper."

One important pressure group helped to focus the Assembly's attention on the church-state issue. The delegates knew that during Easter week, in Coethen, a group of theological leftists composed of rationalists, "Lichtfreunde," and some theologians from Halle and Jena, had proposed a radical plan for church unity in Germany. They had suggested that the national church be built from the ground up; autonomous congregations would elect delegates to district, provincial, territorial, and finally national synods, and church authorities would serve at the pleasure of these representative bodies.

Other formative pressures affected the Frankfurt delegates as well. During the early phase of the revolutions, there seemed to be little public support for the "Christian state" and its close alliance between throne and altar. Though more radical groups, such as the "Lichtfreunde," wanted total separation of church and state, the majority of confessionalists, mediating figures, and church liberals favored independence for the church, although they wanted to avoid any endorsement of separation of church and state that seemed to promote a religionless society. Lacking the American denominational system, they could not disestablish

237

the church through political surgery, and assume that a "social" establishment would nurture religion in society. Nevertheless, with the exception of many conservatives, evangelicals favored more independence for the churches, or less arbitrary interference by princely governments.

In fact, most Protestant liberals viewed the revolution primarily as a church-political event. They concentrated on the revolution's church-political consequences, and saw it as their task to solidify their theological and ecclesiastical positions through a constitutional structure. Since they felt oppressed by ecclesiastical structure and authoritarian church officials, they also interpreted attacks on political oppression through church-political lenses. Their leading journal, the UNIVERSAL CHURCH NEWS, said that the "great events of this day" were as important for the churches as for the state. "The state was not free, but the Protestant church was even less free than the state," therefore, "living and true members of the church greet the results of recent battles with jubilation." Protestants in the mediating camp also generally welcomed the revolution, but they differed from the liberals in one important way. They laid less emphasis on the need to guarantee the church's new freedom through a presbyterial-synodal constitution.

The one factor that distinguished liberal evangelicals from both the mediating and conservative groups was their heavy stress on constitutionalism in the ecclesiological, as well as the political, realm. They were just as concerned with the question of constitutional church structure and representative organs as with the course of the revolution itself. Their journal advised clergymen to permit themselves to be nominated for office in local and national parliaments, advice not ordinarily given in conservative and mediating periodicals. But the underlying assumption was that the nomination and subsequent election of liberals would ensure the church's just treatment in its relations with the state. Larger political problems seemed to be of less importance.

At the Frankfurt Parliament most delegates, who were largely from the upper middle classes, followed a line of thought compatible with the views of these theological liberals. Few words of defense for the "Christian state" were spoken by

238

anyone, including the sixteen Roman Catholic and sixteen Protestant clergymen who held seats. At the same time, the extreme left wing had little success in calling for total separation of church and state. The Hessian zoologist, Carl Vogt, claimed to speak for the left wing when he said that every church was a drag on civilization. Denying even the possibility of a democratic church, he endorsed full separation of church and state, since that would be a step toward annihilating all that was called "church"; religious freedom should imply the right not to belong to any church, he said. But his argument failed to elicit much positive response.

Roman Catholic leaders in the German states seemed to favor independence for the church rather than separation of church and state, primarily because many civil problems, including marriage and education, included religious factors. A Prussian general named von Radowitz, chairman of the Catholic Association in the Frankfurt Parliament, reassured Protestants that independence for churches would not necessarily work to their disadvantage, even though they lacked a papal protector. He argued that independence for both confessions would not separate church and state, but would guarantee that the state's relations with the church would be guided by law. He felt that Protestants could continue to give certain prerogatives in church life to their governments.

Some Protestants at the Assembly agreed with Pastor Karl Zittel of Baden, when he argued that independence for the churches might work to the advantage of the Roman Catholics, but most felt that the new freedom would more than compensate for state protection. In any case, full and total separation of church and state did not seem to be a live option; most delegates agreed with Pastor Karl Jurgens of Brunswick, that German political life would always have a Christian basis, as church and state cooperated for mutual benefit. The solution was clear: make the church less dependent on the state, and give official Protestant and Catholic churches the kind of freedom that had been accorded in recent years to new religious societies like the "Lichtfreunde." The fact that more than half of the Assembly's delegates traveled to Cologne in mid-August, 1848, to participate in the Colonge Cathedral Festival, at which the Vicar of the Empire and the Prussian king stood

239

side by side, showed that they did not intend to strike a crippling blow against the churches.

But no action was taken on the question until after a radical right-winger made a compact with radical leftists. A young Swabian pietist pastor named Christoph Hoffmann, whose father founded the Korntal settlement in Wuerttemberg, had been elected to the Assembly with 5,800 votes against his opponent's 3,300. In the bitter electoral contest, a poet portrayed Hoffmann's opponent, David F. Strauss, as a long-legged bird whose giant steps to Frankfurt would ensure progress and eternal sunshine; Hoffman was pictured as a bird of the night, an owl hooting in the dark. Hoffmann gave his first speech at Frankfurt on August 25, 1848; assuming that the nearness of the End required the separation of good and evil, he argued forcefully for full separation of church and state. Since the new state would be unchristian, he argued, it should not retain the slightest degree of control over the church. Supported only by the extreme left, his proposal died in a crushing vote of 99 to 357.

In short order, the Assembly approved proposals on basic religious rights. Everyone was to be given full liberty of faith and conscience, and one could not be forced to reveal one's religious convictions or to join any religious society. All restrictions on freedom of worship were removed. Another paragraph stated that one's civil rights were not conditional upon, or limited by, the religion professed; the question at issue were the requirements levied against Jews. In the paragraph dealing most explicitly with church-state relations, it was agreed that new religious societies could be formed without any approval by the state; churches would be permitted to administer their affairs independently, but they would be subject to state laws, like any other organization; no religious society would receive any special privilege, and there was to be no state church. No one was to be forced to participate in a religious act; civil marriage depended only on civil registration, and church marriages were to occur only after the civil act. Official registries would be kept by civil authorities, and oaths were to read, "True, so help me God." But since the Parliament's Constitution and Bill of Rights soon met the same untimely fate of the Assembly itself, most of these grand plans came to nothing, even

240

though they had been voted by the delegates.

One other major issue was the relationship between church and school. Once again, Hoffmann rose to speak. Basing his remarks on the supposed liberal assumption that parents were directly responsible for educating their children, he argued that if schools were placed under direct state control, not under the control of independent congregations, those people who remained true to the church would be forced to break relations with the state since the schools would become a "paradise of despotism." "Those people will subject themselves to penalties, they will bleed if necessary, but they will not obey," he said. He reminded the assembly that rejecting his argument meant rejecting the views of 24,000 people in Baden and Wuerttemberg who signed a petition he held in his hands. But he was not persuasive, and the Assembly voted 316 to 74 to take the schools out of the hands of the clergy and put them under the state's general supervision. After this vote, a number of Roman Catholic delegates lost interest in the Assembly, and many distinguished clerics, including Bishop Wilhelm von Ketteler, soon left Frankfurt with Hoffmann.

A National Church?

It was, of course, the issue of national unity that provided the broad framework for discussion of a national church. But the more immediate influence for evangelicals was Frankfurt's implied promise, or threat, of independence for the church.

Many who talked about a national church believed that independence would open the way for—and in fact necessitate—more interaction among Protestants on the national level. In this way, the political liberals' correlation of freedom and unification influenced Protestant discussion of the church's independence and national unity. But before we examine specific Protestant plans for unity, and the formation of a pseudo-national church in the voluntary Inner Mission, we will summarize how some Protestant preachers talked about national unity in this period.

In their sermons, a number of evangelical pastors publicly

supported proposals for German unity. Included in this group were Karl W. Schultz of Wiesbaden, Konrad Rudel of Nuremberg, and Johann C. B. Wilhelm of Neustadt an der Orla. Others endorsed the general idea of national unity while rejecting the freedom movement, and opposing the proceedings at Frankfurt, specifically the election of Austrian Archduke John as the Parliament's titular head. But usually they tempered their endorsement with pessimism about the chances of achieving national unity.

Frankfurt's selection of Archduke John as regent complicated matters, and opened for consideration once again the "Grossdeutsch/Kleindeutsch" question ("Great" or "Small" Germany, with or without Austria). His election not only represented a temporary victory for Great Germany, but his Catholic affiliation ignited controversy between the two confessions. As might be expected, the awakened Prussian preacher, F. W. Krummacher, supported the Small Germany approach. "Enter beloved Prussia," he said to Berliners in May of 1848, "into the great German fraternal alliance of race and state. . . . You have a special calling for the whole fatherland." In general, Protestant clergymen in Prussia did not applaud John's election to the post late in June, 1848, and some publicly condemned the action. But in Thuringia, a different spirit prevailed. Johnann F. T. Wohlfarth of Rudolstadt applauded the choice on the seventh Sunday after Trinity, showing from John 1:6 that this John, just like John the Baptizer, preached repentance, so that people could follow law and order properly, and secure a better future for themselves and their children.

In Wuerttemberg, Strauss' campaign against Hoffmann gave the author of THE LIFE OF JESUS (1835) the chance to enunciate his national views. His speeches and articles demanded that political liberalism facilitate the development of Christianity into a purely humanistic religion; German unification was the prerequisite. In one speech he paraphrased a biblical quotation to make his point: "Seek unity first, and all the other things will be added to you." But the national unity he envisioned it was not a republic like France. A monarch would head the empire, and the territorial states would preserve the monarchical principle as well. According to Strauss, the Prussian king was best suited for this position of leadership. Discussing the related problem of the Jews, he suggested that they receive

242

full civil and political rights in exchange for their continuation as a distinctive race. But this could happen only if, through blanket religious freedom, all churches broke up into sects.

The Hessian confessionalist, August Vilmar, was equally adamant in rejecting a republic. The unified empire he proposed was even more authoritarian than Strauss.' He used his periodical to urge the re-establishment of the German empire, but did little more than glorify the past, even though he advised the Prussian king to accept the proffered crown in 1849. He summarized his position rather well in April, 1848:

> If an emperor and an empire come to Germany, then a longer and probably more comfortable future is in store for spiritual matters and for the church..... But if the republic is victorious, then the last stages will probably happen very quickly, perhaps in a few years, and the final cleavage will occur in our lifetime. So lift up your eyes to the Lord of glory, the Lord of victory! He comes!

Vilmar soon became one of the leading reactionaries in Hesse, in part because his support for the empire in 1848 was not a liberal proposition in the first place.

As German Protestants addressed the question of national unity in 1848, the majority seemed to reject democratic and revolutionary means for attaining unity, but national unity itself was not problematic. If in the future ways could be found to secure unity without the revolutionary processes employed in 1848, they were certain to gain the support of most German Protestants. That proved to be true in Bismarck's revolution from above.

Of more immediate significance to most churchmen was the institutional problem that the church would face if national unity and the church's independence both materialized. As we reflect on discussion surrounding this subject, we may come to think that churchmen were merely reacting to political developments, and making contingency plans. In great part that was true, but others made a positive contribution to the search for national unity, and expressed nationalist sentiment through their plans for an independent national church.

In 1848 and 1849, a number of church figures offered proposals for structuring an independent national church for Protestants. In TWELVE THESES ON THE PRESENT AND FUTURE OF THE CHURCH (1848), Michael Baumgarten (1812-1889), a theology professor at Rostock, demanded full separation of church and state, and an assembly of all interested parties and groups, including Roman Catholics, to reorganize the church, much like the politicians were debating political questions at Frankfurt. Karl A. Hase (1800-1890) of Jena, one of the century's foremost church historians, had attended the radical Easter week meeting at Coethen, but he did not fully agree with the proposals offered there. His work, THE EVANGELICAL PROTESTANT CHURCH OF THE GERMAN EMPIRE (1849), described some of the proposals he laid before the Frankfurt assembly earlier. Hase agreed with left wing radicals on the need to rebuild the church from the bottom up, but he did not think that the imperial church should be confessionless, or that congregations should be autonomous. The "Zeitgeist," he said, should not be allowed to throw out the Scriptures and the Holy Spirit. He had visions of a "Protestant German people's church in which the great, tender principles <of our faith> might arrive at a firm conviction about the religious characteristics of the Evangelical Church." At the top of a synodal structure he urged a national council that would make binding administrative decisions, but remain advisory on theological matters.

Mediating figures who were less radical than Hase agreed that a democratic and synodal constitution was desirable, but they laid greater emphasis on the confessional basis of a national church. The Bonn theologian, Isaac A. Dorner (1809-1884), published three open letters urging a national German evangelical church with Nitzsch's ordination oath as its confessional basis, adopted in 1846 by the Prussian general synod. He argued that a confession has life only if the church from time to time renewed itself though a confessional act.

A Prussian lay official from Bonn, named Moritz von Bethmann-Hollweg (1795-1877), suggested that laymen and clergy of all kinds gather and discuss the church's future rather informally, apart from any set doctrinal basis. He felt that territorial churches should be free to accept or reject any advisory resolutions that the group might adopt.

These efforts culminated in an ecclesiastical "Vorparlament" of sorts that met for the second time in June of 1848, in Sandhof near Frankfurt. Since the conference coincided with the publication of the Frankfurt Assembly's first draft on Human Rights, the matter of providing some national structure for independent evangelical churches seemed all the more pressing. Participants included such prominent churchmen as Bethmann-Hollweg, Dorner, Ullmann, Hundeshagen, Zimmermann, Palmer, and a "gymnasium" teacher of strong Lutheran convictions named Philipp Wackernagel (1800-1877).

Wackernagel and Bethmann-Hollweg proposed that a "free assembly of German evangelical notables," a "Kirchentag," meet in Wittenberg to work toward organic unification of all the Protestant German churches. Invitations were published in the EVANGELICAL CHURCH NEWS and the UNIVERSAL CHURCH NEWS, two papers of differing theological positions which both accepted the union church. According to the invitation, the meeting on September 21 would "discuss the status of the Evangelical Church in its present difficulties." A proposal to create a confederation of churches, or a church league, had been offered at about the same time in a Berlin pastoral conference by the lay theologian J. F. Stahl.

About five hundred clergymen and laymen attended the unofficial "Assembly for the Creation of a German Evangelical Church League" in Wittenberg on September 21-23, 1848. But events in Frankfurt provided an immediate agenda, despite the fact that Bethmann-Hollweg, who had chaired the conference of territorial church representatives, suggested that the conference's unfinished work should be completed in Wittenberg. Several days before the Assembly opened, two rightist delegates in Frankfurt had been murdered in uprisings there. In response, Ernst Ludwig von Gerlach urged the Assembly in Wittenberg to declare revolution unlawful and a sin against God, since it defied governmental and divine authority. Instead the delegates adopted a more moderate proposal from Hengstenberg, designating the Sunday after Reformation, November 5, as a day of repentance for all social orders and classes.

As the delegates struggled over the question of union, confederation, and confession during the first session, the planned confederation appeared to be running aground. After lunch, Johann H. Wichern demanded that "practical questions" should come under discussion since they were directly related to the question of church confederation among the territorial bodies. The acting chairman, Bethmann-Hollweg, asked him to discuss these matters in greater detail the next morning, but once more the session was filled with endless speeches on doctrinal issues. The afternoon session went little better for Wichern, despite the pledge of the co-chairman, Stahl, that practical issues would surface.

In the realm of church polity, the assembly at Wittenberg did not write a constitution for Germany's evangelical church, nor did it revive the "corpus evangelicorum," even though it claimed that "the <proposed> evangelical church league is not a union of . . . confessional churches, but an ecclesiastical confederation." The adopted resolutions were victories for Stahl, who wanted the confessions of the churches to retain their force in any proposed league. But the proposal for a German confederative church came to nothing since the conservative counterrevolution and its corollary, non-related territorial churches, soon overshadowed it.

The most promising result of the conference was an ingenious political solution to the problem of creating some kind of national bond among evangelicals, without destroying the territorial integrity of the churches. The "Inner Mission," proposed by Wichern, was given institutional form by this rump group of unofficial delegates to an unofficial conference. The rather amorphous nature of the Mission allowed it to be all things to most people, and as a result, it was the single most important accomplishment of the Wittenberg "Kirchentag."

The eminent German historian Franz Schnabel has called Wichern "the most forceful and impressive personality, on the whole, that Protestantism produced in Germany in the nineteenth century." During the first half of the century, Wichern (1808–1881) prepared himself for broad participation in Protestant church life. Like some of his contemporaries, he grappled with the doctrine of ecclesiology, while dabbling at the same time in Germany's emerging social problem. His primary teachers were Schleiermacher, Neander and Luecke; they greatly influenced his ecclesiological views. But the writings of Stahl, Puchta, and Bunsen, as well as his experiences in the awakening in Hamburg, also played an important role.

Wichern's first full analysis of the revolution, an article published in April of 1848, showed more interest in the moral and spiritual conditions that led to revolution than in its social and political origins. Wichern charged that if church and state had followed a slightly altered course in the preceding months, the results would have been different. The time for action was at hand, he wrote; those who wanted to rescue nation and church were to take courage and vigorously prosecute the work of the "inner mission," even though it had no organizational structure. "The inner mission," he wrote,

> is truly patriotic when it presses the sword against those who rise up against the church. Fatherland and church—both of them can vanish in these troubled times, but only in order to rise again more glorious than before. After a time of suffering, the inner mission will celebrate an even more glorious resurrection.

Wichern said that the same enemy was attacking these institutions under different disguises; revolution shook the state, while atheism stalked the church.

After some backstage maneuvering, Wichern was allowed to speak about his "inner mission" three times at the Wittenberg Assembly, on Thursday, Friday, and Saturday. In his second speech, partly recorded verbatim, he informed the delegates that "the inner mission merely wishes to serve church and state, as well as the other divine institutions. . . ." Asked for a fuller description of the "inner mission," and concrete plans for its organization, he returned on Saturday to describe his proposal in detail. He said that for fifteen years he had envisioned an alliance of faith and love, an association generated by the fatherland that would exhaust its energies serving church and state, for the sake of God's kingdom. Perhaps, he added, his idea would catch fire at Wittenberg. He hoped that when the Assembly established its Continuing Committee, it would include a commission to organize and launch the proposed inner mission on a national level. He recommended that the mission's organizational committee should serve as a clearinghouse, publicizing charitable work already underway and stimulating new cooperative endeavors.

Wichern's dramatic appeal at Wittenberg secured an initial victory for him. The conference finally authorized the creation of a voluntary organization, or at least its steering committee, to assist church and state as they labored to advance God's kingdom. The "Kirchentag's" Provisional Committee on Inner Mission soon met, and appointed ten prominent laymen and clergymen to the permanent Central Committee for the Inner Mission of the German Evangelical Church, but not before full monarchical rule was reinstated in Prussia. Among the appointees were Stahl; Bethmann-Hollweg; Heinrich von Muehler (1813-1874), later Prussia's minister of ecclesiastical affairs; Ernst von Senfft-Pilsach (1795-1882), a close advisor to the Prussian king; and Wichern, who remained a theological candidate all his life. The committee, which was composed of Prussians except for Wichern, quickly showed its influence at home; in March of 1849, Prussia granted full franking privileges for all mail sent or received by the committee. For Wichern's benefit the committee established two headquarters, in Berlin and in his home town, Hamburg.

The Protestant conference at Wittenberg preceded by several months the Roman Catholics' National Bishops Conference, the first to be held since the collapse of the empire in 1806. The Wittenberg Assembly was broadly representative of German evangelicals, although neither the extreme left wing nor the right wing Old Lutherans were present. In fact, a group of confessionalist Lutherans gathered for a counter-conference in Leipzig that summer.

In sum, the Wittenberg "Kirchentag" was a meeting of mediators, evangelical pastors and laymen whose doctrinal positions did not require them to reject the Prussian union or unions in other territories. The decision to press for a confederation of territorial churches in a church league, and the failure to adopt any new confessional basis at Wittenberg, permitted even such theologically conservative neo-confessionalists as Stahl and Hengstenberg to work with others, and to agree to hold another "Kirchentag" the next

year. But since a church league did not materialize, the
real beneficiary of the conference was Wichern's Inner
Mission, which now assumed institutional form. Inner
Mission meant the practice of charity, not arguments over
doctrine.

UNCERTAINTY IN THE MIDDLE

Liberals who were active in the revolutions, including some
churchmen, set in motion the effort to disestablish the
church, or at least to make it independent. They also
searched for a national church that would complement in some
way the liberal dream of a liberalized, unified Germany. But
just as in most upheavals, there was also a middle group of
clergymen who did not necessarily endorse all the more
radical proposals, nor did they want public identification
with conservative evangelical forces that were satisfied
with the status quo. Because of its ambivalence, the
position of the middle group did not offer much of a sense
of certainty and security to those in the mediating camp.

Clergymen in the mediating camp faced difficult times during
the revolutionary period. The latitude of their theological
position made it difficult for them to define their
political goals as sharply as conservative Protestants.
Generally they supported legitimate authority, although
their halfhearted endorsement of the status quo, or the
status quo with minor modifications, included some critical
elements. One is reminded of the preacher in the
principality of Hohenzollern, deep in southern Germany below
Wuerttemberg, who was ordered to preach a sermon on the
occasion of Prussia's purchase of the principality in 1849.
His sermon outline took cognizance of the prevaling power
structure, as well as the mixed feelings of the people.
"Beloved in Christ," he said, "I will speak to you today
about two points: how we should rejoice that we now have
become Prussian, and how on account of our sins we have
deserved no better than this."

Middle-ground Protestants interpreted the revolution as a
divine judgment on human failures, and little more than

249

that. Clearly, the Christian could accept this judgment without participating in the revolt against authority. But mediating periodicals indicated that a distinction must be drawn between the revolution itself, and the human rights it advanced; in this sense, the revolution was also a judgment against authorities. The middle party's ambivalence was especially apparent in statements about church-state relations. On the one hand, the journal QUESTIONS OF THE TIME endorsed separation of church and state, and the non-confessional nature of civil rights; on the other hand, it warned that such moves could create a chasm between social and political spheres, and endanger "culture and morality, humanitarianism and civilization." The middlers' position over against revolutionary currents seemed generally to be more negative than positive.

But in one regard the mediating party distinguished itself in clear fashion from liberal churchmen. It emphasized constitutional government more than a constitutional church, which the liberals pursued. Men in the mediating group wrote that the people had decided to turn the monarchical state into a constitutional monarchy. This approach enabled them to preserve their views on the state's divine origin without ignoring powerful undercurrents of human liberty. Conservatives usually stressed the king's appointment by God, to whom alone the king was responsible; men in the middle stressed the king's responsibility to God in the light of his relationship with his subjects.(6) This made the citizen responsible in some areas, as Dorner argued in a meeting at Stuttgart when he said that Christians bore political guilt not only for participating in revolution, where that had been the case, but also for their political inactivity and sluggishness.

In sum, the mediating group focused attention on the moral and spiritual context of the day's political events. While endorsing constitutionalism, most of their periodicals argued that politics could not solve the day's problems since the causes lay deeper. Formal political questions could not be answered without referring to the moral and spiritual dimensions of the human situation, since the religious culture of the state and its citizens was determinative for an effective political structure. For example, on second Easter Day in 1848, Leopold I. Rueckert (1791-1871) of Jena preached that Christ alone could ensure the nation's deliverance, because sin was the basic problem, and unrest merely its symptom.

In their own eyes, the mediating group's ambivalent position enhanced their importance for church and state, but in practice it aided the conservatives' effort to roll back the revolution as quickly as possible. Since it influenced a sizable block of German Protestants, the mediating party was largely responsible for Germany's inability or failure to address political questions on political terms. Despite their willingness to accomodate the modern world theologically, during the upheaval at midcentury they were as unwilling as the conservatives to undermine the prevailing religious charter. They looked at revolution much like Wichern viewed the church's role in the emerging social question: the church was the Good Samaritan summoned to bandage society's wounds, not the Jacobin, intent on restructuring society.

Bishop David Neander of Prussia personified the mediating position on March 18, 1848, while the battle raged in the streets of Berlin. He tried to bring an end to the uprising by leading a delegation of city officials to the royal palace. After agreeing with the barricaders to negotiate if the king responded affirmatively, he was abruptly turned away by the king.

CONSERVATIVE COUNTERREVOLUTION

By the fall of 1848, it was clear to many that the German revolutions had failed to turn the corner. The collapse of Vienna's revolutionary regime in October was a clear signal that the German states would reject revolution. Prussia followed suit almost immediately, and in less than a year her troops were extinguishing the last sparks of revolt in the southwestern states, after bringing order to Frankfurt. After the autumn of 1848, initiative and attention shifted once more to the territorial states.

The way the counterrevolution began is not difficult to understand. As artisans and others tried to radicalize the

251

revolution in order to achieve some of their most important social and economic goals, the glue between the liberal movement and its supporters became too brittle to hold together the tenuous coalition. The most important factor in the failure of the revolutions was the collapse of the alliance between liberal leaders and their lower class supporters; it was a natural and almost inevitable consequence when conservative forces filled the vacuum. Monarchs, armies, and conservative masses seized the initiative, and in the process the states that had no constitution learned how to absorb one.

Especially in Prussia, the largest Protestant state, clergymen and evangelical churches played important roles in this counterrevolutionary process. Church polity was structured so that it met the letter of the new constitution, but preserved the traditional relationship between church and state. An important new institution, the High Church Council, became the chief administrative arm of the supposedly independent church, but functioned directly under the king. The church press also rallied to conservative causes, opposing democratic church polity and liberal political movements. And as the Inner Mission grew rapidly, an increasing number of local societies defended orthodoxy and distributed information on the dangers of communism. In sum, the churches made a major contribution to the counterrevolutionary movement in order to preserve intact the unwritten religious charter, and to defend the alliance between church and state in its darkest hour.

Conservatives in Prussia were forced to organize in order to protect their interests in 1848, just as they had coalesced under the pressure of Hardenburg's reforms in 1810-11. It was a wrenching experience to follow the liberals into party politics and political organizations, but largely under the influence of Ernst Ludwig von Gerlach, a party was finally organized to marshall conservative power in the halls of Prussia's new parliament. In the spring of 1848, conservatives exerted little influence in the election that produced Prussia's first assembly; only one-tenth of the 402 deputies were clergymen, most of them Rhenish Roman Catholics and sectarian leaders. But the future looked better for the conservatives in June, when the ministry called out the civil guard to put down an uprising at Berlin's arsenal.

Before 1848 the conservatives had been active as a party only in Prussia's evangelical church. This is one reason why the counterrevolution assumed visible form in the church at an early date. The parliaments in Frankfurt and Berlin were targets of semonic attacks by conservative pastors in Elberteld, Halle, Brandenburg, Stettin and elsewhere. Pastor Friedrich Sander of Elberfeld gathered a nucleus of conservatives and publicly condemned the liberal movement, while clergymen in the provinces condemned the Berlin pastors for participating in the burial of revolutionaries in March. Meanwhile, conservative political clubs sprouted in July and August of 1848. Composed mostly of estate owners, officers, veterans and clergymen—although the social spectrum was somewhat wider in Posen and Westphalia—the clubs bowed to the exigencies of the moment, and supported a constitutional monarchy as a bulwark against republicanism. They distributed tracts such as the one entitled, "Dr. Martin Luther Against Insurrection and Rebellion."

With these and other activities of churchmen in mind, the French historian Jacques Droz summarized the church's aggressive counterrevolutionary role in these words:

> There is no doubt that one of the most effective
> counter-revolutionary forces were the churches.
> By influencing conscience to reaffirm loyalty and
> obedience, by opposing democracy as a manifestation
> of liberal thought and radical philosophy, and, as
> a result, by linking the political struggle to de-
> fense of orthodoxy, the churches rendered extra-
> ordinary service in the cause of supporting the gov-
> ernments.(7)

His statement has special pertinence for Protestants in Prussia. After the uprisings, the masses had every reason to confuse orthodoxy with the reactionary political movement of the fifties.

Church Polity and Constitutionalism

During the early days of the revolution, a great deal of interest was expressed in Prussian church polity. Max von

Schwerin, who was married to Schleiermacher's daughter, held the office of Minister of Ecclesiastical Affairs from March 19 to June 15, 1848. He set the tone for his work in a speech before the United Diet early in April, which indicated that since the king wanted equality for all faiths, state leadership of church groups was no longer appropriate. That month he issued an order that permitted German Catholics and "Lichtfreunde" groups to hold services in territorial church buildings. He also abolished the Supreme Consistory, a somewhat autonomous body independent of the ministry that the king had established in January, and assumed its responsibilities as a political minister responsible to the assembly. These actions threw fear into the hearts of many Protestants, not merely those who were conservatives.

Schwerin soon appointed a commission of clerical representatives and laymen from his department to address the question of the church's structure as an entity independent of the state. The commission met only once, but it was unanimous in recommending a presbyterial and synodal polity structure that would give voting rights to all members of the territorial church. According to the commission's plans, laymen would outnumber clergymen in the territorial synod by a ratio of four to three. It was clear that church polity would be one of the fields on which the larger political battle over constitutionalism would be fought.

The impact of political events on church-political discussions was great. This was evident, for example, in an unofficial gathering of pastors in Berlin that met every other week between July of 1848 and May of 1849. Bishop David Neander issued the invitation, which was accepted by all the regular pastors in Berlin's three circuits, together with their superivisors, and other pastors serving in non-parish positions (including the theological professors Otto von Gerlach and Nitzsch, but not Hengstenberg). Attendance was spotty around the sixtieth session, and again toward the end.

This so-called "Berlin Synod" was not a gathering of radical leftists as much as a series of meetings attended by mostly older pastors. Neander himself was 76 years old, and a number of others had been born in the eighteenth century.

This was one reason why political events set the tone of the meetings. Early in the agenda, the pastors laid plans to memorialize the Frankfurt Assembly and the Prussian king, but this never happened. In the eighth session the synod seemed to have a consensus that a "constituting" assembly should be called for Prussia's territorial church, since the king's role was unclear and congregations were not equipped to provide much input. The question about who should vote in proposed church elections stirred heavy debate in the Berlin Synod, and the group turned its attention to the role of confessions in the local and territorial church to mark time, while the larger political questions—of which church voting rights were a subset—were answered elsewhere.

The king's promulgation of Prussia's constitution late in 1848 sparked a desire in the Synod to speak some "word" to congregations in view of constitutional provisions for an independent church, but the nature of that "word" was not easily decided. In fact, no "word" was issued before the Synod adjourned in May of 1849, after attendance plummeted. It was clear that the Synod would go nowhere, and it adjourned of its own will before church authorities forced its adjournment.

This Synod achieved nothing because it lacked decisive leadership and relied on the larger political context for direction. It was never meant to be more than a pastoral debating society, under semiofficial auspices. It was an exercise in "freedom within authority," and its participants shadowed larger political developments with finesse. Verbosity was valued more than action in times that cried out for evangelical leadership.

Things were not much better on the larger church scene in Prussia. Political pressures moved church political decisions to the right in reaction to Schwerin's proposals for constitutional polity. The new minister of ecclesiastical affairs, von Ladenburg, served intermittedly as acting minister before filling the office permanently between November of 1848 and December of 1850. He moderated earlier church polity proposals with the suggestion that the government's ecclesiastical administration would retain power until a self-sufficient organization could be created for the church. Seeking advice from consistories and theological faculties, he learned that most of them rejected the idea of a constituting synod to create such an autonomous polity, and representative polity in general. The theological faculty at Berlin indicated that it was contradictory to refer in the same breath to universal suffrage and truly <i.e., spiritually> representative church government, since democratic principles would soon destroy the church's biblical and confessional foundation. It was apparent that church polity would have to wait for larger political decisions, specifically the question of how the monarchy would absorb constitutionalism.

Political dissatisfaction in Prussia during the revolution focused on the monarchy's absolutist powers. The revolutionaries, and eventually some moderate conservatives, hoped to gain a participatory role in politics through a republic or a constitutional monarchy. The question of a constitution was as old as new Prussia. On several occasions, Frederick III had promised to promulgate a constitution, but one delay followed another. And when Frederick William IV addressed the opening session of the United Diet in April, 1847, he reiterated the throne's bottom line position:

> I am impelled to the solemn declaration that no
> power on earth shall move me to transform into a
> conventional and constitutional relationship that
> bond between princes and people, whose intrinsic
> worth it is which renders us so mighty, and that
> neither now nor ever will I allow a scribbled sheet
> of paper to intervene, like a second providence,
> between our God in heaven, and this land of ours,
> to rule us by paragraphs.

Prussia's popular assembly, which was more radical than the Frankfurt Parliament, voted in October of 1848 by 217 to 134 to strike the phrase "by the grace of God" from the king's title. This laid the ax to the root.

Neither the Prussian king nor his conservative advisors waited for this decision to initiate counterrevolutionary activity, but it added drama and immediacy to their work. The king was among the last to understand that he could stage a successful "Putsch" on his own behalf; although he had the tactical power, he at first lacked the will power. But his backbone stiffened during a trip to Cologne in

August, 1848, to celebrate the anniversary of the cathedral's reconstruction program. While an officer reported that "the king's carriage was plastered with manure in Duesseldorf," Frederick received a warm welcome in Cologne while the imperial agent, Archduke John, got a lackadaisical reception. This, as much as his counselors' advice, probably influenced Frederick to turn toward counterrevolution.

In the same month that the king travelled to Cologne, a group of landed aristocrats assembled for a "Junkerparlament" in Berlin. In this forum, landowners hoped to compete with the Frankfurt Assembly and defend their prerogatives. They quickly firmed up support among peasants on their estates, among small townspeople, and among a small number of artisans. Protestant clergymen flocked to their assistance, partly because some of the "Junkers" were patrons of their churches, and patriotic groups and conservative pastoral societies soon mushroomed throughout Prussia.

We have already noted that by the fall of 1848, particularism once more had the upper hand as the initiative passed from Frankfurt to the states. The prevailing motto appeared to have been, "cujus regio, ejus revolutio" ("whoever rules, his is the revolution"). In Prussia, the king's kitchen cabinet of ultraconservative advisors and personal friends were plotting their next move. Dubbed the "Camarilla," and described by Ludwig von Gerlach as the "king's advisors when he wants to be rid of his ministers, but cannot," this circle included Ludwig's brother Leopold, Edwin von Mantueffel, H. H. von Kleist-Retzow, Baron Senfft von Pilsach, Georg von Bauch, Ludwig von Massow, Keller, Stolberg, Niebuhr, and others. The group opposed any concessions, and urged the use of force against revolutionaries.

In November the king appointed a new ministry with the conservative Count Brandenburg at its head. The conservative coup ensued with the forced adjournment of the assembly on November 9, and its transfer from Berlin to the small town of Brandenburg to reconvene in fifteen days. When some of the deputies defied the order, more than ten thousand fresh troops marched into Berlin on November 11 in a show of force. Two days later, Prussia was declared in a state of siege, and on December 5 the king dissolved the assembly and promulgated a constitution that promised more than it delivered.

Church-related issues had contributed to the rising conservative tide, especially concern over a constitutional provision proposed by the assembly that assigned supervision of public schools to public authorities, instead of to ecclesiastical supervisors. In provincial Saxony, evangelical clergymen feared that this would result in sectarian teachers taking over religious instruction in state schools. This issue also attracted conservative Roman Catholics to the largely Protestant conservative movement in Prussia. In the fall of 1848, Roman Catholic ecclesiastical authorities in the Rhineland began moving away from the liberals, and especially in Silesia they attached themselves openly to the conservative movement because of the proposed separation of church and school. In their conference at Wuerzburg, the Roman Catholic bishops upheld the right to inspect and direct schools where Catholic doctrine was taught; while they wanted independence for the church, they did not want separation of church and state. This argument was compatible with the thoughts of many Prussian Protestants.

The constitution promulgated by the Prussian king in December of 1848 was a rather liberal document. Political considerations, including Prussia's desire to lead a unification movement among German states, provided the rationale for this action. The constitution guaranteed civil and political rights without regard for religious affiliation, abolished church patronage, recognized only civil marriages as legally valid, and freed schools from ecclesiastical supervision by placing them under educational authorities. The most important article on religious matters was the twelfth:

> The Evangelical and the Roman Catholic church, like every other religious organization, order and admin- ister their affairs autonomously, and continue to retain ownership and use of the institutions, endow- ments, and funds allotted for furthering their acti- vities in worship, education, and charity.

While the article provided for the independence of the

Evangelical and Roman churches, it was more prescriptive than the pertinent Frankfurt paragraph in that it formally distinguished these churches from other religious groups, giving them a slight advantage.

In January of 1849, the king created an autonomous section within the ministry of ecclesiastical affairs to handle internal Protestant affairs. It was later to become the High Church Council. This was the start of a revisionist process through which the best of two worlds would be retained: the king continued to exercise controlling leadership in the evangelical church, while the church purportedly continued to mature in its independence. The unwritten religious charter could not be destroyed by a small band of liberal constitutionalists, at least not in Prussia.

The new elections in February of 1849 provided a vote of confidence for the king's actions, and the right wing achieved a comfortable majority in both Prussian houses. In a circular letter published early in January preparatory to the elections, such eminent conservative evangelical laymen as Bethmann-Hollweg, Bismarck, Stahl, Savigny, Ludwig von Gerlach, and others offered the following advice:

> The clergy should be obliged to demand votes <from their congregations> along the lines of obedience to law and authority and faithfulness to the king, as well as attention to the right and the neighbor's possessions. They should make these appeals through their moral authority, and through all means of instruction that are compatible with the law, and with the esteem of their office.

Evangelical pastors openly supported conservative candidates in the election; some campaigned from the pulpit, while others opened election day with appropriate hymns and prayers in the churches where balloting occurred. One district in Minden-Ravensberg responded by electing a Protestant pastor named C. Huchzmeier to the Prussian parliament.

The conservative takeover in Prussia was complete. In orchestrated fashion, the government went through the motion of signalling its liberal intentions, but soon troops from other states joined the Prussians in quelling new revolutionary outbreaks. In March of 1849, Frederick William IV decorously refused the imperial crown voted by the Frankfurt Assembly. In May and June the radicals made one last effort to regroup in the southwest, but disunity, and the presence of Prussian troops in Dresden, Frankfurt, and elsewhere in the southwest, spelled their doom. The collapse of the Rastatt fortress in Baden was the beginning of the end of Germany's philosophical approach to politics.

By 1850 Prussia was fully capable of swallowing constitutionalism, especially since the constitution of December, 1848, was revised appreciably in the new constitution promulgated by the king in 1850. While the parliament's deputies debated the final wording of the constitution in the fall of 1849, during the same period that Prussian clergymen lost their exemption from the class tax, the king had the final word in formulating the constitution that prevailed in Prussia until 1918. While taking his oath to the constitution of February, 1850, the king struck the keynote with these words: "For in Prussia the king must rule, and I rule not because it is also my good pleasure to do so—God knows that!—but because it is God's command." He ruled through a three-class voting system that elected the deputies of the lower chamber. One third of the deputies were elected by five percent of the eligible voters, one third by fifteen percent, and one third by the remaining eighty percent.

The constitution glossed over some difficulties in the 1848 document. It left to future legislation the problems of church patronage and civil marriage. Article Twenty-Four was appropriately ambiguous about separating church and school: "As much as possible, confessional circumstances are to be taken into consideration in establishing public schools." The article on church independence was taken over verbatim from the 1848 document, but the new article that preceded it left little doubt that full separation of church and state was not contemplated: "The Christian religion will lay at the basis of those areas of the state that are related to the practice of religion, without prejudice to the religious freedom guaranteed in Article 12." In June of 1850, the minister of ecclesiastical affairs made a move toward autonomous church polity by instituting a "Gemeindeordnung" (congregational rule) for each parish.

260

Elected by heads of households, the church council was to supervise the congregation's worship and property and represent the congregation in school matters. But since the program was unacceptable to conservatives, who had an inbred dislike of anything democratic, it was cancelled by the new Minister of Ecclesiastical Affairs, Karl Otto von Raumer (1805-1859), who took office in December of 1850.

Von Raumer held the office during what came to be known as the "Reaction" in Prussia, from 1850 to 1858. He "discovered" the truth that the territorial prince ruled the church not as head of state, but as chief member of the church. In this sense, the church's constitution was the "church law of the territorial prince." Most Protestants seemed to be satisfied that the constitutional provision for an independent church could be implemented effectively in this way; it was assumed that as head of the church, the king was functioning differently than as head of state. The High Church Council was instituted in 1850 so that the church could handle its internal affairs autonomously, but, as we shall see below, this was little more than a facade. In addition to cancelling the "Gemeindeordnung," von Raumer also put a stop to the creation of a synodal structure. The liberal church historian Hase called this manipulation of the constitutional provision a "scornful treatment of the legal autonomy of the church."

The king's response to the constitutional provision for an independent Protestant church was a royal decree that he issued on June 29, 1850, establishing the High Church Council ("Oberkirchenrat"). He picked five lawyers and five clergymen to serve on this high-level commission charged with administering the church's internal affairs. As president he appointed Rodolf von Uechtritz, a Silesian jurist with a pedantic zeal for order, who had chaired the evangelical section of the Ministry of Ecclesiastical Affairs. This section had begun to manage the church's internal business, but now was dissolved.

Officially the Council was responsible for the church's internal affairs, but its composition and nature ensured that internal matters would not be decided without consideration of administrative repercussions. This, of course, was a two-way street. The chief of chaplains of the Prussian army was one of the clerical appointees; in his person he represented both the chaplain's corps, which like the rest of the army was under royal control, and the "military church" to which the chaplains ministered. The king created the Council as supreme bishop of the church, but as territorial prince in a constitutional government, he administered the church's external affairs, as well as through a minister responsible to the parliament. The relative impotence of the independent church's Council can be measured by its budetary allocations; while 100,000 "Thaler" were budgeted for all evangelical consistories in Prussia in 1849, only 16,000 "Thaler" were allocated in 1851 for the Council's activities.

The king created the Council partly to distract those who wanted independent church polity. This movement reached alarming proportions in 1848. The independent evangelical section of the Ministry of Ecclesiastical Affairs was supposed to serve provisionally until a constituting synod was held, but the Council's formation dealt a death blow to this ideal. The royal decree constituting the Council stated that such a synod was neither advantageous nor legally required for the church's independence; the territorial ecclesiastical administration would seek to be not only supervisory and jurisdictional in nature, but also to serve the church as it was epitomized in its principal member, the king. The Council was the answer to an important question: How could a constitutional monarch, whose ministers were responsible to parliament, continue to exercise his authority over the church as chief bishop? The solution was so effective that after 1918 people joked that only two conservative institutions outlived the monarch, namely, the High Church Council and the Social Democratic Party. The Council lasted for 101 years.

Acting in compliance with the king's empowering order, the Council made one of its first orders of business in 1850 to formulate a new parish constitution for the eastern provinces. The arrangement provided that the church council or presbytery was to be chosen by the pastor, the patron, and representatives from the consistory, not elected by heads of households. But most clegymen in the east rejected even this proposal, arguing that it smacked of liberalism, incited the revolutionary spirit, and weakened the office of the ministry. In essence, this optional plan was shelved for another twenty-five years in the eastern provinces.

Meanwhile, von Raumer continued to insist before the new Prussian parliament that the creation of the High Church Council filled the constitutional requirement for an independent Protestant church. He asserted that state authorities had no right to interfere with the constitutional structure of the evangelical church, although that was happening all along, just as the chambers had no authority to pass resolutions regarding the evangelical church's polity. But he insisted that the Council submit a copy of its minutes to him as Minister; this insistence stirred deep resentment in Uechtritz, who felt it necessary to report directly to the king. Such bureaucratic infighting confused the real issue, namely, the church's independence, and although the Council took some steps in that direction, it functioned under the shadow of the bishop-king.

Developments in church polity in other German states differed little from the Prussian giant during these years, even though some states already had constitutions for as long as twenty or thirty years. Nowhere was a fully independent church achieved. Steps toward a more representative church order were taken in Hanover, but arrested early in 1849. Some advances occurred in Thuringia, and in Wuerttemberg, lay members joined the pastors' councils after 1851, and after 1854 diocesan synods began meeting annually. But Sixt Karl Kapff helped keep the movement in check during the revolutionary years with his emphasis on the firm unity of church and state, consistory and monarchy. In Oldenbourg, a new constitution in 1849 separated church and state, and generally put church administration into the hands of a synod. But conservatives issued a new constitution in 1853 enabling the grand duke to function as the church's head through a High Church Council.

In Hesse, the confessionalist Vilmar, a church administrator, was no friend of territorial church government. But his kind of independent church government was no less conservative and reactionary because of its strong emphasis on the ministerial office. Under the skillful leadership of Kliefoth, the High Church Council in Mecklenberg temporized earlier liberalizing efforts, much as had occurred in Prussia. In 1849 Lutherans in Bavaria witnessed the unification of the two general synods of the consistorial areas of Ansbach and Bayreuth, and the strengthening of lay involvement in synods, as well as a relaxation of strictures against voluntary societies; Reformed congregations were given their own synod in 1853. But everywhere it seemed that democratization of church government was not all that popular. One is reminded of the question that a pastor from Dessau asked Ernst Ludwig von Gerlach as they returned by rail from the conference at Wittenberg in September of 1848. How, he asked, should he address the issue of democratizing church government, when not a single educated layman in his area was a Christian? It was easier to accept the status quo even if, as in Prussia, the constitution guaranteed the church's independence.

Church Press

The counterrevolution gained momentum slowly. But one factor that contributed markedly to its success, especially in Prussia, was the popular support given to the crown in conservative periodicals, including those edited by churchmen. A corollary was their opposition to basic reforms in church polity. The unwritten religious charter lay at the basis of this dual attack.

In 1848, Hengstenberg's EVANGELICAL CHURCH NEWS consistently rejected plans for elective representation in church polity. The paper also commented on political events that had religious ramifications—and for Hengstenberg, they all did! Although the paper never had more than 1,000 subscribers, its influence was extensive during the revolutionary years. Soon after the March uprising in Berlin, the NEWS provided this analysis: "Now finally everyone can understand it. Events of the last week have revealed loudly and clearly that state and church, law and Scripture, are inexorably connected. We cannot divorce ourselves from one without offending the other." Enemies of the church were political demagogues, and enemies of the state were also enemies of the church, Hengstenberg argued. In mid-April the paper urged all evangelical pastors to boycott all revolutionary activity, and not to assist revolutionary forces. Invoking Luther, the writer argued that revolution was a heinous sin against God and man since the dynasty provided structure for the state, and the state for the people. On April 22, Hengstenberg charged that revolution was nothing less than large-scale Gallicanism, systematically destroying Germany's moral fibre; insurrection was not Teutonic. He added that "Christianity opposes all revolution. Some day those clerics who recently bestowed the church's benediction on the Berlin rebels <at their burial> will be judged very severely."

While not a church periodical, the NEW PRUSSIAN NEWS (NEUE PREUSSISCHE ZEITUNG) was another important conservative mouthpiece. It was initially financed by the Russian ambassador in Berlin, members of the "Camarilla," and other Prussian "Junkers." The paper was nicknamed the "CROSS GAZETTE" (KREUZZEITUNG) since its masthead included the motto, "With God for King and Fatherland," together with the Iron Cross, the patriotic medal first offered during the War of Liberation. Time after time its issues charged that nationalism, liberalism, and democracy would lead Prussia down the primrose path to communism and anarchy. Editors and contributors argued for continued close cooperation between church and state, noting that for its part the church would continue to uphold the state's authority. Openly anti-Semitic, the CROSS GAZETTE firmly supported Prussian particularism in opposition to German unification at Prussia's expense. One frequent contributor was the lay theologian, Ernst Ludwig von Gerlach, who wrote in 1848 that the revolutionary battle lines did not separate Christians and non-Christians, but proponents and opponents of Christianity. One of his monthly political reviews observed in 1849 that "the German is really not simply a member of one nation in opposition to other nations, but in still another sense, like other Christians, a cosmopolitan citizen, partner in the kingdom of God. The kingdom of God is his fatherland."

With the inauguration of freedom of the press during the revolutions, a number of Christian Sunday papers appeared, and they too contributed to the impetus of the conservative movement. Meanwhile, in Wuerttemberg the CHRISTIAN MESSENGER prefigured the reaction of the fifties with a major statement in March, 1849, that firmly opposed revolutionary and liberalizing tendencies. It argued that absence of fear of God had led to present difficulties; parties and political changes would bring no solution. Revolution lacked a biblical basis since the Bible urged

265

people to honor authorities, especially such an excellent one as Wuerttemberg's king. Kapff, one of the authors of the article, served for a time in Wuerttemberg's assembly as a monarchical-conservative deputy, and joined about 700 pietists in the short-lived Christian Political People's Society in 1849.

The PILGRIM FROM SAXONY provided conservative readers in Saxony with a consistent anti-revolutionary line, blaming the uprisings on rationalist control of church and school. In provincial Saxony, the chief conservative paper was the POPULAR NEWS FOR TOWN AND CHURCH (VOLKSBLATT FUER STADT UND LAND). Soon after the uprisings in Berlin, Ernst Ludwig von Gerlach and Hermann Wagener appointed as editor a reactionary named Friedrich von Florecourt. The paper's strong endorsement of conservative causes was reinforced in 1849 by the appointment of Philipp von Nathusius, a pietist industrialist, as editor.

Inner Mission

Some auxiliary societies of the newly organized Inner Mission also published periodicals to further their goals, both eleemosynary and political. Such papers appeared in the Prussian provinces of Silesia, Prussia, and Pomerania. The same sort of message was trumpeted in FLY-LEAVES (FLIEGENDE BLAETTER), the journal that soon became the official mouthpiece of the Central Committee of the Inner Mission. Less than a year after it first appeared in 1844 under Wichern's editorial pen, the journal had 1,500 subscribers. By early 1849 the press was running 2,000 copies for delivery throughout Germany, and by September, 1854, over 3,000 copies of each issue, and 7,000 copies of its popular supplement, were being mailed. Wichern inaugurated the supplement in 1850 to provide the masses with more "devotional" discussions of the Mission's goals.

A number of Evangelical Societies were organized in many parts of Prussia in the fall and winter of 1848. Their lay and clergy members actively defended orthodoxy, supported the benevolent work of the Inner Mission proposed by Wichern at Wittenberg, and opposed some of the provisions of the proposed Prussian constitution. Karl Gutzkow was not writing in the sand when, in the novel entitled DIE RITTER

VOM GEISTE (1850-52), he portrayed a Berlin salon frequented by representatives of the Inner Mission as a nerve center of reactionary propaganda in 1848. Conservative politicians viewed these societies, as well as the Protestant clergy, as natural allies.

The Inner Mission was slowly gathering power and influence in 1848 and 1849, and in the process Wichern was able to use his rhetorical skills on behalf of the conservative counterrevolution. In May, 1848, he had portrayed communism as attacking the foundational principles of state, church, and their cooperative partnership, from which the kingdom of God would emerge. Atheistic and anti-Christian spiritual forces unleashed by the devil were bent on destroying all trust in authority and all reliance on the ideas of justice, truth, and freedom, he said. He added that the Inner Mission would defend the state against these enemies without reward since the Mission was deeply anchored in freedom, and lived only to serve.

A citizen of the free city of Hamburg, Wichern had been inching toward the Prussian king for some time. His first royal audience in 1843 was followed by another in November of 1849, after the cancellation in 1848, and a third some days later. He discussed penal reform at length with the king in the fall of 1850. Ordered by the king to assess the effectiveness of Prussia's penal system, he toured prisons in all Prussian provinces in 1852 and 1853, and, as we shall see below, became a tireless prison reformer.

But the work of the Inner Mission was not limited to the activities of one man. Wichern made good his promise at Wittenberg to publish an extended discussion of the Inner Mission's assignments. In his full-scale study of the subject, entitled DENKSCHRIFT (1849), he proposed the following activities for Inner Mission societies throughout the land: stimulating and coordinating prison work and penal reform; distributing Bibles and tracts; nurturing home devotions and Bible study; establishing evangelical presses, libraries and newspapers; employing colporteurs, traveling evangelists and street preachers; employing theological candidates while waiting for parish assignments; caring for the poor, sick and aged; founding children's homes and societies for prison visitation; recruiting and training workers for all aspects of Inner Mission activity;

267

confronting moral issues in society, such as drunkenness, prostitution and illegitimacy; sustaining a ministry to migrant workers, factory workers, day laborers and young people; increasing the supply of adequate housing; stimulating local congregations to charitable work; creating workingmen's associations; and caring for the German diaspora throughout Europe and across the Atlantic.

A number of societies and institutions in the German states were already involved in some of these activities, but Wichern hoped to provide an organizational focus to stimulate fuller participation, and increase the number of local societies and agencies. His memorandum insisted that the Inner Mission's activities should concentrate in three divinely instituted areas: church, state, and the family unit. His discussion of the interdependence of these three orders left little doubt about the counterrevolutionary impact of the Mission:

> The free adoption or disavowal of these orders of God remains the nation's final choice of salvation or destruction. With the renunciation of these orders, the state, church and society break up into wild, anarchical chaos. . . . But with the reaffirmation of these orders, or with the return to them, chaos vanishes in the same way.

According to Wichern, God's hand was the source of state, church and society.

The Inner Mission seemed to grow as the counterrevolution gained ground. Wichern reported in the spring of 1849 that fifty-nine agents and five correspondents throughout Germany were serving the Mission's cause. Thirty-six of the agents were from the provinces of Prussia, together with four of the five correspondents; the total included important church figures such as Richard Rothe in Baden, and Friedrich Fabri in Bavaria. By August of the same year, the numbers of agents and representatives climbed to 116 and 16 respectively. Wichern wrote in FLY-LEAVES in March of 1849 that revolutionaries seeking to destroy God's kingdom, His throne, and His ordinances had been foiled through the Mission's progress. He added that "our fatherland is still not lost if the church raises the banner of the eternal King and Savior." In June he had noted that the Mission was gaining ready acceptance wherever pastoral conferences and provincial synods met.

In the meantime, a number of local societies were affiliating with the Inner Mission's Central Committee. Twelve societies had entered into agreement with the Committee by April of 1849, and by August the number doubled. Five years later Wichern announced that ninety-eight societies and institutions were affiliated. Later it was his practice to speak of local societies that had no official affiliation with the committee as part of Germany's "inner mission," although he did not include them in his statistical tabulations. While no one has fully analyzed the political impact of these societies and their local auxiliaries during the years of revolution and reaction, the groups were probably the staging area for many of the shock troops of counterrevolution and reaction in a number of states, especially Prussia.

The annual meeting of the "Kirchentag," during which Inner Mission activities were also considered, provided another opportunity for conservatives to garner support. The notables who assembled in 1849 passed a Declaration of Thanksgiving, Confession and Prayer to God for coming to their rescue in 1848. The declaration lamented the calamities that would befall everyone if church disestablishment occurred, as seemed so imminent at the time. It urged people to confess the sins that brought them to that point in time, and requested that congregations focus on such problems during the Reformation season.

In southern Germany as well, various Protestant societies gave impetus to counterrevolutionary pressures. In its annual report in 1849, Wuerttemberg's Bible Society assured the king that by distributing Bibles, it hoped to nurture "respect for the king as the divinely appointed one, reverence for all authority, obedience to the law, good manners, morals, loyalty, patience, self-abnegation, public spirit and fraternity." The implication was that the Bible stood on the side of the counterrevolutionaries. In northwestern Germany, especially in Bergerland and the Ruhr area, thirty-six pastors organized the Evangelical Association in the summer of 1848 to combat "de-christianizing" influences that had recently manifested themselves. The association used evangelization, literature

269

publication, Bible groups, city missions (the first was organized in Breslau in 1855), and house visits to attain its goals.

PATTERNED RESPONSES TO REVOLUTION

At this point it will be helpful to examine how most churchmen responded to revolutionary events, in order to see how their responses meshed with their allegiance to the unwritten religious charter. Without claiming that they alone were responsible for the successes of the counterrevolution, we can trace their responses to revolution to the focal point, as well as their theological interpretation of revolutionary activities, which seemed to carry great weight in public opinion. That was the prevailing consensus about the church's responsibility to the state, and its function in society.

Evangelical churchmen and lay leaders, particularly those in the conservative wing, contributed to the failure of the revolutions of 1848-49. Their patterned responses involved three elements: they avoided the temptation to immediately reject revolutionary advances; they avoided the real issues at stake as portrayed by the revolutionaries; and they provided a theological interpetation of the revolutionary thrust for freedom.

The conservatives were well trained for their initial response to revolution. The religious charter they cherished prepared them to adjust rapidly to political changes; that was part of the agreement. If a new kind of government emerged, it was relatively simple to switch allegiance, as long as this new government demanded obedience; this was a critical element in the unwritten charter. Perhaps it was possible to buy some time, as long as evangelical conservatives did not reject all the initial achievements of the revolutionaries.

The conservatives' call to "wait and see" rang from one end of Germany to the other. Early in the revolution, the important Swabian evangelical, Immanuel G. Kolb, asked his

270

Protestant brothers in Baden not to overthrow the new powers with force, since some pietists saw the End as near. One of them refused to run for election to the Frankfurt Assembly, not because of the nature of the parliament, but because he would have to take an oath to do so. In Hesse, Vilmar's HESSIAN PEOPLE'S FRIEND announced that the adopted changes in governmental structure came through God's will, and a Christian could accept them "without transgressing a commandment of religion or of conscience." Vilmar heartily endorsed moves aimed at achieving German unity. And in Leipzig, Adolf G. Harless took a positive attitude toward the March uprisings as a way of moderating the absolutist state. In May of 1848 he commended the parliament that was to meet in Frankfurt.

Avoiding real political issues was also implicit in the unwritten charter. Churches were to occupy themselves in their own niche; within prescribed boundaries, churchmen had some latitude, as well as the right to continue debating confessional differences. In the revolutionary period, the way to avoid issues was to discuss what consequences would follow from this or that political change. For example, Protestant liberals concentrated their attention on church polity in preparation for an independent church, since for them the revolution was a church-political event. Another way to consider consequnces was to discuss the formation of a national church.

Churchmen also contributed to the rupture of the alliance between middle class liberal leaders, and artisans and lower class musclemen who had generated the uprisings. They avoided the major issues raised by the leaders, namely, shared power, by turning their attention to church polity (liberal Protestants), or the spiritual and moral context within which political constitutionalism was emerging (middle ground Protestants). They addressed the problems of the lower classes through a first-aid coalition called the Inner Mission, whose primary purpose was to bandage the wounds of society, not to treat the patient as a whole social person. Their concentration on the symptoms of deeper problems helped dissolve the alliance, and all the while, conservative churchmen avoided the real issues by couching their responses in terms of obedience to God and king.

The most significant contribution by Protestants to the failure of the revolutions was that they provided a theological interpretation of the movement for freedom. In the process, they encouraged the conflation of theological and political conservatism. But this was understandable since it was part of their assigned responsibility within the religious consensus. While liberal and middle-road clerics at first performed their duty in an indirect way, the conservatives did not hesitate to use their most influential arguments once the initial shock wore off.

Theological interpretations of the revolution fell into two basic categories, radical and conservative. Since the German clergy included few radicals, the majority joined the other camp, although only a small number verbalized their conservative theological interpretations of revolution. They argued that revolution was destroying divinely ordained institutions, and one could participate only at the cost of disobeying God and His appointed authorities. Little wonder that in 1848, the Protestant painter Alfred Rethel (1816-1859) created a woodcut of 10,000 prints, entitled "Also a Death Dance." It showed death at work in the 1848 uprisings; God sustained life through the institutions He ordained for mankind, and efforts to wreck them led to death.

The year 1848 was seen as the heyday of rationalism, the culmination of its onslaught against state and religion. Hengstenberg's EVANGELICAL CHURCH NEWS portrayed rationalism as the enemy of both; arguments levelled against this destructive force echoed motifs from the early Awakening. Since atheism was the power behind democracy, church and state were engaged in a survival struggle with revolution. Hengstenberg wrote that monarchy was a distinctly Germanic political contribution that contrasted markedly with the "poison" of the Gallican state. The rationalists' ultimate political objective was to eliminate the monarch and inaugurate a republic, in the same sort of atheistic coup that proposed to ignore God and His church.

The conservatives' theological interpretation of the revolution did not prevent them from accomodating some of the revolutionaries' demands. Conservatives in Prussia accomodated constitutionalism at different levels, Stahl more quickly than Ludwig von Gerlach; but they followed the king's lead, and had few objections once he promulgated a constitution. As long as the contextual fabric of obedience remained intact, they could accede; this fabric was the basic theological foundation of their politics. But at all costs, the connection between obedience to God and obedience to the king had to be retained, since this was the most critical element, the linchpin, in the religious charter. The citizen's cooperation with the monarch was acceptable if he invited it, but activity against the monarch was a transgression against both him and God.

By 1850 in Hesse, even Vilmar's tune had changed. He summarily offered his readers a conservative theological interpretation of the day's events: "The battle of our day and of the future is really no national, political battle, but in the most strict sense a divine battle ('Gotteskampf')." That same year in Wuerttemberg, Kapff published a rigidly conservative theological interpretation of the revolution; within a few months, over 8,000 copies of the small book had been distributed. And although liberal and mediating Protestants were not as openly supportive of the conservative counterrevolution as the conservative Protestants, the former's emphasis on church polity, and the latter's stress on the spiritual and moral context, supported the conservative position by default.

In the 1870s, the Roman Catholic Church in Germany engaged in a struggle with the state known as the "Kulturkampf." Roman Catholic resistance to state pressure provided a data bank of experience that was drawn upon when the Nazis assumed power sixty years later.

German Protestants had the chance to engage in their own kind of "Kulturkampf" in 1848. But because they refused to join forces with liberal and revolutionary forces, in most cases they avoided conflict with the states' governments. This was one of their last opportunities to hone the skills of resistance, before the ultimate resistance was demanded in the social and political revolution that Adolf Hitler engineered in the twentieth century. In 1848, vested interests turned most evangelicals against revolution and deprived them of valuable experience in the art of resisting.

Any number of phrases are apt descriptions of these vested interests, including "throne and altar," "pastor and patron," and "church and state." Equally applicable is our term, "unwritten religious charter," or "religious consensus." For Protestants, the revolutions of 1848 were the crucible test of the state's capacity to assign the church its proper social role. Evangelicals ensured that the church would continue to model "freedom-within-authority" for society, although a few faltered along the way. The number of radical preachers was small; slightly larger, but even more vocal, was the percentage of conservative stalwarts. After sensing what was most advantageous, those who for a while floated down the middle of the river soon rowed to the right bank.

The responses of evangelicals to the tremors from Frankfurt, together with their discussion of church independence and a national church, pointed toward eventual rejection of revolutionary goals. Counterrevolutionary movements assumed identifiable form within the churches with the formation and rapid growth of the Inner Mission; church polity modifications that met the letter, but not the spirit of constitutional provisions for church independence; and strong support for conservative views in most church periodicals. Along with the patterned responses of most churchmen to the revolutions, these activities preserved the unwritten charter intact in the dark hours of 1848–49. And in the fifties, the labors of evangelical churchmen were well rewarded.

NOTES

CHAPTER VI

(1) The upheavals of 1848–50 have been categorized in a number of ways. After discussing the "period of preparation" in the forties, Veit Valentin spoke of the "first outbreak and apparent victory" of the liberal forces (March to June, 1848), the "social-revolutionary and national threat, consequently the beginning of the counter-revolution" (June to November, 1848), the "second outbreak" (November to April, 1849), and the "victory of the counter-revolution" (November to April, 1849). See his 1848, CHAPTERS OF GERMAN HISTORY, tr. Ethel Talbot Scheffauer (London: George Allen & Unwin, 1940). Leonard Krieger simplified this schema by dividing the revolution into three phases: the dovetailing of popular and liberal movements in uprisings against authority in the spring of 1848; the separation of the political liberal movement from its supporters in society, from the summer of 1848 to the spring of 1849; and the passing of initiative from the liberals to the masses and the monarchs, between revolts in May, 1849 and the "humiliation" at Oelmuetz in November, 1850. See his THE GERMAN IDEA OF FREEDOM, HISTORY OF A POLITICAL TRADITION (Boston: Beacon Press, 1957), pp. 273–340.

(2) Theodore S. Hamerow, "1848," in THE RESPONSIBILITY OF POWER, ed. Leonard Krieger and Fritz Stern (Garden City, NY: Doubleday & Company, Inc., 1967), p. 147.

(3) Friedrich Meinecke, "Lack of Unity Among Disaffected Classes," in THE UNIFICATION OF GERMANY, 1848—1871, ed. Otto Pflanze (New York: Holt, Rinehart and Winston, 1968), p. 32.

(4) Ibid., p. 36.

(5) The Concert of Europe can be assigned some responsibility for the outcome of the revolutions in the German states. The Great Powers, each in its own way, and in pursuit of its own interests, used diplomacy to deny unity to the German states, although the domestic situation probably had a greater impact on the outcome.

(6) Horst Zillessen, PROTESTANTISMUS UND POLITISCHE FORM (Guetersloh: Verlagshaus Gerd Mohn, 1971), p. 93.

(7) Jacques Droz, LES REVOLUTIONS ALLEMANDES DES 1848, Publications de la Faculte des Lettres de l'Universite de Clermont, Ser. 2, Fasc. 6 (Paris: Presses universitaires de France, 1957), p. 481.

CHAPTER VII

REWARDS FOR RESERVISTS

In 1853 a church visitation commission made a visit to the
town of Elbing in East Prussia. When a frightening summer
storm struck the area, the darkened skies, lightning and
thunder terrified the 3,000 people attending the worship
service with the committee. The preacher stopped preaching,
and the crowd huddled together in fear. But when the members
of the visiting commission sang out the first strains of the
familiar hymn, "Stay Near Us With Your Grace, Lord Jesus
Christ," the organ and congregation sooned joined in.
According to the commission's report, it seemed as if "oil
had been poured on the waters." Devastation was everywhere
after the storm; roof tiles and window sashes lay all around
in the bright sunshine. But inside the large church, the
people and their distinguished visitors had been safe.

Safety from the storm was one reward for ecclesiastical
reservists who had been faithful during the revolutionary
years. In the main, the churches had faithfully defended the
status quo, and especially in Prussia they received
appropriate recognition during the "reactionary fifties"
(1850-58). This decade of close cooperation among
monarchical, conservative, and ecclesiastical forces showed
that, despite pommeling in the revolutionary years, the
unwritten religious charter remained intact, and the
alliance between throne and altar seemed stronger than
ever.

While bedrock conservatism prevailed, a sense of uneasiness

permeated the decade. Many felt that the abortive
revolutions settled little; unnerving social, economic,
political, intellectual and religious currents now made it
all the more important for the church to fulfil its
chartered responsibilities. Now more than ever, the church
had to be a state-approved model for society! Among all
social institutions, it could provide the clearest example
of free persons living responsibly within boundaries
delineated by authority.

During the revolutions, most of the churches compromised the
little prophetic power they had left. In fact, their
support of the status quo stimulated the growth of social
and political realism. In the fifties, culture and society
seemed to be less directly influenced by philosophical and
ideological considerations, and more immediately influenced
by "realistic" appraisals of social and political
developments. Meanwhile, relations in Prussia between
church and state were governed by an ideology whose time had
come. Conservative philosophy saluted that relationship
with the phrase, "the Christian state."

Most of the states dutifully rewarded the churches for
faithful service as social models during the revolutionary
upheavals. Church and state functioned cooperatively to
instill and nurture a conservative spirit in society, which
was the third—and distinctly inferior—party in their
triangular relationship. Two things happened in the process:
the church continued to function effectively as a social
model; and simultaneously, its modeling function became a
channel for rewarding the services that had been rendered in
revolutionary times.

But the church's continuing alliance with the state required
that it ignore the new material powers in society, or merely
note them in passing. Wichern's Inner Mission usually
bypassed basic social problems, and addressed the
implications of social issues indirectly. The theological
and spiritual challenges of these new social forces took
second place to a more pressing question: What were the
consequences of these challenges for the church as an
institution? The consensus seemed to be that, whatever
their true nature, the implications were extremely grave for
the church as a social entity. As a result, the fifties
were a time to "hold onto nurse."

As we review the triangular relationship that flourished in the fifties among monarch, preacher and social conservative, we will concentrate on parish and institutional church life. The story centers in Prussia, not only because it was the center of social and political reaction, but because this state had nearly six times as many Protestants as any other territory.

After a cursory look at how this triangle was personified in Prussia's newly created ecclesiastical visitation committees, we will examine the monarch's, conservative theorist's, and the preacher's contributions to the religious reaction of the fifties. It is clear that the Inner Mission was a microcosm of the kind of church-state cooperation that prevailed for the pedagogic benefit of the wider society. The chapter's final section investigates the church's broader relationship with society and politics, in the light of two powerful forces that were stirring in the fifties, namely, social change and nationalist sentiment.

THE REACTIONARY TRIANGLE

In Prussia at least, the most striking social reform of the reactionary decade was the completion of rural emancipation. When the king agreed to agricultural reform in 1850, he was issuing an emancipation proclamation for 640,000 peasants, more than twice as many as had been emancipated between 1811 and 1848. The conservatives were rewarding their friends by eliminating external personal servitude in the East, although social and financial restraints persisted. The conservatives also gave increased support to the artisans' guild system, so that migrants to urban centers would confront some type of united front more akin to their rural background.

In the light of these developments, it is not surprising that a novel church project was launched in the largely rural areas of the eastern provinces. The formation of "vistitation committees" to inspect churches and schools helped shore up conservative support in these parts.

Personified in these visitation commissions, the reactionary triangle of the fifties was composed of ecclesiastical bureaucrats representing the monarchical state, pastors representing the church, and aristocrats representing an ordered, conservative social structure. Church and state cooperated in nurturing a conservative, reactionary spirit in the larger society.

The first general visitation of churches was prompted by a request from the consistory in Breslau in 1852, and that autumn a commission visited the diocese of Nimptsch-Frankenstein.(1) The other church provinces in eastern Prussia followed the example with visitations in 1853. Early in 1854 the High Church Council in Berlin regularized these "extraordinary" visitations. In a document entitled "Instruction for Conducting General Church and School Visitations in the Provinces of Prussia, Brandenburg, Pomerania, Silesia, Posen and Saxony," the Council added the responsibility of visiting schools, religious institutions and jails.

According to the Council, the body charged with administering internal church affairs directly under the supervision of the "summus episcopus" (the king), the visitations were responsible for "strengthening and fortifying evangelical faith and confession, and, with the greatest possible speed, strengthening or restoring traditional evangelical morality in the congregation." Grievances were to be identified and remedied, especially those caused by the church's internal affairs. After evaluating "the total spiritual condition of the congregations, and those who work in them," the commission was to send its report to the provincial consistory, with a copy to the Council in Berlin.

The High Church Council's memorandum in 1854 included over a hundred questions to be used by commission members in their visitations. The questions covered such subjects as devotional life in the parsonage; the pastor and patron's confessional commitment; school children's familiarity with the Bible; locations of weddings and baptisms (church or home); use of private confession; local observances of Sunday as a day of rest; bigamy; ratio of legitimate to illegitimate births; drunkenness; temperance societies; dancing and the participation of school children in this practice; spiritual admonition; progress in developing a parish church council; the patron's involvement in church life; success in the use of rhythmic songs; use of agenda and liturgical appointments; length of sermon; religious instruction in school as preparation for confirmation instruction; pastor's opinion about church maintenance, and the building's general suitability; the "pastor's visit to the school, his participation in instruction and his relationship to the school teacher;" the pastor's special wishes relating to the school; and the implementation of church discipline on the occasion of the baptism of an illegitimate child, desire for the Lord's Supper by a public sinner, the burial of an unchurched person, or marriage when the female's virginity had been violated ("Deflorierte"). The last question to be asked of the pastor had the ring of an oath: "Have <you> answered these questions according to <your> best knowledge and conscience, and with sincerity, as before God?" The questions permitted the commission members to put their finger on some complicated problems, and occasionally they took advantage of the opportunity to assist the pastor in providing "pastoral" admonition aimed at rectifying a given situation. Under pressure from the visitation commission, commonlaw marriges were often legitimatized.(2)

The visitation of churches and schools allowed three interested parties to share in a common venture: ecclesiastical bureaucrats from the territory, pastors, and aristocratic laymen. While the enacting order was issued by the purportedly "independent" arm of the church, the High Church Council, the burden of the work fell to the provincial consistory and its ecclesiastical bureaucrats, the general superintendent and his superintendents. The commissions were composed of pastors and laymen representing the Council, and members or employees of the consistory, the bureaucratic "state" arm of the church charged with external affairs and personnel. For example, the commission that visited the diocese of Mohrungen in the province of East Prussia in 1856 included three pastors and eight laymen representing the Council, and four other "spiritual" members from the administrative branch of the church, including the general superintendent, two superintendents, and a member of the consistory.

That the visitations were a cooperative effort between

281

church and state is clear from the commission's composition. In view of the High Church Council's immediate supervision by the king, which violated the constitutional provision for an independent church, one hesitates to suggest that "church" existed as an independent body. But given the realities of the Prussian situation, this can be viewed as a cooperative effort between "independent" and territorial administrations of the church.

Social conservatism was apparent not only in the nature of the cooperation itself, but in the social status of the laymen who were appointed to the commissions. The commission that visited the diocese of Mohrungen in 1856 included among its eight laymen, or "secular assistants" as they were called, a member of the province's chief governing council, two chairmen of rural district councils, and five manorial lords. Only the member of the chief governing council and one chairman accompanied the team at all times, but the six other laymen divided the visit into three equal parts. Close cooperation between officals of church and state ensured that peasants were free to attend the special services at each site. In a district paper, the chairman of the rural district council requested that estate owners release their workers from obligations on days when the commission visited a local parish.

The team visited twenty-five congregations in the diocese. The commission noted that organs enlivened worship services; only two congregations had not experienced the philanthropy that had recently provided most of the others with organs. The commission tagged four pastors as "especially gifted and impressive preachers," but balanced the ticket with the names of three others who were unsatisfactory because of doctrine or other reasons.

After several years of experimentation, it was determined that expenses were too high to carry on such an intense schedule of visitations. The High Church Council ordered in 1856 that each province limit the number of visitation commissons to one or two a year. In 1858 the number of people on the commissions was also reduced to cut costs. The visitations seemed to be patterned after the visits made to congregations during the Reformation era, when the prince ruled the church as chief bishop. But the publicist Hengstenberg had a more precise dogmatic purpose in mind when he wrote in his paper in 1853 that the commissions should put an end to clerical involvement in Freemasonry.

Most clergymen visited by these commissions in the eastern provinces of Prussia seemed to have been cut from the same piece of cloth. Conservative and proper, these semi-officials of the state were excellent representatives of the status quo. After most of them had gone beardless for several decades, the church administrators made it official: pastors were prohibited from sporting a full beard because it was a token of unchurchly sentiment. Their street clothes were to be compatible with their position, and were to give no offense to the pastoral office. The government laid down provisions for appropriate liturgical apparel, and warned that unauthorized use of vestments was punishable by a fine of 100 "Thaler" or three months in jail.

But at least the clergymen were not forced into military uniforms, unless they agreed to serve as army chaplains. In 1858, Prussia's minister of war and the minister of interior agreed on regulations that exempted students of evangelical theology from military service, although pastors were still obliged to loan their horses to the army upon demand.

Pastors were expected to obey divinely ordained authority and, in accord with the law, to speak out against those intent on destroying society. Prussia's territorial law authorized confidential communication between clergyman and parishioner; breaking confidentiality could bring the loss of one's pension. But if the pastor knew of circumstances that posed a very grave danger to the state, he was required to divulge the information. It was also appropriate to break confidentiality if his cooperation was required to apprehend a criminal.

The pastor received a rather meagre salary for his work except in the Rhineland, where each congregation was responsible for the pastor's support. But even this plan had inequities. Pastoral salaries in that area in 1859 ranged from 1,400 "Thaler" in Duesseldorf and 1,200 in Elberfeld, to 300 in Loevenich and 250 in Ronsdorf. The poor pastor in Kircherten had to live on an annual salary of 82 "Thaler."

Prussian law prevented pastors and their families from supplementing their income with any kind of commercial activity. With special permission from their superiors, they could engage in agricultural work or small-time farming. Pastors were also legally restrained from getting involved in the complex question of royal hunting grounds and hunting parties. Fees for performing baptisms, weddings and funerals added to their income; strict parish boundaries helped keep finances straight, and poaching on another's territory was illegal unless permission was granted. Local courts handled the proceedings if a pastor wanted to sue for uncollected fees, and legal forms for this process were readily available.

Marriage fees added to the clergyman's income, but he was not free to marry anyone who asked. Special dispensation was required to marry two adulterers who caused the dissolution of their previous marriages. A nobleman could marry a female from the peasant or "burgher" class only in a marriage "of the left hand," but an aristocratic female could marry a man from the lower classes, as well as a nobleman who had give up his nobility.

The most difficult fee-related question was a proposed marriage between Christian and Jew. Territorial law prohibited marriages in which the non-Christian was prevented by the principles of his or her religion from being subject to Christian marital laws. A very complicated case arose in Silesian Glogau in the fifties, when an evangelical Prussian army officer married a Jewish woman, who was a member of an independent German Catholic congregation in the city. After their marriage in 1850, it became known that she was Jewish, but she had not been baptized even though she was a member of this free congregation. She was baptized in 1853 after permitting two children to be be baptized earlier at birth, but in 1854 the state's attorney announced that a clergyman would have to marry them, since he did not recognize their earlier union. The ensuing court proceedings highlighted the importance of the "Christian state," and the clergyman's pivotal role in the marriage contract. A related problem was the question of who determined the dogmatic position of such an independent congregation. Prussia's Supreme Court ruled that in view of the circumstances the original marriage remained valid, not because the woman thought herself to be a Christian when she first married, but because she was subsequently baptized.(3)

THE MONARCH'S CONTRIBUTION

After the revolutions of 1848, the monarchical principle remained in force in all the German states. In most, the prince or monarch courted the church as one of the supporting girders of his rule. This was especially true in Prussia, where all signs of Frederick William IV's earlier liberalism vanished. The monarch did not always personally endorse actions aimed at solidifying relations between throne and altar, of course, but there is little doubt that he approved of most. Religious instruction in the schools, programs of church construction, and the Evangelical Alliance showed that the state was interested in perpetuating the reactionary triangle of the fifties, and with it, the unwritten religious charter. As he assisted the preacher, the monarch served his own interests, as well as those of social and political conservatives. This dynamic within the reactionary triangle made it easier for the church to fulfil its assigned role as model for society.

During the revolutionary period, conservatives and many churchmen challenged attempts to separate church and school, arguing that such a move would be injurious to both. The constitution of 1850 prescribed that "with the introduction of public schools, confessional conditions are to be taken into consideration as much as possible." Religious instruction was arranged by the religious groups, and supervision of schools was in part the responsibility of church officials under the Minister for Ecclesiastical Affairs, von Raumer.

In the fifties, the place of religion in the schools continued to be a subject of debate in many German states. The curriculum for Prussia released in 1856 required each "gymnasium" to continue offering two hours of religious instruction weekly. A few years earlier a group of philologists meeting in Erlangen had supported this practice in their theses on a "Christian Gymnasium," arguing that the teaching of classical studies did not conflict with Christianity. "Living Christian faith does not exclude the kind of love for humanity that is found in classical literature," they said in a self-serving statement aimed at protecting their jobs, while conservative Christians looked for witches.

School reform under conservative principles was a hallmark of the reaction in most German states. In Prussia, the "Three Regulations" (1854), authored by privy councilor Ferdinand Stiehl, tried to exorcise from teachers' seminaries and elementary classrooms the spirit and instruction that supposedly incited the uprisings of 1848. The regulations' stated purpose was to guarantee a continuing relationship between church and school.

The regulation that von Raumer issued to teachers' seminaries acknowledged that it was impossible to provide a universal curriculum for teacher training which would be mechanically accurate in all details. But it offered a number of guiding principles for administrators of these institutions. The teachers' seminary trained a student to become "a teacher for evangelical Christian schools, which have the assignment . . . of educating youth IN A CHRISTIAN, PATRIOTIC WAY OF THINKING." But it was not necessary to inculcate a special system of pedagogy or educational methodology in the training school. "The doctrine of sin, human helplessness, the law, divine salvation, and sanctification is a pedagogy which needs only a few additional secondary propositions from anthropology and psychology for the elementary teacher's use."

The basis of religious instruction in the teachers' seminaries was to be God's Word, Luther's SMALL CATECHISM, and the HEIDELBERG CATECHISM; later, as teachers in elementary schools, students would merely elucidate these materials. In teaching the mother tongue, teachers' colleges were to use materials dealing with church life, Christian morals, patriotism, and nature, not the classics. In history and geography, the teachers' seminaries were to stress important personages of the past and present who had served their nation faithfully, and to inculcate love and respect for the ruling family. Cultural history was to include special reference to the important role of

Christianity. The regulations closed with an unmistakably clear instruction:

> Impractical reflection and subjective experiments, with little meaning for simple and healthy education on a popular level, are not to be perpetrated on these <students>. Holding firmly to Christian foundation in life and discipline, the <teachers' seminaries> will train themselves more perfectly to become what they should be: nuclei for pious, loyal, intelligent teachers who stand close to the people, who in self-denial, and according to God's will, have the desire, calling, and competence to embrace growing young people in love.

The regulation for elementary schools issued at the same time was firmly opposed by Friedrich Diesterweg, one of the day's leading educational figures. But his opposition did not interfere with implementation in the elementary schools, which enrolled 97 percent of the school-age children in Prussia in the sixties. The regulation insisted that it was time to "eliminate the unauthorized, superfluous, and that which misleads;" it was time to return to fundamentals, in which "the needs and the worth of a truly Christian popular education" are known and appreciated.

Popular life had to be formed on the basis of eternal realities and "on the foundation of Christianity, which in in its legitimate churchly form should permeate, cultivate, and support the family, the area of vocation, community and state." The regulation read like an Inner Mission tract, emphasizing that elementary schools needed to prepare a person for practical life in family, church, calling, community and state, not inculcate some kind of abstract system.

Each week, twenty-six class hours were to be divided among religion (6), reading (12), arithmetic (5), and singing (3). The regulation recommended that singing classes use church hymns and good patriotic songs; liturgical choirs should be formed, and teachers should rehearse the hymns to be used the next Sunday in church. The Holy Scriptures were to be the basis for religious instruction in Christian living. Younger children were to learn the Lord's Prayer, morning and evening blessings, and table prayers; older

287

students were to investigate the common church prayer, parts of the church liturgy, at least thirty hymns, the weekly gospel lesson, and the chief parts of the Catechism.

This type of conservative educational reform did not take hold of schools in independent Hamburg until the turn of the century. But many of the German territories experienced a reaction similar to Prussia's in the fifties, and education was affected. The Prussian monarch had a deep personal interest in church-school relations, and the regulations of 1854 left little doubt about the government's position.

During the period of the reaction, the Christian state had to guard itself against those trying to infiltrate the educational system with sub-Christian and sub-patriotic teaching. It also had to preserve the integrity of the specifically Christian honors and awards that its monarch bestowed. That was why Prussia hesitated when the powerful Jewish banker in Frankfurt, Meyer Carl von Rothschild, asked through Prussia's amabassador Bismarck that he might be awarded the Order of the Red Eagle, third class. While his specific request was to be named court banker, Bismarck indicated what his real desire was. He was granted the title of court banker, but his other request was more difficult to fulfil since it involved bestowing and wearing the Christian cross. Bismarck had the difficult assignment of awarding Rothschild the oval-shaped insignia of the third class especially designed for non-Christians; he never wore it. When Rothschild received the second order in oval shape, people in Berlin gossipped that he wore the sign of the cross. Bismarck advised the government this usually was not the case; on rare occasions when he did wear the order, the cross was in a buttonhole, but, Bismarck added, that was not out of character for an emancipated Jew who had received a number of orders.

The king continued to show interest in Jews in the Holy Land, and in the Prussian-English bishopric in that area. Politically, this matter was less volatile than the Rothschild case. In 1853, army chaplains and court preachers organized a society to advance Protestant work in Palestine, especially the care of Germans who lived in the area. But their best efforts, including a new journal for the society, failed to bring a vibrant response among evangelicals in Prussia.

288

No more successful was the attempt to fund a new cathedral in Berlin, although Heydt, the Minister of Trade, Industry and Public Works, made valiant efforts in the fifties. He told provincial presidents that a new cathedral should symbolize the generation of peace inaugurated by Frederick William III and his son, and that the population should rally to its support with sacrificial offerings. His specific objective was to secure gifts from men of commerce and from railway magnates. Failing miserably, he tried a moralistic approach in 1858, arguing that the cathedral would recognize the role of the kings in European peace. But his effort to concretize the throne-altar alliance in a new edifice was unsuccessful. The royal dynasty still had no place to lay its head in death, at least not a national cathedral like Westminster.

While the king continued to share a concern for church buildings and for the church triumphant, especially its monarchical members, he was also dedicated to the church militant and the church catholic. His adamant support of the Evangelical Alliance, when it met in Berlin in 1857, grew out of his religious convictions, and his desire to give a clear witness to Prussia's leadership role among German Protestants.

The story began in London with the organization of the Evangelical Alliance in 1846. It was a voluntary organization of individual Christians that included such evangelical luminaries from Germany as Christian G. Barth, August Tholuck, and Johann G. Oncken, who about this time established the first Baptist church in Germany, in Hamburg.(4) After the Alliance met in London in 1851, some of its German participants formed a paper committee of the Alliance in northern Germany that included two important members of the Awakening in western Germany, Treviranus of Bremen and Krummacher of Elberfeld. But by the end of 1851, Berlin had become the focus of the movement in Germany. The articles of incorporation of the German branch included a set of nine rather fundamentalistic doctrinal statements. This branch became the steering committee for the international meeting held in Berlin in 1857.

When the Alliance met in Paris in 1855, representatives of free and independent churches in Germany, though not from

Prussia, complained about the trickery, imprisonment, and general oppression they suffered. Some of the complaints accurately portrayed conditions in Mecklenberg, royal Saxony, and Wuerttemberg. The Alliance passed a resolution to send a deputation to the Prussian king to ascertain what help he might give, and later that year the king received the delegation in Cologne. He extended an invitation for the Alliance to meet in Berlin in 1857, partly to show Prussia's liberal spirit.(5) Prussia's invitation should be viewed in the light of her power struggle with Austria over German unity since, as a Catholic state, Austria could not invite the Alliance, or play the protector's role for middle-state Protestants who were in the Alliance.

Sixt Karl Kapff of Wuerttemberg was asked to draw up the invitation for the meeting in Berlin. It was signed by such notable figures of the earlier Awakening as Tholuck, Fliedner, the presidents of the provincial synods of Rhineland and Westphalia, and some important professors. Stahl demanded that the conference not meddle with internal church affairs in Prussia, while Wichern showed some scepticism about the meeting, fearing that an amorphous international organization might swallow the Inner Mission.

In September of 1857, over 1,000 pastors and 300 laymen gathered for the eight-day meeting in Berlin. Two thirds of the registered laymen came from Berlin, while 111 Berlin clergymen attended the meeting. The provinces of Brandenburg had 260 delegates while the Rhine Province had only 54, although none of the participants were official representatives. The Prussian king attended many sessions; in his absence he was represented by the recently retired ambassador to England, Bunsen. Also attending were the liberal professor, Daniel Schenkel, and some Freemasons. The great variety of doctrinal positions was one reason why the Lord's Prayer was not prayed publicly during the conference, although many attended the official communion service at its close.

Public debate focused on the rights of free churches. Pointing to the sad shape of spiritual affairs in Germany, some pleaded for the governments to give greater freedom to the free churches. Stahl and Hengstenberg left Berlin during the conference in a demonstration against the protests and participation of free church representatives.

That same month, Stahl delivered a vitrolic speech against the Alliance at the "Kirchentag" in Stuttgart.

While the rest of Germany experienced economic recession, the Prussian king transported the delegates from Berlin to Potsdam in special trains, to entertain them at the palace with a two-hour audience and reception. He, his wife, and his brother, the future William I, mixed with the delegates, and then the pleasantries ended with the singing of "A Mighty Fortress" and a prayer. One of the concrete results of the conference was the publication of a paper, entitled the NEW EVANGELICAL CHURCH NEWS. It soon became a mouthpiece for the High Church Council in Berlin, advocating broad-based church union quite unlike the narrow ecclesiological views offered in Hengstenberg's EVANGELICAL CHURCH NEWS.

The pivotal role that the monarch played in sustaining the reactionary triangle of church, state, and social-political conservatism was all the more apparent in Prussia when the "New Era" dawned in 1858. After Frederick William IV was incapacitated by a stroke, the crown prince, the future William I, acted as prince regent. In his inaugural speech to his "New Era" ministers in November, the prince alluded to rampant orthodoxy that was destroying the evangelical union in Prussia. He indicated that this union should be maintained and extended, without violating the confessional viewpoints that were protected by the various decrees.

Hengstenberg and his party were the targets of the prince regent's broadside, partly because in 1854 he had infuriated the crown prince with a vitrolic attack on Freemasonry, a movement dear to the prince after he joined in 1840. Reviewing events of the previous year in the first issue of EVANGELICAL CHURCH NEWS in 1859, Hengstenberg reminded his readers that Psalm 146 advised people to "put no confidence in princes" since they were mortal; he warned that the "enlightened" spirit would surface again and destroy the spiritual achievements of the last fifty years. Speaking before the Evangelical Society in Berlin in 1860, Hengstenberg lauded the spiritual character of Frederick William IV, but indicated that the devil was loose once again; he would make gains unless the state continued to find the rationale for its existence in God's kingdom, and turned to the church for moral guidance. When the prince was crowned in 1861, Hengstenberg saw reason for hope, proclaiming that the crown "comes only from God." But his continuing attacks on the king, and references to political affairs in sermons in the Cathedral Church and in the parliament's opening session, did not endear him to the monarch. The king directed the Minister of Ecclesiastical Affairs to remedy the situation, and nudged Bismarck to take similar action in 1863 and 1866.

In Wuerttemberg, the trappings of the New Era did not deflect the church from the reactionary course it had been following in the fifties. A pietist named Kapff, who had become an important ecclesiastical official, led the way in seeking even closer relations beteen church and state. During the revolution he supported the king and the conservative counterthrust, and late in 1849 he tilted toward Prussia in the question of German unity with the claim tnat Austria had shut herself out of Germany. He said that God "speaks out over our apparently hopeless chaos and says, 'Let there be light and peace and unity.' Trusting Him, we cry out: 'Let it be so in all of Germany!'" After the revolution, the pietists in Wuerttemberg tried to gain full control of the territory's church government, opposing those who favored representative church polity. Wuerttemberg's politicians were little influenced by Kapff's rhetoric, even though he was an early spokesman for the reaction. Elected to the parliament in 1851, he proposed that sessions should begin with prayer. His resolution was adopted, but then overturned after his opening prayer was filled with personal vendettas. But in 1852, Kapff succeeded in persuading the consistory to adopt the north German practice of an annual day of penitence and prayer; he and others were miffed when the king refused to close the court theatre during the observance. He was less successful in securing the passage of Sunday blue laws and limiting the use of oaths, but the Bible and hymnbook continued to be counted as elementary school texts because of his efforts.

CONSERVATIVE THEORETICIANS

The social philosophy of the "Christian state" came into

full bloom in Prussia during the fifties. Acting in the role of social philosophers, conservative theoreticians provided the platform and rationale for Protestantism as political principle, and politics as Christian patriotism. For them, society was the product of the interaction of church and state; the "Christian state" and society were coterminous. They felt that it was necessary to reassert the validity of the religious consensus that had weathered revolution, and they issued pages of documentation for the claim that the preservation of God's creational orders depended on close church-state cooperation. This was another way to reaffirm the church's state-assigned role as model for society.

After the revolutions in 1848, one major challenge confronting the conservative theoreticians was to adapt their idea of the Christian state to Prussian constitutionalism. Their answers varied, but most agreed that czarist Russia was a bulwark against revolution, despite its absolutist tendencies. Some eschewed this interpretation of the international scene, just as many in Prussia's House of Deputies judged as too doctrinaire the proposals advanced by the archconservative theoretician and politician, Ernst Ludwig von Gerlach (1795-1877). For example, in 1856 the House defeated his proposal to repeal the constitutional article that guaranteed civil and religious rights without regard for religious persuasion, and the next year, by a vote of 134 to 173 it rejected his legislative proposal to limit divorce to cases that had Scriptural justification.

Gerlach was an important conservative theoretician, although his unbending attitudes diminished his political stature as time passed. A Reformed lawyer with strong theological interests, he was the presiding officer of the appelate court in Magdeburg, and on several occasions an elected member of Prussia's House of Deputies. His political theory owed much to Karl Ludwig von Haller, but he was even more heavily indebted to the famous legal historian, eclectic theoretician, and converted Jew, Friedrich Julius Stahl. Stahl's professed Lutheranism led to some important differences between the two. Gerlach was more theocratic in orientation than Stahl, who held that only at the end of time would God's total rule in church and state be restored. As a student of Augustine, Gerlach elucidated God's kingdom as a political system, describing the parallel between Prussia's monarchical state and the theocratic state portrayed in I Samuel 8:7. For him, the importance of historical law lay in its objective basis in the creational orders.

Gerlach despised attempts to divorce religion and politics. Politics was a kind of "applied" or "practical" theology for this lawyer, who tried to give "political form" to his "consciousness of God." While he modified the platform of the conservative party in Prussia, of which he was a founder, in order to keep contact with realty, he never deviated from his basic premise that political theory was an extension of theology. God's kingdom provided the integrating framework for the two realms, since its communal and organic structure ruled out religious subjectivism and radical, revolutionary individualism in politics. Gerlach accepted constitutinalism, but preferred "staendisch" or estate constitutionalism, with representation for universities, churches, social classes, the Jews as a group, and other classes. He described the statesman's primary responsibility as cultivating the seed of organism in whatever form he found it, in order to overcome unrestrained appeals to the masses and individuals.

Gerlach held that the ruling family could establish a constitutional political system in the state if it chose, but at all costs a constitutional system had to preserve the monarchical principle, since monarchy was more firmly rooted in the human spirit than republicanism. He added that "monarchy is the noblest political structure . . . since it is the universal political framework. It is also the political arrangement of Christ's kingdom in the narrow sense." He opposed any form of revolution from "above" or "below," since both revolutionary movements broke with the true legal principle of rule by divine right. Neither monarchical nor democratic absolutism could appropriately identify and fulfil the monarch's primary task in God's plan, namely, to reflect the image of the Eternal King to his subjects.

He held that the great mission of the age was to "Christianize" the kingdom of God, a world-historical entity encompassing all Christian and non-Christian states, and all forms and levels of civic authority. After man's fall into sin distorted theocratic rule, God reorganized His world plan and created the state as the kingdom of power, and the church as the kingdom of grace. Perfect theocracy was the unified goal sought by the Christian church, and every Christian state.

Gerlach understood the most important question of his day to be eminently more theological than symptoms might indicate. That question centered in the nature of God's kingdom: Was God the Ruler of heaven and earth, or was the world god? Gerlach felt that the proponents of pantheism were distorting the great ideas of freedom, progress, and human rights. Christians had to be electrified by the vision of God's kingdom to seek victory in this struggle. A proper understanding of "rule by divine right" leads one to grasp important Christian truths, and helps him understand the wild attacks on all principles of authority, human and divine, he said.

Friedrich Julius Stahl (1802-1862) was probably the greatest theoretician of the Christian state in these decades. Converted from Judaism to Christianity in his native Bavaria in 1819, he continued to be influenced by Jewish thought thoughout his life, and maintained close friendships with converted Jews such as Gerhard P. Ewald, and Karl F. Neumann, a professor in Munich. Called to teach in the faculty of law at Berlin in 1840, he was never fully accepted in the inner circle of political conservatives. He served as vice president of many of the "Kirchentagen," president of the Berlin Pastors' Conference, and as a member of the High Church Council from 1852 to 1857, and he was elected to several territorial diets.

Stahl provided an alternative in the northern states to the restorational theorist, Haller. He accepted the sovereignty of the state as an unassailable assumption, viewed constitutionalist and nationalist thought and sentiment as historical and conservative forces, and provided a unified perspective for the conservative movement in Prussia in such works as DER PROTESTANTISMUS ALS POLITISCHES PRINZIP (1853), and DER CHRISTLICHE STAAT (1847; 2nd ed. 1858). The romantic idea of "Persoenlichkeit" (personhood) provided the point of embarkation for delineating the relationship between God and the monarch. Stahl welded Hegelian state absolutism and Lutheran confessionalism to form a protective shield against popular control of politics and morals. His slogans were not caricatures of his views: "Knowledge must be converted!" "Authority, not majority!" "Solidarity of conservative interests!" "Tolerance is a child of disbelief!"

Stahl advised conservatives to adapt to constitutionalism, and to espouse it for the sake of their principles. He turned upside down Gerlach's strict respect for the law, suggesting that since the king had promulgated a constitution, it was now legally binding for all. But he did not advocate a figurehead king; though accepted as a reality, ministerial responsibility should be sharply limited. Despite his efforts to adapt to the changing political scene, he remained in the good graces of conservatives because of his respect for the divine origin of authority, and his commitment to the monarch's integrity.

In church affairs, Stahl thought that the monarch's administrative responsibility for external matters had to be executed through a minister. But with equal vigor he defended the High Church Council as the supreme bishop's direct line to the church's internal affairs. He was less enthusiastic about the constitutional provision for civil and political rights, irrespective of religous affiliation. He granted that a constitutionalist state could make this decision, but his experiences as a converted Jew, and his religious convictions, made it difficult for him to accept this paper principle. He argued that it did not abrogate the reality of a Christian state.

One of the most forceful political descriptions of the Christian state was a lecture he gave that was subsequently published as an article, entitled "What is Revolution?" (1852). Stahl defined revolution as "the founding of the entire public order on the will of men instead of on God's order and dispensation," "the most manifest sin in the political realm" since it is a "foundational annulment of God's order." Revolution included demands for popular sovereignty; freedom from God's commandments; equality without regard for divinely ordained differences among men; separation of church and state, under the assumption that each one believes what he wishes apart from revelation; a new political structure that disregarded the divine structure that developed historically; and a call for national unity that would destroy divinely created states. Stahl wrote that communism was the final stage of revolution; men who disregarded the dispensation of God could not be expected to respect the property rights of others. The root of revolution was rationalism, "an opposing faith in men" that idolatrizes humanity and seeks to emancipate men from God. Stahl added that "only Christianity is able to put an end to revolution. Christianity is the original pattern for that kingdom of freedom whose empty caricature is revolution." Christianity nurtured a "yearning for the creation of a great commonwealth, which should be a kingdom of the Lord, a protection for all individuals in their freedom and purity."

Most conservative theoreticians of the Christian state saw nationalism as the chief opponent, since in their minds it was connected inextricably with revolution. Many showed continuing allegiance to the Holy Alliance by firmly opposing any sort of power politics on the part of Prussia, and by touting Austria as a German state. Principles came first, then the realities of the day, and, naturally, Christian principles served as the foundation for political theory.

But the supposed absence of self-interest and self-service on the part of social conservatives was more apparent than real. Essentially they provided a religious-political theory for the east Elbian "Junkers," and others in the society who were trying to adapt to new political, social, and economic circumstances without yielding their favored position in society. The theoreticians were also refurbishing the alliance between throne and altar, tested so severely in the years of revolution. Conservative political theory anchored in Christian principles, and the rising tide of Lutheran confessionalism in the fifties and sixties, provided a sense of social stability in the face of many changes. The emphasis on confessional doctrines and objectivity in creational orders helped arrest subjectivist undercurrents, and social and political revolution. As a result, under Bismark's leadership moderate conservatives gained the time that was required to execute a revolution from above. But for the present, the reactionary triangle of monarch, pastor, and conservative theorist continued to function with the ideology of the "Christian state."

297

A CHURCHLY CHURCH

The major contribution of the church to the reactionary triangle was to be "churchly" in fulfilling the expectations of others. In these years, most evangelicals tried to serve the state and society by shoring up religion in the private realm. Credence was given to the Awakening's narrow description of the church's nature and function. In general, the church's response to the reaction of the fifties was that it engaged in an ecclesiological reaction of its own, concentrating on spiritual matters, and crossing few boundaries into other areas. In territorial churches and in parishes, in worship services and in the Prussian High Church Council, in church periodicals and in forms of piety, eyes focused on the restrictive and delimiting assumption of the unwritten charter: when in doubt about the advisability of speaking or acting in non-religious areas, do the purely spiritual thing, and trust God and the state to take care of the rest.

Territorial Church Life

In the realm of faith, the territorial churches continued to ply the tried and true. In their sermons, most preachers discussed narrow doctrinal concerns or exposited texts around the polarities of confession and faith, scarcely referring to special problems of religious and moral life in the modern age, the congregation's condition, or the fields of nature and history. Lacking contact with reality, their sermons probably could have been preached in any century. The biblicism that was prevalent in the Awakening invaded most pulpits, and sermon topics, such as "Nicodemus' Night Visit to the Lord," "The Great Last Supper of the Lord," and "A Spiritual Test for Jesus Christ," were standard fare. The style of preaching contrasted markedly with the practice of Schleiermacher and others earlier in the century.(6) Biblical exegesis seemed to have displaced homiletics, and preachers were satisfied with textual exposition instead of the riskier work of correlating the text's message with contemporary life. Sometimes they received assistance from

298

"Reisepredigtern" (traveling preachers) or assistant pastors, many of whom were candidates awaiting placement in a position. At midcentury the four territorial churches of Prussia, Hanover, Mecklenberg and Holstein had a total of 3,165 candidates awaiting calls; some had to wait as long as ten or fifteen years for a parish to serve.

Prussia's state church had more than five times as many Protestants as any other state. This was one reason why the course of the ecclesiastical reaction and the fate of the religious charter in Prussia were determinative for most other Protestants in Germany. In 1862, her territorial church membership numbered 11,026,608.(7) Next in size were Saxony (2,171,148), Hanover (1,630,618), Bavaria (1,283,867), and Wuerttemberg (1,178,501). All of the remaining twenty-seven territorial churches in the German Confederation had fewer than one million members; the smallest of these was Hesse-Homburg (20,066), and the largest the Electorate of Hesse (614,688). Though Prussia's Protestant church was large, it had only three million more members than the population of New York City in 1970.

Piety in the territorial churches might be measured by comparing the average number of communions administered to each member (including children, although they did not commune). German Austria led the list in 1862, with 1.09 communions per member annually:

German Austria	1.09	Baden	.68
Electorate of Hesse	.82	Hanover	.64
Schaumburg-Lippe	.82	Prussia	.52
Waldeck	.80	Mecklenberg-	
Bavaria	.76	Sterlitz	.28
Saxony	.72	Holstein	.29
Wuerttemberg	.70	Frankfurt a/M	.18

Some of these averages were undoubtedly due in part to the pastor-to-people ratio, which varied greatly from one territorial church to another. For example, in Holstein and Frankfurt the ratio was 1:2,788 and 1:2,206, respectively, in 1862. The larger churches had ratios of 1:1,968 (Prussia, with a high of 1:3,104 in the province of Prussia, and a low of 1:103 in provincial Saxony); 1:1,981 (Saxony); 1:1,400 (Hanover); 1:1,183 (Wuerttemberg); and 1:1,102 (Bavaria). Some of the medium sized churches fell in the same range

(Baden, with 1:1,204), while some of the smaller churches
had excellent ratios, such as 1:843 in Saxony-Weimar, or
1:977 in Waldeck.

These factors, together with varying birth rates, meant that
pastoral care loads differed from one territory to another.
The time that pastors had to spend baptizing and marrying
people, for example, differed from place to place, as these
figures indicate:

TERRITORY	AVERAGE NUMBER OF BAPTISMS/CLERGYMAN	AVERAGE NUMBER OF MARRIAGES/CLERGYMAN
Holstein	88	21
Saxony	86	18
Prussia	75	17
(Highest: E. Prussia)	(134)	(30)
(Lowest: Saxony)	(40)	(9)
Frankfurt	64	15
Wuerttemberg	45	10
Hanover	43	11
Bavaria	37	9
Hesse-Homburg	30	9
Saxony-Weimar	28	7

Marriages and baptisms bring to mind the keeping of birth
records and the question of illegitimate children, which
seemed to obsess state and church officials. Between 1850
and 1861, the ratio of illegitimate to legitimate births in
Prussia was 1:10.95. The ratios of the provinces differed
greatly, partly because illegitimacy was socially
respectable among some peasants and farm workers; it showed
that a woman was fertile, and marriage often occurred after
an illegitimate birth. While this social approbation was
morally distasteful to most evangelical clergymen, its
effect is clear. In heavily rural Silesia, the ratio in
these years was 1:7.9, about the same as provincial
Brandenburg's 1:7.81, and provincial Saxony's 1:9.25. Some
smaller areas had even higher averages; at midcentury one
parish in the Silesian diocese of Parchwitz baptized one
illegitimate child for every two born in wedlock, while in
1858 the reports of visitation commissions to the diocese of
Rastenburg in provincial Prussia indicated that in five
congregations, the ratio of illegitimate to legitimate

children was 1:3, 1:4, 1:5, 1:6 and 1:7.

Church services were held on a regular basis in various territorial churches—when enough people appeared for worship. In 1850, three "average" church districts in Mecklenberg failed to conduct 228 divine services because no one came to church. In general, church attendance was poor; at midcentury, scarcely 50,000 of Berlin's 420,000 inhabitants regularly attended Protestant services. Communion attendance was spotty as well, as the figures above indicate. Wichern reported that some congregations of 3,000 members communed only sixty to eighty people each month, but in the East Prussian town of Schloppe, at midcentury a congregation of 5,500 members had an annual communion attendance of 5,600.

In 1852 Prussia's High Church Council revised the General Prayer used in worship to include references to the conversion of Jews, missions, and obliquely, the new experiment in Jerusalem. "Accompany also in Thy grace, with the power of Thy Holy Spirit," the revision read,

> the preaching of the Gospel among Jews and heathen;
> bless each of Thy servants assigned to this work,
> and according to Thy great promises, permit the
> kingdom of Thy beloved Son to increase and expand so
> that the time comes, for which we wait expectantly,
> when the fullness of the heathen is attained, and
> Israel too—converted to Thee—will be blessed.

In Prussia, the church balanced Jewish emancipation with liturgical references to the need for conversion.

Delegates from the church administrations of most territories continued to meet regularly, as they had met in Berlin in 1846, but their cooperative efforts rested on a voluntary basis, with little hope for a unified evangelical church prior to national unity. The Evangelical Church Conference, or Eisenach Conference of German Evangelical Church Governments, met in 1850, 1851, and 1852 in Eisenach, and usually annually thereafter. Stuttgart's court preacher, Karl von Grueneisen, was the first president, and a moving force in the Conference. This purely advisory body discussed such topics as clerical life, the congregation's role in securing pastors, church government, mixed

301

marriages, catechetical instruction, wartime activities, and domestic and foreign missions. The Conference assisted organizations dedicated to religious art, collected statistics, revised Luther's translation of the Bible, prepared a hymnal, and arranged lectionaries for home and church, but it did not grapple with the most serious issues facing the churches. The Conference's early retreat into strictly ecclesiological concerns set the tone of its meetings for the rest of the century. Neither Prussia nor Austria participated in the Conference until 1866.

Parish Life and Economic Recession

A brief glance at a major urban parish in Silesia will show us how a congregation occupied itself in "churchly" matters. It also enables us to pose the hypothesis that a religious depression preceded the economic depression of 1857.

St. Elizabeth's was the largest Protestant parish in Breslau, in Prussian Silesia. Between 1848 and 1864 its membership rolls increased from 28,000 to 34,000 members. Its endowment totalled over 150,000 "Thaler," and its edifice was worth about the same amount. The church's thirteenth century structure suffered misfortune in 1857 when the collapse of two pillars destroyed the chancel, but the building was again operational within a year. Although the city's magistrate was the official patron of the parish, the Prussian king provided funds in 1858 for painting some of the church's glass ornamentally.

Three pastors headed the parish staff of nearly thirty people. They supervised three deacons and a lector, and among themselves divided the preaching schedule, liturgical services, and pastoral acts such as marriages, baptisms and funerals. Among the fifteen "endowed" sermons, some were supposed to deal with Christ's washing of His disciples' feet, baptism (in April), thunderstorms (in June), the Holy Scriptures (in June), harvest (in August), forbearance in distress (in September), and a sermon on schools. That the church was big business is apparent from the size of the auxiliary staff, which included a cantor, two organists, two instrumentalists, treasurer, steward, several servants, three masons, a bell ringer and two assistants, three guards, four grave diggers, and—strike a blow for women's liberation!—three cleaning women. Hopefully the staff at St. Elizabeth's was more discrete than the organists and cantors at another location, who were chastised in a report from around 1860 for shamefully sneaking out of a service during the sermon.

St. Elizabeth's was included in the first of the three ecclesiastical districts administered by the royal consistory in Silesia. While the population in the first district, which encompassed Breslau, increased from 700,000 in 1853 to around 767,000 in 1865, the number of communions administered only increased slightly, from 423,000 in 1853 to 429,000 in 1865. In 1855, communion attendance in the district dropped to 382,000, and in the other two Silesian districts as well, the lowest communion attendance for the twelve years between 1853 and 1865 was recorded in 1855. Something was afoot. Perhaps a religious depression preceded the economic downswing of 1857, much as in the United States a religious depression preceded the economic depression of the late 1920s.(8)

The data, from Silesia at least, lends credence to the hypothesis. The statistical evidence is not airtight, but there is reason to believe that at least in Silesia some sort of religious depression foreshadowed the economic recession and panic of November, 1857. Whether the same phenomenon occurred elsewhere is not clear, but perhaps this hypothesis helps explain some of the data.

As reported in Protestant church records for provincial Silesia, suicides increased substantially in 1854, 1855 and 1856, and then receded. The number of Protestant suicides per year between 1853 and 1865 was as follows:

1853	292	1860	319
1854	362	1861	367
1855	457	1862	293
1856	416	1863	363
1857	326	1864	273
1858	340	1865	353
1859	320		

It is possible that in 1857 the economic recession provided another means to work out private frustrations, or to channel these frustrations away from suicidal tendencies, but a malaise of spirit preceded the recession.

The economic dislocation of 1857 may also have affected the rate of illegitimate births. In the present day some may not construe illegitimacy as a religious problem, but the fact that church authorities and clergymen carefully tabulated the ratio between illegitimate and legitimate births indicates the importance they attributed to the subject in that age. For them, more was involved than state requirements; the ratio signalled the relative health of religion and morals in an area. Among evangelicals in Silesia this ratio changed from 1:8 in 1853-56 to 1:7 in 1857, where it remained through 1859. In 1860 the number of illegitimate births increased again, altering the ratio to 1:6, where it stayed through 1865. The shifts of 1857 and 1860 may have been due to arithmetical calculations that turned fractions into whole numbers, but social and economic forces undoubtedly contributed to the variation in the number of illegitimate births.(9)

CHURCHLY PRESS AND CONFESSIONAL COMMITMENT

One sign of the churches' preoccupation with "churchliness" in the fifties was the appearance of many new papers and periodicals. Congregations and societies of all kinds began publishing papers in support of their causes, and a number of new party periodicals appeared. Some might interpret this phenomenon as a sign of life and vitality, but I interpret it as evidence of the ingrown ecclesiological spirit of the reactionary period. The prevailing sentiment seemed to be that the church was an isolated fortress, largely unrelated to the surrounding terrain, except for the monarchical and conservative edifices that abutted its walls. One might venture outside on some mission of charitable Good Samaritanship, or engage other churchmen in heated doctrinal debate within the fortress. New periodicals nurtured such attitudes, but they did little to encourage an encounter with problems on the slicing edge, where church met world.

The one exception was the liberal PROTESTANTISCHE

304

KIRCHENZEITUNG (PROTESTANT CHURCH NEWS), which appeared in 1854 under the editorship of Heinrich Krause (d. 1868). The names of its associate editors hint at the paper's purposes: Karl A. Credner, professor at Giessen; Theodor W. Dittenberger, a Badenese liberal who moved to Weimar in 1852 because of the reaction in Baden; Heinrich Eltester; the historian Karl A. Hase of Jena; Ludwig Jonas, a student of Schleiermacher; Karl H. W. Schwarz, who cooperated with Ruge, served in the Frankfurt Parliament, and was later co-founder of the Protestant Union; Karl L. A. Sydow, Berlin preacher and student of Schleiermacher; and Karl Zittel, liberal churchman and political publicist in Baden. The paper's platform insisted that no human authority could control the freedom of personal faith, that German Protestants should unite in a non-dogmatic union based on common faith, and that evangelical Christianity should pursue the correlation between faith and science. But it is clear that the prevailing reactionary atmosphere contributed to the periodical's appearance, and while the paper seriously addressed the relationship of faith and science, its primary purpose was to provide an intra-church forum for the liberal wing. Without doubt, this paper was the exception rather than the rule.

The second new paper of major significance was the PROTESTANTISCHE MONATSBLAETTER FUER INNERE ZEITGESCHICHTE (PROTESTANT MONTHLY FOR CONTEMPORARY TIMES), first published late in 1852. Earlier, a Congress of the Inner Mission pointed out the need for a journal for people in "upper classes" who were interested in all phases of religious life and faith. While not an official journal of the Inner Mission, the paper encouraged a cooperative spirit among parties for the sake of German Protestantism. The paper's introductory editorial suggested that the left wing was populated by enemies of unbelief who opposed Christian principles; on the right, Rome's attacks on the Protestant world were being decried; in the middle there was an abundance of indifference toward human need, prejudice against the Christian life, and an arrogant party spirit. The monthly represented the broad, union-oriented middle, and in the process it took few risks. It owed its birthright to the reactionary period, and to the mediating theological position that tried to maintain the support of educated classes for the institutional church. It was a periodical for the consciences of people still working in

305

the institutional church.

Cut from the same bolt of cloth was the NEUE EVANGELISCHE
KIRCHENZEITUNG (NEW EVANGELICAL CHURCH NEWS), mentioned
above. Originally an informational organ for Germans in the
Evangelical Alliance, it supported the union in opposition
to Hengstenberg's EVANGELICAL CHURCH NEWS and its party's
adamant confessionalism. Columns were filled with reports
from correspondents, not devotional pieces or theological
treatises. The fact that it appeared in 1859, soon after
the New Era was announced, is significant; in seeking to
promote unity in the union church, especially in Prussia, it
mirrored the approach of the new Prussian king. But its
roots lay in the struggle between confession and union
during the reactionary period, and it too was a church organ
for churchmen, promoted by German delegates who attended the
Evangelical Alliance in 1857.

These and other periodicals indicated that the church's
primary responsibility was to be the church itself. This
seems to have been a guiding maxim during the reaction, both
because it correlated well with the conservative world view,
and because it meshed with the confessional emphasis on
church and pastoral office that was becoming so prominent.
Wichern, too, threatened to turn the Inner Mission's
resources on the church unless it renewed itself, and
deserted the rationalistic practices that were strangling
it. In a major address at the "Kirchentag" in 1857, he
claimed that,

> Only insofar as the church attains the principles of
> the divine kingdom in its confession and life can
> and will it carry on Inner Mission; insofar as it
> neglects or diametrically opposes and disavows these
> ordinances will it, as an opponent, become an object
> of Mission.

The conference accepted his argument in its portrayal of the
Inner Mission. One resolution said that, "in order to aim
toward the coming of God's kingdom, the <Inner Mission> at
the same time nurtures a true church spirit." Another
asserted that individual works, societies, and institutions
would not create the Inner Mission; it was a more churchly
entity that included such confessional emphases as "the
Christian's work at his post and in his calling, as part of

306

the universal priesthood," as well as "the work of the clerical office" and "the renewed apostolic diaconate."

In its work during the fifties, Prussia's High Church Council showed that the church's primary responsibility was to the church itself. This was especially true in the Council's response to the new churchly forces of confessionalism. But we must remember that the Council was immediately subject to the chief bishop, who also happened to be the head of state. In this light, it was acting responsibly in 1851 when it released from office Pastor Ludwig Hildenhagen of Provincial Saxony for his involvement in revolutionary activities in 1848. Three years later, the Council sponsored a campaign to finance memorial tablets for churches; the tablets listed the names of those who gave their lives in 1848-49, while being "faithful in their duty to king and people, law and order." Meanwhile, in 1851 conservatives in Prussia's lower house blocked a liberal move to examine the Council's constitutionality; liberals argued that the Council reported directly to the king, but was supposed to serve an independent church.

The Council's major challenge during the reaction was to give the appearance of being reactionary, without becoming revolutionary. The problem was simple: How could the Council acknowledge the renewed vitality of confessionalism, without destroying the administrative church structure that was called the union? At the king's direction, the Council tried to walk the tightrope between destroying the creation of Fredrick William III, or betraying the confessionalists. Either extreme seemed to endanger the monarchical principle, the first because the monarch had created the union, and the second because confessionalists and the orthdox party had been stalwart defenders of the throne during revolution.

Conservatives faced much the same problem as they debated the question of constitutionalism. Some insisted that the constitution promulgated by the king required that the electoral process represent individuals, but others opted for a "staendisch" or estate system of representation. The question remained for the High Church Council: Could the rising tide of confessionalism receive its due without destroying the union church? Should Prussia's Evangelical Church, created in a revolutionary way when Frederick William III promulgated an administratively unified territorial church, be dissolved in favor of a "staendisch," or confessional arrangement?

At Reformation time in 1850, the Council signalled a change in emphasis in a pronouncement that stressed its role in protecting the confessional integrity of components in the confederative union church:

> We wish to maintain and cultivate the union as a holy legacy, but we do not want to, and should not, do this at the expense of degrading confession, which in like measure we know we are obligated to protect in its own right.

This pronouncement gave a positive twist to the negative description of the union's confederative character which had been offered by Frederick William III in 1834. "The union intends and signifies no surrender of the prevailing confession of faith," the king wrote then, "nor does it abolish the authority that the symbolic books of both evangelical confessions have had to date."

The king issued a cabinet order in 1852 directing the Council to protect the interests of both confessions. It was time to "give the assurance that in the control of the evangelical territorial church, just as in supervision of the communion which by God's grace is associated in the union, the two evangelical confessions should be maintained; similarly, the autonomy of each of the two confessions should be guaranteed." The king said that while the Council had members of both confessions who agreed to cooperate, it was understood that questions dealing with the internal affairs of one confession would not be addressed by Council members from the other confession.

Some interpreted this order as reversing previous policy. The cry arose that the territorial union was gravely endangered; Rhenish evangelicals in particular rallied to the union, partly because it had been a success in the Rhineland, where over 400 of 450 congregations participated by 1852. Influential figures, such as Tholuck, Bunsen, the historian Heinrich Leo, and the theologian Julius Mueller, argued that Frederick William III's edifice was being dismantled under pressure from extreme orthodox evangelicals.

The clamor led the king to issue another cabinet order to the Council in July of 1853, stating that the previous order was not to be interpreted as endangering the evangelical union. "Confessional particularisms" could be tolerated only as long as they did not harm the union itself. Despite this moderating statement, the long and laborious journey toward confederative union had been completed. The territorial church would not split into separate, independent confessional bodies, but neither would the kind of confessional union envisioned by the territorial synod in 1846 be foisted on Prussia's Evangelical Church.

The early reaction to Frederick William III's liturgical agenda, in the twenties, takes on added significance when understood from the perspective of the reactionary fifties, and the confederative union of Prussia's "churchly church." Since the agenda struggle raised the question of the king's control over internal church affairs, it foreshadowed events between 1848 and 1850, when an "independent" church structure became a constitutional necessity. Under the Minister of Ecclesiastical Affairs, the royal consistory continued to be the legal and administrative religious unit of a "confessionless state." But when the king formed the High Church Council, he had direct intelligence and advice on such religious questions as doctrine and worship. This was how the state exerted control over ecclesiastical affairs through "church law" rather than "state law." The agenda conflict in the twenties was clearly the opening volley in this decisive battle. In the case of the confederative union, the king's recognition of the integrity of each confession was another in a series of actions enabling him to retain control over the church, under the guise of the supposedly independent High Church Council. The unwritten charter was alive and well in the fifties, especially in the conference room of the "churchly" High Church Council. The Council helped portray the church as a model for the broader society, a model that showed well how to practice "freedom within authority."

WICHERN'S INNER MISSION: MICROCOSMIC TRIANGLE

While the previous chapter described the origin and early stages of Wichern's Inner Mission, we will examine it here as a microcosm of the reactionary triangle of the fifties. According to this theory, the Inner Mission's purpose was to extend God's kingdom by preserving and reviving the two basic institutions, church and state. The Mission was their point of intersection; it sought to achieve goals that would stabilize society and preserve the "Christian state." As an organizational manifestation of the reactionary triangle, it assisted the church in its assigned modeling function.

Wichern's theoretical description of the Inner Mission, his organizational work in this charitable organization, and his ardent efforts as a penal reformer, represented the three sides of the reactionary triangle in his own person. Social conservative, pastor, and governmental official—and he was all three—worked in the Inner Mission to enable the church to fulfil its state-assigned responsibility as model for society. Even though he was never ordained, Wichern fully embodied the role of pastor.

According to Wichern, the most important factor in the advancement of God's kingdom was the voluntary association of Christian people, who would prompt church and state to fulfil their divine assignments.

God's will for all reality was manifested in His kingdom. On earth the kingdom functioned through the "Volk," usually organized in national groupings, or the Inner Mission. These instruments in turn affected the course of the two major orders of creation, church and state. The Inner Mission (i.e., the "Volk") ensured that church and state were properly aligned over against one another, and that they were moving deeper within the boundaries of God's kingdom.

From another perspective, Wichern envisioned the revitalizing power of the divine kingdom, flowing through the channels of the "Volk" and the Inner Mission, to the two major institutions of creation, church and state, and their foundational social unit, the family. The Inner Mission, the "Volk" in action, enabled these orders to achieve their objectives in God's kingdom and to cooperate peaceably to each other's advantage, thereby enlarging the boundaries of the kingdom on earth.

Church, state and Inner Mission were assigned the task of extending the boundaries of the divine kingdom. Of the three, the Inner Mission was at the same time the weakest and the most powerfully equipped for the task. Its catalytic role placed it in this ambivalent position. In January 1847, in his introduction to the fourth series of his paper, FLY-LEAVES, Wichern promised in the following months to designate which movements the inner mission approved, and which it condemned. He would accurately depict the inner mission for what it was, not a type of shriveled philanthropy, but "an expansion and realization of the Christian kingdom, one of the most buoyant manifestations of the awakened community that is again rousing itself to life, and to full and comprehensive consciousness." The inner mission, he continued, is a "Christian activity in the Christian state and in the Christian church," young and somewhat inexperienced, but dedicated to its task out of devotion to God's kingdom.

The revolution of 1848 did not significantly alter Wichern's views of church, state, and Inner Mission, or their role in the expansion of God's kingdom. The founding of a national organization in 1848 was an early sign of counterrevolution, as indicated in the previous chapter. In 1856, his editorial introduction to a new series of FLY-LEAVES equated the kingdom's advance with the Inner Mission's successes. The Inner Mission dedicated itself to reviving "the holy orders of life in church and state, whereby a people called Christian can be gathered in order to become truly Christian people within these orders . . . ." Church and state were the two primary creational orders; God's kingdom manifested itself in the two foundational orders through the instrumentality of so-called "charitable institutions."

But Wichern was too much of an activist to limit his Inner Mission involvement to theoretical and organizational aspects. He worked zealously to excite interested people at annual meetings, and to involve representatives of charitable agencies affiliated with the umbrella orgagnization that was now formally called the "Inner Mission." One sign of his success was the size of each fall's annual meeting, which convened in different German cities. People came as interested individuals, not official representatives. The three "congresses" of the Inner Mission in 1849, 1850, and 1851 were held concurrently with the "Kirchentag"; this carried on the tradition of the Wittenberg conference in 1848. The two events were combined in 1852, and the minutes of the joint conference issued as a unit. In 1853, the third and fourth sessions of the "Kirchentag" took up issues of the Inner Mission. That pattern prevailed in succeeding years, as the meetings moved to different cities to attract new faces. In 1854, sixteen hundred delegates attended the "Kirchentag" in the famous St. Paul's Church in Frankfurt, site of the Parliament in 1848, and 1,400 were present in Stuttgart in 1857. These figures show an increase of nearly 300 percent over the 500 delegates who came to Wittenberg in 1848.

Wichern was deeply committed to the charitable impulse that lay at the core of the Inner Mission. His home for destitute children at Horn, near Hamburg, was an early example for others. He paraded figures showing that between 1833 and 1845, only about five percent of the children released from his family-oriented institution got into trouble with the law. He said that between 1846 and 1867, the number fell to about four percent, which favorably compared with the ten percent of children who escaped from the institution, or were taken back by their parents before it was deemed opportune.

The problem of staffing the "Rauhe Haus" at Horn with supervisory personnel produced a training program for workers, and soon some of his assistants there were being prepared for a wider range of service in their diaconate. At first the training society was called the "Aid Institute," but eventually it took the name "Bruederanstalt" (Brothers Institution). Established in 1842, it started a training program late in 1843. Trainees who desired work in prisons or social institutions received a year and a half's instruction while they gained practical experience as overseers in the "Rauhe Haus."

In February of 1844, the Prussian king funded two three-year scholarships for future teachers or juvenile wardens with 120 "Thaler." After lengthy negotiations, Wichern announced in June of the next year that the king had authorized six new scholarships, and in 1847 the treasury agreed to provide twelve for the next six years. Recipients would serve at the discretion of the Prussian government.

Relations continued to improve as time passed. At first the king endorsed each brother appointed to serve in the Prussian penal system, but in 1851 he gave a blanket endorsement to all endowed trainees.

The rate of recruitment and placement climbed rapidly. Six trainees enrolled in 1843, and by 1849, fifty to sixty brothers left the institution annually. In 1852, eighty-eight brothers had been assigned by November; thirty-four became assistants in houses of refuge, while the others worked in homes for the aged, congregations, schools, prisons and other institutions. By the middle of 1853, Wichern's official "brotherhood" consisted of 142 individuals, thirty-eight of whom remained at Horn. Thirty-three brothers were assigned during the early months of 1855; 137 brothers were in positions of service, while thirty-six remained in training. Thirty of the 137 worked in prisons, fifty-three in humane societies, fifteen in city missions or with the poor, fifteen in education, and nine in colonial preaching missions, while the rest were variously employed. Penal work took on greater importance for the trained personnel in the fifties. Eighty-eight of the 513 trainees released between 1845 and 1855 entered prison work, but only 132 of the total trainees were members of the official "brotherhood." By the end of 1861 the brotherhood numbered 212 members, with forty-three still at Horn; sixty were employed in seven different penal institutions.

This brief statistical summary of Wichern's training efforts shows that he successfully recruited, trained, and placed a large number of workers. The Prussian government gave substantial assistance to the institute through scholarships and penal jobs. Wichern's claim that church, state and Inner Mission could profitably cooperate in many areas suddenly seemed to ring true.

In January 1857 the king issued a cabinet order calling Wichern to service as a penal advisor in Prussia's Ministry of Interior. Previously, Wichern made a number of penal inspections at the king's request. The same day of the order, Wichern was seated on Prussia's prestigious "Oberkirchenrat" (High Church Council). With high hopes, he left Hamburg for Berlin in February; he then made it a

313

practice to live in Berlin from October to June. As a member of the Council and an advisor for penal affairs, he embodied the personal union that had been the Inner Mission's trademark for some time. In a "round-robin" letter to brothers of his order, he rejoiced at his good fortune. Now he could fully exercise his responsibilities as a trained clergyman, and at the same time participate in governmental deliberations, occupy a seat on the Council, and serve as the chief spokesman of the Inner Mission. In the case of penal reform, Wichern's theory about the proper relationship of church, state, and Inner Mission became functional, as did the reactionary triangle.

One reason he urged Inner Mission involvement in penal reform was that the prisoner represented, in miniature, all the various types of rebellion against state and authority. He thought that penal reform, and work with released prisoners, could help neutralize the revolutionary spirit rampant in the criminal world. Soon after joining the High Church Council, Wichern published a series in FLY-LEAVES that described the need for penal reform in general, and the church's responsibilities in particular. In 1858 and 1859, he used official channels to alert prison chaplains to their churchly duties, urging them to be less anxious about their status as civil servants. In the Council, he helped revise regulations governing the spiritual care of convicts, while in the Ministry of Interior he compiled new reporting forms for prison chaplains. By early 1859 the Council reached an agreement with Prussia's Department of Justice, guaranteeing worship services and spiritual care for prisoners in local court prisons.

Wichern also worked to alert the public to the prisoner's plight. In 1860 he submitted a proposal to his governmental superior, suggesting that wider distribution be made of the annual reports of penal officials, chaplains, and doctors, since a wider availability of information would facilitate prison reforms. After the Minister of Interior approved the plan, the first report was published in 1861.

Wichern also ordered a thorough review of custodial practices in prisons, and tried to improve the quality of prison personnel. Two important reforms fall to his credit: the extension of the solitary cell system in Prussian institutions, and the upgrading of prison

314

personnel. He felt that the first goal was dependent on the second, arguing as early as 1850 that prison reform depended more heavily on the spirit of the personnel than the system of incarceration.

At the time, most prison guards in Prussia were retired servicemen, who received employment as a stipend after twelve years of military duty. Wichern reasoned that for most of them, guard duty involved the largely negative qualities of punctuality and exactness. Since prison employees were ordered not to speak with prisoners, they patterned their relationships with convicts after the policeman-criminal model. But Wichern thought that Christ's sanguine principle, "You visited me," should guide prison workers. In 1844 he explained that these words contained "the principle of all penal and custodial care." Employees infused with this spirit would neither relax discipline, nor ignore their superior's orders; at the same time, they would have a distinctively Christian outlook.

Wichern claimed that true penal reform involved dissolving the old penal community and creating a new one. Properly used, the solitary cell system could help break the old bond; this was primarily the state's responsibility. Communal incarceration merely deadened consciences; it could not break the grip of evil. Isolated from his family, the convict found satisfying human relations in this "school of the criminal," and only the solitary system could shatter the walls of this "community of criminals."

He added that only Christian personnel could guarantee that the solitary system would produce a new community. They had the responsibilty of leading the prisoner through the shadows of solitary confinement to the community of new life, which they exemplified. Christian nurture sanctified imprisoned conscience, presented it with viable alternatives, and prepared the way for a speedy return to society.

Wichern's first attempt to implement this reform plan was at the "Rauhe Haus," when some "criminal children" were admitted as residents, although the effort was acknowledged as a temporary measure. But soon his brothers were assigned as trainees to prison work in the Prussian system. The government took a decisive step in 1856 and staffed the new

cell and communal prison in Moabit, a suburb of Berlin, with
Wichern's trained brothers. Modeled after the Pentonville
prison near London, the prison's 508 cells were arranged
according to the panopticon priciple.

On Reformation day that year, Wichern commissioned
twenty-two brothers for the task. By December, only two
previous employees remained at Moabit; thirty-eight brothers
and their supervisors were the new staff. Hand-picked
prisoners under forty-five years of age were moved to the
prison for the experiment, and the next year, administrative
responsibility for the complex was transferred from the
police president's office in Berlin to the royal government
in Potsdam. In a rush of enthusiasm, the brothers prepared
to share their common life with four hundred prisoners.(10)

In the experiment, the brothers allowed the solitary system
to exert its full impact. Prisoners could communicate only
with non-prisoners. Prisoners were masked whenever they left
their cells. Even worship services were "solitary." The
Moabit chapel had 233 individual "prayer-stools;" all the
convicts could see the altar at once, but were unable to see
one another. Each morning the brothers sang hymns and
offered joint prayers at the center of the panopticon, and
in the evening their devotional services included hymns,
Bible readings, and the Lord's Prayer. Wichern monitored
the program from his office in Berlin.

In 1859, the violent, accidental death of one of the
prisoners at the hands of a brother stirred vicious rumors,
and further antagonized liberal opponents to the experiment
at Moabit. Wichern emphasized that the prisoner was
incarcerated in the communal section of the prison, but
cries of outrage came from the liberal press and the House
of Deputies. Matters were not helped by the fact that
Wichern, a native of non-Prussian Hamburg, had been
appointed to a strategic and lucrative position in the
Prussian government. But for the House of Deputies, a more
significant point at issue was whether the government could
institute the solitary system by fiat, without prior
legislative approval. Wichern's chief opponent in the house
was Schulz-Delitsch. Literary attacks were levelled by J.
A. Mittermaier, a professor at Heidelberg, and Franz von
Holtzendorff, a political liberal and penal authority at the
University of Berlin. Wichern was strongly supported by two

conservative deputies, Lette and Vinke, and also spoke before the House himself.

The challenge turned into a fiasco when the Moabit experiment became enmeshed in a budgetary squabble, precisely at the time when the budgetary subcommittee of the House was in violent disagreement with the crown. This shouting match, in turn, was part of the larger constitutional struggle that tested Prussia's political fiber in 1861-62. In 1863 the House rescinded the "Rauhe Haus'" annual subsidy of 2,040 "Thaler," and cancelled the government's contract with the board of directors as of the end of the year. Nine brothers were commissioned in the first four months of 1863, but not one entered penal work.

While the various institutions affiliated with the confederation called the Inner Mission engaged in many charitable enterprises, it is important to note that much of Wichern's energy in the fifties went into penal reform. In his mind, prisoners were small-time revolutionaries who could easily become big-time, and he was committed to arresting this process. The fifties provided an excellent climate for his experiment at Moabit; church, state, and a conservative spirit of charitable reform cooperated toward this goal. But their cooperative effort was surely not aimed at the most grievous of all social ills. In fact, penal reform, though a necessity, was at this time an effort by conservatives to rehabilitate one of the most repressive institutions of the state. Their efforts showed that in Prussia the religious charter was alive and well, at least in the tightly controlled environment of the prison.

CHURCH, SOCIETY AND POLITICS

It would be inaccurate to give the impression that peace and tranquility prevailed everywhere in German culture and society in the fifties. Kant's era of perpetual peace had not yet arrived. That much is clear from the glowing coals of two fires that soon flared into major conflagrations: national unification, and social change accompanying modernization.

317

As we take a final look at the reactionary triangle in the broad context of society and politics, we will note that the evangelical church made a faltering witness to certain emerging social and political forces. It refracted its responses to these challenges through the prism of the unwritten religious charter. This prismatic, refractory process was itself a facet of the interaction of governmental official, pastor, and social conservative that we have called the reactionary triangle. The fifties were something of a "last hurrah" for the religious charter since, as the next chapter indicates, political nationalism soon modified the consensus about the church's social role in imporant ways.

Social Undercurrents

During the fifties, most of the German churches followed a simple maxim in their relations with the broader society: do not disturb the peace, and provide as much support as possible for such basic social institutions as monarchy and family. One author suggests that during this period, the church "emigrated" out of Protestant society. "Churchly Protestantism" was in danger of rejecting "secular Protestantism" as its illegitimate child, and in the process laying itself open to charges of being anti-socialist.(11) One important result was that the emerging socialist movement lost contact with the church.

In 1858, Pastor G. F. Reimann published a utopian tract that portrayed the church's social responsibilities as understood by many. Touted as a Biblical description of the millennial kingdom, the booklet sketched the outline of Christ's earthly kingdom when He would return to reign after a thousand years. The author wrote that Palestine would be the center of that kingdom; agriculture and gardening, trade and the arts would flourish, as Christian culture flowed out from this people of God to all peoples. Peace would take the place of international strife; movements for political freedom and constitutionalism would disappear, as would sectarianism in the Christian church. Freemasons and Jesuits, political parties and revolutions would be problems of the past. Sickness would be curtailed, and the length of human life extended. Society would lose its open sores, including houses of prostitution, dance floors, card games, and lotteries—in short, "everything that one still cultivates in service of the world."

This social utopia may not have been acceptable to all German Protestants at the time, but it did strike a resonant chord in many. The church's social responsibilities revolved around preserving certain sacrosanct traditions, preaching against private vices, and nurturing cooperation between church and state to ameliorate certain conditions, and to strengthen society's foundational unit, the family.

Many thought that the church's primary social responsibility was to preserve Sunday as a day of worship and rest. Under churchly pressure in the fifties, the old Prussian provinces prohibited railway builders from working on Sundays and church holidays, except in dire emergencies. Pay windows had to close an hour before Sunday services, and remain shut until an hour after services. Similar prohibitions against Sunday work applied to construction workers on canals and roads, servants, and young people over twelve; legal transactions, such as executions, auctions, or delivering summonses, could not occur on Sunday.

Wichern and his Inner Mission societies had a somewhat larger vision of the church's social responsibilities, but most of their activities centered around the reforms of privatistic vices, or the nurturing of traditional social mores. Speaking to the Congress of the Inner Mission in 1856, for example, Wichern described the proper role of women in the family structure. As her husband's helpmate, she saw to it that he was won for God's kingdom and the church, he said. She shielded her children from the bitterness and strife of ecclesiastical parties, while she taught them the decency of "German piety" and avoided false legalism. But while "the home is and remains the woman's first calling," she did not have to resign herself to being a homemaker. Only her familiy duties limited her love; beyond that, she was free to join societies or become a missionary helper or deaconess. The woman with "no time" for these affairs was probably incapable of rendering true service in her family unit as well, he added.

In 1851 Wichern discussed what he considered to be a related problem, namely, prostitution. He insisted that the solution of any social problem depended on the energetic cooperation of church and state officials. In this instance, he advised civil officials to continue heeding the church's conscience, pursuing a policy that had secured rich rewards. Meanwhile, urban clergymen should speak out on behalf of their members, by exposing the houses of ill repute that preyed on their parishioners. Wichern was convinced that such cooperative action could eliminate prostitution, and advance the cause of God's kingdom.

His basic assumption was that the social structure was slightly out of balance. The "social problem" resulted from the breakdown in cooperation among the components of society; the root cause of imbalance was moral and spiritual decay, compounded in turn by industrialization. The solution lay in re-establishing organic wholeness and re-affirming each class' corporate responsibility. Wichern told the Congress at Stuttgart in 1850 that the workers' problem could be solved if God's Word and the doctrine of universal priesthood were preached to all.

He sounded like a mouthpiece for many Protestants when he deliverd a lecture on poverty in 1855. His audience at Berlin's Evangelical Society for Churchly Goals included the Prussian king. Wichern argued that the cooperative efforts of church, state, and voluntary agencies could deal effectively with the problem of poverty.

His running battle with the foremost evangelical proponent of cooperatives, Victor Aime Huber (1800-1869), was more than a personal feud. Huber's thinking on self-help cooperatives followed the contours of group need and group response, while Wichern showed more interest in private philanthropy. For this reason, Wichern was unable to understand Huber's claim that cooperatives were not charitable organizations, and one suspects that the majority of Protestants agreed with him.

In 1857 Wichern delivered a scathing review of Huber's latest book on cooperative housing. He asserted that the Inner Mission took the high road; in agreement with basic Christianity, it addressed problems in all areas of life—official, private, social, ecclesiastical and governmental. Housing concerns were not necessarily foreign to the Mission's work, he wrote, but people had to be alert

320

to the moral and religious ramifications of this and other problems. He felt that Huber expected housing cooperatives and home construction to accomplish more than these programs were designed to handle.

Wichern's tendency to moralize and spiritualize social problems was symptomatic of the church's understanding of its social responsibilities in the fifties. Because of this assumption, his treatment of the housing problem at the Congress in Bremen in 1860 did not lead to spectacular results. After his speech, only seven factory workers in Wuppertal volunteered to help eliminate severe housing shortages.

Cultural materialism added more fuel to the social fires of the fifties. Before the end of the century, Karl Vogt, Ludwig Buechner, Jacob Moleschott, and others published a stream of books written from a materialistic perspective. In 1854, Vogt and Rudolf Wagner waged a battle in the Conference of Scientists over the relation between faith and science. Vogt, who had been a deputy at Frankfurt, pushed a hard materialistic line, while Wagner discussed such questions as the soul's immortality and the origin of human society, claiming that scientific advances did not necessarily spell the doom of religious doctrines. Some scientists remarked that Wagner should have been registered for attendance at the "Kirchentag" assembly, which was meeting at the same time in Frankfurt.

There was more fireworks at the annual science meeting in Karlsruhe in 1858. Some speakers claimed that scientists had turned the material world into an idol, thereby invalidating their attack on religion; another asked whether there was an irreparable breach between science and faith, or whether the inexplicable still left room for belief; another argued that scientific progress strengthened true belief in God. Rudolf Virchow took the young Turks' position, claiming that religion was a private affair; there was little reason to waste time in public argument about a problem that would be solved in one's private study. But the question was far from answered, and soon the churches faced a culture with materialistic biases sharply focused by the conditions that accompanied industrialization.

The pessimistic works of Arthur Schopenhauer (1788–1860)

321

achieved prominence in the fifties, a few years before the author died. What was most attractive was the pessimism of personalism. Schopenhauer insisted that the individual exercised himself in the private sphere of life, not in the larger social and political realm. Fuerbach's views came into greater public appreciation at the same time as well.

One evangelical group embodied this pessimistic spirit in a unique way. The movement was organized in Wuerttemberg by Christoph Hoffmann, the son of the founder of the Korntal settlement. After returning in 1849 from Frankfurt, where he served as a delegate, this cleric collected a group of people who were dissatisfied with the state church and with political authority. His announced objective was to bring together the people of God, and to lead the new Israel to Jerusalem, there to erect God's state. At the Salon, a school for boys near Ludwigsburg, he was drawing up battlelines with the territorial church by supporting the principle of separating church and state. But Hoffmann soon concluded that the establishment of a "church" at Salon was not the answer to the problem. A new form of "Christian folk life" was needed. It could not be created in Germany or anywhere else in the west, but only in Palestine.

Chairing the organizational meeting of the "Friends of Jerusalem" late in 1854, Hoffmann invited participants to sign one of several petitions for the Federal Diet of the German states in Frankfurt. Heads of 419 families, including fourteen Roman Catholics from Baden, eventually signed the petition that was sent to the Diet. It described Germany's condition in dramatic and pessimistic terms:

> The feeling of being close to the living God has
> been torn away from our people, and they have looked
> for their spiritual nourishment in confessional
> battles, in the desolate maxims of the falsely-named
> Enlightenment, and in other unprofitable products
> of human arrogance. This fall from the living God
> has deprived us of all vigor, and transformed us
> from a people who cared for one another into a dead
> mass that can only be held together by force, and by
> encroaching governmental machinery run by a horde of
> civil servants.

The members of the group were convinced that the beginning

of a "folk life grounded in God's law and Spirit must be made in Jerusalem and in the Holy Land." The time for action was at hand. The petition noted that these were not the foggy notions of a group of dreamers:

> May the honored Federal Diet, therefore, consider this matter not as the idea of several well-meaning dreamers, but as a bond of unity between the German princes and the people, as an opportunity for the German nation to develop power along lines pleasing to the Lord Jesus, King of kings and Lord of lords.

But on December 14, the Diet approved a subcommittee report that recommended that the petition not be considered because it concerned matters beyond the Diet's jurisdiction. Meanwhile, Bishop Gobat, Wichern, Johann Gess, Kapff, and Johann C. Blumhardt wrote letters and articles encouraging Hoffmann to reconsider his plan.

Once more in 1859, the organizing committee petitioned the Diet, indicating that "the conditions of our time prove that the apostacy prophesied by the apostles is at hand." The German people need not stand idle while emigrants were scattered everywhere without rhyme or reason; rather, a program should be established that provided "room for natural expansion." It was God's plan, the brief continued, to use the Holy Land as a place where His people could gather as an example for the nations, so that His law became the basis for true civilization. The Diet accepted the memorandum without issuing a reply.

Hoffmann then used an estate he purchased near Marbach as a point of embarkation. His troubles with the territorial church mounted; after being suspended from office, he and ten others living on the estate were excommunicted in 1859. In 1861 the group was organized as the "German Temple," with the announced goal of salvaging the crumbling family structure, teaching the proper use of possessions, alerting Germany to the importance of colonizing the Holy Land, educating German youth in true piety, and creating a central German power. The first colonists settled in the Holy Land in 1866, followed by others in 1867, 1869, 1870 and later. By 1884, more than 937 colonists affiliated with the German Temple were in the Holy Land.

The Temple was organized to operate as an independent religious and political entity in Wuerttemberg, although it never gained political recognition. Adherents were deeply concerned with social fragmentation and the breakdown of authority; filled with pessimism, they felt that Germany's days were numbered. God's kingdom, complete with its hierarchy of political values and social priorities, could be fully manifested only on foreign soil, in Palestine. But the burning question of national unity played a subliminal role in the Temple's development. The use of the word "German" in the name was significant; the people of the Temple claimed to have a saving word for the problem of national fragmentation, for Germany's emerging social question, and for the great number of emigrants.

Theocracy, Nationalism and Diaspora

In the fifties, the churches had two complementary goals in the political realm: support the monarchy, and endorse political activities that perpetuated the reaction. In 1855, a speaker for the Berlin pastoral conference discussed these issues in simple terms when he indicated that "THEOCRACY is the beginning and end of God's kingdom: whenever a nation is truly Christian in all its parts, there the unity of church and state is already firmly rooted in reality." The same issues were broached in the careful phrasing of the petition inserted in the General Prayer, when Prussia's House of Deputies was in session: "Look down in grace on the legislators of our land, who once again are assembled around the throne of our king."

Religious support for reactionary policies was one reason why a new religious group, called the Irvingites, got a foothold during the fifties. This British movement was imported through the efforts of the English "apostle," Thomas Carlyle, and his most important German disciple, a one-time professor at Marburg named Heinrich W. J. Thiersch (1817-1885). The group claimed that the "beast" of Revelation was loose, and the End was at hand. One important convert in Prussia was Hermann Wagener, who served as editor of the KREUZZEITUNG for several years, and was recognized as the major spokesman for the paper's archconservative Prussian clique. The Irvingites claimed they could remain within the territorial churches, but encountered opposition from Prussia's High Church Council regarding their participation in communion and marriage ceremonies. The movement succeeded in establishing a number of cell groups in provincial Silesia, Prussia and Pomerania, especially in the cities of Berlin and Koenigsberg. By 1852 the number of "sealed" in north Germany exceeded 1,000; the congregation in Berlin numbered 400. When the Lord failed to appear in 1855, and three "apostles" died, including Carlyle, the movement lost much of its appeal.

During this decade, many churchmen preferred to ignore the issue of nationalism or, more precisely, to theologize it. It was thought that the churches' most critical national assignment was to fight against unbelief; among Protestant liberals, this meant struggling against constraints of conscience.(12) The net result was a tendency to ignore popular nationalist sentiment, in favor of watching governmental and monarchical leadership move toward unification at its own speed. The one exception was the way many churchmen reflected on the conscience-related problem of nationalism in an area where they were not directly involved, namely, the dutchies of Schleswig-Holstein.

Nearly a hundred pastors in the dutchies supported the revolt against the Danish king during the revolutionary period. As long as Prussia endorsed the movement, evangelicals in Germany made few negative comments about the illegitimate behavior of colleagues supporting the provisional government. Some of the more liberal church periodicals in Germany endorsed the action of clergymen in Schleswig-Holstein, claiming that preachers were not exempt from the just claims of social community and nationalism. Even Hengstenberg's EVANGELICAL CHURCH NEWS referred to the dutchies as a "field of honor."

But Hengstenberg took the field against the pastors in the dutchies after Prussia deserted the provisional government late in the summer of 1848, lashing out against them in the first issue of his journal in 1850. The other side was forcefully argued by a mediating professor from Bonn, August Dorner, in a powerful speech at the "Kirchentag" in Stuttgart in 1850. Dorner insisted that if authorities deserted the sphere of morality, Christians were not released from their obligation to authority. Authority was not the person but the office; sometimes the people were properly incited to "active resistance," and since they had a deep interest in the people's welfare, evangelical clergymen were obliged to respect their action. Others, including the Bavarian theologian Johann C. K. Hofmann, and the church historian Hase, supported positions similar to Dorner's, while Stahl and right-wingers in Prussia took the opposite view.

The issue was complicated by Danish rescripts in 1851 and 1854 requiring that, in mixed areas of the dutchies, worship services were to be conducted in German and Danish, and confirmands were to be instructed in Danish. As the fifties passed, even the more conservative evangelicals in Germany seemed to support German nationalist sentiment in the dutchies because of this turn of events. In 1857, Stahl referred to a "matter of law" in the area, as well as a matter of "German national duty and German national guidance." The issue was far from settled when the New Era dawned in 1858, but it was clear that the dutchies would play a significant role in the future for politicians in Germany, because of the political capital that could be accrued from mining the complex Schleswig-Holstein problem.

Most German pastors who participated in the debate over Schleswig-Holstein did not suffer professional harrassment for supporting German nationalism. This was not true for the one hundred pastors in the dutchies who were relieved from office, including one of Claus Harms' leading disciples, Michael Baumgarten (1812-1889). Forced to leave the dutchy when the Danes came in 1850, Baumgarten took up residence in Mecklenberg as a professor at Rostock. Kliefoth emerged as his chief opponent, while others baited him with the challenge of providing scriptural grounds for revolution. Through Kliefoth's efforts, he was thrown out of his teaching position in the mid-fifties, and banned as a heretic from the pulpits of Mecklenberg. Despairing of the church's uncritical political views, he eventually entered the field of politics.

Nationalist sentiment persisted in the fifties, and it was evident that more was yet to come in the drama of national unification. Some church periodicals supported such innocuous national cultural gatherings as the "Schillerfest" in 1859. Other people examined the nationalist ramifications of emigration as a problem for the churches.

Scattered across Europe, and flung across the Atlantic, the German diaspora provided an excellent opportunity for joint action between church and state. Like colonial mission fields, the diaspora was ripe for harvest—if only someone would hire and equip the workers. In the case of the colonial mission, mission societies forced the states and the territorial churches to cooperative action. As far as Wichern was concerned, for the diaspora the catalytic task fell to the Inner Mission.

The number of German emigrants held rather steady at about 10,000 persons a year between 1835 and 1845, but in the mid-forties that number increased sharply, peaking at almost 50,000 in 1847. European states began identifying and protecting citizens who lived outside their native borders, a practice that was overtly nationalistic, and covertly imperialistic. German churchmen also showed increased concern for the welfare of German immigrants in the United States, and for German journeymen working in France, Switzerland and elsewhere in Europe. The four and a half million Germans who emigrated to the United States between 1851 and 1900 included a good number of the 1,000 pastors sent to North America between 1800 and 1877 by the German churches.

When the "Kirchentag" met in Berlin in 1853, Wichern faced the issue of the diaspora squarely. He urged the German churches to cooperate in ministering to German colonists wherever they could be found, but their cooperation hinged on a single goal: to help the colonists build God's kingdom anew at construction sites already available. Emigrants were to dedicate themselves to "loyally nurture and preserve the German mother tongue and German life and morals, for the honor of the Divine Name," he said.

At this occasion and others, Wichern used the phenomenon of emigration to focus attention on Germany's political disunity, and the inability of the independent states to care for emigrants. He was convinced that if the Inner Mission successfully arrested the drift toward atheism and communism among thousands of journeymen on foreign soil, church and state alike would profit when these men returned home. Similarly, emigrants to foreign countries performed a ministry to the people at home by appealing to them to break

327

down their haughtiness and particularism, in a unified effort on the emigrants' behalf. Their appeal, and the reply in the mother country, would demonstrate that God's kingdom was taking in a ripe harvest all over the world.

But emigration and the care of emigrants was only the tip of the iceberg. The problem of national unification remained to be solved, and Wichern's appeal for ministry to emigrants did little more than sensitize some in the church to the problem. The decisive shift in international relations that accompanied the Crimean War in the late fifties showed that the spirit of the Holy Alliance was dead, once and for all. Earlier in the decade, Russia successfully intercepted Prussia and Austria as they followed a collision course toward war over constitutionalism in electoral Hesse, and the resulting treaty at Oelmuetz temporarily defused the issue. But the Crimean War spelled the end of federative polity among the major nations of Europe, and a final test of will between Austria and Prussia over national leadership seemed imminent. When, how, and with what weapons the battle would be fought were still to be determined, but such a major adjustment in political relations among the German states was sure to have serious repercussions for the territorial churches.

During the fifties the population of the German states increased nearly ten percent, from 35,900,000 to 38,000,000. Not all of the nearly forty million people were Protestant ecclesiastical "reservists" who had performed well in the upheavals of 1848. But those who were received their due rewards in the fifties, a remarkable decade for the "Christian state."

A solid alliance among church, state, and social conservatism flourished in Prussia until 1858, and even then it did not disintegrate. That alliance surfaced at such civil-religious events as the service in the royal court commemorating the king's birthday in 1855. One of the prayers identified the hierarchy in religion, society and political structure that was the alliance's stock-in-trade:

Lord God, Thou who hast promised Thy church that

kings would see to her care, guide the king's heart
so that it is like a stream of water in Thy hand,
and channel whatever Thou choosest, that through
him Thy kingdom may be expanded.

The congregation closed the service with this response: "O
Lord, advance Thy kingdom on earth in our land, so that we
may become Thy subjects."

The reactionary triangle of the fifties was a clear
manifestation of the power of the unwritten religious
charter. Social and political conditions were conducive to
the church's serving as a model for the broader society. In
return, the state distributed rewards and social recognition
to the church, as part of its continuing effort to keep
society under control; and most social conservatives
strongly approved of these developments. This was a decade
for the church to be "churchy," and it was—with the Inner
Mission providing a helpful assist.

But two problems hovered on the horizon like storm-clouds,
and no amount of gainsaying by the parties of the
reactionary triangle would make them go away. In succeeding
years, national unity and social issues came to the fore.
Since the reactionary triangle continued to exert some
influence, the question of national unity was ultimately
addressed first; the result helped shape both the form and
the content of the second question. But the process of
addressing the first question shifted the dynamic within the
reactionary triangle, and church and state made several
minor modifications in the unwritten charter as a result.

CHAPTER VII

(1) Walter Hubatsch, ed., DIE EVANGELISCHEN GENERAL-KIRCHEN UND SCHULVISITATIONEN IN OST- UND WESTPREUSSEN 1853 BIS 1944 (Goettingen: Vandenhoeck & Ruprecht, 1970), p. xii.

(2) Ibid., p. 761.

(3) K. G.Boche, DER PREUSSISCHE LEGALE EVANGELISCHE PFARRER; EINE UEBERSICHTLICHE DARSTELLUNG DES PREUSSISCHEN EVANGELISCHEN KIRCHENRECHTS (4th ed.; Braunschweig: C. A. Schwetschke und Sohn, 1869), pp. 128-34.

(4) Only about fifty of the 800 leaders in attendance came from the continent; more than eighty made the trip from the United States. In succeeding years, mission work, a week of united prayer, and defense of religious liberty were hallmarks of the Alliance, but in general the association had a difficult time attracting interest on the continent. Non-German churches did show interest in Wichern's Inner Mission; in 1851 the committee of the British Evangelical Alliance sent six representatives to the "Kirchentag" in Elberfeld, to swell the total attendance to more than 2,000.

(5) Erich Beyreuther, DER WEG DER EVANGELISCHEN ALLIANZ IN DEUTSCHLAND (Wuppertal: R. Brockhaus, 1969), pp. 29, 38.

(6) Paul Drews, DIE PREDIGT IM 19. JAHRHUNDERT, Vortraege der theologischen Konferenz zu Giessen, 19. Folge (Giessen: J. Ricker'sche Verlagsbuchhandlung, 1903), pp. 31-35.

(7) Prussia's eleven million Protestants (including

8,500 soldiers stationed outside her borders, and 12,500
French Reformed) easily outnumbered her Roman Catholic
population of 7,000,000. Statistical reports from 1861
indicate that the two percent of the population that was not
Protestant or Roman Catholic included a variety of religious
groups:

Jews	251,145	Anglicans	250
Old Lutherans	36,648	Brockhausians	160
Mennonites	13,725	Darbyites	153
Free (Indepen-		Edwardians	136
dent) Congregat.	7,735	Mezelians (Luth.)	123
German Catholics	6,125	Nazarenes	100
Baptists	5,452	Methodist (Berlin)	60
Moravian Brethren	4,536	Beerians (Luth.)	55
Irvingites	2,822	Muslims	3
Seehosian (Luth.)	2,082	Quakers	1
Netherland (Ref.)	1,923	Dissidents "who	
Other Luth. Separa-		belong to no party"	300
tists	1,000		
Philopponians (Rus-			
sian-Greek sect)	940		
Russian Orthodox	263		

(8) See Robert T. Handy, THE AMERICAN RELIGIOUS
DEPRESSION, 1925—1935, Facet Books, Historical Series, ed.
Richard C. Wolf (Philadelphia: Fortress Press, 1968).

(9) Another set of religious statistics dealing with
the intermarriage of Roman Catholics and evangelicals in
Silesia hints at a slowdown in the mid-fifties. The
following table indicates the number of mixed marriages
solemnized with a Catholic husband or wife in each year:

YEAR	TOTAL MIXED MARRIAGES	CATHOLIC HUSBAND	CATHOLIC WIFE
1853	1,545	1,175	370
1854	1,393	1,090	303
1855	1,305	993	312
1856	1,475	1,099	376
1857	1,970	1,477	493
1858	1,990	1,551	439
1859	1,677	1,288	389
1860	1,668	1,250	418

1861	1,568	1,219	349
1862	1,830	1,423	407
1863	1,996	1,481	515
1864	1,927	1,519	408
1865	2,343	1,860	483

(10) The thirty-one brothers assigned to Moabit made up the Ebenezer "Konvent" in Wichern's brotherhood. The "Konvent's" six sections appropriately bore the names of biblical figures who suffered imprisonment: Joseph, Micah, Jeremiah, Daniel, John the Baptizer, and Silas. At Moabit the men regularly met to discuss their work, but Wichern assured the Minister of Interior that their meetings were valuable therapy sessions, not religious gatherings.

(11) Theodor Strohm, KIRCHE UND DEMOKRATISCHER SOZIALISMUS; STUDIEN ZUR THEORIE UND PRAXIS POLITISCHER KOMMUNIKATION (Munich: Chr. Kaiser Verlag, 1968), p. 26.

(12) Joachim Rohlfer, "Staat, Nation, Reich in der Evangelischen Kirche Deutschlands im Zeitalter der deutschen Einigung, 1848—1871" (unpublished dissertation, Goettingen University, 1955), p. 93.

CHAPTER VIII

IMPERIAL SERVANTS

A ceremony in the Hall of Mirrors at Versailles inaugurated
the German Empire in January, 1871. It was a glittering
occasion for officialdom, but not for the people. Military
uniforms were the order of the day. Seven high ranking
military chaplains were present, including the nephew of the
Minister of War, the court preacher, and army division
chaplain Rogge, complete with the Iron Cross on his collar.
Rogge's speech drew attention to the century and a half that
lay behind this important moment for Prussia's dynasty;
during this period, God led "the kingdom <of Prussia> from
the smallest and most insignificant beginnings to ever
widening borders," and greater influence among the earth's
peoples. Rogge's second point touched on humility. Surely
the Hall of Mirrors was a reminder of what happened when the
monarch became an idol, since God appropriately rewarded the
French kings when they turned the Hall into an idolatrous
temple of their earthly power. The division chaplain closed
his remarks by referring to God's providential activity:

> In the work we see finished before our eyes today,
> in this hour and in this place, we see the goal
> achieved that God's providence has appointed for
> us in the history of our fatherland and royal
> dynasty, since that coronation at Koenigsberg that
> we recall today.

The empire was a reality, and within several months every
liturgical agenda in Prussia reflected that fact in new

intercessions for emperor and empire, added to the General Prayer by the king's order. The same was true in other states as well.

The decade of the sixties stood in marked contrast with the slow-moving fifties. After recovering from the economic bust of 1857, Germany's economy experienced sustained growth that did not falter until the early seventies. The growing cities showed that a new industrial society was emerging, but the most feverish activity was reserved for the realm of politics. In the sixties Prussia fulfilled an earlier king's promise that she would "merge" into Germany, but the truth of the matter was that Germany merged into Prussia, under the leadership of Otto von Bismarck. One way or another, the German states attained the imperial unity that received religious sanction in the Hall of Mirrors.

Most German Protestants accepted Bismarck's revolution from above as the best means of solving the national problem with the least amount of social disruption. A few dissidents offered criticism, some of it based on religious grounds, but most objections quickly evaporated in view of the serious threat posed by growing numbers of industrial workers. The churches' native ability to adjust to new political conditions made for a bright future. After national unity was achieved, the churches continued to function within the political compromise that underlay the new empire.

This chapter traces how the Protestant churches performed their task of imperial servanthood. It examines how the churches fulfilled their role as social models, while the German states attained nationhood and imperial unity. The churches' responses to liberalism's "final test" in Prussia, early in the sixties, set the pattern for their participation in the political ballet that ended with national unity; the responses of conservative, liberal, and mediating parties differed more in form than in substance, as they interpreted Prussia's constitutional crisis and the problem of the Danish dutchies, and provided humanitarian and religious assistance to the fighting force. Despite the hesitation of a few archconservatives, Protestants seemed to welcome Prussia's sudden defeat of Austria in 1866. Prussia's subsequent annexation of several territories opened the way for some vocal confessionalists to voice their anti-Prussian bias. But the war against France in 1870-71 brought little dissent. It showed that the unwritten religious charter was still viable; clergymen of every stripe gave the signal for patriotic involvement, and helped generate patriotic zeal. This event led to a significant alteration in the religious charter. The churches were given the added responsibility of lending moral support to conservative nationalism, as institutionally embodied in the empire. During their long march toward nationhood, Protestants had become imperial servants.

PROTESTANT CHURCHES AND LIBERALISM'S FINAL TEST

The response of evangelical leaders to Prussia's constitutional crisis in the early sixties was a weathervane of their reaction to many of the tumultuous political events of the decade. Included in these later developments were approval of Prussia's interference in the affairs of the dutchies of Schleswig and Holstein, and direct religious ministrations to the fighting forces in the three major wars of the decade. No less significant was the religious rationale that Protestantism supplied for Bismarck's use of nationalist sentiment on behalf of Prussian conservatism. But in order to understand these civil-religious activities, which were part of the church's expected responsibilities under the religious charter, we need to set them in the context of the emerging dualism between Roman Catholic Austria and Protestant Prussia, and to review the Prussian constitutional struggle in some detail.

In the years after the midcentury revolutions, political dualism between Prussia and Austria intensified as relations deteriorated. The two powers on the northern and southern ends of Germany sparred over the leadership of a unified German nation. Each used commercial and economic policies to attract the other German states to its side, and in the German Confederation they offered reform plans aimed at giving one or the other the edge. In 1863-64, Bismarck lured Austria into his capricious plans for the dutchies of Schleswig-Holstein with the tantalizing bait of a dualistic "balance;" Austria accepted, since she had no alternative to Prussia's totally annexing the area. Other facets of the intensifying struggle included Prussia's relative inactivity during Austria and France's crisis over Italy in 1859, Prussia's military reforms, the popularity of academic studies of Prussia as "Protestant champion" of Germany, and Austria's efforts to consolidate her empire through financial reform and the Bach administrative system. As federative polity disintegrated in Europe, at the same time that Civil War tested the federalist fabric in the United States, the traditional dualism between Austria and Prussia took on a nationalistic earnestness that was rather new. The middle German states were being forced to choose their lot.

The crisis between Austria and France in 1859, over the Italian question, had several important repercussions in the German states. One was the widespread renewal of nationalist sentiment, since many feared a French invasion of the Rhineland. Some middle class people, who favored a liberalized Prussia at the head of a strong Germany, organized the German National Union. Although its membership reached 25,000, the group made no appreciable political impact, nor did it become a mass movement. The subsequent course of events soon made its conflation of nationalist and liberal principles an anachronism, although the liberal movement was revitalized.

In Prussia, one important result was the regent's decision to strengthen the army through military reforms. Though he opened the windows of the "New Era," the crown prince stood by his calling as Prussia's foremost soldier. In 1859 he created a military cabinet, through which he supervised the army directly without interference from the House of Deputies' minister. This arrangement paralleled the church structure created some nine years earlier, the High Church Council, independent of the Minister of Ecclesiastical Affairs. Thus, at about the time a large liberal majority was elected to the House (1858), the regent, who ruled as his brother lay dying, pursued a course of military reform apparently unacceptable to the liberal majority. The majority's election reflected the impact of major economic changes in Prussia's three-class voting system, but more significant was the fact that the revolutionary forces of German liberalism were exhausted before industrialization made its lasting imprint on most of the masses.

Prussia's liberals maintained a firm majority in the House, while conservative strength plummeted in the early sixties. The king's proposed army reform was greeted with little acclaim, especially since General Roon wanted to eliminate the citizen militia, a sacrosanct creation of liberal reformers earlier in the century. The king also proposed an extension of military draft service from two to three years, so that the army would serve as the "school of the nation." Since liberals feared that military force might be used to reverse minimal constitutionalist gains, they could not consider the king's plans dispassionately. After presenting his proposals, the king proceeded to implement certain sections, creating new regiments toward the end of 1860, and dedicating their standards at the tomb of Frederick the Great in 1861 as a provocative gesture. The army's reorganization was now assured, regardless of the parliament's action.

In the meantime, the liberal majority in the House reacted timidly. Each year the liberals had voted the necessary military appropriations, while withholding approval for the army's reorganization. Finally in 1862, the budgetary committee refused to pass the army's current budget, and the House concurred in its action. This turn of events brought a constitutional crisis, since the assembly was charged with appropriating funds. The issue was not army reform as much as the liberals' desire to share in the responsibility of power; for his part, the king feared that the parliament was trying to control the monarchy's single most important institution and mainstay.

Threatening to abdicate, King William was counseled by Roon to name Otto von Bismarck as minister-president, and eventually foreign minister. Traveling from his diplomatic post in Paris, Bismarck assumed office in September, 1862. Some years earlier he indicated his unwillingness to dance to bureaucratic music, but now the tune was his to call. A strange twist of fate brought this foreign affairs expert to power in the midst of a domestic crisis. But since the vortex of the domestic storm was the army, the king's primary instrument of foreign policy, the choice of Bismarck was a happy one, even though some saw him as a last resort. His strong commitment to the monarchy tempered his radical reputation in foreign affairs, including his reasoned rejection of partnership with Austria.

Bismarck threw the liberals into disarray. He accused some of trying to overthrow the monarchy, when actually they were trying to influence it. In a show of force, he ruled without a budget, applying the "gap theory" to the constitution to legitimate his action. He argued that if the constitution failed to give explicit directions, the monarch had to fill the vacuum; without a budget from the House, the monarch had to spend the levied taxes that accrued in increasing amounts due to growing industrialization. An immediate show of force bought the time needed to fend off the liberal thrust; a concerted effort to convince the liberals of the monarch's wisdom came later in the international realm.

In the ensuing struggle, the liberals suffered from a number of disadvantages. They were uncertain of their goal. They feared that too sharp a confrontation would bring a military coup, and then Prussia's fragile constitutional system would collapse. They were uncertain about the extent of their popular support. And, many of them were extremely susceptible to governmental pressure since they were governmental employees. Of the 352 deputies elected in 1862, 183 were employees of the government, including eighteen clergymen and eighteen retired civil servants. Bismarck exerted pressure on the deputies by requiring them to pay the cost of substitutes while they attended sessions. Nine non-judicial officials suffered vocational harrassment, including transfer and, in one case, dismissal from office; eight of them were part of the extreme liberal or left-center faction, and one had served on the budget commission. The government moved with dispatch against the deputies serving in judicial posts, transferring or dismissing eleven out of seventy-five for disciplinary reasons in a few years; three had been members of the budget commission. In addition, Bismarck secured a royal press edict in 1863 that aided the conservative press, and placed strict controls on the liberal press.

A "People's Church" in the Protestant Union

How did Protestant churchmen respond to what is sometimes

called the "final test" of German liberalism? As barometers of opinion, church periodicals provide a satisfactory answer to that question. We would suspect that liberal churchmen who did not emigrate after 1848 were gun-shy, and not apt to repeat their mistakes, in view of the liberals' defeat at that time. At the same time, parliamentary skirmishes probably attracted conservative churchmen to the monarch's position. To test our hypothesis, we will review the mediating party's response, then turn to the conservatives, and finally consider the liberals' proposal for a "people's church" in the Protestant Union organization.

Already during the upheavals at midcentury, Protestants in the mediating party demonstrated a disinterest in political affairs. During the constitutional struggle, they continued their hands-off policy so they could play a mediating role, although no one invited them to do so. They were joined by their liberal colleagues, who generally had little to say about the political mechanizations of the constitutional struggle. While recognizing the political significance of the battle, they were not prepared to enter the fray or encourage others to take decisive positions.(1) The number of clergy deputies in Prussia's House fell from seven percent in 1849 to six percent in 1862, and about one percent in 1866. The better part of valor was to watch from the sidelines.

Wichern exemplified the kind of response that most of the mediating group offered. He wrote in FLY-LEAVES in 1860 that one of the Inner Mission's tasks was to counteract factionalist enemies of God's kingdom by nurturing fraternal peace. In 1862 he again renounced party spirit in church and state, and urged Christians to extend God's besieged kingdom into all areas of life. Speaking to churchmen in Brandenburg that autumn, he attacked modern opponents of religion who sowed seeds of dissent in social, religious and political spheres of life. He added that conflict always accompanies the creation of any new structure, but men perform a divine service only when their opponents were truly God's enemies. Wichern said much about conflict in these years, but little was directly applicable to Prussia's constitutional crisis.

The conservatives offered more forthright advice. "The Prussian clergy," said a spokesman at the regular June meeting of pastors in Gnadau in 1862, "can presently take their place only with the conservatives, who are not a party but people who represent the true folk that gathers around its king. Contemporary democracy is nothing more than the modern manifestation of anti-Christianity." No less direct was the advice printed in provincial Saxony's conservative PEOPLE'S PAPER FOR TOWN AND COUNTRY. The day after the House refused to budget money for army reorganization, the paper told its readers that the real issue was sovereignty. Who would rule? The king? Or "the demagogues who know how to create a majority in the House of Deputies?" The "wildly democratic" majority, which was disrespectful of the king's person, was set on ruling Prussia through parliament. The paper proposed an interesting solution to the budgetary quandry. According to constitutional theory, without a budget Prussia ceased to exist, and "then it existed only in practice." That was the solution.

In separate speeches in Berlin early in 1863, Hengstenberg of the EVANGELICAL CHURCH NEWS and Ernst Ludwig von Gerlach indirectly supported the conservative minority in the House. Hengstenberg argued that a non-believing Christian could be a democrat in the contemporary understanding of the term. For the Christian, the state was a "moral creation with a calling in god's kingdom;" the state could never accept the majority's will as a guiding principle superior to moral order. Gerlach asserted that any constitutional system had to preserve the monarchical principle at all costs; "monarchy is the noblest political structure . . . for it is the universal political framework. It is also the political arrangement of Christ's kingdom in the narrow sense," he added. Both absolutism and democracy tried to replace rule by divine right with the rule of the fallen creature, man.

Prussia's High Church Council played a conservative role in the constitutionalist struggle by issuing memoranda when political elections occurred. The first appeared in April of 1862, when the king called new elections after the deputies refused to pass the military money bill. The Council advised pastors that as servants and preachers of God's Word, they had a special responsibility if "a case arises concerning the power and rights of the crown based on the recognized territorial constitution, over against the opinions and designs of political parties." The Council added that it did not intend to turn pastors into party leaders, but neither could it relieve them of their responsibility during these elections. Their behavior could bring profit or injury to themselves and the church, but they could not avoid their responsibility to king and fatherland. This duty showed itself in a "childlike submission to authority under God's holy ordinance," and in the election of delegates who were morally responsible to God and Jesus Christ, officials who recognized moral accountability before God, and an eternal goal above and beyond their political goals. The consistory in Breslau was even more explicit; it urged Silesian pastors to cooperate "so that the result of the approaching territorial election suits the intentions of His Majesty, the King." But these efforts had little effect. The conservatives continued their losing streak, dropping from fifteen seats to ten seats; the liberals won 284 of the 325 seats, with the Progressives, the strongest faction, retaining more than 100 seats.

Things went no better for conservatives after the election early in 1863. On Easter Sunday, many pastors in Koenigsberg deleted from the General Prayer the petition for the parliament, in an act that had the marks of a political demonstration. A number of orthodox pastors also informed the king of their support, and told of their difficulty interceding for parliament because of the House's sin against the Fourth Commandment. Bismarck arranged a royal audience for one group; waiting in the palace reception area for the meeting to occur, one pastor sentimentally remarked, "Oh, how exquisite it is here! How beautiful it will finally be in heaven!"

Heaven was still to come, and so was political unity for Germany. But in liberalism's most crucial test, the constitutionalist struggle, it was becoming apparent that German Protestants could absorb a revolution more easily from above than from below. The conservatives who rallied around the besieged monarch gave the clearest witness. If they could enlarge their conception of the dynasty to encompass all of Germany, and if at the same time liberals could be realigned in a way that separated liberalism from nationalism, a revolution from above could become a reality. Inasmuch as the constitutionalist struggle in Prussia foreshadowed this possibility, the signals that came

341

from churchmen augured well for the future: there was a vocal right, and a left and center that had learned something about power in the midcentury upheavals.

Bismarck's manipulation of Prussia's foreign relations threw both liberals and conservatives into disarray, and at the same time forged German unity under Prussia's leadership. Like their predecessors earlier in the century, most Prussian liberals were nationalists, who hoped that German unity would bring liberalized constitutionalism to the German states. Meanwhile, conservatives supported a Prussian state patriotism that centered in monarchical power and the army's supportive role. Bismarck, a revolutionary figure, imposed his will on both groups, remolding their conceptions of nation and state so that the two were not mutually exclusive. Henry Kissinger noted that this complex new order had something for everyone, but Bismarck alone held the reins:

> Too democratic for conservatives, too authoritarian for liberals, too power-oriented for legitimists, the new order was tailored to a genius who proposed to restrain the contending forces, both domestic and foreign, by manipulating their antagonisms.(2)

In 1863, over 500 delegates gathered to observe the fiftieth anniversary of the Battle of Leipzig, and to lay the cornerstone of a great "national monument." These middle class representatives came from over two hundred cities to press the claim for a unified, constitutionalized Germany. But even at this gathering, the idea of power intruded itself into speeches, and soon the tumultuous events of the sixties interrupted the monument's construction. The answer to the question, "Whose power will stand at the center of the new German nation?", was not a national monument in Leipzig, but Prussian leadership.

Supposedly, the Protestant Union was established by liberal Protestant churchmen in 1863 to give encouragement to Prussian liberals in the constitutional struggle. But since the Prussian liberals were somewhat unsure of their goal, the founding of such an "auxiliary" organization is open to other interpretations as well. We recall that in the revolutionary upheavals of midcentury, Protestant liberals were less interested in political events per se than in their ramifications for the church. This is perhaps the most promising key to understanding the Union's origins.

The Protestant Union pointed up a problem that the churches had refused to address straightforwardly, the question of national unification. Since they would play no direct role in the process of unification, the most the churches could expect was to claim some involvement by virtue of Protestantism's place in the wider culture, and this, in turn, raised the question of a national church. The Protestant Union was one of the earliest discernible forms of the cultural Protestantism that prevailed in the last quarter of the century. The cultural Protestantism it espoused was a liberal manifestation of the nationalism that was later de-liberalized and Prussianized; since Prussia was the largest and most powerful Protestant state, cultural Protestantism implied a "small Germany" ("Kleindeutsch") solution to the national question.

Meeting in the late fifties in Gotha, German liberals had proclaimed that the substance of national political unity was more important than its form. Protestant liberals who joined the Protestant Union made similar noises, indicating that the most important goal was national unity; if it had to occur in state before church, so be it. They intended to pursue a brand of "political Christianity" that would enable political unity to overcome the disunity of the German territorial churches.

Acting on impulses provided by an essay by Richard Rothe (1799-1867), entitled "For Direction Regarding the Contemporary Assignment of the German Evangelical Church" (1862), as well as his own commitment to Protestantism as unbridled freedom, a theologian from Heidelberg named Daniel Schenkel (1813-1885) worked to expand the liberal era of church government that he helped inaugurate in Baden in 1861. He was convinced that the people's church should be based on popular spirit, not on some kind of doctrinal formulation. Schenkel spearheaded a preliminary meeting at Durlach in August of 1863, which set an organizational meeting of the Protestant Union at Frankfurt am Main the next month. One hundred representatives from throughout Germany attended the meeting, including Karl Schwarz, Rothe, Johann C. Bluntschli, Heinrich Ewald (one of the "Goettingen

343

Seven"), and Rudolph von Benngsen, later a leader of the National Liberals. The Union drew its strength from Baden, the two Hesses, Nassau, Saxony, Gotha and Hanover; Protestants in Prussia offered little support, except for a few of Schleiermacher's disciples from Berlin.

The assembled clergymen, professors, officials, doctors, lawyers, merchants and teachers hoped to turn the "pastor's church" into a "people's church" by harmonizing German Protestantism with the day's cultural advances. Free inquiry, and the question "What is truth?" were to be paramount as they "transform<ed> the church, in the spirit of Protestant truth and freedom, into a German national church based on confession to Christ, the only Master," and on the free will of its members.

Rothe struck the keynote as he addressed the group. "If the times demand civil freedom and national satisfaction little by little, they therefore seek these possessions with such a deep thirst because they are nothing less than the conditions of a dignified human existence, and a truly moral wholeness, both for the individual and for the nation as a whole." As a disciple of Hegel, Rothe was convinced that religious advance occurred within the context of a moral state. "The moral commonwealth, the modern state," he said at the meeting, "has done much more to bring mankind into a condition adequate to Christ than all the churches from Jerusalem or Rome, from Wittenberg or Geneva. This is historical fact." He added that "by all means I live in the firm conviction that the invention of steam engines and railways has brought a far more important positive advancement to the kingdom of Christ than the ingenious reasonings of dogma at Nicea and Chalcedon." In no small part, the Protestant Union was an embodiment of Rothe's liberal theology.(3)

In 1864 the Protestant Union faced difficult times when Schenkel's CHARAKTERBILD JESU created such a furor in Baden. The High Church Council and the General Synod interceded on Schenkel's behalf, acknowledging the validity of Rothe's theological opinion that administrative ecclesiastical authorities did not have the power or responsibility to endorse or condemn a theological method. Despite its small size, the Union was gravely affected by these developments. In Prussia, the general superintendents advised pastors not to join this liberal society, but Schenkel came to the Union's defense in the UNIVERSAL CHURCH NEWS:

> Whoever rejects the Protestant Union because it has national purposes in mind, because it has decided to struggle for the foundation of a German Protestant Church, because it may bring the blessings of the GERMAN Reformation to the full appreciation of the GERMAN people, such a one really must first learn the basic elements of Christianity; he must come to recognize above all that if one does not love his people, he also cannot rightly love men, or the One who above all else went into bitter death for His people.

Another author wrote in the paper that the "structural elements of the state change, but the people remain; the folk is the form in which the other finds life." But the writer failed to say that the Protestant Union was essentially a cadre of Protestant shock troops, preparing the Protestant world for revolution from above. If its rhetoric were de-liberalized, its emphasis on Protestant culture strengthened the hand of supporters of Prussian leadership in the national cause.

The Union held its first Protestant Day at Eisenach in 1865. One of the statutes adopted there echoed motifs enunciated by the church historian Hase in 1848, when he called for unity among Germany's evangelical churches. But the raw political realism of the sixties gave an ironic twist to words such as "freedom" and "cultural development." The statute said, "On the basis of evangelical Christianity, a German Protestant Union is formed among such German Protestants as strive after a renewal of the Protestant church in the spirit of evangelical freedom, and in harmony with the collective cultural development of our time." What it meant to say was that a revolution from above was underway, and Protestants should not stand idle in the marketplace.

God's Gift: The Danish Dutchies

The Danish dutchies of Schleswig and Holstein were a focus

345

for intermingling nationalist sentiment and dynastic power during the sixties. The struggle over the dutchies exposed Protestant churchmen to the workings of a revolution "from above," though at the time many were unable to discern the meaning of events. Meanwhile, political liberals in Prussia saw how a government could function without a legal budget while making progress toward one important goal, the unification of Germany.

We need not describe the intricate series of events that produced an international crisis over the dutchies in 1863, when the Danish king died without a heir. But it should be noted that shortly before his death, the Danish parliament adopted a new constitution making Schleswig an integral part of the kingdom, altering earlier international agreements. When a German duke claimed the two dutchies after the king's death, a number of smaller German states rallied to his side; the basis of their argument was the dutchies' largely German population.

Prussia's Bismarck had little interest in forming another small German state in the north. Bismarck eventually decided that the solution was to annex the dutchies. He opposed the smaller states' action, and supported an international treaty that would keep the dutchies in the Danish kingdom, while making special provisions for them at the same time. This appeal to international law allowed him to take Austria in tow, and prevent her from endorsing the nationalist claims of the smaller German states. When the Danish government failed to respond to Austria's and Prussia's ultimatum, the two powers declared war in January, 1864, on behalf of the dutchies. The basic question remained even after the Danish phase was over: Who would own the dutchies?

Many Protestant pastors in the dutchies were Germans, and they faced a dilemma when the new Danish king was crowned in November of 1863. Four-fifths of the clergymen in the southern dutchy of Holstein refused to take the new oath of allegiance; all but two pastors performed their duty in the northern dutchy of Schleswig. In most parishes, the General Prayer included petitions for the new king and his family.

Pastors in the German states were given their clearest chance to discuss the politics of the dutchies in detail with this question about taking oaths. Most published reports commended the pastors who refused to take the oath; only the Prussian conservatives seemed opposed to that decision. Some liberal nationalists, such as the ex-dutchy pastor Michael Baumgarten, of Mecklenberg, claimed that pastors supported the true monarchical principal by endorsing Holstein's true monarch, the German duke Frederick, and refusing an oath to the Danish king. Theirs was the "high responsibility" of defending the monarchical principle "in its original purity and power," Baumgarten wrote in a memorandum to "my former pastoral colleagues in Holstein."

Nationalist zeal for the dutchies also surfaced among some southern churchmen. One periodical in Wuerttemberg said that it affirmed the princely principle, as well as the people's rights and demands. In Bavarian Erlangen, the confessionalist von Hofmann joined a society supporting nationalist goals for the dutchies. In speeches to the society, he argued that autonomy for the dutchies would be a step toward national unity. In middle states such as Saxony, a groundswell of support emerged for the German prince who claimed the dutchies. The Saxon court preacher Liebner described to the parliament early in 1864 the "deep, great, magnificent feeling that now runs through our German people." If it kept its moral basis and firm connection to law, the feeling would bring democaracy of the highest order. "Then welcome, democracy, blessed democracy! May you never desert us," he added. His indirect support for the dutchies' independence from Denmark hinted at the approval for the revolution "from above" that was gathering strength under a liberal disguise.

Conservatives endorsed the dutchies' move for independence from Denmark because their world view was, at the same time, all-embracing and elastic. But they did not all arrive at the same conclusion at the same time. Early in 1864, the UNIVERSAL CHURCH NEWS commended clergymen in the dutchies who resisted the Danish king, adding that "the conservative principle reveals itself in the entire movement for Schleswig-Holstein." Surely a cooperative effort of Prussia and Austria could not be radical! Conservative papers such as Saxony's PEOPLE'S PAPER FOR TOWN AND COUNTRY at first ignored the nationalist question, with the suggestion that Denmark was well advised to disintegrate as an autonomous state. Most conservatives seemed at first to dispute the clergy's right to refuse the oath as long as their actions had nationalistic overtones; together with many Lutheran confessionalists, they continued to equate nationalism and revolution, in the light of midcentury experiences. Pastors were not patriots but servants of God, Hengstenberg reminded readers of the EVANGELICAL CHURCH NEWS early in 1864.

But as the plot thickened, conservatives showed a willingness to endorse Prussia's plans for annexing the dutchies. Simply put, they were influenced by the successes of Prussia's power politics. After Prussia and Austria agreed in the Gastein Convention of 1865 to a de facto division of the joint administration of the dutchies, conservatives found themselves marching in step with Prussia and her monarch. Since Prussia retained sovereign rights over Holstein through her peace treaty with Denmark in 1864, Bismarck could at any time open up the whole question of the dutchies with Austria. And while Austria continued to be blamed for selling out German interests in the dutchies, Prussia waited for the inevitable annexation.

Once the Gastein convention assured that the German duke would have no place in the dutchies, Hengstenberg's EVANGELICAL CHURCH NEWS dropped its resistance to Bismarck's plans. If it came to Prussia's annexing the dutchies, at least the act would have the appearance of more legitimacy—through war and Austria's cooperation—than if some mere German duke replaced the Danish king. The Reformed conference that met in Rhenish Barmen in 1865 made a statement that most German Protestants of the time probably could have endorsed: "After weapons lay silent for fifty years in our Fatherland under God's gracious providence, the sword once more had to be drawn last year in war for the just cause of an oppressed segment of our German brotherhood. God the Lord has given a glorious victory to our weapons!" That may have been true, but then it was equally true that He had also given them a shrewd political leader named Bismarck, who used the affair to extend Prussia's hegemony over the German states.

One German conservative consistently resisted the effort. Ernst Ludwig von Gerlach, the Reformed lawyer-magistrate with the makings of a lay theologian, was disinclined to accept Bismarck's handling of the Schleswig-Holstein affair. His older brother Leopold (1790-1861), a Prussian general and confidant of Frederick William IV, was the first of the brothers to tangle with their old friend. Since Bismarck owed him so much, including his initial appointment as Prussia's diplomat to the German Federal Diet, the widening gap between the two indicated the revolutionary character of Bismarck's activity. In 1857 Bismarck rejected Leopold's claim that politics had to be practiced under the aegis of principle and dogma; he said that he would not allow the state to be bound to ideological principles, in a way that allowed men to force their own goals and convictions on the state. Bismarck's conception of the statesman's ethic was the pursuit of "pious" politics firmly anchored in the demands of reality, and subject to the total needs and demands of the state, not to a theory molded by arbitrary and illusory dogmatic convictions.

On January 12, 1864, shortly before Prussia and Austria went to war against Denmark, Leopold's brother, Ernst Ludwig, lashed out at Bismarck's plan of action in the NEW PRUSSIA NEWS. The article, which soon appeared as a pamphlet, interpreted the candidacy of the German duke as a ploy for German liberals. Gerlach warned that the full implementation of Prussia's plans would be grossly immoral. His private efforts to win Bismarck to his views were unsuccessful. Later that year he labelled Prussia's military action a "violent and premature measure," since she forced her will on the dutchies. In October he said that Prussia suffered from "territorial greed," a "shortsighted, suicidal sin and hypocrisy" that "calls down God's wrath on us."

In the fall of 1865, at the regular Pastoral Conference in Gnadau, Gerlach commented on a recent sermon that justified war against Denmark. He said that in such areas, clergymen had no more expertise than laymen. But he added that sermons could legitimately discuss the majesty of divine law as it applied to politics, and call into question the law of power and self-interest that had lately been held in such high esteem. Apparently, Gerlach felt that preaching had to promulgate legitimatism or it was not legitimate.

But as Bismarck's policies showed evidence of success, and as the military campaign in Schleswig-Hostein vindicated the king's proposals for army reform, the majority of Prussian conservatives cast their lot with Bismarck. By early 1865, the conservative party backed him almost to a man. In view of his increasingly precarious position among conservatives, even Gerlach began tempering his remarks. When Prussia signed the Gastein Agreement, he warned in the NEW PRUSSIAN NEWS against the "lust of annexation," but distinguished between lust and legally sanctioned annexation when designed to protect the dutchies from the revolutionary plans of German democrats.

Bismarck had welded nationalist sentiment to the crown, while seducing Austria into taking his bait in the dutchies. The great distance between Schleswig and Austria made it unlikely that she could administer the dutchy effectively. He knew that at any time he could raise the question of the dutchies as a pretext for war with the Austrians. They had been maneuvered into an untenable position, and the final blow was merely a matter of time.

Ministry to the Front

The four decades between 1830 and 1870 probably witnessed more advances in the science and practice of warfare than any previous comparable period in human history. Most of the changes occurred in the sixties, a period that witnessed the tactical use of railways, and a number of other technological innovations. Under these conditions, and especially under Wichern's leadership, the churches tried to provide religious and humanitarian assistance in the decade's three major wars, in 1864, 1866, and 1870-71.

Wichern rarely wrote an introductory editorial in the popular SUPPLEMENT of his journal, FLY-LEAVES, but in 1864 he altered his practice, and discussed the possibility of war with Denmark over the dutchies. He noted that it was not his purpose to play politics with the situation, but neither was he anxious to see Germany's honor disgraced. He wanted to ensure that "amid all these events, God's kingdom receives no injury; that our nation must be pointed toward this goal, namely, that it must guard this HEAVENLY refuge which has been entrusted to it—next to and under those EARTHLY endowments—with full commitment to faith." Men should recognize and confide in the final Judge, who through the scourge of war "wants to capture men's hearts and their

political structures . . . for Himself and His kingdom."
Wichern seemed to echo preachers of the "Erhebung" period,
who were apt to glorify war because it turned people's
hearts to spiritual concerns. War played a role in his
understanding of how God used church and state, or in this
instance, rivalry between states, to advance His earthly
rule.

With the consent of the Prussian government, brothers from
Wichern's training institutions in Hamburg and Berlin served
as paramedical personnel and humanitarian envoys during the
war with Denmark. The institution at Berlin assumed the
added burden of caring for "helpless children" of Prussian
"fathers and heroes, who gave their lives in the war for
king and fatherland." This work was done in the name of
God's "kingdom of peace on earth," Wichern reported in
1864.

The chaplain corps also provided religious ministrations to
the troops during the war with Denmark. Sixteen permanent
chaplains, and twelve newly activated reservists, ministered
to the Prussian troops who took the field against Denmark.
One chaplain gave a touching account of the communion
celebration that followed the Prussians' victory at the
Dueppel fortifications. Hospitalized veterans trooped to the
altar in clean clothes, some without arms and legs, some on
crutches, and some with bandages on their eyes. It was, he
recounted, a Supper for the "crippled, lame, and blind."

Once more in 1866 the air was filled with war rumors, this
time of a civil, fraternal war between Austria and Prussia.
Writing just weeks before the war broke out, Wichern
claimed, amid the nation's many divisions, to see the
outline of an indestructible community of faith. Conflict
could not destroy this communion, since its members were
knit more closely than ever by the pressures of the day. He
added,

> Would to God that the quarreling among the Lord's
> confessors—often so insignificant and wretched,
> and a curse for the evangelical church—falls deaf
> before the cannon thunder, and those who are one
> in Christ extend their hands to stand united in
> prayer, and to work for the coming of His kingdom,
> and if it be God's will, to fall together! The

351

community of the faithful is the seed for the
future community of peace in our fatherland.

With war looming on the horizon, Wichern discerned a peace
sign indelibly imprinted on the foreheads of those whose
hands were raised in confession and supplication. But with
his next breath, he discussed the kind of relief work that
war would require of Christians. He seemed to suggest that
when civil war cut an area into pieces, the role of the
Inner Mission was to bring healing, so that events would not
retard the growth of God's kingdom.

In that year, Wichern published recruitment notices in his
FLY-LEAVES for field hospital personnel, and men who would
render humanitarian service. He also invited Protestant
pastors to accept a three-month minimum tour of duty,
suggesting that the need was urgent since some brothers had
been drafted for military service, and his corps was short
of help. While he hoped that this activity would "build the
kindom of peace" while God's judgment of war swept across
Germany, Prussia's lightning victory over Austria limited
this effort in time and scope.

Military chaplains once again took to the field in 1866.
When her troops supported the Austrian cause, Saxony named
the Leipzig professor, Gustaf A. Fricke, as Chief of
Chaplains in 1866, since Saxony did not retain a
"Feldpropst" during peacetime. During the war, Prussia
fielded forty-five permanent chaplains, and thirty
volunteers and reservists, to minister to troops and
hospitals. One chaplain described the service on the day
after Prussia's victory at Koeniggraetz. The king and his
troops gathered to bury a general, along with others killed
in the battle. The sermon text came from the Old Testament:
"The noblest in Israel have been slain on your mountain.
How the heroes have been killed in action!" On another
occasion soon after the war, the king gave Prussian army
chaplains this advice: "Reverend pastors, you have
undertaken an important and difficult vocation. I thank you
for that. This campaign was short and victorious, and for
that we have to thank your prayers in part. I know that
many at home have prayed for the success of our weapons. On
our knees we must thank God that He has given us such
success so quickly. But appropriate humility, no
arrogance—preach that to the people!" Johannes T. R.

Koegel, one of the court preachers, did in fact warn against Prussia's growing pride in that year of success.

As a result of the war in 1866, a special Fund for Strengthening Evangelical Ministry in the Field was created under the Ministry of Ecclesiastical Affairs. The Fund originated in Pomerania, and received royal sanction in mid-June as a depository for offerings from all provinces. By the beginning of World War I, the Fund's assets totaled over 150,000 "Mark."

Wichern had a premonition for war, although it took no soothsayer to know that war with France was inevitable. A month before the Franco-Prussian War in 1870, he spoke before the "Kirchentag" in Eisenach, distributing printed theses as part of his presentation. The sixth thesis warned that in times of peace, the church should prepare for wartime labors of love, including recruiting men and women to nurse sick and wounded soldiers. "Efforts must be made at all times to arouse and cultivate in congregations a living, patriotic frame of mind that puts aside all vested interests, and is evaluated only in terms of God's kingdom." His fifteenth thesis advised church officials to arrange days of confession, prayer and thanksgiving, and to provide liturgical forms of expression for patriotism, as they nurtured the popular opinion that "war itself, as well as its cessation, should serve to test, humiliate, refine and morally strengthen our people, and in all to advance God's kingdom." True to his promise, Wichern once again rallied a sizable contingent of military field deacons for service in the war against France; three hundred and sixty workers participated in the campaign against Germany's archenemy. We will discuss the involvement of chaplains in a section below.

Wichern interpreted war as a scourge on an immoral people, but he proposed to salvage its blessings for God's kingdom wherever possible. War seemed to be an extension of life's conflicts, and since in days of peace, the church, state, and Inner Mission were linked in mortal combat against the deadly foe, there was no reason to terminate that alliance during a military campaign. War was undesirable, but the alliance's collapse would be even more calamitous for the progress of God's kingdom. In addition, a hundred charitable acts in wartime were more valuable than none in peacetime. He urged church and state to cooperate for the welfare of the combatants.

Bismarck's Religion and German Nationalism

More than any other individual, it was Otto von Bismarck (1815-1898) who bore responsibility for the decade's three wars. A university graduate and one-time judicial administrator in Aachen, this Prussian "Junker" soon left bureaucratic service out of dissatisfaction, and retired to his family estate. After serving in several official and unofficial parliamentary bodies at midcentury, he was appointed as Prussia's ambassador to the German Confederation, to Russia, and to France, before assuming Prussia's highest domestic post in 1862.

The theologian Schleiermacher confirmed Bismarck as a young man, but the confirmation bore little fruit until he experienced a renewed prayer life at the deathbed of a good friend's wife. The religious awakening in his native Pomerania surrounded him, especially after 1843. A diary entry by Ernst Ludwig von Gerlach in October, 1846, gives some insight into his character:

> Ate with Otto Bismarck: State and church must be wholly separate, etc. Senfft said I answered more vehemently than was my custom. Otto Bismarck returned at midday to Trieglaff. Bismarck said later that it was fine to argue with me as long as one did not oppose me, for then I came to my own aid and contradicted myself. . . . After supper at Senfft's, an evening hour as in old times; very satisfying; much wine. . . . Moritz <von Blanckenburg> remarked that O. Bismarck seeks stability and sincerely wants to believe, but cannot.

After his "conversion," Bismarck's individualism asserted itself in his religious practices. He favored action over contemplation, and found the biblical book of James to be of great value. He prayed regularly, and had a special fondness for the Lord's Prayer; he regularly read the Bible and two devotional aids, a Moravian book of daily devotions (after 1864), and a compendium of Luther's quotations. He

354

attended church and received communion rather regularly until he became minister of state, then refused to attend communion publicly for fear of becoming an "animal in a zoo." He took up the practice of communing with his family at least once a year in private, and no longer attended divine services.

Bismarck's strong dislike for the British statesman Gladstone was partly due to Gladstone's liberal views, as well as his insistence that a Christian program should be implemented in politics. Bismarck eventually had to make peace with German liberals in order to accomplish his revolution from above, but his political schema left little room for a distinctively Christian program, although he claimed that a Christian statesman was obliged to serve the state and preserve the ordained order. He held that God in some way guided affairs to accomplish His will, but he was equally convinced that no man could know God's will for certain. The undeveloped agnosticism of his individualistic faith permitted him to practice a form of "Realpolitik" that was morally anchored in the state's self-interest, and in the preservation and extension of Prussia's military monarchy. "We are not in this life to be comfortable," he wrote to his wife in 1851, "but we put ourselves and our resources in debt to serve God, the king, and the state." "Without me there would not have been three great wars, 80,000 men would not have met their death, and parents, brothers, sisters, and widows would not sorrow. . . . In the meantime, I have settled this with God," he told a visitor in 1878. Near the end of his life, he felt estranged from God, comparing himself to Peter as he began sinking in the waters. But he prayed that God would not take him from life without restoring his "faith-minded attitude toward Christ."

The relationship between Bismarck's religion and his political-nationalist views is not an easy one to delineate, although it is clear that his agnosticism facilitated his "realpolitisch" approach. Scholars disagree as to whether he generated his own kind of German nationalism or Prussian expansionism, which helped him succeed at home and abroad, or whether in a masterful way he mounted and rode the tidal wave of nationalism already underway. No one doubts his native ability to weigh the political potential of nationalist sentiment. His major American biographer, Otto Pflanze, contends that it is a "fiction of nationalistic historians" to portray Bismarck as riding the waves of a nationalistic movement that finally peaked in 1870. Rather, nationalism began to move the masses only under his stimulation. "It is a fact of fateful significance," he added, "that German national sentiment could gain momentum to overcome the particularist loyalties of the German people only in combination with Prussian militarism and Hohenzollern authoritarianism." The German historian Otto Becker took the opposing view, but the weight of the evidence lies with Pflanze, who aptly summarized his position by quoting the elder Bertrand Russell:

> It was only though Bismarck that German patriotism became respectable and conservative, with the result that many men who had been liberal because they were patriots became conservative for the same reason.(4)

This view of German nationalist sentiment, under Bismarck's stimulation, is compatible with a recent description of the growth of nationalism before 1848 in response to the needs of German modernization.(5)

Like any good "Junker," Bismarck was committed to monarch and state, not to German culture as such. What was German was Prussian, and he was a German because he was a Prussian. For this Prussian "Junker," Weimar was distantly removed from Berlin, and he could scarcely imagine a Prussian monarch without the desire to expand Prussia's territory. He described the power of the German nation as residing in the Prussian monarch, and every political tool, including universal suffrage, could serve that monarch. Because of Bismarck's intrigue, the socialist Liebknecht later described the imperial constitution as a "fig leaf for Prussian absolutism."

When it was necessary, Bismarck used his "Junker" background to put him in the good graces of the "Junker" military aristocracy. This group was an influential element in the Prussian power bloc, but he never aligned himself so closely with it that he could not disengage. Sometimes he even opposed the militant zeal of General Moltke and the king himself, such as in 1866. But he joined in the critical decision to address the national question first, and then take up the social question, although in reality much of

Germany confronted both issues at once. This decision was important for the "Junker" class, and it directly affected the response to the second issue.

One of the fateful ramifications of this decision was that Prussia's traditional class structure lay at the basis of the new nation state. The social ferment that accompanied industrialization, including the growth of an industrial class, was sure to bring trouble. In point of fact, the social movement soon became chief among the "imperial enemies." In addition, since Protestantism was so closely associated with Prussia and her traditional social structure, Roman Catholics experienced much the same fate in the new empire. But during the decade of unification, Bismarck played the traditional classes against the middle classes in order to build a state with advantages for both: a new Prussianized Germany.

It is simplistic to claim that Bismarck was converted from Prussian patriotism to German nationalism. It is probably more accurate to report that he distinguished between legitimatism and conservativism with the elimination of three crowns in 1866, and also amputated nationalism from liberalism. He showed great patience in waiting for the right time to act, but displayed great impatience when it was necessary. He artfully disguised his use of liberal and nationalist sentiments for his own purposes, by constantly asking that the unjust injuries he suffered be redressed, and he skillfully used nationalist sentiment in support of monarchical conservatism.

RESPONSES TO AUSTRIA'S DEFEAT

Bismarck was forced to do battle on two fronts: with the liberals, to show that his policies could bring national unity; and with the conservatives, to show that he was not set on destroying Prussia's traditional social structure, and their privileged place in it. The war with Austria in 1866, that "fraternal" war between two giants, made a decisive impact on both groups, as well as religious spokesmen within them. Bismarck's genius was that he seemed to give something to everyone except a small group of vocal conservatives, but for them he kept the crown intact. That was why most Protestants welcomed Prussia's defeat of Austria in 1866, and there is little question that the prevailing consensus between church and state helped build acceptance of the "realpolitisch" perspective.

In final analysis, the conflict between Bismarck and the lawyer and lay theologian, Ernst Ludwig von Gerlach, centered in the question of the legitimacy of power. Ultraconservatives such as Gerlach viewed legitimacy as a moral value that transcended the claims of power. Bismarck held that power had its own legitimacy; properly computed, power entailed elements of self-limitation. Conservatives insisted that only a superior doctrine, a moral principle that lay beyond power itself, could restrain force. Given the argument on both sides, Prussia's war with Austria either would lend greater credibility to Bismarck's claims, or weaken even more Gerlach's case against a political theory that was a self-fulfilling prophecy.

Gerlach continued to hope that somehow the moral force of the old Holy Alliance would heal the breach between the two sisters, Austria and Prussia. Early in 1865, his annual political program called for a return to the happier days of the old Alliance. He wrote that men should realize once again that "the condition and basis for the unification of Germany is harmony between Prussia and Austria." A fraternal war was incomprehensible and unchristian. When conflict seemed imminent, the only recourse was to reaffirm the Holy Alliance's moral and political principles, since they were anchored in the divine kingdom. If the German people wanted to remain Christian, there was no other basis for relations between the two powers.

Gerlach broke fully with Bismarck when war erupted in June, 1866. While this war did not unite the German states under Prussia in a single stroke, it set the process of unification on an irreversible course, and brought the two men to irreconcilable positions.

In May of 1866, Gerlach's article in the NEW PRUSSIAN NEWS, entitled "War and Reform of the Confederation," unequivocally rejected Bismarck's policy, and appealed to the Austrian emperor and the Prussian king, over the head of

358

"Count Bismarck," to seek a compromise between Prussia's need to expand, and Austria's need to preserve her prestige. Both had to resist revolution; armed conflict would be counterproductive, since there could be no Germany without either. Gerlach bitterly denounced Bismarck's proposal to enact universal suffrage, and rejected any policy that sought a higher law than the Ten Commandments.

In a final effort to reverse Bismarck's policy, Gerlach forwarded copies of the article with an accompanying letter to Roon, Bodelschwingh, Itzenplitz, and Bismarck, then travelled to Berlin to discuss the issues with Itzenplitz, Bodelschwingh, von Thile, and Frederick William IV's widow. His discussions led to nothing, although he tried to create a peace cabinet paralleling the old "Camarilla."

On the eighteenth of May, he met Bismarck in what Gerlach called that "lacerating interview." At one time, Bismarck claimed that Gerlach's pamphlet hurt him more than the assassin's bullet that bounced off his rib cage the same day the pamphlet was published. But when Gerlach asked his old friend to continue their personal friendship despite political differences, according to his account, Bismarck replied "neither with word nor handshake." The two parted ways and concluded a long friendship. Downtrodden, Gerlach returned to Magdeburg the next day; the experience was particularly painful since he was the godfather of Bismarck's oldest son.

Gerlach was not the only conservative to fear the effects of this "fraternal" war in 1866. Before hostilities commenced, Karl von Bodelschwingh, Prussia's Minister of Finance, called Bismarck's inflammatory moves brutal and atheistic. Justun von Gruner, Bethmann-Hollweg, and others also opposed the policy. Clemens C. Perthes, son of the famous evangelical bookseller, Friedrich A. Perthes, wrote his old friend Albrecht von Roon, the Minister of War, to warn of the consequences of Bismarck's plan. Edwin von Manteuffel, the Prussian general who was administering Schleswig, feared only that Prussia might have to retreat in the face of the enemy.

But Bismarck's propaganda mill was not idle. Heinrich von Muehler, the Minister of Ecclesiastical Affairs, organized a meeting for Prussia's clergy in Berlin on May 4. There the king spoke movingly of his love for peace, and blamed Austria for the impending war. After the meeting, provincial Saxony's PEOPLE'S PAPER FOR TOWN AND COUNTRY portrayed Gerlach and his associates as troublemakers who sowed distrust for the king and Bismarck, his Minister of Foreign Affairs.

Bismarck continued to gain the confidence of less doctrinaire conservatives. On June 1, Eberhard Stolberg chaired a large gathering in Berlin. Moritz von Blanckenburg, who headed the list of speakers, said that Gerlach did not speak for the conservative party; Prussia's power politics were appropriate for the time. On the war, Blanckenburg said that he was neither "feudal nor conservative, neither Gerlachian nor Bismarckian—but once and for all 'Prussian!'" Conservative party leaders instructed the NEW PRUSSIAN NEWS to stop publishing Gerlach's articles, and on June 16 he severed all relations with the paper that he helped found.

A small number of vocal conservatives continued to resist Bismarck's policies, but they could not turn the tide. The short war with Austria in the summer of 1866 brought quick victory to Prussia with its strategic, unique use of railways for mobilizing troops and executing plans. In September, Gerlach published his first openly anti-Bismarckian pamphlet, a brochure with six editions in one month. His "Annexations and the North German Confederation" accused Bismarck of grand larceny for annexing Hanover and the electorate of Hesse. He claimed that the deposed dynasties' oaths of allegiance had been violated, and the German Confederation destroyed. Prussian patriots had to ask themselves, "What would it profit my fatherland if it lost its soul, after gaining the whole world?"

Bismarck was little affected by such idle chatter. It came months too late to influence the parliamentary elections coinciding with the war. Several weeks before the balloting for electors on July 3, Prussia's general superintendents issued a strongly conservative election memorandum to all clergymen. The general superintendent of Silesia urged all pastors to exercise their "holy ministerial responsibilities" in word and deed in order to silence the political voices that were raised against king and fatherland. He wrote that, for the citizenry, the election would be as decisive as any battle; clergymen should call their parishioners' attention to the fundamental principles of "biblical politics," so that they elected electors who accepted God as Lord. Most of these recommendations followed an instruction from the High Church Council to all Prussian consistories, asking pastors to rally the people around the royal throne in this time of distress.

The electors were chosen on June 25, and they gathered to elect parliamentary deputies on the same day that Prussia scored its remarkable victory over Austria at Koeniggraetz (Sadowa). This election on July 3 brought overwhelming victory to the conservatives, whose delegation in the House rose from 38 to 142 deputies. But the Progressives and left-center liberals still held 148 seats, though their bloc was substantially reduced from 253. While the Prussian clergy's activity was not the most decisive factor in the election, it did not harm the conservatives' cause. For example, the conservative platform in Minden-Ravensberg included such planks as retaining religious instruction in elementary schools, prohibiting civil marriage for those who legally quit the church, and having "no Jews as authority over the Christian folk."

More important than the election results was the indemnity bill that Bismarck soon presented to the new parliament. This ex post facto gesture of reconciliation was a request to the House to grant indemnity to the government for conducting business without an approved budget. The bill passed by a three to one majority. The significance of the act was that the liberals acknowledged their defeat in the constitutional struggle, in exchange for imminent national unity. Early in 1867, a National Liberal Party was organized to support the government's foreign policy. It played an important role in the North German "Reichstag," the parliament of the North German Confederation of states that replaced the German Confederation.

The Prussian king took action to involve the churches directly in the war effort, and in the election, by setting a Day of Repentance and Prayer a week before the election, on June 27. The church press reported that at no time since 1815 were churches as crowded in town and country as on that day. Half the churchgoers in Berlin reportedly could not find a seat. People came for guidance in the middle of a perplexing war, but the parliamentary electors were also treated to homilies on the clear necessity to stand up for God, fatherland, and church.

Protestants seemed to welcome Austria's defeat. The PEOPLE'S PAPER FOR TOWN AND COUNTRY called the war a campaign against democrats and liberals, and urged its readers to thank God that Prussia's might and her king remained unharmed, ready to confront the real enemy at home. The lay church leader, Bethmann-Hollweg, wrote in a letter to Ernst Ludwig von Gerlach in December of 1866 that, while he was ready to repent for Bismarck's misdeeds, he was also ready to acknowledge that if God permitted a "revolution from above" to change state relationships drastically, the subjects should adjust to new relationships. He was referring specifically to the end of monarchies in Hanover and the electorate of Hesse.

The PEOPLE'S PAPER was much less hesitant to applaud the war's outcome, since it was seen as a Protestant victory. The paper portrayed the war as a struggle between evangelical freedom and the Hapsburg's oppressive hand; great sacrifices were required to retain that freedom, and as a Protestant state, Prussia had to take the lead. The paper dutifully reported an eyewitness's account of the Prussian king falling to his knees in prayer for an hour, and calling on the King of Kings to help in time of great need. The editor added that "several days later came the victory near Koeniggraetz." Undoubtedly the journal would not have published Ernst Ludwig von Gerlach's diary entry for July 21, which said: "There is a religious element in this war. Personally, I do not want Germany to be Prussian-Protestant-Freemason, nor that she be non-Roman. Dualism is the real Germany."

Hengstenberg kept his views on the war rather private until, at the end of the year, he published his overview of the year 1866 in the EVANGELICAL CHURCH NEWS. First he lamented the energy poured into the war, while the church militant expended so little on behalf of the "heavenly war Lord." Disclaiming the need to vindicate all of Prussia's actions, he refused as well to agree with those who found her fully responsible for the war. He reported that according to the king, Prussia certainly had no intention of creating war, but added that the king's first counselor may have had other ideas. Nevertheless, if the spirited state of Prussia now had a mission for Germany, she should follow the Apostle's advice: "Whoever has an office, let him attend to it." Hengstenberg also viewed the war as a pitched battle between Protestantism and Roman Catholicism; it would have been unfortunate for the evangelical church, he said, if the plan to relegate the Prussian king to his earlier status as "Marquis of Brandenburg" had succeeded. Friedrich Fabri, mission supervisor of the Barmen Mission, also warmly endorsed the Prussian victory.

The Protestant Union reflected on the war's consequences when its delayed meeting occurred at Cassel in September, 1866. One resolution stated that the exclusion of Austria, and the separation of the south German states, did not destroy the Union's goal of creating a united church in Germany. Rather, the cause of a national church was aided by excluding a power that harbored ultramontante and Jesuit movements.

But the reaction among southern Protestants did not universally favor the Prussian victory. During the war, few southern churchmen took the side of Prussia; Kapff in Wuerttemberg, and Holtzmann and Hausrath in Baden, were among the more vocal in this group. Even after the war, in October, the maverick Swabian biblicist, Johann T. Beck, called on individual Prussians to repent of their immoral and unchristain behavior. Others accused Prussia of transforming her belief in providential calling and hegemony over Germany into an article of saving faith; as proof they cited the Prussians' decision to destroy those who would not believe—namely the Austrians—with fire and sword, like heretics. A less pointed condemnation of Prussian activity came from an anonymous author, who answered one of Fabri's pro-Prussian tracts late in the summer of 1866. Perhaps it was true, he argued, that aflame with life and zeal, Prussia was called to lead the way to German unification, but "there are other, better ways" to attain that goal than war with Austria.

Soon after the war, however, among most Swabian pietists the balance shifted in favor of a "small Germany," with Prussia at the head. The way was paved by their theological interpretation of God's will in this event. "God certainly has willed a new order of things in Germany," Kapff wrote in September. "He has willed that the visibly strongest power rules in Germany, but He has not willed this power's unlawful instruments of power." Kapff acknowledged that it was difficult to discern why God gave the victory to Prussia, but clearly He was using this power to overcome some of the moral and spiritual deficiencies of people. For this reason, Kapff added, "we will meet our northern brothers halfway in the spirit of Christian love." The aged editor of the CHRISTIAN MESSENGER, Phillip Burk, failed to fall into step with most of the other pietists, and as a result, his publisher relieved him of the editorial duties he had performed since 1831, and named Kapff's son as the new editor. Most pietists seemed to feel that only an alliance with conservative, monarchical Prussia could succeed in repelling the forces of democracy and revolution. Many of them campaigned for the election of candidates from the liberal German Party ticket in the "Zollparlament" elections, but none of these Prussian-oriented candidates were elected in Wuerttemberg.

TERRITORIAL ANNEXATIONS AND CONFESSIONAL RESISTANCE

The Prussian court preacher Wilhelm Hoffmann published a book in 1868, entitled GERMANY THEN AND NOW IN THE LIGHT OF GOD'S KINGDOM, in which he discussed Prussia's national calling. He insisted that the Prussian church had the mission of uniting German Protestantism, by subsuming the principle of territorial churches to the principle of a national church. Hoffmann was sure that the annexation of Hanover was due to God's judgment.

Prussia's annexation of Hanover, Hesse, Nassau, the city of Frankfurt, and earlier, Schleswig-Holstein, raised the ticklish problem of their churches. Would they be subject to Prussia's administrative ecclesiastical structure for Protestants? Would the Prussian union church include areas such as Hanover and Hesse, where strong Lutheran confessionalism flourished? Protestants in the annexed territories were filled with anxiety in the fall of 1866. But like the churches in the provinces of Prussia, their churches received a royal order to conduct a Service of Peace on November 11. The agitation of von Hoffmann, Professor Emil Hermann, and others for a national church, presumably under Prussian leadership, did little to calm the waters. The solution to the problem was an example of the churches' modeling "freedom-within-authority" for the larger society, and it took a shrewd politican like Bismarck to pick his way through the minefield toward a solution.

Early in 1867, Prussia's High Church Council issued a memorandum to secular and ecclesiastical officials, including superintendents and pastors, describing how Prussia's evangelical church should integrate the churches in annexed lands. The position paper noted that a national church was desirable, but it was unclear how it might be achieved at present. People needed to build on realities, not some future dream, and the greatest reality was the largest Protestant church in Germany, Prussia's union church. Its remarkable unity in confession, worship, and polity provided a solid foundation for future developments; the elements of zealous confessionalism should not be allowed to polarize evangelicals even more. The paper added that a Lutheran confessional church would be an offense to the "German national element;" now was the time to capitalize on the impetus toward unity provided by the union in Prussia.

But the Council was not in a position to speak the last word on this critical political problem. Lutheran and Reformed confessionalists soon published a number of rebuttals, although the Council seemed to have had the support of King William I, who, we recall, was rather pro-union and anti-confessionalist in his "New Era" days. The Minister of Ecclesiastical Affairs after 1862, Heinrich von Muehler (1813-1874), began drafting a new church constitution for all the provinces, including the annexed areas, but he too faced the critical question of how to incorporate the newly annexed churches into Prussia's ecclesiastical administration.

The most important input was provided by Bismarck. His political goal in church affairs apparently was to have an independent church without any state administration, but the king continued to oppose these plans. Taking half a loaf rather than none, Bismarck prevented the churches of the annexed areas from being forced into the Prussian union church, and subjected to centralized authority, although he was unable to give them complete autonomy. His solution was to place the churches under the Minister of Ecclesiastical Affairs for administrative purposes, but they had no responsibility to the High Church Council. This policy paralleled political arrangements within the North German Confederation; the churches retained some autonomy, but were still administratively subject to the Prussian Minister of Ecclesiastical Affairs. In Hanover, electoral Hesse, and Schleswig-Holstein, this solution prevented the separation of large confessional groups from the state church.

The rising confessionalist tide in Prussia, the annexed areas, and the southern states, continued to have the markings of a political resistance movement. For some Protestants outside of Prussia, confessionalism demonstrated an anti-Prussian spirit; opposition to the Prussian union church was also a rejection of Prussian leadership in the national question. The same forces were at work in Prussia, but the union church intensified the more specifically religious element.

Confessionalists created an organizational focus in 1868 in the General Evangelical Lutheran Conference in Hanover, an organizational precursor of the Lutheran World Federation. One of the conference's leaders was Christoph E. Luthardt (1823-1902), a professor at Leipzig who defended Lutheran rights when Prussia annexed territories in the sixties. Its 1,500 members decided to publish a paper, and in the fall of 1868, Luthardt assumed editorship of the new GENERAL EVANGELICAL LUTHERAN CHURCH PAPER. In the first issue he enunciated the conference's position in unmistakably clear terms, noting that church "union is not a product of history, but a break with history." The union was a "revolutionary moment," he added, "for what is revolution other than a break with history?" Lutheran confessionalists feared that the political revolution being imposed from above would thrust the Prussian union church upon them as well. The confessionalist movement in Prussia's union church finally published its own periodical in 1870, entitled LUTHERAN CHURCH PAPER, but like most other confessionalist journals, it was meant for theologians rather than lay people.

Some confessionalists in the annexed territories were outspoken opponents of Prussian power moves in the sixties. In electoral Hesse, Vilmar drew on Haller's restorational theory to support his argument against Prussia. He spoke of satanic Prussian politics, and the expansion of an antichristian world monarchy, and was especially troubled by Hengstenberg's support of Bismarck's policies. Vilmar feared that Prussia was yielding to pan-Slavism, which attacked "Germanism" from the east, while "Celtic Romanism" mounted an attack from the west. We have already mentioned the opposition of the Reformed lay theologian, Ernst Ludwig von Gerlach, who received some support from Lutherans in Bavaria and Wuerttemberg. Meanwhile, the Roman Catholic bishop Ketteler, the historian Jacob Burkhardt, and the political theorists Constantine Frantz also registered their opposition to Bismarck's policies.

In Schleswig-Holstein, the host committee for the "Kirchentag" chose the theme of the annexed churches for the conference at Keil in the fall of 1867. Wichern noted that this was the group's first meeting in the dutchies, but he was happy with the invitation since everyone had the same goal, namely, to build God's kingdom among the people of the nation. The dutchies' political fate had been sealed, but the church question remained unresolved. The new chairman of Prussia's High Church Council gave the conference a vigorous defense of the territorial principle, implying that the annexed churches should become part of the Prussian union. The conference showed that fear of the union church was not as strong in the dutchies as some had supposed, and the next month the Prussian government made a final decision on the church question. It directed that the churches remain under the control of the Ministry of Ecclesiastical Affairs, but not the High Church Council. Internal affairs were handled by a consistory at Kiel chaired by a layman.

The annexation of Hanover shows how complex the problem was for the church. Confessionalists saw an early sign of woe in the royal order issued on October 24, 1866, requiring churches in the annexed territory to make regular intercessions for the Prussian dynasty. Intercessions for England's George V had been cancelled three weeks earlier. Part of the new intercession was mandatory, and part left to the discretion of the pastor, the second part being largely an embellishment of the first. In December, the king

367

responded to a request from Hanover's consistory for his views on the church; his reply bore Bismarck's imprint. The king assured his new subjects that he did not intend to ignore their confessional commitments, but neither would he ignore his commitment to Prussia's union church.

All clergymen in Hanover were required to take an oath of allegiance to the new king in January of 1867. When some pastors seemed unwilling to accept him as an authority from God, the territorial consistory reminded them that an oath of conscience was appropriate, since King George V had yielded his authority. But a group of non-juring clergymen emerged that included the Old Testament orientalist scholar Heinrich Ewald, who had been one of the "Goettingen Seven" in the thirties; Pastor Ludwig Grote-Hary, who became a radical agitator in succeeding years; and six other pastors in office, five of whom were forcibly retired. Fearful of inciting the largely Lutheran Welf population, the government moved more harshly against the one Roman Catholic priest who refused to take the oath than against the Lutherans. A sizable number of Welf nobility showed renewed interest in church matters after 1866, favoring the vibrant witness of confessionalism.(6)

The Prussians did insist that the military church in Hanover become part of the administration of their union church, although they allowed Hanoverian soldiers to choose Lutheran pastors for certain rites if that was their wish, as often was the case. Clearly, the king's interest in keeping the army as the monarch's instrument of power had repercussions for the military church.

In the meantime, a small group in Hanover continued agitating for admission into Prussia's union church, despite the king's announced decision not to place the Hanoverian church under Prussia's High Church Council. The king addressed this issue in the spring of 1867, and again in September, but the group's agitation, as well as editorial comments in certain journals, continued to disturb Lutherans in Hanover. The territorial consistory, established in April of 1866, administered internal church affairs in the new province. Less acceptable for Hanoverian Lutherans was the way their independent monastic fund, which originated when church properties were secularized during the Reformation, was used for a number of philanthropic projects after 1866. The money budgeted for these projects was no longer available for church use.

NATIONAL UNIFICATION AND THE RELIGIOUS CHARTER

Between 1866 and 1870, Protestants from all points of the theological spectrum endorsed national unification. Some continued to broach the problem indirectly through the question of a national church, but others were more direct. In 1868, the PROTESTANT MONTHLY said that the ethical spirit of modern Germans searched for national unification, and this spirit was ready to scale political and ecclesiastical obstacles to achieve a "vigorous community, one that restores its parts to full unity, and complies with churchly-religious national sentiment." In June of that year, the dedication of a Luther Monument in Worms provided another occasion for the confluence of Protestant and nationalist sentiment. In 1869 the "Kirchentag" held its annual meeting, appropriately, in the southern state of Wuerttemberg. In his address, Wichern stressed that the mission of the Reformation would be complete when the folk church became a reality, and he implied that national unity and the folk church were corollaries.

But some confessionalists continued to resist the idea that German unification should occur under Prussian leadership. Reviewing Hoffmann's book, GERMANY THEN AND NOW IN THE LIGHT OF GOD'S KINGDOM (1868), early in 1870, a Lutheran journal suggested that while Hoffmann found the basis for unification in "a German king and a German state <Prussia>," a more desirable basis was a "German emperor and a German empire." The king implied absolute rule, the emperor limited control; the state implied centralization, the empire, decentralization.

The war with France in 1870 crystallized opinion, just as it brought the southern states into national unity with the North German Confederation. The outbreak of hostilities in July led to a decisive battle at Sedan in September, where the Germans were victorious. By January of 1871, the German Empire was a reality, but the initial victory celebration

369

was delayed until March, and the official observance did not occur until June.

During the nineteenth century, the struggle for liberation in 1813, and this war in 1870-71, were probably the two most significant occasions for Protestant clergymen to encounter the masses in the greatest numbers. Both experiences occurred in a patriotic context. In the first event, a limited number of pastors participated with lay people in the common experience of patriotism; a much larger percentage of pastors and people shared in the surge of emotion in 1870-71, when sermons often contained references to the earlier war.

These two patriotic experiences played significant roles in forging a common experiential bond between pastor and parishioner. That fact helps explain the effectiveness of the religious charter during the century. In both instances, a patriotic trigger set off an experiential explosion. And in both instances, the state perpetuated its subordination of society to the state's governing power, effectively channeling the forces of patriotic nationalism toward its own ends. Apparently, the religious charter was functioning effectively; the clergy received the signal to be patriotic, and to respond to their parishioners' patriotic sentiments, particularly in 1870-71.

But the Franco-Prussian War, and the process that led to national unity, modified the unwritten religious charter significantly. The war gave German Protestants the chance to validate, in a religious way, the revolution "von oben" that had been underway for some time. A new stipulation was added to the religious charter: it was now the churches' responsibility as well to lend moral support to conservative nationalism. The charter's basic structure remained intact; its social function was to model "freedom-within-authority" for the larger society. This was evident not only from the state's continuing subjugation of society, but also from the fact that the church's halfhearted effort to become popular or folkish ("volkisch")—a "people's church"—had been successfully diverted by the new stipulation. But in addition, and as a subset, the churches' popular calling or mission was to support the nationalist sentiments that centered in the new empire's emperor. In sum, the earlier appeals of some churchmen to conjoin nationalism and liberalism were now disallowed, and attempts to be folksy or popular were firmly linked to nationalist support for the ruling dynasty, especially in Prussia.

German Protestants experienced two long-term results from the drive for unification that ended with the Franco-Prussian war. First, they became incapable of mounting a campaign against the new religion or ideology of nationalism. This was as true in the last quarter of the nineteenth century as in the fourth decade of the twentieth century. After carrying the torch for another religion, could they readily throw off the National Socialist scourge? The data in the final pages of this chapter describe why this question must be answered in the negative.

The second consequence was no less significant, as we will see in later chapters. Since the churches acccepted the decision to face the national question before addressing the social question, although the two arose somewhat concurrently, they had to abide by the consequences of that decision. One was to continue addressing the social question within the nationalist framework, and ultimately, to view social dissidents and social agitators as "enemies of the empire." The churches' participation in the struggle for unification meant automatic estrangement from the emerging socialist movement. The feeble efforts of some churchmen to establish rapport with socialist workers were doomed by the new nationalist stipulation in the religious charter.

Preaching Repentance and a Taste of Victory

When the French declared war on July 19, 1870, the North German "Reichstag" greeted the announcement with sustained applause. The Reformed synod of the Elberfeld district was meeting in western Prussia at the same time, and on the twentieth of that month it sent the Prussian king a message that it would pray for king and army, since "God is our Refuge and Strength, a timely help in trouble." Two days earlier, the Rhenish consistory reminded the congregations of the Rhineland that "Germany's old hereditary foe" was rising up to attack. The report added that when fathers and brothers took the field with the slogan of their ancestors in 1813, "With God for King and Fatherland!", civilians on the home front should support them with "the weapons of prayer" in their homes and churches, in order to "implore the Lord of Hosts for the victory of our weapons."

On July 21, the Prussian king ordered that all public business should cease on Wednesday, the twenty-seventh, while churches conducted prayer services on behalf of the "pressing needs of the time." Bremen and Hamburg held a Day of Repentance and Prayer that same day, Wuerttemberg and Thuringia four days later, Saxony on August 3, and Bavaria and Mecklenberg on the seventh. In the Lutheran order of things, it seemed appropriate for an order of repentance to accompany the outbreak of hostilities; only in the light of God's searching judgment of men could His affirmative vindication be seen. Thus a statement of repentance could easily become a rhetorical question: "We have deserved the scourge of war because our sins were many," became, "Do we not have the right to make war with France?"(7)

On the appointed days of prayer and repentance, churches in many places overflowed with worshippers. Pastors in Berlin had to organize additional services; people were turned away at Koenigsberg for lack of space; churches overflowed in Leipzig; in the Bavarian Palatinate, attendance rivaled that of high church festivals. But services were not held everywhere, and some people complained because of variations in dates. The Marburg consistory's invitation was something less than a call to repentance: "Declare a holy war, call your troops to arms! Beat your mattocks into swords and your pruning-hooks into spears. Let the weakling say, 'I am strong,'" said the summons, as it quoted the prophet Joel.

Sermons on the day of repentance ranged from radical denunciations of the war, to an innoncuous summons for moral repentance. The first type was rather infrequent, although Pastor Schwalb in Barmen demanded repentance from German Protestants who "have done nothing to avert this terrible, unchristian war." He charged that their studied neutrality was as despicable as the Roman Catholics gathered in Rome to declare the pope's infallibility. Milder in tone, but still critical, were the sermons of the Erlangen confessionalist, Karl A. G. von Zezschwitz, and a few other preachers. But the majority appealed for repentance without casting aspersions on the war effort, or discussed the general need for moral repentance. Some liberal clerics used the chance to discuss the war as a turning point in the process of national unification, but most preachers apparently ignored the war in their generalized remarks. Their silence affirmed the actions of their legitimate governments.

In Wuerttemberg, the pietist leader Kapff told his congregation that the Christian should humble himself under God's mighty hand, in fear and faithful obedience, in confession and repentance, and in silent trust. The Prussian court preacher Koegel addressed a crowd in the Berlin cathedral on the Pauline theme, "Often Pressed Down, Never Overcome!" In Schleswig-Holstein, provost Neelsen in Ploen recommended that his congregation pray with stalwart trust and good conscience for victory in war.

The days of repentance and prayer provided an opportunity for civilian ecclesiastical forces to take to the field. Consistories soon inaugurated weekly devotions and prayer services in many places for the duration of the war. Services were held on Wednesdays, and sometimes another weekday; one rural community had devotions at 5:45 A.M., and in other places an evening hour was used. The services often provided a communications network for good news, as well as bad.

Another way of institutionalizing the church's intercessory activity was to revise the liturgy for the war's duration. In Prussia, the General Prayer was revised in the late summer of 1870 to include petitions for "our German fatherland" and victory in war, but another petition tempered the impact with its request for divine grace, in order that "we show ourselves as Christians over against our enemies." Similar revisions were made in the agendas of most German churches, including Wuerttemberg's and Bavaria's. Many church officials had provided pastors with special prayers for the Day of Repentance and Prayer, and they followed up with pertinent material for the victory celebration on June 18, 1871.

Although the German troops won several minor victories in the war's early days, the first major victory, with a resounding impact at home as well as on the front, was the French defeat at Sedan early in September of 1870. Over 100,000 Frenchmen became prisoners of war; even an amazed

Bismarck described Napoleon as "the one whom God's powerful hand has thrown down," in a letter to his wife.

In many cases, the sermons preached on September 4 and September 11 portrayed the victory at Sedan as a turning point in history. The printed sermons that remain, if they are characteristic, point to an obvious change in mood. While earlier sermons from the war gratefully recognized the rising spirit of patriotism, they seemed to treat current developments in an offhand, superficial way. Sermons dealing with the Sedan victory, on the other hand, displayed a much deeper and stronger religious consciousness. The preachers appeared to have experienced the numinous, and to have seen God's hand at work in world events. "World history is world judgment," said one. "Yes, world judgment has happened right before our eyes. A victory above all victories has been given to us," said another. The words of the king's telegram announcing the victory—"What a turn of events, through God's Providence!"—was the message of many preachers on those September Sundays. Some even insisted that the power of God's judgment should bring widespread repentance, or else He would turn on the victors.

Another characteristic of the September sermons distinguishing them from earlier ones was their forthright discussion of God's righteous judgment against the French nation. Some claimed that only France's leadership stood condemned; the human bond with the French people was closer than it had been for some time, they claimed. But others argued that the political chaos accompanying France's defeat at Sedan was indicative of a problem much deeper than the leadership alone.(8)

The printed sermons that remain from the war, most of them from the first three months, show that a new homiletical form, or "Gattung," originated with the war, or at least attained clarity of expression in that experience. Sedan was an important factor in structuring that form. After the victory, most people felt that the war's decisive phase was over, and only with Christmas, and the realization that many of the nation's troops would be fighting on foreign soil for some time, did the preachers once again turn their attention to the war. The first victory celebration in March of 1871, and the official celebration in June, interrupted the apparent decline of interest in January and February.

The primary characteristic of the new homiletical form or "Gattung" was the sermon's shattering contemporary character. In 1870, one homiletical journal gave a straightforward answer to the question, "What should be preached, and how should it be preached?" It replied, avoid abstractions and that which battles with the air, deal with "given situations," and "express a view on the present war." Many other journals gave similar advice to a generally receptive clergy audience. Political, ethical, and religious questions related to the war were taken up in Sunday sermons. Preachers used more popular vocabulary, and chose their texts with more liberty.

The war sermons intercepted a homiletical method that had been largely textual, analytic and devotional. Preachers customarily used stated pericopes as texts, and gave close attention to the doctrinal content of their biblical exegesis. Sermons contained few references to contemporary events, and every effort was made to culivate the service's devotional atmosphere. There were exceptions, of course, but this seems to have been the prevailing homiletical style.

The new kind of preaching in 1870-71, however, had its prototype in the way some preachers responded to the liberation struggle in 1813-14. For this and other reasons, preachers in 1870 were more apt to rehearse the events of the earlier years than the more recent war with Austria, as they searched for a reasonable historical parallel. But the situation in 1870 was clearly different from 1813-14, and that was why the new form of preaching was something more than a warming up of left-overs. The population was less receptive to using the earlier campaign's religious themes to interpret events under the canopy of a sacred cosmos. Then, too, there was less of an inclination to "repent," and more of a sense of deserving victory. Sermons preached during the Franco-Prussian War made sense to a people that was achieving national unity, and attaining a sense of self-sufficiency, although they appreciated knowing that God was on the other end of their deserved blessing.(9) In sum, the pace of secularization was much more advanced by the seventies, and in their sermons, preachers used religious language to discuss secular autonomies. That which began as repentance tasted more like victory each day, and Sedan seemed to be as decisive a turning point for the preachers as for the troops in the field.

Tools in the Hand of a Mighty God

During the war with France, German Protestants were convinced that God was working through men to do His will. He was providing them with victory over an immoral enemy, deserving of defeat. He was using the church to minister to the needs of combatants. And He was accepting gifts—the offerings of the wounded, and the ultimate sacrifice of the dead—on behalf of the nation.

Preachers described the war as a "holy work," a "holy act of self-defense," a "holy battle." Pastor Johannes Bachmann of Rostock loaded his sentences with numinous references: "It is a war for God's honor and the protection of His kingdom, a holy war in which the Holy God stands on our side, in which our watchword can be: Here is Immanuel! Here the sword of the Lord and of Gideon!" The words of detractors, such as Pastor Lechler of Leipzig, who asked how someone could prosecute a "holy war" when "he himself is unholy," were mostly lost in the rising crescendo. Most preachers favored texts from the Old Testament, which were more readily applicable without the intervening step of cultural translation, and these texts often served as the basis for exhuberant claims.

Few doubted that God's hand guided events, since He held the fate of nations in his hands. The call for radical repentance by Pastor Schwalb of Bremen had an ironic ring: "God gives the victory; world history teachers us that. Undeniably, He does not always give it to the most pious or most just people, but to the strongest, bravest, best-led people." Most preachers seemed to agree with Pastor Schmieder's conclusion, that "victory is always certain for the just, and for him who protects the just matter." Victory, it was almost universally assumed, came from God; behind the scourge of war was the saving love of the Lord of Hosts.

Most sermons were theocentric rather than specifically christological in orientation. Had the war continued for a longer period, it is possible that preachers would have more

376

readily appropriated the comfort afforded by certain christological formulations. In a careful study of these war sermons, one scholar concluded that there was a definite correlation in the sermons between critical tenor and christological content.(10) In any case, many preachers subsumed religious to nationalist sentiment, and preserved this imbalance through the theocentric orientation of their sermons. The revelatory nature of events they witnessed firsthand provided the incarnational or christological element, not a dogmatic constraint or formulation that was integral to their theology. Some provided running accounts of the most recent events on the warfront; the pulpit became a communications center, as preachers provided the latest information on the war, sometimes received from returning troops or periodicals. In the early phases of the war, when information was scarce, Pastor Romberg in Wittenberg and Pastor Kadelbach in Leipzig were two of the day's leading reporters.

New Year's sermons provided an excellent opportunity to reflect on divine guidance during the last six months. Many preachers commented that the past year had been a time of marvelous revelation from God, and they encouraged parishioners to see themselves as part of a people that had been greatly blessed. Some expressed the hope that, in view of God's revelatory activity, the year 1871 would produce a special religious awakening. The theme of praise reappeared early in February, when homileticians such as Court Preacher Koegel in Berlin used texts from the Psalms to encourage hearers to "bless the Lord" for the fall of Paris. Less poetic, but more to the point for the occasion, was the southern preacher Frommel, who used a text from Jeremiah to discuss the theme, "Woe to the Splendid Crown of the Drunks!" Kapff of Wuerttemberg was no less straightforward in attributing victory to God when in the spring he preached a sermon observing the cessation of hostilities.

Most preachers were convinced that God was granting victory over an enemy that suffered from grave moral and religious deficiencies. Few of them would have accepted the satirical and chastising words of the rector of the University of Berlin: "We have no other thoughts than war, war, war to the knife, until the last drop of blood, until the last 'Thaler;' . . . war against this immoral, peace-murdering people of the French!" More in keeping with the tenor of the times were sermons that portrayed Frenchmen as morally inferior, and deficient in Christian truthfulness, discretion, and other Teutonic virtues. In December of 1870, Kapff summed up the feelings of many when he wrote in the CHRISTIAN MESSENGER, "God has endowed our people with the most excellent gifts. . . . From this point on, let all mimicking of the French be damned!"

Preachers interpreted the collapse of Paris as the fall of sin city, a modern Babylon or Rome with too much sin, debauchery, lust, unbelief and revolutionary zeal. Even the graying Young Hegelian, David F. Strauss, participated in the condemnation. In a heated exchange of correspondence with the French writer Renan, he satirized French culture as inferior to Prussian character. Meanwhile, an atheistic scientist named Karl Vogt laughed from the sidelines. In his POLITICAL LETTERS, he asked sarcastically how both sides could confidently storm heaven with prayers, sermons, blessed candles, and votive offerings. He gave a slight edge to Prussia since her well-oiled system of prayer, obedience, and taxation—otherwise known as "God, King and Fatherland"—had always produced good results in the past, but he did not discount France's religious resources.

The war's victors were largely Protestant, and the vanquished Roman Catholics. Surely that was a sign that God was accomplishing His will through men, the Protestant preachers said almost unisionally. Journals spoke of waging war with a people that "hated Protestants," and plundered Germany for three hundred years. Early in 1871, the influential Badenese theologian, Adolf Hausrath, wrote that the war was a victory of "German culture over ultramontane spiritual slavery," of "the Protestant spirit over the Jesuits." One sermon after another portrayed the victory over France as a culmination and extension of the Reformation; Luther and Melanchthon "stood in our ranks and conquered with us in those glorious days for Germany." The NEW EVANGELICAL CHURCH NEWS warned that nations that oppose the Gospel "must die."

According to the preachers, the French emperor's desire to rule the world was as immoral as the pope's claim to infallibility. The "great liar on the Tiber," the "Roman whore," was obviously cooperating with Paris in an alliance that linked the spiritual Babylon with its secular counterpart. Some German Protestants argued that when God permitted Germany to overthrow Rome's favorite daughter, France, His real target was the pope.

This war added new fuel to old confessional rivalries. Some felt that God's gift of victory over Catholic Austria merely foreshadowed His new assignment for Prussia, the conquest of Catholic France. Many German Protestants traced a direct line from Wittenberg in 1517 to Paris in 1871. But what was appropriate for a Protestant preacher to say was wrong for a Roman Catholic priest; a Roman Catholic congregation in Paderborn stormed the pulpit when a Jesuit preached that the war against France was a war against Catholicism, and troops finally had to restore order. The "Kulturkampf" that soon erupted in the new German Empire was presaged in the anti-Catholicism of the Franco-Prussian War.

Another way God worked through men, it was thought, was to provide chaplains to minister to sick and wounded troops, and to bury the dead. The Prussian army began the war with sixty-two regular chaplains, but eighty reservists soon joined the active corps for field duty. More than ninety chaplains served the wounded in field hospitals, while thirty more worked in base hospitals. Another thirty-six made rounds in hospitals back in Prussia, while twelve were chaplains for prisoners of war. One field chaplain died in battle, four hospital chaplains died of infection, three were wounded, and five were taken prisoner. The other German states also provided chaplains for their troops, but Prussia's program was extremely well organized under Peter Thielen, the field provost who held office from 1862 to 1887. When the war ended, the emperor sent him a telegram commending the chaplains, and the ornamental relief that adorned the victory hall in Berlin included his representation. One of the most popular chaplains of the war was the powerful preacher Emil Frommel (1829-1896); he was subsequently appointed a court preacher in Berlin.

These chaplains counseled wounded and dying soldiers, who were regarded as instruments of the Lord. Sermons praised them for sticking to duty, wherever it led. In Leipzig, the Lutheran theologian Kahnis assured his hearers that since this was a just war, "whoever falls in this war falls in the line of duty for a just cause." Rogge of Barmen portrayed the battlefields as "the Lord's harvest fields," and

hospitals and graveyards as "seedplots of His kingdom."
Another said that the dead had given their sacrifice, and
"inherited the kingdom of glory under the flag of the
Savior." A number of preachers commended those killed in
action for fulfilling Jesus' word, that the one who lays
down his life for his friends has the greatest love. A few
of the preachers restrained themselves at this point,
indicating that no one died justly without justifying faith,
and stating that those killed in battle had suffered God's
judgment.

THE SEDAN FESTIVAL: THE EMPIRE AT PRAYER

During the war, diplomats and preachers use the word "Reich"
(empire, kingdom) with a variety of meanings and
connotations. "Reich" could mean God's kingdom, the new
German Empire, or both. It was a verbal coin, traded on
several markets. In the trading process, diplomats and
preachers wrangled over all sorts of questions. Would the
new nation's leader be called "emperor?" Was the new nation
a revival of Germany's medieval empire? How was the heavenly
kingdom related to this political entity, if at all?

While debate continued, most Protestants seemed to agree
that the empire's baptism by fire, the victory at Sedan,
should be observed regularly. The Sedan Festival became an
annual day of prayer for the empire, and an occasion for
Protestants to remember their status as imperial servants.
Through this renewal ceremony, the Protestant churches
acknowledged their chartered responsibility to foster the
spirit of conservative nationalism.

The printed sermons that remain show little interest in the
proclamation of the German Empire at Versailles on January
18, 1871. The occasion lacked the impact of such
unforgettable experiences as the victory at Sedan. People
expected the declaration, and some sermons in December
referred to its imminence. But since the proclamation was
something of a formality, it received little comment in
published sermons.(11)

As indicated above, the proclamation ceremony was not designed for public involvement. Among the handful of civilians present were several parliamentary deputies from Berlin, and some nurses from a nearby hospital. This was the ceremonial consummation of the revolution "from above," and the people's role remained unchanged: be obedient, or uninvolved, if that was the order of the day. The army's custom of creating the emperor in the late Roman Empire seemed to flourish once gain, and the parallel was not lost on some confessional Lutherans. "Truly, an emperor of the <medieval> Holy Roman Empire and an emperor of the new German Empire are two very different things," a Hanoverian paper for confessionalists said early in 1871, before the proclamation was issued. After the proclamation, the paper attributed the naming of the German emperor to the need to satisfy a popular fantasy: "People do not want a president of the German Confederation, or a duke of the Germans, but an emperor." Bismarck had been listening, and although he resisted the title when the North German Confederation was organized in 1867, he yielded to south German influences at this time.

The German princes who gathered at Versailles attended divine services in the chapel of Louise XIV's magnificent palace. In December, a delegation from the North German Confederation stepped before the Prussian king, and asked him to accept the crown offered by the German princes. A Jewish professor, Eduard Simson, headed the delegation, but this time he was more successful than when he discussed the imperial crown with William's brother in 1849. The proclamation ceremony in January occurred not in the palace chapel, but in the famous Hall of Mirrors.

For some, the idea of God's kingdom stood in sharp contrast with the war and the empire it created. "If God's kingdom were to come to us, as we pray daily in the Lord's Prayer," Pastor Koehler of Friedberg preached, "if the Spirit of Christ ruled in our hearts, and His word and will were everywhere acknowledged as the highest law, how could there then be war?" Johann Christoph Blumhardt of Wuerttemberg insisted that the pulpit was not the place to vent one's spleen for or against France; he insisted on proclaiming God's kingdom through deeds of love. Another pietist from Wuerttemberg, Karl Werner, agreed that the war would not bring spiritual renewal. "Such diverse elements have cooperated," he said, "in the common effort to see a unified Germany arise, and to work together toward that end with power, that it is noteworthy if, in the attempt, one should not be tinged with and infected by a mode of thinking that is foreign to God's kingdom." An important theologian and church official from Hanover, Gerhard Uhlhorn (1826-1901), offered a similar disclaimer in a wartime sermon; he insisted that for the Christian, one's fatherland was a divine gift that he valued properly only if he loved his heavenly homeland. "Only the one who knows God's kingdom," he added, "who loves all men as they are called to this kingdom—only he can also love his people aright."

But many other preachers easily made the transition from the heavenly to the earthly in this time of revolution "von oben." A preacher from Tuebingen named Palmer insisted that the true Christian identified the call of his fatherland with the kingdom's call, and this equipped him to leave father, mother, wife and child. "According to God's will and counsel," said a preacher in Frankfurt, there was no doubt that "also the events of our day should advance His kingdom." Another offered a rather broad maxim: "To the extent that, as Christians, we are moved by our love for the fatherland, at the same time we work for the furtherance of God's kingdom in our midst." One pastor entitled his book of war sermons THE GERMAN EMPIRE AND GOD'S KINGDOM (1871), and Johannes Thikoetter of Bremen argued that "God has designed an important mission for the people of the Reformation, in regard to the reconstruction of His kingdom on earth."

When the empire was proclaimed in 1871, people debated whether it was something new, or something reconstructed. Since the idea of Providence was involved, their debate was a facet of the theologians' discussion about the relation between God's kingdom ("Reich") and Germany's empire ("Reich"). Bismarck and the Prussian king gave the impression that the empire was a reconstituting of the old, with minor modifications. The proclamation in January announced that "the German princes and the free cities have unanimously called on us to renew and assume, with the restoration of the German Empire, the German imperial office that has been vacant for more than sixty years." The proclamation added, "We hope to God that the German nation will be given the ability to fashion a propitious future for the fatherland, under the image of its ancient glory."

Later in the century, the historian Heinrich von Treitschke and others tried to show how the two empires were continuous. Treitschke emphasized that the "old empire was a crumbling national monarchy, but the new empire is an emerging national monarchy." Monuments were constructed in 1873, and in 1892-97 as well, using royal figures to stress continuity in the imperial office. But the new and old breathed different spirits, though less than seventy years intervened. The German historian Golo Mann claims that "without the words 'Emperor,' 'Empire,' and 'Chancellor,' unification would not have been nearly as pleasurable. It must be added that these words alone linked the Reich of the Hohenzollerns with the Holy Roman Empire."

Another important issue was whether or not to give the Prussian king the title "Kaiser" (emperor). Bismarck recognized better than the National Liberals the magnetic quality this title held in the southern states; properly manipulated, this issue would facilitate national unity and centralization. He also knew that the title might help establish Prussian hegemony in the "Bundesstaat," despite the opposition of some southern princes. Thirty years later, the empire's foremost constitutional authority, Paul Laband, emphasized the importance of the title and the imperial symbol when he explained that for the German people, an empire without a "Kaiser" was like a body without a head. Bismarck skillfully meshed the old with the new in a way that enabled him to hold the reins of state. The terms "Kaiser" and "Reich" were ambiguous enough to allow legitimists to cooperate with those of strong nationalist conviction.

But the empire's true anniversary was not the proclamation of imperial union, or the attribution of the title "emperor" to the king of Prussia. It was the Sedan Festival, and anniversary festivities began even before the Empire was officially proclaimed. On September 1, 1870, Berlin's famous Brandenburg gate was decorated and illuminated to celebrate the victory at Sedan. Huge letters reproduced the king's announcement of victory: "Sedan—What a Turn of Events through God's Providence!"

For Protestants, the annual celebration in succeeding years was a strange mixture of Prussian patriotism and German nationalism, the old and the new in the context of the empire. Since the Sedan Festival was the empire at prayer in thanksgiving for victory, this national Protestant festival showed the vitality of the new stipulation in the religious charter.

Agitation for a national festival in 1871, to commemorate the victory at Sedan, originated with the Protestant Union in Berlin. In March of that year, eighty-eight well known men, mainly clergymen and professors from Berlin and Heidelberg, petitioned the emperor for a national festival. The group included Daniel Schenkel, Franz von Holtzendorff, Franz Hermann Schulze-Delitzsch, Johann C. Bluntschli, Heinrich von Treitschke, Wilhelm Gass, Friedrich Nippold, and Michael Baumgarten. Their brief argued that all religious confessions could easily "join together in a common prayer of thanksgiving for the reconstitution of the empire, thankful to the Providence that governs in eternal righteousness." They emphasized that Protestants, Catholics, and Jews could offer thanksgiving in their own tradition, and decorate graves with oak leaves or spruce twigs, but a common thankful spirit would permeate all activities. Several prominent church papers, as well as the German Protestant Union, endorsed the idea.

After the emperor replied that he preferred to leave this decision to popular spontaneity, a Protestant clergyman took the lead in a movement that produced annual celebrations after 1873. Friedrich von Bodelschwingh (1831-1910), the director of the Bethel institute for epileptics in Rhineland-Westphalia, outlined his plans for a national festival at a large meeting of the Inner Mission in Bonn in June of 1871. His proposed program for celebrating God's miracle at Sedan included the participation of churches and schools. Evidently, his experience as a military chaplain during the war made a lasting impression.

The Sedan Festival was observed annually throughout the empire until 1914. Worship services, patriotic services, school ceremonies and a parade in Berlin helped perpetuate the tradition, and special poems added a folk touch to this "Christian folk festival." But the "Kulturkampf" in the seventies helped accentuate the problem of minorities in the empire: In view of Austria's exclusion, would the empire respect the civil rights of Roman Catholics? Or of the

384

fourth estate? Or of non-German groups, such as Poles, Danes, and people in Alsace-Lorraine? Roman Catholic papers jokingly referred to the national festival as "St. Sedan's Day" or "Satan's Festival," and in 1874, Bishop Emmanuel von Ketteler forbade his clerics to participate in the festival. The socialists also adamantly opposed it, since most felt that the empire was not theirs.

But most Protestants appeared content with Prussia's domination of the new "Reich." The imperial constitution was structured in her favor; the empire's flag was not the tri-color of 1848, but an artistic creation, with Prussia's colors predominating. And the empire had no official national anthem until 1922, after its demise. But many Protestants annually recalled the day of divine judgment at Sedan, when Napoleon III stood condemned before his judge, the Prussian king.

"Almighty, merciful God, Lord of the heavenly hosts," Prussian Protestants prayed in 1870,

> we humbly seek Thy powerful help for our German
> fatherland. March out with the German armies and
> sanctify their weapons for conquering the enemy.
> Lead us to victory, and give us grace also to show
> ourselves as Christians over against our enemies.

Added to the General Prayer after the intercession for Prussia's royal provinces, these petitions were offered by imperial servants before the empire was established.

The sixties were a decade for bold, chauvinistic words among Protestants. National unification, and the events preceding it, modified their unwritten charter; in view of national unity, many assumed that it was the churches' unequivocal responsibility to endorse conservative nationalism. This was to be their primary "folkish" or popular assignment, not some wild-eyed appeal to the traditional alliance between liberalism and nationalism, or some "social" mission to suffering and oppressed people. Their imperial assignment was to sanction nationalism with religion. This was one very specific way to model "freedom-within-authority" for the broader society.

Protestants pointed the way with their response to liberalism's final test in Prussia. Their nearly unanimous approval of political developments in Schleswig-Holstein, and of Austria's defeat, prepared them psychologically for the campaign against France. In succeeding years, a kind of rigorous Protestant imperialism found expression in politics, theology, and religious culture. The Sedan Festival symbolized the decade's political achievements, as well as the Protestant commitment to imperial servitude in the new empire.

NOTES

CHAPTER VIII

(1) Horst Zillessen, ed., VOLK, NATION, VATERLAND; DER DEUTSCHE PROTESTANTISMUS UND DER NATIONALISMUS, Veroeffentlichungen des Sozialwissenschaftlichen Instituts der eKidO, Vol. II (Guetersloh: Guetersloh Verlagshaus, 1970), pp. 151, 184.

(2) Henry A. Kissinger, "The White Revolutionary: Reflections on Bismarck," DAEDALUS (Summer 1968) <Proceedings of the American Academy of Arts and Sciences, XCVII,3>, p. 888.

(3) Influenced by Schleiermacher and Hegel, Rothe thought that God's kingdom would find its fullest manifestation in a Christian state that was a religious and moral entity. He coordinated Hegel's philosophy of history with Schleiermacher's emphases of nature's latent potential, and God-consciousness as the focus of religion. He agreed with Hegel that God's kingdom reached its fulfilment in concrete civil society, but also insisted that the church would dissolve in the process. Integral to his argument was the claim that morality consisted of uniting personhood and material nature, inasmuch as each had a claim on the other. Through the developmental process of His kingdom, God's Spirit became a part of the world; creation was the vehicle through which God achieved potentiality. The world moved in tandem with God's Spirit as it attained its goal in His kingdom, and this process was the structural framework for morality. Thus, the history of universal salvation had its parallel in the sphere of each individual. Man's moral process, which increased self-spiritualization, paralleled the process in God Himself; while man's moral activity was especially concerned with his physical nature, it was also the process through which God reached fruition within Himself. While both church and state were moral communities,

the church was destined to merge into the state since it more perfectly embodied the moral nature of God's kingdom.

(4) Otto Pflanze, BISMARCK AND THE DEVELOPMENT OF GERMANY; THE PERIOD OF UNIFICATION, 1815—1871 (Princeton: Princeton University Press, 1963), p. 13. See also Otto Becker, BISMARCKS RINGEN UM DEUTSCHLANDS GESTALTUNG, ed. and supplemented by Alexander Scharff (Heidelberg: Quelle & Meyer, 1958), p. 464, where Becker argues that "the father of the German state was the German war <between Austria and Prussia>. What it set in motion, the force of the magnetic power of victory and the people's sentiment for national unity brought to completion."

(5) See Robert M. Berdahl, "New Thoughts on German Nationalism," AMERICAN HISTORICAL REVIEW, LXXVII (1972), 76-78.

(6) Wolfgang Raedische, DIE EVANGELISCH-LUTHERISCHE LANDESKIRCHE HANNOVERS UND DER PREUSSISCHE STAAT 1866—1885 (Hildesheim: August Lax, 1972), p. 108.

(7) Karl Hammer, DEUTSCHE KRIEGSTHEOLOGIE, 1870/1918 (Munich: Koesel Verlag, 1971), p. 16.

(8) Paul Piechowski, DIE KRIEGSPREDIGT VON 1870/71 (Leipzig: A. Deichert'sche Verlagsbuchhandlung, 1917), pp. 30-33.

(9) Ibid., pp. 190-91.

(10) Ibid., p. 89.

(11) Ibid., p. 24.

(12) Golo Mann, THE HISTORY OF GERMANY SINCE 1789, tr. Marian Jackson (New York: Frederick A. Praeger, 1968), p. 196.

CHAPTER IX

THE FLAG AT FULL STAFF

It was a significant moment for German Protestantism in the eighteen-sixties, when church and state agreeably modified the unwritten religious charter without signature or vote. They added another assignment to the church's modeling task, namely, to cultivate moral and religious support for the empire's conservative nationalism. As a result, churches propagated a spirit of Protestant dominance and cultural imperialism in church and state alike.

In the seventies, eighties, and nineties, the imperial flag flew at full staff over Protestant churches. Imperialistic Protestantism knew few boundaries. It concretized itself in Jerusalem in 1889, when the new emperor dedicated the Church of the Redeemer to symbolize German Protestant presence in the Holy City. The dedication occurred on Reformation Day, appropriately enough. The parade to the church resembled a military exercise; a large contingent of Turkish troops preceded the German emperor and his wife, who were followed, in turn, by German officers. At the church doors, the president of Prussia's High Church Council presented the keys to the emperor, and then the Prussian king marched into the sanctuary to the strains of the German chorale, "Rejoice, Daughter of Zion! Your King Comes to You!"

An imperialistic spirit dominated church life. People felt the full force of a Protestant national ethos that was the religious corollary of the political compromise underlying the new empire. And cultural Protestantism exuded a triumphalist spirit that permeated Protestant activities at home and abroad.

Protestant cultural imperialism colored mission theory and colonial missions. It assumed the form of brick and mortar in countless new and rebuilt churches. The cultural Protestantism of Ritschl and other theologians enunciated the theological ramifications of Protestantism's good fortune in Germany. A coterie of divergent forces coalesced in an imperialistic crusade against Roman Catholicism, which has come to be known as the "Kulturkampf." And while some Protestants tried unsuccessfully to form a national church for the empire, others turned to the more practical task of arranging for church taxes, and aligning church polity with the empire's political structure. That few clergymen were willing or able to resist this massive tide of Protestant imperialism is not surprising.

The one area not penetrated by Protestant imperialism was the social question. That was no accident, since the Germans addressed the national question first, with important consequences for the social question, and since many who became interested in the social question seemed disinterested in religion. In the main, the responses of Protestants to the social problem were unrelated to Protestantism's major thrust in the last third of the century. Subsequent chapters will discuss the faltering efforts of some Protestants to address the social question, as well as the Protestant imperialistic zeal that sometimes informed anti-Semitism.

ONE CHURCH FOR THE NATION?

Even before the Franco-Prussian War, the Prussian Minister of Ecclesiastical Affairs broached the question of a national evangelical church with Bismarck. Early in 1870, Ludwig Muehler reminded the chancellor that Lutheran confessionalism, "against which Luther himself protests," had secured a large following in the last thirty years in Hanover, Mecklenberg, Saxony, and Bavaria. He warned in his letter that the movement "stands on the same footing as

political particularism." Then he added that, in opposition
to confessionalism,

> the idea of one evangelical united church, which
> does not vitiate the individual confessions, and
> which has found a response in the Lutheran
> Churches of Schleswig-Holstein, Wuerttemberg,
> Oldenbourg and Thuringia, as well as our eight
> provinces—this idea has the same power in eccle-
> siastical circles that the national idea has in
> political circles.

Bismarck jotted this comment on Muehler's proposal for a
united evangelical church "for all of Prussia, and
additionally, all of Germany": "Would be very nice, but not
possible by means of legislation."

Some Protestants hoped that the war with France would bring
a general moral and spiritual revival, and others added that
one of the revival's fruits might be a national evangelical
church. But reality did not attain the vision. Kapff,
Gerok, and other pietists in Wuerttemberg complained that
national unification brought no moral or religious rebirth
of the German people. When the Bible Institute in
Hamburg-Altona issued an invitation to all German Bible
societies to establish a "common German Bible society,"
Wuerttemberg's society accepted the invitation in principle,
but dropped the idea after referring it to the Prussian
Bible Society, which had reservations.

By 1876, mirroring the pessimism that accompanied the
financial crash several years earlier, many agreed with
court preacher Adolf Stoecker's analysis of events. In a
speech entitled "The Religious Spirit in Nation and Army
During the French War," he noted how swiftly religious zeal
ebbed after the war, even though the Lord fulfilled
Germany's millennial dream and created "one nation, one
house, one army." He added with some surprise that "since
the war, spiritual life is worse than before." The war gave
people the chance to reject materialism and affirm
traditional spiritual values, but people probably "expected
too much for the kingdom of God from the experiences," he
said.

Immediately after the war, however, pessimism was not the

order of the day. Many churchmen responded to national unity with plans to coordinate national and ecclesiastical life in a national evangelical church. In the fall of 1871, Bethmann-Hollweg, Hoffmann and Wichern led the way in an effort to solve the problem of a national church. That year's "Kirchentag," held in Berlin on October 10-12, discussed a united evangelical church for all territories and confessions. Most of the 1,500 unofficial delegates at the "October Assembly," including 1,300 pastors, came from the "mediating" camp. Some moderate Lutherans attended, as well as such prominent Lutherans as Wangemann, Kahnis, and von Hofmann, but hardline confessionalists such as Harless, Luthardt, Uehlhorn, and Kliefoth were not present. In his appeal to the assembly, Wichern argued that a united evangelical church would be the most effective instrument for God's kingdom in the new empire. Willibald Beyschlag later remarked in his memoirs that it seemed natural to form an evangelical church confederation while the nation rode the crest of unification, but there was still not enough momentum.

Although the meeting had the new emperor's support, most officials kept their distance. Evening sessions conducted by two pietists from Wuerttemberg were well attended, but the work sessions were unprofitable. The star attraction was Chief of Staff Helmuth von Moltke, the general who once refused to join the German branch of the Evangelical Alliance because he felt that the nine fundamentals of the Alliance's platform were too constrictive. Moltke failed to create an aura of unity for what the socialist Franz Mehring called a "hypocrites' conference," and the meeting adjourned without results. No way was found to synthesize the three views of a national church advanced by Lutherans, liberal Protestants, and the mediating party. The proposition of the provost, Brueckner, to unite the territorial churches in a German "church convocation" was unacceptable because of centrifugal, particularist forces.

One last effort to raise the flag over a national church came when the "Kirchentag" met at Halle in 1872. Wichern addressed the issue squarely, claiming that the October Assembly had been called in 1871 because God's kingdom left no room for party strife. He reminded his listeners that for forty years God had been regenerating His people, the chosen of His kingdom; before the eyes of all, God's kingdom had rescued the German nation from its foreign and domestic enemies. The Inner Mission's Central Committee was merely trying to give visible form to newfound national unity when it authorized that meeting in Berlin, he said. He promised that God's kingdom would continue its march, despite human foibles, and the Inner Mission was dedicated to accomplishing this goal: "<to build> the old and perpetually new kingdom of God and of His Christ in the new German empire."

Wichern and others felt that the empire opened new avenues for the advancement of God's kingdom, so long as the nation was a "worthy" sanctuary for its honored guest, the kingdom. A unified evangelical church could manifest the unity that God bestowed on His kingdom's recent conquests. But the "Kirchentag's" failure to achieve any sort of unity in 1872 was a serious blow. This was the last time the unofficial gathering convened, since the possibility of a national church or church confederation seemed even more remote than when the "Kirchentag" first met in 1848.

It is not surprising that this unofficial body was unable to create a unified evangelical church. The idea of a national church ran counter to the religious charter that serviced the German territorial churches; most of the initiative for making important decisions lay with the states. Territorial churches encouraged particularism and a conservative outlook, and a national church structure, especially one created from the bottom up through the "Kirchentag," would have caused problems. In addition, the process that led to German unity differed materially from the give and take of the "Kirchentag." The formation of a national church from the bottom up, in an empire just formed from the top down, would have been something of a revolutionary anomaly. The churchmen's flag had nationalist insignia, but the governments saw it more as the tricolor of 1848 than the imperial flag, with its predominant Prussian colors. In sum, the failure of the national church movement embodied the power of conservative imperialist nationalism better than a unified church might have.

With the eventual disintegration of the "Kirchentag," the zeal for a unified national church waned. Official representatives of the territorial churches continued to use the Eisenach Conference as a forum, and although this group accomplished some projects, little happened to bring a national church into existence. In 1903, the Conference created the German Church Committee as a kind of continuation committee with executive power between conferences, and this committee took up relations with other religious communions, church-state questions, and the care of German emigrants until it became another group in 1922.

REALIGNING POLITY AND ASSESSING TAXES

One way to raise the imperial flag, or at least acknowledge the new political entity called the German Empire, was to align territorial church polity with elements of the political compromise that lay at the basis of the new national state. If the religious charter was still intact after unification, and it was, one would expect to find the churches taking cues from political and governmental leaders, and adjusting the structures of state churches to the political realities articulated in the constitutonal and political framework of the "Reich."

While modifications in church polity were not the same in each territory, they seemed to mirror in some degree the constellation of political forces on which the empire rested. That was why provisions for church taxes were an important component of the realignment process. Liberals were able to interpret regulated church taxes as a step toward the separation of church and state, as long as a person could renounce church membership officially and be relieved of the tax. For conservatives, the creation of a solid financial tax base for church support implied a continuing close relationship between church and state.

The basic political compromise that undergirded the new empire was composed of a number of elements. Many of them had corollaries in ecclesiastical polity developments in the sixties and seventies. Since Germany addressed the question of national structure before the social problem, the churches appropriately gave polity structure priority over social mission. Adjustments in polity signalled their endorsement of the political compromises that were required

for unification; their earlier hesitancy toward limited
representative government vanished. A trade-off emerged;
ideological support for conservative nationalism allowed
them to relax the polity structure.

Political unification originated in a revolution from above,
and in many cases, adjustments in church polity followed a
similar pattern. In Prussia's eastern provinces, for
example, the church bureaucracy provided impetus for change,
despite the resistance of many pastors and most
parishioners. In many northern church governments, lay
representatives usually came from aristocratic stock, and
sharply defined limits of suffrage made church polity only
partly representative. In addition, Prussia's church
bureaucrats continued to name a substantial number of the
voting delegates in many synodal assemblies.

The German Empire owed its founding to Prussian hegemony,
and Prussian preeminence continued into the twentieth
century, when 75 percent of the imperial map, and forty of
its sixty-five million inhabitants, were Prussian. Prussian
hegemony influenced church polity negatively, through
Prussia's lukewarm attitude toward a national evangelical
church. Prussia's conservatism was elastic only when
Prussia was sure to profit from the exercise of stretching,
as in the case of national unification. But a unified
national church would probably have been more difficult to
supervise, and Prussian politicians, especially Bismarck,
did not want to duplicate the problem of a united Roman
Catholic church. Prussian policy was served by preserving
centrifugal, conservative territorial churches that she
could influence and control more readily than a national
body or confederation. Consequently, church polity
modifications proceeded on a territorial, not a national
basis. There was little reason to disturb the territorial
basis of the century's religious charter.

Another element in the imperial compromise, one deriving in
part from the victory over Austria in 1866, as well as a
long series of historical precedents, was that the empire
was Protestant in name, if not by constitutional provison.
One result was the "Kulturkampf" of the seventies. But as
we shall see below, Bismarck could not prosecute the
"Kulturkampf" with Roman Catholics, in order to pacify his
liberal constituents, without levying many of the same

provisions against Protestants. As a result, the other edge of the "Kulturkampf's" knife pressured some territorial churches into making polity adjustments. This was especially true in Prussia itself, where the battle was fought more vigorously than in much of the rest of the empire. In sum, polity adjustments were necessitated by the Protestant character of the empire, and Bismarck's effort to keep the liberals in tow by attacking Roman Catholicism.

The new empire was shot through with dualisms. One of the most significant was the dualism between political and military authority, which the constitution allowed by requiring a military appropriations bill only once every seven years. Since most of the imperial budget's receipts came from fixed tariffs and excise taxes, this formality was not likely to spawn a constitutional crisis. A similar dualism characterized most of the polity arrangements in the territorial churches, especially Prussia's. Church-political authority was formalized in a tightly knit electoral process that produced district, provincial, and territorial synods or assemblies. But the church bureaucracy, equivalent to the army directly under royal control, was not open to the political pressure of elected church representatives. Meanwhile, church taxes were collected as a surcharge on income taxes, accumulating to be spent for buildings and other necessities as determined largely by the bureaucracy.

A final element in the "Reich's" political compromise was the working arrangement forged between agriculture and business, land-based trade and industrial commerce, or in Prussia, the largely "Junker" east and the industrialized west. All agriculturalists were not conservatives, and neither were all businessmen liberals; but the compromise that was arranged between the two groups was an important factor in creating national unity, and in providing political stability in the empire. The inauguration of regular church taxes after national unification can be understood as a way of providing a financial counterbalance to church patronage, which was largely dependent on the largess of landowning aristocrats. Taxation put church financing on a business level, although patronage was not totally eliminated.

Some adjustments in church polity occurred in the sixties, but the largest church, Prussia's, delayed major changes until the seventies. In 1861 a new church constitution was created in Baden as part of the "New Era." Adopted by a general synod convened for that purpose, the constitution contained presbyterial and synodal provisions, and also permitted congregations to elect their pastors. The High Church Council was no longer responsible to the Minister of Interior; residency alone conferred church membership; the established church was effectively ended, although cooperation between church and state continued. Baden's general territorial synod was composed of twenty-four clerical and twenty-four lay members, along with seven appointed by the grand duke.

In the city state of Hamburg, the New Era brought impetus for change as well. The question of separating church and state arose once again in 1859; a new constitution in 1860 permitted religious groups to govern themselves, an important provision for Lutherans, who had been governed by the city's Senate and College. A new church constitution was finally adopted late in 1870, during the war with France. Parish councils and a synod were integral parts of the new order, as was a nine-man church council to administer the Lutheran church. But the old order was effectively tied to the new, since the Lutheran members of the Senate were collectively designated as advowson, or "Patronat." The Senate chose two senators for the church council, and also ratified church laws and appointed pastors. While this constitution legally ended the Senate and the Sixty's control of the church, the "Patronat" once more tied the church to the state or Senate; it became the equivalent of the monarchical "head member of the church." The church's autonomous government was more an apparition than a reality, but some degree of representative government was inaugurated. In financial matters, the endowment that previously supported the churches in Hamburg provided insufficient revenue, and so a church tax was instituted in 1886. In nearby Bremen, a church tax was fiercely debated in 1911-12, but church taxes were not adopted until 1922, and then implemented the next year.

Rhenish-type church constitutions were adopted in Wuerttemberg in 1854 and in royal Saxony in 1868. In Wuerttemberg, diocesan synods of pastors and elders met annually, and a territorial synod was created in 1867. A form of church tax, self-imposed by believers, prevailed for some time before a legal church tax was codified in 1878. In Saxony, a territorial consistory took control of the state church in stages between 1868 and 1874, but the state retained inspectional rights. Territorial synods met every five years; they included lay representatives after 1868. Saxony collected compulsory church taxes before most other states in the German Confederation. One section of the kingdom imposed taxes as early as 1838; they were modified in the early forties and extended to other areas. The right to tax rested with congregations, and the governmental treasury financed the cost of synodal meetings. No territorial-wide church tax was imposed before 1906.

The Lutheran and Reformed churches of Hanover made hesitant steps toward self-government and church taxation in 1848, 1864, and in the 1880s. Progress was slower among Lutherans; in 1864 they anxiously questioned the effects of synodal and presbyterial polity on pure doctrine and the pastoral office. The anxiety level was raised even higher by a law in 1873 that provided for legally exiting from the church, and avoiding payment of church taxes. In Bavaria, the High Church Council was separated from the Ministry of Interior in 1860, and the next year a new church constitution adopted synodal and representative provisions. These two states differed little from the others in one point: the system of dyarchy did not function any more effectively in ecclesiastical Germany than in colonial India.

Synodal church government was established in the grand dutchy of Hesse in 1874, in Schleswig-Holstein in 1876, in Anhalt in 1875-78, in Nassau in 1878, in Hesse-Cassel in 1885, and in Frankfurt am Main in 1899. Mecklenberg and some areas of Thuringia failed to adopt this type of polity.

The largest territorial church, the Evangelical Church of Prussia, inaugurated important polity changes in the seventies, although some progress had been made in the fifties and sixties. When Bethmann-Hollweg became Minister of Ecclesiastical Affairs in the New Era late in the fifties, he set out to strengthen the presbyterial-synodal structure and to give the church greater autonomy, but the High Church Council was less cooperative. The effort faltered, even though parish councils were required in the light of special allowances for each province. District synods were once again ordered into existence after 1861. The prince regent's orders to strengthen the presbyterial-synodal stystem brought few results in 1860 and 1861. The tempo slackened after Muehler assumed the chief ecclesiastical post in 1862, even though he wanted to develop some degree of autonomy for the church. The slow process of creating congregational councils in 1858-60, and district synods in 1861-64, culminated in provincial synods for each of the six eastern provinces in 1869.

The most rapid advance toward representative polity in Prussia came under the chief ecclesiastical bureaucrat, Adalbert Falk, in the seventies, a decade during which Bismarck earnestly sought liberal support. The "Kulturkampf" was a major stimulus for this advance, but equally important was the work of Emil Hermann (1812-1885), a jurist whom Falk called from Heidelberg to design a program of polity changes in 1873 and 1874. Hermann served as president of the High Church Council from 1872 to 1878; his polity proposals received the approval of the court preacher, Wilhelm Hoffmann, but Theodor J. R. Koegel (1829-1896), who was first named court preacher in 1873, vigorously opposed the plans. Koegel claimed that the polity proposals placed the union church's confessional standard in jeapordy; his position was strengthened in 1879, when he was named to the High Church Council.

But plans were drawn and implemented despite some resistance. In 1873, the king promulgated an order on congregational structure and provincial-synodal organization for the six eastern provinces. He was acting in his capacity as "one who bears the burden of territorial church government;" he was offering the opportunity "to available forces in the church to participate more freely than heretofore in the service of ecclesiastical life," although he noted that neither the union nor the church's confessional position—whatever that was—were affected. Church councils, headed by the pastor and composed of four to twelve elders elected by the congregation, or appointed by the patron, were responsible for supervising the congregation's religious and moral affairs and charitable endeavors. District or circuit synods met annually; they were composed of elected and appointed members, including the chief ecclesiastical bureaucrat of the area, the superintendent; provincial synods met every three years at the consistory's call. The provincial synod was composed of royal appointees, a faculty representative elected from the theological faculties of the province, and delegates elected by the district synods. It was characteristic of the times that the composition of these groups was carefully prescribed, but their duties and responsibilities were minimally or vaguely described.

In 1876, new legislation in Prussia transferred all functions previously administered by the Ministry of Ecclesiastical Affairs and the government to the High Church Council and the consistories. State authorities retained only the right of general governmental inspection. The previous year, an extraordinary general synod created an ordinance for a territorial synod; the ordinance received royal approval in 1876 for Prussia's nine older provinces, though not for the newly annexed territories. The territorial synod was composed of 150 members elected by the provincial synods, as well as faculty members, the general superintendents (twenty-four in number in 1904), and thirty representatives appointed by the king. The tendency of provincial synods to elect older, more conservative men assured that the pyramid system did not produce a radical territorial synod. All laws passed by the synod had to be approved by the king, who also had the right of calling a synod into session. A meeting every six years was assured.

While the church polity structure in Prussia was modernized somewhat with ostentatious modifications, the ecclesiastical structure continued to parallel the political structure. Initiative and control rested with the monarch. Pastors headed parish councils, and royal superintendents chaired the district synods. In provincial synods, the royal consistory closely monitored the elected president, while the High Church Council carefully supervised the territorial synod. Leadership rested in the hands of theologians and jurists who had the king's confidence; representative polity and elective reform seemed like so much window dressing. If one asks whether things changed materially in seventy years, the answer is no, except that minor modifications were required to make ecclesiastical polity more palatable as interest in representative polity spread. Royal decrees in 1886 and in the 1890s made slight adjustments once more, but the basic dyarchical structure remained. It was automatic for delegates at the Prussian territorial synod to respond affirmatively at the closing session in 1879, when the synod president urged them to join his rousing cheer for their "summus episcopus": "Our emperor and our king! Long may he live!" In case there were stragglers in the crowd, the cheer was repeated three times.

Polity modifications in Prussia did not endanger the close relationship between church and state. The state continued to regulate the church's fiscal matters, and the House of Deputies had to approve each appointment on every consistory. In addition, new synods meant additional financial expenditures had to be secured through a compulsory church tax, which, in turn, cemented the church-state tie.

Polity changes between 1873 and 1876 gave congregations in Prussia with more than 500 souls the authority to levy church taxes for specific purposes. In addition, district, provincial, and territorial synods were able to levy taxes on congregations to finance their meetings and support other activities. Originally, the provincial and territorial church units in Prussia were limited in their taxing power to collecting and spending no more than four percent of the income tax paid by the evangelical population, although no clearly codified law on church taxes was passed in Prussia until 1905-06. Exemption from the church tax was granted to patrons who otherwise supported the church, pastors in the territorial church, church officials, and widows of pastors and church officials. Included among these "officials" were university lecturers serving in theological faculties, ecclesiastical accountants, organists, cantors and janitors. Teachers in Prussia were exempted from the tax until 1880. In addition, people who legally left the territorial church were exempted from the tax, as were Old Lutherans and Mennonites. Baptists and the Netherland-Reformed paid the tax unless they declared themselves outside the territorial church. Church laws had to be drafted delineating the various kinds of mixed marriages, so that the appropriate tax could be collected.

In 1909, the state empowered the church to raise the rate of the church tax to a surcharge of not more than eight and one-half percent of the income tax paid by evangelicals. One percent was placed at the disposal of provincial units, and seven and one-half percent alloted to the territorial church. The larger sum was distributed as follows: five percent for supporting retirees and widows of pastors; one and one-half percent for creating new pastoral positions, building churches, and training pastors; one-half percent for financing auxiliary pastors; one-fourth percent for strengthening pastoral work in urban and industrial areas, where parishes were severely threatened; and one-fourth percent for the pastoral care of Germans outside of Germany.

In summary, polity adjustments permitted the Prussian church to continue functioning in its chartered role as society's best model of freedom within authority. The representative ecclesiastical pyramid of district, provincial, and territorial synods, with parish councils at the base, exemplified the kind of political "freedom" permitted by the state in the political system. Protestant polity gave quite a different witness and impression than the unending demands of the Catholic Center party, which urged that Prussia's constitutional article on church independence be inserted in the imperial constitution as well. The steady character of Prussian church polity also contrasted markedly with the raucous clamor of socialist agitation. In sum, the German territorial churches' satisfaction with dyarchical polity was a vote of confidence—patriotic, conservative, and nationalist—in a political system that offered some self-government within strict limits defined by authority.

THE CLERICAL MOLD

Is it asking too much to expect that Protestant clergymen would resist the growing tide of religious imperialism at home and abroad? The answer is yes. The processes that incorporated an imperialistic cultural strain into the religious consensus also molded a rather docile Protestant ministerium, intent on cultivating, not questioning, religious triumphalism.

Church life in the sixties and seventies was hardly a seedplot for revolutionary thought and activity. The

402

consistory at Koenigsberg reported in the mid-seventies that an extraordinarily high number of clergymen in the area had been sick; their illness was partly due to the harsh climate. The report added that in many cases, poor morale was credited to annual incomes of only 3,000 "Marks," and substandard housing. This was inadequate income, especially when the pastor had a wife and children. As late as 1869, Prussian pastors had to secure the consistory president's permission to marry, and this mothering did little to encourage autonomous thought and life.

Middle class magazines continuously sniped at the parson's image. The family-oriented "GARTENLAUBE" experienced phenomenal growth between 1853 and 1881, expanding from 5,000 to 378,00 copies. The liberal journal popularized scientific achievements, and paid little attention to religion with the exception of such "Lichtfreunde" pastors as Uhlich and Balzer, who tried to accomodate religion and scientific progress. The magazine was quick to endorse the "Kulturkampf," and regularly attacked Wichern's home for destitute children near Hamburg. Conservative clergymen found some redress in a conservative Christian magazine named "DAHEIM," which encouraged middle class people to retain their loyalty to church and king. In 1886 this journal printed communiques from the battlefield in support of Prussia over Austria; it also defended Wichern's "Rauhe Haus" against its competitor's attacks, and printed religious stories and recommendations for religious novels.

Some candidates for the pastoral office seemed somewhat disinterested in assuming office after completing their training. The consistory in Koenigsberg reported that in 1874, sixty-eight of its sixty-nine candidates were so preoccupied with their work in schools and tutorial positions that they could not be shaken loose to take a parish position. As a result, one parish remained empty for a year and a half, and most candidates engaged in work that was only distantly related to their intended profession.

The pastor's public life was closely monitored. After 1871, imperial law provided severe punishment if a clergyman engaged in any activity that might be construed as fomenting revolution:

A clergyman or religious official who, in the

practice of his vocation, or in giving directions for that practice, makes a declaration or presentation concerning the larger affairs of state in such a way as to endanger public peace, whether publicly before an assembly, or in a church, or in another place appointed for religious meetings, such a one will be imprisoned or confined for a term of up to two years.

For that matter, the report of the Koenigsberg consistory, mentioned above, also indicated that parish councils were often not effective sounding boards for the complaints of pastors, especially in Prussia's eastern provinces. The report noted that elders were slow to assume responsibility as overseers of congregational faith and morals.

Much of the pastor's time was spent fulfilling legal requirements. In most areas he kept the official record of vital statistics until the mid-seventies, and in Prussia he performed such semi-disciplinary duties as notifying the local judiciary each year of the names, mother's names, and birthdays of all illegitimate children.

In large cities, the sheer size of parishes made the pastor's workload almost insurmountable. Despite the rapid growth of Berlin's population, only seven new churches were constructed in the sixties. Congregations were sometimes as large as the population of such major towns and cities as Stettin, Magdeburg, Stuttgart, and Karlsruhe, although most churches in Berlin seated no more than 1,000 people. Parishes of over 100,000 people had three or four pastors at most. On Second Pentecost Day in 1875, one Berlin pastor performed 230 baptisms and some twenty marriages, in addition to an evening service.

PROTESTANT IMPERIALISM AND THE "KULTURKAMPF"

The "Kulturkampf," the conflict that erupted between the Roman Catholic Church and the German empire and territorial states in the seventies, was the most poignant manifestation of the Protestant imperialist spirit that swept across

Germany in the last third of the century. During the battle, the Protestant flag flew at full staff over the newly unified German nation. The growing strength of the predominantly Catholic Center Party, and Bismarck's determination to reward the National Liberals, added fuel to the fire. For Roman Catholics, the struggle was another in the series of exercises that prepared them to deal somewhat more effectively with the Third "Reich" than Protestants.

National unity ended much of the flexibility built into the German political system, since the unification process bent nationalism to serve the purpose of established governmental power. Society's claims on the state now were carried by groups that, by definition, were extraneous to the state: political Catholicism, and political socialism. In Germany and other European states, it was a natural step to focus liberal agitation against Roman Catholicism; this meshed with Bismarck's efforts to reconcile liberals to "Junker" rule. The political compromise leading to unification, and Protestantism's place in the new order, were configured for a struggle against Roman Catholicism. The ensuing "Kulturkampf" affected Protestants in such areas as polity and the church's role in essentially civil rites such as marriage, but the brunt of the burden fell on Roman Catholicism.

Bismarck was no special friend of Roman Catholicism. As early as 1854, he remarked in a letter that

> it is not a Christian creed, but a hypocritical, idolatrous papism full of hate and cunning, which conducts an unrelenting struggle with the most infamous weapons against the Protestant governments, and especially against Prussia, the worldly bulwark of the evangelical faith. The struggle goes on in practical affairs, from the cabinets of the prince and their ministers, to the feather-bed mysteries of the married set. Here in the city and diet <at Frankfurt>, and at nearby courts, 'Catholic' and 'enemy of Prussia' are identical in meaning.(1)

The Syllabus of Errors, promulgated by the pope in 1864, excacerbated his fears with its condemnation of liberalism and countless other secular heresies. For some, the declaration of papal infallibility during the Franco-Prussian War suggested that the Syllabus was a prospectus for the Catholic Church in all of Europe, and states aborning, such as Germany, had a perfect right to protect themselves.

But Bismarck's dislike of Roman Catholicism and his struggle in the "Kulturkampf" were not theologically motivated, although, of course, there was no question of his commitment to the Protestant culture, as long as that commitment brought political dividends. Rather, what prompted the "Kulturkampf" was the growing political strength of the so-called "reichsfeindlich" Center Party, which was conservative and Catholic in the main, and Bismarck's courtship of the National Liberals in the seventies.

Bismarck viewed the party as revolutionary in the way it mobilized the masses toward objectives that he considered inimical to the empire. During November and December of 1870, the Center was busy rebuilding itself, and in the "Reichstag" election several months later it won seventeen seats. While it did not try to reverse the process of unification, it was concerned with strengthening the individual states, in view of the emerging power of the imperial government. Its platform in 1870 included a strong emphasis on particularism:

> Germany is the fatherland of Germans. But since the nation is made up of popular components from north and south, east and west, even so, Germany has never been a centralized, unified state, but a multifaceted empire . . . . The uniformity of a unified state, and the leveling regulations of an all-controlling center <centralized imperial government> militates against popular spirit.

Bismarck feared that the Center might become a rallying point for nationalist groups that did not easily fit into the new state: the Welfs in Hanover, Danes in the upper part of Schleswig-Holstein, the Poles in the east, and some people in the newly annexed area of Alsace-Lorraine. When the Center showed interest in the Polish problem, it concerned him greatly since Roman Catholics predominated among the Poles.

406

Bismarck was committed to preserving Prussia's monarchical state authority and the new nation state. The Center's growing strength, as well as the socialists' magnetism, seemed to challenge Prussia directly, since both parties apparently wanted to parliamentarize the monarchical state. The Center's insistence that the imperial constitution should include a provision for church independence was added evidence, not only of the party's particularist interests over against the empire, since it was supposed that this would protect the Catholic Church, but of its zeal for constitutional and parliamentary government. The nation state was susceptible to attack not only because the Center Party attracted divergent groups of non-German extraction, in addition to many Germans, but because Roman Catholicism appeared to be an international force, much like international socialism. Those centrists interested in addressing the social issue compounded the problem. No less despised by Bismarck was the party's interest in seeing the pope's temporal possessions restored in Italy; that for him was not a parliamentary problem or, for that matter, a concern for the secular government. The dogma of papal infallibility (1870) also made the Center a special threat to the empire, since the doctrine seemed to undermine the civic loyalty of Roman Catholics.

The severe economic depression in 1873 demanded a political scapegoat, and Bismarck was not about to offer himself. If he intended to court the liberals, one likely candidate was the conservative and largely agrarian interests represented by the Center. The most profitable political tact would be one that echoed progressive and liberal tenets. A broadside attack on the religious and ecclesiastical foundations of the Center Party also met that qualification.

One other factor played an important role: Bismarck's goal of isolating France, so that she could not ally with other powers and mount a war of revenge. Their recent defeat made Austria and France prime suspects for collusion, and he wanted no fifth column at home to render assistance. An attack on the Center and on Roman Catholicism would emphasize, almost subliminally, Bismarck's fear of a religiously-based alliance between these two major powers.

As far as Bismarck's liberal supporters were concerned, the schools were an ideal place to draw the battle lines. For some time, liberalism had been trying to remove religious instruction from the schools, and exempt them from ecclesiastical supervision. In 1868 the Progressive Party in Minden-Ravensberg vigorously attacked the institution of the confessional school; an awakened evangelical pastor in Berlin named Gustav Kack (1806-1870) took up the challenge, accusing the progressives of accepting the Copernican world view in opposition to the Bible.

The Prussian Minister of Ecclesiastical Affairs, a conservative named Muehler, played no role in this election battle, but his opposition to the formation of confessionless schools in Breslau at the same time showed that he was unfit to serve as Bismarck's orderly in the imminent "Kulturkampf." The magistrate of Breslau offered plans for a vocational school and a "gymnasium," and requested permission to make both institutions confessionless, so that the greatest number of students could attend. Muehler replied that while one or both could be organized in accordance with the principle of parity, which would provide religious instructions and a teaching staff from both Protestant and Catholic confessions, there was no way to circumvent the practice of 400 other Prussian schools of this kind, and establish these institutions as confessionless schools.

The debate continued for several years. Bismarck refused to get involved, claiming he was too busy. Muehler reported that he finally secured a hearing with Bismarck in 1868, during which Bismarck said that he felt the higher schools should be confessionless, although he warned Muehler not to make his views known to the king. Whether Muehler's memoirs can be trusted is debatable, but the problem in Breslau was resolved in any case. The magistrate agreed to organize both schools as "Simultantschulen," schools with confessional parity for evangelicals and Roman Catholics alike, although non-Christian students were also admitted. But the agreement provided that Jewish teachers could be hired only if they were not in a supervisory post.

In the fall of 1871, Muehler presented Bismarck with a number of legislative and administrative proposals dealing with education and ecclesiastical administration. He insisted that the state could throw off its subordination to the church in three ways: it had to make provisions for

legally exiting from the church; it had to require civil
marriage (although he indicated that some precautionary
practical measures would still be required, so that the
church could continue its disciplinary practices); and it
had to secure from the church the unconditional surrender of
supervisory function for the schools. He noted that two
additional steps were necessary to stop the encroachment of
the Roman Catholic Church; the state must require prior
approval of pastoral letters on political matters, and it
must outlaw the Society of Jesus in the whole empire. Since
the well-being of the Evangelical Church should also be
guaranteed, he proposed that the program of representative
polity should be consummated in an imperial, not a
territorial synod. Muehler reminded the political leader
that a convocation of all the evangelical churches in
Germany was a necessity "over against the firmly organized
Catholic Church."

The fuse that set off the "Kulturkampf" was the refusal of
certain Roman Catholic teachers to accept the teaching of
papal infallibility. But Bismarck had no firm ally in
Muehler, the man most responsible for executing his church
policies. In addition, Muehler's friendship with the royal
couple, especially the empress, was no consolation to
Bismarck, although Muehler followed orders in the middle of
1871, and eliminated the Roman Catholic section of the
Ministry of Ecclesiastical Affairs. It was argued that this
department was a papal instrument within the Prussian
government, more inclined to seek the welfare of the Roman
Catholic Church than the state's.

The first signs of battle appeared in 1871, when Roman
Catholic professors in some universities, and some Catholic
teachers in lower level schools, asked whether they had to
submit to the recent declaration on papal infallibility.
Conflict ensued between teachers and ecclesiastical
officials in Cologne, Breslau and Ermland. In the area of
Ermland, the lines were clearly drawn when teachers refused
to submit to the bishop's orders. The question was clearly
framed: Should "missio canonica" have legal ramifications
for the state, whose teachers were involved in this
problem?

Muehler was dismissed from office in 1872, since his face
was an old one. Three months earlier Bismarck addressed the

House of Deputies in a speech that signalled the opening of the "Kulturkampf." He accused a "confessional parliamentary party" of creating a "political assembly," adding that if all other groups adopted the same principle, an evangelical party would also have to be organized. "Then," he said, "we would be standing on all sides on incommensurable bases," because theology would have become the standard of political debate. "After my return from France," he added, "I have been able to interpret the formation of this splinter group only as a mobilization of party against the state."

His new Minister of Ecclesiastical Affairs, the Silesian Adalbert Falk (1827-1900), seized the gauntlet. But while Bismarck was chiefly interested in battling the Center Party, Falk's emphasis fell on rectifying legal relationships between church and state. A jurist who grew up in a Lutheran parsonage, he served in the Prussian House of Deputies in the sixties, and followed a liberal course amenable to the government. There was a measure of truth in the way the old conservative war-horse, Ernst Ludwig von Gerlach, characterized Falk's theological views in a parliamentary debate in 1875, that "the state is God, and the present Minister of Ecclesiastical Affairs is its prophet."

Sentiment and Prescriptive Legislation

Liberal support for Bismarck's war was axiomatic. One liberal legislator used the term "Kulturkampf" to describe the battle, and most liberals fell in line with Bismarck. Many Protestants were drawn to the government's position.

Protestant sentiment against Rome had a long and involved history, but anti-Catholicism was heightened by such recent events as the wars against Austria and France, and the unification of Germany. Even before the empire was formed, Protestants celebrated a national festival of sorts when the famous Luther statue was dedicated in Worms in 1868 with a number of notables present. The "Kulturkampf" seemed to show the effectiveness of the most recent modification of the Protestant religious charter; in exchange for Protestant support of conservative nationalism, the rallying point for national unification, the state was moving against the power of Rome. And Protestants supported the move.

The differences among church parties at the time helps us understand why Bismarck's moves garnered widespread support among Protestants. The confessionalists had been organized for some time. In such areas as Hanover, they did little to encourage success in the "Kulturkampf," since they feared that they might become the next target of the Prussian liberals. Other groups of confessionalists were more amenable to using the terms "German-evangelical," "German Protestant," and after unification, "Protestant German Empire." In March of 1872 Bismarck spoke of an "evangelical emperorship," a term widely used by some National Liberals. This phrase was not especially politically volatile—or useful—when it indicated the traditionally Protestant faith of the Prussian monarchy, but during the "Kulturkampf," it helped pit the new empire against Roman Catholicism.

The church party that paralleled the National Liberals in politics was formed in 1873 with the help of a theologian from Halle, Willibald Beyschlag (1823-1900). The "Middle Party," or "Evangelical Union," represented those who wanted a firm connection between Protestant Christianity and culture. The party's platform frequently referred to the Reformation, and demanded freedom for academic theologians and those responsible for the church's teaching. One plank clearly endorsed the "Kulturkampf:"

> We think that our evangelical church is obliged, according to the Lord's will, to be subject to authority, just as each individual Christian. We desire that the church, serving the people best in every available way, and mindful of its required obedience, should cooperate with the state that nurtures and protects it. It is of special importance that it support the state, in its present difficult battle against the Roman hierarchy, with all the weapons of justice.

In Hanover, this party received the special support of Falk and the provincial president; it unsuccessfully tried to combine confessional commitment and support for Prussia. The party's major strength lay in old Prussia. Beyschlag created a paper for the party, the GERMAN EVANGELICAL PAPER (1874), which proved to be one of the century's last programmatic Protestant journals. The Middle Party

411

distinguished itself from the Protestant Union, which also supported the "Kulturkampf," by adhering more closely to a confessional position, and by not appealing for a national church.

The fourth major Protestant party, the "Positive Union," was formed in 1876 in reaction to the Middle Party, and the repercussions of the "Kulturkampf" within Protestantism. The Prussian court preacher Koegel was its founder; much of its support came from courtly circles and east Elbian nobles, who were often church patrons. The party's platform referred to the evangelical church's "well-established place in the elementary school," and insisted that ecclesiastical administrative organs should influence the appointment of theological professors. The party also stressed the need to integrate representative polity with consistorial and governmental church administration.

The first legislative act in the "Kulturkampf" was an imperial law passed late in 1871 at the urging of Bavaria. It prohibited the use of pulpits for political purposes. Only one other imperial law dealt directly with the "Kulturkampf;" most of the pressure was exerted in the largest Protestant state, Prussia, where the new minister, Falk, proposed legislation on educational matters. Rejecting the claim of some preachers after the Franco-Prussian War, that France's problems were due to the de-christianization of French schools and their separation from the church, Falk proposed that the state supervise both the content and the personnel of religious instruction. Religious instruction continued to fill four or five of the twenty or thirty class hours each week, depending on the level in the primary grades. Prussian legislation in March of 1872 gave the state total supervision of the schools. The move turned some conservatives against Bismarck, but also increased liberal support.

The second imperial law was passed in July of 1872. It banned the Jesuit Order and similar orders from "the areas of the German Empire." In April of the next year, the Prussian legislature altered the Prussian constitution, once more subjecting the autonomous government of churches and religious groups "to the laws of the state and the legally ordered supervision of the state." This change laid the groundwork for the famous "May Laws," passed the next month in Prussia. The blow was aimed at the Center Party, which tried to get the unrevised constitutional provision into the imperial constitution.

The four May Laws (1872) covered a number of points. The first required priests and ministers to attend a German high school, and then to study at a German university. Candidates had to pass an examination on philosophy, history, and German literature before a state board. Church authorities had to inform the state of all appointments, any of which the state could veto. The second piece of legislation regulated papal jurisdiction over the Roman Church in Prussia. Church discipline was transferred to German agencies, and the clergy was required to inform the state of all church penalties. Both church members and the state could appeal church penalties in a special royal court established for that purpose. The third law forbade the publication of penalties imposed by the church. The fourth provided for legal withdrawal from churches in Prussia.

Subsequent legislation in Prussia rested on this foundation. In May of 1874, a series of laws was adopted that permitted the government to restrict the movement of a deposed cleric who continued to function as a priest; he could be banned. Another enabled the state to appoint an administrator for properties in a diocese without a bishop; local patrons, or a meeting of parishioners called by the mayor, would appoint a local priest to the vacant bishopric.

Elected parish boards were to administer the property and finances of a parish, according to a law passed in 1875. After a papal encyclical declared Prussia's ecclesiastical legislation invalid, and released Roman Catholics from obedience under the pain of excommunication, new legislation in April revoked all state funds for the church's support. Five weeks later, another law outlawed all monastic orders except those involved in hospital work.

Among other legislative acts were laws that made civil marriage obligatory in Prussia (1874), and transferring responsibility for keeping vital statistics to civil agencies (1874). The next year the empire adopted parallel legislation. What began as an attack on the Center Party ended as an attack on the Roman Catholic Church, with some

413

important consequences for Protestants as well.

Resolving the Struggle

Protestants of every stripe seemed at first to support the "Kulturkampf." Some argued that freeing the state from ultramontane oppression was a completion of Luther's work. Others honestly took to the field for freedom of thought and conscience, or would not desert the government's position in Prussia because of the church's longstanding subservience to the state. Since the Protestant Union repeatedly stressed the Protestant character of German culture, it was not surprising in 1871 to hear Schenkel describe the confessional struggle against Catholicism as a "battle of culture with the barbarism that menaces New Germany." Emil Friedberg (1837-1910), a Protestant canonist at Leipzig who was a member of the scholarly commission that Falk appointed to draw up the May Laws, interpreted these laws less as an attack on the church than on the state. Since the time of Frederick William IV, he said, the state had too warmly fostered the church's influence. After Bishop Ketteler closed a polemical statement against Friedberg with the words, "May God preserve our German fatherland from the evil these <May Laws> are capable of producing," Friedberg concluded his response with a parody: "May God preserve our German fatherland from the evil that such laws can set aside."

In September of 1873, Emperor William I seemed to voice unequivocal support of the "Kulturkampf" in a letter to the pope. He wrote that "a segment of my Catholic subjects," incited by clerical leaders, had formed a political party that threatened to destory confessional peace in Prussia. As a "Christian monarch," he felt constrained to fulfil his royal calling against such servants of the church, "so that they, no less than the Evangelical Church, recognize the commandment of obedience to civil authority as an emanation of the divine will revealed in us." In response to an earlier papal note, he added that he did not believe that every baptized person belonged to the pope. The evangelical doctrine that "the majority of my subjects recognize" identified Jesus Christ as the only intermediary between God and the individual, he wrote.

Another manifestation of support for the "Kulturkampf" occurred in 1875, when the Monument to Hermann was dedicated in the Teutonberg Forest. The emperor joined a number of princes, Germans from America and other countries, and local dignitaries in a mighty celebration of power. Earlier plans to sing "Praise to the Lord" were scrapped in favor of "our Protestant hymn," Luther's "A Mighty Fortress." National power and anti-Roman Catholicism seemed to hang from the same hinge: Protestant freedom of spirit.

The Koenigsberg consistory's annual report in 1875 indicated that pastors in this east Prussian district had adjusted rather well to the secularization of marriage, and the transfer of vital records to civil agencies. Some pastors decided to eliminate perquisites, or lower their marriage fee, in order to continue serving the poor. A major problem arose, however, when an evangelical married a Jewess in a civil ceremony; the husband later took a pastor to court to determine why a church wedding could not be performed as well.

As the battle peaked, some Protestants showed increasing opposition to the "Kulturkampf." One of the sharpest critics of the Empire and of the battle was the Protestant Konstantin Frantz, whose RELIGION OF NATIONAL LIBERALISM (1872) portrayed nationalism as a new heathenism. Frantz pointed to the "Kulturkampf" as evidence that Germany now embodied Hegel's power state. As early as 1872, when the Prussian "Landtag" was deliberating the school laws, lobbyists presented a number of petitions urging defeat, and once more in 1873, Protestant clergymen in Hanover opposed the May Laws. After these laws were passed, six hundred clergymen petitioned the Prussian king not to promulgate them.

The old war-horse, Ernst Ludwig von Gerlach, strongly opposed the "Kulturkampf," portraying it as a struggle between "universal Christianity" and a "national Jupiter." The Center Party secured his election as the oldest member of the House in 1873. He represented a safe Roman Catholic district near Cologne, and became the party's spokesman in some of the debates, but in 1874 the government fined him for slander in his brochure CIVIL MARRIAGE AND THE IMPERIAL CHANCELLOR. He resigned his judicial position at the appeals court in Magdeburg, and asked whether he could suffer imprisonment as well. The empress' influence on her husband was one reason why Bismarck began losing the emperor's support in this battle with the Center Party, and now with the Church.

William I never supported Bismarck unequivocally, and as the struggle moved toward a radical stage and the government grew unsure of its footing, the emperor was even less supportive. One court preacher, Koegel, tried to form a "Camarilla" or kitchen cabinet with the court to counterbalance Bismarck; though unsucessful, he influenced the emperor's views. The winds of change were blowing; earlier elections hinted that the liberal tide was waning, and the conservatives' victory in Minden-Ravensberg in the elections of 1879 was an unmistakable sign. The party had won no elections after 1873, but its platform now contained a very important plank: "If it is to be that the emperor is to be given what is due the emperor, and <if we want> order and good morals, peace and concord <to> return, then one must also give to God what is God's."

The "Kulturkampf's" effects on Roman Catholicism were paradoxical in nature. The more the hierarchy suffered, the more lay people seemed willing to hold to their position. National elections in 1873 and 1874 augured well for the Center Party, which doubled its representation in the "Reichstag" in 1874. All Roman Catholic bishops in Prussia were imprisoned or in exile by 1876, and by the next year, 1,400 of the 4,600 parishes in Prussia were without priests. Very few of the faithful joined the "Old Catholic" movement, even though in some states it received the government's financial assistance and support. The battle with the church was at a standstill because of the hierarchy's firm resistance, and laity's dogged support.

Protestants also felt the effects of many of the laws. In addition to Prussia, Baden and Hesse were the two states that prosecuted the battle most vigorously. In Prussian Hanover, the special "cultural examination" required of all ministerial students apparently affected the enrollment pattern. The number of pastoral candidates slipped sharply from 35, 39, 33, and 34 in the years 1873-76, to 23 in 1877 and 18 in 1878. The new examination probably contributed to this decrease, since graduates would have enrolled in the program of studies after the passage of the May Laws in

416

Another identifiable consequence was the decreasing number
of church weddings and baptisms in a time of demographic
increase. After the new civil regulations were inaugurated
in 1874, only about 20 percent of Protestant marriages were
solemnized in churches subsequent to a civil ceremony, and
only about 50 percent of the babies born in 1874-75 were
baptized.(3) The number of church weddings in Berlin dropped
from 11,531 in 1873, to 2,647 in 1875. As a result of the
transfer of vital records to civil officials, baptisms in
Berlin plummeted from 32,073 in 1873, to 19,291 in 1875.
Although the percentages of church marriages and baptisms
inched upward again, the statistics showed the willingness
of a segment of Berlin's population to disassociate itself
from the church when given that option.

In Hanover, the new marriage laws brought a schism in the
territorial church. Some conservative Lutherans withdrew
because they would not accept the new text of the agenda,
which removed the word "ehelich" ("matrimonially," legally)
from the marriage formula: "Thus I, an ordained servant of
the church, pronounce you matrimonially <legally> joined
together." The Hanoverian synod revised the formula, but the
Lutheran group in Hermansburg used the revision to explain
its withdrawal. Another consequence of the "Kulturkampf" was
that Protestants now could legally resign from or exit the
church. Although the number of people who legally withdrew
from the church remained a relatively small percentage, the
numbers climbed appreciably in the early decades of the
twentieth century. The number of legal withdrawals in all
the territorial churches ranged between 1,800 and 6,300 per
year from 1884 to 1905 (with 1,600 in Prussia alone in 1900,
for example). In 1906, the total was 17,400; from 1907 to
1913, withdrawals from all the territorial churches climbed
from 14,300 to 29,300 (with 19,000 in Prussia in 1908, and
20,500 in 1913). By the end of World War I, 240,000
withdrew in one year (1919).

It was no easy matter to resolve the "Kulturkampf." Bismarck
was adept at shifting much of the blame onto Falk, insisting
that in some cases he had not even read the legislation.
Discussing the situation earlier with Bishop Ketteler, he
offered these words in response to the bishop's question
whether a Catholic could be saved: "Certainly a Catholic

layman, but a cleric is more of a problem." Bismarck was hinting that the question and the answer were neither to be taken seriously, nor dismissed lightly. Falk had waged the battle on one line, while initially at least, Bismarck thought along different lines. One reason why it was difficult to end the battle was that people had different impressions of what the struggle was about.

Although Falk held office until mid-1879, the preceding year was decisive for a number of reasons. The emperor continued to question the wisdom of this struggle against the church, but more pressing issues influenced Bismarck. Both the agrarian and the industrial sectors clamored for protective tariffs, and he became aware that to accomplish this objective, he needed a new parliamentary base without the National Liberals. Two attempts to assassinate the emperor in 1878, one of which wounded him gravely, opened the way for legislation outlawing the virulent Social Democratic Party; by innuendo, the socialists were accused of these anarchistic acts. At the same time, conservatives were gathering strength in the "Reichstag." All signs indicated that Bismarck should re-establish relations with the Center Party, and party leaders such as Windhorst were not joking when they said that "extra centrum nulla salus" ("no salvation outside of the Center"). In addition, a new pope had been elected in 1878. Leo XIII was a capable diplomat, who skillfully made concessions so that Bismarck could conclude the battle as if it had been a cabinet war.

Legislation in 1880, 1882, and 1883 lessened the severity of many laws passed during the "Kulturkampf," and concerted efforts were made in 1886 and 1887 to rescind the legislation that lay at the heart of the battle. It might be argued that 1887 marked the end of the struggle, although legislation remained in force to neutralize the Prussian constitutional article on church autonomy, to give the state exclusive supervision of schools, to prohibit the pulpit's use for political purposes, and to require civil marriage. A modified anti-Jesuit law was also retained; it was revised in 1904, and abolished in 1917. But it seemed like a symbol of peace already in 1880, when the emperor joined German princes in the dedication of the completed cathedral in Cologne.

What began as a political struggle against the Center Party

became an effort to impose on Roman Catholics some elements of the Protestant religious charter. The resistance of Roman Catholics stiffened for a number of reasons, including their theological resources, their heirarchical structure, the Center Party's resurgent strength, and political conservatism's growing attraction in the late seventies. Many Protestants wanted to see a symbolic national flag fluttering over every Roman Catholic church in the empire, but others recognized that religious oppression in the name of liberalism would complicate their lives as well.

At this point in the century, the comparison between Roman Catholic and Protestant communities was striking. Accustomed to their place in the social and political power structure, Protestants seemed unable, and in most cases unwilling, to offer resistance except though theoretical or theological argument. On the other hand, Roman Catholics seemed to burn with the same zeal that ignited during the Cologne Troubles. The two groups responded quite differently to the ominous threats and encroachments of the Nazi regime several generations later, and their responses were greatly influenced by their history and training during the previous century.

Continuation Committee

Some Protestants were not as adept as Bismarck in rapidly shifting their religious convictions and cultural emphases. Anti-Catholicism retained its magnetism despite efforts to end the "Kulturkampf," or, more precisely, because of these moves. The Evangelical Confederation ("Evangelische Bund") of 1886 was formed while the legislative substructure of the "Kulturkampf" was being dismantled.

Some years earlier, a pastor named Sander in Elberfeld called for a Protestant society to protect Protestants against the dangers of Roman Catholicism, but this effort met little success. The time was much riper in 1886, especially since the 400th anniversary of Luther's birth three years earlier stirred a new Protestant consciousness. An organizational meeting was set for Erfurt, the same meeting place for an irenic gathering of certain Protestants and Roman Catholics in 1860. Among the founders of the Evangelical Confederation at this meeting were Willibald

Beyschlag, whose Middle Party was the left-of-middle counterpart of Koegel's right-of-middle Positive Union; Gustav Warneck (1834-1910), a missiologist from Halle; Gustav A. Fricke (1822-1908) of Leipzig; and Friedrich Niepold (1838-1918), a church historian who vigorously opposed ultramontanism and supported the Old Catholic movement.

The Confederation held that Protestants could no longer rely only on the state for protection against the renewed strength of Roman Catholicism. "Protestant self-consciousness" had to be nurtured not only in view of Catholic incursions through mixed marriages and proselytizing, but because the common cultural inheritance from the Reformers needed public recognition. The "Bund" wanted to assist the state in finding an appropriate relationship with the church, especially the Roman Church. Its platform insisted that Rome's powerful unity gravely threatened the splintered churches in "German evangelical Christianity." And although the "Kulturkampf" was ending, "the struggle with Rome continues; it will continue 'as long as one heretic stays in the land,' or as we understand it, until the truth of the Gospel achieves victory in all of Germany." In a sense, the "Bund" was a self-appointed "continuation committee" for the "Kulturkampf."

The Confederation tried to achieve its goals through planned events, annual meetings, and a vigorous publishing program that included brochures, statements and papers. Its members interwove national-cultural and Christian-Protestant emphases, and made anti-Catholicism a religious and patriotic duty. The "Bund's" first published pamphlet (1887) asked what should be done with a third of the population that was systematically indoctrinated "to undermine true patriotism," and to place state law under the judgment of the supposed vicar of Christ. The solution would be found in a group committed to "German Christian conscience" that integrated faithfulness to God, to evangelical faith, to fatherland, to emperor, and to territorial prince. In 1907, a publication insisted that a kind of Germany had to be created free of outside influences, so that a unified national, economic, political, and religious life would emerge, based on Protestantism's cultural power. Several years earlier, the Confederation expressed anxiety over moves to relax the anti-Jesuit laws. In 1912, a speaker at the annual meeting denounced the same enemies of the "Reich" that Bismarck fingered in the seventies, the Social Democratic "Reds" and the Catholic "Blacks."

As the century ended, the Confederation continued to emphasize the need for a united German church. In 1899, Beyschlag published a book entitled THE NEED FOR A CLOSER CONNECTION AMONG GERMAN PROTESTANT TERRITORIAL CHURCHES. Meanwhile, relations with Roman Catholics improved little, partly because the Confederation's publishing program aggravated the situation. A Catholic book, entitled 'THY KINGDOM COME TO US,' A PROTESTANT PASTOR'S FAMILY ON THE WAY TO THE CATHOLIC CHURCH (1890-93), was answered by THY KINGDOM OURS REMAINETH; A COLLECTION OF LECTURES BY EVANGELICAL PASTORS FOR DEFENDING GERMAN PROTESTANT INTERESTS IN A BATTLE WITH ROME; A HANDBOOK FOR FRIENDS OF THE EVANGELICAL CONFEDERATION (1896).

Popular response to this new group showed that it had struck a raw nerve. The year after it was organized it claimed a membership of 10,000 persons, with 7,000 lay members. By 1890 the membership stood at 100,000, by 1904 at 240,000, and when war broke out in 1914, it claimed a roll of 500,000. The group encouraged the annual observance of Luther's birthday on November 10. During its early decades, it was preoccupied with counteracting Roman Catholic political power. Toward the end of the century, encouraged by the "Away-From-Rome Movement" ("Los-von-Rom Bewegung") in Austria, it focused attention on the problem of acculturating Roman Catholic converts. In Prussia alone, about 100,000 persons converted from Roman Catholicism to Protestantism in the two decades preceding 1914. Ten to twelve Roman Catholics converted for every Protestant who changed confessions.

This "Bund" embodied some of the religious imperialism that blossomed soon after the nation was united. It was a pressure and propaganda group that accepted the basic tenets of the unwritten religious charter, even though many of its members urged greater autonomy for the church. With the creation of national unity, cultural Protestantism emerged as a powerful force; it was the religious corollary of nationalism. The national counterpart of the religious charter, which continued to function primarily in a territorial context, was cultural Protestantism. As a

421

strong proponent of cultural Protestantism both in its negative (anti-Catholic) and positive (pro-Reformation) forms, the Evangelical Confederation was an organizational manifestation of the religious charter written large.

RITSCHL AND CULTURAL PROTESTANTISM

Ritschlianism was a theology for the rising Protestant bourgeoisie of the new empire. Albrecht Ritschl (1822-1889), who after 1864 taught at Goettingen, provided a theological basis for the strong, active, disciplined individual. As the most articulate form of cultural Protestantism, his work took theology out of the sphere of ontology, and thrust it into the realm of morality.

Ritschl poked at the weaknesses of a speculative rationalism based on Hegelianism. A friend of the union, he located the church within the orb of God's kingdom, and understood church unity as an ethical quotient first and foremost. His theology was attractive to an age hungry for facts; he carefully pointed to God's revelation in Christ as sufficient. His grasp of the concrete made him a pragmatist of sorts. This was clear even in non-theological matters; losing his wife to death after a short marriage of ten years, he turned both his living room and bedroom into a study.

Ritschl was preoccupied with Luther as a formative figure in German culture and Protestant history. In an address observing the 400th anniversary of the Reformer's birth in 1883, he asked a rhetorical question that defined his understanding of Luther's importance: "For where else can one find already prepared the basic premise of all scientific research—that the human mind has power over the world and is of higher value than the world—save in Luther's religious idea of the freedom of the Christian?" But as David Lotz has carefully demonstrated, Ritschl felt that the mature Luther "dissolved the original secular and social context of justification," and "surrendered both its telic relation to life in the world and its anchorage in the community's transpersonal consciousness of God's ever-present grace."(4)

It was with the consequences of this dissolution that Ritschl wrestled. He tried, Lotz argues, "to unfold the epoch-making cultural implications resident within that much maligned doctrine of justification by faith and its practical correlate of Christian liberty." That was why he assumed that Protestantism ultimately links itself with cultural progress. His festival address in 1883 argued that Luther's basic concern was that "a formation of character can be achieved" by religious edification, and by well-rounded education, "which will make it possible to reach the highest ideal of fulfilling one's duties toward one's fellowmen."(5)

Luther's Christian freedom, he argued, did not involve a religious independence from communal norms and considerations, nor did it propose a weakening of the power of the state. Ritschl thought that Protestantism was immature, and the Reformation incomplete, because both theology and churchly practice failed to build on the Reformation's genuine religious and practical impulses. His own day's world view, based on natural science, showed all the more clearly the need for a Protestant apologetic. He wrote in a letter in 1873 that Christianity was both a religion and a system of morality:

> I have become convinced that a certain consequence
> of reconciliation which heretofore I have always
> located within the province of ethics—namely,
> sonship of God, freedom from and over the world—
> must form as leading a point of view for dogmatics
> as the idea of the kingdom of God. These are surely
> the two chief aims of Christianity in a practical
> religious and moral reference. Both are lacking not
> only in the traditional dogmatics, but also in the
> presentation of the Protestant Confessions. With
> the idea of the kingdom of God one cannot get fur-
> ther than that Christianity is a doctrine of moral-
> ity; its nature as a religion can be upheld only
> through the other idea.(6)

Given these assumptions, one can understand Ritschl's desire to get Protestantism over its "teething problems," as he said in a festival speech in 1883:

I should like to advance the thesis that to date
Protestantism has not yet emerged from its age of
teething problems, but that its independent course
will begin when—on the basis of a thoroughgoing
comprehension of its practical root ideas,—it
reforms theology, fructifies churchly instruction,
shores up the moral sense of community and achieves
political resoluteness for the actualization of
those spiritual riches which one of her greatest
sons once acquired for our nation.(7)

Ritschl's cultural Protestantism was a response to currents
of his age, especially the growing power of political
Catholicsm and the raging battle of the "Kulturkampf." He
said in his festival speech in 1883 that if all Protestants
became Catholics, and all national governments became
obedient to the Roman See, "the sword and fire will stand
ready at hand to effect the desired peace of the
cemetery."(8) He was less than enthusiastic about the claim
that the ascetical character of Roman Catholicism had been a
positive force in history.

On the other side were those who attacked the paltry
contributions of the Reformation, both in doctrine and
life. Contemporaries such as Paul de Lagarde and Jacob
Burkhardt, as well as Friedrich Nietzsche, scorned
Protestantism, insisting that it simply marked the beginning
of the end of ancient and medieval Christianity. In this
light, Lotz notes, it is ironic that Ritschlianism has
become a synonym for modernism, "when Ritschl devoted almost
his entire career to investigating, expounding and defending
a doctrine that the 'moderni' regarded as a dead issue."(9)
His major works, including the three volumes of THE
CHRISTIAN DOCTRINE OF JUSTIFICATION AND RECONCILIATION, and
his INSTRUCTION IN THE CHRISTIAN RELIGION, appeared after
1870 in his mature years.

This proponent of cultural Protestantism influenced a full
generation of theologians. Central to his theology was the
idea of God's kingdom, and he tried—some say
unsuccessfully—to anchor his understanding of the kingdom
firmly in Christology. His two major intellectual
influences were Kant and Schleiermacher.

Ritschl posited God's kingdom as a "correlate" of God's

love, arguing in the festival speech in 1883 that "in the Christian religion trust in God is decisively informed by the idea that the aim or purpose of the world is the association of men in the kingdom of God; that the order and course of the world are subordinated by God to that purpose . . . ."(10) Every activity on behalf of God's kingdom was always and only a reaction to God's activity; forgiveness of sins prompted man's activity and set his will on the right path. Ritschl's identification of God as love permitted him to fill God's personhood with meaning in a way that he hoped would avoid the pitfalls of metaphysics. Ritschl was concerned to avoid the dichotomy between religious consciousness and moral purpose that he found in Schleiermacher. He tried to show that Jesus' messianic consciousness was inherently connected with the creation of God's kingdom of moral ends.

He argued that through their moral pedagogy, church and state together were responsible for the progress of God's kingdom in history. The state's civil ordinances, including the social orders of the family and vocational calling, were channels or structures through which the kingdom was extended. Ritschl claimed that Augustine erred in equating the church with God's kingdom. The Reformers rectified the problem somewhat by interpreting the state as a direct divine order, and the church as Christ's kingdom, the communion of believers, but they too soon fell into the old trap. The church was not to be equated with God's kingdom, and therefore, legally the church's existence depended on the order maintained by the state, not the other way around. For this reason, Ritschl adamantly opposed any theology or theory of natural law that offered a foundation for an ecclesiastically-based political party, such as the Catholic Center, or such other parties as the Progressives or Social Democrats. His theological work informed the sermons of such students as a pastor named Schwarz, who preached these words:

> How may we separate our faith from our most holy
> obligations as citizens, our Christianity from our
> love of the fatherland? Both are one, indivisibly
> one. The fatherland, the people to which we belong
> . . . is our most holy heritage and right, with
> regard to which we have to raise up ourselves with
> our small selfhood. Only in it and with it can we

be what we are, and fulfil our human and Christian obligations.

Ritschl's cultural Protestantism portrayed Christianity as an ellipse with two foci: God's gracious initiative in Christ's restoration of sinners to fellowship, on the one hand, and the moral imperative of discipleship in the kingdom, on the other. That kingdom was within and above history, rather than at the end of it; its only code of ethics was love. His understanding of God's kingdom was a powerful effort to unite Kant's two realms in a theological system dominated by the doctrine of justification, without at the same time ignoring Kant's kingdom of moral ends. His theological system raised the flag of Protestant imperialism over a generation of theologians and preachers.

MISSIONARY THEORY IN AN AGE OF IMPERIALISM

In the final third of the century, missionary theory was another way that Protestant imperialism, or the imperialistic spirit of cultural Protestantism, showed itself in Germany. Sometimes it seemed almost impossible to distinguish between the church's mission and the nation's colonial responsibilities, and missionary theory displayed a great deal of confusion in this area. The challenge was clear: to integrate some of the day's most powerful forces, including nationalism, colonialism, confessionalism, the "Kulturkampf," and economic trends, into a working theory of mission. In addition, developments in church polity, and the bourgeoisie's growing commitment to the idea of progress, had to find a place in mission theory, or else the practical work of missions would suffer. It was feared that failure in this effort would adversely affect the outreach of Protestant mission to foreign fields.

It is not true that a nationalist flag was superimposed on every page of missionary theory written during this period. Rather, cultural Protestantism made an impact on the ways that Protestants construed their programs of missionary outreach. Concerted efforts were made to coordinate the day's most powerful currents with the theory or theology of

426

foreign missions. A brief examination of theory at two of the most important mission societies, located in Basel and Barmen, and a review of the work of several prominent missiologists, bear out the fact that, in its modified nationalist form as cultural Protestantism, the religious charter of the Protestant churches renewed and reshaped missionary theory.

From 1850 to 1879, the director of the Basel Mission Society was Joseph Friedrich Josenhans (1812-1884). Although Basel was headquartered on Swiss soil, most of its support came from southern Germany, especially the Swabians. During Josenhans' directorship the society was racked by internal strife. Like his predecessor, Josenhans invoked the idea of God's kingdom to encourage support of foreign missions, but by this time the symbol's apocalyptic connotation had been infused and secularized by the idea of progress. In one speech, Josenhans noted that "the kingdom of God is prepared and firmly anchored, but still not perfected. . . . Missionary leadership is charged with the task of working together to bring God's kingdom to consummation." His references to the kingdom often echoed the progressive and naturalist ideology that was the hallmark of Friedrich Fabri, the inspector of the Barmen Mission.

Two problems plagued the Basel Mission during Josenhans' tenure. The first was the complicated situation that resulted when Christian F. Spittler (1782-1867) withdrew support from Basel, and established the St. Chrischona Mission School nearby. Spittler's school was the first step in a plan to send out streams of Christians all over the world who, like the early apostles, would be free of churchly and confessional ties.

The second problem was the spirit of factionalism generated by growing nationalism in Germany and Switzerland. Since the mission drew some support from neighboring Swiss citizens, some felt that France's rising influence in Switzerland was a test of German honor. Should a separate south German mission society be established, they asked? Josenhans tried to counteract this divisive spirit at the mission's jubilee celebration in 1874, when he said:

> One has examples of missions that have gone under
> . . . we Swiss and Germans assembled here cannot

> hide from it: we are much more in danger of a
> schism than a mission that belongs to a single
> nation; and our mission will disintegrate if Swiss
> and Germans let their patriotic feelings gain
> control and assume a higher value than love for
> the Lord and for the kingdom of God. Our mission
> has this one beautiful, magnificent characteris-
> tic, namely, that it really is a mission of God's
> kingdom, and not the mission of a single church or
> nation.

He offered another exhortation at the last conference he
chaired, in 1878:

> Now we can still shake hands with one another and
> say, "You Germans and Swiss, we do not want our
> nationality to interfere with the work of God's
> kingdom, but let us stay united!" . . . if this
> work is to continue in true unity, it is impor-
> tant that our distinct nationalities take a back
> seat in favor of kingdom-nationality.

Since both confessionalism and nationalism threatened the
missionary enterprise along similar lines, Josehans felt
obliged to apply the idea of God's kingdom in both cases. He
argued that true catholicity should not allow national
barriers or confessional differences to divide people, whose
awakened religious spirit pursued the cause of foreign
missions.

Theodor Oehler (1850-1915) succeeded Josenhans, and served
as director until 1915. Even more than Josenhans, he
provided naturalistic interpretations of the apocalyptic
conception of God's kingdom, which had so faithfully served
as the mainspring of the mission's support in Wuerttemberg.
The kingdom continued to have eschatological connotations in
Oehler's speeches, but in the main, he portrayed God's reign
as a natural development that scarcely distinguished between
the kingdom's growth and world history. Eschatology played
little part in missionary theory or missionary practice.
Oehler invoked the image of the kingdom to defend Basel's
supra-confessional stance, but he modified and weakened the
argument somewhat by suggesting that one integral purpose of
mission work was to establish churches. In 1898, he wrote in
the Basel MAGAZINE that "mission work should pursue the

business of Christ's kingdom; it should extend the kingdom of God, and this it does by establishing churches in which God's kingdom organizes itself in its terrestial form."

Missionary theory up north in the Barmen Mission Society followed a similar course. Friedrich Fabri (1824-1891), inspector of the mission from 1857 to 1884, was an ardent proponent of cooperation between missionary and colonial interests. His mature theology tried to mold apocalyptic anticipation into a coherent system of theosophy. He had a tendency to retreat to the supposed simplicities of the apostolic age, hoping thereby to avoid questions about the historic confessions of the Reformation. Success in this effort would open the way for a mission society to seek one simple and important goal: "kingdom immediacy" with the apostolic church.

Two guiding principles governed Fabri's theology and missionary theory. He was convinced that the apostolic age had reappeared in a novel way in his day, and he sensed a sort of eschatological or apocalyptic expediency in the movement of history. The overarching motif of God's kingdom held together his longing for the past and his concern for the future. For example, he noted in the mission's report in 1862 that "the duty of the faithful to pursue missions" could only be implemented if it were successfully demonstrated "how and where <this duty> had its special significant place in the execution of the divine kingdom plan."

He confronted the problem of confessional rivalry among Barmen's missionaries, and avoided a split between workers of the two confessions, by stressing that the missionary was first a citizen of God's kingdom, and only then a representative of Lutheranism, or of the Reformed communion, or of the union. In the mid-seventies he invoked the symbol of God's kingdom to explain the society's new governmental structure, which was created as a result of legislation during the "Kulturkampf." His annual report in 1874 described the kingdom as a voluntary creation of free enterprise quite distinct from the state; he claimed that the principle of free association appeared in Christian circles long before it found wider acceptance in social and political circles, or in joint stock companies.

Fabri was a tireless proponent of colonialism and the role of missions in colonization. He gave the impression that in colonial areas, at a comfortable distance from home, mission societies and institutional churches could interact effectively. After retiring from Barmen, he published a number of colonial studies to supplement his earlier works. His strange mixture of theosophy and apocalypticism enabled him to infuse a racist ideology of colonial imperialism with eschatological views. At the General Mission Conference in Berlin in 1868, he announced that he preferred to "put off until the time of the millennium the entrance of all peoples into the new city <of unity>. The future of the Asiatic peoples appears to be very problematic for me." During the interim, the diffences between people and races were insurmountable. Fabri held that the white man was under divine commission to rule the world.

Another major missionary theorist was the great missiologist, Gustav Warneck. His UNIVERSAL JOURNAL OF MISSIONS provided a focus for a group that included Reinhold Grundemann (1834-1924), Theodor Christlieb (1833-1889), Franz M. Zahn (1833-1900), Charles Buchner (1842-1907), Julius Richter (1862-1940), Johannes Warneck (1867-1944), August Schreiber (1839-1903), Theodor Oehler (1850-1915), and Carl Mirbt (1860-1929). Toward the end of the century these men tried to integrate mission, confession and church, and to relate the sum of the equation to new situations facing missions. In general, they were more positively inclined than the liberals toward the old pietist institutions, and the confessional mission societies.

In his journal, Warneck used the symbol of God's kingdom to portray how the naturalistic, progressive evolution of the world's history served God's mission to the heathen. At the end of the century his multi-volume EVANGELICAL TEACHING OF MISSIONS suggested that God's sovereign reign opened all mission doors; God fashioned history to fit plans for missions, just as He changed history through missions.

More of an academician than a practitioner, Warneck had close ties with several mission societies, especially Barmen. His practical interests led him to design and publish a supplement for a wider audience than the UNIVERSAL JOURNAL reached. In 1878 he published a recent speech to a student mission festival, in which he explained the journal's motto, "And this gospel of the kingdom will be preached throughout the whole world as a testimony to all nations; and then the end will come" (Matthew 24:14). He noted that in the course of the century, the number of German mission workers had increased from 200 to 2,300, but Christ's promise of victory was the most heartening fact of all.

There is little doubt that cultural Protestantism made an impact on missionary theory. Academic missiologists and directors of mission societies were busily creating a model for missions that incorporated secular and semi-secular autonomies that could not be ignored. It was quite natural to use the idea of God's kingdom in this process since it was open to a number of interpretations, but the observer of missionary theory is struck by how often this idea was loaded with naturalistic and evolutionary connotations. Even in this area of mission theory, where some of the most conservative Protestant thinkers functioned, the flag flew at full mast. Through the good auspices of cultural Protestantism, missionary theorists endorsed the idea of cross-fertilization between the church's outreach and contemporary currents of thought, including colonial ideology.

COLONIAL MISSIONS

At mid-century, territorial churches began moving closer to the independent mission societies in Germany, but widespread cooperation failed to develop until the mid-seventies. One factor in this development was the rising interest in colonialism; foreign missions won the support of many in the churches because missions and colonial expansion seemed inseparable. With this in mind, the mission historian Wilhelm Oehler referred to 1885 as a "milestone in the history of German missions:"

> How much missions continued in their own isolated
> box may be seen from this fact: events like the
> Revolution of 1848 and the establishment of the
> German Empire in 1871, which moved people deeply,

431

basically had little effect on missions. Missions
were faced with new questions and tasks for the
first time when Germany became a colonial power,
especially after 1885. And it is a strange coincidence that around the same time, two new mission
movements had disputes here and there with the old
societies, which for almost seventy years had been
the supporters of missionary work . . . . So in
more than one way, the year 1885 can be reckoned as
a milestone in the history of German missions.(11)

Already in 1879, Theodor Christlieb (1833-1889), professor
of practical theology at Bonn, and a close friend of both
the Barmen and Basel missions, urged the delegates of the
Prussian General Synod to ponder the importance of Germany's
growing fleet. He said,

Gentlemen, we are happy that in these days German
warships carry the German flag even to the most
distant shores and islands. Let us do our part
for self-expansion, in active competition with
many non-German churches, so that where the peace
flag of missions is unfurled, with the dove holding
an olive branch in his mouth, the Gospel messenger
representing the German evangelical church is not
absent—at least not in the major provinces.

The Evangelical Mission Society for German East Africa,
later known as Berlin III, had its beginnings in 1886 in the
flush of colonial excitement. About the same time, a chair
for missions was established at the University of Hamburg,
although this merchant city's university had no theological
faculty.

German mission societies were involved in mission work on
foreign soil long before the colonial era, of course, as we
have seen in a previous chapter. But the colonial era had a
major impact. Among the new mission stations opened after
mid-century were the Hermannsburg Mission's posts in Natal
in South Africa (1854), and in Tyransvaal (1860). The Natal
effort was a miserable failure, even though it began as a
self-sufficient congregation with strong lay support. The
Rhenish Missionary Society began work in Sumatra in 1861,
and most of the other societies were engaged in operations
on foreign soil by the time Germany was unified. In 1866,

432

German evangelicals took the lead to invite representatives from Scandinavia, France, and Holland to the Continental Missions Conference in Bremen, but the quality of their missionary workers remained inferior. According to one report, only about 25 of the 500 German missionaries in service in 1877 were university-trained, and more than half of them came from Leipzig University. Finances were another difficulty, especially with the economic crash of 1873. The Barmen mission collected over a million "Thaler" between 1863 and 1875, but at the end of the period it still faced a deficit of 135,000 "Thaler." When the society celebrated its fiftieth anniversary the next year, the attending representative of the Moravian Brethren sadly announced that he could present no gift since his agency faced a deficit of 100,000 "Mark."

Bismarck finally brought Germany into the colonial race on a small scale, acting almost exclusively to please the merchants. In the eighties, the constellation of international relations on the continent made it possible to secure colonies without serious reprisals, and France's cooperation in the so-called German-French "colonial marriage" was extremely important. But Bismarck did not want a large fleet, and took every precaution to avoid confrontation with the British.

Togo and the Cameroons became German colonies in 1884. The Hamburg merchant Adolf Woermann had secured property in the area of the Gulf of Guinea. Although the North German Mission Society of Barmen had been working in Togo since 1847, it had been coordinating its efforts with British missionaries in the area. The lay president of the society, whose brother headed a trading company in the area, exerted pressure on the mission to fill Togo with German missionaries, but the society's director was hesitant about wrecking good working relations with the British, despite elusive governmental promises of 3,000, 4,000, and 10,000 "Mark" subsidies each year to support the project. The director claimed that the amount was insufficient, but the society finally entered the field in earnest in 1890, after an English-German agreement located two of its stations in the area. Roman Catholic missions ensued as a result of negotiations between the German government and the papacy.(12)

In the Cameroons, the English Baptist Mission had to make way for the Basel Mission Society in 1886. The previous year, a mission conference in Bremen had come to this decision. The German government was anxious for the arrangement to be implemented, since the Baptists did not hide their displeasure after Germans attacked Duala and destroyed many of the missionary structures. Financial plans were completed in 1886 to purchase Victoria, a Baptist stronghold, and the next year it became part of the Cameroons.

In June of 1884, Britain recognized the German colony of Southwest Africa, where a Bremen merchant had acquired territory. German missionaries from the Rhenish Society had been working there and agitating for colonial status for some time. Mission inspector Fabri of Barmen provided important coordinating functions between missionary and colonial interests in the area.(13) The missionaries were instrumental in arranging treaties with some African leaders, and the Bremen merchant Luederlitz favored them over Roman Catholics in return. Missionaries interpreted the discovery of gold in 1887 as a gift of "God's gracious hand." When native Christians in one part of the colony asked that the mission's major church and school be closed, missionaries appealed for armed strength to overcome such "arrogance," but the government sent only a small detachment.

German East Africa (Tanganyika) grew out of the plans of an adventurous pastor's son, Carl Peters, of Hamburg, who founded a "society for German colonization" in 1884. The next year he received an imperial patent of protection, and opened the new colony. In 1886 the Evangelical Mission Society for German East Africa was formed in Berlin. Also known as Berlin III, or the Bethel Mission, the society floundered until Friedrich von Bodelschwingh came to its rescue in 1890. Because it was closely associated with colonial interests, the society's station in Dar es Salaam suffered heavy damage during an uprising in 1889. Also active in the region were the Lutheran society from Leipzig and, after 1891, the Berlin Mission Society (Berlin I), which also engaged in work in Southern Rhodesia (1892-1906), South China (after 1882), and North China (1898-1924).

There were other colonial efforts and missionary endeavors

as well. The New Guinea Company had been making territorial acquisitions in northeastern New Guinea, and in 1885 these territories became protectorates, called Kaiser-Wilhelm-Land and Bismarck-Archipelago. The next year, Loehe's Lutheran Mission in Neuendettelsau began work in the region, along with the Rhenish Society. After two German missionaries were murdered in China, the Germans received a ninety-nine year concession on the Kiaochow territory in the Shantung peninsula. Cooperating with the China Inland Mission, the Liebenzeller Society began working there and in Hunan in 1899, while the Barmen Society entered Chekiang and Kiangsi in 1890; the Chrischona Pilgrim Mission entered Kiangsi in 1896, while Berlin I worked in Kiatschou. Two missionaries from the Basel and Rhenish societies had begun work in Kwangtung province in 1847. In 1889, a German merchant named Carl Polnick took the lead in creating the German-Chinese Alliance Mission, which cooperated with the China Inland Mission. Early in the twentieth century, an institute for medical missions was opened in the German town of Tuebingen.

It is not necessary to chronicle all the adjustments the older societies were required to make to understand the impact of colonialism on the missionary enterprise. Nonetheless, we should at least mention the new and important roles played by education, medicine, and women in mission work. By 1913 the relationship between foreign missions and colonial power was so close that a three and a half million "Mark" anniversary offering, collected in honor of the emperor, was designated for use in colonial missions. In addition, the new alliance produced a subtle shift in the motivation for foreign missions. It was argued that since the empire now included a number of heathen territories, missions could no longer be regarded as a voluntary pursuit; rather, they were the duty of all members of the territorial churches.

The so-called "liberal circle" of missiologists and missionary proponents, including F. W. Nippold (1838-1918), Heinrich Bassermann (1849-1909), Adolf von Harnack (1851-1930), H. Kesselring (1852-1919), and Otto Pfleiderer (1839-1908), understood colonial activity as a divine right given to Christian people, especially those in the German territorial churches. Working with others, this nucleus organized the German Evangelical Protestant Mission Society in 1884—in Weimar, of course. The society's foundation was the "gospel of Jesus Christ;" its objective was to "extend Christian religion and culture among non-Christian peoples." Kesselring provided a ringing challenge at the first meeting: "The enduring, visible church has ONE great assignment, and that is to penetrate all humanity with the blessed gospel, to transfigure it into the kingdom of God."

In theory and practice, missions were a flagpole for the flag of cultural imperialism, as Protestant national ethos found another expressive channel. The unwritten religious charter was being applied on a national level, as Protestants reconfigured it to accomodate national unification and colonial imperialism.

THE EMPEROR'S SACRED SOIL

The man who assumed the emperorship in 1888 can be cast in the role of a crusader with little difficulty. At the center of his crusade was an encrusted, yet ardent form of nationalism, which for many people replaced idealism as a life-integrating force. His imperialistic zeal helped raise the flag of Protestant Germany in remote places. A strict loyalist, he dismissed Bismarck from office in 1890 and set out to rule in his own right. He showed appropriate sorrow at the ex-chancellor's death in 1898 by declaring a day of mourning, but relatives arranged to have the coffin closed before the emperor arrived so that, it was rumored, he could not view the man to whom he had brought such grief.

But William II seemed more interested in the sacred soil of the East than the "dirt to dirt, ashes to ashes" of dead chancellors. Above all else, he was a religious crusader, with religious and political interests in the Near East. In the fall of 1898, with a large contingent of religious, financial, and economic experts in tow, he sailed to the area on his ship, the HOHENZOLLERN. He stopped in Istanbul to discuss with the Turkish ruler the proposed German railroad to the Persian gulf, ignoring for the moment the Turks' horrible persecution of Armenian Christians, in which over 200,000 were massacred between 1894 and 1896. Nor did he seem to fear that his foray into this area might antagonize Russia, although the Czar was less certain. It was possible to placate the English by giving them partial control of the proposed railway.

The next stop was Jerusalem, where the emperor dedicated the new Church of the Redeemer as a symbol of German-Protestant presence in the Holy City. The German Temple colonies included about 1,400 people, and some additional Germans resided as well in the Holy Land. The church's dedication festival was set for Reformation Day, October 31. A high church official accompanying the emperor on his tour kept meticulous records, since these historical events were making a "laudable confession of true German faith" in its "historical importance for the German Empire and the German church."

The loquacious emperor seldom passed up an opportunity to speak, and this dedication was opportune. "Jerusalem, the respected city in which we stand," he said in the church,

> calls to memory the redemptive activity of our Lord and Savior. . . . The world-renewing power of the gospel that went out from here pulls us to follow it; it reminds us of a vision of faith of Him who died on the cross for us, of Christian toleration, of works of selfless neighborly love for all men. . . . Light came to the world from Jerusalem, and in its reflection our German people has become great and powerful. What the German people have become, they have become under the banner of the cross of Golgotha, the true sign of self-sacrificing love. As for almost two millennia, so also today the cry rings out from here into all the world . . . peace on earth! . . . And while on this festive day I repeat the vow of my ancestors, now asleep in God, "I and my house, we will serve the Lord," so I seek the same solemn promise from you all. Let each one see to it in his position and calling that all who carry the name of the crucified Lord pursue their business in the sign of his praiseworthy name, to victory over all the dark powers that originate in sin and self-service.

The symbol of the Golgotha cross was inextricably associated with the greatness of the German nation, of that he was certain. Even the bells of the new church reminded him of the fatherland. The recorded account of his visit noted that the bells of the Church of the Redeemer struck the same notes as the bells of the great Emperor William Memorial Church in Berlin, but the Berlin church's "d, f and a" were not as pure or beautiful, nor were its chords as full as those produced by the new bells donated by the emperor.

The emperor passed through Beirut and Damascus on his journey. While at sea, he probably preached to those on board his ship, as was his custom; he was adept at applying biblical passages to Prussia and her challenges. He could expect to be greeted by Protestant clergymen with some enthusiasms upon returning home; not only had he journeyed to the Holy Land, but in 1898 he was partly responsible for the passage of legislation that gave Prussian clergymen a raise in pay.

CHURCH CONSTRUCTION AND RENOVATION

The construction of public buildings has traditionally helped groups of people define their identity and manifest their public pride. The last decades of the nineteenth century were no exception in Germany, since in this period Protestants built churches with a zeal probably unmatched in their history. The willing participation of the new emperor and of the governments, especially in Prussia, does not hide the fact that, through an exercise in civic and national pride, church construction was also a dire necessity, as far as the institutional church was concerned. Growth in population and in the size of cities gave urgency to the need for more churches.

Protestants showed the wealth and power of their new empire with brick and mortar; their churches were "public buildings" in the true sense. They celebrated the unwritten religious charter's new imperialistic and nationalistic theme. And since 60 percent of the forty-five million Germans in 1880 were Prussian, and 62 percent of the sixty million in 1905, Prussia's concern for church construction and renovation was characteristic of Protestants in the rest of the nation.

The two proposed structures in Berlin that attracted the most attention were a memorial church for Emperor William I, and a new Westminster-type cathedral that was to serve as a burial crypt for the royal family, and as a religious focus for national life. Plans for the memorial church originated in 1878, when the emperor decided to build a "Thanksgiving Church" after narrowly escaping assassination. General von Ollech of the army gave a progress report to the Prussian General Synod when it met in 1879; he indicated that the project originated "because men wanted to honor the God who had blessed the German nation with such a wonderful sovereign." Over 20,000 "Mark" had already been collected, and "faithful fellow-workers in God's kingdom have also partly promised us furnishings for the church's interior." Rather than the zoological gardens, a building site was chosen in Wedding, a Berlin suburb where 25,000 workers were said to be without a church. The building was finished in 1884; it became an anti-socialist symbol, since many believed the unsubstantiated rumor that the emperor's attempted assassins had been Social Democrats.

But the real Emperor William Memorial Church was still to be built. It awaited the financing that was provided by the Church Building Society, organized in 1890 with the new empress as patron. Chamberlain Ernst Freiherr von Mirbach was very active with this group, which became a receptacle for gifts aimed at political influence. Known in courtly circles as the "church conqueror of Berlin," Mirbach was a master at gathering donations from Jewish bankers, the presiding official of the "Reichstag's" Social Democratic bloc, and anyone else who wanted good press at the court. It was understood that Empress Augusta Victoria would learn the contributor's name and the size of the gift. Scandal almost wrecked the society when the bank that held its deposits nearly collapsed, but it survived and financed thirty-two churches in Berlin, and eleven in the suburbs.

The Memorial Church was finally dedicated in 1895 at a cost of three and a half million "Mark." According to Mirbach, the sum included 74,000 "Mark" from non-Protestants, including 19,000 from Jews. The new emperor insisted on memorializing his grandfather with monuments, and the church boosted the number of monuments dedicated during the reign of William II to 328. It was the most impressive of them all. Its cornerstone was laid in 1891, as part of a pompous military ceremony viewed by the emperor on Berlin's magnificent "Kurfuerstendamm." Four years later, the dedication occurred on September 1, the anniversary of the Sedan victory. The Emperor William Canal had opened in June, and the foundation stone for a large monument to the deceased emperor was laid in August. The church's dedication seemed to climax these events. Court preacher Wilhelm Faber's sermon on that occasion exemplified his homiletical maxim, namely, "a sermon on German soil must also bear the German imprint."

The "Dom" or Cathedral in Berlin was finally finished in 1905, after the cornerstone was laid in 1894. After the war with Austria in 1866, the Prussian king issued a cabinet order to build a new cathedral. The parliament discussed the subject at great length in the seventies; a number of deputies wanted to construct a Westminster-type "holy crypt" for the dynasty, while others argued for a burial place for all the nation's great figures. Finally in 1892 the "Landtag" allocated funds for the 10,000,000 "Mark" project. Dedicated with great pomp, the edifice was built in late Renaissance style to seat 2,000 people. It was nearly 350 feet long and 375 feet high.

The renovation of the Castle Church at Wittenberg was helped along by the Luther renaissance in the century's last decades. The four hundredth anniversary of the Reformer's birth in 1883 brought all sorts of festivities, and youth from nearly every "gymnasium" in Germany gathered in Erfurt to honor the Reformer. In autumn, Crown Prince Frederick took his father's place, kneeling in silent meditation before Luther's grave. In a festival speech, the famous historian Treitschke called Luther a "Christian German colleague in battle," who was "blood of our blood," since "Protestantism was always our safest border guard" when Germans clashed with foreigners.(14)

The Castle Church in Wittenberg underwent major renovation between 1885 and 1892. As a symbol of power, the northwest tower was transformed into a church steeple eighty-eight meters high. Plans were to top the steeple with a replica of the imperial crown, but a cross was placed there instead. In the course of the renovation project, seven stone masons were fired for trying to organize a Social Democratic club—the first—in Wittenberg. The emperor appeared for re-dedication ceremonies on Reformation Day in 1982, along with the six evangelical princes of the German states, and representatives of the free cities of Luebeck, Bremen and Hamburg. The proclamation of the emperor and princes noted that "in evangelical communon with one another, we have called on the almighty and gracious God in fervent prayer to protect the blessings of the Reformation for our evangelical people, and to increase fear of God, love of neighbor, and civic loyalty in our lands."

Protestant cultural imperialism was not the only reason for building and rebuilding churches in this period. In the Rhineland, one hundred and thirty-eight new congregations joined the existing 333 congregations between 1815 and 1909, and most of them needed new church buildings. The conversion of Roman Catholics, and the influx of Protestant soldiers and officials into Prussia's new western provinces, were two reasons for the Protestant growth there. Seventy-one of the new congregations were formed after 1880, thirty-eight between 1890 and 1899 alone. In other areas, population increases also created the need for new churches. In the kingdom of Saxony, the average clergyman in Dresden served 6,000 members in 1900, but even the sixty-six new churches built in the kingdom between 1886 and 1900 did not keep pace with the growth of population.

Prussia's High Church Council authorized the collection of free will offerings in 1852, and every year thereafter, for church buildings, property, parsonages, organs, bells, and personnel. Each annual collection in the 1870s averaged 340,000 "Mark." The amount designated for church property and buildings increased markedly between 1872 and 1878, from 17,850 "Mark" in 1872, to 23,303 in 1876, and 62,881 in 1877 and the first quarter of 1878. The evangelical church was struggling to provide new buildings and to renovate old, but it lagged far behind the population bulge.

Berlin was a showcase for all that was wrong. In the mid-seventies, only ninety-six clergymen, including part-time assistants, served the city's 850,000 people, while twenty-four additional pastors ministered to 600,000 people in the suburbs. Provincial churches were asked for a special free will offering to support the work in Berlin since, according to census figures of 1871, only 20 percent of the people were native Berliners. Some argued that the dearth of churches was responsible for the low number of baptisms, weddings and funerals. Only 67 percent of the children born in 1877 were baptized, and only 31 percent of the marriages in Berlin were solemnized by evangelical pastors that year. At St. Mark's parish, only one hundred and sixty-one of 2,884 members who died that year were buried by a pastor. The other major cities fared little better. While 80 percent of the marriages in Berlin were not blessed by the church in 1874, the same was true of 75 percent in Stettin, and almost 66 percent in Magdeburg. Church buildings may not have been the full answer, but they were being built nonetheless; twenty-five churches were in various stages of construction in Berlin in 1892.

The province of East Prussia scheduled a special building program to coincide with the 200th anniversary of the Hohenzollern dynasty in 1901. A number of churches had been built in the nineties to accomodate the new parishes being formed, partly by dividing large churches. Thirty-eight congregations had more than 5,000 souls on their rolls in 1896, but by 1901, that number dropped to twenty-six. Forty-eight new parishes were formed between 1885 and 1904, and forty-five churches, nine chapels, and three prayer halls were built. Several of these churches were constructed as part of the special Jubilee Church Program in 1901, which financed twelve churches and two chapels between 1901 and 1912. East Prussian pastors heard in 1901 that two men had already contributed 100,000 "Mark" toward the Jubilee Offering, but more than forty congregations needed worship facilties. This memorandum compared the zeal of the Roman Catholics with the evangelicals' lack of fervor, and indicated that parishes without church buildings were ripe for disintegration, or takeover by sectarians or Roman Catholics. The province's chief governmental official chaired the Offering Committee; its membership included church officials, judiciary officers, mayors, and top ranking military officers.

The dominant church architectural style toward the end of the century was "authentic" German Gothic, endorsed by the Eisenach Conference in 1861. The preferred floor plan was a crucifix. The Reformed offered the so-called "Wiesbaden

Program" in 1890, which portrayed the church building as the assembly point of the worshipping congregation, the celebration of the Supper in the middle of the congregation, and equality between pulpit and altar. But the Wiesbaden Program was not very influential in East Prussia and other areas of Lutheran strength in the east, although it had some influence in western regions.

In addition to those mentioned above, the more important Protestant church buildings constructed after mid-century included the basilican "Goldenstedt" Church in Oldenburg (1864); the basilican St. Thomas in Berlin, with 1,500 seats for a congregation of 38,000 souls (1869); Elizabeth Church in Langenhagen, designed by Hase, the creator of Hanoverian Gothic style, and architect of over one hundred churches (1869); St. Peter's in Altona (1883); Emmaeus in Berlin (1893); the basilican Garrison Church in Hannover (1893); the shipmen's church in Berlin, built on a boat to accomodate one hundred and twenty river and canal workers (1904); and the Luther Church in Karlsruhe (1907). The cathedral in Bremen was renovated in the nineties at a cost of two and a half million "Mark," and the third edifice for St. Michael's in Hamburg was dedicated in 1912, with the emperor present.

The question of modernization attracts historians and social theorists with remarkable magnetism. It is the basal hypothesis of many contemporary historical studies; it provides a paradigm or scientific model that people may use to understand their past in terms of their present. The dissolution of the feudal or "ordered" age, and the birth of the new, is apparent in most areas of modern life. Change has become the byword in society, politics, economics, artistic expression, culture, religion, intellectual life, and theology. An hour with Michelangelo's paintings, and another with Picasso's, gives one enough grist to grind for several years.

In his important small work, GERMANY CONFRONTS MODERNIZATION, GERMAN CULTURE AND SOCIETY, 1790-1890 (1972), Robert Anchor argues conclusively that in this period, Germany failed to negotiate the transition from a

443

traditionalist to a modern society. It seems as well that in the seventies, eighties, and nineties, German Protestants failed to accomodate to the modern world, including the novelty of national unification. That much is clear from our late twentieth-century perspective.

But the interesting fact is that German Protestants thought that they were making the transition successfully. At least they spared no effort to accomodate their churches to the decades' new cultural and political currents. That is the significance of cultural Protestantism in Germany. It was an unsuccessful effort to adjust to modernity, but those caught up in this multifaceted effort imagined just the opposite.

The Protestant flag, the flag of cultural imperialism, flew at full staff, as Protestants tried to incorporate the basic modification that national unification brought to the religious charter in the sixties. Since the charter was essentially territorial in origin and application, apparently the only way to graft it onto the new nation was to protestantize the culture shared by the territories, and to culturalize their Protestantism. Thus, cultural Protestantism was nothing more or less than the enlargement, the nationalization of a religious charter that was originally designed for territorial application.

It was a valiant endeavor, this effort to make Protestantism synonymous with Germany. It reached to the Near East, with the emperor's dedication of a church on the sacred soil of the Holy Land. It touched foreign missions deep in Africa and in other places, where German colonialism was making a faltering beginning. It rebounded back to Germany, where missiologists and directors of mission societies revised missionary theory for an age of imperialism.

It also directly affected life in the church. Protestants tried, but were unable to surmount the territorial divisions that barred a national evangelical church, although perhaps this failure reflected the new empire's basic conservatism more adequately than a unified church might have. But they did join in a cultural battle against Roman Catholicism, the "Kulturkampf," until it became obvious to some that they too might suffer in the scrap. Even after Bismarck called a halt to the battle, some Protestants created a "continuation

444

committee" of sorts. Their pastors filled a professional role that scarcely prepared them to function as cultural critics; the clerical mold pressed with more force as cultural Protestantism extended its influence. Church polity was realigned to parallel more adequately the social and political forces of the new empire, and a new regulated form of financial support for the church, the church tax, assumed that all the culture owed its religious spokesmen a debt. Church construction and renovation proceeded at a phenomenal pace, since religious edifices were viewed as public works in a Protestant culture.

The most influential theological representative of these decades was Albrecht Ritschl. He clarified the theological ramifications that resulted from updating Protestantism, finishing the Reformation, applying religion to practical daily problems, and grafting the religious charter onto a culture and society that had recently been unified politically. Perhaps unconsciously, he explained more clearly than anyone why this massive thrust of Protestant imperialism failed to penetrate Germany's most serious and pressing problem, the social problem.

If Bismarck stood for "Realpolitik," Ritschl represented "Realtheologie." While giving the appearance of a modernist with his challenge that Protestantism must accommodate itself to the progress of culture, he carefully delimited the scope of the church, if not its theology. Any challenge to state or political power was off limits, since the state no less than the church was pressing forward with a pedagogy of God's kingdom. Such a challenge might come from anemic or natural-law-oriented Roman Catholics, but not from Protestants.

Ritschl's cultural Protestantism explains why the social problem was largely ignored by the Protestant flag-raisers of the last decades, unless they were merely interested in ameliorating the sufferings of people ground up by society, as some were. To wrestle with the social problem, one had to come to grips with the social power structure that underlay the empire's basic political compromise. In terms of the religious charter, now expanded to the national scene as Protestant imperialism, that would have been suicidal.

No wonder so few ventured down that alley. No wonder the

NOTES

CHAPTER IX

(1) Otto Pflanze, BISMARCK AND THE DEVELOPMENT OF GERMANY; THE PERIOD OF UNIFICATION, 1815—1871 (Princeton: Princeton University Press, 1963), p. 368.

(2) Wolfgang Raedische, DIE EVANGELISCH-LUTHERISCHE LANDESKIRCHE HANNOVERS UND DER PREUSSISCHE STAAT 1866—1885 (Hildesheim: August Lax, 1972), p. 126.

(3) Erich Beyreuther, KIRCHE IN BEWEGUNG; GESCHICHTE DER EVANGELISATION UND VOLKSMISSION (Berlin: Chrislicher Zeitschriftenverlag, 1968), p. 131.

(4) David W. Lotz, RITSCHL AND LUTHER, A FRESH PERSPECTIVE ON ALBRECHT RITSCHL'S THEOLOGY IN THE LIGHT OF HIS LUTHER STUDY (Nashville: Abingdon, 1974), pp. 40, 194.

(5) Ibid., pp. 168, 196.

(6) Ibid., p. 67.

(7) Ibid., p. 201.

(8) Ibid., p. 198.

(9) Ibid., pp. 162, 164, 170.

(10) Ibid., p. 191.

(11) Wilhelm Oehler, GESCHICHTE DER DEUTSCHEN EVANGELISCHEN MISSION (2 vols.; Baden-Baden: Wilhelm Fernholz, 1949—51), I, 162-63.

(12) Heinrich Loth, "Die politische Zusammenarbeit

447

der christlichen Mission mit der deutschen Kolonialmacht in Afrika," ZEITSCHRIFT FUER GESCHICHTSWISSENSCHAFT, VII, 6 (1959), 1340.

(13) Ibid., p. 1341.

(14) In academic circles, Heinrich Boehmer (1869—1927) and Georg A. Buchwald, superintendent in Rochlitz, provided impulse for Luther renaissance studies. The incomparable Weimar Edition of the reformer's works began appearing in 1883, while a test edition of a revision of his Bible translation was published for public evaluation. The Eisenach Conference had begun updating and revising this translation in 1855, but heavy criticism of the test edition delayed publication of the official revised edition until 1892, when it appeared under the auspices of the Conference of German Evangelical Churches.

CHAPTER X

MISDIRECTED ZEAL

The attempts of German Protestants to constructively address
the emerging social question seemed doomed to failure from
the beginning. Their religious charter prevented
evangelicals from confronting the problem in an effective
way; their target should have been the state, but the
charter allowed no direct attack on the warp and woof of the
social and political structure. As a result, most of their
zealous efforts were misdirected.

They grappled with the symptoms of social issues, but not
the underlying, foundational problem itself. In fact, when
they acquiesced in first turning their attention to the
national question, and only then the social, they reinforced
the religious charter, which implicitly subjected society to
the state, and the social realm to the political. The basic
message that issued from Protestants was that the new
working class should accept subjugation and endure the
ravages of industrialization, just as they themselves
yielded to authority in the authoritarian relationship with
the state.

As a group, Protestants were inclined to show charity to
those who were suffering the social fallout of
industrialization and urbanization. There were those who
showed some dissatisfaction with this response, or at least
asked the appropriate questions. But they will occupy us in
the next chapter. Their words and works were not enough to
turn the tide.

449

To understand the Protestants' responses to heavy industrialization after 1870, we must turn back to earlier decades, when the groundwork for industrialism was being laid. The general pattern of Protestant response also took shape in these years, since their religious charter significantly influenced their mission to the emerging working class.

EARLY INDUSTRIALIZATION

Industrialism in the German states did not follow England's pattern precisely, nor did it begin as early. German industrialism was restrained by a number of social, political and economic factors. The Napoleonic wars gave an even greater lead to Britain since domestic consumer demand in the German states was no stronger while, at the same time, the early industrialists often invested in older, secondhanded machinery, instead of the new machines then available in Britain. David Landes concludes that "emulation of Britain was probably harder afer Waterloo than before."(1)

In the German states, the decades between 1820 and 1860 were really a preparatory period for rapid industrialization. Nonetheless, it is helpful to isolate factors that led to the emergence of industrialism in the early fifties. Long-term environmental factors included the states' social and political composition, their geographical features, and the availability of select resources. More immediate influences included the elimination of internal tariffs, improved transportation, the acquisition of mineral and fiber resources, sustained population growth, new consumer markets at home and abroad, the growing availability of capital and labor, and a resolute spirit of entrepreneurship.

The British dominated the textile market for a number of years. If a German manufacturer wanted to enter the market, it was largely a matter of whether or not the English would accept him as a competitor. This consideration, and the fact that German manufacturers were able to bypass several earlier stages of industrialization, meant that in Germany the most important stimulus toward industrialism devolved from the most practical application of mining and smelting skills, namely, railway construction.

Artisans who worked with fiber resources had been an important part of Germany's social, political and economic life for a long period. This was one reason why the "Junkers" and others who could amass capital were more inclined to mine metals—often on their own lands—than to construct fiber-related factories. The other option entailed greater risk, and could lead to undesirable results, socially and politically.

Between 1834 and 1837, the number of spinning mills in Saxony rose almost 40 percent, from 91 to 130. But since the British controlled the market, increased textile production did not serve the catalytic function that it did in England. Instead, the transportation industry, especially railroads, jarred loose the necessary capital in the late thirties and forties. German railway trackage more than doubled between 1845 and 1850, to 5,822 kilometers. This percentage increase exceeded all other areas of the continent.(2)

A comparison between hand and mechanized spinneries shows that increased textile production was not the stimulus for industrial takeoff in Germany. Hand spinning suffered heavy losses to mechanical processes in the fifties, and by the early seventies, hand spinners played an insignificant role in Germany's textile industry. This was true despite the fact that, in the area covered by the customs union ("Zollverein"), the number of mechanized weaving looms merely increased by 2,864 units, from 5,000 to 8,000, between 1849 and 1858. In sum, the mechanization of textile manufacturing followed rather than preceded the transportation revolution in Germany.

One reason for this development was that by 1850, urbanization still had not greatly stimulated consumer demand. British imports and hand manufacturing were able to saturate the textile market. Cotton yarn production in the "Zollverein" states showed a gradual upswing between 1834-35 and 1848-49, from 92,274 hundredweight to 281,938, but

451

production doubled between 1850 and 1857, and then shot up to 1,170,312 hundredweight in 1860-61. A lucrative home market, and gains in the field of transportation, helped mechanize the textile field. Few of the entrepreneurs who tried to build large factories like the British survived the depression of the late forties, but the next decade was different.

Front line casualties of this development were the full and part time weavers, whose looms ran under muscle power. In 1846-47, the "Zollverein" contained 133,245 looms owned by full-time weavers, with 45,000 in Prussia alone. Another 300,000 looms were used for part-time work by farmers and others, including 280,000 in Prussia. By 1861 the number of looms used full-time dropped nearly 20 percent. On the other hand, agricultural losses and economic difficulties contributed to the rise in the number of part-time looms, from 220,000 in 1834 to 290,000 in 1861, with 265,000 in Prussia.(3)

Textiles and other manufactured goods were freely transported across territorial lines under the aegis of the "Zollverein," or tariff union, formed by Prussia in 1834. On New Year's eve, long lines of wagons lined up at border checkpoints, as merchants anticipated the benefits of the tariff union the next day. German industrialism profited even more from the union after additional states joined its ranks, and later, Bismarck used Prussia's leadership in the union, together with her commercial and economic strength, to good advantage in forging national unity.

But the single most important impetus for large-scale industrialization in Prussia and the other states came from a revolutionary transformation in transportation. The transportation revolution, especially the use of steamboats and railways, stimulated the mining of ore and coal, and led to the formation of additional joint stock companies. Through the consolidation of capital, these companies extended the industrial revolution to other fields, and the railway boom of the forties helped attract much needed foreign capital as well.

Production rates in iron and mining industries showed a sharp increase between 1822 and 1847. Between 1822 and 1834, mining production jumped about 33 percent, while the corresponding increase between 1835 and 1847 was 162 percent. Growth in the iron industry was 61 and 138 percent, respectively, for the same periods. In the "Zollverein" states, the use of pig iron increased almost 350 percent between 1834 and 1847. But despite an early start in Silesia, Germany was the last western European country to develop a modern iron industry.

Steam engines increased production and consumed new coal and iron stocks at the same time. In 1837, Prussia's 421 steam engines produced a total of 7,507 horespower, but by 1846, her 1,139 engines turned out over 21,000 horsepower. The steam engine was the linchpin between coal and ore, and the new transportaion system.

The key to railway development was the locomotive, "steam on wheels." At first most locomotives were imported; 166 of the 245 engines in Germany came from England in 1842, 12 from Belgium, and 29 from the United States. After ten years the ratio changed appreciably; 679 of the 1,084 locomotives were German-made. By 1848, Germany's railway map resembled a number of self-contained circles, with Berlin, Leipzig, Hanover, Hamburg, Cologne, Frankfurt, and Munich as focal points. In another twenty-five years the systems were fully integrated. In the interim, some medical men warned that the speed of passenger trains could bring illness or mental derangement, while religious figures claimed that long railway tunnels would produce immorality.

Early industrialization in the German states set a pattern: industry was distributed throughout the countryside much more than in Britain. This was partly due to reliance on water power, and the scattered pattern of metal deposits and mines. In Westphalia in 1858, 19 of 49 spinning mills, 49 of 57 blast furnaces, 158 of 167 steel plants, and 15 of 28 machine factories were located in the open countryside, often in swollen villages.(4)

WEITLING AND MARX

Some early signs of the social consequences of

industrialization appeared already in the forties. The starvation of weavers in Saxony, agricultural collapse, and economic depression indicated that a new movement was underway. But there seemed to be few signs that the church would take interest in the large new working class that was soon a reality. Philosophical idealists claimed that the church was essentially superfluous for philosophy, but at the same time, the idealists had little place for social ethics in their thinking. Traditionalists wanted the church to retain its authoritarian structure and orientation, in order to serve as a prop for the state and an example for society. One exception during the forties was the pseudo-theologian and utopian socialist, Wilhelm Wietling (1808-1871).

Although he hinted several times that he was about to assume the mantle of the messiah, Weitling was not an evangelical churchman. Born in Magdeburg as the illegitimate son of a French officer, and reared in poverty, he never received more than an elementary education. He was raised a strict Roman Catholic until age twelve, and soon took up tailoring and advanced to the rank of journeyman. An early socialist and acquaintance of Karl Marx, he had good rapport with German workers in Switzerland, especially artisans, in the late thirties and early forties. He sensed some of the new pressures under which craftsmen were working; his own craft of tailoring was being taken captive by capitalist forces, even though the trade itself was not distinguished. In 1842, the first large store in Germany to sell ready-made clothes opened in Berlin.

Weitling used the idea of God's kingdom to acquaint German workers with the bliss of utopian socialism at a time when they were still receptive to religious symbolism. He hoped that the image would carry meanings of mixed significance that referred both to the spiritual and material world. His theory held that such a kingdom would be established, when the self-serving monetary system of the rich was destroyed and replaced by an effective and humane form of communism. The eclipse of the golden age would bring the curse of private ownership, the source of man's ills; in the future, he said, utopian communism would reconstitute the earth as a paradise, and re-establish unity among people. His terrestial utopia was attainable if the proper moral guidelines were fulfilled, and if it were preceded by a miraculous uprising.

His romantic utopia was anchored in a personal conviction about the unity of mankind. He first encountered emerging industrialism as a journeyman tailor, but his religious recources were inadequate for the task when he used them to rectify social ills. Weitling was essentially a romantic figure who awaited the reappearance of the golden age and its instant solutions.

Weitling's weakness was also his strength. Though inadequately anchored, his commitment to religion made his brand of communism attractive and understandable to certain workers. Marx realized, through Feuerbach's earlier work, that in Germany at least all criticism had to begin with the criticism of religion, because of the prevailing idealist spirit. Weitling reinforced that argument by relying on religion to make his communistic solution palatable to workers. His work created the first semblance of solidarity among some German artisans, even though the socialist movement soon passed him by. His reliance on ritual, and his emphasis on Christian brotherhood, won for him the confidence of some workers long before others earned it. He was in an enviable position to understand and be understood, since his work as a craftsman, and his station in society, were being challenged by indeterminate forces that threatened to render him and others obsolete. More than that, his use of religious imagery helped temper his communist theory; that somehow seemed to involve God in the righteousness of the cause, and the inevitability of its victory.

He was a transitional figure in every sense. In the tradition of idealism and romanticism, he tried to forge a coherent relationship between the material and the spiritual before such a position became wholly untenable. But his theory already showed that a new realism was beginning to sweep the continent at midcentury, a realism that stressed the component parts over the whole.

Weitling was also a transitional figure in that he experienced only the early stages of industrialization. Since German industrialization was only beginning to gain momentum when he appeared on the scene, his description of social ills, heavily influenced by French thinkers, was not fully congruent with the German or Swiss scene. His personal experiences equipped him to speak about the artisan's problems; since the new industrial worker's plight was still unclear, Weitling seemed content to blame all ills on private ownership and a money-based economy. He offered an interim report on the effects of early industrialization, but even that report was inadequate for all the workers being caught up by the new forces of change.(5)

With the publication of THE GOSPEL OF A POOR SINNER (1845), Weitling became "intellectually unemployed" as far as his contribution to socialist literature is concerned. Exiled from Switzerland, he travelled to Germany and then to London. He and Marx had a dramatic clash in Brussels on March 30, 1846, that brought his expulsion from the communist elite. He journeyed to the United States, returned to Germany in the summer of 1848, and then made his way back to his new American home in August of 1849 via London.

Weitling's confrontation with Marx was inevitable. His religious appeal on behalf of communism was out of step with Marx's economic theory. His biographer, Carl Wittke, sympathetically portrayed his religious commitment in this way:

> He rejected the doctrine that made self-interest the sole motivation of life. He believed that man had an inner desire to do good and a potentiality for self-sacrifice which could be developed by training in morality and religion; and he desired to use religion to achieve a kind of communism which would be like the good life of the genuine Christian and give men a faith which would help them to penetrate the black night of their despair.(6)

Weitling was convinced that man's nature was essentially good; man was the chief actor, the creator of history's drama. Progess was a law of nature, but men had to execute and administer that law in the form of utopian socialism.

Several years after his confrontation with Weitling, Karl Marx (1818-1883), the proponent of "scientific socialism," wrote in a newspaper that "the social principles of Christianity have had time to develop for eighteen centuries, and they need no further development through the Prussian <church> consistorial council." As a man of twenty-five in 1843, Marx married Jenny von Westphalen in an evangelical church in Kreuznach. He was born of Jewish parents in the western town of Trier, and baptized in 1824 as a young boy, together with six siblings. Their evangelical baptism in heavily Roman Catholic Trier was a symbol of their father's commitment to the province's new rulers, the Protestant Prussians. But Marx's evangelical training did not take as deep a root as in his associate, Friedrich Engels; unlike Engels, he failed to manifest a crisis of faith when he became the chief spokesman of scientific communism.

His CRITIQUE OF HEGEL'S PHILOSOPHY OF RIGHT (1843) argued that "religion is the sign of the oppressed creature, the sentiment of a heartless world, and the soul of soulless conditions. It is the OPIUM of the people." His oft-quoted reference to opium was probably prompted in part by the recent "opium war" of the British in China, but there were other influences as well. While discussing the sermons of the Wuppertal preacher, Friedrich Wilhelm Krummacher, in 1828, Goethe called Krummacher's revivalistic homilies "narcotic sermons" that were suitable to "lull to sleep the inhabitants of that region in the face of their physical and spiritual hardships." This idea was taken up by the Young Hegelians and by Moses Hess, who referred to religion as "Schnaps" for the people.(7)

Marx was influenced by the Young Hegelians, especially Feuerbach, while on his way to an economic-social philosophy, but he then superseded them. He agreed with their claim that people had to be politically emancipated from the Christian state, writing in 1843 that,

> man emancipates himself POLITICALLY from religion by expelling it from the sphere of public law to that of private law. Religion is no longer the spirit of the STATE, in which man behaves, albeit in a specific and limited way and in a particular sphere, as a species-being, in a community with other men.

But he noted that while political emancipation represents progress, "it is not, indeed, the final form of human

457

emancipation, but it is the final form WITHIN the framework of the prevailing social order."(8) Marx's goal was to emancipate man FROM the framework of the prevailing social order.

He contended that in Germany the criticism of religion was the premise of all criticism since man makes religion, religion does not make man. He wrote in his CRITIQUE that "the abolition of religion as the ILLUSORY happiness of men, is a demand of their REAL happiness. The call to abandon their illusions about their condition is a CALL TO ABANDON A CONDITION WHICH REQUIRES ILLUSIONS. The criticism of religion is, therefore, THE EMBRYONIC CRITICISM OF THIS VALE OF TEARS of which religion is the HALO." Criticism of religion was necessary since "religion is only the illusory sun about which man revolves so long as he does not revolve around himself." Philosophy's task is to "unmask human self-alienation in its SECULAR FORM now that it has been unmasked in its SACRED FORM." That is why "the criticism of heaven is transformed into the criticism of earth, the CRITICISM OF RELIGION into the CRITICISM OF LAW, and the CRITICISM OF THEOLOGY into the CRITICISM OF POLITICS."(9) Marx was convinced that if criticism of religion were carried to the end, man would come to see that "MAN IS THE SUPREME BEING FOR MAN. It ends, therefore, with the CATEGORICAL IMPERATIVE TO OVERTHROW ALL THOSE CONDITIONS in which man is abased, enslaved, abandoned, contemptible being . . . ." In this way the status quo would be overthrown by philosophy. The section of society that would lead the way would have no traditional status in society, but only human status. The proletariat "can only redeem itself by a TOTAL REDEMPTION OF HUMANITY," and thus the proletariat is the heart of an emancipation of which philosophy is the head.(10)

While he gave Feuerbach credit for breaking up the old philosophy, Marx claimed that he did not go far enough with his criticism. Feuerbach's discussion of man in a religious world and in a real world was not complete, since he failed to determine what self-contradictions in the secular realm produced the religious world. The secular basis of the religious world "must itself, therefore, first be understood in its contradiction and then, by the removal of the contradiction, revolutionised into practice." The problem with Feuerbach was that he did not investigate the "religious sentiment" as a social product, as Marx wrote in another of the THESES ON FEUERBACH: "Feuerbach, consequently, does not see that the 'religious sentiment' is itself a SOCIAL PRODUCT and that the abstract individual whom he analyzes belongs in reality to a particular form of society."(11)

It was on this basis that Marx set out to explore the social conditions that lay underneath religious sentiment, as well as the whole structure of human society. His effort to forge a "scientific socialism" centered in a Hegelian dialectic that had a material rather than a spiritual base. He understood the new working class to be the beginning of the proletariat revolution that would totally restructure human society, and liberate persons to be human. While his writings apparently had little effect on workers during Germany's early industrial period, he dramatically influenced the development of the Social Democratic Party, which in the seventies posed a threat to Bismarck. With the possible exception of Wichern, churchmen at midcentury seemed largely to ignore him. In any case, his proposal for finding a place for the emerging industrial working class differed appreciably from the charitable approach of churchmen, and the paternalism of Engel's father, a factory owner who subsidized his workers' wages with gifts of sugar.

POPULATION GROWTH, URBANIZATION, AND INDUSTRIAL EXPANSION

Steady population growth was one of the most important concomitants of industrialization in Germany. The precise relation between population growth and industrialization is, of course, a matter of conjecture, but as Peter Stearns indicates, it can be assumed that "without population growth the industrial revolution would have been unnecessary; without a radically new industrial structure population growth could not have been sustained. The two forces were intertwined in their occurrence and effects."(12)

Demographic statistics are open to manipulation and distortion, but that Germany participated in the general

459

growth of European population between 1800 and 1900 is without question. Europe's total population increased from 180 million to 400 million. Within the boundaries of what came to be the empire, Germany's population surged at a rate surpassing France's and England's growth: 24 million in 1800, 25 in 1810, 26 in 1820, 29 in 1830, 32 in 1840, 35 in 1850, 38 in 1860, 41 in 1870, 45 in 1880, 50 in 1890, 56 in 1900, and 65 in 1910. Prussia's population was especially youthful and vigorous; 45 percent of her people were less than twenty years old in 1868.

A significant factor in the demographic revolution was the sharp increase in urbanization. Between 1820 and 1870, more than 40 million acres of land in Prussia were removed from common cultivation, most of it in the eastern region. This consolidation of land contributed to the flight to the city. In 1815, four out of five Germans live in rural communities of less than 2,000 inhabitants, but by 1850 this ratio had decreased to two out of three. The number of Prussians living in towns of more than 2,000 increased from 27 percent in 1849, to 32 percent in 1871; by 1871, 36 percent of the German population lived in towns of more than 2,000 people, and by 1910 this percentage nearly doubled to 60 percent. One week during 1882, a rural pastor in Minden-Ravensberg complained that the previous week, forty of his 1,300 parishioners had moved away. While in the rest of the continent the number of localities with more than 4,000 inhabitants increased by 70 percent between 1880 and 1900, in Germany the percentage of increase during this twenty-year period was 130 percent.

Since the total percentage of people in rural areas changed little during the century, most of the population growth made its impact in towns and cities. Large cities expanded rapidly between 1850 and 1910, as an urban population of ten million grew to forty million. In 1870, Germany had only eight cities of more than 100,000, but by 1900, forty-one shared this distinction, with five over a million. Seven more were added in the next decade, so that 21 percent of the population lived in cities of more than 100,000 by 1910; twenty years earlier, about 10 percent met this qualification. The Krupp industries in Essen contributed to that town's phenomenal growth, from 4,000 people in 1800 to 100,000 a century later. After an increase of 30 percent between 1841 and 1850, Berlin's population increased nearly

100 percent between 1850 and 1870.

The rapid growth of industry and commerce were able to absorb the enlarged work force and satisfy consumer demands, although the social tremors of sudden urbanization persisted long into the twentieth century. A million and a half people emigrated from Germany between 1871 and 1885, but emigration dwindled after 1890, and was negligible after 1900. Between 1816 and 1871, Prussia's population in the agrarian east increased by 90 percent, while the more heavily industrialized south and west increased only 23 percent. But between 1871 and 1890, the situation reversed itself; the south and west increased by 79 percent, while the east chalked up a minimal gain of 26 percent. It is at best risky to estimate the total number of factory workers in Prussia at any given time, but Heinrich Bechtel calculates that less than a half a million were at work in 1846; 1.1 million out of a total of 5 million workers were employed in industry in 1867, and 9.8 million industrial and trade workers were numbered among the total of 22 million wage earners in Germany's population of 62 million in 1907.(13)

Industrial expansion began in earnest in the fifties and sixties. Coal production doubled between 1850 and 1860, while the production of pig iron more than doubled in the same period. The 1,416 steam engines of 1845 increased to more than 10,000 in fifteen years. Henschel's famous firm in Kassel produced two locomotives in 1848, 13 in 1865, 41 in 1868, 42 in 1870, and 123 in 1873. By that year the firm had manufactured more than 400 engines, two-thirds of them in the last three years. Railway trackage in 1840 covered only about 500 kilometer, but by 1855 the total was 8,000, and by 1875 more than 28,000 kilometer of track were in use. By 1850, passengers and freight would move from Aachen to Breslau, and from Kiel to Munich, although some transfers were required. Between 1850 and 1873 the compound annual rate of increase for railway mileage, coal consumption, steam power, and the production of pig iron registered between 5 and 10 percent. Germany's iron industry grew at the rate of 10 percent per year between 1850 and 1869, and although the British still held the lead in total production, the rate of increase exceeded theirs, as well as France's.(14) Meanwhile, the amount of imported cotton yarn fell appreciably between 1840 and 1867, demonstrating that a modern, mechanized industry was emerging to fill this need.

Population increases also helped create a vibrant market at home before colonialism began. Germany's iron production quadrupled, from 41 pounds per capita in the sixties to 170 pounds in 1890. The workers' share in the gross national product decreased by 55 percent between 1870 and 1900, but this decrease was accompanied by a sharp upturn in the consumption of certain necessities, reflecting the net gain for workers in the depressed prices of the time. Meat consumption increased from 59 pounds per capita in 1873 to 105 in 1912; consumption of coffee, tea, sugar and tobacco climbed from 12 pounds per person in 1880 to 34 pounds in 1900, while per captia beer consumption increased from 78 liters in 1872 to 123 in 1900.

The emergence of the joint stock company ranks high on the list of significant contributions to the development of German industrialism. Taken together, the early connection between industrialism and the propertied class, intimate dealings between banks and industries, the formation of cartels, the inauguration of protective tariffs in the seventies, and the joint stock company, determined the course of industrialization in Germany. Between 1850 and 1859, 107 new joint stock companies were established in Prussia; only 37 had been organized in the five preceding decades. Much of the accumulated capital flowed into mining and smelting, laying the groundwork for future industrial growth. It is unnecessary to chart the growth of financial resources at length, but it should be noted that Prussia's victory over France in 1871 markedly increased the amount of available capital. Some of the five billion "franc" reparation payment went to repay the national debt, and this released substantial amounts of private capital that led to frantic and speculative investments. Germany's involuntary participation in the worldwide crash of 1873 followed quickly.

Because to a large extent she was able to bypass textiles in her industrial development, and because she was capable of absorbing foreign technological advances in mining and transportation, Germany was in a position to break new ground in the fields of chemicals and electricity. In the eighties, these industries experienced phenomenal growth. No provision was made to count electrical workers in the census

462

of 1882, but by 1895 this new category included 26,000 employees; by 1906-07, the industry employed 107,000. Germany soon dominated the field of electrical research. Her rapid development of electrical technology had ripple effects in related industries, and the same was true of chemicals.

In the main, industrial expansion paralleled the accepted political model. Authoritarian control and directorial power was vested in a small circle. As the century closed, most industries had more than sufficient resources of capital and labor. By 1895 the average coal mining company employed over 800 men, a rather sizable average for any industry in any country at the time. Large concerns dominated the textile industry as well. By 1895, more than 90 percent of all spinners were controlled by 300 spinning companies, with 70,000 workers. The growing size of corporations, and the formation of interlocking interests in cartels, assured that economic recession would travel at a high rate of speed. In the economic downswing of 1873-74, employment in iron smelting works dropped off by 40 percent, and by 1876 nearly half of Germany's blast furnaces were idle.

CHARTERED RESPONSE

Protestants responded to emerging industrialization and its attendant social consequences with almost programmatic precision. The unwritten religious charter helped them realize that the positive nationalist consequences of industrialization were more significant than the negative social consequences; that was one reason why they commonly turned their attention to the problem of national unification rather than to the social problem. In turn, the process of settling the national question, and national unification itself, reinforced the religious charter and helped deflect the attention of Protestants from social issues. At the same time, those Protestants who showed an interest in industrialization and its social consequences learned quickly what was and what was not an appropriate response on their part.

The Elberfeld district of the Evangelical Church, located in the Ruhr region, where industrialization was advancing at a rapid pace, provides us with a microcosmic view of the church's relation to the new social problem in the second half of the century. Before midcentury, for this evangelical island surrounded by Roman Catholics, all social problems were at the same time the church's problems. Most Protestants were of Reformed vintage, but the Lutherans too were committed to a sense of social responsibility, nurtured in part by the Protestants' minority status. Things changed in the fifties, the decade of reaction.

In 1855, the district's presbyterial conference adopted three programmatic theses defining the relationship between ecclesiastical and civil efforts to relieve poverty. "Ecclesiastical care of the poor and the civil program for the poor should not be conflated with one another, since they are distinct from each other in a fundamental way," one thesis read. It continued, "in such a conflation, ecclesiastical concern for the poor cannot achieve its right, power, and life, and as a result, it atrophies and gradually dies." Another thesis asserted that a self-sufficient ecclesiastical program for the poor had to be created to achieve properly ecclesiological goals. This statement signalled a reaction to previous policy, since the district was concentrating on specifically ecclesiastical concerns as they related to social issues. A special deacon and deaconess program was established to spearhead the church's ministry to the poor.

The more that workers in the area became conscious of their status as a new group, the more difficulty the church had in relating to them. One reason was that the worker was being treated as an object, with no voice on the governing board of agencies that were created to serve him. A paternalistic spirit prevailed, as the families of factory owners and merchants assumed positions of leadership in church agencies designed to care for the poor. The agencies' goals were middle class, or at least "churchly" goals, not objectives formed with the help of those receiving ministry. For example, the school set up for young female factory workers emphasized domestic skills, such as needlework, knitting, mending and darning. Meanwhile, the working people's needs and feelings seemed to be summarized more adequately in a poem published in the Elberfeld daily in 1855:

> You address the poor man in an honorary way
> As brother in the Lord's house:
> Then lock him <out> with the bann of culture
> Simultaneously before the door,
> Out of your intellectual companionship, your company,
> From your tables and your festivals.

By 1884, the synod of Elberfeld had gone full circle in extricating itself from any social involvement that was not explicitly oriented toward a manifestly religious goal. In that year the synod decreed:

(1) The church in its organs does not enter into the social movement insofar as it is of an economic nature;

(2) On the other hand, the church engages in the social movement insofar as it is of a religious, that is, insofar as this movement is carried along by men's souls, which need pastoral care, and insofar as the religious factor has a great, if not the greatest, importance.

(3) In this capacity, the church has no other means than those which it has traditionally used, namely, Word and sacrament, nurture of faith and love.

(4) Corresponding with this, the church brings means into the gravity of the situation with great zeal, in order to awaken and promote faith and love.(15)

One reason, then, why Protestants took a dim view of addressing the social ills of industrialization was that the reactionary atmosphere of the fifties encouraged institutions, including the church, to concentrate on basic tasks. At the same time, industrialization was beginning to flourish, and Protestants seemed to sense that the nature of the "poor" was changing. This provided sufficient reason to withdraw from long-standing social commitments. At a deeper level, of course, the religious charter encouraged the churches to leave to the states what was not specifically assigned to them as their responsibility, and that apparently included the problems of the new poor. To ameliorate the social problem with charity did not require that one challenge or question the course of industrialization, or the basic framework of the emerging social structure. But for some, even that approach seemed dangerous, unnecessary, or unworkable.

There were other reasons why the churches were not inclined to enter the fray. Lutheran confessionalists could appeal to the doctrine of God's two kingdoms, and the need to distinguish between the church's and the state's responsibilities. One has the suspicion that the social problem did not bother great numbers of Protestants, especially Lutherans, precisely because their doctrinal system relieved them of any anxiety over the question. Others transferred to the anonymous, industrialized city their vision of the prince as a paternalistic, charitable ruler, who was interested in his subjects' welfare; they mistakenly imagined that someone or some corporate entity in the new urban environment would express the kind of personal concern shown by some princes in tiny municipalities, or "Junkers" on estates. In addition, the curse of particularism once more gave the territorial churches reason to believe that someone else would handle the social problem of another state or territory. So-called "church-steeple politics" meant that responsibility extended only so far as the steeple's shadow in the case of the parish, or to the border in the case of the territorial church. It was always someone else's responsibility, but at base the churches' response, or lack of one, was politically programmed by the nature of the religious charter.

When conservative politicians in Prussia clamored for such reforms as supervision of female and child laborers, no work on Sunday, and a restricted number of working hours, they knew that their clientele were the artisans who were suffering under industrial advance. In the fifties, they tried to repay the artisans who had held firm against revolution in 1848, but giving greater status and power to the guilds once again was merely a stopgap measure. Nevertheless, the paternalistic, almost eleeomosynary attitudes of conservative politicians seems to have set a pattern for the way that churchmen related not only to hard pressed artisans, but to new factory workers as well. A religious atmosphere was piped into the lodging house for itinerant artisans founded in Bonn by C. Perthes in 1854; it became a model of churchmen's charitable involvement in one

466

part of the social problem.

The conservative social theoretician, Victor Aime Huber (1800-1869), wanted to add a fourth social institution to the "sacred three" of the conservatives, the monarchy, church, and family. He believed that cooperatives were the sort of self-help that workers could engender, with some help from social superiors. Factory workers in particular could strengthen their families and contribute to stability by forming housing cooperatives, he said. Huber was one of the few conservatives who was interested not only in agricultural and artisan laborers, but in mill workers and factory hands. Although he appealed to Christian principles to support cooperative verntures, he failed to achieve more than token relief for the poor and the new working class. Especially in the fifties, his proposals had too much of a radical ring for his conservative friends in Prussia; in a previous chapter, we noted that he could not interest Wichern or the Inner Mission in cooperatives.

Among the conservative social theorists in Prussia in the fifties were Friedrich Julius Stahl, Georg W. Raumer, Wilhelm H. Riehl, a Roman Catholic named Joseph Maria von Radowitz, Heinrich Leo, Theodor Lohmann, and Hermann Wagener. Most agreed that since a person's social welfare depended largely on his personal morals, his physical needs could only be met through charity, not through legislation or technical adjustments in the economic system. The historian of the early Protestant reaction to the social question, William O. Shanahan, indicates that "no involvement in man's temporal fate was considered possible unless it suited God's providence."(16)

In southern Wuerttemberg in the fifties, a mystical moralist named Gustav Werner (1809-1887) centered his activities in factories rather than guilds. Without radical roots, Werner's Christian socialism of love did not achieve its goal of an industrial utopia. But his vision was extraordinary; his achievements endured into the twentieth century.

While studying at Tuebingen, Werner was attracted to Swedenbourg's revelations, and influenced by reports of Oberlin's accomplishments. Serving as a pastoral assistant in Waldorf near Tuebingen, he established a child rescue institution in the late thirties; he subsequently moved it to Reutlingen, and also formed a primitive Christian communist community. Then he travelled widely in search of funds to support the struggling paper factory which the community operated. His fundamental principle, "What does not become practical has no value," was aimed at combining Pauline doctrine and Johannine love, in order to overcome the "sickness of business." His travels irritated territorial churchmen until finally in 1851 his theological candidacy was rescinded. In 1863, a financial crisis forced Werner to declare bankruptcy, but the new attention he garnered as a result brought him additional support. He finally succeeded in making the factory the Lord's battlefield, although his two factories soon had to hire wage earners because there were not enough communal laborers. Today, two factories and a number of charitable and educational institutions continue to operate in Reutlingen.

A correspondent from Wuerttemberg wrote in 1852 that Werner enunciated one major theme in his travels and preaching: in the new stage of development, Christianity had to recognize Christ as King in all areas of life, not merely as Prophet and Priest. In the King's kingdom, the church could become a community of love and righteousnes, he argued.

Werner was committed to concretizing God's kingdom in an industrial environment. He wrote,

> The time has come for God's kingdom to be fully realized on earth, and the simple precepts of this reign should also be employed in all earthly relationships. This will work itself out on two sides: the spiritual condition of men will be refined, and their external condition improved.

Dedicating his paper factory in 1851, he said that the work performed inside, including the "lovely music made by the roaring wheels," was "dedicated to the glory of God, the advancement of His kingdom, and the deliverance of brothers; and it shall never serve secular purposes, but shall be and remain a vessel of holiness." His journal, entitled PEACE MESSENGER, A PAPER FOR THE KINGDOM OF GOD, integrated socialistic and eschatological themes into a theological framework. Another manufacturer, the pious Karl Mez of

Baden, also tried to create Christian fellowship in his silk factories, but Werner's uniqueness was that he directed attention to factories "when most Protestant-conservatives persisted in thinking of labor problems only in terms of crafts and guilds."(17) Ultimately, he did little to change the river's course.

Many Protestants responded to the social question on the basis of a working assumption: industrialization was, if not a direct act of God, at least His will. The Lutheran doctrine of God's two kingdoms reinforced this unconscious and sometimes conscious acceptance of industrialization, and its social consequences, as divinely willed. In addition, a significant sign of the age's secularity was the transformation of the doctrine of Providence into the principle of "laissez faire," a major component of early classical liberalism. The ethical corollary of this coordinate was that, while impersonal forces or major economic changes could alter the social structure, Protestants were hesitant to accept responsibility for monitoring such change, much less question its validity. The chartered response to social problems was to ignore them, or to treat the symptoms instead of the disease.

WICHERN

The ambivalence of some evangelicals, as they saw industrialization mature, but worried about its social consequences, was best exemplified by the Inner Mission's founder, Johann Hinrich Wichern. Speaking at Barmen in 1860, he sounded a cautionary note against industrialism, but offered caritative Christian concern for those being ground on its millstones. He said:

> We must guard against two extremes: against high-flown optimists, who see the best part of human history and of God's kingdom brought to consummation at the industrial exhibitions in London and Paris, and against pessimists, who see only black, who claim that the world will be brought to ruin—or has been brought to ruin—by industry. A cir-

cumspect, Christian-social view demands something
entirely different. It recognizes that in and of
itself, industry is a matter of disinterest for
God's kingdom, and can just as easily develop for
good as for evil, depending on the spirit in which
it is managed. As the great task to be performed,
it sees something different that is brought forth
through the whole industrial process, something
that is more than profit and riches, namely,
CHRISTIAN WORK, which will be a furtherance of
Christian life, not a hindrance.

This Christian work was the work of the Inner Mission, an
association of charitable institutions which a twentieth
century scholar has called "the sanitation squad that picked
up and cared for those wounded in economic battle."(18) We
have discussed the Inner Mission in an earlier chapter.

Wichern delivered his most comprehensive statement on the
social question in 1871 before a crowd of 1,500 delegates at
the "October Assembly" of the Inner Mission, in Berlin. He
argued that "true socialism" was not incompatible with God's
kingdom; the kingdom supported its cause. The critical
issue was to define socialism. He claimed that the
individual was deprived of his sense of community in
"pseudo-socialism;" this person had neither a past nor a
future. Marx and Lassalle's movement was ethically bankrupt
and theologically pantheistic since it had no regard for
law, fatherland, or family. Christians were obligated to
struggle to the death with pseudo-socialists.

But Wichern added that while rampant scepticism often
clouded the issue and made the task seem impossible, the
contemporary age was summoned to solve the social problem.
Church, state, school, the arts, the sciences,
economics—all had to join hands to find a solution, since
social insecurity would quickly bring the collapse of
religion and morality. A solution was attainable only under
the aegis of God's kingdom; "yes, it is attainable only
under the power of God's kingdom," he said.

For him, the social issue centered in the question of the
one and the many. He told his hearers that in this sense,
Christianity was prepared for battle; its "socialism"
integrated the individual and the Redeemer of the cosmos.

470

With this unchanging Head, the organism moved through evolutionary contortions in history, on the way toward consummation. The organic communion was not the church per se, but the place of salvation, where Word and sacrament were at work. It had both a past and a hope-filled future, since this "historically-evolving entity constructs an emerging kingdom, God's kingdom." Wichern contended that a moral solution to the social problem was concealed in this Christian conception of true socialism.

He used the idea of God's kingdom to forge a link between the three Christian responses to the social problem, and to explain the ramifications of each: confronting the pseudo-socialists directly, giving a clear witness to the foundation of true socialism, and acting practically in areas of special need. He advised the Assembly that "we cannot rest in this impending conflict with the socialists until Christianity, God's kingdom, successfully attains its goal," and wins its opponents with love. Love could show the socialists the self-destructive nature of their resistance.

Wichern insisted that the church should confess its guilt, lack of love, and failure to provide moral direction. It should eliminate infighting, witness to God's activity through the preached, printed, and practiced word, and bind up the wounds of family life in order to restore health to a broken society.

He isolated six specific areas of social concern for the church: the impoverished condition of artisans; Sabbath sanctity; the poverty of day laborers and wage earners, especially in rural areas; prostitution; the proletariat; and the actions of owners and bankers, especially their cheating of workers. He asked the Assembly to petition Germany's evangelical churches to encourage members to address these social ills. In addition, the churches should assist congregations and other groups in prompting programs of social education "for the creation and expansion of the divine kingdom's true socialism in their own midst."

Wichern ended his speech with an example of his rhetorical skill. After a passing reference to General Helmuth von Moltke, the architect of Prussia's victory over Austria and France, he summoned his audience to the task with the ringing assurance that God would not desert His kingdom in such a critical time. The military and political successes of 1870-71 were not imaginary; God was standing at the side of the Germans, who now had a new empire and a Protestant "Kaiser" for all the world to see. They had no reason to fear the impending battle with the socialists. "This is not a secular but a divine kingdom, not the standard of an earthly king and emperor, but the banner of the Eternal King and Absolute Lord, who unfolds His glory upon us." In its history, God's kingdom had negotiated some important curves, and "we stand in one of these scallops, in one of these developments! If we go into it in Christ's spirit, then both the social mission of our national life and our people's history will move ahead in an ideal way." The battle with the French was merely the first round; the next step too had to be taken under Christ's banner.

In summary, Wichern did not deviate from his accepted theological and political views when he addressed the social issue. He was convinced that the social order's validly structured components needed slight realignment, and by definition, the Inner Mission could not perform this task alone. All the creational orders, including church, state, and family, were responsible for restoring the balance, and thereby advancing the kingdom's borders in an industrialized world. This solution applied whether the problem was poverty, prostitution, employee-employer relations, or the Sabbath's sanctity.

The "pseudo-socialists," the most recent enemies of God's kingdom, and other embittered subjects of the world's kingdom, would continue to oppose any constructive realignment of the social orders. But Wichern was confident they could not prevent the world's regeneration, since the "true socialism" of God's kingdom was rapidly penetrating all spheres of life. In 1871 he gave the added assurance that the German empire, the German-national manifestation of God's kingdom, would enable the nation to face its social problem with a united front, instead of with the empty promises of particularism.

But in final analysis, Wichern was a better orator than troubleshooter. His conception of God's kingdom made it easier to gloss over the essential nature of the social problem, and this in turn predetermined the type of solution he offered. By arguing that only Christianity's "true socialism" gave persons a meaningful history, and a hope-filled future, Wichern was asserting that the only present deserving to exist was the one that existed; the alliance between throne and altar was a divine work, an integral part of God's plan for healing the ills of society. The solution of Germany's social problem lay in strengthening this alliance between religion and culture, and enlarging its spheres of influence in the workaday world.

SABBATH SANCTITY, CITY MISSIONS, AND THE INNER MISSION

The chartered response of Protestants to the human consequences of industrialization can be traced in the blue law and charitable efforts they pursued. This was the reaction of most mainline Protestants. The other track was a resonse to the respose: Protestant reaction to the challenge and program of the Social Democrats. We will investigate that second track in the following chapter.

Throughout the century, Protestants showed deep interest in preserving Sunday as a day of rest and worship, but this was an item of special concern after midcentury. Protecting the Sabbath's sanctity, legally if necessary, was part of a larger campaign to bring the city worker to divine services; it was assumed that, in turn, he would be won for the church. This ministry to workers was carried out as much for the church's benefit as for theirs. The zeal with which conservative Protestants tried to protect Sunday matched their political counterparts' interest in protecting and extending the rights of artisan guilds.

In 1837, the Prussian government authorized the provinces to preserve Sundays and Holy Days for rest and worship, but little affirmative action was taken. Stricter ordinances were levied in some other states, but clergymen constantly complained of the raucous and disturbing events that interfered with the sacred hours of Sunday. In 1850, the Prussian government received a petition asking that factory work and rail travel be suspended on Sunday; the new rail transportation system, and the non-stop nature of industries such as iron smelting and commercial baking, brought urgency to their request. Shanahan contends that "keeping the Sabbath holy was literally the cornerstone of Protestant-conservative efforts to deal with the social problems of industrialism."(19)

The church press brimmed with stories about Sabbath-breaking, and the need to sanctify the holy day. The influential conservative NEUE PREUSSISCHE ZEITUNG featured a front page editorial on the question in 1851, and a year earlier, Wichern's influential FLY-LEAVES listed the newspapers and organizations that were agitating for proper observance of the Sabbath. Matters seemed in even worse shape when the Prussian general synod met in 1879. The High Church Council reported that the growth of textile factories and industry in general had appreciably diminished the Sabbath's sanctity. The report indicated that in Saxony and the Rhineland, scarcely one out of ten people attended church on Sunday; church bureaucrats blamed managers of the railway industry, post office, and telegraphic system for making Sunday a day of work.

Another response to industrialization that was not much less "churchly" was the formation of city missions, although in most instances, the missions were not at first directly affiliated with the territorial churches. Evangelists, church buildings, and points of contact had to be provided if workers were to sanctify the Sabbath, and affiliate with the church. That was the essential task of the city missions, although sometimes they also provided charitable relief.

Most of the new city dwellers came from the countryside. Germany differed from France and Britain in that railroads were already functioning when land reform brought an exodus of poor peasants. This meant that emigrants did not have to huddle in great numbers in the nearest towns; they could choose a place where industry was flourishing, or travel directly to emigration ports. Their departure often produced an identity crisis in their old village, and some village parsons tried to develop deeper communal consciousness among those who remained. Pastors such as G. Frenssen, K. Hesselbacher, and E. Gros preached their sermons in "Plattdeutsch" in parts of lower Germany, in order to relate more closely to the people.

But people kept moving to larger towns and cities, and in the move they were apt to lose their connection with the church. Since the territorial churches had no national organization, they were unable to coordinate efforts to follow people to the city. In addition, most city parishes were so large, and the facilities and personnel so inadequate, that the new city worker was often lost in the shuffle. Since the church was a state church, the belief persisted that a person belonged to the church even if he had no parish connection for years. Artisans at first were probably hurt most severely by the growth of cities; while industry squeezed them out of their jobs, they offered a low profile, and were not as readily identifiable in large cities as the new industrial workers.

In 1853, Wichern suggested to the "Kirchentag" meeting in Berlin that street preaching and the division of large urban parishes might counteract some of the problems accompanying urbanization. He was right about the need to divide the large parishes. In 1862, the overall ratio of pastors to people in Prussia was one pastor for 1,800 people, but few urban parishes had even this salutary ratio. In 1810, Bremen's 35,000 inhabitants were pastored by eighteen Protestant clergymen, each with an average load of 1,900 people. A century later, Bremen had 220,000 inhabitants, but only 30 pastors; each Protestant clergyman had an average soul-load of 7,300 people. Berlin was even worse. Over 700,000 people moved to the city in the decade following the Franco-Prussian War, and by 1892 the city had more than two million inhabitants. Meanwhile, in 1879 each of the ninety-six Protestant clergymen (including assistants) in the city had an average soul-load of 9,000 souls, while the twenty-four clergymen in the suburbs had an average load of 25,000 people. Since only 20 percent of the city's population was native-born in 1871, the number of emigrants to Berlin was staggering.

Wichern called the capital a "spiritual cemetery." His first effort to create a city mission occurred in Hamburg in 1848. It was patterned after the London City Mission; three brothers from his "Rauhe Haus" distributed Bibles and literature, and worked unsuccessfully to get artisans to witness to artisans. Ten years later he formed a city mission in Berlin, but once more his attempt floundered. Berlin's general superintendent, Brueckner, took up the challenge, but it was not until he surrendered control to the court preacher, Adolf Stoecker, in 1877 that the effort caught hold. Stoecker began with two clergymen and nine lay assistants, but he was able to add to the mission staff as financial assets increased. His connections at the court helped swell financial receipts from 11,000 "Mark" in 1877 to seven times that amount in 1882, and over 200,000 "Mark" a short time later.

City missions were soon operating in Bremen and Breslau (1856), Stuttgart (1868, with a new start in 1889), Leipzig (1869), Dresden (1874), and other urban areas. By 1885, Germany had more than twenty-five active city missions. Other modes of witness also appeared. In 1876, for example, the cathedral congregation in Bremen transferred the suspended Sunday afternoon service from the cathedral to the newly built seaman's yard, where the cathedral's pastors conducted services on a rotating basis.

One of the city mission's major problems was lack of worship facilities. Germany's evangelical churches simultaneously faced a sudden growth in population, and massive emigration to the cities. The shortage of financial capital was one reason why they could not build the religious edifices that were suddenly required in large cities in the last third of the century. Stoecker marveled that 250 churches were reportedly built in Chicago between 1870 and 1890, after the great fire; in the same period, only two new churches were constructed in greater Berlin. But after the church tax in the capital was increased, five new churches were built during the next allocation period. Much of the city mission work continued to occur in rented quarters, which gave an unchurchly impression in the light of German Protestantism's liturgical tradition. This factor did little to attract the new emigrant.

The churches' major response to industrialization and its human consequences was the so-called "sanitation squad," the Inner Mission. An earlier chapter traced its origins, and discussed the congresses that met annually in cities throughout Germany. The institutions and societies that voluntarily affiliated with this national organization pursued a number of evangelistic, charitable, and educative activities. Some were aimed specifically at artisans, men engaged in railway construction, and the new industrial workers. Included in the Inner Mission's work, or, more precisely, the work of groups making up the Mission, were Bible and tract circulation; campaigns against drinking, prostitution, and gambling; ministry to prisoners and released convicts; youth organizations; rest homes for sailors; rescue missions; itinerant preaching; educational institutions of all kinds; work among German emigrants; Sunday Schools; the publication of Sunday papers; city missions; witness to railway construction workers; and paramedical assistance during war. Wichern refused to assign the problem of poverty to the Inner Mission alone, since he defined the Mission as a free association of institutions and societies, designed to support and complement the ordered institutions of church and state, not to displace them.

In the seventies, the Inner Mission turned its attention toward people who worked on rivers and canals. It provided evangelical witness and service through publications, divine services, and homes and schools for the workers' children. An early response to that terrifying monster, the locomotive, was the "Bahnhofmission," a railway travelers' assistance program first created to protect women and young girls while traveling. The Mission's central committee showed an interest in this work in 1884, and ten years later the first of these missions was established in the Berlin train station. The work mushroomed, and a national organization was created in 1897. In 1910, and interconfessional commission was formed to coordinate the efforts of evangelicals and Roman Catholics, who entered the field in 1985. The mission lobbied for laws and regulations to protect the traveler, and soon extended assistance to children, men, and aged persons.

One specialized form of Inner Mission work emerged in Bethel bei Bielefeld, when in 1872 Friedrich von Bodelschwingh (1831-1910), of Sedan Festival fame, assumed leadership of a deacon training center and an institution for epileptics. Showing great evangelical warmth, he built and staffed a complex of widely respected institutions that cared for epileptics, trained workers, taught theological students, and sponsored foreign mission enterprises, including the Bethel Mission.

In the last decades of the century, the Inner Mission was the catalyst for the formation of a number of national organizations formed along functional lines. Institutions with similar interests now affiliated with others of the same kind.

The Mission found some of its severest critics among confessional Lutherans, such as Loehe, who charged that its caritative emphasis diluted pure doctrine and gnawed at the church's doctrinal purity. A more radical kind of criticism came from a small group of evangelicals who felt that the mission was doing too little too late. Paul Goehre, who later participated in the Christian socialist movement, appreciated Wichern's early work, but levelled this charge against him and his mission: "It is CHARITY, not social action, that <he> performed; help for the individual, not help for the masses, which alone is effective against the widespread need of our time; patchwork, not lasting, fundamental assistance through social reform for the entire nation." In his review of the Mission, Shanahan adds that

> the mode of Wichern's social method, more anxious to succor infirm and dejected individuals than to assist able-bodied and spirited men caught in a desperate situation, had serious consequences for the Inner Mission. Christian social action, without being suppressed, nevertheless remained subordinate to repetetive charity.(20)

It took the Social Democrats to stimulate another course of action among some Protestants.

The Inner Mission's guiding philosophy was summed up late in the century in a pamphlet by Theodor Lohmann, a strong proponent of protective labor legislation, and a ministerial director in the imperial Ministry of Interior in 1890. The Mission's central committee published the popular brochure in 1885, and it was republished five years later. Lohmann wrote:

> Just as the church has fought continuously, with special force, those sins that prevail and that have chiefly hindered the building of God's kingdom in a given time and under given circumstances, so

in the present era it has to promote with special
seriousness the Christian teaching of the USE AND
ABUSE OF TEMPORAL POSSESSIONS, especially where
economic and social dissension threaten to control
the people's feelings and thought. In this context
the church must apply that Christian teaching to
different economic circumstances.

Lohmann argued that rich and poor should realize that true
liberation comes not from earthly goods, but from nurturing
the moral possessions through which God's kingdom was
attained. The lower classes in particular should recognize
that equality before God did not entail equailty of
possessions. Capital and labor should learn to cooperate in
order to preserve the social fabric; on the other hand, the
attempts of the church and the Inner Mission to solve the
social problem should not rely on laws or regulations. Only
a strengthened moral life could revitalize the Christian
perspective, and bring a solution. Economic and social
dissension could not be overcome, he said, "unless <they>
succeed in permeating the life of the whole culture folk
again more forcefully with the Christian world view, which
sees the goal of all cultural development in the
construction of God's kingdom on earth."

Lohmann's philosophy was echoed by a consistorial officer in
Dessau, named Duncker, who spoke to the annual assembly of
Saxony's Provincial Committee for the Inner Mission at Halle
in 1890. His speech, subsequently published, showed that in
1890 not everyone in the Inner Mission dismissed
cooperatives, as Wichern had done some decades earlier.
Duncker indicated that people who were united in God's
kingdom, and filled with unifying love, could not look on
their neighbors as strangers. Although contemporary social
and economic conditions encouraged them to seek only their
own ends, their communal interests should not be ignored.
Christ's gospel, the "right salve and the right Physician
for the social sickness of our time," prevented Christians
from endorsing the "dog-eat-dog" philosophy of Social
Darwinism. Duncker encouraged his listeners to support the
efforts of Raffeisen and Freiherr von Broich to create
cooperatives, and to extend the idea of cooperatives from
housing, savings, and consumer associations, to production
facilities that would preserve the valuable contributions of
artisans and craftsmen.

479

The Inner Mission was the single most important response of Protestants to industrialization. Its caritative philosophy deprived it of the kind of reforming or revolutionary zeal that was necessary at the time, although one hesitates to estimate the kind of success that such an effort would have enjoyed, had it been more widespread among Protestants. In any case, the Mission was one way that some degree of social consciousness was cultivated among Protestants. In addition, it channeled the voluntarist energies of laypeople in a constructive way during this "century of the masses." One of the most important, but least understood, factors in the movement was its contribution to nationalist sentiment. Wichern soon became a national figure, and the Inner Mission a national organization, and an historian has difficulty thinking that the attraction of this centripetal movement came only from its evangelical, eleemosynary goals. The Inner Mission was a way of hoping for and working toward a united evangelical church and a unified state, before either were realities. That was one of its reasons for success, and also why its response to industrialization coincided so well with the provisions of the Protestants' unwritten religious charter.

Alfred North Whitehead, the great philosopher, once said that most modern history can be told around the polarities of "steam" and "democracy." Encountering industrialization and its social consequences, German Protestants were challenged to bring an evangelical witness to "steam." They misdirected their zeal, in part because of the unwritten religious charter under which they functioned. They gave a caritative response to the social question that was framed most clearly by Karl Marx.

Industrialism brought a number of social changes, including such attendant factors as rapid urbanization and substantial demographic growth. For example, on an average, twenty-five of every one hundred newborn children died in infancy, but by the end of the century the percentage dropped to 20 percent. Meanwhile, Germany's net reproduction rate jumped from 100 per 1,000 in 1840 to 150 per 1,000 in 1880, while average life expectancy increased from thirty-seven years in the seventies to forty-two years by 1900. We have already taken note of other social and economic changes that accompanied industrialization in the second half of the century.

Industrial growth undoubtedly affected the church in one way that is difficult to document, but highly probable nonetheless. Before industrialization, church work was one channel used by ambitious young men who wanted to escape the constraints of peasant or burgher life, especially since in Prussia the officer corps was a "Junker" monopoly, while the bureaucracy offered some civil service posts. New occupational opportunities in business and industry probably deprived the church of progressive leaders, who might have encouraged it to face the social question more squarely in these decisive decades.

Most Protestants made a chartered response to the social problem. Their reaction was molded in great part by the church's assignment in the unwritten religious charter. As the state's chief social model on how to exercise freedom within authority, the Protestant churches were responsible for administering charity, and showing concern for people who were humiliated, crippled, destroyed, or ostracized by the forces of industrialism. Any additional response would call into question the unwritten religious charter that monitored relations between churches and states. Wichern recognized this contract's limitations, and proposed activities in the Inner Mission that respected its boundaries. No less acceptable were such Protestant activities as the campaign for Sabbath sanctity, and the formation of city missions. The curious shift in social ministry in the Elberfeld district between 1850 and 1895 showed how adjustments had to be made for the unwritten religious charter to retain its validity.

But the full story has not yet been told. The caritative concern and misdirected zeal of Protestants—their target should have been the unwritten religious charter and the social structure supported by the state—was their major response to the social problem. Another response was the feeble effort of some churchmen to blunt the attraction of Social Democracy. That response to a response is the subject of the next chapter. No more successful than the misdirected zeal of most Protestants, at least the projectile was aimed

NOTES

CHAPTER X

(1) David S. Landes, THE UNBOUND PROMETHEUS; TECHNOLOGICAL CHANGE AND INDUSTRIAL DEVELOPMENT IN WESTERN EUROPE FROM 1750 TO THE PRESENT (Cambridge: Cambridge University Press, 1969), pp. 124-47; quotation from p. 147.

(2) Hans Mottek, "Einleitende Bemerkungen—Zum Verlauf und zu einigen Hauptproblemen der industriellen Revolution in Deutschland," in STUDIEN ZUR GESCHICHTE DER INDUSTRIELLEN REVOLUTION IN DEUTSCHLAND, ed. Hans Mottek, Veroeffentlichungen des Instituts fuer Wirtschaftsgeschichte an der Hochschule fuer Oekonomie Berlin-Harlshorst (Berlin: Akademie-Verlag, 1960), pp. 30, 38.

(3) Horst Blumberg, "Ein Beitrag zur Geschichte der deutschen Leinenindustrie von 1834 bis 1870," ibid., pp. 67-68, 73.

(4) Landes, p. 188.

(5) Weitling's romantic effort to find a golden age in the past was not foreign to many early industrialists, who sometimes peered into the past with as much concentration as into the future. This was clear from architectural designs and ornamentation. Many smoke stacks on German steamships were designed to look like Greek columns, and the connecting rods on engines were equipped with Corinthian capitals. The exterior surface of the copper works built at Sangerhausen in 1835 was neo-Gothic, and the iron works built at Gliewitz in 1841 was patterned after the classical style. See Heinrich Bechtel, WIRTSCHAFTS- UND SOZIALGESCHICHTE DEUTSCHLANDS (Munich: Verlag Georg D. W. Callway, 1967), p. 364.

(6)   Carl Wittke, THE UTOPIAN COMMUNIST; A BIOGRAPHY OF WILHELM WEITLING (Baton Rouge: Louisiana State University Press, 1950), p. 107.

(7) Alexander Evertz, "Die Religionskritik von Karl Marx," BEIHEFT NR. 15 DES MONATSBLATTES DER NOTGEMEINSCHAFT EVANGELISCHER DEUTSCHER (Sachsen bei Ansbach, 1973), p. 10.

(8) Robert C. Tucker, ed., THE MARX-ENGELS READER (New York: W. W. Norton & Co., Inc., 1972), p. 33.

(9) Ibid., p. 12.

(10) Ibid., pp. 18, 22-23.

(11) Ibid., pp. 108-109.

(12)   Peter N. Stearns, EUROPEAN SOCIETY IN UPHEAVAL; SOCIAL HISTORY SINCE 1800 (New York: Macmillan Company, 1967), p. 66.

(13) Bechtel, p. 329.

(14) Landes, pp. 193, 219.

(15)   Hewart Vorlaender, EVANGELISCHE KIRCHE UND SOZIALE FRAGE IN DER WERDENDEN INDUSTRIEGROSSSTADT ELBERFELD, Schriftenreihe des Vereins fuer Rheinische Kirchengeschichte, Nr. 13 (Duesseldorf: Pressverband der Evangelischen Kirche im Rheinland, 1963), pp. 5, 10-11, 24-25, 112-113.

(16) William O. Shanahan, GERMAN PROTESTANTS FACE THE SOCIAL QUESTION; THE CONSERVATIVE PHASE, Vol. I (Notre Dame: University of   Notre Dame Press, 1954), p. 136; see also pp. 239-301.

(17) Ibid., pp. 190-91.

(18) Gottfried Kretschmar, DER EVANGELISCH-SOZIALE KONGRESS; DER DEUTSCHE PROTESTANTISMUS UND DIE SOZIALE FRAGE (Stuttgart: Evangelische Verlagswerk, 1972), p. 11.

(19) Shanahan, p. 267.

(20) Ibid., p. 88.

CHAPTER XI

RESPONDING TO THE CHALLENGE OF SOCIAL DEMOCRACY

In the final third of the century, the Social Democratic party was the the most important catalyst in crystalizing the alternate response of evangelicals to industrialism. The nature of the party implied that charity was not the way to address the social problem. This posed two critical questions for Protestants. Could they support efforts to re-design the social structure, or re-weave its fabric? Could they endorse the assumptions behind the Social Democratic platform in its most radical form? The religious charter implied a negative response to both questions, and its continuing influence among evangelicals made it very difficult to establish any rapprochement with the new party.

But some clerics, notably Todt, Stoecker, Naumann and Blumhardt, hesitantly entered the arena with varying proposals. Meanwhile, official and unofficial statements by church authorities and voluntary groups left less and less room for maneuvering, and often repeated the basic tenets of the unwritten charter as they were interpreted to define the church's responsibility in the social question. Several clerics were disciplined for joining the new party's ranks; most Protestants kept their distance, and failed to engage the Democrats in dialogue.

The nature of the workingman's problems changed drastically
as the century progressed. Initially the major problem was
the displacement of artisans by machines, but soon it was
clear that new industrial workers could not take for granted
a livable wage, adequate housing, and good working
conditions. Germany's rapid urbanization and industrial
momentum alerted many workers to this array of problems in
the last quarter of the century. Low wages and their
payment "in kind," poor housing conditions, the immediate
effects of economic recession, and the exclusion of the
working class from social and political power bases, were
symptoms of a deeper malaise. A growing segment of society
was restless to find its place, and the Social Democrats
offered their assistance to the distressed.

On the other hand, government hostility and large
corporations limited the success of the newly formed trade
unions. In 1895, trade unions included only 260,000 of the
nearly eight million male laborers in Germany. Collective
bargaining got off to a slow start, unable until 1906-14 to
secure the place it had acquired in Britain a generation
earlier.

As pressure mounted, the imperial government moved to pacify
workers. In 1871, employers were forced to pay all expenses
from on-the-job accidents. In the late seventies, Bismarck
terminated the "Kulturkampf" by forging an alliance between
agriculturalists and industrialists, in order to deal with
the growing power of the workers' party, the Social
Democratic Party. Protective tariffs were part of the new
design, and the Catholic Center's support was crucial. The
anti-socialist law of October 18, 1878, proscribed all
public activity by the Social Democrats except in the
"Reichstag," effectively driving the party underground.

Bismarck's new social security program, the most advanced in
Europe, included such landmark measures as health insurance
(1883), and old age disability insurance (1888). This
social legislation was designed to make workers more
passive, endear them to the government, and defuse the
Democrats' propaganda. Addressing the "Reichstag" in 1881

on the question of social insurance, Bismarck said that "the principle of compulsory insurance entails the state taking over the insurance. . . . If this is communism, as the previous speaker said, and not socialism, then that is a matter of indifference to me. I call it practical Christianity in legislative action—but if it is communism then communism has been practiced to a high degree for a long time in the communities and by compulsion on the part of the state."(1) His reference to Christianity was probably aimed at discrediting the Social Democrats, but many workers credited them with creating the climate that led to the legislation.

At midcentury, Marx and the early socialists were unable to secure a political footing in Germany, partly because industrial workers made up a rather insignificant percentage of the work force. But by the end of the century, industrialism had almost totally transformed the social scene, and the potential for a mass socialist movement was greater. According to J. H. Clapham, "since in no European country was the laboring man better educated, and at the same time divided by a wider social gap from the 'upper' classes, the possible became the actual with astonishing speed."(2) In 1877, the Social Democrats polled 493,000 votes, 10 percent of the total; in 1890, after the twelve-year ban against them was lifted, they polled 1,427,000 votes.

Bismarck's decision in 1866 to ally with the moderate liberals in effect created a working alliance between the landowning aristocracy and the capitalist bourgeousie. Shifting political alliances in the mid-sixties effectively shut out the emerging laboring class from the political process. Its only alternative was to find its own leadership and ideology. In the course of events, the Social Democrats organized a party at Eisenach in 1869, although earlier groups with Marxist and socialist orientations had been formed. The prime feeder for this new independent political party was the radical Union of Workers' Societies, led by Wilhelm Liebknecht and August Bebel. In 1875, the Eisenachers combined with the more moderate General Association of German Workingmen, which was organized by Ferdinand Lassalle in the sixties. The program adopted at Gotha that year declared that "religion is a private matter," and demanded that all Sunday labor be prohibited.

It also proposed that all educational processes be removed from church control. These planks were also included in the Erfurt Program of the Social Democrats in 1891, although it made no reference to Sunday work.

Matters worsened for the Social Democrats after they gained amazing electoral support in 1877. In May of the next year, a deranged ex-Social Democrat tried unsuccessfully to assassinate the emperor. On the same day, Bismarck asked his advisors to design measures against the Social Democrats. He was once again turning toward the right for support, and the Democrats gave him the opportunity to challenge the patriotism of other left-wingers. But, as expected, the first anti-socialist law failed to pass the legislature.

Early in June, the emperor was seriously wounded by a shotgun blast from another assassin. Bismarck immediately dissolved the "Reichstag" and called for new elections, throwing the Social Democrats on the defensive. The results showed a marked shift to the right, although the Democrats did surprisingly well. The major Protestant paper in Elberfeld lamented the local election of a Democratic legislator, since all could see that the attempted assassination was the work of "state-destroying Social Democracy."

In all probability, the Protestant churches contributed to the electoral shift in 1878. Three days after the assassination attempt in June, Prussia's High Church Council issued a memorandum to all points, explaining that this episode was the sign of "the deeply imbedded sickness, and especially the religious and moral defects, of popular life." Pentecost was to be observed as a day of repentance. Even earlier, the Reformed presbytery in Elberfeld set June 6, a weekday, as a day of repentance and prayer. In Wuerttemberg, the influential CHRISTIAN MESSENGER concluded that the two assassination attempts were a more serious blow to Germany than the loss of a war. For years, the Christian press had warned that the Social Democrats were gathering power as they rode the crest of unbelief, the article continued, and now the fruit was ripening. Shortly before he died several months later, Prelate Kapff warned fellow pastors in Wuerttemberg that the Social Democrats were the "degeneration of the German people."

Bismarck said in 1848 that "only soldiers can help against democrats." In 1878, he turned the "Reichstag" against the Social Democrats, suppressing their organization and depriving their legislators of an organizational basis. By a margin of two to one, the parliament decided in October to prohibit "societies which aim at the overthrow of the existing political or social order through social-democratic, socialistic, or communistic endeavors."(3) Despite Bismarck's efforts, the Democrats still could field candidates for elections; in fact, elections provided the movement with its only means of self-preservation.

The Democrats disbanded their organization and floundered until covert legal and illegal structures were created. By 1884 a healthy recovery was evident, and once again they won almost ten percent of the total vote. More repressive tactics were instituted again in 1886, but their fortune was related to the improving economic status of the workers. The price depression of the century's final quarter contributed to the welfare of workers, and while the English working class achieved its greatest gains in the seventies and eighties, the eighties and nineties brought heavy gains for German workers. Using an index of 100 for 1913, statisticians calculate that real wage earnings for all industries in Germany reached a level of 84 in 1875, then dropped to 70 in 1880 and 1881, before climbing steadily in the 1880s, to 75 in 1882-83, 80 in 1884, 83 in 1885, 85 in 1886, and 87 in 1887.(4)

Early in 1890, the "Reichstag" refused to renew the Socialist Law after four earlier renewals. In February the party received 20 percent of the popular vote, making it the strongest vote-getting party in Germany. Bismarck was forced from office in March. Outlawed for twelve years, the party emerged much stronger than before.

CHALLENGE TO RELIGION

The challenge which the party put to the church was, on the one hand, ideological, and on the other, a tactical strategy designed to call the prevailing value structure into question. Religion was addressed in whichever way proved to be most profitable for the party. Lassalle portrayed himself as a religious reformer following in Luther's footsteps. Others satirically denounced the idea of God's kingdom, and portrayed Jesus as the first socialist.

By the seventies, the atmosphere was loaded with charge and countercharge between representatives of religion and party spokesmen. A student of the conflict, Vernon Litdtke, notes that many Christians were gravely offended by the strident atheism of some Social Democratic leaders. Albert Dulk wrote in VORWAERTS that religion was "the most powerful enemy of socialism," the "main bastion of anti-socialism, of reaction, the breeding ground of all social evil." The anarchist leader, Johann Most, lambasted Christianity, and encouraged members of the working class to exercise their legal right to quit the church. Some spokesmen wrote theoretical essays explaining the rationale for choosing socialism over Christianity. Litdke concludes that

> the socialsts' militant atheism attracted more attention and created more resentment than either their economic or political theories. It offered a clear instance of value confrontation, and illustrates strikingly how alienated the Social Democrats were from the beliefs and assumptions of the dominant classes.(5)

In his book, entitled CHRISTIANITY AND SOCIALISM (1874), Bebel wrote that "Christianity and socialism are as opposed to one another as fire and water. The so-called good core of Christianity, which I do not find in it, is not Christian but altogether humanist <in nature>, and that which truly makes up Christianity—its doctrinal and dogmatic odds and ends—is foreign to humanity."

Of course, not all Social Democrats were atheists. In fact, the tiny Thinkers Society of Atheists formed in Berlin in 1865 could attract only twenty-four members by the end of the year. Nonetheless, materialistic philosophy made heavy inroads for atheism among educated people after 1850. Buechner's POWER AND MATTER (1855) became the bible of the new materialism, and Darwin's ORIGIN OF SPECIES provided a plausible evolutionary explanation for organic life. Haeckel proclaimed the new atheistic religion in 400,000 copies of WORLD ENIGMA (1879).

The Social Democrats insisted that "religion is a private affair." Their position had antecedents in the Prussian "Landrecht" and the best of Prussian legal and political theory, but the motivation for protecting private religion differed in the two cases. Prussian law allowed confessional differences to exist because unanimity of religious conviction was no longer necessary or possible within the state, but this guarantee did not extend to religious groups or communities, which were still controlled entities, except for various sectarian groups legally protected under the general law governing associations. The Democrats' support of this principle was an effort to undercut the communal and social consequences of religion, by relegating it to the strictly private realm.

One of the earliest autobiographies of a Social Democrat gives a striking illustration. Bromme wrote that his parents hung pictures of a number of people in their home, including William II, Field Marshall Moltke, Bismarck, Bebel, Liebknecht, Marx, and Lassalle. In addition, his mother insisted on having pictures of saints, and his father yielded to her request, although she probably was not a regular church-goer. Her religion was a private affair.

In sum, the Democrats' position on religion pointed to one of the ironies of Prussian life and culture. Earlier, when confessionalists and others tried to influence the territorial church by insisting that it had to have a confessional basis, church bureaucrats and state officials reminded them that religion was a private affair. But now, in turn, the Democrats were twisting the argument against all religious practice, in order to exclude it from the public realm.

Not all Social Democrats were satisfied merely to dismiss religion as a "private matter." Hardliners such as Liebknecht seemed to agree with Marx's CRITIQUE OF THE GOTHA PLATFORM (1875), in which Marx wrote,

> If one desires at this time of the "Kulturkampf" to remind liberalism of its old catchwords, it surely could have been done only in the following form:

493

Everyone should be able to attend to his religious as well as his bodily needs without the police sticking their noses in. But the workers' party ought at any rate in this connection to have expressed its awareness of the fact that bourgeois "freedom of conscience" is nothing but the toleration of all possible kinds of RELIGIOUS FREEDOM OF CONSCIENCE, and that for its part it endeavors rather to liberate the conscience from the witchery of religion. But one chooses not to transgress the "bourgeois" level.(6)

Liebknecht argued in Erfurt in 1891 that "the new religion for the masses is social democracy," and in the new socialist state there would be no room for religion as a private matter.

The revisionist line that won the day, and opened the way for some Protestant figures to seek rapprochement with the movement, was supported to some degree by Bebel. In this matter, he was more of a middle-roader than some others. At Cologne in 1876, he said that the party supported full freedom of religious practice: "We say that religion is each man's private affair, and no state whatsoever . . . has the right to favor one religious persuasion over another." Later he answered critics, who asked why one Democrat was encouraging workers to leave the church legally, by saying that the party was not atheistic.

An even more revisionist line flowed from the pen of Karl Hoechberg, in an article co-authored by Bebel in THE FUTURE (1878). The authors wrote that one could be a Social Democrat with a Christian perspective, just as readily as one could simultaneously oppose Social Democracy and the church. About the same time, a Democrat named Bethany wrote in the SOCIAL DEMOCRAT that both Christianity and socialism sought the material and spiritual well-being of humanity. Georg von Vollmar, who led the south German wing of the party, attacked the hardliner's stand on religion at the Erfurt Conference in 1891, asking whether the party was promulgating too many absolutes, instead of offering a workable platform that did not resemble a new religion. And at the party's Congress in 1904, Eduard Bernstein charged that the Erfurt plank misstated a good thought, since it meant to argue that the adherents of all religious and philosophical positions should have the same right and freedom to believe; religion was "no private matter, but a public matter of great importance."(7)

In sum, the party moderated its position on religion as part of its strategy to gain followers, but in the process it presented an even greater challenge to Protestants than if it had followed some of its more radical spokesmen. The churches reacted in a variety of ways to the challenge laid down by the Social Democrats. On an organizational level, a number of memoranda and position papers were issued. On an individual level, some Protestant leaders tried to build bridges to the new party. In both cases, the unwritten religious charter provided the guiding assumptions for response. Precisely what happened will be described in the pages that follow.

TODT AND STOECKER

It was not easy to get the churches talking about the social issue, or the challenge of the Social Democrats. A synod meeting at Elberfeld in 1869 was scheduled to discuss the question, "What Does the Evangelical Church Have to Do with the Sizable Workers' Movement?" Instead, the conference concentrated on the issue of confessionless schools in the Protestant union. But the next year the synod heard an excited speaker complain that

> the hammer of industry, the wheels of locomotives
> have increasingly called forth a new world that
> wants to offer no room for the erection of the
> temple of the living God. The idols of industri-
> alism have taken thousands into their service....

Meanwhile, representatives of the Inner Mission engaged in public dispute with members of the Social Democratic party. When the Mission distributed a well-written religious tract on social questions to workers in 1872, the Democrats offered an immediate and vigorous response. And in Elberfeld, the REFORMED WEEKLY explained that centuries earlier, Calvin opposed democracy and offered a theological rationale for his position. Amid all the clamor and the silence, two evangelical pastors, named Todt and Stoecker, took the initial steps to evaluate the attraction of Social Democracy.

In 1873, the Prussian court preacher, Adolf Stoecker, issued a challenge in the NEW EVANGELICAL CHURCH NEWS. Could anyone present the composite social doctrine of the New Testament? Four years later, Rudolf Todt (1837-1887), a pastor in Barenthin, published a study he said was prompted by Stoecker's request. Entitled RADICAL GERMAN SOCIALISM AND CHRISTIAN SOCIETY; AN ATTEMPT TO PRESENT THE SOCIAL CONTENT OF CHRISTIANITY AND THE SOCIAL TASKS OF CHRISTIAN SOCIETY ON THE BASIS OF AN INVESTIGATION OF THE NEW TESTAMENT, its second edition appeared in 1878. A theologically-grounded critique of radical socialism, Todt's study did more than take issue with the socialists' supposed atheism.

Todt advised Christians to implement their social theory through a political party, since the Gospel was not limited to the sanctification of individuals. "The Gospel," he wrote, "not only wants to sanctify individual souls, but to renew the world as well in which these souls should live, complete with its political and social orders, and to transform it into God's kingdom." The kingdom was to be the criterion for evaluating all human existence; its power subordinated all social and political processes to theological interpretation, and it opened the way for a continuing creation. In concrete terms, Todt affirmed the need to separate church and state.

In reaction to Todt's book, Prussia's High Church Council issued a memorandum in November, 1877. It explained that Christianity did not entail any legal order that was valid and authoritative for all time; it added that while the church had a sincere interest in people and their moral goals, it was ill-equipped to enter the field of politics, to glean directives from the gospel to solve contemporary problems, or to serve as a court of arbitration. It was self-evident, according to the statement, that pastors would not participate in "political diatribes."

Todt and others were not dismayed. With the help of Stoecker and two economists, Adolf Wagner and Rudolf Meyer, Todt established the Central Society for Social Reform on a

Religious and Constitutional-Monarchical Basis. The membership of this theoretical study group never exceeded 1,000 persons, but drew representatives from most of the German states. The participation of a prominent Jewish banker from Koenigsberg showed that it was not anti-Semitic. The STATE SOCIALIST appeared the next January, but by 1880 the number of subscribers dropped from 1,500 to 400, and Stoecker gradually disassociated himself from the group, since he favored action over theory.

The adult life of the Lutheran pastor, Adolf Stoecker (1835-1909), bridged the period of reaction, industrialization, and national unification after 1850. In many ways, Stoecker was caught between the times. In the final quarter of the century, he wrestled with the socialists' understanding of the causes and consequences of the social problem, and tried to fashion a brand of "Christian socialism" that met all the needs of people, including their spiritual needs. But since he understood God's kingdom to be a transcendent entity that critically judged the world, and social intercourse in it, he appealed to the divine kingdom only as an integrating social force with transcendent roots. His attempt to make industrialism livable and humane presupposed a moral order, anchored in divine law.

Like many other theological candidates, Stoecker went to work as a tutor in Neumark and elsewhere while awaiting a parish assignment. In 1862 he travelled extensively in Germany, Switzerland, and Italy, until a pastorate in Altmark opened in 1863. Three years later he moved to the industrial town of Hamersleben, where he tried to rally a largely unchurched congregation. He stayed there until 1871, when be became a divisional chaplain in the army after the Peace of Frankfurt. In 1874 he became a Prussian court preacher.

In Hamersleben he met for the first time some of the social problems that accompanied industrialization. An editorial position with the NEW EVANGELICAL CHURCH NEWS also stimulated his interest in social problems, but his theology changed little during this period. His biographer, Walter Frank, describes his theological rigidity in these words:

Stoecker's churchly model—and his ecclesiastical

497

stance always remained the decisive motivation of his work—belonged entirely to the restorational period. . . . In his case there was no RELIGIOUS DEVELOPMENT. Once, in early youth, the true faith fell on this man; thereafter he held firmly to it without doubting in the least, and struggled for it.(8)

The "man in the middle" was wrestling with problems that had no easy solutions. The major problem was to determine the role of a free church in a Christian state. On a personal level, that problem appeared in Stoecker's attempt to fill the dual role of preacher and politician. On both levels, the focus of the problem was the day's massive social upheaval.

Stoecker was convinced that all human interaction pivoted on a religious basis. He enunciated this conviction in a speech before the "Reichstag" on December 14, 1882. "It is my political conviction that a single great struggle permeates our whole age: either a Christian world view <will prevail>, or not! And I believe that neither our political nor our social difficulties will be overcome without the reassertion of this Christian perspective." But his commitment to this principle implied that the gate would swing both ways: winning the masses for the monarchy would bring a religious revival, and the opposite was no less true.

Stoecker wanted the church freed from state control. He claimed that this would allow it to exert greater influence on the state, and to re-establish its "volkisch" base. This arrangment would also reap rewards for the state; he said in 1878 that "the state will first have a helper in the church if the church is a real power in the nation's life." In a speech at Gera in 1881 he noted that "we no longer want to build our religion, our true church, on the protection of state power, although the help given us by the state is highly regarded. We want to build our church on the faithful conviction of a Christian people."(9)

Stoecker turned to the idea of God's kingdom to straddle the gap between a static-conservative society, and one radically restructured to incorporate the new working class. The image helped him portray the church as a divine force empowered to resolve the social problem, which had its

498

origin in a materialistic world view. The church's freedom, brotherhood, and equality were a celestial basis for reconciling class differences on earth. Reflecting God's kingdom, the church could nurture a reconciling spirit among those who had vested interests in the social problem. Reconciliation would bring a "better world," and enable rich and poor to live at peace. He said that respect for God's social order had to be stressed among workingmen, but at the same time, the established order had to make room for the disinherited.

Early in January, 1878, Stoecker attended a meeting of workers in the famous Ice Cellar in north Berlin. The court preacher stood toe to toe with a thousand Social Democrats, and engaged in lively debate with Johannes Most, a member of the "Reichstag." Fifty of those who attended the tumultuous meeting remained behind to form the nucleus of the "Christian Socialist Worker's Party." By the end of the year, Stoecker's party included 3,000 in its ranks.

The party's platform advocated such reforms as national labor associations; obligatory pensions for widows, orphans, invalids, and the aged; prohibition of Sunday labor; abolition of child labor; higher wages and an eight-hour work day; protection from unsafe and unhealthy conditions; and a progressive income tax. But soon Stoecker's mode of operation became clear. He portrayed the Social Democrats as a foil for his own brand of Christian socialism, and used the workers' plight as another backdrop for his moral and religious principles. The court preacher stood among the workers, but it is questionable whether this experience had any effect on him.

The "Reichstag" elections in the summer of 1878 brought a decisive defeat for his new party. Before the elections, his meetings attracted as many as 2,000 people, but after the vote they did well to attract a hundred persons. The reason for the decline is evident: Stoecker's party culled only 1,400 votes in the three districts of Berlin where it fielded candidates, while the Social Democrats collected 56,000 votes. The party's poor showing was largely due to Stoecker's inability to create a functional political machine; he lacked organizational skill. In addition, his call for a "political diaconate" did not strike a responsive chord; his appeal for a return to church, monarch, and fatherland held little attraction for most workers. But in the campaign he discovered his rhetorical skill, which he subsequently used to good effect.

Prompted by his party's dismal showing in these elections, and the new imperial law suppressing the Social Democrats' organization, Stoecker started seeing a new constituency in the lower middle class. While estabishing this new power base, he discovered the magnetic appeal of anti-Semitism, affiliated with the conservative party in Berlin, and transformed his initial electoral defeat into nationwide popularity. He largely forgot the workingman, although he continued to refer to his condition in efforts to stimulate a national religious revival.

After Stoecker's party suffered its major defeat in 1878, it became evident that churchly elements were anxious to disassociate from his movement. The Inner Mission's central committee quickly divorced itself from him, and pointedly advised member societies to keep their distance as well.

Under a new president, Ottomar Hermes, Prussia's High Church Council was also charting a new orthodox and conservative course for the church's response to the social problem. After the "Reichstag" passed the Socialist Law, the council issued a memorandum in February of 1879, entitled "Address to Clergymen and Parish Church Councils of the Evangelical Territorial Church, with regard to Their Orientation toward the Dangers That Have Arisen out of the Socialist Movement." It advised pastors to watch their step as they brought the gospel of peace to all people, including those caught up in the excesses of the socialist movement. Since they were "preparing the way for the kingdom of heaven in the world," their pastoral office required them to be circumspect; the pastoral office would be irreparably harmed if it were used for political ends. Noting the spiritual decay manifested by the socialist movement, the church should re-commit itself to its primary task:

> to stimulate the practice of a way of thinking
> among all classes that finds its focus in benevo-
> lent, active love for the cooperative forces of
> men, and to proclaim to the wealthy and the suffer-
> ing that the operative mode of life in God's king-
> dom is the only way to achieve well-being and peace

in exchange for goods.

Jesus and his apostles did not demand the creation of a new social order, the memorandum noted, but let these matters rest with heathen authorities; therefore, the church's servants had no right to support social and political theories, or to demand that others accept them. This general rule was equally applicable to questions of taxation, length of military service, unemployment insurance, and the redistribution of private property. Like Christ and the apostles, the church's servants should wait for the fraternal spirit of love to redress any grievance. The memorandum did not mention Stoecker's name, but it was written between the lines. The "Address" was a restatement of the religious charter as it applied to the social question.

Stoecker held the horrible spectre of Social Democracy before the public, even after the party was suppressed. In Brunswick in 1880, he noted that the Democrats' reference to social injustice and misfortune touched a sensitive nerve. He knew from personal experience that workers' wages were often inadequate; he had seen many breadless tables and visited many needy families. But only a religious renewal could rectify a situation that involved poverty, immoral behavior, and religious backsliding, as well as social injustice and misfortune. Workers and craftsmen suffered because society pursued materialistic goals; those with plenty paid little attention to the poor and needy. According to Stoecker, his new party's name, "Christian Socialist," showed that its members wanted moral reform and an end to the materialist spirit. But the word "Workers" had been dropped from the party's title.

Stoecker increased his attack on materialism, and stressed religious and moral reform. With greater emphasis than before, he served those ends by highlighting the workingman's problems. He was adjusting to the times, yielding to the pressure of the High Church Council, and appealing to artisan and lower middle class people with his anti-Semitic propaganda. At the same time, he pointed to the conditions of the working class to emphasize the degradation of a materialist society.

In an address in Stuttgart in 1881, Stoecker charged that

materialism was "the father, and avarice the mother of socially disruptive ideas." He insisted that proponents of these ideas were trying to press on the people a "debased world view with reference to themselves and God's kingdom." But the idea of God's kingdom was a powerful counterweight; it united the two concepts, "Christian" and "social," into an all-encompassing unity that could motivate and permeate the nation's life. This "Christian-social" combination would help conservatives counterbalance the National Liberals' overemphasis on freedom, without destroying their proper emphasis on national unity. They could show that the church embodied freedom's truest form, and that valid social principles involved a spirit of fraternity and community. "Our power and goal should be the kingdom of God," he added; "if we have the Christian world view, then we have already implemented the first word of conservatives, the word 'authority.'"

Although he was defeated in the race for a seat in the "Reichstag" late in 1881, despite Bismarck's assistance, Stoecker claimed a moral victory in a post-election address to the party faithful. He insisted that the fifty thousand supporters of the six candidates in his party helped restrain the Progressives and vindicated the Christian Social Party's platform, which urged social reform, moral and religious renewal, and strong opposition to Jewish influence and power. Several months later, Stoecker praised the emperor when he urged the "Reichstag" to take up the social question at once. He interpreted the emperor's statement as an endorsement of the "Christian folk life" that he had long supported. For the last thirty years of his life, Stoecker served almost continuously as a member of the "Reichstag."

But his political activities were causing him increasing difficulty at the court. In the spring of 1889 he was ordered to refrain from political activity in Berlin, as a condition of continuing to hold his appointment as court preacher. After four near-dismissals, he was finally released from the position in November, 1890, because of a strong anti-Semitic speech in Baden. He preached his farewell sermon at the court on December 28. Six years later he also left the conservative party.

It is no surprise that Stoecker portrayed the working class

as an object of paternalistic charity. He showed his true colors in deleting the word "Workers" from his party's title, and allying himself with the conservatives. He argued that the two remaining elements of the party's name, "Christian" and "social," were unified at the deepest level because both manifested God's kingdom. That transcendent kingdom could influence temporal life through the church, which channeled the kingdom's reconciling power to earth. The prevailing theme was reconciliation, not utopia.

The historian Eckart Schleth offers an adequate evaluation of Stoecker's efforts in these words:

> Adolf Stoecker's merit is that he put before the church the living embodiment of the problem "Christ and world" with such urgency, that from that time on it could not strike it from its consciousness. He saw that out there in the world something lay in wickedness, and he knew that he had been called to lend a hand. And so he rattled at the doors of the old fortress of paternalism in church, state, and society, but he did not take his leave from them, shouting, as it were, out of the window. . . . In the question of a controlling framework suitable for the social structure that was emerging through industrialization, and for the industrial worker's new existential feelings, he brought us no further along.(10)

Stoecker was ensnared in the problem of freedom and authority, an issue that held special significance for Germany throughout the nineteenth century. For him, God's kingdom was the idea that reconciled the two forces. The social question focused attention on the church's need for greater independence; he hoped that independence, in turn, would make the church a more effective instrument of authoritarian reconciliation in a society jolted by industrialization.

EVANGELICAL-SOCIAL CONGRESS AND EVANGELICAL WORKINGMEN'S SOCIETIES

The year 1890 was a momentous one for Germany and for Stoecker. The "Reichstag" refused to renew the Socialist Law, Bismarck resigned, the new emperor stressed the need to improve conditions for the working class, and Stoecker was fired from his post as a court preacher. In 1890 as well, Stoecker founded the Evangelical-Social Congress, but not without some stimulation.

One of the day's accepted axioms was that Protestant churchmen gave greater or less public attention to the workingman's plight, depending on signals from governmental authorities. This was implicit in the unwritten religious charter. "Caritas" or charity was dispensed almost uninterruptedly, but more serious dialogue depended on the government's approval. Prussia's High Church Council gave a mixed signal in 1879, when it urged clergymen to walk with care; in April of 1890, responding to the emperor's recent emphasis on improving working class conditions, it gave a different signal in a circular letter.

The letter said that the church was not called to solve the social problem, but it could not stand idle while a large group of people were being estranged from the gospel. In addition, the nation's moral fabric was being weakened as anti-Christian movements gained strength. The Council encouraged all pastors to confront workers openly in "eyeball-to-eyeball" discussions whenever possible, and to help them overcome their prejudice against the church—and, we might add, against the emperor. Clergymen who felt inadequate for the task were urged to get help from a neighboring pastor. "Everywhere it will be the task of pastors," the letter continued,

> to set the aforementioned needs <of the worker and his family> firmly before all eyes, to seek relief for them, to awaken the active participation of ecclesiastical organs and congregational members who are owners in solving them, and to point them in the right direction.

The day after the emperor issued his proclamation, Stoecker declared, half in jest, that "overnight the world has become Christian-social."

That year Stoecker organized a study conference for theologians, pastors, and laymen, to stimulate the church's involvement in the social problem. Assisted by Adolf Wagner (1835-1917), Ludwig Weber (1846-1922), and Adolf von Harnack (1851-1930), he founded the Evangelical-Social Congress on May 28, 1890.

Stoecker first envisioned a "Christian-Social Congress," but changed his mind after consulting Weber, who convinced him that the second choice would meet with more success among people who were active in the Evangelical Society, or "Bund." The first meeting in Berlin was attended by eight hundred men, representing a variety of evangelical parties and factions. Most were pastors, but laymen and professors also joined. Between 500 and 1,000 people attended each of the first six annual meetings. In 1891 the Congress clarified its purpose, agreeing that

> the Evangelical-Social Congress has set as its task to investigate the social conditions of our nation without prejudice, to calculate the moral and religious claims of the gospel, and to make these more fruitful and effective than heretofore in today's economic realm.

Most of the conference addresses were issued as brochures, and all annual proceedings were published. Some speakers gave full support to the emperor's efforts to win over the working class. In 1890, Pastor von Bodelschwingh of Bethel proposed a plan that would stabilize the family life of working people by providing homes and garden plots. He asked the emperor to erect safeguards against speculation, and to charter credit unions that would assist workers in purchasing their homes. The emperor's positive attitude, he said, originated in currents of grace from on high; the hearts of the royal pair "beat with love and warmth for the true welfare of the most wretched and poor."

Some conservative participants were unwilling to admit women to the Congress' deliberations. When for the first time a woman addressed the group in 1895, the conservative theologian, Martin von Nathusius (1843-1906), severed his affiliation. But Stoecker, no less conservative, served as one of her panel respondents.

One receives the impression that the Congress' deliberations were little more than vents for steam generated by academicians and would-be academicians. The Congress proposed that theologians and clergymen gain familiarity with the resources available from the studies of national enonomists. Panels included such eminent social scientists as Wagner, Max Weber, and Ernst Troeltsch, and theologians such as Harnack, Julius Kaftan, Otto Baumgartner, Wilhelm Hermann, and Martin Rade. Adolf Deissmann, the historian Hans Delbrueck, and Theodor Heuss also participated. Harnack was the group's president from 1903 to 1911. Since about 40 percent of the Protestant theological students in Prussia around 1900 were sons of university graduates, we are better able to understand why the Protestant clergy had a greater propensity toward theoretical discussion of the social problem, as well as a more conservative social and political orientation, than the Roman Catholic clergy.

In 1890 and 1900, the Congress discussed housing needs in city and country. In 1890 it adopted a resolution requesting the church to "destroy the image that the Christian faith is inimical to the energetic cultural strivings of the working sector, and to do all in its power in order to bring the truth of the gospel to acceptation, distinct as it is from any ancient or modern orientation toward nature." In 1896 and 1897, the Congress discussed unemployment and the right to work, the social responsibility of private ownership, and the welfare of the middle classes. Each year it debated the question of the relationship between Social Democracy and Christianity. At the first assembly Wagner argued that this movement was not the product of agitators, "but the total result of modern economy and, not the least, the failure of the educated classes." Especially after Stoecker withdrew from leadership, the Congress concentrated on this question. Martin Rade led the discussion in 1898, but the high point came in 1910, when more than 1,500 participants gathered for debate in Chemnitz, the stronghold of radical socialism.

Stoecker's work in forming the Congress in 1890 helped him bear the shock of dismissal as court preacher that year, but his popularity suffered another blow five years later. As he returned from Friedrichsruh, where he brought greetings to the aged Bismarck on his eightieth birthday, the Social Democratic paper FORWARD published a letter that he had written to Freiherr von Hammerstein seven years earlier, while Bismarck was still in office. The letter questioned Bismarck's usefulness to the emperor. Stoecker's prestige plummetted with this disclosure, and the emperor tried without success to divest him of his title as court preacher.

No less disturbing was another proclamation issued by Prussia's High Church Council, after a meeting of consistorial presidents and general superintendents late in 1895. The memorandum to all clergy fingered Stoecker as titular head of a radical group that was trumpeting the workers' cause, in ways that brought dishonor to the pastoral ministry. It endorsed the memoranda of the Council in 1879 and 1890, but failed to reiterate the more positive and progressive recommendations about the church and the social question found in the document from 1890. Once more, authorities emphasized that social and political activities could easily distract the church from its primary mission, the saving of souls. The Council described the fundamental basis of national life in terms of "fear of God, loyalty to the king, and love of the neighbor," and urged the church and its servants to exert their influence indirectly in order to advance these goals.

On February 28, 1896, Emperor William II sent a telegram to his tutor, Georg Ernst Hinspeter of Bielfeld, describing his dislike for Stoecker, and his relief at seeing him leave the conservative party:

> Stoecker is finished, just as I have predicted for years. Political pastors are an absurdity. Whoever is a Christian is also social; Christian-social is nonsense and leads to arrogance and intolerance, both of which are diametrically opposed to Christianity. Pastors should be concerned with the souls of their congregations and with nurturing neighborly love, but should leave politics out of the picture, since it does not concern them.

With the emperor's approval, on May 15 the short telegram was published in the POST, a paper owned by a famous industrialist from the Saar region, Frieherr von Stumm-Halberg.

507

The choice of von Stumm as the publisher was an apt one. He ardently opposed socialism of any kind, including so-called "Christian socialism." Speaking to his employees at Neukirch, he once indicated that if workers successfully overthrew their employers' authority, church and state would be next to fall. He said that he lagged behind no one in his effort "to look after your material and spiritual welfare to the best of my knowledge and conscience, and to apply that practical Christianity for which I feel myself to be responsible before God." He wanted to make sure that his workers would "remain unreceptive to the lures of the Social Democrats and other false prophets," since "that is the best welfare provision that I can give and leave you." He promised his workers that they would flourish if they remained firm in their "old, unshakable loyalty to our monarch," in their Christian love to neighbors, and in their fear of God, "whatever denomination you belong to."(11) He insisted that he had a right to know before the fact if an employee intended to marry.

Stoecker was also encountering difficulty in the Evangelical-Social Congress during these years. Theological problems emerged as early as 1892, with Harnack and the young Friedrich Naumann pulling two ways, but both opposing Stoecker's conservative orientation. Naumann's "young Turks" emphasized the need to work at the social question "from below" in order to implement the spirit and words of Jesus. Stoecker continued to seek redress in an ecclesiastical context.

In mid-1896, Stoecker, Weber, and Nathusius issued an invitation for a new study group, to be called the "Church-Social Congress." Writing in three journals, they argued that the growing power of liberals in the Evangelical-Social Congress posed a grave threat. Their conduct showed "the impossibility of joint activity, just as their agitation there tends to throw out reprehensible slogans among the masses, to stir up class bitterness, incite dissatisfaction, and set human passions in motion for the alleged purpose <of furthering> God's kingdom."

Stoecker was asked to resign from the vice presidency of the Evangelical-Social Congress in order to show that the Congress was in no way connected with his political activities, which by now were heavily permeated by anti-Semitism. A small number of conservatives left the Congress with him, and the Evangelical Workingmen's Society also took refuge under the new umbrella congress.

The Evangelical Workingmen's Society was a conservative Christian response to the organizing power of the Social Democrats. Weber, who helped Stoecker organize both congresses, was extremely active in the effort to create workers' societies among evangelicals. In 1890, he discussed at the Evangelical-Social Congress the need to expand the number of societies, and was supported by Pastor Dietz of Messel, near Darmstadt, who applauded their patriotic character. "On earth, the EMPEROR remains number one," Dietz said at the meeting, adding that "the precondition is assuredly faithfulness to the heavenly King. A truly pious man has never been found manning the barricades."

Workers' societies seemed to be one way to implement Stoecker's earlier call for ecclesiastically sanctioned groups that would reconcile class differences, and to restore societal health by rooting out materialism. From small beginnings in the Rhineland and Westphalia in 1882, more than 350 societies had a membership of 80,000 by 1896. The Evangelical Worker's Society of Germany was formed as an umbrella organization in 1890. Its central committee included representatives from the Inner Mission and the Evangelical-Social Congress, until Stoecker left the Congress.

Weber, the Samuel Smiles of Germany, was the right man to lead this movement. One of his most popular pamphlets carried a "Smilean" title: SELF-HELP, STATE HELP, AND DIVINE HELP. His bourgeois philosophy, that God helps those who help themselves, was appropriate fare for societies whose members included more conservative artisans, owners, and clergymen than industrial workers. Weber encouraged workers to control their spending, provide for retirement, organize consumer unions and building associations, and demand that the government institute shorter working weeks, safety measures, and a day off on Sunday.

From the start, a strong religious atmosphere permeated the workers' societies, and many leaders were pastors. Sick and benefit societies provided some self-help relief, but the

509

groups also published songbooks of patriotic and religious songs and hymns. Until about 1890, most societies had some affiliation with the strongly anti-Catholic Evangelical Society, and society meetings often offered advice on mixed marriages, and the education of children from these unions. As the battle against Rome faded, the Social Democrats became the target, and the societies stressed the need for workers and owners to reconcile their differences. A national HANDBOOK in 1892 reminded readers that Social Democracy could not claim to speak for the worker; as evidence, it quoted a recent Social Democratic calendar that said that man descended from the ape. Anti-Semitism was another powerful weapon for use against this "troublemaker;" the same brochure claimed that the party was "one of the best missionary forces that Judaism could wish to have."

The societies' program took up the five basic "diseases" of modern life. In the social realm, the societies sought to destroy the barriers that divided people on differing social levels. In economics, members were challenged to reconcile employer and employee, while carefully noting housing conditions and encouraging economic living. Societies tried to cultivate patriotism, and asked members to oppose all immoral practices, especially drunkenness, gambling, cursing, and materialism. The societies' religious goal was to support the evangelical faith, and renew popular life through a moral and religious revival.

The cultivation of patriotic attitudes was seen as an important goal, since it would sharply distinguish members from the internationalism of the Social Democrats. When five to seven thousand workers convened in Elberfeld in 1890, they sent a laudatory telegram to the emperor after hearing speeches, singing songs, and toasting his health. Earlier that day, four worship services accommodated the crowd.

The societies faced an identity crisis in 1892. Traditionalists resisted attempts of younger leaders to recapture earlier interest in industrial workers, the kind of zeal that Stoecker showed early in 1878. The next year, a split was narrowly averted when pastoral leaders, meeting in conjunction with the Evangelical-Social Congress, adopted a new platform. It was heavily influenced by economic theory, and included social-political and social-practical sections, while omitting any reference to the cultivation of religious faith. Instead, a new goal was proposed for the Evangelical Workingmen's Societies: "We see the goal of our work much more <than such nurture> in the development of Christianity's world-renewing power in contemporary economic life." This goal was difficult to implement since the program lacked specific proposals, and the societies continued in their traditional, conservative views.

The evangelical workingmen's societies were ideally structured to fulfil the unwritten religious charter that governed Protestant church life in Germany. Their effectiveness was partly due to their limited membership, but they embodied the best "chartered" tradition as they responded to the new world created by industrialization. Their affiliation with Stoecker was no accident, since he too was trying to counteract the Social Democrats, and reinvigorate the reactionary Christian state, in order to solve the social problem in a paternalistic way. His effort to mold the religious charter to the challenges of industrialism depended on a populist church that did not materialize. The Social Democrats influenced his response, but he controlled that influence while using it, like the Jews, as a foil for his conservative answers to the social problem.

The intellectualized response to the social problem by the Evangelical-Social Congress also perpetuated the precepts of the unwritten religious charter. Todt's rhetoric was no more dangerous than the academic steam released at its regular assemblies; in fact, both were innocuous. Proponents of the unwritten charter encouraged academic discussion that did not become political, and the Congress was a debating society that eased the consciences of informed academicians and sensitized churchmen, without committing them to anything more than caritative concern. It was better to talk than do nothing, especially under the state's encouragement.

But others pushed off into the night with less concern for the dangers ahead. Their voyages—one is tempted to call them suicide missions—were lonely journeys, more satisfying for the participant than effective. Their stories must be told, not so much to rehearse their heroics as to explain the minimal results of their labors, and, by contrast, to demonstrate the response of most Protestants to the challenge of the Social Democrats.

NAUMANN: CHRISTIAN SOCIALISM TO SOCIAL DARWINISM

In his career, Friedrich Naumann (1860-1919) recapitulated the development of German Protestant theology from the collapse of idealism to the Great War in the twentieth century. Naumann first formulated a theological position along Ritschlian lines; this led to exegetical investigation, and deep regard for Jesus as an historical person. Eventually he accepted the cultural Protestantism espoused by Harnack and the liberal school, emphasizing the individual.

Naumann took a more radical position on the social question than the court preacher, Stoecker. Disenchanted with the socialists' utopian schemes, he posited God's kingdom as the organizing framework for a community that originated in time, but consummated itself in eternity. With this perspective, he described what might be called God's "futuristic kingdom" as a human creation. But a theological crisis, partly due to Johannes Weiss' studies about Jesus' eschatological preachment of the kingdom, and partly to his travels in Palestine, crushed his efforts to formulate a viable brand of Christian socialism. In the end, he returned to the more traditional position—with strong social Darwinist overtones—namely, that Christians had to address the problems of industrialization individually. His was a journey from Christian socialism to social Darwinism.

After hesitating initially to enter the ministry, Naumann served as chief assistant to Wichern's son in the "Rauhe Haus" before accepting a pastorate at Langeberg, near Zwickau in Saxony. In 1890 he became a pastor for the Inner Mission's association in Frankfurt am Main. Upon entering the ministry, he immersed himself in the question of the church's social responsibility. He concluded that socialism and the Inner Mission complemented one another, and that Marx and Wichern were counterparts, especially since Wichern prophesied that the Inner Mission would soon enter a new stage.

Late in 1888, Naumann published an extended study of the interdependence of socialism and the Inner Mission in the liberal journal, CHRISTIAN WORLD (CHRISTLICHE WELT). The histories of Marxism and the Inner Mission belonged together, he concluded; the first provided an eschatological theory that met human needs, while the second was oriented toward charitable activity. The goal in history toward which both were striving he called the "socialist state," or the "future state," whose full manifestation hinged on Christian elements embodied in the Inner Mission. The chief remaining obstacle for Naumann was his feeling of uneasiness with the Social Democrats, whom he viewed as heretics of both true socialism and Christianity. He proposed to solve this problem by tracing the origins of socialism and the Inner Mission to two primal figures, Marx and Jesus.

In 1889 at Leignitz, Naumann addressed the general assembly of the Silesian Provincial Society of the Inner Mission. Using the image of God's kingdom, he offered the best of two worlds, that of Jesus and of Marx: the Social Democrats' platform for this world, and the eternal verities of the spirit for the life consummated above.

Naumann's artfully chosen title for his long speech, "What Do We Do against Faithless Social Democracy?", undoubtedly disarmed his audience. He also made the speech more palatable for his listeners by referring frequently to God's kingdom as he described the Democrats. But he insisted that Christians had no right to oppose their platform, especially its approach "from below," from the perspective of the poor. Their futile and immobilizing vigil for a chiliastic utopia was quite another matter. He claimed that God's kingdom alone met all the needs of people, which was not true of an ethical optimism that merely marked time, until utopia suddenly appeared.

In observations about Naumann, Hermann Timm described this speech as an act of "theological aggression," since Naumann substituted the idea of God's kingdom for the socialist state he envisioned in 1888. This turn of events severed the previous connection between socialist theory and philanthropic practice, and attributed to true socialism the right, in Timm's words, to be "the eschatological theory of the Christian world design." Naumann's conception of God's kingdom now corresponded theologically with Ritschlian

513

thought, but he loaded the idea with socialistic content and meaning. Ritschl's idea of the kingdom was not limited to a single dominant motif, nor was it so specifically related to socialism.(12)

In view of his revised description of socialism as the most vibrant force in God's kingdom, Nauman needed to reevaluate the Inner Mission's role. He issued this reevaluation under the pretext of seeking wider circulation for a tract on the church's mission published by the Inner Mission, namely, a pamphlet by Theodor Lohmann, entitled AUFGABE DER KIRCHE UND IHRER INNEREN MISSION GEGENUEBER DER WIRTSCHAFTLICHEN UND GESELLSCHAFTLICHEN KAEMPFEN DER GEGENWART . . .(1885). The tract was republished in 1890, and the church and Inner Mission were the focus of articles written by Naumann between August, 1889, and January, 1891.

A major thrust in these articles was Naumann's call for deeper Christian knowledge. He recommended that Christian acquaintance with Jesus on the soteriological or redemptory level should move to the historical level, and realistically appraise His preachment of God's kingdom. "No formulated program is projected for us in Jesus Christ. In Him we meet more than that—the spirit from which every era should take its program." His teaching of God's kingdom eliminated all divisions among people based on differences of wealth. The only "party spirit" in God's kingdom was love, which created solidarity with the poor, and made people brothers in economic life; its absence was sin. The church's mission, Naumann added, was to preach the kingdom that "overcomes the world," and to play the role of "the reconciling power that announces divine peace." As reconciler, the church should rely on consciences bound by faith, rather than its organizational power.

In the fall of 1890, Naumann assumed his duties as pastor for the Inner Mission in Frankfurt. Later that year he hinted that his recent interpretation of the Inner Mission's program statement was an effort to formulate new theological tools. He added that since Christians lacked the theological tools to engage the Social Democrats, they should preach Jesus' teaching of God's kingdom. Even without instructions from the consistory, the pastor was a prophet to his contemporaries when he preached God's will as manifested in the kingdom.

514

Three years later, Naumann issued his "magnum opus" on the relation between the industrial age and God's kingdom. "The Christian in the Age of the Machine" appeared in the CHRISTIAN WORLD in 1893, and was republished with other essays the next year. Naumann wrote that technological advances of the machine age manifested God's kingdom on earth. The kingdom would soon engulf the whole earth; the machine was integral to its expansion.

He added that machines had to serve the kingdom's goals. Christian missions would benefit directly from interaction with industrial societies, and machines would reduce the world's suffering. Responsibility for problems in the age rested not with the machine as much as with the economic system, which prevented equitable distribution of products. The problems should be solved by altering the economic system, not delaying technological advance. He ended his article by stressing the double meaning of the second petition of the Lord's prayer, "Thy kingdom come!", in the machine age.

For as short time, Naumann seemed to revel in his discovery that socialism was the moving force in God's kingdom. The peak of excitement was the article entitled "The Christian in the Age of the Machine," but a subsequent article failed to draw on the idea of the kingdom. One or both eventualities probably deterred him. He may have encountered the recent studies of Johannes Weiss, stressing the apocalyptic and eschatological character of Jesus' preachment of the kingdom, in opposition to the cultural interpretation in the Ritschlian school. Or he may have sensed that his heavy emphasis on will, with its social Darwinian connotations, was incompatible with his understanding of God's kingdom as a community of love. Subsequent developments indicate that social Darwinism influenced his thinking appreciably, although at this juncture Weiss may have been a more important factor.

In any case, an article in THE FUTURE (DER ZUKUNFT) early in 1894 was important for several reasons. In the piece, Naumann relegated the Christian-social movement to the realm of inexplicable mysticism; he stressed historical determinism more than before; he reinterpreted Jesus' social interest, finding Him more concerned with unemployment than

515

blindness; and he urged his readers to hold to Jesus and Marx, without inextricably committing themselves to a program that would soon be outdated. In the period that followed, Naumann turned his attention increasingly to study of the historical Jesus. Together with other influences, this shift led to the full collapse of his Christian socialist views, brought a drastic realignment of his conception of God's kingdom, and produced a rigorous distinction between religious and political spheres.

One factor that encouraged Naumann's active involvement in politics was the publication of his paper, DIE HILFE (THE ASSISTANT), early in 1895. The paper was subtitled "Divine Help, Self-Help, Fraternal Help" until 1902, when the masthead became "A Weekly for Politics, Literature and Art." The journal's weekly run was 6,000 copies in 1895, 12,000 in 1896, and 12,500 in 1912. Naumann's publication drew a strong protest from conservatives, including Frieherr von Stumm-Halberg, who attacked it in the "Reichstag" in 1895 as an organ of the Social Democrats. Von Stumm advised fellow magnates to fire any worker who subscribed.

This weekly brought to a head the long-standing argument between Stoecker and Naumann. Among other things, Naumann was rebelling against Stoecker as his theological father-figure. Together with Paul Goehre (1864-1928), the Evangelical-Social Congress' general secretary from 1891 to 1894, and other "young Turks," Naumann had agitated for the Congress to forsake Stoecker's conservative anchorings, and establish closer relations with the Social Democrats. He publicly opposed Stoecker's anti-Semitism, and understood marriage and family life as purely social phenomena. To the dismay of Stoecker and his cohorts, who depended largely on the landed aristocracy for support, Naumann and the young Turks urged land reform in East Prussia with the slogan, "Land for the Masses!"

In the nineties, Naumann's work in the Congress put him into contact with a group of men, largely professors, who opened a new range of experiences for him. Among them were Adolf von Harnack and Max Weber (1864-1920). Harnack's influence came later, but Weber and Rudolph Sohm (1841-1917), a respected scholar of church law, influenced him appreciably by mid-decade.

Naumann's relations with Weber intensified as time passed. One result was that he no longer interpreted the socialist movement within a theological perspective. Socialism became essentially a political question to be evaluated in the framework of the nation's international role.

Sohm undermined Naumann's position from the other side. Addressing the Congress of the Inner Mission in 1895, with Naumann as a listener, Sohm distinguished sharply between Christianity and the civil and political sphere. Negatively speaking, Christianity could provide no applicable norms for the state's codified law. "The 'Christian state'—away with it. . . . Away with Christian law, with the Christian state! The state is secular, naturalistic, and the law equally so," he argued.

These men, and perhaps Johannes Weiss, radically altered Naumann's views. His zeal for Christian socialism waned appreciably. This uncertainty was compounded when the emperor turned a cold shoulder to Christian socialism in 1896. In the meantime, Naumann was having great difficulty steering the Inner Mission toward a proposed linkage with socialism. The growing cleavage in his mind between Christianity and politics made it difficult to think in terms of a "merciful state law," or a Christian form of socialism. In 1897 he resigned from the ministry and moved to Berlin. On October 7 he wrote to the liberal editor, Martin Rade, "The idea of 'Christian-social' has been pursued politically to its end, and it leads to nothing. This experience may have some historical value, but is painful for the one who was the subject of the experiment."

Under Weber's influence, Naumann set out in 1986 to forge a political alliance to benefit the power state, in terms of national and socialist goals. He argued that socialism could help strengthen the empire internally; at the same time, since he was an imperialist, he accused the Social Democrats of inconsistency at this point.

In what later proved to be a major political mistake, Naumann composed a catechism for the new National-Social Association (1896). First published in the ASSISTANT (1897) and then issued separately, the pamphlet provided a running commentary on the association's principles, and stressed the group's support for power politics in the international realm, and social reform at home. Naumann emphasized that without strong national commitment among the masses, the nation could not remain an international power; but unless it expanded its world markets, social reform was a pipe dream. A well-equipped fleet for the colonial empire was compatible with a constitutional monarchy. Naumann denied that Christianity had any political or economic program of its own, and restricted religion to "spiritual folk life."

With increasing frequency, Naumann's public speeches oscillated between the gospel of political "conflict," and the pietistic and individualistic Good News of personhood manifested in Jesus. In 1899 he blamed theologians of ethics for not charting the church's course in the social problem. He urged a strongly realistic approach: the Lutheran church should endorse the lowest common denominator, composed of only three social reforms, namely, preserving Sunday as a day of rest, better housing, and the right to collective bargaining. He added that most pastors had some experience with these three issues; in addition, they did not invalidate Protestantism's free spirit, which originally was not, and never should have become, a paternalistic system.

Naumann visited Palestine late in the summer of 1898, and experienced the squalor and backwardness of the land. For the first time, he grasped the enormous gap between the conditions of Jesus' life and those of contemporary Germany. These experiences reinforced his conviction that modern Christianity was unrelated to socialism. The journey finalized the divorce between religion and politics.

Politically, Naumann was not driven to this conclusion until he identified the domestic ramifications of international relations. After committing himself to the theory of self-interest in international relations, he identified as well the importance of political realism on the domestic front. Bismarck used the fulcrum of foreign affairs to unify Germany; Naumann used international relations to drive a wedge between religion and politics at home. One modern scholar notes that as long as he ignored Germany's international relations, he could concentrate on renewing state and society, and maintaining a balance between Christian ethics and politics. But international relations appreciably clarified his conception of the state's internal power structure.(13)

In subsequent years, Naumann gravitated closer to Harnack's theological views. He wrote that the basic religious question for Christianity was a simple query: "Is Jesus a conquering personality for me?" He confessed that while doctrinal commitments could not stand the test of his personal experiences and trials, "the Person at the center stood firm." Several times in the ASSISTANT he called himself Harnack's student. His affinity for Harnack reinforced his belief that religion was more important than the organized church. As a result, he made God's kingdom the special province of religion, and insisted that the kingdom would be built by people who discovered their true nature in Jesus Christ.

When the Great War struck, Naumann remained true to his principles. In 1915 he showed contempt for those who supported national or military causes with their preaching, reminding readers in the ASSISTANT that concepts could not encapsulate many of life's experiences. Three years before his death, he issued the sixth unaltered edition of his LETTERS ON RELIGION. The appendix suggested that he changed his mind in some specifics, but in general concurred with the first edition's conclusions: Christian socialism was a non-entity, and Bismarck and Tolstoy could never shake hands in agreement.

In the end, his conception of God's kingdom permitted him to live with himself. It soothed the seared conscience of a guilt-ridden chauvinist, who was disgusted with his earlier nationalism. He believed that the Christian was committed to humanity, while the politician wrestled with human pride and national units to provide the necessary synapse between humanity and the individual. Christianity and social Darwinism coexisted in Naumann's personality, but no room remained for Christian socialism. It succumbed to the power state.

Naumann's political activities in the twentieth century showed him to be a mature politician, less captivated by nationalism than earlier. During World War I, his best seller, MIDDLE EUROPE (1915), surveyed Germany's relations with the nations of central Europe. Elected to the National Assembly at Weimar after the war, he left his mark on the new constitution's Fundamental Rights and Duties. His untimely death interrupted a promising political career.

BLUMHARDT

One clergyman who joined the Social Democratic party was Christoph Blumhardt (1842-1919). A maverick figure from Wuerttemberg, he was cut from the same cloth as his father, Johann Christoph Blumhardt (1805-1880). Christoph was born in Moettlingen. In 1869 he entered the ministry with his father in an old castle in Bad Boll, assuming leadership of the small private spa in 1880. From 1900 to 1906, he represented the Social Democrats in Wuerttemberg's parliament.

Students of Christoph Blumhardt point to four periods in his adult life. Each had a motif, and, we might add, a corresponding reference to God's kingdom. Up to 1888, he uncritically assumed his father's message and mission under the theme, "Jesus is victor!" The next period, one of retreat and critical analysis, reached to 1896; its motto was, "Die, that Jesus may live!" In this time Blumhardt made a concerted effort to reject religious hypocrisy. He entered the political arena as a legislator in the third period, which extended to 1906; "You men are God's" was the motto of his religious humanism. The fourth period centered in meditative prayer and patient anticipation of the Lord's coming. "God's kingdom comes!" was its characteristic theme.

Blumhardt's early description of life's chaos, and God's peace for His allies, was linked with the same woman who prompted his father's awakening. In his case, the death of Gottliebin Dittus in 1872 was significant. Since she lived with the family at Bod Boll, her death was a signal for the whole family to renew its spiritual life. Death was more than chaos, Christoph claimed; it also opened the way to see God's rule firmly established, and that was why His kingdom and the resurrection were synonymous terms.(15)

During this period, Blumhardt did a great deal of public

preaching, since he believed that through preaching God would conquer the kingdom of darkness with His kingdom of light. In the seventies and eighties he attracted large crowds, and preached to thousands of people at more than twenty appearances in Berlin.

In the second period, Blumhardt levelled widespread criticism, and portrayed himself as a change-agent. Preaching in 1891, he noted that people were capable of forming the soil of God's kingdom, although at the time no fertile plot was offered by Christianity, or the depressed social conditions of the day.

Because he felt that the community at Bad Boll was limiting God's reign too narrowly to matters of sickness and health, Blumhardt lashed out at the guests' hypochondria. In 1888 he tired of public preaching, and the number of healings in his presence diminished. A circular letter to friends suggested that a selfish streak had invaded the spa; people interested only in the restoration of their health were thwarting God's history, he wrote.

Blumhardt engaged in a massive rejection of organized Christianity. He stripped every "churchly" element from the mansion at the spa, donated his pulpit to a tiny church, refrained from administering communion and baptism, and sometimes ignored a regular preaching schedule. The lordship of God was not a magnification of human existence, nor was Christ's victory attainable by human beings, he contended.

The third period extended from 1896 to 1906. Until he actively joined the Social Democratic party in 1900, Blumhardt prepared the theological groundwork for the step. Subsequent political activities opened no new vistas, so the period must be seen as a unity.

This was a time to give a clear humanitarian witness: "You men are God's!" Blumhardt felt that the institutional church failed to witness to God's kingdom, preferring instead to discuss confessions and doctrines about which people had little concern. Given these circumstances, "we must begin to speak of God's kingdom in a new way," by proclaiming that God's kingdom "was and will be the rulership of justice, of order, of power, of law, of all that is of God in creation.

This, my friends, is what moves us men, and this must come into being." God was active in human affairs, although society resisted Jesus' living power. Blumhardt shouted his second slogan once again, this time for the whole world to hear: "Die, that Jesus may live!"(16)

Since the institutional church showed little eschatological anticipation and futuristic hope, Blumhardt turned instead to the proletariat and the socialists, who in his thinking embodied these important qualities. Like his father, Christoph saw "signs" of the impending victory, including the Russian czar's search for peace, hygenic efforts to eliminate the common communion cup, and most importantly, the socialist struggle against capitalism.(17)

His third phase began in the fall of 1896. Three years later he described in words what his actions of that year meant: "In Jesus peace should come to earth, in Jesus society and an arrangement of society should come into existence in which one is not suppressed by others."(18) In the summer of 1899 he participated in a workers' meeting in the heavily industrialized town of Goeppingen, to protest legislation limiting the right of employees to organize. Tagging the bill a "crime against justice," he declared solidarity with the workers. That fall he joined the Democrats in supporting factory employment for married women. Invited by the party members of Goeppingen to explain his views, he urged them to recognize that their enemy was the church, not Christ. "Surely the Christian world order is not Christ's order," he said. "Jesus was a socialist" who was always "down there" with people, and His invitation to "twelve proletarians to be His disciples" was sufficient reason for him to join the proletariat. He noted that emperor and nation deserved sacrifices, but insisted that under no circumstance should they be human sacrifices; Social Democracy intended to give life, not take it. It sought a just order, not a revolutionary bloodbath, and he would do all he could to contribute.

The workers applauded warmly, but his appearance created a sensation in the press. The BASEL ADVERTISER criticized his "act of folly." Some evangelicals claimed that he had fallen from the faith. One pietist paper coined the maxim that "a believing Christian cannot be a Social Democrat, and a convinced Social Democrat cannot remain a Christian," even

522

though the southern Democrats were usually less radical than their brothers up north, and ordinarily retained legal membership in the church. Immediately after the meeting in Goeppingen, the royal consistory in Wuerttemberg asked Blumhardt to voluntarily resign from the territory's ministerium. He yielded to pressure and resigned, although he remained a member of the church until his death.

Blumhardt described his rapprochement with the Democrats in these words:

> All my life I have believed in and striven for God's kingdom and His justice on earth. Now all this is expressed in this alliance of mine with the great workers' movement. . . . Their fight is represented by social justice. It sets thousands of hearts afire everywhere. I see a sign of Christ in it; for Christ too wants a humanity which is wholly penetrated by justice and truth, by love and life. In the spirit I am united with this struggle. Let us not judge. Movements, even revolutions, have to be. Do not be afraid. Rather believe that our time, more than any other, is called to bring us closer to God's kingdom.(19)

While he failed to say that by joining the Democrats he was pointing precisely to where God's kingdom would strike, he hinted that with his help, the Social Democrats would create God's new community on earth.

Running as a Democratic candidate, he was elected as the Goeppingen district's representative in the Wuerttemberg assembly. He served from 1900 to 1906, although he was not the first southern clergyman to join the party.(20) He and four other Social Democrats boycotted the opening session, when the king appeared for the festivities. He joined in debate over agriculture and the church's role in the schools; he supported the proposal to transfer supervision from the church, arguing that religion and morality existed outside the church, and laypersons could sometimes do more than clergy for morality among the masses. But in 1902 he refused to run for a seat in the imperial "Reichstag," and showed signs of weariness with debate and parliamentary maneuvering.

Probably the structural parallel of hope—his own eschatological hope for God's intervention, and the Democrats' hope of achieving a more acceptable social order in the future—motivated Blumhardt to join the party. Later the important religious socialist, Leonhard Ragaz, argued that it was Blumhardt, not the religious socialists that followed him, who first idealized the socialist movement, since he saw in it an advancement of God's kingdom. The structural parallel collapsed when Blumhardt realized that the socialists had no obligation to link the fulfillment of their dreams to the realization of God's kingdom. According to the theologian Gerhard Sauter, Blumhardt's concession to the Marxist-economic emphasis of society over the individual was merely the rigorous application of his father's system of cosmic priorities. The Democrats' sense of anticipation was equivalent to the terrestial "holy time," which his father said would precede the "parousia."(21)

After serving six years in the territorial parliament, Blumhardt resigned his seat and made an extended visit to Palestine, so that the party would not impose candidacy once again. Sickness overtook him, and he returned seriously ill. During this fourth phase of his life, he dropped nearly all social references in his speech, but maintained a connection with the Social Democratic party until his death. During public worship it was his custom to pray only the first three petitions of the Lord's Prayer, but he anticipated Christ and His kingdom with joy. Lines from a sermon in 1914 offer an insight into his thinking at the time:

> What is God's kingdom? It is not Christian insti-
> tutions, although the kingdom of God can reside in
> them. Kingdom of God is power of God, rule of God,
> revelation of God in life, the creation of new
> hearts, new ways of thinking and new feelings so
> that we will be turned toward what is right. King-
> dom of God—oh who can comprehend what it means
> when God rules! It is entirely too big for Chris-
> tians of our day!(22)

Blumhardt's efforts to create solidarity with workers in the Democratic party was anchored in his understanding of God's kingdom; the new socialist movement signalled the kingdom's arrival. But his theological stance also helped bring to an end his service as a party legislator, after he tired of legislative deliberations. While resuming preaching and witnessing, he waited for God's rule to intervene and change the structures of society.

It would be uncharitable to suggest that, for Blumhardt, the unwritten religious charter merely took more time than for most to have its effect. It was, after all, his driving theology that led him to retreat once again from active politics. Nevertheless, the religious charter programmed Protestants not to accept his religious and political witness from within the workers' party ranks. The unratified agreement between Protestants and the states contributed to the overall ineffectiveness of this preacher-politician, and soon his lonely voice was no more effective in the area of social concerns than it later was in support of pacifism. Blumhardt was out of joint with the times, in part because the charter retained such great influence.

This is not to ignore his enormous influence on some twentieth century theologians. His thought combined two impulses in a tension that his successors found unable to sustain. He stressed both God's rule and revelation, and the Word of God lived out in a social context. One strand of his thinking affected Barth, Brunner, Bonhoeffer, Thurneysen, Cullmann, and the theologians of hope, especially Paul Schuetz. Barth retained the strong socialist emphasis, which he never fully lost, until World War I, when his COMMENTARY ON ROMANS maintained that religious socialism was not a new appearance of God's kingdom, but a reappearance of man's. Barth's work in succeeding years showed that his visits to Bad Boll were not without effect, but he no longer fully accepted Blumhardt's counsel.

Blumhardt's second impulse flowed most clearly into the religious socialism of theologians in pre-war Switzerland, and post-war Germany. Tillich and Wuensch were the German counterparts of such Swiss pastors and theologians as Howard Eugster-Zuest (1861-1932), Hermann Kutter (1863-1931), and Leonhard Ragaz (1868-1945).

Religious socialism in pre-war Switzerland offered a religious interpretation of socialism. Kutter called socialism a judgment of capitalism, and Ragaz the promise of a reordered world. Religious socialists interacted with Social Democrats without feeling the need to refer to God explicitly, since He was bringing His will to fruition in His own way. After 1895, Eugster-Zuest corresponded extensively with Blumhardt, and then followed him into the Social Democratic party, while also showing solidarity with workers in their strikes. Kutter visited Blumhardt and remained on good terms until 1901, but the two parted ways when Kutter identified the Social Democrats as the bearers of God's future kingdom, while not insisting on the need to identify himself with them existentially.(23) As an influential Swiss preacher, Kutter gave public witness to his thinking, arguing in his popular book, SIE MUESSEN (1904), that God's promises were being fulfilled among the Social Democrats.

Ragaz' relations with Blumhardt were complex, but there is little doubt about Blumhardt's influence. His book, DAS EVANGELIUM UND DER SOZIALE KAMPF DER GEGENWART (1906), provided a sense of direction and purpose for religious socialism in Switzerland, but the movement soon found its focus in the journal entitled NEUE WEGE (1906). Kutter and Ragaz eventually separated, but between 1912 and 1920, religious socialism influenced the Social Democratic party in Switzerland. Kutter aptly summarized the religious socialists' position—and pointed to Blumhardt's impact—when he observed that the Social Democrats were revolutionary because God is revolutionary; they pressed toward the future because God's kingdom was coming with new structures.

Enlarged in the sixties by the experience of national unification, the unwritten religious charter bracketed the two major responses of Protestants to the social question. National unity helped them understand that their primary "folkish" responsibility was to sanction conservative nationalism, not to waste energy on irrelevancies, such as ministering to social upheaval caused by rapid industrialization and urbanization. As a result, one chartered response to social problems was the "misdirected zeal" of many charitable efforts, as we saw in the last chapter; the other was the limited hearing given to those who offered moderate rejoiners to the Social Democratic challenge.

But the new working class, and others unable to express their hopes, kept an eye out for spokesmen. The Social Democrats articulated their hopes with varying degrees of authenticity, especially after party restraints were lifted in 1890.

The next chapter explains how the uneasiness of "little people" foreshadowed a nearly universal slide into cultural subjectivism. Discontent, disillusionment, and alienation spread to the middle classes, while intellectuals asked whether rationality was as foundational for thinking as they once thought. The churches were unable to make full use of their theological and religious resources, in part because of earlier failures to penetrate the social problem. As the century closed, foundations collapsed on all sides, while many Protestants rallied to anti-Semitism, and continued to lay their blessing on a bloated form of nationalism.

NOTES

CHAPTER XI

(1) W. M. Simon, ed., GERMANY IN THE AGE OF BISMARCK (London: George Allen and Unwin LTD, 1968), pp. 201-202.

(2) J. H. Clapham, ECONOMIC DEVELOPMENT IN FRANCE AND GERMANY, 1815—1914 (4th ed.; Cambridge: University Press, 1966), p. 326.

(3) Vernon L. Lidtke, THE OUTLAWED PARTY: SOCIAL DEMOCRACY IN GERMANY, 1878—1890 (Princeton: Princeton University Press, 1966), p. 337.

(4) Ibid., p. 178.

(5) Ibid., pp. 68-69.

(6) Robert C. Tucker, ed., THE MARX-ENGELS READER (New York: W. W. Norton & Co., Inc., 1972), p. 397.

(7) Theodor Strohm, KIRCHE UND DEMOKRATISCHER SOZIALISMUS; STUDIEN ZUR THEORIE UND PRAXIS POLITISCHER KOMMUNIKATION (Munich: Chr. Kaiser Verlag, 1968), pp. 71-77.

(8) Walter Frank, HOFPREDIGER ADOLF STOECKER UND DIE CHRISTLICHSOZIALE BEWEGUNG (2nd ed.; Hamburg: Hanseatische Verlagsanstalt, 1935), p. 19.

(9) Stoecker's interest in an independent church was sparked by the Roman Catholic model. Generally he approved of the "Kulturkampf" against Rome, and hoped that an independent evangelical church would emerge. Civil marriage and the freedom not to baptize children were not inherently evil, he said; the extent of these practices merely showed

528

the power of unbelief and the great need for evangelism. But at the same time, he opposed the growing influence of liberal polity and doctrine in the evangelical church during the "Kulturkampf." Despite this irritant, he committed himself to working for a free church, since that was the only way the church could effectively address the social question and assume leadership among the masses.

(10) Eckart Schleth, DER PROFANE WELTCHRIST; NEUBAU DER LEBENSFORM FUER DEN INDUSTRIENMENSCHEN (Munich: Chr. Kaiser Verlag, 1957), pp. 41-42.

(11) Simon, ed., p. 205.

(12) Herman Timm, "Friedrich Naumanns theologischer Widerruf," THEOLOGISCHE EXISTENZ HEUTE, ed. K. G. Steck and G. Eichholz, Neue Folge, CXLI (Munich: Chr. Kaiser Verlag, 1967), pp. 18-19. See also the author's article, "Friedrich Naumann: From Christian Socialist to Social Darwinist," JOURNAL OF CHURCH AND STATE, XVII,1 (Winter 1975), 25-46.

(13) Juergen Christ, STAAT UND STAATSRAISON BEI FRIEDRICH NAUMANN (Heidelberg: Carl Winter Universitaetsverlag, 1969), p. 27.

(14) The older Blumhardt studied at Tuebingen, taught briefly at the mission training institute in Basel, served as a pastor in Swabian Moettlingen from 1838 to 1852, and then organized a health community in a castle at Bad Boll where he lived until his death. He experienced a spiritual awakening in Moettlingen in the early forties while ministering to a young woman who was very sick. Her experience of a miraculous healing became at the same time his primal religious experience, and provided the impetus for an awakening in the small congregation. Soon Blumhardt encountered trouble with church officials, and published THE STORY OF THE ILLNESS OF GOTTLIEBEN DITTUS as a rejoiner. He also authored a popular history of missions. In 1848 he narrowly missed being elected against his will to the Frankfurt Parliament. In 1852 he purchased an old resort in Bad Boll, resigned his parish post, and moved there to form a healing community while awaiting God's visitation. In the sixties, a visitor reported that the guest list included persons from Norway, Holland, Denmark, France, Switzerland, Prussia, Saxony, Russia, Baden, Bavaria, and Wuerttemberg.

Blumhardt corresponded with people all over Germany and ministered to his private community until he died.

(15) Eduard Thurneysen, CHRISTOPH BLUMHARDT (Zurich: Zwingli Verlag, 1962), p. 79

(16) R<obert> Lejeune, CHRISTOPH BLUMHARDT AND HIS MESSAGE, tr. Hela Ehrlich and Nicoline Maas (Rifton, NY: Plough Publishing House, 1963), pp. 142-51. The sermon was preached in 1896.

(17) Ibid., pp. 158-68; Gerhard Sauter, DIE THEOLOGIE DES REICHES GOTTES BEIM AELTEREN UND JUENGEREN BLUMHARDT, Studien zur Dogmengeschichte und systematischen Theologie, ed. Fritz Blanke et al., Vol. XIV (Zurich: Zwingli Verlag, 1962), pp. 183-89.

(18) Ernst Staehelin, ed., DIE VERKUENDIGUNG DES REICHES GOTTES IN DER KIRCHE JESU CHRISTI (7 vols.; Basel: Verlag Friedrich Reinhardt <1951—65>, VII, 255.

(19) Lejeune, pp. 65-69.

(20) Ibid., pp. 71-72.

(21) Sauter, p. 137.

(22) Staehelin, VII, 258.

(23) Markus Mattmueller, "Der Einfluss Christoph Blumhardts auf schweizerische Theologen des 20. Jahrhunderts," ZEITSCHRIFT FUER EVANGELISCHE ETHIK, XII (1968), 233-46.

CHAPTER XII

FOUNDATIONAL COLLAPSE

> If wartime bread is scarce,
> Give us each day the enemy's death
> And for them, mountains of anguish.
> With merciful patience
> Forgive each bullet and slash
> That misses its mark.
> Keep us from the temptation
> To execute Thy divine judgment
> All too mildly with our wrath.
> Deliver us and our allies
> From the hellish foe
> Since we are Thy earthly servants.
> Thine is the kingdom, the German nation,
> And power and glory must be ours
> Through Thy iron hand.

This poem, entitled "Hurrah and Hallelujah!", was written by Pastor Dietrich Vorwerk in 1914. It can be read as satire on the Lord's Prayer, but apparently it was written to instill fierce loyalty to God and country. We might debate whether or not the poem was Christian, and whether or not it signalled moral and religious collapse. But there is little question that Protestant foundations were cracking and collapsing in a number of places as World War I approached.

In the pre-war decades, the churches were fired upon from

many quarters, while conflict and unrest erupted on all
sides. Rapid industrialization brought social upheaval and
divided social classes even more widely. In general, highly
educated people and the working classes showed little
interest in religion and the churches. The greatest
percentage of active Protestants were found in the middle
classes—a highly volatile social and economic group—and
among aristocratic and peasant people of the hinterlands.
But nationalist ideology and religious and racial
anti-Semitism competed for the attention of those who were
still attracted by Protestant Christianity. Meanwhile,
theological conservatives battled the liberals in Germany's
phase of the "modernist versus fundamentalist" controversy.
After war shook the foundations of state, culture, and
church, things were never the same again.

As powerful centrifugal forces whipped through politics,
culture, and society in the pre-war decades, it seemed that
the church's modeling role for society would soon be a thing
of the past. For a variety of reasons, what we have called
the unwritten Protestant charter was coming to its end. The
state was adrift, careening under the emperor's unsteady
hand. Apparently incapable of harnessing social and cultural
forces, let alone economic and political power, states and
governments seemed less and less adept at using the church
as a "freedom-within-authority" model for society. Though
limited in its impact, social pluralism called into question
the political assumption that one's chief duty was to live
"freely and responsibly within authority." This development
affected the welare of the Protestant charter as well.

In addition, theological pluralism reared its head in parish
situations, just as it had on theological faculties.
Churches no longer presented a monolithic public image,
although, of course, their monolith had never been as
indestructible as it appeared to be. Theological pluralism
helped undermine the basis of the unwritten agreement
between church and state.

But probably the most significant development was the
growing conviction of many that the church was irrelevant to
their lives. For many workers and highly educated people,
this had been the case for some time. But now middle class
people as well channeled their energies into secular
religions and other interests, including nationalist

ideology, materialism, and anti-Semitic movements.

This chapter reconstructs the story of foundational collapse in the pre-war decades, beginning with the intellectual upheaval of the nineties. During these years, church life offered a number of paradoxes, but a sense of malaise permeated ecclesiastical affairs. Liberal theologians met limited success in their efforts to pour a palatable form of Protestantism into a fluid culture; liberalism's drift made the conservatives' obfuscation all the more attractive to some. And while religious and racial themes punctuated the virulent anti-Semitism of these decades, the interplay of the movement's two sides showed not only that foundations were cracking; the anti-Semitic movement laid new footings as well for the devastating anti-Semitism of the twentieth century. War was the one place where all seemed well. Once more, Protestants rallied around the flag, and preachers and people joined in prayer for the fatherland. More than any other event, the World War showed the extent of foundational collapse. For the unwritten Protestant charter, it is the story's denoument.

FINDING A REASON

Nineteenth century German culture was a post-Enlightenment culture. Though in many ways it overstepped the rational and often rationalistic boundaries of the "Aufklaerung," the emphasis on reason and rational inquiry persisted. But in the century's last decades, thinkers searched for a "reason" to fill the gap that remained when systems and assumptions no longer were deemed adequate. Their search led down unexplored paths, demolishing many post-Enlightenment assumptions.

In the final third of the century, many German intellectuals indicted their age, and questioned their own ability to systematize new forces in society and in the world of thought. Uriel Tal, a professor at Tel-Aviv University, suggests as well that the intellectuals' profound disillusionment with the liberal heritage and the promise of rational inquiry turned them against liberalism, humanism, and the legal, social, and economic foundations of Jewish emancipation.(1)

In his pivotal intellectual history of the period, H. Stuart Hughes points to a number of themes that emerged. Scholars showed deep interest in the problems of consciousness and the role of the unconscious, while in philosophy, literature, historical studies, and psychology, great importance was attributed to the meaning of time and duration. Intellectuals asked foundational questions about the nature of knowledge, and stressed the need to penetrate beyond the fictions of political action. It was a heady and paradoxical time during which self-doubt and indictment flowed from the same pen. Around 1890, a noticeable shift occurred as intellectuals began emphasizing subjective rather than objective data, and seriously questioned the "false objectivity" of the natural sciences. "From 1890 to 1914, then," Hughes concludes, "we can detect in Germany two complementary and contradictory processes—a cultural revival and the beginnings of a 'secession of the intellectuals.'"(2)

Social fragmentation and new popular movements gave greater urgency to the search for a "reason," while complicating the search at the same time. Between 1900 and 1905, Germany experienced its highest absolute birth rate in history, but for Protestants, the parents alone presented enough of a problem, even without their newborn children. For many, the failure of Protestant imperialism to meet the social challenge heightened the sense of incompatibility between "subjective" religion and "objective" life in society; it also left open the way for new secular religions to satisfy the working people's longing for subjective certainty. Some middle class people found their "reason" for living in religious or racial anti-Semitism. The church's earlier failure to penetrate the workers' social problem was being replicated in another social group, as virulent anti-Semitism invaded the church's heartland, the middle classes. Meanwhile, the nation and its national ideology was the one constant in the day's social upheaval. The chauvinistic zeal of some Protestants permitted others to equate Protestantism with cultural and political nationalism; more often than not, the result was a passionate commitment to the nation and the "German God."

Things were not much better in the political realm, where the ship of state seemed to drift aimlessly. After dismissing Bismarck in 1890, the new emperor took the reins in his own hands. It was probably no accident that he spent about a third of his time on his yacht, since he was more adept at commanding a boat than steering the ship of state. With national unity a reality, for what "reason" did the state exist? Fritz Fischer's GERMANY'S AIMS IN THE FIRST WORLD WAR (1961) stirred widespread debate among historians about whether national expansion was a national objective. But is it not proper to ask whether a state that was disinclined to open the second front, namely, the expansion of domestic liberties, had viable goals other than the expansion of its borders?

In this atmosphere of growing subjectivism and social and political uneasiness, the popularized Darwinism of H. P Haeckel's monism met the needs of many. Haeckel's "reason" was the "biogenetic law," through which the individual's development recapitulated the race's history. His best-seller, DIE WELTRAETSEL, pitted materialism against idealism. In a tour de force, he stretched the rationality of the Enlightenment until it dissipated into a world view that explained everything. A Monist League was formed in 1906 to spread the new gospel; a scientist from Leipzig named Wilhelm Ostwald served as president. After the famous Protestant theologian Adolf Harnack attacked Ostwald for promoting a world view composed of "beetle legs" and "electrified substances," he officially withdrew from the territorial church, and set an example for others in the League.

The previous chapter discussed how Friedrich Naumann's writings signalled the passing of the post-Enlightenment century. Concluding that religion had little to do with the social realm, he found the "God of the world" and the "Father of Jesus Christ"—Bismarck's and Tolstoy's worlds—to be irreconcilable; it is impossible to reconcile a person's impulse to rule and to suffer in love, he argued.

In their search for a new "reason," some theologians attacked the Christian humanism of cultural Protestantism. In FROM REIMARUS TO WREDE (1906), later re-titled THE QUEST OF THE HISTORICAL JESUS, Albert Schweitzer (1875-1965)

535

claimed that Protestant theologians had distorted the historical Jesus. Schweitzer wrote that the world-negating expectation of God's imminent kingdom dominated Jesus' career, and by his death he tried to force that kingdom into coming. But Schweitzer did not pursue his "reason" to the end since, paradoxically, he held that Jesus partly wanted to destroy the eschatology by which he lived in order to free people from it.

Johannes Weiss (1863-1914) also refuted the older liberal interpretations of Jesus and his message in a book entitled JESUS' PROCLAMATION OF THE KINGDOM OF GOD (1892), in which he interpreted Jesus' message in terms of futuristic or "consistent" eschatology. With others in the "Religionsgeschichtliche Schule" (religious-historical school, or history of religions school), founded by Paul Anton de Lagarde (1827-1891) of Halle, he asked whether Christian foundations were as exclusively Christian as many had argued, in view of the influence of other religions.

The search for a "reason," sometimes leading beyond the borders of rationality, hinted that the end was near for the Protestant charter. German Protestants had arrived at an unofficial consensus that they would model for society the kind of "freedom in authority" that the institutional church symbolized. This unwritten agreement between church and state was a legacy of the Enlightenment, although, as we have seen, the people of the nineteenth century made their own imprint on it as well. In general, this consensus about the church's social role rested on a foundation of order, rationality, and accountability; one accepted principle of the "Aufklaerung" was that the church should assist the state in its appointed goals. This foundation served its purpose well during the post-Enlightenment century, but the search for a new "reason" at the end of the century foreshadowed its collapse. Numerous signs pointed in that direction, especially since Protestant churches were ill-equipped to offer a satisfying "reason" for life and living.

PARADOXES OF CHURCH LIFE

It is an apparent contradiction to say that, at the end of the century, churches were flourishing while Protestantism was dying, but both statements are accurate. Paradoxes and extremes permeated church life. Pious commitment coexisted with superficial religiosity, while overworked pastors and lazy clerics drew the same pay for a day's work; each year thousands of children entered the church through baptism, while thousand of adults legally terminated their membership.

The records of congregational visits to East Prussia, the place of religion in elementary schools, a broader look at church life, and new evangelistic movements provide some insight into the anomalies and paradoxes of church life. The intensity of these paradoxes shows that the church was finding its social role increasingly more difficult to fulfil, just as culture and state were giving a greater number of mixed signals about the church's expected role.

Congregational Visits

Just as they had for some time, teams of ecclesiastical bureaucrats and laymen continued visiting congregations in East Prussia. The records of their congregational inspections between 1883 and 1904 point up some of the paradoxes of church life in this backward, agrarian province of Prussia.

Visiting teams lavished praise on the spirit and work of some pastors, but had no kind words for others. The team visiting the diocese of Prussian Holland in 1883 reported that the two youngest pastors were the most unsatisfactory of all; one in particular gave no indication of a sense of transcendence in his words or works. On the other hand, the team captain described Dr. Weihe of Smazin as a model pastor; coincidentally, he had just returned to the ministry after twenty-eight years as a manorial lord. According to visitors to Scheoneck in 1890, Pastor Zuwachs' 300 baptisms, fifty communions for the sick, and 200 burials in eighteen widely separated cemeteries brought him to the brink of "performing the <pastoral> office mechanically, which is its death." Visitors to the diocese of Flatow in 1884 complained about Pastor Becker's laziness and indifference; when asked about visiting the sick, the Koenigsdorf pastor answered, "Now and then—but must do more of it." He was incompetent in other duties as well, and one visitor noted that his small library, filled with trivial books, held only one theological volume. And even then, the pages of Schleiermacher's THE CHRISTIAN FAITH remained uncut. "He must first learn what it means to work," the general superintendent warned.

A report in 1885 accused Pastor Riedel of Putzig of being soft on Rome. His apathy was all the more alarming since his congregation's size plummeted from 2,000 people in the forties to 900 at that time, apparently because of defections to Roman Catholicism. Riedel failed to pacify his visitors by remarking that people in the lower classes were the ones who were converting. Even more disconcerting to the inspectors was their discovery that this bachelor's housekeepers, his mother and his sister, were both Catholics. Apparently the church councils that were supposed to assist pastors in overseeing congregational work were not any more zealous than some pastors. Visitors reported that in 1891 only about half of the councils in the diocese of Rosenberg met monthly; the others met irregularly or when called.

The visitors looked long and hard for family stability as a highly desirable social dividend of religion. The rate of illegitimate births in the northern half of the Roseberg diocese disturbed the visitors as it climbed from 13 percent in 1888, to 15.4 percent in 1889, and 15 percent in 1890. Troops stationed in the area received some of the blame. But the visitors' stop in Prussian Holland in 1883 showed how the church could build family solidarity. In nearly all the parishes, the heads of households proceeded to the altar during special services to discuss with the inspectors their responsibility for home devotions, morals, Sabbath sanctity, and other matters. The church's patron, usually a nobleman, led the way to the altar, while the men of the congregation gathered in rows behind him. "Where traditionally the same spirit prevails in courtly castles and parsonages, the spirit of Christian faith and Christian morals," the visitors reported, "where patron and pastor have worked together for decades, yes even centuries, there under divine blessing the tree of community life grows and blossoms under Christian influence . . . ." But reality did not always match the vision. In 1904, visitors to the diocese of Thorn reported that a "very restricted number of families" conducted daily devotions, although mealtime prayers were frequent.

The report from Thorn said that Bible classes, mission study classes, mission festivals, children's worship services, young men and young women's societies, and a diocese-wide Gustavus Adolphus Society were functioning in many places. Sometimes these and other religious activities were instruments of cultural imperialism, through which non-German groups were "initiated" into the empire. Visitors to the diocese of Heydekrug noted in 1885 that some Lithuanian Protestants refused to use tobacco because the Apocalypse referred to smoke, but they were not afraid to use snuff, because God gave man life by blowing into his nostrils. The report suggested that it was time for the Lithuanians to catch up with modern culture, adding that religion would play an important role in bringing them into German culture, "to which <they> must be introduced."

Compulsory Religious Instruction

Just as paradoxical as certain phases of East Prussian church life were the views of some Protestants on compulsory religion in schools. For a few, the relation between church and school no longer seemed as natural and inviting as it once was, while others stressed the traditional alliance more emphatically because of the unevenness of life. Some viewed the admission of young women to German universities in 1900 as another sign of decadence.

The states continued exercising inspectional control over elementary schools, but in general they relied on ecclesiastical functionaries for this work until 1919. The arrangement was reassuring to some conservatives, and disconcerting to some liberals. In any case, it allowed church and state to monitor how effectively religion was being used for patriotic ends, and enabled the state to regulate religious instruction directly. Toward the end of the century, schools were battlefields over the question of religion's place in the culture.

Prussia fired the opening volley in 1882, partly because

right-wing Protestants and Roman Catholics in Lippstadt opposed the Darwinism of an upper level teacher. The government then reduced the number of natural science units in the upper schools' curriculum. Elementary school controls were tightened as well in 1889, when the emperor instructed the schools, above all else, to "lay the foundation for a healthy view of governmental and societal relationships by nurturing divine fear and patriotism." He wrote that firm patriotic and religious foundations would endear students to established powers, and reduce the influence of radical parties. He was especially bothered by current "socialistic and communistic ideas," and urged that religious instruction take up the moral questions which radical groups posed.

The Prussian "gymnasium" promoted a Christian-German educational ideal until the World War. Students received two hours of religious instruction each week in 1901, as had been the rule throughout the century. "Gymnasium" graduates nurtured a strong religious-patriotic ideal in some universities as well. Organized in 1881, the "Kyffhaeuserverband" united students who wanted to defend "Christianity, monarchy, and German character." Students joined others in observing the quadricentennial of Luther's birth in 1883, by reading and reviewing works on Luther by two dramatists, Hans Kerrig and Otto Devrient.

Clearly, the schools were lightning rods for the question of the place of religion in culture. Inspectors of parishes in East Prussia were disturbed in 1885 when a pastor in Katz reported that "he occupied himself with the school as little as possible, since school matters leave no room for the pastor." Even more disconcerting was his failure to evaluate the local teacher, over whom he exercised inspectional responsibility. But religionists often failed, even where they tried to exert influence. Despite conservative resistance, some two hundred and seventy-three teachers in Bremen recommended in 1905 that strict religious orthodoxy not be forced on elementary students. They were especially interested in avoiding contact with the Old Testament, since in their view it presented students with Syrian-Arabic Bedouins, rather than a vibrant Germanic heritage.

Hamburg, the base of a large Social Democratic contingent, had its share of conflict over religious instruction in schools. After several decades of relative peace, the Elementary Teachers Society proposed an end to all religious instruction in the eighties. After 1890 it was possible to exempt from instruction all unbaptized children, children of religious dissenters, and children of parents who did not belong to the established Lutheran church. Around 1905 an educational reform movement, which stressed self-sufficiency and spontaneity as primary educational goals, once again attacked compulsory religious instruction, describing it as an obstacle to emancipation, a "prejudice inimical to culture." Social Democratic leaders offered the same argument.

Three factors interacted between 1903 and 1906 to eliminate compulsory religious instruction in Hamburg's elementary schools. First, biological studies were pitted against religious training. One consequence was the formation of the Monist League in Hamburg in 1906. Second, the demand of teachers in Bremen in 1906 to end religious instruction had an impact in nearby Hamburg. Third, opponents of religious instruction succeeded in politicizing the question in Hamburg; they exerted more influence than their small number suggested. The way was cleared for the secularization of schools after 1918, and while some liberal Lutherans in Hamburg acceded to the development, the conservative Church Society complained that religious instruction was liberal, monistic, and materialistic. This small minority stressed parental rights, and the need for solidly confessional religious instruction.(3)

Massive culural shifts and social changes brought pressure to bear on elementary schools in Germany. Given these circumstances, the question of religious instruction was a nerve nodule of some importance. Voices arose on all sides of the controversy, and the only unanimity was the deep difference of opinion that existed. Prussia resisted the elimination of compulsory religious instruction for the longest period, but even there it was a matter of time. Deep-seated differences about religion in the schools was another signal that the Protestant charter was in trouble.

Rebirth or Rigor Mortis?

Statistics are known to lie, or more precisely, liars are

known to use statistics. A person studying religious history faces this problem too, and that is why a number of interpretations can be offered about statistics on Protestant church life at the close of the century. The same holds true for other data about church life; from one perspective, it seems that the churches were enjoying a fair amount of prosperity; but from another, it is clear that they were living off the dividends of a previous age.

The paradox is that both were true. It was as if two sides of a triangle remained standing without a base, although in a short time they collapsed into a straight line. Social, political, economic, cultural and intellectual changes were making a major impact, and a number of landmarks were passing over the horizon as German society moved toward an uncharted future. One of these landmarks was the consensus about the church's role as a social model. Church life on a broad scale helps us understand what happened, although, paradoxically, the evidence shows signs of both rebirth and rigor mortis.

Protestant churches made superficial and significant changes as a result of social pressures they felt. For example, Berlin's consistory decided in 1890 that confirmands should wear only black clothes at the confirmation ceremony. The reason, it was said, was not to distinguish Protestant from Roman Catholic confirmands, or to show the day's solemn character. Rather, since white clothes usually indicated the parent's wealth, black clothing supposedly would keep social and economic differences to a minimum.

Another pressure point for the churches was the growth of business and commerce on Sunday. After the High Church Council told the Prussian territorial synod in 1879 that the Sabbath's sanctity was endangered everywhere—it blamed railway, postal, and telegraph system managers for making Sunday a day of work, and lowering church attendance to about ten percent in provincial Saxony and the Rhineland—the convention expressed interest in legislation to protect the Sabbath. The imperial "Reichstag" passed a law regulating work on Sunday in 1891.

The growing interest in women's rights brought other changes. Female church workers got their own Bible schools toward the end of the century in Berlin (1896), Bad

542

Freienwald-Oder (1898), Stuttgart (1910), and Dresden (1913). A number of books and articles appeared on the question of women's rights and their religious duties. Most seemed to suport the woman's traditional homemaking role, rather than radical or socialist views, but among the exceptions were Wilhelm Gamper's DIE FRAUENFRAGE UND DAS CHRISTENTHUM (1893); Albert Kalthoff's "Die Frauenfrage," in AN DER WENDE DES JAHRHUNDERTS, KANZELREDEN (1889); and DIE RELIGION UND DIE FRAU, SIEBEN VORTRAEGE, GEHALTEN BEIM 5. WELTKONGRESS FUER FREIES CHRISTENTUM UND RELIGIOESEN FORTSCHRITT, edited by Gertrud Baeumer in 1910.(4)

Pastors came in for their share of criticism by writers and social critics. Toward the century's end, the literary works of Gerhard Hauptmann portrayed ministers as less than heroic figures, although some pursued worthwhile goals, including social welfare and fraternizing with the suffering. But most of the time they seemed unable to achieve their life's goals. Hauptmann's drama, "The Weavers" (1892), compared an older pastor's theological rigidity and social obscurantism with the social insight and courage of a young theological candidate. His novel, THE FOOL IN CHRIST, EMANUEL QUINT (1910), featured an enthusiastic fool who wandered in and out of the lives of pastors without finding the spiritual authenticity he sought. They lacked all prophetic qualities; snatched away from them, the "secret of God's kingdom" resided in naive enthusiasts, such as Quint. Hauptmann wrestled with the paradox that some German pastors showed marks of religiosity, but failed to mirror a depth of spirituality.

Social change moved the churches to organize new voluntary groups and to refurbish old ones. Already in the seventies, the Inner Mission began supporting Sunday School societies and publishing Sunday School literature. By 1910, reportedly 9,000 Sunday Schools were functioning. Many met on Sunday afternoon, like the one in Gumbinnen in East Prussia; it had an attendance of 300 in 1887. The Mission also supported new schools for women and handicapped people, and continued its work with prisoners and released prisoners. In the area of foreign missions, several new mission societies were formed in Schleswig-Holstein and Wuerttemberg. The Basel Mission Society sent its first two medical missionaries into service in 1885-86, and mission groups created special programs for women in other nations, especially China.

By the early nineties, more than 235 journals and religious papers kept Protestants informed on religious life, theological matters, home and foreign missions, and official and unofficial events in church life. One hundred and eighteen of these periodicals printed 1,400,000 total copies of each issue. Ninety were popular publications, such as Sunday weeklies; eighty-eight were published by societies such as the Inner Mission or foreign missions groups; and fifty-one were organs of territorial or provincial churches. Individuals in the Inner Mission organized a number of evangelical press associations toward the end of the century, to help Christians confess their faith in daily life. The first was formed in provincial Saxony in 1891, followed by the Evangelical Press Association of Westphalia (1907) and of Wuerttemberg (1912). Under the leadership of August Hinderer, the Evangelical Press Association of Germany (1910) became the hub of these associations. Its goal was to bring a Christian interpretation of contemporary issues, especially the social problem, to the attention of the public press, in order to influence public opinion. The Evangelical Press Association for Germany was created in order to "have the potential in the daily press to illumine all contemporary questions in the light of the Christian moral world view."

Another important voluntary movement were the new church chorale societies that Heinrich A. Koestlin helped to organize. The first appeared in Wuerttemberg in 1878, followed by others in Baden, the Palatinate, and elsewhere. By 1900, the Evangelical Chorale Society for Germany (1883) had more than 50,000 members. The chorale societies found encouragement in a rash of newly published hymnals and chorale books that often included authentically classic Protestant hymns and chorales from the Reformation. The chorale societies were not church choirs, but volunteers who were interested in music on a more intense level.

Religious statistics can never summarize all the spiritual assistance and religious edification that people received and shared during this period, nor can they conclusively prove whether the church was suffering from rigor mortis or stirring to new life. But statistics can indicate some of the difficulties that Protestant churches were facing at the time, as well as the minimal participation of Protestants in most phases of church life.

The percentage of people who attended church was seldom higher than the percentage of American colonists who were church-goers at the time of the American Revolution, namely, less than ten percent. Although American Protestants scored appreciable gains in the area of church attendance by the end of the nineteenth century, among Protestants in Germany, the consistent trend was downward. In 1892, the committee visiting German Eylau reported that only about 250 of the 5,000 Protestants in this area of East Prussia regularly attended church, while in nearby Loetzen, the figure was 700 of 11,000. Both areas had fewer than ten percent attending church. Attendance in provincial Silesia was not much better toward the end of the century; about ten percent of the nominal Protestant population in Breslau went to church, and five to six percent in Goerlitz. Leignitz's Protestant population of 46,000 was served by two churches with 3,000 seats, and on Sunday they were usually half full or full. In royal Saxony, about three and one-half percent of Dresden's 300,000 Lutherans attended church. One church historian estimates that in large cities, only about three percent of the population attended church.(5)

Figures for annual communion attendance were not much better. Royal Saxony seemed to be something of an exception, with 48 percent of its Lutherans reportedly communing some time in 1874, and 46% in 1900. The fourteen churches (75,000 members) of the East Prussian diocese of Elbing had an average annual communion attendance of 26 percent in 1912. By contrast, twenty years earlier, the diocese of Carthaus had no congregaton with fewer than 56 percent of its members communing at least once annually.

Baptism remained popular, despite the states' assuming responsibility for keeping vital statistics, which allowed people to avoid the rite if they chose. The number of baptisms dropped in some places when this legislation was enacted in the seventies, but the custom, which included the traditional baptismal party, prevailed. In Silesian Leignitz, 94 percent of the children of Protestant parents were baptized in 1875, and by 1900 the figure climbed to 98 percent. In royal Saxony, 95 percent of the children of Protestant parents were baptized between 1876 and 1898, but seven percent of the nominal Protestant children refused the rite of confirmation during the same period. In Berlin, 26 percent of the children were unbaptized in 1880, but in 1893, only 12 percent of the newborn infants remained unbaptized. Marriages and funerals showed a similar upward trend in Berlin; in 1880, fifty-eight percent of the marriages were performed by civil authorities, but by 1893 the figure dropped to only 36 percent. In 1880, eighty percent of the funerals were performed without religious rites, but by 1893 the percentage decreased to 63 percent. Berlin's city mission was partly responsible for these changes; the same was true in other major cities, where twenty-seven city mission societies were operating by 1887.

New liturgical agendas provided the liturgy for regular services, baptisms, weddings and funerals. Despite spirited protests from Spitta, Smend, and other liturgical experts, Prussia issued a new agenda in 1894, after the king insisted on his right to revise the liturgy. Hesse's new agenda appeared in 1904, and other state churches revised their liturgies as well. Most new agendas eliminated prayers for the dead, an item that many agendas included earlier in the century.

Apparently the most appropriate vocal inflection for speaking or chanting the Sunday liturgy was the "ministerial tone." At least that was implied by the commission that visited churches in East Prussia near the end of the century. Their reports often commended the use of a firm, strong voice in liturgy and preaching. In 1887, the visitors criticized the pastor in Judtschen for using a conversational tone in liturgy; the "extraordinarily sorry liturgy" he conducted "lacked all solemnity and majesty." The pastor may have been more human than the visitors thought appropriate, since he also instituted short services for children.

One other set of statistics illuminates church life in the century's closing decades. The number of people who legally terminated their membership in territorial churches increased as the years passed, although the total never represented more than a fraction of one percent of the total legal membership. Bewteen 1884 and 1905, the number of official withdrawals from all the territorial churches fluctuated between 1,800 and 6,300 each year. It rose to 17,400 in 1906 (with 12,000 in Prussia alone), then hovered between 14,300 and 29,000 up to 1914. After plummeting to between 3,700 and 8,700 during the war—it was unpatriotic to quit the church during this national crisis!—the number of withdrawals leaped to an astounding 250,000 adults in 1919.

Despite the relatively small number of legal withdrawals in the last quarter of the century, preachers and church publications viewed the phenomenon with alarm. In 1892, Elberfeld's REFORMED WEEKLY lamented the fact that twenty-seven people in the area recently terminated their church membership. These "foolish Galatians" looked to the church to solve their social problem, when in fact people gathered in church to pray and hear God's word, said the periodical. But withdrawals continued to occur even while new congregations were being established, sometimes by dividing old ones. Between 1891 and 1904, fourteen new congregations were created in East Prussia alone.

Occasional signs of rebirth could not hide the fact that Protestantism was big business, and in view of circumstances, it was a major challenge just to keep the churches financed and functioning. A vocational census for the empire in 1883 showed that Germany had 40,000 pastors, priests, and church officials working in all confessions, including Roman Catholicism. Assuming that Protestant and Roman Catholic churches were distributed equally throughout the different demographic units, Protestantism's overwhelmingly agrarian and small-town complexion was apparent. Even at this late date, the majority of church workers in all confessions performed their duties in small towns or rural areas. The census provided the following data:

SIZE OF COMMUNITY	NUMBER OF CHURCH WORKERS (All Confessions)
100,000+	1,819
20,000—100,000	2,757
5,000—20,000	4,341
2,000—5,000	5,591
under 2,000	25,296

Most pastors continued serving very large groups of Protestants. In 1905, each clergyman in provincial Saxony had an average congregation of 1,600, while in Wuerttemberg the ratio was 1:1,350. Hamburg's population of 900,000 in 1900 reportedly included 800,000 Lutherans; one hundred pastors, forty churches, and three chapels served the group. In 1911, Prussia had 9,620 pastors in office (about one-half of all of the Protestant ministers in Germany), and 8,390 parishes; twenty-four general superintendents and 639 superintendents provided supervision. Nearly 12,000 churches and 4,300 other buildings were set aside for religious use. In 1910, the minimum annual salary of a Prussian pastor was 2,260 "Mark," the equivalent of about $565 at the time.

In Prussia and elsewhere, most clergymen performed their duties as faithful government officials. The state's ecclesiastical bureaucracy curbed the church's use of its system of self-government. The golden jubilee publication of the High Church Council in 1900 touted this feature as a positive factor in Prussian church life. The publication stressed that the state's ecclesiastical bureaucracy played the most important role in church polity, followed in turn by church synods and presbyterial systems.

On a national scale, the territorial churches defended their prerogatives, even at the cost of not having a national church. There was little likelihood that a religious rebirth would occur at any expense to the territorial churches. The Eisenach Conference continued functioning as an evangelical federal diet, without legislative power. It limited its work to revising Luther's Bible translation (completed in 1892); gathering church statistics; publishing a songbook and prayerbook for the army (1890); arranging a united celebration of Reformation Day, and in northern Germany a Day of Humiliation and Prayer at the end of the church year; and several other projects. In 1903 the Conference created the "Deutsche-Evangelische Kirchenausschuss" (Standing Committee of the Territorial Churches), with headquarters in Berlin. This commission of fifteen members was charged with conducting relations with non-German churches and supervising the religious welfare of Germans abroad, but the territorial churches had to ratify its decisions. The Conference insisted that "the ecclesiastical-governmental rights of the territorial princes remain intact." After 1908 the senior official of Prussia's territorial church served as the committee's president.

Church life was filled with signs of death and rebirth in the pre-war decades. But a body's twitch can just as readily signify the muscular stiffening that accompanies rigor mortis as it can indicate life. Church life was loaded with paradox, as the revival movement toward the end of the century attests.

Revival Movement and the Free Churches

Rooted in a resurgence of old German pietism, a major revival movement spread through Protestantism in the pre-war decades.(6) This movement's story, together with developments in the free (non-territorial) churches, heightens the impression of paradox in church life.

The roots of the "Gemeinschaftsbewegung" (alliance movement) reach back to seventeenth-century pietism, a religious movement that was perpetuated by the "Stundenleute" of Wuerttemberg, and other small groups, which in turn created organizational alliances between 1857 and 1873. But a major impulse for this renewed religious zeal late in the century came from American and British revival movements. Through printed sermons, and sometimes their personal visits, Robert Pearsall Smith, Edward Irving, Charles Spurgeon, Charles Finney, Dwight Moody, and others carried the good news of God's grace to Protestants in Germany.

These revivalists enunciated the kinds of themes that became standard ones for the people of the "Gemeinschaftsbewegung:" the gospel demands repentance and decision for Christ; precise differences distinguish the converted from the unconverted; God's people make willful changes in behavior in their search for a perfect, holy life (an ethical optimism that in some ways paralleled certain Ritschlian emphases); the Christian is obligated to pray fervently; people practice the doctrine of universal priesthood by supporting foreign missions and evangelizing for Christ; and eschatological matters are of great importance.

Robert Pearsall Smith led the way with a revival tour in 1875. After hearing his message of sanctification at Oxford in 1874, several pastors invited him to visit Germany the next year. Smith preached progressive holiness at revivals in Berlin, Basel, Stuttgart, Frankfurt am Main, and elsewhere, attracting opposition as well as crowds up to 8,000 people.

In 1881, the first extended evangelistic effort came to Berlin when court preacher Stoecker invited the American evangelist Friedrich von Schluembach (1842-1901), a native German who had moved to the United States at age seventeen. This Methodist preacher showed Berliners and people in other cities the kind of revivalistic services that made Moody famous in America. Stoecker insisted that he speak to the weak and the faltering, not the committed.

Schluembach also played an important role in new evangelistic programs for young men in large cities. Societies for young men had been functioning in many areas since the century's second quarter, but they were ill-equipped to assist young men in cities. In 1875, some two hundred societies formed regional organizations, and in 1882 Schluembach attended their "national festival," which stressed the need for Bible study among university and "gymnasium" students. Bible study clubs began meeting in a number of places, and especially after 1909 the movement flourished, with over 300 societies in 200 towns and cities.

But Schluembach and others recognized that these Bible study groups were not meeting the need to evangelize young men in large cities. He viewed the Young Men's Christian Association (YMCA) as a model, partly because he was one of the group's important leaders in North America. With the assistance of Eberhard von Rothkirch (1852-1911), he was instrumental in organizing the first "Christlich Verein Junger Maenner" (CVJM, Christian Society for Young Men) in Berlin in 1883. At the end of its first year, this lay-led group had more than 600 members, and soon a number of CVJM societies emerged as headquarters for evangelistic efforts in other major cities. Some complained that the groups' "Methodist" practices were theologically unsound, but the tide ran on. Berlin's CVJM provided the impetus for another evangelistic effort, called the "Deutsche Christliche Studentvereinigung" (DCSV, German Christian Student Union). It was formed in 1890 for evangelism among students by students. Count Eduard von Pueckler was its major leader until 1911.

If there was any one organizational impetus for the modern "Gemeinschaftsbewegung," it was probably the German Evangelistic Society, founded in 1884 by Theodor Christlieb, a theological professor in Bonn, and Jaspar von Oertzen (1833-1893), the chief lay leader of the City Mission in Hamburg. With this society they proposed to achieve Wichern's goal of evangelizing Germany. But, as indicated, a number of evangelistic efforts were already underway before this society was formed, and the "Gemeinschaftsbewegung" was too multifarious a movement to be strapped into any one organizational structure.

The movement continued to grow as individuals, especially laypersons, organized evangelistic efforts and formed cells and groups of "born-again" Christans. In the main, the "Gemeinschaftsbewegung" was a lay movement in which people tried to implement Christlieb's guiding principle: "In the church, if possible with the church, but not under the church." The territorial churches usually tolerated the revival, with varying degrees of enthusiasm. In sociological terms, most participants came from the bourgeoisie and the middle social strata; they were people who found little feeling of community in the territorial churches. The alliance grew rapidly in the nineties, when a variety of revivalistic and evangelistic methods paid their dividends.

Foremost among the movement's revivalists were Elias Schrenk (1831-1913), the German Evangelistic Society's chief evangelist after 1884. Schrenk conducted revivals in Bern, Frankfurt, and throughout Germany. Another revivalist, Otto Stockmayer (1838-1917), performed prayer healings, but opposed the excesses of pentecostals. Christian Dietrich (1844-1919) of Stuttgart was an important evangelist, as was Theodor Jellinghaus (1841-1913), the movement's unofficial theologian, and the founder of an important evangelistic training school near Berlin.

The "Gemeinschaftsbewegung" eventually found an unofficial organizational focus in 1888, when the German Evangelistic Society invited a number of leaders to a conference in Gnadau. Subsequently, the "Gnadau Pentecost Conference" was held annually, first at Gnadau and then in other locations. Many of the old pietist groups sent representatives to these meetings, as did the newer evangelistic groups; the agenda included inspirational talks, Bible study, prayer, sharing, and discussion of evangelistic techniques. The Conference organized the German Committee of Evangelical Communal Edification and Evangelization, as well as other groups.

Interest in holiness and personal sanctification became so intense in the "Gemeinschaftsbewegung" between 1904 and 1909 that it nearly shattered the movement. Exported from the western United States via Norway, speaking in tongues surfaced for the first time in Germany in 1907, in Hamburg and Kassel. Spirit baptism and speaking in tongues created such pentecostal fervor in Kassel that the police had to restore order. In Silesia, nearly half of the Alliance's groups split off and entered the pentecostal circle. The next year, fifty pentecostals from throughout Germany held a major conference in Hamburg. The "Gemeinschftsbewegung's" crisis ended only after fifty-six of its major leaders signed the "Berlin Declaration" (1909), which labelled tongue-speaking and other pentecostal activities as "demonic." After World War I began, people in the "Gemeinschaftsbewegung" closed ranks more fully with the territorial churches, although most had not legally withdrawn from the church. The passing of time and the pressures of war undoubtedly were factors in this development.

Some people in the Alliance joined the various free or independent (non-territorial) churches that experienced growth during the pre-war decades. Reportedly by 1914 the various free churches had 150,000 members, including 28,000 Methodists and 43,000 Baptists. The free churches' rather dismal growth record—their total membership numbered about half of the people who legally withdrew from Protestant churches in 1919—points to the state churches' hammer-hold on German Protestants. The churches had no real competition or "loyal opposition," and that was one factor in their inability to meet many of the challenges of the nineteenth century. The Evangelical Lutheran (Old Lutheran) Church, which began in Breslau before mid-century, garnered only 60,000 members by 1918, up ten thousand since 1860. The other Lutheran free churches, including the Evangelical Lutheran Free Church in Nassau, were no more successful. Baden's religious statistics for 1900 tell the story well. The Protestant territorial church numbered 700,000, and there were 1,100,000 Roman Catholics; the free churches had only 4,200 members (1,600 Lutherans, 400 Reformed, 600 Mennonites, and 1,600 others).

For some time, some of the free churches were closely connected with the "Gemeinschaftsbewegung." That was true of the Irvingites (including the new Irvingites), also called the Catholic Apostolic Church. The Pentecostals organized another free church after they separated from the "Gemeinschaftsbewegung." Their leaders included the Silesian preacher, Eugen Edel (1872-1951).

The Pentecostals were not the only group that owed its origin to American influence. After an abortive start in 1876, the Seventh Day Adventists made a more stable beginning in 1888, with Ludwig R. Conradi's help. The small group used colportage and other means to multiply; its one thousand members in 1897 increased fourteen-fold by the war. Among other American groups that made small inroads were the Mormons (1861), Christian Scientists (1899), Jehovah Witnesses (1903), and Salvation Army (1896). William Booth found a number of Salvation Army corps already operative when he visited for the first time in 1891. Jacob Junker (d. 1901) was an important worker after joining the group in 1889.

The Methodist church started with English impetus in the south, and American influence in the north. Before mid-century, a Swabian named Gottlieb Mueller carried English Methodism to his homeland, but the groups remained in the territorial church until 1872. A native of Bremen named L. S. Jakoby brought American Methodism to his home, conducting his first service in Bremen in 1849. His two hundred followers spread the news to other cities, and by 1886 there were 11,000 in the group. After Wesleyan Methodists from the south united with the American-influenced northerners, the number of German Methodists climbed to 25,500 by 1908.

Influenced by English Baptists, Johann G. Oncken (1800-1884) began working in Hamburg in 1823. The Sunday School played an important role in early efforts. A visiting American finally baptized Oncken in the Elbe River in 1834, and then, with eight others, he organized the first Baptist congregation. Church and civil authorities opposed his work, and even imprisoned him until the atmosphere changed in 1843. In 1837, a copperplate engraver named G. W. Lehmann (1799–1882) organized the second group of Baptists, in Berlin. The group had 800 members by 1870. Baptists formed a federation at mid-century, and by the eighties Germany counted 31,000 Baptists in her borders.

Other free churches and religious groups also made small beginnings, including counterparts of American Unitarians, and free thought movements. At mid-century, the German branch of the Evangelical United Brethren Church, the Evangelical Association, began witnessing in Wuerttemberg and Baden. Another group, the "Evangelical-Johannine Church," was not officially organized until 1926, but its founder, Joseph Weissberg, began prophesying and reportedly performing miracles in Berlin at the turn of the century. He claimed to contact departed spirits and to exorcise devils. The group grew phenomenally, and by 1934, 400 congregations reported a membership of 100,000. August H. Hain, a visionary who claimed to be God's sixth incarnation, established a small community, called "Shepherd and Flock," among industrial workers in Saxony late in the century. He and his followers (600 in 1913) were perfectionists who looked for the period of Sabbath rest, when the world would attain its goal. Johann E. Keller organized another millennial band in Berlin, claiming that Israel's ten lost tribes wandered to Europe as Germans.

Religious life in the pre-war decades featured a number of paradoxes, esoteric movements, and polarizing currents. A cursory glance at religious statistics, Protestant church life in East Prussia, the debate about religious instruction in schools, and revivalist and free church movements shows the abundance of deep sentiments, extremes, and extremists of all kinds. The churches were floundering in their effort to project a clear image of "freedom within authority" to the society.

There were at least three reasons why the unwritten Protestant charter was in trouble. First, increased religious pluralism failed to hide the sloth of many leaders and laypersons, nor did it prevent the outcropping of religious zeal outside of normal institutional boundaries. The net result was that the churches transmitted a garbled message to society. Second, rapid changes in society and culture made it more difficult for the churches to make contact with their social target. Finally, ineffective political leadership contributed to the confusion. The next section explains as well how the failure of liberal theologians to revitalize cultural Protestantism dealt a severe blow to Protestant foundations, and to the uncodified charter.

LIBERALISM ADRIFT

Proponents of cultural Protestantism faced increasing difficulty as they tried to interpret Christian theology for their culture. Some felt more comfortable expressing their opinions in academic halls than in parish pulpits. But a phase of the "modernist controversy" erupted nonetheless when several pastors were charged with heresy in celebrated "Faelle," or cases. The liberals' growing uncertainty foreshadowed the end of cultural Protestant theology, announced so triumphantly by Karl Barth after the end of World War I. The unwritten Protestant charter now faced theoretical as well as practical problems, since foundational collapse endangered its theoretical undergirdings, which reached back to Schleiermacher, Hegel, and others.

Liberal Theology

The difficulties of traditional philosophy in the second half of the century complicated liberal efforts to coordinate religion and culture in a meaningful way. In the seventies, eighties, and nineties, Protestant imperialism was an important factor in the emperor's visit to Jerusalem, colonial missions and mission theory, the "Kulturkampf," and church renovation and construction. It also flowed in the veins of Ritschl and other cultural Protestants. But theological liberalism was being forced to use history rather than philosophy as its point of contact with culture, and that shift dramatically affected its fortunes.

The Ritschlian school continued making a major contribution

through the work of Theodor von Haering (1848-1928), who modified Ritschlianism in a conservative direction; Johann Wilhelm Hermann (1846-1922); Julius Kaftan (1848-1926); Karl Holl (1866-1926); Ferdinand Kattenbusch (1851-1935); Richard Adelbert Lipsius (1830-1892); Adolf von Harnack (1851-1930); and others who showed Ritschl's influence. The Lutheran church historian, Friedrich Loofs (1858-1928), mined the history of dogma and vigorously opposed Haeckel's monism, while Friedrich Rittelmeyer (1872-1938), and Christian K. L. Geyer (1862-1929), represented cultural Protestantism in Bavaria, founding a journal entitled CHRISTENTUM UND GEGENWART in 1910.

The historical interest of many Ritschlians deserves further consideration. Ritschl set his followers on course by stressing God's revelation through concrete manifestations in the phenomenal world, and vigorously opposing any hint of mysticism. Cultural Protestant theologians took up the use of history as an apologetic tool since, on the one hand, the philosophical age was past, and on the other hand, the Prussian "school of historians" was acclaimed for rehearsing the story of Prussia's expansion on behalf of Germany. Much like Treitschke, Mommsen, and other "political" historians, who were interpreting Prussia's history positively by constructing a catalog of military and political successes, these theologians tried to throw a positive light on Christian history. Their discussion of Christian history, and their historically-informed Biblical studies, could give the masses some credit without disturbing social and ecclesiastical equilibrium. In their hands, history became the great "leveler," much as secular historians interpreted Prussia's role in the quest for German unity.

Heavily indebted to history, this idiosyncratic form of cultural Protestantism was not without its dangers to the church, as the eccentric church historian, Franz C. Overbeck (1837-1905), showed. As a teacher at Jena and Basel, he advocated a rigorously secular interpretation of church history, especially its early origins. His friendship with Nietzsche, and his indefatigable criticism of both orthodox and liberal theology, as well as his professed atheism after about 1870, did little to endear him to Protestants. He wrote in a document published posthumously that "there is nothing miraculous in the church's history," and argued that for modern Christianity, "the most spiritual and real need rests in doing it."

At one time this established scholar had been a close friend of a young instructor named Adolf Harnack, but their ways soon parted. Harnack became one of the century's most celebrated historians and theologians, while Overbeck remained aloof from church battles and drew little positive response. Despite his success, the church withheld nearly all official recognition from Harnack, even refusing him the privilege of examining students of his who entered ecclesiastical service. His only direct contribution to church life was membership in the Evangelical-Social Congress, in which he was also an officer. But still he exerted overpowering influence through his scholarly and professional work.

A gifted scholar who reportedly could memorize a page of Greek text after reading it slowly, Harnack was less interested than Overbeck in trying to write presuppositionless history. He argued that history gives no absolute judgments, which arise only subjectively from feeling and will. As an historian he worked on three levels, pursuing source criticism, presenting the data, and reflecting; he felt most comfortable with the third. His approach made him the last grand representative of nineteenth century Protestant theology in Germany, and he is more intelligible in terms of predecessors and teachers, including Ritschl and the eminent historian from Tuebingen, Ferdinand C. Baur, than his successors, especially Barth.

Harnack began his career teaching in Leipzig, Giessen, and Marburg, but he exerted his greatest influence in Berlin, where he was called to teach in 1888. Prussia's High Church Council opposed his call to the university since some churchmen objected to his views, which supposedly included criticism of miracles, and rejection of conventional understandings of Jesus' virgin birth, resurrection, and ascension. But Harnack retained the support of the theological faculty and Ministry of Education, and after Bismarck's cabinet recommended the appointment, the emperor signed the official document. Though he was no match for Harnack, the conservative scholar, Adolf Schlatter (1852-1938), was called to the faculty five years later as a counterbalance. During negotiations about his own call, Harnack wrote a memorandum to the Ministry of Education that summarized his views in a helpful way. "Neither exegesis nor dogmatics," he wrote,

> but the results of church-historical research will
> break the power of the traditions which are now
> burdening the consciences of men. Cardinal Manning
> once made the following frivolous statement: "One
> must overcome history by dogma;" we say just the
> opposite: Dogma must be purified by history. As
> Protestants we are confident that by doing this we
> do not break down but build up.(7)

Harnack taught at Berlin until 1921, when he took emeritus status, but teaching was only part of his work. The Prussian Academy of Sciences elected him to membership in 1890, and Mommsen enthusiastically welcomed this embodiment of cultural Protestantism. Soon the prestigious group asked him to write its bicentennial history. In 1906 he became the Director General of perhaps the most important library in Germany, the Royal Library in Berlin. Five years later he was named president of the Emperor William "Gesellschaft," a foundation that sponsored pure and applied scientific research that was not being pursued by university scholars. William II invited him to court, and he was the last scholar ennobled by Prussian royalty. In 1921 he declined to serve as Germany's ambassador to the United States.

Harnack influenced an inordantly large number of students, including Dietrich Bonhoeffer. He wrote more than 1,600 works of varying sizes, concentrating his energies in early Christian, reformational, and Protestant subjects. Despite his prodigious accomplishments, he is most often remembered for a lecture series delivered in Berlin in 1899-1900, which was stenographically recorded and published as WESEN DES CHRISTENTUMS (WHAT IS CHRISTIANITY?, 15th ed. 1950). He created a major stir with the claim that the Christian religion is one thing: eternal life in the midst of time, not an ethical or social arcanum for general improvement. His popular description of Christianity criticized those who identified it with dogma, or equated it with the gospel about Jesus. The gospel is the good news that God is our Father and we are His children, he wrote; it is the higher righteousness of the commandment of love; it is God's kingdom and its coming in the individual's life in justice, righteousness, love, and other values; it is the value of the individual soul and eternity's invasion of time. Jesus was a heroic figure, a founder who led men to his Father.

Harnack challenged Protestants to seek an ecumenical unity that was not based on dogmatism or doctrinal authoritarianism. He also encouraged them to throw off dogmatic burdens about Jesus' personhood, and insisted that Protestants "clearly decide" against the Old Testament's canonicity.(8) But Barth and others soon showed that Harnack was speaking to an aristocratic age of cultural Protestantism that was past. His inability to win a place in the church was symptomatic of a deeper chasm between church and culture that liberal theologians could not bridge, despite their substantial accomplishments.

Historical and dogmatic theology were not the only concerns of liberal theologians at the end of the century. They also pursued biblical theology. Their work was often based on the textual criticism of other scholars, who were not always favorably disposed toward liberal Protestantism. Among the important "lower textual" critics, who sometimes by choice or necessity also took up "higher" criticism, were Friedrich C. von Tischendorf (1815-1874), who discovered the Codex Sinaiticus, and published eight editions of the New Testament; Bernhard Weiss (1827-1918), Johannes' father, and an important textual critic; and Christoph Eberhard Nestle (1851-1913), whose New Testament Greek text was first published by the Bible Society in Stuttgart in 1898. Lagarde worked on the Septuagint, while Seligmann Baer and Franz Delitzsch published the Hebrew Bible in installments, omitting some books. Rudolf Kittel (1853-1929) made the most important contribution in Old Testament textual studies, with critical editions of the Hebrew text in 1906 (1st ed.) and 1912 (2nd ed.). In subsequent editions, this text has remained standard in Christian circles to the present.

In the hands of liberal scholars, as the century progressed, Old Testament biblical theology tended to dissolve into the religious history of Israel. Following the lead of Wilhelm Gesenius (1785-1842), Heinrich Ewald (1803-1875), Ferdinand Hitzig (1807-1875), and Johann Karl W. Vatke (1806-1882), scholars such as Julius Wellhausen (1844-1918) and Friedrich Delitzsch (1850-1922) stressed historical over theological themes in Old Testament studies, as did Augustus Kayser.

559

Rudolph Smend initiated a series on Israel's religious history in ALTTESTAMENTLICHE RELIGIONSGESCHICHTE (1893), which was continued by Giesebrecht (1904), Loehr (1906), Klautzsch (1911), Marti (1907), and others. Gustav Hoelscher's GESCHICHTE DER ISRAELITISCHEN UND JUEDISCHEN RELIGION (1922) epitomized the purely historical works. Conservative Old Testament scholars naturally leaned more toward traditional theology. They included Johann Keil (1807-1888), Johannes Bleek (1793-1859), H. A. C. Haevernick (1811-1845), Gustav F. Oehler (1812-1872), Franz Delitzsch (1813-1890), and Martin Kaehler (1835-1912).

Developments in New Testament studies were closely linked with the emergence of historical-critical methods, and the "history of religions school." After Strauss presented new hypotheses earlier in the century, and drew a rejoiner from F. C. Baur, New Testament studies tended to concentrate on such important figures as Jesus and Paul. In 1863, Heinrich J. Holtzmann delineated the figure of the "historical Jesus," and subsequently liberals pursued this line of research with special interest. Holtzmann's NEW TESTAMENT THEOLOGY (1866-99), and Karl Heinrich von Weizsaecker's study of early Christianity, were rejected by conservatives such as Bernhard Weiss, Theodor Zahn and Schlatter. Meanwhile, religious-historical research threw new light on Christianity's Jewish and Hellenistic connections, while form criticism began to affect New Testament studies, as it had Old Testament work. In a pamphlet entitled TASK AND METHOD OF SO-CALLED NEW TESTAMENT THEOLOGY (1897), Wilhelm Wrede (1859-1906) urged that the history of religion of primitive Christianity replace New Testament theology. Among others, Heinrich Weinel and Julius Kaftan took up his proposal, while Wilhelm Heitmueller (1869-1926) and Wilhelm Bousset (1865-1920) also stressed the importance of history of religions for study of the New Testament. Conservative opponents included Paul Feine.

But the most important contribution to the study of Christian origins came from Albert Schweitzer, whose epochal work was mentioned earlier. He questioned the liberals' total reliance on history in New Testament studies by posing the hypothesis that, historically speaking, Jesus' most descriptive characteristic was his apocalyptic sense. Together with Johannes Weiss, Schweitzer dealt a death blow to Protestant liberalism; he argued that since a supra-historical outlook dominated Jesus, theologians needed to look beyond history. This proposal set the stage for shifts in theology after World War I. Schweitzer claimed that in WHAT IS CHRITIANITY?, Harnack almost "entirely ignores the contemporary limitations of Jesus' teaching, and starts out with a Gospel which carries him down without difficulty to the year 1899." He concluded that Jesus remained an enigmatic stranger who should be permitted to return to his own age; in that way, he summoned a person to his own contemporary mission. Schweitzer's uncommon life provided his own commentary on the concluding lines of his major work:

> He comes to us as One unknown, without a name, as of old, by the lake-side, He came to those men who knew Him not. He speaks to us the same word: "Follow thou me!" and sets us to the tasks which He has to fulfil for our time. He commands. And to those who obey Him, whether they be wise or simple, He will reveal Himself in the toils, the conflicts, the sufferings which they shall pass through in His fellowship, and, as an ineffable mystery, they shall learn in their own experience Who He is.(9)

But for the present, the intitiative in biblical studies remained with the history of religions school. The "Religionsgeschichtliche Schule" did much to split the hermeneutical question about the Bible into two tenses, "What did it mean then?", and "What does it mean now?" Among the school's founders were Lagarde, Gunkel, Bousset, Weiss, Wrede, Albert Eichorn (1856-1926), and others. The philologist Richard Reitzenstein also pursued Old Testament studies from this perspective. The school generally held that the two testaments were less firmly linked together than had previously been assumed; it was claimed that the New Testament's development hinged more on Hellenistic influence than on post-exilic Judaism.

One clear sign of the growing influence of this new historical-religious school was the famous "Bible-Babel Battle" of 1901. In that year, the Assyriologist Friedrich Delitzsch, an anti-Semite, discussed the recently unearthed Code of Hammurabi in three lectures in Berlin. A number of churchmen protested when he emphasized that the discovery would surely have radical consequences for traditional understandings of the Old Testament. The press soon took up the battle, as did a well-known pantomimist. Interest was high since the emperor attended the first lecture, held in his Berlin palace, and then invited Delitzsch to discuss matters with court preacher Dryander present. The emperor quickly silenced rumors that he was deserting the faith by releasing a personal confession that was published in the press; but his confession broached the question of "revelation" in a way that caused discomfort to many theologians, including Harnack.

One other influential member of the history of religions school was Ernst Troeltsch (1865-1913), a professor at Heidelberg and Berlin, who sought to relate Christianity and culture in the broad context of religious history. Insistent that all religions were dependent on their cultural setting, he rejected dogmatic theology's supra-historical and absolute truth claims. Troeltsch explored themes that emerged from the intersecting of historicism and religion; he is best known for his major study of the interrelation of Christianity and civilization, THE SOCIAL TEACHING OF THE CHRISTIAN CHURCH. The sociologist Max Weber influenced him appreciably in Heidelberg, and the historian Friedrich Meinecke in Berlin. At a time when neither theology nor history seemed to offer sound footing, he searched for a solid foundation. Following the important philosopher, Wilhelm Dilthey, he tried to pursue subjects that offered spiritual substance, but like Dilthey, he realized that relativism could bring one to the precipice of unassailable scepticism. His effort to countermand scepticism with ethics was less successful than he might have liked.

Rade's "CHRISTIAN WORLD"

Cultural Protestantism's most important voice in these decades was not one or another academician or scholarly work, but the journal entitled CHRISTIAN WORLD. Its pages included articles by Troeltsch, Gunkel, Bousset, Rittelmeyer, Harnack, and many other important liberals. Its founders hoped to spread Ritschl's insights on the Reformation, and Harnack's important discoveries on the early church, and soon the paper became the chief organ of the Ritschlians. But in contrast with the THEOLOGISCHE

LITERATURZEITUNG (1876), which Harnack and Emil Schuerer established for criticism of theological works, its founders wanted to inform the "educated bloc," not merely theologians, about the pressing problems of modern Christianity. Martin Rade (1857-1940) was the editor of the CHRISTIAN WORLD until 1932.

The CHRISTIAN WORLD'S founders in 1886 included Rade, Loofs, Paul Drews (1858-1912), and Wilhelm Bornemann (1857-1946), all Ritschlians. The editorial group at first succeeded in making it a paper for the whole of Protestantism rather than a church party rag. Early issues focused on the social problem, with articles by Naumann, Goehre, and others who knew the subject well. Then the paper followed the times, and began covering the history of religions movement. Its strong defense of Harnack in 1888 moved it closer to the stereotype of a church party paper, and its defense of pastors accused of modernism pulled it sharply to the left, where it remained. Despite good intentions, it had become a party paper; all doubt was removed when the Association of Friends of the CHRISTIAN WORLD was formed in 1904. The group had 1,000 members a year later, and the WORLD had 5,000 subscribers. The paper supported "free Protestantism," and the spiritual freedom it called the gift of Protestantism.

Rade worked as a parish pastor until 1899, when he resigned to edit the paper full-time. For a short period early in the new century he also taught at Marburg. His editorial position provided impetus for the important theological encyclopedia, DIE RELIGION IN GESCHICHTE UND GEGENWART. His articulate editorials in the WORLD included one that severely criticized the Germans for being too cowed by authority when a "dangerous fissure" opened in foreign relations, after the emperor held a disastrous interview with the DAILY TELEGRAPH in 1908.

Modernist "Cases"

The heresy charges brought against several pastors in celebrated "Faelle," or cases, provide a clearer understanding of the fate of liberalism in these decades. Legal charges against theological insurgents provided little reassurance that the church was the state's model for society, its pattern for "freedom within authority." The unwritten Protestant charter was showing signs of wear; things seemed to be coming apart.

The problem had its origin back in the eighteen-twenties, when the liturgical agenda of Prussia and other states made the Apostles Creed obligatory in certain services and ceremonies, including ordinations. The battle over the Apostles Creed in the second half of the century was part of the continuing opposition to the agenda as an instrument of governmental control, but the opposition now included strains of theological modernism as well. Some liberals questioned the Creed's declaration of "fides historica," just as they questioned its traditional emphasis on saving faith, and its purported Greek metaphysics and dated world views. The battle over the Creed showed that theological pluralism was raising the level of stress in parish life. In addition, some who opposed the Creed were caught up in the subjectivistic spirit that was influencing culture in these years.

Several cases involving the Creed erupted at mid-century, but the struggle intensified in the late seventies when two old pastors, Adolf Sydow (b. 1800) and Emil G. Lisco (b. 1810), delivered lectures in Berlin on aspects of the Apostles Creed. After an investigation, Lisco was reprimanded; the consistory suspended Sydow from office, although the High Church Council, under Falk's urgings, later reduced his sentence to a "sharp reprimand." In the eighties, cases occurred in Saxony, Schleswig-Holstein (where Luehrs was released from office in 1881), Nassau, and elsewhere; in most of the suspensions or reprimands, parts of the Creed were involved. Those who opposed Harnack's call to teach in Berlin in 1888 also exploited the issue.

A major stir was created by charges brought against Christoph Schrempf (1860-1944), a thirty-one year old Swabian cleric from Leuzendorf, who had been influenced by Weizsaecker's biblical studies. Although the church in Wuerttemberg required the use of the Apostles Creed only in baptismal ceremonies, Schrempf attempted to elminate it there as well. He told his congregation that parts of the creed, including the phrases "conceived by the Holy Ghost," "born of the Virgin Mary," and "resurrection of the body," were unacceptable to him, and to many in the territorial church. After the congregation petitioned the consistory, he was released from office in 1892. In 1909 he left the territorial church and organized a group of freethinkers. He was known for translating and editing the works of Kierkegaard.

Harnack and the emperor offered different responses to this event in southern Germany. While Harnack refused to advise his students on how to eliminate the Creed from the Prussian agenda, his published remarks on the Creed in the CHRISTIAN WORLD created a storm of controversy. He reiterated what he had said in his scholarly writings for some time, namely, that the Creed should be replaced by a more adequate representation of modern Christian belief. But until this was done by a general synod, not individuals, theologians should busy themselves offering valid new interpretations. Only two phrases, he said, caused him immediate difficulty; they were "conceived by the Holy Ghost," and "born of the Virgin Mary." Liberals did not find this advice totally acceptable, and neither did conservative church papers. Unofficial groups of all kinds met to give their opinions on the issues involved.

In October of 1892, the young emperor gave a speech to the German princes in commemoration of Luther's "Theses," in which he championed the orthodox position. He made a public confession in "Jesus Christ, God's incarnate Son," and asked all servants of the evangelical church to remain faithful to the Word of God as expressed in the spirit of the Reformation. Prussia's High Church Council then issued a circular to the general superintendents deploring Harnack's views, and reaffirming the church's confessional position and liturgical use of the Creed. The High Church Council in Baden, on the other hand, took a more moderate course by refusing to act against Pastor Georg Laengin, despite the appeal of 300 parishioners.

Prussian church officials also acted firmly when they released the new "Agenda" in 1894. In 1891, a liturgical commission had recommended that the Apostles Creed not be used in the ordination formula, but a newly constituted commission later recommended just the opposite. In a compromise designed to satisfy the middle and the right at the expense of the left, the new agenda's ordination formula repeated the earlier agenda's commitment to the faith of the scriptures and the "three Christian creeds," but then the ordinand was to recite the Apostles Creed.

A rash of dismissals, reprimands, and other disciplinary action against clerics followed during the nineties, and the first decade of the twentieth century. Some involved the pastor's theological views on the Apostles Creed; others were related to a pastor's social or political views and activities; still others showed the growing impact of cultural subjectivism within the churches. Pastors were involved in Silesia, Hesse, Baden, Pomerania and Berlin, Mecklenburg, Hanover, Wuerttemberg, and other areas. In 1905, the Senate in Bremen ordered Pastor Oskar Mauritz to rebaptize at least 600 people with the Trintiarian formula, which he had omitted for a lengthy period. He was attracted by Haeckel's monism.

Theological unrest was probably one reason for the precipitous drop in the number of ministerial students in Prussia between 1900 and 1907. In Prussia's nine old provinces, the number plummeted from 4,536 to 2,228. Meanwhile, the number of fully-trained candidates for the ministry decreased by about 50 percent between 1895 and 1907; it is doubtful that the ranks dwindled so rapidly because the candidates took pastoral positions, even though clerical salaries had inceased. The number of official withdrawals from territorial churches also rose appreciably in 1906.

Cologne was the stage for the next major "case" in the struggle over the Apostles Creed. Karl Jathro (1851-1913), a pastor inclined toward the aesthetic, attracted large crowds to his sermons, and was praised by writers in the CHRISTIAN WORLD for trying to make Christianity intelligible to modern people. He publicly discussed a number of subjects, including the significance of the Lord's Supper and the meaning of "church," from a decidedly subjectivistic point of view. After receiving complaints, including the claim that he used his own creed in confirmation classes, the consistory began an investigation in 1907. Jathro claimed a special affinity for Harnack, to whom he wrote that "you and I, we are doubters, we who no more believe in the old Christology, we dare no longer affirm anything objectively valid about God."

His case was prolonged until the Prussian General Synod

passed a new Heresy Law ("Irrlehrgesetz") in 1910. It provided that judgment be rendered by a collegium of thirteen, including representatives of the High Church Council, the General Synod, professors of theology, general superintendents, and the provincial synods. This court of arbitration was to provide an alternative to legal sentencing that involved disciplinary consequences, and was to ensure prominence for the theological aspects of a case.

The next year, Jathro's case was placed before this "Spruchkollegium." Assisted by two defense counsels, he defended his position on God, sin, Christology, and other doctrinal points, but the court voted eleven to two to release him from office. On his return to Cologne, Jathro's congregation rallied to his cause, collecting 50,000 signatures in his support. He died two years later of blood poisoning after an auto accident. His conviction created a major division among liberals; Rade and Harnack approved of the new method for handling such cases, and Harnack asserted that Jathro had overstepped himself. But not all agreed.

One who failed to agree was Gottfried Traub (1869–1956) of Dortmund, a young pastor who had been one of Jathro's defense counsels. A strong supporter of the CHRISTIAN WORLD, he lashed out verbally and in print at the teaching and authorities of Prussia's territorial chuch. The traditional legal process was used to release him from office, and he became director of the German Protestant Conference, an organization formed in 1909 through the merger of the Protestant Union and several other liberal groups. His patriotic service during the war rehabilitated him in the eyes of authorities, and he later resumed his pastoral functions.

Liberal academic theology, as well as these "cases," showed that theological liberalism was adrift in the century's final decades precisely because it had "gone public," and appealed to a wider circle than its traditional haunt, the halls of academia. This development contributed to the foundational collapse of the unwritten Protestant charter. The public was no longer receiving the kind of unisional message about "freedom within authority" that the churches had customarily provided throughout the century. The boundaries of freedom and authority were shifting, for both church and state.

But paradoxical as it may seem, Protestants showed near unanimity in two areas. They were areas that contributed to the foundational collapse of post-Enlightenment, nineteenth century German culture, and to the emergence of National Socialism. Anti-Semitism and nationalist zeal survived the shocks the culture received, and provided new footings as well.

ANTI-SEMITISM

The historian Friedrich Heer called the decades between 1870 and 1914 the "incubation period of anti-Semitism." There is debate about precisely what "incubated" during this time, but there is little doubt that German society was an incubator.

In his important study of late century anti-Semitism, Professor Uriel Tal describes modern anti-Semitism as a "bifurcated movement," "the confluence of two streams—the continuation and product of anti-Jewish Christian tradition, and at the same time antagonistic to Christianity itself, including its biblical Jewish sources, its eschatological conception, and its ethical theological elements." He found it advisable to speak of "Christan anti-Semitism," and "anti-Christian anti-Semitism."(10)

Tal's description enables us to focus on the two sides of anti-Semitism, as well as their interaction and cross-fertilization. Anti-Semitism shows the magnetism of subjectivism in these decades of social and cultural upheaval. Anti-Semitism also helped undermine the foundations of post-Enlightenment, nineteenth century German Protestantism, while paradoxically preparing the way for horrible new developments in the next century.

Christian Anti-Semitism

Wilhelm Marr apparently coined the phrase "anti-Semitism" in 1879 in his book THE VICTORY OF JUDAISM OVER GERMANISM, but

the concept was older than Christianity. For centuries, some
Christians had erroneously accused Jews of being
"God-killers." The Protestant record in Germany was as
blemished as the rest of Christian history; people in later
centuries often echoed Luther's tirades against the Jews.
During the second empire, religious anti-Semitism was not a
spotty phenomenon, but a widely accepted ideology among
many, including such reputable people as pastors and
professors.(11)

It was, as Pastor J. de le Roi complained to a pastoral
conference in Berlin in 1880, the Jews' "atrophied
religiosity" that disturbed many Protestants. But
educational and liturgical formulations constantly
reiterated the more serious accusation: that the Jews killed
Christ, the Son of God. Some Christians made the startling
accusation even more contemporary by accusing Jews of
ritually murdering Christians, especially children, through
the centuries. "Will anyone who knows history still deny,"
Stoecker asked rhetorically in the "Reichstag" late in the
century, "that Christians, especially children, have died by
the hand of Jews for centuries, from fanaticism or
superstition?" Pastor Carl Mommert's RITUAL MURDER BY
TALMUDIC JEWS (1895) described the motives of Jews
purportedly involved in the deaths of one hundred and
fifty-nine Christians through the centuries.

Anti-Semitism took hold forcefully after the economic crash
of 1873, for which Jews were mistakenly blamed. Two years
earlier, Prussia's High Church Council issued a circular
about "converting to Judaism," which urged Protestants not
to fall back under the "yoke of slavery" from which
Christianity freed them. Anti-Semitic religious ideology
had tremendous magnetism when reinforced by economic stress;
Christian anti-Semitism was a movement to be reckoned with.

The campaign against Jews rested primarily on the idea of
the "Christian state." So popular during the restorational
fifties, as we discovered above, the concept was
rehabilitated for new purposes in these years. Political
conservatives, and they included many Protestants, adapted
the idea to the unwieldy social, political, and cultural
realities of the time. "The central symbol for these
destructive, antiorganic manifestations," says Tal, "was the
Jews . . . ." Meanwhile, the conservatives' two protective

mechanisms, the authority of the aristocratic class, and the state churches' autonomy and independence, seemed to be gravely endangered.(12)

Viewed from our twentieth-century perspective, even such an innocent document as the citation for Bismarck's honorary doctorate at Giessen University in 1888 had anti-Semitic markings. Referring to his use of the term "practical Christianity" as a rationale for the social reforms of the early eighties, the citation described him as a statesman who recognized that "the Christian religion alone can redeem the social order."

Christian anti-Semitism turned on the idea that Jews were foreigners in the Christian state. Stoecker said in 1879 that Jews walked more willingly in the financial district of Jerusalem Street in Berlin than in the streets of Jerusalem; they remained "a people within a people, a state within a state." In a lecture in 1881, an army chaplain in Cologne named Heinrich Rocholl warned that the Jews were trying to de-Christianize the state and its elementary schools, and limit the church's influence on youth. A Protestant missionary to Jewish people in Berlin named Daub levelled the same accusation.

As early as 1866, the platform of Minden-Ravensberg's heavily Protestant Conservative Party included the plank that "no Jew <should serve> as authority over the Christian 'Volk.'" In 1892, the platform of the Christian Conservative Party in Westphalia contained the following paragraph:

> We want to see legally recognized the right of the German people <to have> Christian confessional elementary schools and Christian government, and especially for this reason <we demand> the exclusion of Jews from all governmental offices, and from the education and instruction of Christian children.

Christian conservatives in Pomerania, Silesia, and royal Saxony adopted the same provision.

Defense of the "Christian state" was a high priority for the anti-Semitic court preacher, Adolf Stoecker, whose response to the social problem we discussed above. His amalgam of ideas allows no easy distillation, nor is it possible to explain his ambivalence between forms of racial and religious anti-Semitism. But Tal provides assistance with his analysis of Stoecker:

> His demands and his proposals for the solution of the Jewish question constitute a complex system of theological, biblical, pietistic, and racial motifs. But the basic aim that he inflexibly pursued from the time when he first turned his attention to social problems was the defense of the Christian nation against the inroads of Leftist ideology. This singleness of purpose stemmed from his Conservative Protestant world view, according to which it was the task of the German Empire to realize in the empirical political sphere those ideals which, after Israel's defection and deep betrayal, passed from Israel in the body to Israel in the spirit, that is, from the Jews to the Christians.

Stoecker held in tension his theological view that the Jewish question could be solved only when Jews renounced their faith, and the racially-based conclusion that the problem was insoluble as long as Jews continued to exist in the flesh. "He did not characterize the Jewish question as racial," says Tal, "and yet he found it to be rooted in the racial and ethnic peculiarity of the Jew."(13)

Stoecker was elected to the Prussian House of Deputies in 1879, where he served uninterruptedly until 1898. In 1881 he was also elected to the national "Reichstag," where he held a seat until 1893, but was then re-elected in 1898. These elective offices were a forum for the religious anti-Semitism he espoused on behalf of the Christian state. In addition to Stoecker, four other Protestant pastors sat as anti-Semites in the "Reichstag," and one in the House.

Stoecker's popularity soared in the eighties, and next to Friedrich von Bodelschwingh, probably no other church figure was as well known among German Protestants. The law curtailing Social Democratic activity in 1878, as well as his election to parliamentary bodies, and the High Church Council's memorandum in 1879 instructing pastors to eschew party politics, helped dissuade him from trying to capture workers in his Christian Social Workers Party. He opened his conservative, anti-Semitic campaign to economically strapped people in the middle classes. Stoecker finally removed "Workers" from his party's title in 1881, but anti-Semitism emerged as a theme two years earlier.

Stoecker floated anti-Semitic propaganda for the first time in September of 1879, in a speech entitled "What We Demand of Modern Jewry." He denounced the capitalistic power of modern Jewry, as well as its intolerant press, and urged Christians and Jews to establish better relations. "Either we succeed in this and Germany will rise again," he concluded,

> or the cancer from which we suffer will spread further. In that event, our whole future is threatened, and the German spirit will become Judaized. The German economy will become impoverished. These are our slogans: a return to Germanic rule in law and business, a return to the Christian faith. May every man do his duty, and God help us all.(14)

His weekly lectures in 1880-81 drew as many as 3,000 applauding listeners. Anti-Semitic topics such as "The Jewish Question" (3,000 in attendance, and 2,000 on several other occasions) outdrew "Is the Bible the Truth?" (500), and "The Old and the New Testaments" (700). His demagoguery fascinated small shopkeepers and others suffering economic and emotional scars from the crash of 1873. Between 1880 and 1884 his oratory gained him a national reputation; his weekly sermons appeared as penny-press pamphlets, in runs of 100,000 copies.

His portrayal of anti-Semitism as the appropriate response to modern Judaism's attack on the Christian way of life kept him from interpreting the Jewish question as simply either a religious or a racial problem. That was one reason why more radical anti-Semitic elements soon outflanked him. But once the anti-Semitic issue was raised, it is doubtful that the people who thronged to hear him were as impressed with his struggle against the enemies of the Christian state, as with his identifying the religious and racial group purportedly responsible for their problems.

His middle class goal, independence for the church, depended on middle class support. The Jews served a double purpose in attracting that support; they were the target of his anti-Semitism, and they bore the onus for materialism, the cause of social and spiritual distress. Until the Jewish problem was solved—and one gets the impression that Stoecker hammered at this issue precisely because it seemed so insoluble—Germany would be plagued with a major social problem, due to the materialism for which he held the Jews responsible. He would not accept the argument that he was making a small percentage of modern Jews, largely editors, represent popular Judaism. While he refused to blame the Jews for the whole social problem, he did not hesitate to say in 1880 that "in the Jewish question lies the expression of the difficulties of our social situation."

Not everyone greeted his words with approval. Arguing against Treitschke that Jewish cosmopolitanism could help integrate diverse Germanic traditions in the empire, the great historian Mommsen said early in the eighties that "Providence knows better than Herr Stoecker why it was desirable to add a certain percentage of Israel in the smelting furnace to temper the German metal."(15) Pastor Paulus Cassel (1821-1892) of Berlin, and others, including Bismarck, also opposed his anti-Semitic propaganda. When Stoecker baited exiled Social Democrats and Jews while visiting London in 1883, the Lord Mayor refused to meet him out of regard for Jewish people.

After a decade of propagating anti-Semitism, Stoecker broached the popular theme once more at a conservative rally in Baden late in 1890. Baden's grand duke immediately complained to the emperor about his court preacher's speech, and it was decided that Stoecker should be fired. A notice to this effect was authorized early in November, and late in December he preached his farewell sermon. By this time, other anti-Semitic forces had passed him by, especially those with racial and anti-Christian bases. Eight years earlier, he had attended the First International Anti-Jewish Congress in Dresden while at the height of his career, playing a leading role among four hundred participants. But the Congress had few important organizational consequences, partly because its portrayal of the Jewish problem, which owed much to Stoecker, left no room for anti-Jewish tendencies that opposed a Christian world view.

Stoecker and other conservatives were not the only anti-Semites in German Protestantism. Liberal Protestants also climbed on the wagon, though somewhat later. German intellectuals, and Jews who supported nationalism, worked toward a common goal in the last third of the century, namely, to assimilate Jews into enlightened, liberal German society and culture. Their common enemies included racial and political anti-Semites, and Protestant and Catholic conservative clerics. But toward the end of the nineties, Harnack and other liberal Protestants, as well as liberal Jews, turned to history as part of the effort to validate their views; they sought what Tal calls "ideological justification" for their existence as distinct communities, and for attainment of self-identity. Tapping historical roots brought a new battle between Christian and Jewish liberals. For example, Harnack stressed Marcion's role as a follower of Paul and a de-Judaizer of Christianity; Old Testament scholars discussed the multiple historical origins of the books they studied, as well as the many cultural strains in the Old Testament. New Testament scholars argued that some epistles were written in the second century under less Jewish influence than had been thought, and Troeltsch described Christianity as the "culmination of all previous religions."(16)

Even the liberal CHRISTIAN WORLD expressed disappointment at the fact that emancipated Jews had failed to enter the national and cultural unity of the empire, based as it was on historical and Christian principles. "Judaism, to be sure, had appropriated the treasures of Christian culture and its material benefits," an article said in 1893,

> but it did not succeed in finding a way of penetra-
> ting the religious-ethical thinking out of which
> this culture grew. . . . No one can be completely
> at home in the life of a nation, or genuinely feel
> that he is participating in its activities, aspira-
> tions, and hopes, as long as he remains untouched
> by the spirit of Christianity...the Jews have not
> reached the point of acknowledging Christianity as a
> vital source of culture; they have appropriated
> Christian culture, but have refused to acknowledge
> that this culture is the product of the religious-
> ethical spirit of Christianity.(17)

Meanwhile, literature courses in the "gymnasia" often used Wilhelm Raak's DER HUNGERPASTOR as an exemplary masterpiece of German literature between 1880 and 1914. The work compared the ethical bankruptcy of a Jewish intellectual with a pastor's praiseworthy hunger for spiritual values.

A few Protestant voices, conservative and liberal, publicly opposed religious anti-Semitism. We have mentioned Cassel, a converted Jew who worked as an evangelist among Jews in Berlin. Michael Baumgarten (1812-1889), a member of the "Reichstag," and at one time a theologian at Rostock, who was deposed in 1858 for his opposition to the state church, published STOECKERS GEFAELSCHTES CHRISTENTUM in 1881. The Reformation historian Heinrich Baumgarten also strongly opposed Stoecker. Franz Delitzsch, a theological professor at Leipzig, whose interest in Jewish missions led to the creation of the "Institutum Judaicum" at Leipzig, and a translator of the New Testament into Hebrew, wrote a blistering rejoiner to the popular anti-Semitic attack on the Talmud by the Catholic professor August Rohling (1871), but Rohling's work appeared in seventeen editions by the year 1922.

Finally, we should note that Hesse's Supreme Consistory issued a circular letter in 1890 that opposed the clergy's support of the political anti-Semitic movement headed by Otto Boeckel. The document said that while the economic practices of some Jewish people deserved criticism, Judaism and the Jewish community as a whole could not be held responsible. It argued that Christian merchants and financiers also participated in some questionable actions. The consistory described the basis of anti-Semitic racial policy as "the fateful dark instincts of the German people, who are led astray," and suggested that the movement would corrupt Christian morality from the inside, and undermine law and order. "A spirit of insurrection and lawlessness, lust and hate thus unloosed . . . could profit only those whose revolutionary plans against the political and ecclesiastical establishment are based on the growing dissatisfaction of large segments of the population," the letter added prophetically.

Anti-Christian Anti-Semitism

After the mid-eighties, racial anti-Semitism with an anti-Christian bias coalesced in an ideology that had wide public influence. Theodor Fritsch and others contended that Christian baptism would not solve the Jewish problem. Among the most outspoken representatives of anti-Christian anti-Semitism were Wilhelm Marr, Otto Glagau, Friedrich Lange, Eugene Duehring, Max Bemer, Adolf Warhmund (who proposed an "idealism of Aryan Christianity"), and others mentioned below. A number of factors contributed to the appearance of this ideology, including religious anti-Semitism, the continuing influence of the Left Wing Hegelians, the growing impact of Schopenhauer's pessimism, and especially the anti-religious and blatantly secular philosophy of Friedrich Nietzsche (1844-1900).

Racial anti-Semitism was a new secular religion that portrayed the "Volk" as a biological and historical "totality," whose vitality pulsed in its blood. Its major proponents included Lagarde, whom we met above, and Friedrich Langbehn (1851-1907), a nondescript writer whose book, REMBRANDT ALS ERZIEHER—VON EINEM DEUTSCHEN (1890), first appeared anonymously before going through fifty editions. The book sharply criticized modern culture, and called for renewed piety based on purely Germanic stock. Lagarde's basic argument was that Germanism needed to swallow Christianity, in order to avert the extinction of the Germanic race. His non-traditional interpretation of the gospel posited man's inherent divinity. He wrote that Judaism was the major obstacle to racial renewal; all traces of its influence had to be erased from Christianity.

Another major figure was Houston Stewart Chamberlain (1855-1927), whose FOUNDATIONS OF THE NINETEENTH CENTURY (1900) raised up racism as the hope of humanity, the goal of its aspirations. He argued that German mysticism and Germanic religion lay at the basis of Germany's great future. Chamberlain's views influenced William II appreciably. With Nietzsche, he also influenced Pastor Arthur Bonus (1864-1941), whose early work, VON STOECKER ZU NAUMANN—EIN WORT ZUR GERMANISIERUNG DES CHRISTENTUMS (1890), laid the groundwork for his labor on behalf of "German Christianity" in the early Nazi period.

Christian, as well as anti-Christian, anti-Semitism failed to achieve significant power at the polls during these decades. For example, in 1881 Stoecker's party gathered only three-tenths of a percent of the total vote in the

"Reichstag" election. At the height of its influence, racial anti-Semitism received less than four percent of the total vote in 1893 and 1898, and this trend continued until 1907. Anti-Semitic representation in the "Reichstag" dropped from a high of eighteen delegates in 1893, to 13 in 1898, 11 in 1903, 17 in 1907, and 7 in 1912. But, as Tal notes, Christian anti-Semitism played an important role in Christian conservative parties and in the other conservative parties; it was "decidedly more widespread and effective than non-Christian and anti-Christian anti-Semitism in the nineties . . . ."(18)

The two sides of anti-Semitism exerted a subtle influence. Permeating the culture and influencing the young, they sowed seeds that were harvested in future decades. Tal correctly indicates that it is inexcusable to suggest that the Christian anti-Semitism of Protestant leaders and followers should not be faulted in part for what happened in the twentieth century. His important study concludes with a paragraph that summarizes the significance of the anti-Semitic movement in the German empire, and delineates the relationship between the movement's two sides. "Racial anti-Semitism and the subsequent Nazi movement," he wrote,

> were not the result of mass hysteria or the work of single propagandists. The racial anti-Semites, despite their antagonism toward traditional Christianity, learned much from it, and succeeded in producing a well-prepared, systematic ideology with a logic of its own that reached its culmination in the Third Reich.(19)

In sum, religious anti-Semitism had a paradoxical effect on the unwritten Protestant charter, while it helped destroy the foundations of post-Enlightenment German culture, and laid new footings. Its acids ate at the civil order of the state, one partner in the agreement that the church serve as a social model. In this it contributed to the charter's end. But it also became a mouthpiece for anti-Semitic religious forces in society which, in their racial form, soon dominated the state itself. In this way, it helped forge an awkward and disastrous arrangment that existed between state leaders and many Protestants during the Third Reich. The cement that held the old and the new together was nationalism, a sentiment that attracted the interest of

Protestants with growing intensity as the century ended.

TO WAR

In the century between 1813 and 1914, Protestants in Germany engaged in war six times, counting the revolutions at mid-century. The most calamitous, of course, was the Great War that began in 1914. In view of the events that overtook German Protestantism in the half century that followed, this war had the most profound impact. The nationalistic and expansionary zeal that lay at its center spread rapidly in the pre-war period, and the faltering "peace movement" among some Protestants did little to arrest the tide of events. Consuming nationalism contributed to the collapse of German culture and society, although in this case, the process of disintegration took longer than in some others.

When linked with anti-Semitism, the appeal of nationalism created a potent ideology for Protestants in the twentieth century. Viewed from the perspective of the alliance between throne and altar in the nineteenth century, the resulting ideology was one of the enduring consequences of the unwritten charter. But when it is understood to have been a secular religion of the rawest type, this ideology spelled the end of rapprochement between Protestant churches and the state. Both interpretations are tenable.

Pre-War Protestant Nationalism

In the final decades of the century, nationalistic Protestants looked back to previous national conquests, and forward to new ones. In 1891, the CHURCHLY ADVISER FOR THE EVANGELICAL LUTHERAN CONGREGATIONS IN ELBERFELD reminisced with pride in an article that traced the happy transition from Wittenberg to Potsdam. Commenting on the biblical passage, "Be of good cheer, my son, your sins are forgiven" (Matthew 9:2), the article recounted the experiences of a divisional chaplain during the Franco-Prussian War, when he came upon a group of defeated and demoralized troops. "In God's name, and empowered by my office," the chaplain began,

"I forgive the sins of those among you who are repentant." After a short speech to the troops, he concluded with the traditional Prussian call to battle, "With God for king and fatherland!" The paper added that the soldiers rose up like lions, and won the next battle. "As the evidence shows, did not this precious, consoling article of the forgiveness of sins pay a real dividend," the paper asked? No less brash was the nationalistic use of religion in 1912, in the centennial FESTSCHRIFT of the Privileged Swabian Bible Institute. "Germany for Germans—that must be the final goal in all Bible matters for all true German friends of the Bible," it said. Paying tribute to British assistance, while, as it were, looking ahead to the Great War, Pastor Risch added that "this honorable duty does not diminish with the sentiment of appreciation that at all times binds us to England."

Some warning against the extremes of nationalism were sounded. Most came from within the circle of the CHRISTIAN WORLD. For example, Julius Kaftan, a liberal theological professor in Berlin, condemned talk about the "old German God," just as he dismissed as irrelevant the supposed cosmopolitanism of Roman Catholicism. True nationalism played a role in Christian morality, he argued, since nationalism was enlarged individualism. While it was a "Christian duty to be patriotic," he added that "national arrogance is a hideous mistake." His brother Theodor also spoke up, strongly opposing a Prussian regulation in 1888, which urged elementary teachers in north Schleswig to use German while teaching Danish children. But this Lutheran preacher's strong denunciation of chauvinistic nationalism (UNTERRICHT IM CHRISTENTUM, 1914) drew little positive response in the first year of the war.

More to taste was an anniversary observance of the events of 1813, sponsored a century later in Hamburg by the Inner Mission. The theme of the congress was "Christianity and Nationhood." The keynote speaker extolled the "holy spirit of patriotic love, which authenticated itself a hundred years ago," while another speaker echoed the sentiments, and praised the "sanctifiction of national renewal through faith." Conservatives especially, but the vast bulk of Protestants generally, affirmed the zealous nationalism that was gathering force in these decades.

579

Protestant ministry to men in the armed forces opened another possibility for turning religion toward nationalist ends. Not all preparations were as haphazard as the new songbook (1912) that the Swabian chaplains presented to their troops in World War I. Many of the melodies were unfamiliar to the soldiers, and the consistory in Stuttgart hastily prepared a new "Field Hymnal" to replace it.

Prussia issued a new regulation governing evangelical ministry to troops in 1902. It updated the regulation of 1832, but left with chaplains the responsibility of inculcating patriotism (paragraph 121). The king appointed a "Feldpropst," or chief of chaplains, to head up the corps of regular and reserve chaplains; after 1888, Adolf Richter replaced Thielen in this position. Each army corps had a command chaplain on the general commander's staff, and under him, individual chaplains served divisions, garrisons, and military institutions. The various armies that fell under Prussian administration, including that of Oldenbourg, Baden, and Hesse, used parts of the new Prussian regulation. The independent armies of Bavaria, Saxony, and Wuerttemberg made their own provisions for religious ministry to troops, some with very few full-time Protestant chaplains. Bavaria had only seven in 1914.

Non-officers in the Prussian army were required to attend church services at the end of the century. Chaplains viewed this requirement as an aid to their ministry and their assignment to instill patriotism. "That the sermons of chaplains stress the soldier's duty, his oath, loyalty, and love of country," said one account of chaplains' work from the period,

> as well as emphasize the significance of authority, and obedience to it, and not to ignore the Bible's pertinent, rich images of battle, service in war, armor, and the victor's wreath—that all is self-understood, just as on the other side the excessive misuse of these images . . . is to be cautioned against.(20)

Chaplains conducted "barracks hours" in the evening which sometimes included religious and patriotic songs, patriotic and moral leadership lectures against cursing, drunkenness, and other sins, and religious devotions. Subordinate officers and their families sometimes attended special programs arranged by chaplains; they might include lectures about a national anniversary, the Emperor William Canal, or comparisons between the battles of Leipzig and Sedan. Special religious papers and supplements were published for soldiers, including the SUNDAY NEWS FOR THE GERMAN ARMY. Bible and tract distribution also helped the chaplain in his work. In 1899, a major Bible society distributed 20,000 New Testaments and 5,000 complete Bibles in the Prussian army. In addition to their work in the field, chaplains also ministered in military hospitals and prisons.

Germany's new fleet brought the need for chaplains on the high seas, and in 1903 the emperor issued the pertinent "Naval Church Ordinance." The army's chief of chaplains exercised supervision over naval chaplains as well. Like army chaplains, they too were imperial officers who belonged to the officers' ranks. Their shipboard services included musical accompaniment if a band was on board; the Apostles Creed closed the service, which never lasted more than an hour. If a ship had no chaplain, its commander or a designated officer conducted an abbreviated worship service. Commanders had a shining example in the emperor, who preached often on his yacht. Naval chaplains also held brief Sunday afternoon lectures, and sometimes short morning devotions during the week. Article twenty-one of their Ordinance required that they care for the religious needs of Germans in foreign ports. The naval chaplains' baptismal registry showed that by the end of the nineties, they had performed baptisms in Havana, Caracas, Shanghai, Yokahama, Singapore, Manila, Lima, Peking, Honolulu, Tonga, Samoa, Casablanca, and other ports.

The Prussian chief of chaplains gave a speech in Potsdam in 1898 at the dedication of the flag of the Third Sea Batallion. His speech showed how easily nationalism and religion flowed together at the time. "To be German means to be pious, the flag says," he said emphatically. "We put our hands together, courageous, of one mind, humble—a living wall around our emperor's throne: one Empire, one people, one God! To be German means to be strong, says the flag." Then he added, "Go out, then, you sleek and splendid flag, and proclaim to the world, say to our brothers out there: The emperor sends you, your God sends you, within and without as a battle banner, to perpetuate and enlarge noble

peace, national honor, and our people's holiest possessions:
German power, German loyalty until death! Amen!"

Peace Movement

It was the wrong time and the wrong place for a peace
movement to gain a foothold. Most Protestants, especially
pastors, were uninterested in the "Friedensfreunde" (Peace
Society) organized in 1892. By 1912, its 9,000 members
included only one hundred and seventeen pastors and three
Roman Catholic priests, this despite the fact that its
roster was usually larger on paper than in fact.

It was the wrong time and the wrong nation. The peace
movement had no living tradition in the territorial
churches, and churchmen did not appreciate having
anticlerical persons as members of the society. Even some
of the most sensitive pastors bristled at the thought of an
end to war.(21) The theologian Friedrich Kattenbusch
published a brochure on behalf of just war, entitled "The
Moral Rectitude of War" (1906), which appeared earlier in
the CHRISTIAN WORLD. "Only in the religious socialism <of
Switzerland>," one scholar concludes, "did opposition
subsequently develop against all theological forms that left
room for war mentality and German nationalism." Christoph
Blumhardt, Leonhard Ragaz, and Karl Barth were among this
minority.(22)

War

As the Great War approached, an increasing number of people
seemed to think that war would bring a solution to numerous
social, political, and even inter-confessional problems. War
did not prove to be the "savior from God's hand" that some
expected. But it did deal the final blow to the collapsing
foundations of post-Enlightenment culture and society, just
as, for decades to come, it influenced political, religious,
and theological history in ways that were less than
constructive.

The process of national unification had modified the
unwritten Protestant charter to make moral support of
conservative nationalism a requirement for the Protestant

582

churches. Each annual Sedan Festival—the empire at prayer—symbolized the fact. The Franco-Prussian War provided many Protestant pastors with the most intense contact with the masses of any time in the century; the so-called War of Liberation ran a close second. That experience repeated itself in World War I, and together with the enduring alliance between throne and altar, these experiences helped sap the capability of German Protestantism to launch a campaign against the religious ideology of National Socialist nationalism in the thirties.

William II set the tone soon after war broke out. He declared that August 5, 1914, would be a day of prayer. "With a clear conscience about the War's origin," he wrote, "I am certain before God of the propriety of our effort." "A Mighty Fortress is Our God" was both a patriotic and religious song in those days, and it was self-understood that the crowd gathering at the Berlin Castle on August 1 would proceed from there to a worship service in the cathedral. On August 4, the "Reichstag" held a special service in the cathedral; Dryander, the vice president of the High Church Council and chief court preacher, was the speaker. He used his artfully chosen text ("If God be for us, who can be against us?", Romans 8:31) to tell attentive listeners, "We go out in battle for our culture against non-culture, for German morality against barbarism."

That month, a number of leading Prussian clergymen, including professors of theology (Loofs, Hermann, Harnack, Deissmann) and proponents of foreign missions, issued a document entitled "To Evangelical Christians Abroad." The signers maintained that "the responsibility for the horrible crime of this war, and all of its consequences for the development of God's kingdom on earth, can and ought to be removed from our nation and its government."

In their comments on the war, Protestant theologians did not always take the stand one might have expected, in view of their theology. Liberal theological views did not necessarily imply liberal political views, and conservative theological views did not imply conservative political views. Nevertheless, cultural Protestants were prone to speak of the war as "divine revelation," or "revelation of God," an idea closely related to their view of the nation as "revelation of eternity." Orthodox and conservative

Lutherans, on the other hand, frequently described the war as divine judgment; the appropriate human response of repentance paralleled rather nicely the Lutheran tradition of obedience to authority.(23)

Traub, for example, was a "radical" in the battle over the Apostles Creed, but his patriotic work during the war rehabilitated him in the eyes of officials. Between 1914 and 1918, Prussia's High Church Council reversed itself and reinstated him in office; the deciding factor was his editing the patriotic EISERNEN BLAETTER, and the emperor's resulting interest in his case.

Pietists in Wuerttemberg might have been expected to support the war effort. Most of them did, offering the theological footnote that God punished Germany for failing to obey His commandments, and sent strength if Germans were pious, moral, and unified. Many of them prayed that God would use this extraordinary means of chastisement to release His kingdom once more within the empire's borders. The CHRISTENBOTEN's special edition for soldiers, "Through Battle to Victory," stressed the two-pronged battle against sin and the enemy.

In 1914, Rade argued in the CHRISTIAN WORLD that the war exemplified the "bankruptcy of Christendom," but not of Christianity. The journal lost over 600 subscribers by March of the next year, although it is less certain that all defections were due to his editorial position. In 1915, for example, W. Stapel published an article in the journal entitled "Why I Pray Not to God, But to the German God."

Critical views also appeared in theologically conservative circles. By 1916, an important teacher-leader in the Hahn (Pietist) Society in Wuerttemberg expressed little hope for victory in war. "A hero's death remains a hero's death," he wrote to others in the society, "and it should be appropriately honored among us as such; but it is not a deed of self-redemption from all burdens of conscience; redemption from all evil is and remains the merit of Jesus Christ." Christoph Blumhardt also criticized nationalistic zeal that was over-extended at the cost of religious faith.

Nearly 2,000 Protestant pastors served as chaplains in the war, some entering the service from civilian status after the war had begun. Prussia and the armies under her administration provided the lion's share, with 1,338 volunteers to augment the small regular staff of 127 chaplains, and 28 naval volunteers to supplement the 28 regular naval chaplains. In addition, eight Old Lutheran pastors became chaplains. Bavaria right of the Rhine provided 242 pastors, and 37 from the left side. Saxony fielded 74, and Wuerttemberg 42 chaplains.

Here and there in the Protestant ministerium could be heard the plaintive lament of a preacher who questioned Germany's involvement in the war, and tested the theological adequacy of chauvinistic nationalism. But these voices were drowned by the majority of those who followed the leader, and praised Luther and Ludendorf as the four hundredth anniversary of the Reformation approached in 1917. Little did they suspect that the end was at hand—and ominous new beginnings as well. Like most German Protestants, they favored executing the war until the inevitable, divinely-ordained victory would arrive.

The pre-war decades found German Protestantism in a crisis of foundational collapse, as post-Enlightenment German culture and society sounded the death rattle. It was clear on all sides that the traditional alliance between throne and altar, and the Protestants' charter to serve as a model for society, had short life expectancies.

The search for a "reason" to fill the vacuum of self-doubt was not limited to academic circles. Religious anti-Semitism, and its step-child, racial anti-Semitism, were part of that subjectivistic search. The same was true for many persons who turned to chauvinistic nationalism in these years with even greater intensity, for those in the "Gemeinschaftsbewegung," and for some pastors involved in heresy cases. Theological liberalism's drift was due in part to the liberals' inability to provide a rationally coherent theological world view; they were incapable of integrating the many new factors that characterized the period. The paradoxical nature of much of church life also showed that the search for a new basis for religious interaction failed to arrest the erosion of the old.

585

Germany's collapse after World War I threw the territorial churches into spiritual and organizational crisis. It was traumatic for a proud nation to experience the unexpected defeat of her army, the collapse of monarchies, and the end of an empire. After the allies concluded their armistice with Germany in November of 1918, Prussia's High Church Council issued a statement of consolation and encouragement that referred ambiguously to "kingdom" and "empire." "We have lost the world war," the statement said simply. It continued,

> We have been forced to accept unprecedented, cruel armistice terms from an arrogant enemy. KAISER and REICH, which have become dear and precious <ideas> to us in a way unequalled in history, are now defunct . . . . Our hearts are numbed and torn with nameless grief, with anxious sorrow. . . . In this most horrible time in German history, we turn to all members of our evangelical congregations with the request that, in the frightful gravity of this difficult hour, we grasp the responsibility, the immensity of our assignment.
>
> Where can we find deliverance and help from the terrible sorrow that engulfs us? Where do we receive the power and courage needed to bear this unspeakable misery?
>
> Germany has not been lost, and the Gospel has not been made captive. The kingdom of Jesus Christ carries in itself the power to preserve and deliver our national life; its citizens are obligated and prepared to serve in the earthly fatherland, and to cooperate in areas where we need to support existing authority and to do justice to new tasks. As a folk-church, then, our evangelical church wants to stand in the middle of this temporal life even if external supports collapse. She is and remains a power on which our people can rely with confidence since she is built on an eternal foundation. Therefore, evangelical Christians, <since> internal dissension has destroyed us, close ranks. Regain your composure in the churches and in all of life—as God's people who joyfully witness to his eternal word; as a band of intercessors fervent <in prayer> day and night, certain that their prayers

receive a favorable hearing; as an army of combatants; as a community that spends itself unflaggingly imitating Jesus. . . . In this day of chaos, our German nation must see a community of Christians that does not flee, but believes; that does not complain, but stands upright; that does not doubt, but hopes.

. . . .
We soon will enter the Advent and Christmas seasons, usually a bright time, but this time a dark one. Many of our people are in grave danger of burying all hope for the fatherland. Hopelessness is death. We want to hold to the comfort that the Lord, who went through death to life, is always in advent. His way is also to be found in the dark waters of this age. Each epoch of world history must also be an epoch in the history of His kingdom. He lives and rules; He will be victorious. He does not let His own in the lurch! The kingdom will remain ours!

A kingdom without an empire was also the theme of a circular release by the general superintendents of the old Prussian provinces, after the Treaty of Versailles was signed in June of 1919. These churchmen echoed the High Church Council's appeal for a spirit of serenity and hope, amid the shocking realities of foundational collapse. They addressed three requests to the evangelical congregations:

> The first is this. Germany's empire and glory are shattered; we face a time of hardship and impotence. But the kingdom of God remains immovable. His foot is also moving in these troubled waters. Therefore let us hold firm to the faith that overcomes the world, a faith in the living God and in the One He sent, Jesus Christ.
> And though we are forced to submit ourselves without defense to our enemy's cruel settlement, still it is impossible to surrender the last, the only thing that remains: our honor and conscience............
> Whatever judgment men may render on the individual acts of our "Kaiser's" reign, the purity of his intention, the integrity of his conduct, the sincerity of his personal Christianity, and his

feeling of responsibility, deeply rooted in this faith—they stand firm. We are unable to protect him with external means, but here is our <second> request: together with millions of German men and women, we call on our congregations, in this time of great need for the "Kaiser" and his gravely-ill wife, herself a faithful model in works of Christian mercy, to surround our German leaders and famous persons with the defense of our intercessions. Men have forsaken us, but the cry of our petition before God can prove to be a powerful force that is mightier than the world's wickedness.

In the third place, as long as God gives life, let us not weary of doing our duty fearlessly, alleviating need, strengthening hope, and practicing love. The center of our faith is our Lord Jesus Christ, our Redeemer. As followers in His train, let us preserve ourselves in His might in order to build the fatherland...........

Over all hoplessness, the "yet" of faith prevails. We have a strong God, a living Savior, an immovable kingdom to which victory belongs! Let us arm ourselves with the weapons of faith and prayer, so that we belong to that band of conquerors!

Down to the bitter end, Protestants knew how to model a stiff upper lip for the "Kaiser" and his defeated empire. But things would never be the same. One partner in their unwritten charter was dead, although his ghost haunted the hills, valleys, cities, and churches of Germany for decades.

NOTES

CHAPTER XII

(1) Uriel Tal, CHRISTIANS AND JEWS IN GERMANY; RELIGION, POLITICS AND IDEOLOGY IN THE SECOND REICH, 1870—1914, tr. Noah Jonathan Jacobs (Ithaca: Cornell University Press, 1975), pp. 68, 75.

(2) H. Stuart Hughes, CONSCIOUSNESS AND SOCIETY; THE REORGANIZATION OF EUROPEAN SOCIAL THOUGHT, 1890—1930 (New York: Random House, 1958), pp. 51, 63-66; quotation from p. 51.

(3) Hildegard Milberg, SCHULPOLITIK IN DER PLURALISTISCHEN GESELLSCHAFT; DIE POLITISCHE UND SOZIALEN ASPEKTE DER SCHULREFORM IN HAMBURG 1890—1935 (Hamburg: Leibniz, 1970), pp. 63-78.

(4) See also other publications listed in Hans Sviestrup and Agnes von Zahn-Harnack, eds., DIE FRAUENFRAGE IN DEUTSCHLAND; STROEMUNGEN UND GEGENSTROEMUNGEN, 1790—1930 (2nd ed.; Tuebingen: Hopfer-Verlag, 1961), pp. 218-26.

(5) Karl Kupisch, DEUTSCHLAND IM 19. UND 20. JAHRHUNDERT, in DIE KIRCHE IN IHRER GESCHICHTE, ed. Kurt Dietrich Schmidt and Ernst Wolf, Band 4, Lieferung R (Goettingen: Vandenhoeck & Ruprecht, 1966), p. 92.

(6) See especially Paul Fleisch, DIE MODERNE GEMEINSCHAFTSBEWEGUNG IN DEUTSCHLAND (3d ed.; 2 vols.; Leipzig: H. G. Wallmann, 1912), and Erich Beyreuther, KIRCHE IN BEWEGUNG; GESCHICHTE DER EVANGELISATION UND VOLKSMISSION (Berlin: Christlicher Zeitschriftenverlag, 1968).

(7) Wilhelm Pauck, "Adolf von Harnack," in A

HANDBOOK OF CHRISTIAN THEOLOGIANS, ed. Dean G. Peerman and Martin E. Marty (Cleveland: World Publishing Company, 1965), p. 106.

(8) Ibid., pp. 108-110.

(9) Albert Schweitzer, THE QUEST OF THE HISTORICAL JESUS (New York: Macmillan Company, 1964), pp. 253, 403.

(10) Tal, pp. 226-27.

(11) Stephan Lehr, ANTISEMITISMUS—RELIGIOESE MOTIVE IM SOZIALEN VORURTEIL; AUS DER FRUEHGESCHICHTE DES ANTISEMITISMUS IN DEUTSCHLAND 1870—1914, Abhandlungen zum christlich-juedischen Dialog, ed. Helmut Gollwitzer, Vol. V (Munich: Chr. Kaiser Verlag, 1974), pp. 3-4.

(12) Tal, p. 148.

(13) Ibid., pp. 252-54.

(14) Paul W. Massing, REHEARSAL FOR DESTRUCTION; A STUDY OF POLITICAL ANTI-SEMITISM IN IMPERIAL GERMANY (New York: Harper and Bros., 1949), p. 287.

(15) Tal, p. 52.

(16) Ibid., pp. 63, 220.

(17) Quoted by Tal, p. 164.

(18) Ibid., p. 300; see also p. 299, and Lehr, pp. 14-15.

(19) Tal, p. 305.

(20) C. Werckshagen, ed., DER PROTESTANTISMUS AM ENDE DES 19. JAHRHUNDERTS IN WORT UND BILD (2 vols.; Berlin: Verlag Wartburg, 1901—02), II, 722.

(21) Reportedly several years before his death in 1910, the influential Protestant pastor Friedrich von Bodelschwingh entered into correspondence with an American steel magnate and philanthropist, Andrew Carnegie. Bodelschwingh was anxious to interest the millionaire in his

many institutions of mercy at Bethel, near Bielefeld, and Carnegie showed a good deal of interest. In one letter, Carnegie spoke of his hope that humanity would soon enter an era of universal peace among all peoples. Bodelschwingh, a former army chaplain, gave a reply unexpected by the American, quoting the New Testament to say that there would always be war, and explaining that God used war as a training and educational instrument. The reply may have cost his institutions millions of dollars.

(22) Wolfgang Huber, "Evangelische Theologie und Kirche beim Ausbruch des ersten Weltkriegs," in HISTORISCHE BEITRAEGE ZUR FRIEDENSFORSCHUNG, ed. Wolfgang Huber, Studien zur Friedensforschung, ed. Georg Picht and Heinz Eduard Toedt, Vol. IV (Stuttgart: Ernst Klett Verlag, 1970), p. 194.

(23) Ibid., pp. 138, 152, 154.

BIBLIOGRAPHICAL NOTES

In preparing this bibliography, it seemed that a catalog of the more than two hundred books and articles consulted in preparing this work would be less helpful than a series of bibliographical notes, organized around the chapter titles. The following notes are a kind of extended reading list for persons who want to pursue certain issues in greater detail. The works are a "selected bibliography"; in no sense is this list exhaustive, either for nineteenth century German Protestantism, or for any of the chapters' major subjects. To conserve space, I sometimes ask the reader to consult the footnotes for full bibliographical information on a work.

A number of more general studies pointed the way for this work, influenced its conception, and informed its content. They are listed here since they do not neatly fit any chapter category. They include the following: J. L. Altholz, THE CHURCHES IN THE NINETEENTH CENTURY (Indianapolis, 1967); Andrew Landale Drummond, GERMAN PROTESTANTISM SINCE LUTHER (London, 1951); Heinrich Hermelink, DAS CHRISTENTUM IN DER MENSCHHEITSGESCHICHTE (3 vols.; Stuttgart, 1951-55); Hajo Holborn, A HISTORY OF MODERN GERMANY, 1648—1840, and A HISTORY OF MODERN GERMANY, 1840—1945 (New York, 1964 and 1969); Johannes B. Kissling, DER DEUTSCHE PROTESTANTISMUS, 1817—1917 (Muenster in Westphalia, 1917); Leonard Krieger, THE GERMAN IDEA OF FREEDOM; HISTORY OF A POLITICAL TRADITION (Boston, 1957); Karl Kupisch, DEUTSCHLAND IN 19. UND 20. JAHRHUNDERT, in Die Kirche in ihrer Geschichte, Ein Handbuch, ed. Kurt Dietrich Schmidt and Ernst Wolf (Goettingen, 1966; 2nd ed., 1975); Kenneth Scott Latourette, THE NINETEENTH CENTURY IN EUROPE, THE PROTESTANT AND EASTERN CHURCHES, Christianity in a Revolutionary Age, Vol. II (New York, 1959); DIE RELIGION

IN GESCHICHTE UND GEGENWART, HANDWOERTERBUCH FUER THEOLOGIE UND RELIGIONSWISSENSCHAFT, ed. Kurt Galling (3rd ed.; 6 vols.; Tuebingen, 1957-61); and Franz Schnabel, DEUTSCHE GESCHICHTE IM NEUNZEHNTEN JAHRHUNDERT (4 vols.; Frieburg im Breisgau, 1927-36).

CHAPTER I

The chapter notes refer to important studies by Bigler, Anchor, and Epstein, and articles by Holborn and Bigler, as well as Andrew Landale Drummond, "Church and State in Protestant Germany before 1918, with Special Reference to Prussia," CHURCH HISTORY, XIII (1944), 210-29.

On calls for church unity in the early decades of the century, one should consult Ernst Schubert, DIE DEUTSCH-EVANGELISCHEN EINHEITSBESTREBUNGEN VOM BEGINN DES 19. JAHRHUNDERTS BIS ZUR GEGENWART, Volksschrift zum Aufbau, H. 6 (Berlin, 1919). George W. Spindler researched the life of Karl Follen in KARL FOLLEN, A BIOGRAPHICAL STUDY (Chicago, 1917); see also Kuno Francke, "Karl Follen and the German Liberal Movement," PAPERS OF THE AMERICAN HISTORICAL ASSOCIATION, Vol. V (1891), 65-84. Guenter Steiger's recent study of the Wartburg Festival is "Die Teilnehmerliste des Wartburgfestes von 1817; erste kritische Ausgabe der sog. 'Praesenzliste,'" DARSTELLUNGEN UND QUELLEN ZUR GESCHICHTE DER DEUTSCHEN EINHEITSBEWEGUNG IM NEUNZEHNTEN UND ZWANZIGSTEN JAHRHUNDERT, ed. Kurt Stephenson, Alexander Scharff and Wolfgang Kloetzer (Heidelberg, 1963), IV, 65-133. Thomas Nipperdey discussed proposals for national religious memorials in "Nationalidee und Nationaldenkmal in Deutschland im 19. Jahrhundert," HISTORISCHE ZEITSCHRIFT, CCVI (1968), 529-85. Several of W. H. Bruford's works, including the recent THE GERMAN TRADITION OF SELF-CULTIVATION: BILDUNG FROM HUMBOLT TO THOMAS MANN (Cambridge, 1975), carefully examine the idea of "Bildung."

Walter Simon adequately described the Prussian reform movement in THE FAILURE OF THE PRUSSIAN REFORM MOVEMENT, 1807—1819 (Ithaca, 1955), while Robert Stupperich discussed church polity during this era in "Die Aufloesung der preussischen Kirchenverfassung im Jahre 1808 und ihre Folgen," JAHRBUCH FUER BRANDENBURGISCHE KIRCHENGESCHICHTE, XXXIII (1938), 114-122. Erwin Muelhaupt chronicled ecclesiastical developments in the Rhineland in RHEINISCHE KIRCHENGESCHICHTE VON ANFAENGEN BIS 1945 (Duesseldorf, 1970).

Prussia's "Erhebung" was the subject of Friedrich Meinecke's important DAS ZEITALTER DER DEUTSCHEN ERHEBUNG, 1795—1815 (Bielefeld, 1913); Meinecke also included valuable information in COSMOPOLITANISM AND THE NATIONAL STATE (Princeton, 1970). Hans Kohn compared the French and German experiences of this period in PRELUDE TO NATION-STATES, THE FRENCH AND GERMAN EXPERIENCE, 1789—1815 (Princeton, 1967). Although it is an uneven work, one should consult Edwin D. Junkin, RELIGION VERSUS REVOLUTION: THE INTERPRETATION OF THE FRENCH REVOLUTION BY GERMAN PROTESTANT CHURCHMEN, 1789—1799 (Austin, TX, 1974). In NATIONALISM AND THE CULTURAL CRISIS IN PRUSSIA, 1806—1815 (New York, 1966), Eugene Newton Anderson discussed early century nationalism in its cultural context. Koppel S. Pinson showed that late 18th century pietism also played an important role in early nationalism in PIETISM AS A FACTOR IN THE RISE OF GERMAN NATIONALISM (New York, 1934). Also important is Georg L. Mosse, THE NATIONALIZATION OF THE MASSES: POLITICAL SYMBOLISM AND MASS MOVEMENTS IN GERMANY FROM THE NAPOLEONIC WARS THROUGH THE THIRD REICH (New York, 1975). Karl Holl's seminal article on religion and the War of Liberation deserves special mention: "Die Bedeutung der grossen Kriege fuer das religioese und kirchliche Leben innerhalb des deutschen Protestantismus," in Karl Holl, GESAMMELTE AUFSAETZE ZUR KIRCHENGESCHICHTE (Tuebingen, 1928), III, 302-384. Arndt was seen as a bridge-figure in the spheres of politics, culture, and religion by Friedrich Seebass in ERNST MORITZ ARNDT, DEUTSCHER UND CHRIST (Giessen, 1958), and by Guenther Ott in ERNST MORITZ ARNDT, RELIGION, CHRISTENTUM UND KIRCHE IN DER ENTWICKLUNG DES DEUTSCHEN PUBLIZISTEN UND PATRIOTEN (Bonn, 1966). In DER EINFLUSS DER BIBEL UND DES KIRCHENLIEDES AUF DIE LYRIK DER DEUTSCHEN BEFREIUNGSKRIEGE (Gelnhausen, 1936), Karl Scheibenberger examined cross-currents between patriotic lyrics and religious literature, including hymnody.

William <Wilhelm> Baur took up broader religious issues in RELIGIOUS LIFE IN GERMANY DURING THE WARS OF INDEPENDENCE

(2nd ed.; London, 1892), while Leopold Zscharnack focused on the activities of clergymen between 1806 and 1815 in "Die Pflege des religioesen Patriotismus durch die evangelische Geistlichkeit, 1806—1815," in HARNACK-EHRUNG, BEITRAEGE ZUR KIRCHENGESCHICHTE (Leipzig, 1921), pp. 394-423. Schleiermacher's responses as preacher and patriot are discussed in Alexander Faure, "Schleiermacher und die Aufrufe zu Beginn der Freiheitskriege, 1813," ZEITSCHRIFT FUER SYSTEMATISCHE THEOLOGIE, XVII (1940), 524-68; Johannes Bauer, SCHLEIERMACHER ALS PATRIOTISCHER PREDIGER, Studien zur Geschichte des neueren Protestantismus, ed. Heinrich Hoffmann and Leopold Zscharnack, Vol. IV (Giessen, 1908); Jerry F. Dawson, FRIEDRICH SCHLEIERMACHER; THE EVOLUTION OF A NATIONALIST (Austin, TX, 1966); and R. C. Raack, "Schleiermacher's Political Thought and Activity, 1806—1913," CHURCH HISTORY, XXVIII (1959), 374-90. The nationalistic sermons of other preachers are reviewed in Adolf Heger, EVANGELISCHE VERKUENDIGUNG UND DEUTSCHES NATIONALBEWUSSTSEIN; ZUR GESCHICHTE DER PREDIGT VON 1806—1848, Neue Deutsche Forschungen, ed. Hans R. G. Guenther and Erich Rothacker, Vol. CCLII, and Abteilung Religions- und Kirchengeschichte, ed. Ernst Benz and Erich Seeberg, Vol. VII (Berlin, 1939); and in Paul Drew, DIE PREDIGT IM 19. JAHRHUNDERT, Vortraege der theologischen Konferenz zu Giessen, 19. Folge (Giessen, 1903).

Magdalene Foltz provided an important bibliography on church unions in "Bibliographie zu den Kirchen-Unionen zwischen Lutheranern und Reformierten in Deutschland," in KIRCHE UND STAAT IM 19. UND 20. JAHRHUNDERT, Veroeffentlichungen der Arbeitsgemeinschaft fuer das Archiv- und Bibliothekswesen in der evangelischen Kiche, VII (Neustadt an der Aisch, 1968), 184-94. In NATIONALKIRCHE UND VOLKSKIRCHE IN DEUTSCHEN PROTESTANTISMUS (Goettingen, 1938), Alfred Adam contrasted the union churches with unfulfilled hopes for a more people-oriented ecclesiastical structure. Johannes Mueller discussed the history of the union in the Palatinate in DIE VORGESCHICHTE DER PFAELZISCHEN UNION, Untersuchung zur Kirchengeschichte, ed. Robert Stupperich, Vol. III (Witten, 1967). Important documents from various church unions are provided in Gerhard Ruhbach, ed., KIRCHENUNIONEN IM 19. JAHRHUNDERT, Texte zur Kirchen- und Theologiegeschichte, ed. Gerhard Ruhbach et al., Vol. VI (Guetersloh, 1967).

Erich Foerester is the most famous historian of the Prussian

Union. His DIE ENTSTEHUNG DER PREUSSISCHE LANDESKIRCHE (2 vols.; Tuebingen, 1905-07) is still extremely valuable. Also important are Walter Geppert, DAS WESEN DER PREUSSISCHE LANDESKIRCHE (Berlin, 1939); Walter Delius and Oskar Soehngen, DIE EVANGELISCHE KIRCHE DER UNION, ed. Walter Elliger (Witten, 1967); and H. J. Schoeps, "Die Preussische Union von 1817," in H. J. Schoeps, UNION UND OEKUMENE; 150 JAHRE EVANGELISCHE KIRCHE DER UNION (Berlin, 1968), pp. 134-70. Otto Hintze discussed the broader political, legal, and social context of this union in REGIERUNG UND VERWALTUNG; GESAMMELTE ABHANDLUNGEN ZUR STAATS-, RECHTS- UND SOZIALGESCHICHTE PREUSSENS, ed. Gerhard Oestreich (2nd ed.; Goettingen, 1967). Among histories of other church unions are Wilhelm Rahe, EIGENSTAENDIGE ODER STAATLICH GELENKTE KIRCHE? ZUR ENTSTEHUNG DER WESTFAELISCHEN KIRCHE 1815—1819 (Bethel bei Bielefeld, 1966); and Heinrich Steitz, GESCHICHTE DER EVANGELISCHE KIRCHE IN HESSEN UND NASSAU, Dritten Teil: Unionen, Erweckungen, Kirchenverfassungen (Marburg an der Lahn, 1965).

CHAPTER II

Delius and Soehngen, Geiger, Sterling, and Walther have written important works on chapter themes. Consult the notes for bibliograpical details.

Especially pertinent for the religious significance of the Holy Alliance are Ernst Benz, DIE ABENDLAENDISCHE SENDUNG DER OESTLICH-ORTHODOXEN KIRCHE; DIE RUSSISCHE KIRCHE UND DAS ABENDLAENDISCHE CHRISTENTUM IM ZEITALTER DER HEILIGEN ALLIANZ, Akademie der Wissenschaften und der Literatur, Abhandlungen der Geistes- und Sozialwissenschaftliche Klasse, Jarhgang 1950, Nr. 8 (Wiesbaden, 1950), pp. 559-852; and Max Geiger, "Politik und Religion nach dem Program der Heiligen Allianz," THEOLOGISCHE ZEITSCHRIFT, XV (1959), 107-125. The history of the Prussian territorial church is discussed in Erich Foerster, DIE ENTSTEHUNG DER PREUSSISCHEN LANDESKIRCHE (2 vols.; Tuebingen, 1905-07); and Robert M. Bigler, "The Rise of Political Protestantism in Nineteenth Century Germany: The Awakening of Political Consciousness and the Beginnings of Political Activity in the Protestant

Clergy of Pre-March Prussia," CHURCH HISTORY, XXIV (1965), 423-44. See also the full bibliography provided by Robert M. Bigler in THE POLITICS OF GERMAN PROTESTANTISM; THE RISE OF THE PROTESTANT CHURCH ELITE IN PRUSSIA, 1815—1848 (Berkeley, 1972), pp. 268-290.

Paul Drews discussed the clerical vocation in detail in DER EVANGELISCHE GEISTLICHKEIT IN DER DEUTSCHEN VERGANGENHEIT (2nd ed.; Jena, 1924). QUELLEN ZUR DEUTSCHE SCHULGESCHICHTE SEIT 1800, Quellensammlung zur Kulturgeschichte, Vol. XV (Goettingen, 1961), ed. Gerhard Giese, includes documents on the interrelation of church, school, and state. Friedrich Weichert recounted the origin of Berlin's Jewish mission society in "Die Anfaenge der Berliner Judenmission," JAHRBUCH FUER BERLIN-BRANDENBURGISCHE KIRCHENGESCHICHTE, XXXVIII (1963), 106-141. Terrence N. Tice provided an excellent bibliography on Schleiermacher in SCHLEIERMACHER BIBLIOGRAPHY WITH BRIEF INTRODUCTIONS, ANNOTATIONS, AND INDEX (Princeton, 1966). Not included because of its later publication is an important work by Martin Redeker, FRIEDRICH SCHLEIERMACHER, LEBEN UND WERK, Sammlung Goeschen, Band 1177/1177a (Berlin, 1968).

CHAPTER III

Works by Beyreuther, Lehmann and Geiger, cited in the notes, should be consulted for more information on the Awakening. Another important study is Friedrich Wilhelm Kantzenbach, DIE ERWECKUNGSBEWEGUNG; STUDIEN ZUR GESCHICHTE IHRER ENTSTEHUNG UND ERSTEN AUSBREITUNG IN DEUTSCHLAND (Neuendettelsau, 1957).

Mack Walker studied early century emigration movements, some undertaken with stated religious goals, in GERMANY AND EMIGRATION, 1816—1885, Harvard Historical Monographs, Vol. CLI (Cambridge, 1964). Specialized studies in this area include Hans Petri, "Zur Geschichte der Auswanderung aus Wuerttemberg nach Russland," BLAETTER FUER WUERTTEMBERGISCHE KIRCHENGESCHICHTE, LVII/LVIII (1957-58), 373-79; Renate Vowinckel, URSACHEN DER AUSWANDERUNG, Vierteljahrschrift fuer Sozial- und Wirtschaftsgeschichte, ed. L. Aubin,

Beiheft 37 (Stuttgart, 1939); and K. Stumpp, "Die deutsche
Auswanderung nach Russland 1763—1862, insbesondere aus dem
suedwestdeutschen Raum, Wuerttemberg, Baden, Pfalz und
Elsass," HEIMATBUCH DER DEUTSCHEN AUS RUSSLAND (1961), II.
Teil, iv-xxiv, 1-34 (1962), 35-80 <with maps>.

The chapter section on "Controlled Dissent at Home" is
supplemented by Heinrich Hermelink, GESCHICHTE DER
EVANGELISCHE KIRCHE IN WUERTTEMBERG VON DER REFORMATION BIS
ZUR GEGENWART; DAS REICH GOTTES IN WIRTENBERG <sic>
(Stuttgart & Tuebingen, 1949); and Fritz Gruenzweig, DIE
EVANGELISCHE BRUEDERGEMEINDE KORNTAL (Metzingen, n.d.
<1957>).

Early figures in the Awakening are discussed in E.
Beyreuther, VORFRUEHLING DER GROSSEN ERWECKUNG. LAVATER,
JUNG-STILLING, OBERLIN, SPITTLER, STEINKOPF UND DIE STILLEN
IM LANDE ZWISCHEN AUFKLAERUNG UND ROMANTIK. DIE ZEIT DER
DEUTSCHEN CHRISTENTUMSGESELLSCHAFT, 1780—1815 (Marburg,
1970); Ernst John Knapton, THE LADY OF THE HOLY ALLIANCE
(New York, 1939); and Francis Ley, MADAME DE KRUEDENER ET
SON TEMPS, 1764—1824 (Paris, 1961); as well as Geiger's
study of Jung-Stilling. Some writings of awakened figures
are reproduced in Otto Weber and Erich Beyreuther, eds., DIE
STIMME DER STILLEN (Kaiserwerth, 1959); and Ernst Staehelin,
ed., DIE VERKUENDIGUNG DES REICHES GOTTES IN DER KIRCHE JESU
CHRISTI (7 vols.; Basel, 1951-65).

Specialized studies of awakenings in local geographical
units include Walter Wendland, "Studien zur
Erweckungsbewegung in Berlin (1810—1830)," JAHRBUCH FUER
BRANDENBURGISCHE KIRCHENGESCHICHTE, XIX (1924), 5-77; and
Otto Wenig, RATIONALISMUS UND ERWECKUNGSBEWEGUNG IN BREMEN;
VORGESCHICHTE, GESCHICHTE UND THEOLOGISCHER GEHALT DER
BREMEN KIRCHENSTREITIGKEITEN VON 1830 BIS 1852 (Bonn,
1966). The importance of Russia for many of the awakened
was the focus of Wilhelm Kahle's study, entitled ZUR
THEOLOGIE UND GEISTESGESCHICHTE DES DEUTSCHEN
RUSSLANDBILDES. EIN BEITRAG ZUR GESCHICHTE DER
DEUTSCH-RUSSISCHEN BEGEGNUNG (Hannover, 1972). A similar
focus is found in Ernst Benz, "Russische Eschatologie,
Studien zur Einwirkung der Deutschen Erweckungsbewegung in
Russland," KYRIOS, VIERTELJAHRESSCHRIFT FUER KIRCHEN- UND
GEISTESGESCHICHTE OST EUROPAS, I (1936), 102-129; and Martin
Brecht, "Aufbruch und Verhaertung; das Schicksal der nach

Osten ausgerichteten Erweckungsbewegung in der nach-napoleonischen Zeit," unpublished paper delivered at XIII Congres international des sciences historiques, Moscow, 16-23 August 1970.

A full summary of theological motifs of the Awakening is found in Max Geiger, "Das Probleme der Erweckungstheologie," THEOLOGISCHE ZEITSCHRIFT, XIV (1958), 430-50; and Friedrich W. Kantzenbach, THEISMUS UND BIBLISCHE UEBERLIEFERUNG, BEOBACHTUNGEN ZUR THEOLOGIE DER ERWECKUNG, Arbeiten zur Theologie, ed. Theodor Schlatter et al., I Reihe, Heft 20 (Stuttgart, 1965). Among the more specialized studies of theology in the Awakening are Horst Weigelt, ERWECKUNGSBEWEGUNG UND KONFESSIONELLES LUTHERTUM IM 19. JAHRHUNDERT; UNTERSUCH AN KARL V. RAUMER, Arbeiten zur Theologie, ed. Theodor Schlatter et al., II. Reihe, Band 10 (Stuttgart, 1968); Friedrich Hauss, ERWECKUNGSPREDIGT; EINE UNTERSUCHUNG UEBER DIE ERWECKUNGSPREDIGT DES 19. JAHRHUNDERTS IN BADEN UND WUERTTEMBERG (2nd ed.; Bad Liebenzell/Wuerttemberg, 1967); and Erich Beyreuther, "Der 'biblische Realismus' in der Schwaebisch-schweizerischen Reichsgottesarbeit um 1800," in DIE LEIBHAFTIGKEIT DES WORTES, FESTGABE FUER ADOLF KOEBERLE, ed. Otto Michel and Ulrich Mann (Hamburg, 1958), pp. 121-34.

The "authorized voluntaryism" of the awakened included a number of missionary and charitable activities. Their zealous commitment emerges in sympathetic treatments by Julius Roessle, in VON BENGEL BIS BLUMHARDT (Metzingen, 1959); and by Alfons Rosenberg, in DER CHRIST UND DIE ERDE; OBERLIN UND DER AUFBRUCH ZUR GEMEINSCHAFT DER LIEBE (Olten und Freiburg im Breisgau, 1953). Wilhelm Oehler provides the most comprehensive study of their missionary activities, as well as missionary work throughout the century, in GESCHICHTE DER DEUTSCHEN EVANGELISCHEN MISSION (2 vols.; Baden-Baden, 1949-51). Johannes Aagaard studied mission work in a broad theological context in MISSION, KONFESSION, KIRCHE; DIE PROBLEMATIK IHRER INTEGRATION IM 19. JAHRHUNDERT IN DEUTSCHLAND (2 vols.; Lund, 1967). Among important histories of mission societies and pivotal missionary figures are Wilhelm Schlatter, GESCHICHTE DER BASLER MISSION, 1815-1915 (3 vols.; Basel, 1916); Julius Richter, GESCHICHTE DER BERLINER MISSIONSGESELLSCHAFT, 1824-1924 (Berlin, 1924); and Wolfgang R. Schmidt, MISSION, KIRCHE UND REICH GOTTES BEI FRIEDRICH FABRI (Stuttgart, 1965).

Christian Stubbe recounted Pomeranian interest in abstinence from alcohol in "Pommern vor 100 Jahren gegen den Branntwein," BLAETTER FUER KIRCHENGESCHICHTE POMMERNS, XX/XXI (1939), 58-65. Martin Schmidt described the views of awakened Lutherans on public life in "Kirche und oeffentliches Leben im Urteil der lutherischen Erweckungsbewegung des 19. Jahrhunderts," THEOLOGIA VIATORUM, II (1950), 48-71.

CHAPTER IV

The chapter's notes refer to works by Brazill, Schlingensiepen-Pogge, Suess, and Welch. These studies cover their subjects very well. Martin E. Marty described the challenge of the German radicals, in the broad context of developments in the United States and Britain, in THE MODERN SCHISM, THREE PATHS TO THE SECULAR (New York, 1969).

Additional information on the Hambach Festival is found in HAMBACHER FEST, 1832—1957, ed. Institut fuer staatsbuergerliche Bildung in Rheinland-Pfalz (Mainz, 1957); and in Veit Valentin, DAS HAMBACHER NATIONALFEST (Berlin, 1932). An important contribution to the understanding of the Young Hegelians is Juergen Gebhardt, POLITIK UND ESCHATOLOGIE; STUDIEN ZUR GESCHICHTE DER HEGELSCHEN SCHULE IN DEN JAHREN 1830—1840, Muenchener Studien zur Politik, 1. Heft, ed. Institut fuer Politische Wissenschaften der Universitaet Muenchen, through Eric Voegelin and Hans Maier (Munich, 1963). More recent studies of Strauss include Horton Harris, DAVID FRIEDRICH STRAUSS AND HIS THEOLOGY (New York, 1973), and Richard S. Cromwell, DAVID FRIEDRICH STRAUSS AND HIS PLACE IN MODERN THOUGHT (Fair Lawn, NJ, 1974). Among important contributions by Ernst Barnikol on Bruno Bauer are "Bruno Bauers Kampf gegen Religion und Christentum und die Spaltung der vormaerzlichen preussischen Opposition," ZEITSCHRIFT FUER KIRCHENGESCHICHTE, N.F., IX (1927), 1-34; and Barnikol's posthumous—and poorly collected—papers, entitled BRUNO BAUER: STUDIEN UND MATERIALIEN (Assen, 1972).

CHAPTER V

Among studies of New Lutheran Confessionalists, the most illuminating is Friedrich William Kantzenbach, GESTALTEN UND TYPEN DES NEULUTHERTUMS (1st ed.; Guetersloh, 1968). Heinrich Laag discussed the Pomeranian Old Lutherans in ENTWICKLUNG DER ALTLUTHERANEN KIRCHE IN POMMERN BIS ZUM MITTE DES 19. JAHRHUNDERTS (Griefswald, 1926). Bavarian confessionalism was the subject of Matthias Simon, DIE EVANG.-LUTH. KIRCHE IN BAYERN IM 19. UND 20. JAHRHUNDERT, Theologie und Gemeinde, ed. Ernst Fikenscher, Heft 5 (Munich, 1961). Claude Welch examined the theology of various confessionalists in PROTESTANT THOUGHT IN THE NINETEENTH CENTURY, Vol. I, 1799—1870 (New Haven, 1972); see also Walter R. Bouman, "The Unity of the Church in 19th Century Confessional Lutheranism" (unpublished Th. D. dissertation, Ruprecht-Karl University, Heidelberg, 1962); and Ulrich Asendorf, DIE EUROPAEISCHE KRISE UND DAS AMT DER KIRCHE; VORAUSSETZUNGEN DER THEOLOGIE VON A. F. C. VILMAR, Arbeiten zur Geschichte und Theologie des Luthertums, ed. Max Keller-Hueschemenger et al., Vol. XVIII (Berlin, 1967). Since there is no recent biography of Hengstenberg, Johannes Bachmann's ERNST WILHELM HENGSTENBERG, SEIN LEBEN UND WIRKEN (2 vols.; Guetersloh, 1876—80) continues to be used. It should be supplemented by recent dissertations on Hengstenberg, such as Hans Wulfmeyer's "Ernst Wilhelm Hengstenberg als Konfessionalist" (unpublished dissertation, Friedrich-Alexander Universitaet, Erlangen-Nuernberg, 1970). Gottfried Mehnert examined Hengstenberg's influential church paper, and other important religious papers during the century, in PROGRAMME EVANGELISCHER KIRCHENZEITUNGEN IM 19. JAHRHUNDERT (Witten, 1972).

Polity developments in the Rhineland come under consideration in Albert Rosenkranz, ABRISS EINER GESCHICHTE DER EVANGELISCHEN KIRCHE IM RHINELAND (Duesseldorf, 1960); and in KIRCHE UND STAAT IM 19. UND 20. JAHRHUNDERT, Veroeffentlichungen der Arbeitsgemeinschaft fuer das Archiv- und Bibliothekswesen in der evangelischen Kirche, 7 (Neustadt an der Aisch, 1968), pp. 46-91 and 144-58. In DAS DOMKAPITEL UND DIE ERZBISCHOFSWAHLEN IN KOELN, 1821—1929 (Cologne, 1972), Norbert Trippen examined the church-political effects of the confrontation between the bishop of Cologne and the Prussian king. Among helpful sources on the "Lichtfreunde" and German Catholics are a dissertation by Catherine Magill Holden, "A Decade of Dissent in Germany; an Historical Study of the Society of Protestant Friends and the German-catholic Church, 1840—48" (Yale University, New Haven, 1954); and an article published under her married name, Catherine M. Prelinger, "Religious Dissent, Women's Rights, and the Hamburger Hochschule fuer das weiblische Geschlecht in mid-nineteenth-century Germany," CHURCH HISTORY, XLX (1976), 42-55.

An important work on church construction is Gerhard Langmaack, EVANGELISCHE KIRCHENBAU IM 19. UND 20. JAHRHUNDERT (Kassel, 1971). The Cologne Cathedral is one of the edifices fully discussed in Ludger Kerssen, DAS INTERESSE AM MITTELALTER IM DEUTSCHEN NATIONALDENKMAL, Arbeiten zur Fruemittelalterforschung, Band 8 (Berlin, 1975). Ingrid Schulze researched the renovation of the Castle Church at Wittenberg in "Die Wittenberger Schlosskirche als Sakralbau und nationale Gedenkstaette im 18. und 19. Jahrhundert," WISSENSCHAFTLICHE ZEITSCHRIFT, MARTIN-LUTHER UNIVERSITAET HALLE-WITTENBERG, Gesellschafts- und Sprachwissenschaftliche Reihe, XVIII (1969), Heft 6, 91-107. Clerical reaction to the bishopric in Jerusalem was the subject of Hans-Joachim Schoeps, "Der Widerstand der Berliner Geistlichkeit gegen die Gruendung des Bistums zu Jerusalem," in GLAUBE, GEIST, GESCHICHTE; FESTSCHRIFT FUER ERNST BENZ, ed. Gerhard Mueller and W. Zeller (Leiden, 1967), pp. 231-43.

William L. Langer provided a broad sketch of different factors in the cultural dissonance of the forties in POLITICAL AND SOCIAL UPHEAVAL, 1832—1852, Rise of Modern Europe, ed. William L. Langer (New York, 1969). In DIE DELITZSCH'SCHE SACHE. EIN KAPITEL PREUSSISCHER KIRCHEN -UND FAKULTAETSPOLITIK IM VORMAERZ, Arbeite zur Geschichte und Theologie des Luthertums, Bd. XIX (Berlin, 1967), Karl Heinrich Rengstorf provided a detailed account of the struggle over Delitzsch's faculty appointment.

CHAPTER VI

The studies of Valentin, Krieger, and Dros cited in the
notes should be consulted. Other important studies on this
period include Friedrich Engels, THE GERMAN REVOLUTIONS,
ed. with an introduction by Leonard Krieger (Chicago,
1967); Theodor S. Hamerow, RESTORATION, REVOLUTION,
REACTION; ECONOMICS AND POLITICS IN GERMANY, 1815—1871
(Princeton, 1958); Lewis Namier, 1848: THE REVOLUTION OF THE
INTELLECTUALS (Garden City, NY, 1964); Frank Eyck, THE
FRANKFURT PARLIAMENT, 1848—1849 (New York, 1968); and
Marjorie Elizabeth Lamberti, "The Rise of the Prussian
Conservative Party, 1840—1858" (unpublished dissertation,
Yale University, New Haven, 1966), which describes the role
of Protestants in the early history of the party.

Walter Delius provided a broad treatment of the church in
the revolutionary period in DIE EVANGELISCHE KIRCHE UND DIE
REVOLUTION VON 1848, Kirche in dieser Ziet, H. 6/7 (Berlin,
1948). Specialized studies include Ernst Schubert, DIE
EVANGELISCHE PREDIGT IM REVOLUTIONSJAHR 1848 (Giessen,
1913); Karl Gerhard Steck, "Revolution und Gegenrevolution
in der theologischen Ethik des neunzehnten Jahrhunderts," in
PROTESTANTISMUS UND REVOLUTION, ed. Trutz Rendtorff,
Theologische Existenz Heute, N.F., Nr. 161 (Munich, 1969),
pp. 27-62; and Eberhard Amelung, "Die demokratischen
Bewegung des Jahres 1848 im Urteil der protestantischen
Theologie" (unpublished dissertation, University of Marburg,
Marburg, 1954).

Otto Leiche discussed the hesitant Berlin Synod that met
during 1848 in "Die Berliner Synode von 1848/49," JAHRBUCH
FUER BERLIN-BRANDENBURGISCHE KIRCHENGESCHICHTE, XXXVIII
(1963), 142-76. Walter Wendland summarized the early
history of the High Church Council in "Die Entstehung des
Evangelischen Ober-Kirchenrats," JAHRBUCH FUER
BRANDENBURGISCHE KIRCHENGESCHICHTE, XXVIII (1933), 3-30.

The bibliographical notes for Chapter VII also discuss the
Inner Mission, but three major studies should be mentioned
here: Erich Beyreuther, GESCHICHTE DER DIAKONIE UND INNEREN
MISSION IN DER NEUZEIT, Lehrbuecher fuer die diakonische
Arbeit, ed. Hans Christoph von Hase, Vol. I (Berlin, 1962);
Martin Gerhardt, EIN JAHRHUNDERT INNERE MISSION (2 vols.;

Guetersloh, 1948), the standard history of the Mission; and Friedrich Oldenberg, JOHANN HINRICH WICHERN (3 vols.; Hamburg, 1884-87), an important early biography of Wichern.

CHAPTER VII

The chapter notes should be consulted for works by Beyreuther, Drews, and Strohm, documents edited by Hubatsch, and Rohlfer's dissertation. In addition, Walter Hubatsch provided a helpful three-volume series of text, pictures and documents on the church in East Prussia, entitled GESCHICHTE DER EVANGELISCHEN KIRCHE OSTPREUSSENS (Goettingen, 1968). Editions of Wichern's works include Karl Janssen, ed., JOHANN HINRICH WICHERN, AUSGEWAEHLTE SCHRIFTEN (3 vols.; 1st ed.; Guetersloh, 1956-62); and Peter Meinhold, ed., JOHANN HINRICH WICHERN, SAEMTLICHE WERKE (4 vols. in 6; Berlin, 1958—69).

Hans Joachim Schoeps sketched informative vignettes of several of the decade's prominent conservative figures in DAS ANDERE PREUSSEN, KONSERVATIVE GESTALTEN UND PROBLEME IM ZEITALTER FRIEDRICH WILHELMS IV (2nd rev. ed.; Honnef/Rhein, 1957). He supplemented the volume in numerous books and articles, including "Der Christliche Staat im Zeitalter der Restauration," in STAAT UND KIRCHE IM WANDEL DER JAHRHUNDERTE, ed. Walther Peter Fuchs (Stuttgart, 1966), pp. 146-65.

Turbulence among intellectuals is the subject of Andrew Lees, REVOLUTION AND REFLECTION: INTELLECTUAL CHANGE IN GERMANY DURING THE 1850'S (The Hague, 1974). Werner Broeker examined Karl Vogt's opposition to religion in POLITISCHE MOTIVE NATURWISSENSCHAFTLICHER ARGUMENTATION GEGEN RELIGION UND KIRCHE IM 19. JAHRHUNDERT. DARGESTELLT AM "MATERIALISTEN" KARL VOGT (1817—1895), Muensterische Beitraege zur Theologie, No. 35 (Muenster, 1973); Owen Chadwick placed this subject in the broader context in THE SECULARIZATION OF THE EUROPEAN MIND IN THE NINETEENTH CENTURY (Cambridge, 1975). Martin Schmidt's study of the church and of emigration, WORT GOTTES UND FREMDLINGSCHAFT; DIE KIRCHE VOR DES AUSWANDERUNGSPROBLEM DES 19.

605

JAHRHUNDERTS (Erlangen, 1953), remains significant.

CHAPTER VIII

The notes of the chapter refer to important works by Pflanze, Raedische, Hammer, Piechowski, and the volume edited by Zillessen. Other significant studies of unification are: Otto Becker, BISMARCKS RINGEN UM DEUTSCHLANDS GESTALTUNG, ed. and supplemented by Alexander Scharff (Heidelberg, 1958); the two volumes by Theodore S. Hamerow, THE SOCIAL FOUNDATIONS OF GERMAN UNIFICATION, 1858—1871, IDEAS AND INSTITUTIONS (Princeton, 1969), and THE SOCIAL FOUNDATIONS OF GERMAN UNIFICATION, 1858—1871, STRUGGLES AND ACCOMPLISHMENTS (Princeton, 1972); Fritz Stern, GOLD AND IRON; BISMARCK, BLEICHROEDER, AND THE BUILDING OF THE GERMAN EMPIRE (New York, 1977); Hans-Joachim Schoeps, BISMARCK UEBER ZEITGENOSSEN; ZEITGENOSSEN UEBER BISMARCK (Berlin, 1972); Hans Rosenberg, DIE NATIONALPOLITISCHE PUBLIZISTIK DEUTSCHLANDS VOM EINTRITT DER NEUEN AERA IN PREUSSEN BIS ZUM AUSBRUCH DES DEUTSCHEN KRIEGES (2 vols.; Munich, 1935); and Theodor Schieder, DAS DEUTSCHE KAISERREICH VON 1871 ALS NATIONALSTAAT, Wissenschaftliche Abhandlungen der Arbeitsgemeinschaft fuer Forschung des Landes Nordrhein-Westfalen, ed. Leo Brandt, Vol. XX (Cologne and Opladen, 1961).

Among the important studies of Protestants during the period of unification are: Fritz Fischer, "Das deutsche Protestantismus und die Politik im 19. Jahrhundert," in PROBLEME DER REICHSGRUNDUNGSZEIT, 1848—1879, ed. Helmut Boehme (Cologne, 1968), pp. 49-71 <first published in HISTORISCHE ZEITSCHRIFT, CLXXI, 473-502>; Joachim Rohlfer, "Staat, Nation, Reich in der Evangelischen Kirche Deutschlands im Zeitalter der deutscher Einigung (1848—1871)" (unpublished dissertation, Goettingen University, Goettingen, 1955); Gottfried Mehnert, DIE KIRCHE IN SCHLESWIG-HOLSTEIN (Kiel, 1960); and Karl Heinrich Hoefele, "Sendungsglaube und Epochenbewusstsein in Deutschland 1870/71," ZEITSCHRIFT FUER RELIGIONS- UND GEISTESGESCHICHTE, XV (1963), 265-76.

Gerhard Ritter discussed the conservative resistance to Bismarck in DIE PREUSSISCHEN KONSERVATIVEN UND BISMARCKS DEUTSCHE POLITIK, 1858 BIS 1876 (Heidelberg, 1913). Ernst Ludwig Gerlach's material from this period is published in Helmut Diwald, ed., VON DER REVOLUTION ZUM NORDDEUTSCHEN BUND; POLITIK UND IDEENGUT DER PREUSSISCHEN HOCHKONSERVATIVEN 1848—1866; AUS DEM NACHLASS VON ERNST LUDWIG VON GERLACH, Ersten Teil: Tagebuch 1848—1866; Zweiter Teil: Briefe, Denkschriften, Aufzeichnungen (Goettingen, 1970).

CHAPTER IX

The works by Raedische, Beyreuther, Lotz, and Oehler cited in the notes are important for some of the chapter's themes. Friedrich Giese's study of church taxes, DEUTSCHES KIRCHENSTEUERRECHT (Stuttgart, 1910), is very helpful. There are many works on the "Kulturkampf," and bibliographies in the following studies will provide helpful suggestions: George Franz, KULTURKAMPF, STAAT UND KATHOLISCHE KIRCHE IN MITTELEUROPA VON DER SAEKULARISATION BIS ZUM ABSCHLUSS DES PREUSSISCHEN KULTURKAMPFES (Munich, 1954); Manfred Stadelhofer, DER ABBAU DER KULTURKAMPFSGESETZGEBUNG IM GROSSHERZOGTUM BADEN 1878—1918, Veroeffentlichungen der Kommission fuer Zeitgeschichte der Katholischen Akademie in Bayern, Reihe B, Forschungen, Vol. 3 (Mainz, 1969); and Walter Reichle, ZWISCHEN STAAT UND KIRCHE; DAS LEBEN UND WIRKEN DES PREUSSISCHEN KULTUSMINISTERS HEINRICH VON MUEHLER (Berlin, 1938). In BELEAGUERED TOWER: THE DILEMMA OF POLITICAL CATHOLICISM IN WILHELMINE GERMANY (Notre Dame, 1976), Ronald J. Ross described the Center's difficulties after 1890. The emperor's journey to the Holy Land is recounted in Erwin Roth, PREUSSENS GLORIA IM HEILIGEN LAND; DIE DUETSCHEN UND JERUSALEM (Munich, 1973), while in THRON UND ALTAR, DIE ROLLE DER BERLINER HOFPREDIGER IM ZEITALTER DES WILHELMINISMUS (Neustadt an der Aisch, 1970), Erwin Roth examined the role of the court preacher in the latter part of the Second Empire.

CHAPTER X

Landes, Bechtel, Wittke, Vorlaender, Kretschmar, and Shanahan have written important works on themes in this chapter, as the notes indicate. Also helpful is the volume edited by Motteck. A new edition of Marx's writings on religion, edited and translated by Saul K. Padover, and entitled KARL MARX ON RELIGION (New York, 1974), supplements MARX AND ENGELS ON RELIGION, introduction by Reinhold Niebuhr (New York, 1964).

Industrialization in Germany is also the focus of these studies: J. H. Clapham, ECONOMIC DEVELOPMENT OF FRANCE AND GERMANY, 1815—1914 (4th ed.; Cambridge, 1966); Hans Mauersberg, DEUTSCHE INDUSTRIEN IM ZEITGESCHEHEN EINES JAHRHUNDERTS; EINE HISTORISCHE MODELLUNTERSUCHUNG ZUM ENTWICKLUNGSPROZESS DEUTSCHER UNTERNEHMEN VON IHREN ANFAENGEN BIS ZUM STAND VON 1960 (Stuttgart, 1966); W. O. Henderson, THE RISE OF GERMAN INDUSTRIAL POWER, 1834—1914 (Berkeley, 1975); and Kenneth D. Barkin, THE CONTROVERSY OVER GERMAN INDUSTRIALIZATION, 1890—1902 (Chicago, 1970).

In addition to the studies mentioned above, the following works discuss the response of Protestants to industrialization and its social consequences: Alexandra Schlingensiepen-Pogge, DAS SOZIALETHOS DER LUTHERISCHEN AUFKLAERUNGSTHEOLOGIE AM VORABEND DER INDUSTRIELLEN REVOLUTION (Goettingen, 1967); Walter Bredendiek, CHRISTLICHE SOZIALREFORMER DES 19. JAHRHUNDERTS (Leipzig, 1953); Karl Kupisch, DAS JAHRHUNDERT DES SOZIALISMUS UND DIE KIRCHE (Berlin, 1958); Guenter Brakelmann, KIRCHE UND SOZIALISMUS IM 19. JAHRHUNDERT; DIE ANALYSE DES SOZIALISMUS UND KOMMUNISMUS BEI JOHANN HINRICH WICHERN UND BEI RUDOLF TODT (Witten, 1966); Richard Grunow, WICHERN—RUF UND ANTWORT (Guetersloh, 1958); Rolf Kramer, NATION UND THEOLOGIE BEI JOHANN HINRICH WICHERN (Hamburg, 1959); and Paul Goehre, DIE EVANGELISCH-SOZIALE BEWEGUNG, IHRE GESCHICHTE UND IHRE ZIELE (Leipzig, 1896). Friedrich Karrenberg provided a broad thematic survey in GESCHICHTE DER SOZIALEN IDEEN DEUTSCHLAND, ed. Helga Grebing, Deutsches Handbuch der Politik, Vol. II (Munich, 1969), pp. 561-694.

CHAPTER XI

The notes refer to important works by Lidtke, Strohm, Frank, Schleth, Christ, Thurneysen, Lejeune, and Sauter, and articles by Timm and Mattmueller, that review facets of the encounter between Protestants and Social Democrats, and related topics. Another important work is Heiner Grote, SOZIALDEMOKRATIE UND RELIGION; EINE DOKUMENTATION FUER DIE JAHRE 1863 BIS 1875 (Tuebingen, 1968). Klaus Erich Pollmann's LANDESKIRCHLICHES KIRCHENREGIMENT UND SOZIALE FRAGE: DER EVANGELISCHE OBERKIRCHENRAT DER ALTPREUSSISCHEN LANDESKIRCHE UND DIE SOZIALPOLITISCHE BEWEGUNG DER GEISTLICHEN NACH 1890 (Berlin, 1973) shows that the Prussian state church could make no effective contribution to easing the social conflict.

Alfred Milatz's bibliography on Naumann, FRIEDRICH NAUMANN-BIBLIOGRAPHIE, Bibliographien zur Geschichte des Parlamentarismus und der politischen Parteien, Vol. II (Duesseldorf, 1957), identifies the early literature on Naumann, including Karl Kupisch, FRIEDRICH NAUMANN UND DIE EVANGELISCHE-SOZIALE BEWEGUNG (Berlin, 1938); Theodor Heuss, FRIEDRICH NAUMANN, DER MANN, DAS WERK, DIE ZEIT (Stuttgart and Berlin, 1937); and Richard Nuernberger, "Imperialismus, Sozialismus und Christentum bei Friedrich Naumann," HISTORISCHE ZEITSCHRIFT, CLXX (1950), 522-48. Also significant are these recent studies: Theodor Heuss, FRIEDRICH NAUMANN UND DIE DEUTSCHE DEMOKRATIE (Wiesbaden, 1960); Kurt Oppel, FRIEDRICH NAUMANN, ZUEGNISSE SEINES WIRKENS, Begegnungen, ed. Theodor Schlatter and Peter Meinhold, Vol. V (Stuttgart, 1961); Wilhelm Happ, DAS STAATSDENKEN FRIEDRICH NAUMANNS, Shriften zur Rechtslehre und Politik, ed. Ernst von Hippel, Vol. LVII (Bonn, 1968); and Paul B. Kern, "The New Liberalism in Wilhelminian Germany" (unpublished dissertation, University of Chicago, Chicago, 1970). Volumes I and V of Naumann's WERKE, edited respectively by Walter Uhsadel and Theodor Schieder (Cologne, 1964), include his RELIGIOESE SCHRIFTEN (I) and POLITISCHE SCHRIFTEN (V).

CHAPTER XII

The notes refer to important works by Tal, Hughes, Milberg, Kupisch, Beyreuther, Lehr, Werckshagen (ed.), Sviestrup and Zahn-Harnack (eds.), and Massing, as well as Huber's article. These studies discuss some of the chapter's themes, as do the articles collected in Hans Joachim Schoeps, ed., ZEITGEIST IM WANDEL, Band I, Das Wilhelminische Zeitalter (Stuttgart, 1967), especially Karl Kupisch's article on civil piety, pp. 40-59.

Two other specialized studies of aspects of church life in this period are Robert Minder, "Das Bild des Pfarrhauses in der deutschen Literatur von Jean Paul bis Gottfried Benn," in AKADEMIE DER WISSENSCHAFTEN UND DER LITERATUR, Abhandlungen der Klasse der Literatur, Jg. 1959, Nr. 4 (Wiesbaden, 1959), pp. 53-78; and Richard J. Evans, THE FEMINIST MOVEMENT IN GERMANY, 1894—1933 (Beverly Hills, 1976). Kurt Hutten examined the various sectarian groups in SEHER, GRUEBLER, ENTHUSIASTEN. DAS BUCH DER SEKTEN (11th ed.; Stuttgart, 1966), while Oswald Eggenberger focused on the free churches in DIE FREIKIRCHEN IN DEUTSCHLAND UND IN DER SCHWEIZ UND IHR VERHAELTNIS ZU DEN VOLKSKIRCHEN (Zurich, 1964).

In DIE PROTESTANTISCHE THEOLOGIE IM 19. JAHRHUNDERT (3rd ed.; Zurich, 1960), Karl Barth discussed the major theologians of the period with remarkable objectivity. Studies on Harnack in English include G. Wayne Glick, THE REALITY OF CHRISTIANITY; A STUDY OF ADOLF VON HARNACK AS HISTORIAN AND THEOLOGIAN (New York, 1967), and his article, "Nineteenth Century Theological and Cultural Influences of Adolf Harnack," in CHURCH HISTORY, XXVIII (1959), 157-82. Johannes Rathje illuminated Rade's world of Free Protestantism in a masterful way in DIE WELT DES FREIEN PROTESTANTISMUS (Stuttgart, 1952).

Among the general studies of anti-Semitism in this period are George L. Mosse, THE CRISIS OF GERMAN IDEOLOGY; INTELLECTUAL ORIGINS OF THE THIRD REICH (New York, 1964); Leon Poliakov, THE ARYAN MYTH: A HISTORY OF RACIST AND NATIONALIST IDEAS IN EUROPE, The Columbus Centre Series: Studies in the Dynamics of Persecution and Extermination (New York, 1974); and Werner E. Mosse and Arnold Paucker, eds., JUDEN IN WILHELMINISCHEN DEUTSCHLAND, 1890—1914 (Tuebingen, 1976). Stoecker and his party's anti-Semitism are treated in Karl Kupisch, ADOLF STOECKER, HOFPREDIGER UND VOLKSTRIBUN, Berlinische Reminiszenzen, XXIV (1st ed.; Berlin, 1970); John C. Fout, "Adolf Stoecker's Rationale for Anti-Semitism," JOURNAL OF CHURCH AND STATE, XVII, 1 (1975), 47-61; Walter Braun, EVANGELISCHE PARTEIEN IN HISTORISCHER DARSTELLUNG UND SOZIALWISSENSCHAFTLICHER BELEUCHTUNG (Mannheim, 1939); Karl Buchheim, GESCHICHTE DER CHRISTLICHEN PARTEIEN IN DEUTSCHLAND (Munich, 1953); and Erich Hoeuer, DIE GESCHICHTE DER CHRISTLICH-KONSERVATIVEN PARTEI IN MINDEN-RAVENSBERG VON 1866 BIS 1896 (Bielefeld, 1923). In THE DOWNFALL OF THE ANTI-SEMITIC POLITICAL PARTIES IN IMPERIAL GERMANY (New Haven, 1975), Richard S. Levy reviewed the collapse of anti-semitic parties.

A brief introduction to religious nationalism is Wolfgang Tilgner's "Volk, Nation und Vaterland im protestantischen Denken zwischen Kaiserreich und Nationalsozialismus (ca. 1870—1933)," in VOLK, NATION, VATERLAND. DER DEUTSCHE PROTESTANTISMUS UND DER NATIONALISMUS, Veroeffentlichungen des Sozialwissenschaftlichen Instituts der eKidO, II, ed. Horst Zillessen (Guetersloh, 1970). Religious nationalism is also treated in Horst Zillessen, PROTESTANTISMUS UND POLITISCHE FORM (Guetersloh, 1971); Paul Wilhelm Gennrich, GOTT UND DIE VOELKER; BEITRAEGE ZUR AUFFASSUNG VON VOLK UND VOLKSTUM IN DER GESCHICHTE DER THEOLOGIE (Stuttgart, 1972); and Reinhard Wittram, NATIONALISMUS UND SAEKULARISATION; BEITRAEGE ZUR GESCHICHTE UND PROBLEMATIK DES NATIONALGEISTES (Lueneburg, 1949). Martin Schian commends the work of military chaplains in DIE ARBEIT DER EVANGELISCHEN KIRCHE IM FELDE, Die deutsche evangelische Kirche im Weltkriege, I (Berlin, 1921), while Roger Chickering discussed the ineffectiveness of the peace movement in IMPERIAL GERMANY AND A WORLD WITHOUT WAR: THE PEACE MOVEMENT AND GERMAN SOCIETY, 1892—1914 (Princeton, 1975).

Two recent works studied specialized aspects of the churches' history between the Great War and 1933. They are Jochen Jacke, KIRCHE ZWISCHEN MONARCHIE UND REPUBLIK; DER PREUSSISCHE PROTESTANTISMUS NACH DEM ZUSAMMENBRUCH VON 1918, Hamburger Beitraege zur Sozial- und Zeitgeschichte, Vol. XII (Hamburg, 1976); and J. R. C. Wright's less enlightening study, 'ABOVE PARTIES'; THE POLITICAL ATTITUDES OF THE GERMAN PROTESTANT CHURCH LEADERSHIP, 1918—1933 (Oxford,

GLOSSARY

Agenda	liturgical book; order of worship
Aufklaerung	Enlightenment
Bildung	formation, education, culture
Burschenschaften	student unions, fraternities
caritas	charity, philanthropy
corpus evangelicorum	organ of the Holy Roman Empire that represented the combined Protestant interests before the emperor, the imperial estates, and the imperial courts
doctrina evangelica	evangelical teaching
Erhebung	revolt, rebellion, uprising
Erweckunsbewegung	religious revival, awakening
Gemeinschaftsbewegung	movement of community; revivalistic or pietistic movement late in the century
Illuminati	Lichtfreunde; Friends of Light; Society of Friends (not related to Quakers)
Junker	aristocratic landowner; country squire; also used as adjective
jus (jura) circa sacra	law regulating external religious affairs
jus (jura) sacrorum	law of religious ceremonies, worship
Kaiser	emperor
Kirchentag	unofficial public gathering of Protestants; sometimes included a congress of the Inner Mission
Kulturkampf	literally, "battle of cultures;" crusade against Roman Catholicism, with important ramifications for Protestants
Landrecht (Allgemeine)	Prussian Territorial Law
Landtag	territorial diet; house of deputies
Lichtfreunde	Friends of Light; Illuminati

Mark	mark; German coin
Oberkirchenrat	High (Supreme) Church Council
Oberpraesident	chief administrator of province
opus operatum	efficacious by the doing of the deed
Patronat	acknowledgment of hereditary rights and obligations of the patron or person who provided lands or funds to build and support a church and its pastor
Plattdeutsch	low-German dialect
Protestantverein	Protestant Union
Realpolitik	politics of realism
Reich	empire, kingdom
Reichsdeputations- hauptschluss	commission of Holy Roman Empire that recommended in 1803 that most ecclesiastical sovereignties be secularized
Reichstag	imperial diet, parliament
Simultantschule	elementary school for children of mixed confessions
Staende	social estates
summus episcopus	rights and privileges exercised by the territorial prince over the state church; jurisdictional and liturgical authority of the prince-bishop
Thaler (Taler)	German coin
Turnvater	father of gymnastics, referring to Friedrich Ludwig Jahn
volkisch	popular, folkish
von oben	from above
Weltanschauung	world view, perspective
Zeitgeist	spirit of the times
Zollverein	tariff union created in 1834
Zollparlament	customs parliament of the Zollverein